TO KEVIN,
FROM THE
"ULTIMATE
DM".

KEVIN J. BYRNE
BEØWULF
09/08/00

DUNGEON MASTER'S GUIDE D&D DESIGN TEAM
Monte Cook, Jonathan Tweet, Skip Williams

DUNGEON MASTER'S GUIDE DESIGN
Monte Cook

ADDITIONAL DESIGN & DIRECTION
Peter Adkison

ADDITIONAL DESIGN
Richard Baker, Andy Collins,
David Noonan

EDITORS
Julia Martin, John D. Rateliff

EDITORIAL ASSISTANCE
Duane Maxwell, Jeff Quick

MANAGING EDITOR
Kim Mohan

CORE D&D CREATIVE DIRECTOR
Ed Stark

DIRECTOR OF RPG R&D
Bill Slavicsek

BRAND MANAGER
Ryan Dancey

CATEGORY MANAGER
Keith Strohm

PROJECT MANAGERS
Larry Weiner, Josh Fischer

CARTOGRAPHER
Todd Gamble

VISUAL CREATIVE DIRECTOR
Jon Schindehette

ART DIRECTOR
Dawn Murin

D&D CONCEPTUAL ARTISTS
Todd Lockwood, Sam Wood

D&D LOGO DESIGN
Matt Adelsperger, Sherry Floyd

COVER ART
Henry Higgenbotham

INTERIOR ARTISTS
Lars Grant-West, Scott Fischer, John
Foster, Todd Lockwood, David Martin,
Arnie Swekel, Kevin Walker, Sam Wood,
Wayne Reynolds

GRAPHIC DESIGNERS
Sean Glenn, Sherry Floyd

TYPOGRAPHERS
Victoria Ausland, Erin Dorries,
Angelika Lokotz, Nancy Walker

DIGI-TECH SPECIALIST
Joe Fernandez

PHOTOGRAPHER
Craig Cudnohufsky

PRODUCTION MANAGER
Chas DeLong

SPECIAL THANKS:
Jim Lin, Richard Garfield, Andrew Finch, Skaff Elias

OTHER WIZARDS OF THE COAST RPG R&D CONTRIBUTORS
Eric Cagle, Jason Carl, Shawn F. Carnes, Michele Carter, William W. Connors,
Bruce R. Cordell, Dale Donovan, David Eckelberry, Jeff Grubb, Rob Heinsoo, Miranda Horner,
Harold Johnson, Kij Johnson, Gwendolyn FM Kestrel, Steve Miller, Roger Moore, Jon Pickens,
Chris Pramas, Rich Redman, Thomas M. Reid, Sean K Reynolds, Steven Schend, Mike Selinker, Stan!,
JD Wiker, Jennifer Clarke Wilkes, Penny Williams, James Wyatt

BASED ON THE ORIGINAL DUNGEONS & DRAGONS® RULES CREATED BY E. GARY GYGAX AND DAVE ARNESON

U.S., CANADA,
ASIA, PACIFIC, & LATIN AMERICA
Wizards of the Coast, Inc.
P.O. Box 707
Renton WA 98057-0707

QUESTIONS? 1-800-324-6496   620-T11551

EUROPEAN HEADQUARTERS
Wizards of the Coast, Belgium
P.B. 2031
2600 Berchem
Belgium
+32-70-23-32-77

First Printing   September 2000

Visit our website at www.wizards.com/dnd

Contents

TABLES

Introduction

You've read the *Player's Handbook*, digested the material inside it, and you're ready to take on a challenge beyond creating a character. You want to be the Dungeon Master (DM). Or, you've been running games for quite some time and know a lot about what you're doing. Either way, this book is going to present you with some surprises and unveil some secrets.

Let's start with the biggest secret of all: the key to Dungeon Mastering. (Don't tell anybody, okay?) The secret is that you're in charge. This is not the telling-everyone-what-to-do sort of in charge. Rather, you get to decide how your player group is going to play this game, when and where the adventures take place, and what happens. You get to decide how the rules work, which rules to use, and how strictly to adhere to them. *That* kind of in charge.

You're a member of a select group. Truly, not everyone has the creativity and the dedication to be a Dungeon Master. Dungeon Mastering (DMing) can be challenging, but it's not a chore. You're the lucky one out of your entire circle of friends that plays the game. The real fun is in your hands. As you flip through the *Monster Manual* or look at published adventures on a store shelf, you get to decide what the player characters (PCs) take on next. You get to build a whole world, design all its characters, and play all of them not played directly by the other players.

It's good to be the DM.

The DM defines the game. A good DM results in a good game. Since you control the pacing, the types of adventures and encounters, and the nonplayer characters (NPCs), the whole tenor of the game is in your hands. It's fun, but it's a big responsibility. If you're the sort of person who likes to provide the fun for your friends, to create new things, or to come up with new ideas, then you're an ideal candidate for DM.

Once your group has a Dungeon Master, however, that doesn't mean that you can't switch around. Some DMs like to take a turn at being a player, and many players eventually want to try their hand at DMing.

ORGANIZATION

The *Dungeon Master's Guide* (DMG) presents information in the order in which you will need it as a DM.

Dungeon Mastering (Chapter 1): This chapter starts out with what it means to be a DM and how to do things such as run a game session, change a rule, or work with the players to make sure everyone has fun. If you've never been a DM, read this chapter first. The information in this chapter isn't the sort that you'll refer to during a game, but you'll want to read and think about the issues discussed here well before you ever sit down to run your first game.

Characters (Chapter 2): This chapter deals with characters. It discusses all the behind-the-scenes stuff about characters that can't be found in the *Player's Handbook,* including running monsters as characters, altering classes and races, advancing in level, special NPC classes, and a new concept called the prestige class that more experienced DMs should check out.

Running the Game (Chapter 3): The next chapter deals with every aspect of managing the action in a game session from combat to skill use. Look to this section to find out more about variant combat rules, the powers of monsters found in the *Monster Manual,* rules for environmental dangers (such as fire, cold, and drowning), and how to determine Difficulty Classes (DCs). You'll refer to this chapter all the time while playing the game.

Adventures (Chapter 4): This chapter starts you on the road to creating adventures by discussing the art of adventure design. It deals with encounters and how to tailor them to your players. It also discusses dungeons and dungeon encounters in depth, provides an example of play, and covers wilderness and town adventures. You'll occasionally refer to this chapter during a game session for its information on traps, the strength of doors, or generating a random encounter in a dungeon, the wilderness, or the city.

Campaigns (Chapter 5): The next logical step in DMing is the campaign. Here you'll find advice on starting a campaign, linking adventures, and handling important aspects such as NPCs. This chapter is useful to read before play starts, but the information about NPCs provides a handy reference during the game.

World-Building (Chapter 6): This chapter takes a step back to look at the joy of world-building. It gets you started in thinking about geography, politics, magic, and more—all of which are important aspects when you create an entire world.

Rewards (Chapter 7): When characters finish an adventure or complete a mission, it's time to hand out rewards to the players (for playing the game well) and their characters (for becoming richer and more powerful). Experience points and treasure are handled in this chapter. The tables you'll find here are useful both before a game (for generating random treasures) and after (for totaling up experience points).

Magic Items (Chapter 8): This chapter covers magic items in depth. It includes rules for creating and identifying magic items and discusses cursed items and artifacts, but the bulk of the chapter is a massive listing of magic items for use in the game. Expect to refer to this chapter all the time once your game gets going—potentially as often as you might refer to the *Player's Handbook.*

GENERAL GUIDELINES

The information in this section also appears on page 275 of the *Player's Handbook,* but it's important enough that it bears repeating here. The rules regarding how to round fractions and how to apply multipliers to damage come into play all the time, and it's vital to use these rules correctly.

ROUNDING FRACTIONS

In general, if you wind up with a fraction, round down, even if the fraction is one-half or larger. For example, if a *fireball* deals you 17 points of damage, but you succeed at your saving throw and only take half damage, you take 8 points of damage.

Exception: Certain rolls, such as damage and hit points, have a minimum of 1.

MULTIPLYING

Sometimes a special rule makes you multiply a number or a die roll. As long as you're applying a single multiplier, multiply the number normally. When two or more multipliers apply, however, combine them into a single multiple, with each extra multiple adding 1 less than its value to the first multiple. Thus, a double (×2) and a double (×2) applied to the same number results in a triple (×3, because 2 + 1 = 3).

For example, Tordek, a high-level dwarven fighter, deals 1d8+6 damage with a warhammer. With a critical hit, a warhammer deals triple damage, so that's 3d8+18 damage for Tordek. A magic *dwarven thrower* warhammer deals double damage (2d8+12 for Tordek) when thrown. If Tordek scores a critical hit while throwing the *dwarven thrower,* his player rolls quadruple damage (4d8+24) because 3 + 1 = 4.

Another way to think of it is to convert the multiples into additions. Tordek's critical hit increase his damage by 2d8+12, and the *dwarven thrower's* double increases his damage by 1d8+6, so both of them together increase his damage by 3d8+18 for a grand total of 4d8+24.

FINAL NOTE

The power of creating worlds, controlling deities and dragons, and leading entire nations is in your hands. You are the master of the game—the rules, the setting, the action, and ultimately, the fun. This is a great deal of power. Use it wisely. This book will show you how.

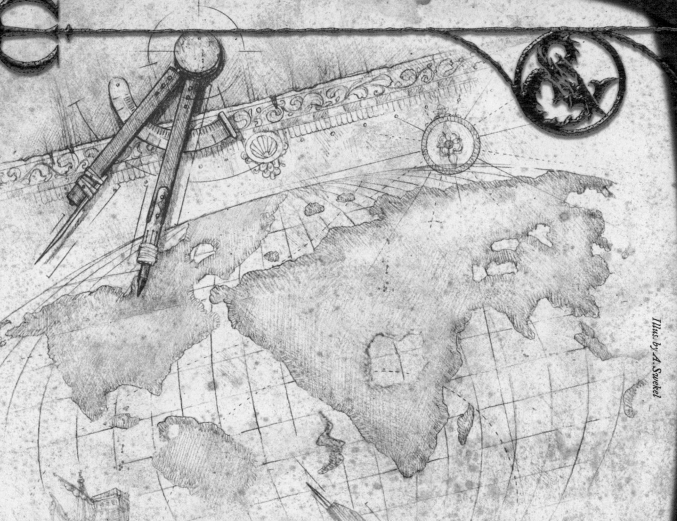

Illus. by A. Swekel

Dungeon Mastering involves writing, planning, acting, refereeing, arbitrating, and facilitating. When you're the Dungeon Master, you're the focus of the game. If the game's fun, it will be to your credit. If it's a failure, you'll get the blame. But don't worry—running a D&D game is not as hard as it may seem at first. (But don't tell the players that!)

Listed below are the different duties of the DM. You'll find that you like some more than others. Like in any hobby, focus on what you enjoy the most, but remember that all the other duties are also important.

PROVIDING ADVENTURES

Your primary role in the game is to create and present adventures in which the other players can play their characters. To accomplish this, you need to spend some amount of time—sometimes a great amount of time—outside the game, preparing. This is true whether you create your own adventures or use prepared adventures that you have purchased.

CREATING ADVENTURES

Creating adventures takes a great deal of time. Many DMs find that they spend more time getting ready for the game than they do at the table actually playing. These same DMs usually find this creation time the most fun and rewarding part of being a Dungeon Master. Creating interesting characters, settings, plots, and challenges to present before your friends can be a great creative outlet.

Creating good adventures is so important that it receives its own chapter in this book. See Chapter 4: Adventures.

USING PURCHASED ADVENTURES

Many published adventures (often called "modules") are available for you to purchase if you don't want to spend the time working on a scenario on your own, or if you just want a change of pace. In a published adventure, you'll get a pregenerated scenario with all the maps, NPCs, monsters, and treasures you need, and an adventure plot designed to make the most of them. Sometimes, when you use an adventure created by someone else, you'll see that it presents challenges you would have never thought of on your own.

Remember, however, that you're the one who has to run the adventure. That means that anything you want to change, you can. In fact, you will often find that you need to make at least small changes to fit the adventure into your own ongoing campaign and get your players into the action. You can have a great deal of fun replacing the villain of an adventure with one the players have already heard of in your campaign, or changing the background of the adventure so that it involves your players' characters in ways that the module's designer never could have possibly imagined.

TEACHING THE GAME

Sometimes it's going to be your responsibility to teach newcomers to the game how to play. This isn't a burden, but a wonderful opportunity. Teaching other people how to play provides you with new players and allows you to set them on the path to becoming top-notch roleplayers. It's easier to learn to play with someone who already knows the game. Those who are taught by a good teacher who runs a fun game are more likely to join in the hobby for the long haul. Use this opportunity to encourage new players to become the sort of gamers you want to play games with.

Here are a few pointers on teaching the game:

- Read the *Player's Handbook* and know the character creation rules so you can help the new players build characters. Have them each tell you what sort of character they want to play and then show them how they can create that hero with the D&D rules. If they don't know what to play, show them the player character (PC) types, briefly describe each, and let them choose the one that appeals to them the most.
- Once the PCs are created, don't worry about teaching the players all the rules ahead of time. All they truly need to know are the basics that apply to understanding their characters (how spells work, what AC means, how to use skills, etc.), and they can pick up most of this information as they go along.
- As long as you know the rules, the game can move along and the players can simply worry about their characters and how they react to what happens to them in the game. Have players tell you what they want their characters to do, and translate that into game terms for them. Teach them how the rules work when they need to learn them, on a case-by-case basis. For example, if a player wants her wizard to cast a spell or the fighter wants to attack, the player tells you what the character attempts and you tell her what die to roll, which modifier or modifiers to add, and what happens as a result. After a few times, the player will know what to do without asking.

PROVIDING THE WORLD

The Dungeon Master is the creator of his or her own campaign world. Even if you use the standard D&D campaign setting or another published setting for the D&D game, it's still your world.

The setting is more than just a backdrop for the adventures, although it's that too. The setting is everything in the fictional world except for the PCs and the adventure plot. A well-designed and well-run world seems to go on around the PCs, so that they feel a part of something, instead of apart from it. Though the PCs are powerful and important, they should seem to be residents of some fantasy world that is ultimately larger than they are.

Consistency is the key to a believable fictional world. When they go back into town for supplies, the PCs ought to encounter some of the same NPCs they saw before. Soon, they'll learn the barkeep's name—and she'll remember them as well. Once you have achieved this level of consistency, however, provide an occasional change. If the PCs come back to buy more horses at the stables, have them discover that the man who ran the place went back home to the large city over the hills, and now his nephew runs the family business. That sort of change—one that has nothing to do with the PCs directly, but one that they'll notice—makes the players feel as though they're adventuring in a living world as real as themselves, not just a flat backdrop that exists only for them to delve its dungeons.

DETERMINING STYLE OF PLAY

The DM provides the adventure and the world. The players and the DM work together to create the game as a whole. However, it's your responsibility to guide the way the game is played. The best way to accomplish this is by learning what the players want and figuring out what you want as well. Many styles of play exist, but a few are detailed below as examples.

KICK IN THE DOOR

The PCs kick in the dungeon door, fight the monsters, and get the treasure. This style of play is straightforward, fun, exciting, and action-oriented. Very little time is spent on developing personas for the player characters, roleplaying noncombat encounters, and discussing situations other than what's going on in the dungeon.

In such a game, let the PCs face mostly clearly evil monsters and opponents and meet clearly good helpful NPCs (occasionally). Don't expect PCs to anguish over what to do with the prisoners, or whether it's right or wrong to invade and wipe out the bugbear lair. Don't bother too much with money or time spent in town. Do whatever it takes to get the PCs back into the action as quickly as possible. Character motivation need be no more developed than a desire to kill monsters and acquire treasure.

Rules and game balance are very important in this style of play. Characters with combat ability greater than that of their fellows lead to unfair situations in which the players of the overpowered characters can handle more of the challenges and thus have more fun. If you're using this style, be very careful about adjudicating rules and think long and hard about additions or changes to the rules before making them.

DEEP-IMMERSION STORYTELLING

The Free City of Greyhawk is threatened by political turmoil. The PCs must convince the members of the ruling council to resolve their differences, but can only do so after they have come to terms with their own differing outlooks and agendas. This style of gaming is deep, complex, and challenging. The focus isn't on combat but on talking, developing in-depth personas, and character interaction. Whole gaming sessions may pass without a single die being rolled.

In this style of game, the NPCs should be as complex and richly detailed as the PCs—although the focus should be on motivation and personality, not game statistics. Expect long digressions about what each player wants his or her character to do, and why. Going to a store to buy iron rations and rope can be as important an encounter as fighting orcs. (And don't expect the PCs to fight the orcs at all unless their characters are motivated to do so.) A character will sometimes take actions against his player's better judgment, because "that's what the *character* would do." Adventures deal mostly with negotiations, political maneuverings, and character interaction. Players talk about the "story" that they are collectively creating.

Rules become less important in this style. Since combat isn't the focus, game mechanics take a back seat to character development. Skills take precedence over combat bonuses, and even then the actual numbers often don't mean much. Feel free to change rules to fit the player's roleplaying needs. You may even want to streamline the combat system so that it takes less time away from the story.

SOMETHING IN BETWEEN

Most campaigns are going to fall between these two extremes. There's plenty of action, but there's a storyline and interaction as characters too. Players will develop their characters, but they'll be eager to get into a fight as well. Provide a nice mixture of roleplaying encounters and combat encounters. Even in a dungeon you can present NPCs that aren't meant to be fought but rather helped out, negotiated with, or just talked to.

OTHER STYLE CONSIDERATIONS

You should think about a few other style-related considerations.

Serious vs. Humorous: How serious you take things becomes an example of how serious the players take things. Jokes and silly remarks can make the game really fun, but they can also detract from the action. If you make funny comments during the game, expect that the players will, too.

Likewise, if you design adventures that are light-hearted, create NPCs that are slightly silly, or introduce embarrassing or humorous situations into the game, realize that it changes the tenor of the game. If the king of the land is a talking dog named Muffy or if the PCs have to find a *brassiere of elemental summoning* rather than a *brazier of elemental summoning*, don't expect anyone to take the game too seriously.

Overall, it's recommended that you play things straight. Don't intentionally insert jokes into the game. There'll be enough joshing around at the table already to keep the game fun. The in-game action should remain fairly serious (although an occasional funny moment is fine).

Naming Conventions: Related to how serious or humorous the game is, character names should be fairly uniform in style throughout the group. Although any character name is fine in and of itself, a group that includes Bob the Fighter, Aldrorius Killraven of Thistledown, and Runtboy as characters lacks the consistency to be credible.

Multiple Characters: You need to decide if each player is going to be limited to one character or can have more than one, and whether a player is allowed to actually run more than one character at the same time. Generally, it's best if you keep to one character per player. However, when players are few, you might allow them to run more than one character just to get the group size up to at least four characters.

ADJUDICATING

When everyone gathers around the table to play the game, you're in charge. That doesn't mean you can tell people what to do outside the boundaries of the game, but it does mean that you're the final arbiter of the rules within the game. Good players will always recognize that you have the ultimate authority over the game mechanics, even superseding something in a rulebook. Good DMs know not to change or overturn an existing rule without a good, logical justification so that the players don't grow dissatisfied (more on that later).

To carry out this responsibility, you need to know the rules. You're not required to memorize the rulebooks, but you should have a clear idea of what's in the rules, so that when a situation comes up that requires a ruling, you know where to reference the proper rule in the book.

Often a situation will arise that isn't explicitly covered by the rules. In such a situation, you need to provide guidance as to how it should be resolved. When you come upon an instance where there seems to be no rule to cover a situation, consider the following:

- Look to any similar situation that *is* covered in a rulebook. Try to extrapolate from what you see presented there and apply it to the current circumstance.
- If you have to make something up, stick with it for the rest of the campaign. (This is called a house rule.) Consistency keeps players satisfied and gives them the feeling that they adventure in a stable, predictable universe and not in some random, nonsensical place subject only to the DM's whims.
- When in doubt, remember this handy little rule: Favorable conditions add +2 to any d20 roll, and unfavorable conditions penalize the roll by –2. You'll be surprised how often this "DM's secret rule" will solve problems.

If you come upon an apparent contradiction in the rules, consider these factors when adjudicating:

- A rule in the *Player's Handbook*, *Monster Manual*, or DUNGEON MASTER'S GUIDE takes precedence over any other published D&D product. These three books are referred to as the core rulebooks. They form the basis of the whole game.
- A rule found in a rulebook overrules one found in a published adventure, unless the rule presented in the published adventure deals with something specific and limited to the adventure itself.
- Choose the rule that you like the best, then stick with it for the rest of the campaign. Consistency is a critical aspect of rules adjudication.

PROPELLING THE GAME EVER FORWARD

While all the players are responsible for contributing to the game, the onus must ultimately fall upon the DM to keep the game moving, maintain player interest, and keep things fun. Remember that keeping things moving is always more important than searching through rulebooks to find the exact details on some point or spending time in long debates over rules decisions.

Even a well-run game can get bogged down sometimes. Perhaps the players have been at it a while and are growing a little tired

The kick-in-the-door style of play.

of the same old thing. Maybe a playing session falls flat for no apparent reason. Sometimes this can't be helped—you're only human. In fact, occasionally you will find it's better to cancel a playing session or cut it short rather than have a poor experience that may set back the whole campaign.

However, there are ways to make an average playing session a memorable one or to spice up a poor one. For example, props can bring sparkling new life to a game. You can make fake parchment from normal paper, "aging" it by wetting it slightly with coffee or tea and then letting it dry to an uneven yellow. Toss in a few creases or small rips, and later when the PCs find a map or a message you can actually hand it to them. Old coins, tarot cards, a battered book in a foreign language, and the like all make wonderful handouts to get players into the spirit of the game.

Another type of visual aid is artwork. In all D&D products, you'll find wonderful fantasy illustrations. Pore through those products, or find a book cover or some other art source to provide you with a picture that fits something the PCs will encounter. Then, when the encounter comes to pass, pull out the picture and say, "This is what you see." While players' imaginations are fertile, sometimes seeing a depiction of something they encounter in the game—a character, a monster, or a place—makes the experience all the more exciting or real. Sometimes you can find illustrations in odd places. Jewelry catalogs can provide visual aids for some magical items or treasure, and sometimes a history book or encyclopedia with illustrations is just as good as or better than a fantasy book.

Of course, you can't always have a prop or a picture of some monster, NPC, or place that you have created. That's when you rely on the DM's best friend: the evocative, exciting description. Pepper your descriptions of what the characters see with adjectives and vivid verbs. Remember that you, and you alone, are the players' eyes and ears. "A dank, dark chamber with moss growing in cracks in the stone walls" is much more exciting than "a 10-foot-by-10-foot room." Throughout the game, continually ask yourself: What *exactly* do the characters see? Do they hear anything? Are there any noticeable odors? An unpleasant tang in the air? Do they feel the chill wind against their skin? Is their hair tousled by hot, damp gusts?

No player will forget a tense battle on a crumbling bridge in the middle of a thunderstorm. The best way to get the players' attention is with gripping action. While not every encounter needs to be life-threatening or earth-shaking, keep in mind how it would all seem in some action movie or exciting book. Villains shout epithets as they fight, and monsters roar menacingly. If a fight with gnolls is exciting, imagine how much more exciting a fight with gnolls on a ledge around a lava pit would be.

It's often a secondary consideration, but some DMs enjoy creating just the right atmosphere for their playing sessions. Music is often a good way to accomplish this. It's sort of like having a soundtrack for your game. Not surprisingly, those who enjoy using music in their games often use soundtracks from adventure movies, although classical, ambient, or other styles work well. Keep in mind, though, that some people find music distracting. Be receptive to what your players like—an atmosphere in which the players can't hear, are distracted, or aren't enjoying themselves is never a good one. Other ways DMs can create an atmosphere are with painted miniatures and dioramas, specially adjusted lighting, and even sound effects. (If the door to the room you are in squeaks, you may want to use that when the PCs open a dungeon door.)

Another element many DMs employ and many players enjoy is for the DM to use different voices when speaking "in character." Practicing several different accents or ways of speaking and assigning them to different NPCs can be a striking way to make those characters stand out in the players' minds.

Once in a while, a little miming of actions can supplement a game that otherwise exists only in your imagination. If an NPC is shriveled and stooped over when she walks, stand up and show the players exactly what you mean. When the ceiling above the PCs begins to collapse, slam your fists upon the table like falling rocks. If someone holds out his hand and offers something to a PC, mime the action—almost every time, the player (assuming the character takes what's offered) will follow your cue instinctively and reach out, miming the character's grasping whatever it is. You could even make a player whose character is invisible sit under the table to remind everyone that they can't see her, but her voice just comes out of nowhere. Keep in mind, though, that this sort of activity can quickly get out of hand. Don't act out your combats, or someone could get a black eye!

Finally, every once in a while, really surprise your players. The NPC they thought was a villain turns out to be a shapechanged unicorn with only the best of intentions. The clue they thought led to the treasure vault turns out to be a red herring (see page 13 for how surprises can overcome metagame thinking). If the PCs are in a dungeon room, and a fire giant is about to storm into the room and attack, keep your voice at a moderate or even soft level while describing the room. Then, suddenly, raise your voice and leap to your feet as the giant enters. That'll get their attention.

KEEPING GAME BALANCE

A lot of people talk about game balance. They refer to rules they like as "balanced," and rules that don't seem to work as "unbalanced." But what does that really mean? All game balance does is to ensure that most character choices are relatively equal. A balanced game is one in which one character doesn't dominate over the rest because of a choice that he or she made (race, class, skill, feat, spell, magic item, etc.). It also reflects that the characters aren't too powerful for the threats that they face, yet neither are they hopelessly overmatched.

Two factors drive game balance:

Good DM Management: A DM who carefully watches all portions of the game so that nothing gets out of his or her control helps keep the game balanced. PCs and NPCs, victories and defeats, awards and afflictions, treasure found and treasure spent—all these aspects must be monitored to maintain balance. No one character should ever become significantly greater than the others. If this does happen, the others should have an opportunity to catch up in short order. The PCs as a whole should never get so powerful that all the challenges become trivial to them. Nor should they be constantly overwhelmed by what they must face. It's no fun to always lose, and always winning gets boring fast. (These types of games are known as "killer dungeons" and "monty hauls," respectively.) When temporary imbalances do occur, it's easier to fix them by altering the challenges than by changing anything about the PCs and their powers or equipment. No one likes to get something (a new magic sword, for example), only to have it taken away again because it was too unbalancing.

Player–DM Trust: Players should trust the DM. Trust can be gained over time by consistent use of the rules, by not taking sides (that is, not favoring one player at another's expense), and by making it clear that you're not vindictive toward the players or the PCs. If the players trust you—and through you the game system—they will recognize that anything that enters the game has been carefully considered. If you adjudicate a situation, the players should be able to trust it as a fair call and not question or second-guess it. That way, the players can focus their attention on playing their characters, succeeding in the game, and having fun, trusting you to take care of matters of fairness and realism. They also trust that you will do whatever you can to make sure that they are able to enjoy playing their characters, can potentially succeed in the game, and will have fun. If this level of trust can be achieved, you will be much more free to add or change things in your game without worrying about the players protesting or scrutinizing every decision.

HANDLING UNBALANCED PCS

Sometimes, though, the unexpected will happen. The characters may defeat a villain, foiling what the villain (and you) thought was an unstoppable escape plan, and gain a *vorpal sword* that you never intended to fall into their hands. PCs entrusted to deliver an artifact to its rightful owner may decide to simply keep it instead. Or, even more likely, the combination of some new acquisition with an item or spell or power a character already has will prove unbalancing in a way you didn't foresee.

When a mistake is made, and a player character ends up too powerful, all is not yet lost. In fact, it's almost never difficult to simply increase the challenges that the character faces to keep him or her from breezing through encounters. However, this way of solving the problem can be unsatisfying, and it can mean that the encounters become too difficult for the other PCs. At the same time, as already noted, it's never fun to lose some aspect of your character (a new spell, a new item, a new power) that turns out to be unbalancing. From the player's point of view, it's not his or her fault.

You have two options:

Deal with the Problem In-Game: "In-game" is a term used to describe something that happens in the story created by the play of the game. For example, suppose a PC becomes unbalanced by using a *wish* spell to give herself the ability to cast all her prepared spells twice rather than once. (This should never happen with a *wish*, but DMs do make mistakes.) An in-game solution might be to have an enemy cleric use a *miracle* to rob her of that newfound ability. Whatever you do, try not to make it obvious that the situation is actually just a tool to balance the game. Instead, make it seem just a part of the adventure. (If you don't, indignant players will get very angry.)

Deal with the Problem Out-of-Game: "Out-of-game" means something that takes place in the real world but has an impact on the game itself. An out-of-game solution to the problem described in the last paragraph would be to take the player aside between sessions and explain that the game has become unbalanced because of her character—things need to change, or the game may fall apart. A reasonable person will see the value in continuing the game, and she'll work with you either in-game (perhaps donating a too-powerful item to an appropriate NPC guardian) or out-of-game (perhaps by erasing the unbalancing power from her character sheet and just pretending it was never there). Be warned, however, that not every gamer is reasonable. Many will hate this level of intrusion on your part and resent giving up a great ability or item their character "earned." Even if they don't tell you to forget it, they'll begrudge the loss. What's worse, after an unfortunate exchange of this type, it will seem obvious and contrived if you try to balance things with an in-game solution. Nobody said DMing was easy.

CHANGING THE RULES

Beyond simply adjudicating, sometimes you are going to want to change things. That's okay. However, changing the rules is a challenge for a DM with only a little experience.

ALTERING THE WAY THINGS WORK

Every rule in the *Player's Handbook* was written for a reason. That doesn't mean you can't change them for your own game. Perhaps your players don't like the way initiative is determined, or you find

that the rules for learning new spells are too limiting. Rules that you change for your own game are called house rules. Given the creativity of gamers, almost every campaign will, in time, develop its own house rules.

The ability to use the mechanics as you wish is paramount to the way roleplaying games work—providing a framework for you and the players to create a campaign. Still, changing the way the game does something shouldn't be taken lightly. If the *Player's Handbook* presents the rules, then throughout the DUNGEON MASTER's Guide you will find explanations for why those rules are the way they are. Read these explanations carefully, and realize the implications for making changes.

Consider the following questions when you want to change a rule:

- Why am I changing this rule?
  - Am I clear on how the rule that I'm going to change really works?
  - Have I considered why the rule existed as it did in the first place?
  - How will the change impact other rules or situations?
  - Will the change favor one class, race, skill, feat, etc., more than the others?
- Overall, is this change going to make more players happy or unhappy? (If the answer is "happy," make sure the change isn't unbalancing. If the answer is "unhappy," make sure the change is worth it.)

Often, players want to help redesign rules. This can be okay, since the game exists for the enjoyment of all its participants, and creative players can often find ways to fine-tune a rule. Be receptive to player concerns about mechanics. At the same time, however, be wary of players who intentionally or unintentionally want to change the rules just for their own benefit. The D&D game system is flexible, but it's also meant to be a balanced set of rules. Players may express a desire to have the rules always work in their favor, but the reality is that if there were no challenges for the characters, the game would quickly grow dull. Resist the temptation to change the rules just to please your players. Make sure that a change genuinely improves your campaign for everybody.

ADDITIONS TO THE GAME

As DM, you get to make up your own spells, magic items, races, and monsters! Your campaign might have a real need for a spell that turns foes to crystal, or a monster covered in dozens of tentacles that drains heat from living creatures. Adding new races, spells, monsters, and magic items can be a really entertaining and rewarding experience.

On the downside, an addition to the game can spoil game balance. As stated earlier, maintaining balance is an important DM responsibility. Most unbalancing factors are actually hasty or ill-considered DM creations. Don't let that happen to you.

One way to judge whether a new skill, feat, spell, or other option is balanced is to ask yourself, "If I add this to the game, is it so good that everyone will want to take it?" At the same time, ask yourself, "Is this so limited that no one will be interested in it?" Keep in mind that it's easier and more tempting to create something that's too good rather than not good enough. Watch yourself.

MAKING MISTAKES

A magic item that allows the characters to move through walls unhindered, giving them easy access to all sorts of places you do not want them to go (at least without great effort), is a mistake. A

4th-level spell that kills multiple foes with no saving throw is a mistake. A race with +4 Strength and +4 Dexterity bonuses is a mistake.

Usually, the mistakes that creep into a campaign are the ones that seem innocuous at first. A 1st-level spell creating a blast of wind that knocks a foe down appears to be fine—until a shrewd player starts using it to knock powerful opponents off the edges of cliffs. On the other hand, you'll know right away that you should never have put a *rod of disintegration* with unlimited uses in that treasure chest, or that you should never have allowed your players to convince you that the game would be more fun if critical hits multiplied all damage by five.

When things get unbalanced, you need to fix things either in-game or out-of-game, depending on the situation and the involved players' personalities. Unbalanced character abilities or items are best handled in-game, but rule changes can only be handled out-of-game. Sometimes it's best for you to admit to the players that you made a mistake, and now it needs to be fixed in order to keep the game fun, balanced, and running smooth. The more reasonable you are, the more likely your players are to be understanding.

RUNNING A GAME SESSION

After everything is prepared, and everyone sits down at the table, you're on. It's your show. Here are some points you should consider, while at the table and before you ever get there, to help the game run as smoothly as possible.

KNOWING THE PLAYERS

Normally, but not always, the DM is in charge of inviting players to play in his or her game. If this is the case, it's your responsibility to know and understand each of these people well enough that you can be reasonably sure that they'll all get along, work well together, and enjoy the sort of game you run.

A lot of this has to do with playing style. Ultimately, you have to know the kind of game your players want to play—and, with players new to the game or a newly formed group, this knowledge may take a while to emerge. Recognize that while you're in charge, it's really everybody's game—and that the players are all here, coming back session after session, because they trust that you'll help them have a fun and rewarding play experience.

Table Rules

One thing that will help everyone, players and DM alike, to all get along is establishing a set of rules—rules that having nothing to do with the actual game but that govern what happens with the people around the table.

The following are some table rules issues that you'll need to deal with eventually. It's best to come up with the answers before you start a regular campaign. You can establish these yourself, or you can work them out with your players.

Nonattending Players: Sometimes a regular player can't show up for a game session. The DM and group are faced with the question of what to do with his or her character. You have several choices:

- Someone else runs that character for the session (and thus runs two characters at once). This is easiest on you, but sometimes the fill-in player resents the task, or the replaced player is unhappy with what happens to the character in his or her absence.
- You run the character as though he or she were an NPC. This might actually be the best solution, but don't do it if running a character and running the game at the same time is too much for you and hurts the whole session.
- The character, like the player, can't be present for this adventure. This only works in certain in-game situations, but if it makes

sense for the character to be absent, that's a handy way to take the character out of the action for a game session. Ideally, the reason for the character's absence is one that allows him or her to jump back in with a minimum of fuss when the player is available again. (The character may have some other commitment, or she might fall victim to some minor disease, for instance.)
- The character fades into the background for this session. This is probably the least desirable solution, because it strains everyone's suspension of disbelief.

Recognize that players come and go. Someone will move away, another's regular life will become busier, and yet another will grow tired of the game. They'll quit. At the same time, new players will want to join in. Make sure always to keep the group at a size that you're comfortable with. The normal-sized group is probably around four players (with the DM as the fifth person). However, some groups are as small as two players, and others as large as eight or more. (Very large groups sometime use a non-player assistant who helps manage player actions, rules referencing, and NPCs to help the DM keep from getting bogged down.) You can also play the game one on one, with just one player and one DM, but that's a very different sort of play experience. (It's a good way to handle special missions such as a paladin's quest for her mount.)

If you can, try to find out from the players how long they're interested in playing, and try to get a modest commitment from them to show up on a regular basis during that time.

Integrating New Players: When someone new joins the campaign, his or her character needs to be integrated into the game (see Chapter 5: Campaigns). At the same time, the player needs to be integrated into the group. Make sure that a new player knows the house rules and the table rules as well as the game rules.

Dice Conventions: When someone makes a roll and the die lands on the floor, do you reroll it or use the die as it lies? What do you do with a die that lands cocked against a book? Are players required to make all die rolls where the DM can see them? There are no right or wrong answers to these questions, but deciding your group's answers ahead of time will save you from arguments later.

Book Use: It's best if no player can reference any book other than the *Player's Handbook* during a playing session. If you allow any other books to be used, establish this as a table rule.

Rules Discussions: It's probably best if players don't question your rulings or established rules, propose new house rules, or conduct discussions on other aspects of the game (aside from what's immediately at hand) during the game itself. Such matters are best addressed at the beginning or end of the session.

Jokes and Off-Topic Discussions: There are always funny things to be said, movie quotes, good gossip, and other conversations that crop up during the game, whether they're inspired by what's going on in the session or completely extraneous. Decide for yourself (and as a group) how much is too much. Remember that this is a game and people are there to have fun, yet at the same time keep the focus on the actions of the characters so the whole playing session doesn't pass in idle chat.

WORKING WITH PLAYERS

Two players want the same magic item. Each thinks his character can use it best or deserves it for what he's done. If the players can't find a way to decide who gets it, you will have to arbitrate or impose a solution. Or, worse, one player is angry with another player for something that happened earlier that day outside the game, so now his character tries to harass or even kill the other player's character. You shouldn't sit back and let this happen. It's up to you to step in and help resolve conflicts such as these. As DM, you're a sort of master of ceremonies as well as an umpire during the game. Talk with the arguing players together or separately outside the game session and try to resolve the conflict. Make it clear as nicely as you can that you can't let anyone's arguments ruin the game for the other players and that you won't tolerate real-world hard feelings affecting the way characters within the game react to each other.

If a player gets really mad when you rule against her, be firm but kind in telling her that you try your best to be fair and that you can't have angry outbursts spoiling everyone else's fun. Settle the matter outside the game session. Listen to her complaints, but remember that you're the final arbiter, and that by agreeing to play in your game she has also agreed to accept your decisions as DM. (See When Bad Things Happen to Good Characters, page 18.)

Sometimes one player's actions ruin the fun for everyone. An obnoxious, irresponsible, troublemaking player can make the game really unpleasant. Sometimes he gets others' characters killed because of his actions. Other times he stops the game altogether with arguments, tantrums, or off-topic conversations. Still other times he might keep everyone from playing by being late or not showing up at all. Ultimately, you should get rid of this player. Don't invite him next time. Don't play the D&D game with someone whom you wouldn't enjoy spending time with in another social setting.

Decide how many players you want in your game, and stick with that decision. If someone leaves, try to get a new player. If someone new wants to join an already full group, resist the urge to let him or her in unless you're sure you can handle the increased number of players. If you have too many players, consider dividing them into two groups that play at different times. If you have too few, you might want to recruit more or have each player play more than one character. (It's good to have at least four characters in an adventuring party.) As a rule of thumb, four to six players is best, although how many you can handle is up to you. Remember that the more players around the table, the harder it will be for you to keep track of everyone and the less time each individual player gets for his or her character's actions.

If one player dominates the game and monopolizes your time with her character's actions, the other players will quickly grow dissatisfied. Make sure everyone gets his or her turn. Also, make sure each player gets to make his or her own decisions. (Overeager or overbearing players sometimes try to tell the others what to do.) If one player insists on controlling everything, talk to him outside the game session and explain that his actions are making things less fun for everyone.

METAGAME THINKING

"I figure there'll be a lever on the other side of the pit that deactivates the trap," a player says to the others, "because the DM would never create a trap that we couldn't deactivate somehow." That's an example of metagame thinking. Any time the players base their characters' actions on logic that depends on the fact that they're playing a game, they're using metagame thinking. This should always be discouraged, because it detracts from real roleplaying and spoils the suspension of disbelief.

Surprise your players by foiling metagame thinking. Suppose there is a lever on the other side of the pit, for example, but it's rusted and useless. Keep your players on their toes, and don't let them second-guess you. Tell them to think in terms of the game world, not in terms of you as the DM. In the game world, someone made the trap in the dungeon for a purpose. Figure out the reasons for what they have done, and the PCs will need to do the same.

In short, when possible you should encourage the players to employ in-game logic. Confronted with the situation given above, an appropriate response from a clever character is "I figure there'll be a lever on the other side of the pit that deactivates the trap, because the gnomes who constructed the trap must have a means to deactivate it." In fact, this is wonderful—it shows smart thinking as well as respect for the verisimilitude of the game world.

KNOWING THE PCS

One advantage that you always have over a professional writer designing an adventure is that you know your players. You know what they like, what they're likely to do, what their capabilities are, and what's going on in your campaign right now. That's why even when you use a published adventure, you'll want to work to ensure that it gets integrated into your campaign properly.

A good DM will always know the following facts about the characters in his or her game:

The Characters' Basic Statistics: This includes class, race, level, hit points, save and attack bonuses, spells, and special abilities. You should be able to look at a monster's hp, AC, and special qualities and be able to judge whether it's a fitting challenge. Compare, for example, the monster's AC with the attack bonuses of the characters in the group—particularly the fighters. When you figure average rolls, can the fighters hit the creature? Do they need above-average rolls? (If so, the challenge will be great.) Do they need a natural 20? (If so, the challenge is almost certainly too difficult.)

CONSIDERATIONS FOR RUNNING THE GAME

The following items are available to enhance your game. They're not for everyone, however.

DM Screen: This is a cardstock screen that stands up on the table between you and the players. It has useful tables and rules reminders on it to speed play. You can also paperclip notes to yourself to it, so you can see them but the players can't. Behind this screen, you can put your maps and notes on the table, and roll dice where the players can't see what you're doing. The only drawback is that a screen creates a wall between you and the players, which can be distancing. DMs who wish to have the information on the screen handy but don't want to set themselves apart from the players sometimes lay the screen flat on the table in front of them, hiding adventure notes underneath.

Computers: There are many reasons to have a computer with you at the table. You can keep all your notes and maps in electronic files easily searched and referenced during the game. There are special DM utility programs that manage NPCs, PCs, monsters, treasure, and other types of information. Some will create random encounters, generate characters, and even generate random numbers. Not all roleplaying groups like them, however, because of the tendency of a computer to draw the DM's attention away from the players and the game. If you find yourself staring at the screen more than at your players, consider scaling back the computer's in-game use and restrict it to generating material between sessions.

Miniatures: Metal or plastic figures can be used to represent characters, monsters, and scenery in the game. You can use them on a grid to show ranges, tactical movement, line of sight, and areas of spell effects. (A vinyl mat with a grid that you can write on with wipe-off markers is especially useful.) Even without a grid, you can use miniatures to show marching order and relative position, or you can use a 1-inch-to-5-feet scale to handle tabletop distances precisely. Sometimes position in combat means the difference between life and death, and miniatures help everyone agree on characters' and creatures' positions. In addition, painting miniatures is fun in its own right. With a little luck, players can usually find miniatures that are posed the way their characters would stand and then paint them so that they match their characters even better.

Counters: If you're not as interested in the visual aspect of miniatures but find the tactical opportunities interesting, you can use any sorts of counters to represent characters and monsters: poker chips, checkers, coins, scraps of paper—anything you want.

Examine the attack bonus of the monster. Look at the damage it can deal. When you compare these pieces of information to the ACs and hit points of the PCs, will the monster be able to hit or seriously damage the characters? Will it almost certainly kill one? If the monster's attack bonus added to an average d20 roll hits the character's AC, and the average damage dealt is more than the PC's total hp, the monster will kill the character. When you look at the save DCs for the monster's special attacks, are the characters likely to successfully resist the attack?

These sorts of questions and analyses allow you to judge monsters, encounters, and adventures and determine whether they are appropriate for your group. Challenge Rating assignments for such things will help, but no one knows your group of characters like you do. (See Chapter 7: Rewards for details about Challenge Ratings.)

Keep an up-to-date record of all the characters, their abilities, spells, hp, AC, etc. One way to do this is to require the players to give you a new copy of their character sheet whenever it changes. This information is helpful to you for balancing encounters and monitoring hit point loss and spell depletion during play. It's also very handy if a player can't make it to a session, enabling you to simply hand the character sheet to whoever is running the character for that session.

The Players' Likes and Dislikes: Some groups hate political intrigue and avoid or ignore it in favor of going down into the dungeon. Other groups are more likely to run from a serious combat challenge. Some groups like adventures with mind flayers and psionics. Some don't. Because of this, you're the best judge, if you're aware of what the group likes and what entices them, whether they will like and partake in a particular encounter or adventure.

For example, a DM might find that the lure of gold motivates the PCs in her group. She knows, then, that in order to get them involved in the adventure she has designed (or purchased), there has to be some treasure involved, and the PCs need to know about it ahead of time. Another group, however, might be interested in heroic deeds. They don't care about money, but if they hear that the duchy's in danger from a storm-controlling wizard, they're off to stop him in a flash.

Nothing's more frustrating for a DM than to create an adventure and provide the PCs with the hook that will bring them into the action, only to have them ignore or even consciously reject it. No one wants to see his or her adventure go unplayed. Know what interests and motivates the group, and you'll be able to avoid this disheartening possibility.

What's Going on in the Campaign: This is an easy one. Since you're managing the events in the game, you need to keep track of what's going on anyway. In this case it's important to always know what the characters are doing and a little about their plans. If the PCs want to leave the area and head into the mountains to find one of the characters' old mentors, you need to keep that in mind when preparing that session's adventure and in planning ahead for future sessions.

Keep a record of everything that's going on in the game. A timeline can help you keep track of when events happened in relation to each other (especially handy for monitoring the activities of recurring villains). Above all, make sure you always have a good grasp of NPCs' names (particularly ones you're forced to make up in the middle of the game) so that the king's name doesn't change abruptly from session to session. And of course you should remember what the PCs have accomplished, where they have been, enemies they have made, and so forth.

KNOWING THE ADVENTURE AND OTHER MATERIALS

You're running the game, so you have to know everything. Well, maybe not everything, but certainly enough to keep things moving. If you know the PCs want to head into the

mountains, it's helpful if, ahead of time, you have looked into how mountain travel affects their movement, what it's like to be in the mountains (possibly through some research in an encyclopedia or travel book), and other considerations (climbing gear, mountain encounters, etc.). If you have a chance to try rock climbing, or if you've done it before, so much the better—there's nothing like personal experience to lend realism to your descriptions.

More to the point, however, you will want to have prepared as much as you can for the adventure ahead of time. You will want to have figured out what will happen when, the layout of the area (both the large-scale landscape and individual encounter areas), what the PCs will encounter if they go to a particular area, how NPCs encountered in the adventure will react to the PCs, and the events likely to happen (such as a conversation or a fight).

When running a published adventure, this preparation often amounts to reading the material carefully and making notes where you need them. Useful points to note might include any or all of the following:

- Page numbers in the rulebook for rules you know you'll need to reference in a given encounter.
- Changes needed to make the adventure fit into your campaign.
- Changes you want to make to please your tastes or those of your group.
- Preplanned actions you want the NPCs to take in a given encounter (ambushes, dying speeches, spell sequences, etc.).
- Reminders to yourself about rules, adventure structure, events that might occur (such as random encounter checks), or the consequences of certain actions.

If you are designing an adventure on your own, your preparation requires (obviously) a lot more time. This preparation might include any or all of the following elements:

- Maps of the area (large scale) and of specific smaller areas where encounters are likely to occur. These can be as simple and sketchy or as detailed as you like.
- A key to the map or maps detailing special areas and what might be encountered there, including foes, allies, treasure, traps, environmental situations, and possibly even written descriptions of what the PCs see, hear, and experience upon entering an area.
- NPC listings that include their statistics and notes on their potential reactions.
- Bookmarks in the rulebooks (or notes listing page numbers) for rules that might need to be referenced.
- Notes on the overall story or plot of the adventure if it is complex.
- Statistics for any new monsters you're introducing.

This preparation can amount to a lot of work. Not every adventure is going to require reams of notes in order to play. It varies from adventure to adventure and from DM to DM. Not every DM likes to prepare detailed notes ahead of time. Some have more fun if they just "wing it." And sometimes a DM would like to be better prepared, but there just isn't time. Find the style of Dungeon Mastering that suits you best.

KNOWING THE RULES

If you know that the tactical aerial rules will be needed to play out the battle where the PCs are mounted on griffons and the gargoyles attack them, review those rules before playing. When rules less often used come into play in the course of the adventure, it slows things down if you have to reread them in the midst of a game. Looking over commonly used rules—such as descriptions for spells you know NPCs or PCs have prepared, or even the basic combat rules—before a game session is always a good idea.

When a player has a rules question, you should be the one best able to answer the question. Mastery of the rules is one reason why the DM is sometimes called the referee.

No matter how well you know the rules, though, a player might remember some point that didn't occur to you. Most players, quite properly, won't lord it over you if they know some rules better than you do. If someone else at the table corrects your recollection of a rule or adds some point you hadn't thought of, thank that player for his help. When people cooperate to make the game better, everyone benefits.

SETTING THE STAGE

It's worth stating again: Once the game starts, it's all up to you. The players are likely to take their cues from you on how to act and react. If you handle the game seriously, they'll be more likely to take it seriously. If you come across with a more relaxed, light-hearted tone, they will crack a few jokes and make side comments of their own. You make the game the way you want it to be.

Recapping

"Last time, you had just discovered the entrance to the lair of the basilisk and learned that a tribe of goblins living nearby apparently worships the creature like a god. You were near the end of your fifth day of traveling through the Thangrat Forest. Mialee the wizard had suffered a great wound while fighting the initial goblin scouts. Krusk wanted to go straight to the goblin's camp and deal with them then and there, but the rest of you talked him into helping you find a suitable place to make a safe and

Adventurers make careful plans regarding their next adventure.

defensible camp. The goblins, meanwhile, were obviously preparing for a fight, based on the sounds you had heard earlier that day. Now, as the sun sets beyond the distant mountains, it seems as though the basilisk itself is stirring within its lair. What do you do?"

In the middle of an ongoing campaign, recapping activity from the previous session (or sessions) at the start of a new session often helps establish the mood and remind everyone what was going on. It can be frustrating to DM and players alike that while in the game the characters continue what they were just doing, in real life the players have lived several days of real time between then and now. They might have forgotten important details that will affect their decisions if they don't get reminders.

Of course, that means that you need to keep notes of what happens so that you don't forget either. At the very least, jotting down a few sentences about what was going on at the very end of a game session and leaving them somewhere where you'll find them right away at the beginning of the next session is always a good idea. You may find that you tend to think about the game between sessions more than the players do, and thus you have a better grasp of the events. You'll quickly get to the point where you won't forget what has happened in past sessions, especially since the adventures you're working on now will often be building off those events.

Describing

Remember that while good description is key to the players' understanding (see page 10), mood is as important as scene. Emotion is as important as sensory data. Tell the players how everything feels. If they have a question, answer it. If their characters don't know the answer, ask them how they're going to go about finding it out.

When only one character experiences something, take him or her aside and describe it to only

Illus. by K. Walker

15

Illus. by W. Reynolds

that player. If she's a scout sent ahead, she'll have to come back and report in her own words what she saw. The other players will then have to see it through her eyes, based on what she chooses to tell them. Of course, occasionally it's okay to describe one character's experience in front of the whole group. Minor details such as what a magic potion tastes like or what one character sees under the bed are probably inconsequential enough to tell everyone.

Such minor details are not inconsequential enough to ignore or forget, though. Don't describe only the important information, or the players will quickly catch on, and the very act of your describing something will give them a clue to its importance. Throw in a few trifling details here and there for flavor as well as to keep them guessing.

Don't prompt their actions. Don't say, "Do you look in the alcove?" At most, say, "Where do you look?" Prompting can give away too much.

For more on describing action, see Chapter 3: Running the Game.

Dungeon Mastering well requires a solid foundation of planning, just like building a castle.

Mapping

If one of the players is drawing a map when the characters explore a new place (and someone should be mapping), give her a break. Describe the layout of the place in as much detail as she wants, including dimensions of rooms. Be willing to repeat a description if needed or even make a rough sketch of the outline of an area.

There are, of course, exceptions to this rule. When the PCs are lost or in a maze, the whole point of the scenario is that they don't know where they are. In cases like these, don't take pains to help the mapper. If they're sneaking through a maze and they get the map wrong, it's all the more fun when they have to backtrack.

SETTING THE PACE

The pace of the game determines how much time you spend on a given activity or action taken by the characters. Different players enjoy different paces. Some pick up every copper piece, some learn it's not worth the game time. Some roleplay every encounter, while some want to skip on to the "good bits."

Do your best to please the group, but when in doubt, keep things moving. Don't feel that it's necessary to play out rest periods, replenishing supplies, or carrying out daily tasks. Sometimes that level of detail is an opportunity to develop characters, but most of the time it's unimportant.

You should decide ahead of time, if possible, how long the playing session will last. This not only allows everyone to make plans around the game but also enables you to judge about how much time is left and pace things accordingly—you should always end a session at a good stopping point (see Ending Things, below). Three to four hours is a good length for an evening game. Some people like to play longer sessions, usually on a weekend. Even if you

normally play for shorter periods, sometimes it's fun to run a longer, "marathon" session.

Referencing Rules

Try to look at the rules as little as possible during a game. While the rulebooks are here to help you, paging through a book can slow things down. Look when necessary (and mark things you'll need to refer to again with a bookmark), but recall a rule from memory when you can. You may not be perfectly correct in your recollection, but the game keeps moving.

Asking Questions

Don't be afraid to stop and ask important questions. If the players seem bored, ask if they would like you to skip ahead or pick up the pace. If you're unsure how they want to handle a situation, ask.

And make sure you ask what their goals are, both in the short term and the long term. The answers to these questions help you prepare adventures and encounters for next time. Remember that some players might want to keep their characters' goals a secret from other PCs in the group, so it's sometimes best to ask the players individually, outside the play session or at least away from the table.

Taking Breaks

When you finish up a lengthy combat encounter or a tension-filled scene, take a break. Particularly in a long playing session, establish a few breaks for food, drinks, trips to the bathroom, or just a little time to relax. During this time, you can take your mind off things for a few minutes, or you can begin to prepare for the coming encounter.

PROVIDING THE ACTION

The players look to you for news of what's going on in the world around their characters as well as for information about what happens when their characters take actions. You have to provide all the answers.

Handling PC Actions

When a player tells you what her character does, give her the result of her action as quickly as possible. Once in a while, it adds tension to leave a player hanging, but that's the exception, not the rule. If a character wants to do something not covered in the rules, do your best to extrapolate from the existing rules to decide how best to handle the unusual situation (see Adjudicating, page 9).

Encourage the players not to slow things down by taking a long time to decide what to do. A character who pauses too long when it's his turn slows things down for everyone. Give him a time limit (such as 30 seconds) when necessary.

The most important point to remember regarding character actions is that each player controls his or her own character. Don't force a character to take a specific action (unless the character is magically compelled). Don't tell a player how his or her character feels about things. Even if an NPC with a high Charisma attempts to persuade a character, no mere die roll should force a character's action (it can, however, foil a Sense Motive skill check). When running an NPC, feel free to lie, trick, cajole, or malign a character, but don't use your authority as Dungeon Master to usurp character control from a player.

Handling NPC Actions

Normally, NPCs should obey all the same rules as PCs. Occasionally, you might want to fudge the rules for them in one way or another (see below), but in general, NPCs should live and die—fail and succeed—by the dice, just as PCs do.

Be as quick—or quicker—to decide what the NPCs do on their turn as the players are when deciding the PCs' actions. To keep things moving, be ready ahead of time with what each given NPC will do. (Since you know ahead of time that the encounter is coming, you can prepare better than the players can.) Jot down NPC strategies right alongside their game statistics.

Still, NPCs are people too. Don't let it be obvious to the players that a particular character is "just an NPC," implying that what he or she does isn't as smart or important as what a PC does. While that might be true, it shouldn't *seem* to be true. In order to make the game world seem real, the people who populate it should act real.

DETERMINING OUTCOMES

You're the arbiter of everything that happens in the game. Period.

Rolling Dice

Some die rolls, when seen by a player, reveal too much. A player who rolls to see if her character finds a trap and sees that she has rolled very poorly knows that the information you give her as a result of the roll is probably unreliable. ("Nope. No traps down that way, as far as you can tell.") The game is much more interesting when the player of a character trying to hide or move silently doesn't know whether the character has succeeded.

In cases where the player shouldn't know the die result, make the roll yourself, keeping dice behind a screen or otherwise out of sight. While this takes some of the fun of rolling dice away from the players (and let's face it, that really is a part of the fun of the game), it helps you to maintain an accurate control on what the player knows and doesn't know.

Consider making the following skill checks for the player where he or she can't see the result:

Bluff
Diplomacy
Hide
Listen
Move Silently
Rope Use
Search
Spot

Do this on a case-by-case basis. When possible, always let the players make the rolls themselves. When it would increase suspense to keep them in the dark, roll the dice yourself.

DCs, ACs, and Saving Throws

Don't tell a player what he needs to roll to succeed. Don't tell him what all the modifiers are to the roll. Instead, tell the players that keeping track of all those things is your job. Then, when they roll the dice, tell them whether they succeed or fail.

This is important so that players focus on what their characters are doing, not on the numbers. It's also a way to hide the occasional DM cheat (see below).

DM Cheating and Player Perceptions

Terrible things can happen in the game because the dice just go awry. Everything might be going fine, when suddenly the players

---

HANDY DM SCRATCH PAPER TRICKS

Here's some advice about what to do with scratch paper during a game.

Combat Matrix: When running a battle, create a quick matrix like the following:

	1	2	3
Arnon	x		*Bless ends*
Barg	x		
Orcs	x		
Skeletons			

The names in the left column are the names of the PCs and NPCs, listed in initiative order (Arnon goes first, Barg goes second, etc.), while the headings across the top are rounds. Space out the names a bit so you can add or move a name if need be. Check characters off (put an "X" in the proper column) as they take their turns each round. In the above example, Arnon, Barg, and the orcs have taken their actions in the first round of the combat. This type of impromptu chart is also handy to keep track of facts such as spell durations (note the entry above for "*Bless ends*" in the column corresponding to the third round).

Wing-It Sheet: Create a "wing-it" sheet. The wing-it sheet stays with your other notes until you need it. On it are items that you might need on the spot to help run the game. Handy DM lifesavers include the following:

- A list of twenty random names. Sometimes, you need to come up with minor characters on the spot, ones you hadn't realized the PCs would interact with. Players pay more attention to "Shalako, captain

of the watch" than just "the captain of the watch." The list lets you quickly give names—and hence potential importance—to each person, town, river, or whatever that the party encounters. Names make things real.

- A more or less random flowchart-style diagram. Imagine a bunch of blank circles with random lines connecting them. When the characters are pursued into the forest, you have a map that works for the chase scene. It works as a cave network, sewer plans, crowded city streets, the diagram of a spur-of-the-moment organization, or even the levels of a villain's plot.

- A few random magic items, spells, or monsters that you haven't used much in your campaign lately, for when you need some new encounter or idea on the fly.

Log Sheet: Start each game session with a blank sheet of paper. Record the date of the session and any starting conditions for the session (the game year, season, etc.). Record PC names on the sheet so that you have them handy and can call each player by his or her character's name. Then, as events happen in the game, make notes on the log sheet. You can keep track of hit points, special conditions such as poison and disease, and other important reminders. At the end of the session you have a sheet of paper that, while not a bona fide log, helps you remember details. You can three-hole-punch the sheet and put it in a binder with all the others from other game sessions, thus creating a file you can refer to later.

If you use graph paper for this sheet, you can mark off squares for timekeeping. Use a slash for a half hour and cross the slash off to make an X for an hour. You can also outline the square corresponding to the time when a spell duration expires.

have a run of bad luck. A round later, half the party's down for the count and the other half almost certainly can't take on the foes that remain. If everyone dies, the campaign might very well end then and there, and that's bad for everyone. Do you stand by and watch them get slaughtered, or do you "cheat" and have the foes run off, or fudge the die rolls so that the PCs still miraculously win in the end? There are really two issues at hand.

Do you cheat? The answer: The DM really *can't* cheat. You're the umpire, and what you say goes. As such, it's certainly within your rights to sway things one way or another to keep people happy or keep things running smoothly. It's no fun losing a long-term character from getting run over by a cart. A good rule of thumb is that a character shouldn't die in a trivial way because of some fluke of the dice unless he or she was doing something really stupid at the time.

However, you might not feel that it's right or even fun unless you obey the same rules the players do. Sometimes the PCs get lucky and kill an NPC you had planned to have around for a long time. By the same token, sometimes things go against the PCs, and disaster may befall them. Both the DM and the players take the bad with the good. That's a perfectly acceptable way to play, and if there's a default method of DMing, that's it.

Just as important an issue, however, is whether the players realize that you bend the rules. Even if you decide that sometimes it's okay to fudge a little to let the characters survive so the game can continue, *don't let the players in on this decision*. It's important to the game that they believe their characters are always in danger. Consciously or subconsciously, if they believe you'll never let bad things happen to their characters, they'll change the way they act. With no element of risk, victory will seem less sweet. And if thereafter something bad *does* happen to a character, the player may believe you're out to get him if he feels you saved other players when their characters were in trouble.

When Bad Things Happen to Good Characters

Characters suffer setbacks, lose magic items, gain ability score penalties, lose levels, and die (sometimes repeatedly). Unfortunate events are part of the game, almost as much as success, gaining levels, earning treasure, and attaining greatness. But players don't always take it well when something bad happens to their characters.

Remind players that sometimes bad things happen. Challenges are what the game's all about. Point out that a setback can be turned into an opportunity to succeed later. If a character dies, encourage the other players (perhaps subtly) to have their characters get the dead character *raised*. If this proves not to be an option, reassure the player of the dead character that there are lots of opportunities in new character types she hasn't yet tried. A bard somewhere will pen a ballad about the fallen character's heroic demise even as the group welcomes her new PC. The game goes on.

It's rare but quite possible that an entire party can be wiped out. In such a case, don't let this catastrophe end the whole game. NPC adventurers might find the PCs and have them *raised*, putting the PCs deeply in their debt (an adventure hook if ever there was one). The players can create a temporary party for the purpose of retrieving the bodies of the fallen adventurers for *raising* or at least honorable burial. Or, everyone can roll up new characters and

start anew. Even that's not really so bad—in fact, it's an opportunity for a dramatic change of pace.

ENDING THINGS

Try not to end a game session in the middle of an encounter. Leaving everything hanging is a terrible note to end on. It's difficult to keep track of information such as initiative order, spell durations, and other round-by-round details between sessions. The only exception to this guideline is when you end a session with a cliffhanger. A cliffhanger ending is one in which the story pauses just as something monumental happens, some surprising turn of events occurs, or just as things get good. The purpose is to keep players intrigued and excited until the next session.

If someone was missing from a session and you had her character leave the party for a while, make sure that there's a way to work her character back in when she returns. Sometimes a cliffhanger can serve this purpose—the PC comes racing into the thick of things like the cavalry to help out her beleaguered friends.

Allow some time—a few minutes will do—at the end to have everyone discuss the events of the session. Listen to their reactions and secretly learn more of what they like and don't like. Reinforce what you thought were good decisions and smart actions on their parts (unless such information gives too much away for the adventure). Always end things positively.

You may want to award experience points at the end of each session, or you might wait until the end of each adventure. That's up to you. However, the standard is to give them out at the end of each session, so players whose characters go up a level have time to choose new spells, buy skills, and take care of other details related to level advancement.

GAME SESSION CHECKLIST

1. Set up the play area. Even if the game's not occurring at your house, you should set up things so that you're happy with where you're sitting and where the players are sitting. You need to have enough room to lay out your notes and books, and so forth. Make sure everyone can hear and see you.
2. Make sure everyone is familiar (or refamiliarized) with his or her character and the current situation.
3. Get a volunteer to keep a map and/or take notes.
4. Determine the marching order of the characters—in general, where they will be in relation to each other during the adventure, so it's always clear who is where. This information can be written down or displayed with miniatures or counters.
5. Describe the initial scene.
6. Ask the players what their characters do.
7. Run through all the events and encounters of the adventure (or that session's portion of the adventure), taking a few breaks as needed.
8. Bring things to a good stopping point or a suitable cliffhanger.
9. End the session.
10. Ask the players what they plan to do next time.
11. Award experience points. Alternatively, this can be done at the beginning of the next session, or once every few sessions (see Chapter 7: Rewards).

A warrior's armor can consist of metal, wood, bone or leather. Anything that will deflect a physical assault.

The magic user is partially protected with anything that is light and offers a degree of deflection.

helmet

neck guard

long bow

A spell casters defence can be from various schools of magic.

ioun stone

crossbow

quiver of arrows

The shield is usually made os metal and wood, and can stop physical damage.

shield

case of bolts

scale mail

Illus. by A. Savekel

C haracters, obviously, are the purview of the players, not the Dungeon Master. That said, however, you can have a lot of influence on the options that players have when creating or advancing their characters. If you want to allow drow and minotaur PCs, that's fine, but you might need a little advice to help you keep such options manageable.

ABILITY SCORES GENERATION

In addition to the standard method for generating ability scores presented on page 7 in the *Player's Handbook* (roll 4d6, discard the lowest die, and arrange as desired), here are eight optional variants you might want to consider using in your campaign:

Organic Characters: Roll 4d6 six times, discarding the lowest die each time. Place in order (Strength, Dexterity, Constitution, Intelligence, Wisdom, and Charisma) as rolled. Reroll any one ability of your choice, taking the new roll if it's higher. Then switch any two ability scores. This method allows some choice but doesn't let a player have all her ability scores exactly where she wants them. A character might have to learn to cope with unwanted clumsiness (just like in real life), or she may have a personal talent that isn't usual in her class (such as a high Strength score for a sorcerer).

Customized Average Characters: Roll 3d6 six times and arrange as desired. This method produces characters more like average people but still allows customization. The player may reroll all abilities if his ability modifiers total –3 or lower, or if he doesn't have any scores of 12 or better.

Random Average Characters: Roll 3d6 six times and place in order (Strength, Dexterity, Constitution, Intelligence, Wisdom,

Charisma). This is the strictest method. It frequently generates virtually unplayable characters, but it makes high scores very special. The player may reroll all abilities if her ability modifiers total –3 or lower, or if she doesn't have any scores of 12 or better.

High-Powered Characters: Roll 5d6 six times, discarding the two lowest dice each time. Arrange as desired. This is just right for a high-powered game where the characters need to be really good just to survive. The player may reroll all abilities if his ability modifiers don't total at least +2 or if he doesn't have at least one score of 15 or better.

The Floating Reroll: Roll 4d6 six times, discarding the lowest die each time. Once during this process, the player can reroll the lowest die instead. Arrange scores as desired. This results in slightly better characters than the default method, allowing players to either improve a particularly bad score or to obtain a very good score. For example, if the player rolled 4d6 and got the results 1, 2, 6, and 6 for a score of 15, she might choose to reroll the 1 to see if she could improve the score (and possibly even get an 18 if the reroll came up a 6).

Standard Point Buy: All abilities start at 8. Take 25 points to spread out among all abilities. For ability scores up to 14, you buy them on a 1-for-1 basis. For abilities above 14, it costs a little more (see Table 2–1: Point Costs for Ability Scores). This method allows for maximum customization, but you should expect each PC to have at least one really good score.

lethal through armor at short ranges.

TABLE 2–1: ABILITY SCORE POINT COSTS

Ability Score	Point Cost	Ability Score	Point Cost
9	1	14	6
10	2	15	8
11	3	16	10
12	4	17	13
13	5	18	16

Nonstandard Point Buy: Use Table 2–1: Point Buy Costs for Ability Scores from the standard point buy method, but the player has fewer or more points for buying scores, as shown on Table 2–2:

TABLE 2–2: ABILITY SCORE NONSTANDARD POINT COSTS

Type of Campaign	Points Allowed
Low-powered campaign	15 points
Challenging campaign	22 points
Tougher campaign	28 points
High-powered campaign	32 points

Default Array: Use the following scores, arranged as desired: 15, 14, 13, 12, 10, and 8. This method is a faster version of the standard point buy method and is good for creating NPCs quickly.

RACES

Sometimes, people are going to want to play cat people, ogres, or drow elves instead of the races in the *Player's Handbook*. The races presented in the *Player's Handbook* provide a great many options for players to choose from, but some DMs want to offer more or different choices, particularly after playing the game for a while. New choices can please the players and give your campaign a unique flavor. An easy way to customize a campaign is to change the races that players can choose from when creating characters.

SUBRACES

Tall, slim halflings are called tallfellows. Sylvan elves are reclusive, tough elves who live in the woods. Mountain dwarves are even sturdier than their more common counterparts. These offshoots of the standard races are called subraces.

The standard D&D character races are divided into subraces to showcase slight differences in appearance, outlook, and adaptation. Other than a few minor differences, members of a subrace resemble members of the race as described in the *Player's Handbook*. Subraces make player choices varied and interesting, but you might also want to create subraces that are limited to NPCs only. A good way to introduce a subrace into the campaign is to create an NPC encounter with the existing characters. By introducing a subrace as an NPC, you demonstrate to the players how you see members of that subrace. Sometimes, players are not interested in playing a new subrace but still appreciate its advent as a new and interesting aspect of your campaign. The major subraces for the *Player's Handbook* races are found under the appropriate entries in the *Monster Manual*.

You also might choose not to allow PCs of subraces. After all, subraces tend to stray from the archetypal races in the *Player's Handbook*, and they complicate the otherwise simple (but important) racial choices. Some of those presented in the *Monster Manual*, such as the drow, duergar, and other evil kinds of creatures, might be inappropriate to your game. The drow, duergar, and svirfneblin might also be too powerful in relation to the other PC race choices.

One consideration you should keep in mind is maintaining a baseline. You might be tempted to drop the standard dwarf altogether in favor of a campaign containing deep dwarves, duergar, derro, mountain dwarves, and any dwarven subraces you add. The advantage to maintaining a common baseline and keeping "just

dwarves" among the choices is that it provides players with a simple choice right out of the *Player's Handbook*. They do not have to look at any other source for information about their character's race unless they want to. While many players eventually appreciate advanced options, a good DM keeps a few choices simple for those who want to concentrate their attention elsewhere.

To create a new subrace, think of a specific aspect of deviation—culture, climate, or physical stature. Then, as you look at the *Player's Handbook* description of the standard race, determine what changes that deviation would cause to this description. A subrace might have different ability score modifications, different free skills (or a +1 or +2 racial bonus to certain skill checks), a different favored class, different languages, or even different special abilities, such as the dwarf's poison resistance or the elf's skill with a bow.

Keep in mind that the standard races have disadvantages to balance their advantages. A subrace should not have a bonus to Strength and a negative adjustment to Charisma without some additional considerations, since Strength is so much more important (in general) than Charisma. Instead, that dwarven subrace you create might have a +2 to Strength and a –2 to Charisma if it also lacks the standard dwarf's darkvision and stonecunning abilities. Alternatively, your dwarven subrace could have +2 to Strength, +2 to Constitution, –2 to Dexterity, –2 to Charisma, low-light vision rather than darkvision, and +2 to Climb checks rather than the stonecunning ability.

In general, strive for balance. Balance an ability score bonus with an equivalent ability score penalty (see Table 2–7: Ability Score Equivalencies). Replace a skill bonus with a bonus to a different skill, a free skill with a different free skill, and a special ability (such as saving throw bonuses or darkvision) with another relatively equal ability. The range of different abilities and skill modifications is great, so you're on your own in finding the perfect mix for your campaign. Look to the subraces in the *Monster Manual* for good examples, and consider the following variations:

Subterranean: Underground-dwelling versions of the standard races might possess darkvision, stonecunning, and a different set of racial enemies. An elf's familiarity with the bow—a weapon more suited to aboveground use—might change to familiarity with a weapon better suited to subterranean use, such as the hand crossbow.

Aligned: A subrace might lean toward one particular alignment, changing its culture and outlook rather than its game statistics. This subrace might have a different favored class or different language options.

Magical: Deviations that have greater or less affinity with magic would change favored classes, ability score modifications (particularly to Intelligence, Wisdom, or Charisma), and even special abilities such as the gnome's free use of particular cantrips.

Focused: Subraces might possess a special attraction to building things, destroying things, theft, battle, particular animals, sailing, nomadic wandering, piety, or virtually anything else that you can conceive. Such a focus probably changes the race's favored class and skill check bonuses and might affect ability score modifications as well.

Wild: Less civilized versions of the standard races would prefer classes such as barbarian and sorcerer and gain bonuses to Wilderness Lore or Handle Animal checks.

Larger or Smaller: Subraces that are larger or smaller than their standard counterparts offer intriguing options. Medium-size halflings or Small elves would use rules and equipment similar to that used by other characters of their new size. Conceivably, a campaign might have Tiny gnomes or Large dwarves. You should be wary of Tiny or Large characters, however, because they alter the campaign in significant ways (for example, new weapons need to be provided for such characters).

Drow

Wild elf

Wood elf

LOCKWOOD

Aquatic: Underwater (or coastal or island) versions of the standard races might have gills to breathe water, a bonus to Swim checks, and an affinity with various forms of aquatic wildlife. Races unable to breathe air are usually too limited for most campaigns. You should also be careful not to simply make aquatic versions of every race and creature, since this rapidly becomes too predictable.

Desert, Mountain, Woodland (Terrain or Climate Types): Finally, climate can change culture and race to create a subrace better suited for the environment in which it lives (desert halflings, polar gnomes, and so on). These subraces differ from their standard counterparts mostly in skill check bonuses or free skills. Just as with aquatic variations on races, this method of diversifying the races can become bland and too pat for many players' tastes if it is overused.

TABLE 2–3: COMMON SUBRACES

Dwarves	Elves
Hill dwarves*	High elves*
Deep dwarves	Aquatic elves (sea elves)
Derro	Drow (dark elves)
Duergar (gray dwarves)	Gray elves
Mountain dwarves	Wild elves (grugach)
	Wood elves (sylvan elves)

Gnomes	Halflings
Rock gnomes*	Lightfeet*
Svirfneblin (deep gnomes)	Tallfellows
Forest gnomes	Deep halflings

*The standard dwarves, elves, gnomes, and halflings described in the *Player's Handbook*.

MODIFYING RACES

Sometimes you may wish to modify one of the common races (those available as PCs in the *Player's Handbook*). Doing this is different from creating a subrace, because it means that the entire common race takes on different characteristics. A campaign might not even use subraces but still have races modified from the rules presented in the *Player's Handbook*.

The main reason you may want to modify the *Player's Handbook* races is to give your campaign a unique or a specific feel. For example, in some campaigns, dwarves never use arcane spells. In others, they may be wizened masters of the arcane arts.

Changes through Limitations

The parameters of a campaign can shape the benefits and restrictions for playing characters of various races. Sometimes, in order to reflect specific roles that you want races to play in the campaign, you can restrict which classes each can choose. Limitations might include any or all of the following:

- Dwarves and halflings cannot be wizards, sorcerers, bards, monks, druids, paladins, or rangers.
- Elves cannot be druids, paladins, or monks.
- Half-elves cannot be paladins or monks.
- Half-orcs cannot be wizards, bards, druids, paladins, or rangers.

The fighter class, the cleric class, and the rogue class are never restricted. Each is considered fundamental to any culture or race, although you can of course create your own exceptions.

It is perfectly acceptable for you to say "In my world . . ." and then describe whatever changes or restrictions you feel necessary.

Be prepared for players to complain if you're denying something otherwise granted to them in the *Player's Handbook* for the choices they make. You're the DM, and it's your campaign. It's important, however, to make sure that the players understand the explanations behind these changes so that they don't feel restricted for no reason. It's often a good idea to balance restrictions with extra allowances—such as greater starting money, free skills, or some other small consideration. Doing this may seem like bribery, but what you're really doing is making a balanced change.

Keep in mind that sometimes restrictions can give a concept more meaning. For example, if you create a new class or prestige class called the elven battlemage, you could logically restrict it to only elves. (Prestige classes are discussed later in this chapter.)

Be careful not to limit one race a great deal more than another. Don't restrict fighter, cleric, wizard, or rogue class selection by race without careful consideration of what effect that restriction might have on player satisfaction as well as on the logic of the campaign. In a setting in which a race cannot be clerics, for example, they must be irreligious as a people. A race with no wizards in a magical world needs some other character class (such as sorcerers or very powerful clerics) to compensate for that absence, or other races will almost certainly best them.

Changes through Addition and Subtraction

Modifying a race by adding or subtracting aspects is just like creating a subrace, but the changes affect the entire race. One DM may find that darkvision is inappropriate for dwarves in her campaign, while another believes that in his campaign elves should never die of old age.

While DMs make such changes to give a unique flavor to a campaign, these changes often end up creating problems with logic or balance. For example, without darkvision for their dwarves, many players opt to play a different race instead, and those who do play dwarves often eventually feel that they made a wrong decision by not choosing, say, a half-orc. Meanwhile, in the game where the DM chose to make elves immortal, no actual game balance issues arise, yet the players grow dissatisfied with the logical incongruity. If elves don't die of old age, they ask, why isn't the world swarming with them by now? These problems are not insurmountable, but they show that change must be well thought out. Balance taking an ability away from a race by replacing it with another. Think through logic problems, and explain them away with a reasonable rationale. For example, elves might have an incredibly low birth rate and fight in many wars against evil, keeping their numbers low despite their biological immunity to aging.

NEW RACES

You can give your players new race options either by using creatures from the *Monster Manual* or new creatures of your own design. In either case, handle this radical change to the campaign with care.

Variant: Monsters as Races

While every monster in the *Monster Manual* has the statistics that a player would need to play, most are not suitable as PCs. Table 2–4: Monsters as Races lists monsters that are easy, difficult, and very difficult to incorporate into a campaign as PCs. Use these lists as guidelines, but don't allow players to play creatures who have an Intelligence score of 2 or less, who have no way to communicate, or who are so different from other PCs that they disrupt the campaign. (The creatures in the Difficult and Very Difficult sections of the table, for example, are too weird for most campaigns.) Some creatures possess strange innate abilities or great physical power, and thus are questionable at best as characters (except in high-powered campaigns). For example, a hill giant dishes out vast amounts of damage, and a PC playing a beholder, with its array of magical powers, is

quite unbalancing. Even something as seemingly innocuous as wings should be considered carefully. The ability to fly can circumvent interesting encounters (particularly outdoors), and it makes skills such as Climb and Jump meaningless. You should not allow such creatures as PCs unless you are running a particularly high-powered game.

Table 2–4: Monsters as Races

Easy (Few Strange Powers)

Race	Level Equivalent
Goblin	Normal
Kobold	Normal
Orc	Normal
Hobgoblin	Normal
Aasimar	Class levels +1
Tiefling	Class levels +1
Lizardfolk	Class levels +2
Gnoll	Class levels +2
Troglodyte	Class levels +2
Bugbear	Class levels +3
Half-celestial*	Class levels +3
Half-fiend*	Class levels +3
Centaur	Class levels +5
Ogre	Class levels +5
Minotaur	Class levels +8

Difficult (Strange Powers or Limitations)

Race	Level Equivalent
Half-dragon*	Class levels +3
Werewolf*†	Class levels +3
Pixie**	Class levels +4
Werebear*††	Class levels +4
Satyr (with pipes)	Class levels +5
Troll	Class levels +8

Very Difficult (Very Large or Very Special Powers)

Race	Level Equivalent
Blink dog	Class levels +4
Ogre mage	Class levels +9
Unicorn	Class levels +6
Hill giant	Class levels +12

*Choose a standard race for the creature's base race.
**Can't cast *Otto's irresistible dance*.
†Character must be at least 2nd level.
††Character must be at least 6th level.

Starting Monster Levels

Creatures such as orcs, kobolds, or goblins make great PCs, since they're humanoid, can communicate, have 1 HD (or less), and don't wield unbalancing special abilities. These characters should be treated normally, with Hit Dice appropriate to their class. Their level equivalent on Table 2–4: Monsters as Races is "normal," which means that, for example, a 3rd-level orc barbarian is pretty much the same as any other 3rd-level barbarian. Some kinds of creatures might be restricted from certain classes (no goblin paladins, for example), but that's up to you.

Other creatures, such as lizardfolk, bugbears, and even ogres, are also simple to add into an otherwise standard campaign, because they have no special powers. However, they are so powerful that their class levels don't accurately reflect their power. Only let a player create one of these powerful characters when you would otherwise allow that player to create a higher-level standard character of equivalent power. Thus, if you would normally allow a player to create a 5th-level character, you can also allow him to create an ogre (with no class levels). If you would normally allow a character to create an 8th-level character, you can allow an ogre with three class levels or a minotaur with none.

If a monster has 1 Hit Die or less, or if it is a template creature (such as a vampire or a lycanthrope; see the *Monster Manual*), it must start the game with one or more class levels, like a regular character. If a monster has 2 or more Hit Dice, it can start with no class levels (though it can gain them later). Lycanthropes are a special case. A lycanthrope should start with at least a number of class levels equal to its animal form's Hit Dice. A PC lycanthrope whose class levels are lower than that is a problem because the ability to assume the animal form's Hit Dice is out of balance with the character's normal abilities.

Even if the creature is of a kind that normally advances by Hit Dice rather than class levels, such as a unicorn, a PC (as an exceptional individual) can gain class levels rather than Hit Dice.

Ability Scores for Monsters

While the *Monster Manual* gives ability scores for a typical creature of a certain kind, any "monster" creature that becomes an adventurer is definitely not typical. Therefore, when creating a PC from the *Monster Manual*, check to see if the creature has any typical ability scores of 10 or higher. If so, for each score, subtract 10 (if the score is even) or 11 (if the score is odd) to get the racial ability modifier. For example, a typical minotaur has a Strength score of 19, so its racial ability modifier is +8 (19 − 11 = 8). Roll the ability score (4d6, discarding the low die) and add the racial ability modifier to get the minotaur PC's Strength score.

For scores below 10, the procedure is different. First, roll the ability score (4d6, discarding the low die), and compare the roll to the monster's average ability score on Table 2–5: Monster PCs' Ability Scores (for Strength, Dexterity, Constitution, Wisdom, or Charisma) or Table 2–6: Monster PCs' Intelligence Ability Scores. For example, the minotaur has a listed Intelligence score of 7, so the player consults that column on Table 2–6. She then rolls 4d6, dropping the low result, and gets a 10. Checking the left-hand column on Table 2–6, she sees that her minotaur PC has an Intelligence score of 6.

The separate table for Intelligence ensures that no PC ends up with an Intelligence score of less than 3. (Optionally, half-orc PCs could use the 8–9 column on Table 2–6 if you wanted to apply this feature to them as well in your campaign.) This is important, because creatures with an Intelligence of less than 3 are not playable characters. Creatures with any ability score lower than 1 are also probably not playable, and you should think twice about letting in any PC with an ability score of less than 3.

A troll trained and equipped as a fighter

Illus. by W. Reynolds

TABLE 2–5: MONSTER PCs' ABILITY SCORES

Dice Roll	— Monster Ability Score (Str, Dex, Con, Wis, Cha) —				
	1	2–3	4–5	6–7	8–9
18	1	4	8	12	16
17	1	4	8	11	15
16	1	4	8	10	14
15	1	4	7	9	13
14	1	4	6	8	12
13	1	3	5	7	11
12	1	3	5	7	10
11	1	3	5	7	9
10	1	2	4	6	8
9	1	2	4	6	7
8	1	2	4	6	6
7	1	1	3	5	5
6	1	1	2	4	4
5	1	1	1	3	3
4	1	1	1	2	2
3	1	1	1	1	1

TABLE 2–6: MONSTER PCs' INTELLIGENCE ABILITY SCORES

Dice Roll	Monster Intelligence			
	3	4–5	6–7	8–9
18	3	6	10	14
17	3	6	9	13
16	3	6	8	12
15	3	6	8	11
14	3	6	8	10
13	3	5	7	9
12	3	5	7	9
11	3	5	7	9
10	3	4	6	8
9	3	4	6	8
8	3	4	6	8
7	3	3	5	7
6	3	3	5	6
5	3	3	5	5
4	3	3	4	4
3	3	3	3	3

Other Statistics for Monsters

Creatures with Hit Dice of 1 or less have normal, class-based Hit Dice and features. Those with 2 or more Hit Dice have statistics based on these Hit Dice plus those for class levels (if any).

For example, an ogre with no class levels has 4d8 HD, a base attack bonus of +3, one feat, and 8 skill points (plus Intelligence modifier). The first HD is treated as maximum, giving her 8 + 3d8 + (Constitution bonus × 4) hit points.

A creature with no class levels has the standard gear for a creature of its kind. A creature with class levels has equipment worth an amount based on the total of those class levels (see Table 2–24: Starting Equipment for PCs above 1st Level).

Experience for Monsters

A creature with only class levels, such as a PC orc, gains XP normally. A creature with class levels plus monster levels, such as an ogre, has a character level equal to his monster levels plus his class levels. A creature starts with the minimum number of XP required to be his level. When creatures gain levels, they add class levels, as in the multiclassing rules in the *Player's Handbook* (with the monster class considered their favored class).

For example, a PC ogre with no class levels could enter the game when any normal 5th-level character would be allowed. The ogre begins at 4th level (because she has 4 Hit Dice) with 6,000 XP (just enough to be 4th level—see Table 3–2: Experience and Level-Dependent Benefits, page 22 in the *Player's Handbook*). Once the ogre earns another 4,000 XP, she becomes 5th level, and she adds a 1st-level class.

Roleplaying Monsters

Many of the creatures in the *Monster Manual* are evil. Not only are these creatures going to have a difficult time in standard settings, such as human cities, but evil PCs might not be what you want for your campaign. However, it's fairly easy to justify how a monster whose kin are evil might be neutral or even good in alignment. See if any of the following background options appeal to your player and fit in with his character concept:

- Reared by humans, elves, dwarves, or another nonevil race.
- Saved from a horrible fate by good-aligned creatures.
- Individually repentant.
- Disillusioned by evil.
- On the run from evil creatures.
- Magically altered or *geased*.

Most NPCs assume that monsters are evil, regardless of the character's actual alignment. Within a human city or an elven town, a goblin or a troll is going to be feared, loathed, or—at best—distrusted. Decide for yourself how much you want to stress the difficulty of playing a monster in civilized areas. The player must decide just how bestial or sophisticated he wants to play the monster character, and how true to the monster archetype the player wants to cling. He may look to you for guidance, so be prepared ahead of time regarding these issues as well. Do you want the minotaur PC to be gleefully terrorizing the little folk or to be struggling to fit in with humans?

Remember that what's good for PCs is good for NPCs. NPC monsters can have classes, exceptional ability scores, and maximum first Hit Dice as well.

Creating New Races

While the creatures in the *Monster Manual* make for interesting PC racial choices, that's not really what they were made for. Most were made to be opponents for the PCs (which is why they're monsters). Thus, some DMs may want to create new races made primarily for giving players new options.

Creating new races is difficult. In general, use the races in the

Player's Handbook as examples and guides. When in doubt, make the new race like one found there. Monsters in the *Monster Manual* weren't created to be PC races and shouldn't be used as models for anything other than monsters and NPCs. If you want to create a catlike race with a great Dexterity, look to the elves as an example. They gain a +2 bonus to Dexterity but suffer a −2 penalty to Constitution. For having such a great benefit as heightened Dexterity, the cat people should have a commensurate penalty as well.

Here's an important secret: Not all of the ability scores are equal. Notice, for example, the half-orc with a penalty in Intelligence and Charisma but a bonus only in Strength. That's because neither a penalty to Intelligence nor a penalty to Charisma by itself is equal to a bonus in Strength. To return to the cat people example: Dexterity is also a very important ability, and thus a Dexterity bonus could not be balanced by a Charisma penalty alone unless some other drawback were added as well.

In general, the following table demonstrates appropriate penalties to match equal bonuses. Notice that sometimes the bonus/penalty trade-off doesn't always work both ways. For example, a bonus in Strength is roughly equal to a penalty in Constitution, but a bonus to Constitution is not equal to a penalty in Strength.

TABLE 2–7: ABILITY SCORE EQUIVALENCIES

Ability Score Bonus	Ability Score or Scores Penalized
Strength	Dexterity
	Constitution
	Intelligence and Charisma
	Intelligence and Wisdom
	Wisdom and Charisma
Dexterity	Strength
	Constitution
	Intelligence and Charisma
	Intelligence and Wisdom
	Wisdom and Charisma
Constitution	Dexterity
	Intelligence
	Wisdom
	Charisma
Intelligence	Wisdom
	Charisma
Wisdom	Intelligence
	Charisma
Charisma	Intelligence
	Wisdom

Of course, there's nothing really wrong with penalizing a more important score than the one getting the bonus. You could create a frail race of kindly, beautiful creatures with a +2 Charisma bonus and a −2 Strength penalty, but be aware that most players will not play such a race. Some might, however, and that's for you to judge. Refer to Chapter 1: Dungeon Mastering if you think you have introduced something into your game (in this case, a new race) that was a mistake because it was either overpowered or not powerful enough.

Basically, the same sorts of guidelines that you must consider when creating subraces or using monsters as races apply to creating new races. Beware of special abilities, particularly movement- or combat-related ones. Remember that size changes many aspects of a character. Benefits should be balanced with drawbacks. Pay strict attention to culture and environment for ideas on how to shape the race.

An interesting avenue you may wish to examine regarding new race creation is the idea of half-breed races. The *Player's Handbook* already presents the half-elf and the half-orc. The *Monster Manual* gives rules on half-celestials, half-dragons, half-fiends, and more mixed races such as the planetouched (aasimars and tieflings).

Half-ogres, half-trolls or elf–orc, orc–ogre (orog), gnome–halfling, or orc–goblin crossbreeds are all interesting possibilities for PC races. You may wish to rule that some crossbreeds are impossible or unfeasible, such as dwarf–elf, halfling–human or gnome–ogre. That's strictly up to you.

CLASSES

A DM should consider carefully the classes in her world, for they define the people who live there. Presented here are ideas for modifying *Player's Handbook* character classes, for special prestige classes, and for NPC classes (which represent everyone who isn't quite a fighter or a sorcerer but who still needs some sort of game mechanics treatment).

MODIFYING CHARACTER CLASSES

Imagine the desert knife fighter, a fighter with a limited weapon selection but early specialization with a knife. Or a fire mage, a wizard with particularly potent fire spells but no access to any spell utilizing water, air, or earth. Or a warrior-priest who functions like a cleric, but with a fighter's weapon selection and attack bonus, fewer spells per day, and no access to healing spells.

If you're like most DMs, the character classes in the *Player's Handbook* are flexible enough to fit most any niche or need, particularly with the possibilities of multiclassing, the variety of feats and skills, and facets such as school specialization for wizards and domain selection for clerics. If you want to create a campaign rich with religion and divine influence, where just about everyone has deity-granted powers, you don't have to overhaul all the existing classes. Instead, you can just say everyone (or most everyone) in that society multiclasses so that they possess at least one level of cleric. You can rule that in such a world, clerical multiclassing has no penalties, and everyone can do it for free (no XP penalties).

This means, of course, that you have modified the class system slightly. Further modifications occasionally allow a DM to create slightly different classes either for variety or to fill a niche created in her own campaign. Various aspects of a class—such as Hit Dice, base attack bonuses, or spells per level—are easy to change. However, even though the numbers are easy to change, you should be aware of the implications. A rogue with a fighter's attack bonus is better than a regular rogue unless her gain in this respect is offset by some loss elsewhere. Likewise, a wizard with more spells per day is also unbalanced in regard to other classes without some significant drawback.

Special abilities are somewhat more complex to alter. Always have a concept with strengths and weaknesses in mind—don't just try to create the class that can do everything. Remember that while the paladin has a lot of special offensive, defensive, and healing abilities, she has neither access to attack spells nor any way to sneak around. The wizard is a great spellcaster but has poor combat abilities. Consider making a swashbuckler rogue with no ability to sneak attack but more combat- and movement-oriented feats, or a druid with fewer spells per day but the capability to shapechange more often.

Remember, however, if you have created a variant class with sneaking and subterfuge capabilities better than the rogue, or a combat-oriented class more adept at combat than the fighter, you have gone astray. Variants should exist for variety and flavor, not to outshine the standard classes. The other point to remember is that making a class worse at something it's already bad at is not necessarily a balancing factor. A wizard with a worse attack bonus or a restriction against taking combat-oriented feats really isn't that much worse off than the standard wizard. (She wasn't likely to get involved in melee if she could help it anyway.) Dungeon Masters who are real sticklers for class balance might want to avoid modifying character classes altogether. It's difficult, and the problems it creates don't usually make themselves evident until the changes are already in play.

Avoiding the Pitfalls

The barbarian and the fighter classes show the difficulty in balancing character classes. Both excel at combat but do so in different ways. The fighter gains more and more combat feats and specialization, while the barbarian attains his prowess in temporary bursts of rage. Take a look at the bonuses and modifications that each gets. Even though their attack bonus progression is the same, a fighter with well-chosen feats outshines the barbarian, even one in a rage. (Once out of his rage, the barbarian's not even close.) This situation is balanced by the other special advantages the barbarian has: an increased movement rate, more skill points, a greater selection of class skills, uncanny dodge, and a more generous Hit Die type. All of these aspects need to be considered when measuring the balance of a character class.

When modifying a class, always take the following steps:

1. Look to see which standard class seems to be most like the end result that you want to create.
2. Look to see if another class has special abilities that can be swapped in exchange for something that this class has in order to create what you want.

BEHIND THE CURTAIN: WHY MESS AROUND WITH CHARACTER CLASSES?

The standard character classes fit into virtually everyone's campaign. They're flexible, and skill and feat selection allow them to be truly customizable. Most character concepts can be covered using the classes as written. Modifying classes is mostly a tool that you can use to tailor things to best fit your campaign. It shouldn't come up that often, since it's rarely necessary.

DMs who create their own worlds may find the classes need some focusing to make them specific to a particular campaign. If, in developing your own world, you design a culture steeped in a long-standing hatred of magic, you might alter the fighter to be a demonslayer and give the class a limited weapon selection and special feats that work best against outsiders. The ranger might become a wizard-hunter, the cleric could be a protector with early access to *dispel magic* and various defensive spells, and all PC classes might be imbued with the ability to use *detect magic* once per day.

Sometimes, however, players come to you and say that they like a certain class, but they want to change a single feature or two. Michele might want to play a ranger with no desire to obtain more than one favored enemy. She wants to play a beast-slayer, and her character hates dire wolves. She's also interested in the paladin's warhorse. You can decide, as a DM, that it's acceptable to trade those ranger abilities for the paladin's mount. In fact, you might decide that it's not a fair trade, and that Michele's character can have the *detect evil* ability as well. (She is, after all, giving up an ability usable at 1st level as well as one that comes into play later for one that she can't achieve until 5th level.) Allowing a player to play the character she wants to play is always a desirable goal. Sure, sometimes it can't be achieved—the player asks for too much, or what she wants doesn't fit with your campaign—but the effort to accommodate reasonable modifications is almost always worth it.

3. Look to all the other classes and match the newly modified class against each one, taking into account the following:

- Hit Dice
- Base attack bonus progression
- Base save progressions
- Skill points
- Class skill list, including exclusive skills
- Weapon and armor proficiency
- Spells per day
- Spell list selection
- Special class features

No class should excel beyond another overall. Pay particular attention to special class features and spells.

Spell Lists for Variant Spellcasters

One fairly easy way to modify an existing character class or, in effect, invent an entirely new one is to modify the spell list of a spellcasting class. Sometimes altering spell lists may seem like mixing and matching the specialty school of a wizard or domains of a priest. And that's not entirely incorrect. Priests with radically different domains or two different specialist wizards *can* seem like entirely different classes sometimes. Altering the mix of spells in a spell list, however, can modify classes to an extent impossible with just specialization.

Switching spell level for various spells, so that the modified class has, for example, faster access to illusion spells but doesn't get key evocation attack spells until later can create an interesting variant. Be wary of this method. The spell lists and the levels assigned to them were designed with a careful balance in mind. Switching a spell up or down more than a single level is probably a bad idea. Don't assume that all spells carry equal weight, either. Making *fireball* and *fly* 2nd-level spells on a spell list and then pushing *see invisibility* and *magic mouth* up to 3rd level to compensate is unbalancing. While *see invisibility* and *magic mouth* are both useful spells, they don't present balance issues as obvious as *fireball* (the first significant multiple-target damage spell) and *fly* (often the difference between avoiding an encounter or not). When trading spells up or down in level, do so with a theme in mind. A caster might be great at divinations and enchantments but poor at any spells with obvious, dramatic effects. Or he may be particularly adept at healing but not as good with spells that affect emotions or minds.

Even if you carefully balance the spells you increase or decrease in level, you're likely to make a spellcaster more powerful. For instance, *fireball* and *lightning bolt* are roughly equivalent spells, but if you create a variant spellcaster with *lightning bolt* as a 2nd-level spell and *fireball* as a 4th-level spell, that character is more powerful than the wizard or sorcerer it was based on.

The most obvious way to create new spell lists is to take spells from the different classes and mix and match. If you combine spells from two classes, you create an interesting but potentially unbalanced new variant class. Beware the all-powerful hybrid: a class with the firepower of a wizard and the healing capacity of a cleric. Don't simply pick the best spells from all the lists and give them to a single caster. As with switching spell levels, a theme for a brand-new spell list helps balance it (especially a theme with both strengths and shortcomings). The new spell list might be strong on offensive spells but lacking in defensive magic, or great with healing and divinations but lacking in movement-related and alteration spells. Casters with access to spells from two different classes should generally have fewer spells available than either of the original classes. Versatility has its price.

Classes for whom spellcasting is secondary—such as the ranger, the paladin, and perhaps the bard—offer an even greater opportunity for manipulation, since their lists are smaller and thus more easily shifted. Subtle changes, such as the paladin of a deity of healing with all curing spells, or a beastmaster ranger with only animal-related spells, are fairly easy to create. Greater changes are also possible, such as the divine bard (the cantor), whose spells are all taken from the cleric list.

The Witch

Here's an example of creating a new spell list for a variant spellcasting class: the witch. A staple of fantasy literature and fairy tales, the witch dabbles in many types of magic—minor illusions, spells dealing with health or life, nature-based magic, simple divinations, and spells that alter the shape and appearance of things—but excels at just a few. Hence, her list is somewhat limited, but it contains wizard, cleric, and druid spells. She uses the sorcerer's Spells per Day table (see Table 3–16: The Sorcerer, page 49 in the *Player's Handbook*), and her spells are based on Charisma. This spell list is designed with these considerations in mind:

Cure Spells: Only the weakest of these, and the witch doesn't have the cleric's ability to cast *cure* spells spontaneously. The witch isn't blessed with a cleric's (or druid's) plethora of healing spells, but she can offer a little aid to those she favors.

Illusions: Only through the middle levels. The witch can trick her foes, but not to the extent that a wizard can.

Divinations: Only the straightforward divinations, such as *clairvoyance* and *scry*, and not even all of them.

Charms: Many. A major niche for this caster.

Form-Changing: Another strong point for the witch. From *change self* to *shapechange*, the witch has most of the spells relating to changing her (or someone else's) form.

Nature: From speaking to animals to controlling the weather, the witch dabbles in this type of magic, if for no other reason than she usually lives a secluded life in the wilderness.

Flashy Spells: Anything from a *lightning bolt* to a *wall of fire* to *Bigby's hand* spells is right out. The witch's archetype doesn't suggest overt attack spells or spells that create massive magic constructs. She doesn't summon monsters, place wards, or teleport from place to place. Her magic is subtle.

Miscellaneous: Spells such as *whispering wind*, *Leomund's tiny hut*, *bestow curse* (and a few other curselike spells), and a few communication spells round out the list. For flavor, the first six levels of the witch's spell list each have thirteen spells.

Witch Spell List

The witch chooses to have access to one of the two spells marked with an asterisk (*). Of the asterisked spells, she cannot cast those of an alignment opposed to her own.

0 level—*arcane mark, cure minor wounds, dancing lights, daze, detect magic, detect poison, flare, ghost sound, light, mending, read magic, resistance, virtue.*

1st level—*cause fear, change self, charm person, command, comprehend languages, cure light wounds, doom, endure elements, hypnotism, identify, silent image, sleep, ventriloquism.*

2nd level—*alter self, blindness/deafness, calm emotion, cure moderate wounds, delay poison, detect thoughts, enthrall, invisibility, locate object, minor image, scare, speak with animals, whispering wind.*

3rd level—*bestow curse, clairvoyance/clairaudience, contagion, create food and water, cure blindness/deafness, dispel magic, Leomund's tiny hut, magic circle against chaos/law*, magic circle against evil/good*, spectral force, suggestion, tongues, water breathing.*

4th level—*charm monster, discern lies, divination, emotion, fear, giant vermin, locate creature, minor creation, neutralize poison, polymorph other, polymorph self, remove curse, scrying.*

5th level—*advanced illusion, attraction, animal growth, avoidance, dream, feeblemind, greater command, greater scrying, magic jar, major creation, mirage arcana, nightmare, seeming.*

6th level—*animate, eyebite, find the path, geas/quest, heroes' feast, legend lore, mass suggestion, mislead, project image, repulsion, Tenser's transformation, true seeing, weather control.*

7th level—*creeping doom, finger of death, insanity, liveoak, repel wood, transport via plants.*

8th level—*antipathy/sympathy, discern location, horrid wilting, polymorph any object, prophesy, trap the soul.*

9th level—*earthquake, foresight, refuge, shape change, wail of the banshee, weird.*

CREATING NEW CLASSES

Of course, it's possible to create entirely new classes, or rather, to alter existing classes so drastically that they're no longer recognizable. For example, you could make the following adjustments to the ranger:

- Limit his weapon selection to resemble the rogue's list of weapon proficiencies.
- Change his favored enemy ability so that he gets it only once and the bonuses come into play whenever the character fights undead.
- Give him the rogue's sneak attack, but change it so that it's usable against undead (and only against undead).
- Change his spell list so that it consists of spells that deal strictly with undead or that are used for subterfuge and sneaking.
- At 3rd level, give him the paladin's smite evil ability, usable only against undead.

Now the class is the undead stalker, a stealthy character skilled in tracking and slaying undead.

This method of mixing and matching abilities from different classes is the best way to go should you want to create an entirely new class. It gives you a starting point and an idea of what you should and shouldn't do to create a balanced character.

PRESTIGE CLASSES

In the City of Greyhawk, a shadowy guild of hired killers wields power and fear like deadly weapons. Only the most ruthless and yet subtle women and men can join the guild as members. These assassins must pass rigorous tests and trials to prove their worth, so that they may learn the art of dealing death as only assassins can. Meanwhile, far to the south, a small, secret cabal of spellcasters called loremasters practice their arts of divination and focus on their deep studies. Only the most talented and deeply inquisitive can join their mystical ranks.

Assassins and loremasters are among the many types of prestige classes. Characters who qualify can choose a prestige class as a multiclass to pick up as they advance in level. Taking a prestige class does not incur the experience point penalties normally associated with multiclassing. Prestige classes allow DMs to create campaign-specific, exclusive roles and positions as classes. These special roles offer abilities and powers otherwise inaccessible to PCs and focus them in specific, interesting directions. A character with a prestige class is more specialized yet perhaps slightly better than one without one.

A newly created, 1st-level character cannot be a member of a prestige class. Abilities granted by prestige classes are inappropriate for 1st-level characters. Prestige classes are acquired only by meeting the requirements specific to each example. This almost always requires—in effect—that a character be at least mid-level (say, around 5th or 6th level). Additionally, the character must meet nonrule-related requirements in-game, such as group membership fees, special training exercises, quests, and so forth.

Allowing PCs access to prestige classes is purely optional and always under the purview of the DM. Even though a few examples can be found below, prestige classes are idiosyncratic to each campaign, and DMs may choose to not allow them or to use them only for NPCs.

Dungeon Masters should use prestige classes as a tool for world-building as well as a reward for achieving high level. They set characters in the milieu and put them in the context of the world.

Creating Prestige Classes

Prestige classes are like regular classes, except that they have requirements that must be met before one can attain the class.

Requirements vary, but here are some general rules. Most characters should have a chance of working toward qualifying. Thus, class or level should never be used as a requirement. A prestige class based around being the champion of Heironeous, for example, wouldn't require a prospective member to be a fighter or a paladin of a given level, although those might seem the most appropriate candidates. Instead, the prestige class might require a base attack bonus of +8. Thus, fighters and paladins at 8th level could take up the prestige class, but clerics and rogues could qualify at 11th level and wizards at 16th level. This requirement then encourages certain types (and levels) of characters but precludes none.

Sometimes, however, prestige classes can be created to be more discriminating. A gnome tinkerer prestige class would require that the qualifying character be a gnome. This sort of restriction further develops the differences in races and helps quantify the game world in very tangible ways.

Examples of good requirements include any of the following:

- Race
- Alignment
- Base attack bonus
- Number of ranks in a specific skill
- Specific feats, including specific weapon proficiencies
- The ability to cast divine (or arcane) spells
- The ability to cast a specific spell
- Specific special abilities such as sneak attack (with a certain number of dice of additional damage), turning/rebuking undead, or evasion

Should a character find herself in a position (changed alignment, lost levels, and so on) where she no longer meets the requirements of a prestige class, she loses all special abilities (but not HD, base attack bonus, or base save bonus) gained from levels of the prestige class.

Prestige classes should offer a number of special abilities, including at least some not available in any other way. Qualifying for a prestige class is difficult, and advancing levels in the new class is a sacrifice, so the rewards should be substantial. When designing a prestige class, look to character class special abilities and use them, modify them, and build upon them for guidelines. A prestige class should be at least as beneficial and powerful as a normal character class, and—if the requirements are high—it might even be more powerful. Always balance the power of a prestige class with its requirements. If the requirements are such that a particular prestige class is not available to characters below 10th level, it can be better than one available to characters at 5th level. (Six examples of prestige classes follow this section.)

Use prestige classes to establish and develop the following themes in your campaign.

Racial Distinctions: Each race might have a number of different prestige classes, ranging from dwarven smiths to halfling scouts to elven warrior-poets.

Cultural Distinctions: If the Torrashi barbarians of the frigid north ride wolves and work with them on their hunts, create a prestige class (wolfriders) that allows a character to speak with and befriend wolves, fight on wolfback, and so on.

Religious Orders: Conceivably, every religion in your campaign might have a prestige class based on being the champion of a specific deity.

Guild or Group Membership: Joining the Band of the Blade, the Slayers, or the Mage's Cabal provides allies and other benefits for those who qualify, making this an obvious way to install a prestige class specific to your campaign.

TABLE 2–8: THE ARCANE ARCHER

Class Level	Base Attack Bonus	Fort Save	Ref Save	Will Save	Special
1st	+1	+2	+2	+0	Enchant arrow +1
2nd	+2	+3	+3	+0	Imbue arrow
3rd	+3	+3	+3	+1	Enchant arrow +2
4th	+4	+4	+4	+1	Seeker arrow
5th	+5	+4	+4	+1	Enchant arrow +3
6th	+6	+5	+5	+2	Phase arrow
7th	+7	+5	+5	+2	Enchant arrow +4
8th	+8	+6	+6	+2	Hail of arrows
9th	+9	+6	+6	+3	Enchant arrow +5
10th	+10	+7	+7	+3	Arrow of death

Arcane Archer

Master of the elven warbands, the arcane archer is a warrior skilled in using magic to supplement her combat prowess. Beyond the woods, arcane archers gain renown throughout entire kingdoms for their supernatural accuracy with a bow and their ability to imbue their arrows with magic. In a group, they can strike fear into an entire enemy army.

Fighters, rangers, paladins, and barbarians become arcane archers to add a little magic to their combat abilities. Conversely, wizards and sorcerers may take this prestige class to add combat capabilities to their repertoire. Monks, clerics, druids, rogues, and bards rarely become arcane archers.

NPC arcane archers often lead units of normal archers or form small, elite units formed entirely of arcane archers. These units are one of the prime reasons that the elves are so feared in battle.

Hit Die: d8.

Requirements

To qualify to become an arcane archer, a character must fulfill all the following criteria.

Race: Elf or half-elf.

Base Attack Bonus: +6.

Feats: Weapon Focus (any bow other than a crossbow), Point Blank Shot, Precise Shot.

Spellcasting: Ability to cast 1st-level arcane spells.

Class Skills

The arcane archer's class skills (and the key ability for each skill) are Craft (Int), Hide (Dex). Intuit Direction (Wis), Listen (Wis), Move Silently (Dex), Ride (Dex), Spot (Wis), Use Rope (Dex), and Wilderness Lore (Wis). See Chapter 4: Skills in the Player's Handbook for skill descriptions.

Skill Points at Each Level: 4 + Int modifier.

Class Features

All of the following are class features of the arcane archer prestige class.

Weapon and Armor Proficiency: An arcane archer is proficient with all simple and martial weapons, light armor, medium armor, and shields. Note that armor check penalties for armor heavier than leather apply to the skills Balance, Climb, Escape Artist, Hide, Jump, Move Silently, Pick Pocket, and Tumble.

Enchant Arrow: At 1st level, every nonmagical arrow an arcane archer nocks and lets fly becomes enchanted, gaining a +1 enhancement bonus. Unlike magic weapons enchanted by normal means, the archer need not spend experience points or money to accomplish this task. However, an archer's magic arrows only function for her. For every two levels of arcane archer the character advances past 1st level in the prestige class, the magic arrows she creates gain +1 greater potency (+1 at 1st level, +2 at 3rd level, +3 at 5th level, +4 at 7th level, and +5 at 9th level).

Imbue Arrow: At 2nd level, an arcane archer gains this spell-like ability, allowing her to place an area spell upon an arrow. When the arrow is fired, the spell's area is centered upon where the arrow lands, even if the spell could normally be centered only on the caster.

An arcane archer

This ability allows the archer to use the bow's range rather than the spell's range. It takes a standard action to cast the spell and fire the arrow. The arrow must be fired in the round the spell is cast, or the spell is wasted.

Seeker Arrow: At 4th level, the arcane archer can launch an arrow once per day at a target known to her within range, and the arrow travels to the target even around corners. Only an unavoidable obstacle or the end of the arrow's range prevents the arrow's flight. For example, if the target is within a windowless chamber with the door closed, the arrow cannot enter. This ability negates cover and concealment modifiers, but otherwise the attack is rolled normally. This is a spell-like ability. (Shooting the arrow is part of the action.)

Phase Arrow: At 6th level, the arcane archer can launch an arrow once per day at a target known to her within range, and the arrow travels to the target in a straight path, passing through any nonmagical barrier or wall in its way. (A *wall of force*, a *wall of fire*, or the like stops the arrow.) This ability negates cover, concealment, and even armor modifiers, but otherwise the attack is rolled normally. This is a spell-like ability. (Shooting the arrow is part of the action.)

Hail of Arrows: In lieu of her regular attacks, once per day the 8th-level arcane archer can fire an arrow at each and every target within range, to a maximum of one target for every arcane archer level she has earned. Each attack uses the archer's primary attack bonus, and each enemy may only be targeted by a single arrow. This is a spell-like ability.

Arrow of Death: At 10th level, the arcane archer can enchant an *arrow of death* that forces the target, if damaged by the arrow's attack, to make a Fortitude save (DC 20) or be slain immediately. It takes one day to create an *arrow of death*, and the arrow only functions for the arcane archer who created it. The enchantment lasts no longer than one year, and the archer can only have one such arrow in existence at a time.

Assassin

The assassin is the master of dealing quick, lethal blows. Assassins also excel at infiltration and disguise. Assassins often function as spies, informants, killers for hire, or agents of vengeance. Their training in anatomy, stealth, poison, and the dark arts allows them to carry out missions of death with shocking, terrifying precision.

Rogues, monks, and bardic assassins make for the classic skulking assassin in the shadows with a blade carrying certain death. Fighters, ex-paladins, rangers, druids, and barbarians operate as warrior assassins, with as much ability to kill in combat as from the shadows. Sorcerers, wizards, and clerics may be the most terrifying assassins of all, for with their spells they can infiltrate and slay with even greater impunity.

As NPCs, assassins work in guilds or secret societies found hidden in cities or based in remote fortresses in the wilderness. Sometimes they serve more powerful evil characters singly or in a group. Occasionally an assassin works alone, but only the most capable are willing to operate without any sort of support or backup.

Hit Die: d6.

Requirements

To qualify to become an assassin, a character must fulfill all the following criteria.

Alignment: Any evil.
Move Silently: 8 ranks.
Hide: 8 ranks.
Disguise: 4 ranks.
Special: In addition, he must kill someone for no other reason than to join the assassins.

Class Skills

The assassin's class skills (and the key ability for each skill) are Balance (Dex), Bluff (Cha), Climb (Str), Craft (Int), Decipher Script (Int, exclusive skill), Diplomacy (Cha), Disable Device (Int), Disguise (Cha), Escape Artist (Dex), Forgery (Int), Gather Information (Cha), Hide (Dex), Innuendo (Wis), Intimidate (Cha), Intuit Direction (Wis), Jump (Str), Listen (Wis), Move Silently (Dex), Open Lock (Dex), Pick Pocket (Dex), Read Lips (Int, exclusive skill), Search (Int), Sense Motive (Wis), Spot (Wis), Swim (Str), Tumble (Dex), Use Magic Device (Cha, exclusive skill), and Use Rope (Dex). See Chapter 4: Skills in the *Player's Handbook* for skill descriptions.

Skill Points at Each Level: 4 + Int modifier.

Class Features

All of the following are class features of the assassin prestige class.

Weapon and Armor Proficiency: An assassin's weapon training focuses on weapons suitable for stealth and sneak attacks. Assassins are proficient with the crossbow (hand, light, or heavy), dagger (any type), dart, rapier, sap, shortbow (normal and composite), and short sword. Assassins are proficient with light armor but not with shields. Note that armor check penalties for armor heavier than leather apply to the skills Balance, Climb, Escape Artist, Hide, Jump, Move Silently, Pick Pocket, and Tumble, and that carrying heavy gear imposes a check penalty on Swim checks.

Sneak Attack: If an assassin can catch an opponent when she is unable to defend herself effectively from his attack, he can strike a vital spot for extra damage. Basically, any time the assassin's target would be denied her Dexterity bonus to AC (whether she actually has a Dexterity bonus or not), the assassin's attack deals +1d6 points of damage. This extra damage increases by +1d6 points every other level (+2d6 at 3rd level, +3d6 at 5th level, and so on). Should the assassin score a critical hit with a sneak attack, this extra damage is not multiplied.

It takes precision and penetration to hit a vital spot, so ranged attacks can only count as sneak attacks if the target is 30 feet away or less.

With a sap or an unarmed strike, the assassin can make a sneak attack that deals subdual damage instead of normal damage. He cannot use a weapon that deals normal damage to deal subdual damage in a sneak attack, not even with the usual –4 penalty, because he must make optimal use of his weapon in order to execute the sneak attack.

An assassin

WAR Z◊◊◊

TABLE 2–9: THE ASSASSIN

Class Level	Base Attack Bonus	Fort Save	Ref Save	Will Save	Special	Spells per Day			
						1st	2nd	3rd	4th
1st	+0	+0	+2	+0	Sneak attack +1d6, death attack, poison use	0	—	—	—
2nd	+1	+0	+3	+0	+1 save vs. poison, uncanny dodge (Dex bonus to AC)	1	—	—	—
3rd	+2	+1	+3	+1	Sneak attack +2d6	1	0	—	—
4th	+3	+1	+4	+1	+2 save vs. poison	1	1	—	—
5th	+3	+1	+4	+1	Sneak attack +3d6, uncanny dodge (can't be flanked)	1	1	0	—
6th	+4	+2	+5	+2	+3 save vs. poison	1	1	1	—
7th	+5	+2	+5	+2	Sneak attack +4d6	2	1	1	0
8th	+6	+2	+6	+2	+4 save vs. poison	2	1	1	1
9th	+6	+3	+6	+3	Sneak attack +5d6	2	2	1	1
10th	+7	+3	+7	+3	+5 save vs. poison, uncanny dodge (+1 vs. traps)	2	2	2	1

An assassin can only sneak attack living creatures with discernible anatomies—undead, constructs, oozes, plants, and incorporeal creatures lack vital areas to attack. Additionally, any creature immune to critical hits is similarly immune to sneak attacks. Also, the assassin must also be able to see the target well enough to pick out a vital spot and must be able to reach a vital spot. The assassin cannot sneak attack while striking at a creature with concealment or by striking the limbs of a creature whose vitals are beyond reach.

If an assassin gets a sneak attack bonus from another source (such as rogue levels), the bonuses to damage stack.

Death Attack: If the assassin studies his victim for 3 rounds and then makes a sneak attack with a melee weapon that successfully deals damage, the sneak attack has the additional effect of possibly either paralyzing or killing the target (assassin's choice). While studying the victim, the assassin can undertake other actions so long as his attention stays focused on the target and the target does not detect the assassin or recognize the assassin as an enemy. If the victim of such an attack fails her Fortitude saving throw (DC 10 + the assassin's class level + Intelligence modifier) against the kill effect, she dies. If the saving throw fails against the paralysis effect, the victim's mind and body become enervated, rendering her completely helpless and unable to act for 1d6 rounds plus 1 round per level of the assassin. If the victim's saving throw succeeds, the attack is just a normal sneak attack. Once the assassin has completed the 3 rounds of study, he must make the death attack within the next 3 rounds. If a death attack is attempted and fails (the victim makes her save) or if the assassin does not launch the attack within 3 rounds of completing the study, 3 new rounds of study are required before he can attempt another death attack.

Poison Use: Assassins are trained in the use of poison and never risk accidentally poisoning themselves when applying poison to a blade.

Spells: Beginning at 1st level, an assassin gains the ability to cast a small number of arcane spells. To cast a spell, the assassin must have an Intelligence score of at least 10 + the spell's level, so an assassin with an Intelligence of 10 or lower cannot cast these spells. Assassin bonus spells are based on Intelligence, and saving throws against these spells have a DC of 10 + spell level + the assassin's Intelligence modifier (if any). When the assassin gets 0 spells of a given level, such as 0 1st-level spells at 1st level, the assassin gets only bonus spells. An assassin without a bonus spell for that level cannot yet cast a spell of that level. The assassin's spell list appears below. An assassin prepares and casts spells just as a wizard does.

Saving Throw Bonus vs. Poison: Assassins train with poisons of all types and slowly grow more and more resistant to their effects. This is reflected by a natural saving throw bonus to all poisons gained at 2nd level that increases by +1 for every two levels the assassin gains (+1 at 2nd level, +2 at 4th level, +3 at 6th level, and so on).

Uncanny Dodge: Starting at 2nd level, the assassin gains the extraordinary ability to react to danger before his senses would

normally allow him to even be aware of it. At 2nd level and above, he retains his Dexterity bonus to AC (if any) regardless of being caught flat-footed or struck by an invisible attacker. (He still loses his Dexterity bonus to AC if immobilized.)

At 5th level, the assassin can no longer be flanked, since he can react to opponents on opposite sides of him as easily as he can react to a single attacker. This defense denies rogues the ability to use flank attacks to sneak attack the assassin. The exception to this defense is that a rogue at least four levels higher than the assassin can flank him (and thus sneak attack him).

At 10th level, the assassin gains an intuitive sense that alerts him to danger from traps, giving him a +1 bonus to Reflex saves made to avoid traps.

If the assassin has another class that grants the uncanny dodge ability, add together all the class levels of the classes that grant the ability and determine the character's uncanny dodge ability on that basis.

Assassin Spell List

Assassins choose their spells from the following list:

1st level—*change self, detect poison, ghost sound, obscuring mist, spider climb.*

2nd level—*alter self, darkness, pass without trace, undetectable alignment.*

3rd level—*deeper darkness, invisibility, misdirection, nondetection.*

4th level—*dimension door, freedom of movement, improved invisibility, poison.*

Blackguard

The blackguard epitomizes evil. He is nothing short of a mortal fiend. The quintessential black knight, this villain carries a reputation of the foulest sort that is very well deserved. Consorting with demons and devils and serving dark deities, the blackguard is hated and feared by all. Some people call these villains antipaladins due to their completely evil nature.

The blackguard has many options available to him—sending forth dark minions and servants to do his bidding, attacking with stealth and honorless guile, or straightforward smiting of the forces of good that stand in his way. Fighters, ex-paladins, rangers, monks, druids, and barbarians make for indomitable combat-oriented blackguards, while rogues and bardic blackguards are likely to stress the subtle aspects of their abilities and spells. Sorcerers, wizards, and clerics who become blackguards are sometimes called diabolists and favor dealing with fiends even more than other blackguards do.

As NPCs, blackguards usually lead legions of undead, evil outsiders, or other monsters to conquer their own doomed demesne or expand their existing territory. Sometimes they serve more powerful evil characters as dark lieutenants. On occasion they operate alone as hired killers or wandering purveyors of ill, destruction, and chaos.

Hit Die: d10.

TABLE 2–10: THE BLACKGUARD

Class Level	Base Attack Bonus	Fort Save	Ref Save	Will Save	Special	Spells per Day			
						1st	2nd	3rd	4th
1st	+1	+2	0	0	Detect good, poison use	0	—	—	—
2nd	+2	+3	0	0	Dark blessing, smite good	1	—	—	—
3rd	+3	+3	+1	+1	Command undead, aura of despair	1	0	—	—
4th	+4	+4	+1	+1	Sneak attack +1d6	1	1	—	—
5th	+5	+4	+1	+1	Fiendish servant	1	1	0	—
6th	+6	+5	+2	+2		1	1	1	—
7th	+7	+5	+2	+2	Sneak attack +2d6	2	1	1	0
8th	+8	+6	+2	+2		2	1	1	1
9th	+9	+6	+3	+3		2	2	1	1
10th	+10	+7	+3	+3	Sneak attack +3d6	2	2	2	1

Requirements

To qualify to become a blackguard, a character must fulfill all the following criteria.

Alignment: Any evil.

Base Attack Bonus: +6.

Knowledge (religion): 2 ranks.

Hide: 5 ranks.

Feats: Cleave, Sunder.

Special: The blackguard must have made peaceful contact with an evil outsider who was summoned by him or someone else to have contracted the taint of true evil.

Class Skills

The blackguard's class skills (and the key ability for each skill) are Concentration (Con), Craft (Int), Diplomacy (Cha), Handle Animal (Cha), Heal (Wis), Intimidate (Cha), Knowledge (religion) (Int), Profession (Wis), and Ride (Dex). See Chapter 4: Skills in the *Player's Handbook* for skill descriptions.

Skill Points at Each Level: 2 + Int modifier.

Class Features

All of the following are class features of the blackguard prestige class.

Weapon and Armor Proficiency: Blackguards are proficient with all simple and martial weapons, with all types of armor, and with shields. Note that armor check penalties for armor heavier than leather apply to the skills Balance, Climb, Escape Artist, Hide, Jump, Move Silently, Pick Pocket, and Tumble.

Detect Good: At will, the blackguard can detect good as a spell-like ability. This ability duplicates the effects of the spell *detect good*.

Poison Use: Blackguards are skilled in the use of poison and never risk accidentally poisoning themselves when applying poison to a blade.

Dark Blessing: A blackguard applies his Charisma modifier (if positive) as a bonus to all saving throws.

Spells: Beginning at 1st level, a blackguard gains the ability to cast a small number of divine spells. To cast a spell, the blackguard must have a Wisdom score of at least 10 + the spell's level, so a blackguard with a Wisdom of 10 or lower cannot cast these spells. Blackguard bonus spells are based on Wisdom, and saving throws against these spells have a DC of 10 + spell level + the blackguard's Wisdom modifier. When the blackguard gets 0 spells of a given level, such as 0 1st-level spells at 1st level, he gets only bonus spells. (A blackguard without a bonus spell for that level cannot yet cast a spell of that level.) The blackguard's spell list appears below. A blackguard has access to any spell on the list and can freely choose which to prepare, just like a cleric. A blackguard prepares and casts spells just as a cleric does (though the blackguard cannot spontaneously cast *cure* or *inflict* spells).

Smite Good: Once a day, a blackguard of 2nd level or higher may attempt to smite good with one normal melee attack. He adds his Charisma modifier (if positive) to his attack roll and deals 1 extra point of damage per class level. For example, a 9th-level blackguard armed with a longsword would deal 1d8+9 points of damage, plus any additional bonuses from high Strength or magical effects that normally apply. If the blackguard accidentally smites a creature that is not good, the smite

---

FIENDISH SERVANT

Upon or after reaching 5th level, a blackguard can call a fiendish bat, cat, dire rat, horse, pony, raven, or toad to serve him. (See the *Monster Manual* for these creatures' basic statistics.) This creature may be used as a guardian (such as a bat), a helper (such as a cat), or a mount (such as a horse). The blackguard's servant further gains HD and special abilities based on the blackguard's character level.

The blackguard may have only one fiendish servant at a time. Should the blackguard's servant die, he may call for another one after one day. The new fiendish servant has all the accumulated abilities due a servant of the blackguard's current level.

TABLE 2–11: FIENDISH SERVANTS

Blackguard Character Level	Bonus HD	Natural Armor	Str Adj.	Int	Special
12 or less	+2 HD	+1	+1	6	Improved evasion, share spells, empathic link, share saving throws
13–15	+4 HD	+3	+2	7	Speak with blackguard
16–18	+6 HD	+5	+3	8	Blood bond
19–20	+8 HD	+7	+4	9	Spell resistance

Blackguard Character Level: The character level of the blackguard (his blackguard level plus his original class level).

Bonus Hit Dice: These are extra d8 Hit Dice, each of which gains a Constitution modifier, as normal. Extra Hit Dice improve the servant's base attack and base save bonuses, as normal.

Natural Armor: This is a bonus to the servant's natural armor rating.

Str Adj.: Add this figure to the servant's Strength score.

Int: The servant's Intelligence score. (The fiendish servant is smarter than normal animals of its kind.)

Improved Evasion: If the servant is subjected to an attack that normally allows a Reflex saving throw for half damage, it takes no damage on a successful saving throw and only half damage on a failed saving throw. Improved evasion is an extraordinary ability.

Share Spells: At the blackguard's option, he may have any spell he casts on himself also affect his servant. The servant must be within 5 feet. If the spell has a duration other than instantaneous, the spell stops affecting the servant if it moves farther than 5 feet away and will not affect the servant again even if the servant returns to the blackguard before the duration expires. Additionally, the blackguard may cast a spell with a target of "You" on his servant (as a touch range spell) instead of on himself. The blackguard and the servant can share spells even if the spells normally do not affect creatures of the servant's type (magical beast).

Empathic Link: The blackguard has an empathic link with the servant out to a distance of up to one mile. The blackguard cannot see through the servant's eyes, but they can communicate telepathically. Even intelligent servants see the world differently from humans, so misunderstandings are always possible. This empathic link is a supernatural ability.

Because of the empathic link between the servant and the blackguard, the blackguard has the same connection to a place or an item that the servant does.

Share Saving Throws: The servant uses its own base save or the blackguard's, whichever is higher.

Speak with Blackguard: The blackguard and servant can communicate verbally as if they were using a common language. Other creatures do not understand the communication without magical help.

Blood Bond: The servant gains a +2 bonus to all attacks, checks, and saves if it witnesses the blackguard threatened or harmed. This bonus lasts as long as the threat is immediate and apparent.

Spell Resistance: The servant's spell resistance equals the blackguard's level + 5. To affect the servant with a spell, a spellcaster must make a caster level check (1d20 + caster level) at least equal to the servant's spell resistance.

has no effect but it is still used up for that day. Smite good is a supernatural ability.

Aura of Despair: Beginning at 3rd level, the blackguard radiates a malign aura that causes enemies within 10 feet of him to suffer a –2 morale penalty on all saving throws. Aura of despair is a supernatural ability.

Command Undead: When a blackguard reaches 3rd level, he gains the supernatural ability to command and rebuke undead (see the *Player's Handbook*, pages 139–140). He commands undead as would a cleric of two levels lower.

Sneak Attack: If a blackguard can catch an opponent when she is unable to defend herself effectively from his attack, he can strike a vital spot for extra damage. Basically, any time the blackguard's target would be denied her Dexterity bonus to AC (whether she actually has a Dexterity bonus or not), the blackguard's attack deals +1d6 points of damage at 4th level and an additional +1d6 points for every three levels thereafter (+2d6 at 7th level, +3d6 at 10th level, and so on). Should the blackguard score a critical hit with a sneak attack, this extra damage is not multiplied.

Ranged attacks only count as sneak attacks if the target is 30 feet away or less. A blackguard cannot make a sneak attack to deal subdual damage. The blackguard must be able to see the target well enough to pick out a vital spot and must be able to reach a vital spot. He cannot sneak attack while striking at a creature with concealment or by striking the limbs of a creature whose vitals are beyond reach.

A blackguard can only sneak attack living creatures with discernible anatomies. Undead, constructs, oozes, plants, and incorporeal creatures lack vital areas to attack. Additionally, any creature immune to critical hits is not subject to sneak attacks.

If a blackguard gets a sneak attack bonus from another source (such as rogue levels), the bonuses to damage stack.

Blackguard Spell List

Blackguards choose their spells from the following list:

1st level—*cause fear, cure light wounds, doom, inflict light wounds, magic weapon, summon monster I*.

2nd level—*bull's strength, cure moderate wounds, darkness, death knell, inflict moderate wounds, shatter, summon monster II*.

3rd level—*contagion, cure serious wounds, deeper darkness, inflict serious wounds, protection from elements, summon monster III*.

4th level—*cure critical wounds, freedom of movement, inflict critical wounds, poison, summon monster IV*.
*Evil creatures only.

Fallen Paladins

Blackguards who possess levels of paladin (that is to say, are now ex-paladins) gain extra abilities the more levels of paladin they possess. Those who have tasted the light of goodness and justice and turned away make the foulest villains.

Dwarven Defender

The defender is a sponsored champion of a dwarven cause, a dwarven aristocrat, a dwarven deity, or the dwarven way of life. As the name might imply, this character is a skilled combatant trained in the arts of defense. A line of dwarven defenders is a far better defense than a 10-foot-thick wall of stone, and much more dangerous.

Most dwarven defenders are fighters, paladins, rangers, or clerics, although ex-barbarians, sorcerers, wizards, and druids can certainly all benefit from the defensive capabilities of this prestige class. Rogues, bards, and monks usually depend too heavily on mobility to really use the abilities of the dwarven defender class to their fullest.

NPC dwarven defenders are usually soldiers in a dwarven citadel, segregated into their own units separate from regular warriors or fighters. Occasionally, a lone, wandering dwarven defender can be encountered on some mission, although he

A blackguard

TABLE 2–12: FALLEN PALADIN BLACKGUARD ABILITIES

Paladin Levels	Extra Ability
1–2	Smite good once per day. (This is in addition to the ability granted to all blackguards at 2nd level, so that a fallen paladin blackguard can smite good a total of twice per day.)
3–4	*Lay on hands*. Once per day, the blackguard can cure himself of damage equal to his Charisma bonus times his level. The blackguard can only cure himself or his fiendish servant with this spell-like ability.
5–6	Sneak attack damage increased by +1d6.
7–8	Fiendish summoning. Once per day, the blackguard can use a *summon monster I* spell to call forth an evil creature. For this spell, the caster level is double the blackguard's class level.
9–10	Undead companion. In addition to the fiendish servant, the blackguard gains (at 5th level) a Medium-size skeleton or zombie as a companion. This companion cannot be turned or rebuked by another and gains all special bonuses as a fiendish servant when the blackguard gains levels.
11+	Favored of the dark deities. Evil deities like nothing more than to see a pure heart corrupted, and thus a fallen paladin of this stature immediately gains a blackguard level for each level of paladin he trades in. For example, a character who has twelve levels of paladin can immediately become a 10th-level blackguard with all abilities if he chooses to lose ten levels of paladin. The character level of the character does not change. This, of course, is in every way a profitable trade for the evil character, since he has already lost most of the benefits he gained from having those paladin levels. However, with the loss of paladin levels, the character no longer gains extra abilities found on this table. Thus, a fallen paladin of 15th level could become a 10th-level blackguard/5th-level paladin with the first three extra abilities on this chart because of those five levels of paladin.

usually guards his words so closely that it's difficult to learn what his quest actually entails.

Hit Die: d12.

Requirements

To qualify to become a defender, a character must fulfill all the following criteria.

Alignment: Any lawful.

Race: Dwarf.

Base Attack Bonus: +7.

Feats: Dodge, Endurance, Toughness.

Class Skills

The defender's class skills (and the key ability for each skill) are Craft (Int), Listen (Wis), Sense Motive (Wis), and Spot (Wis). See Chapter 4: Skills in the *Player's Handbook* for skill descriptions.

Skill Points at Each Level: 2 + Int modifier.

Class Features

All of the following are class features of the dwarven defender prestige class.

Weapon and Armor Proficiency: The dwarven defender is proficient with all simple and martial weapons, all types of armor, and shields. Note that armor check penalties for armor heavier than leather apply to the skills Balance, Climb, Escape Artist, Hide, Jump, Move Silently, Pick Pocket, and Tumble.

Defensive Stance: When he needs to, the defender can become a stalwart bastion of defense. In this defensive stance, a defender gains phenomenal strength and durability, but he cannot move from the spot he is defending. He gains the following benefits:

- +2 Strength
- +4 Constitution
- +2 resistance bonus on all saves
- +4 dodge bonus to AC

A dwarven defender

Arnie

The increase in Constitution increases the defender's hit points by 2 points per level, but these hit points go away at the end of the defensive stance when the Constitution score drops back 4 points. These extra hit points are not lost first the way temporary hit points are. While defending, a defender cannot use skills or abilities that would require him to shift his position, such as Move Silently or Jump. A defensive stance lasts for 3 rounds, plus the character's (newly improved) Constitution modifier. The defender may end the defense voluntarily prior to this limit. At the end of the defense, the defender is winded and suffers a –2 penalty to Strength for the duration of that encounter. The defender can only take his defensive stance a certain number of times per day as determined by his level (see Table 2–13: The Dwarven Defender). Taking the stance takes no time itself, but the defender can only do so during his action. (A defender can't, for example, take the stance when struck down by an arrow in order to get the extra hit points from the increased Constitution.)

Defensive Awareness: Starting at 2nd level, the dwarven defender gains the extraordinary ability to react to danger before his senses would normally allow him to even be aware of it. At 2nd level and above, he retains his Dexterity bonus to AC (if any) regardless of being caught flat-footed or struck by an invisible attacker. (He still loses any Dexterity bonus to AC if immobilized.)

At 5th level, the dwarven defender can no longer be flanked, since he can react to opponents on opposite sides of him as easily as he can react to a single attacker. This defense denies rogues the ability to use flank attacks to sneak attack the dwarven defender. The exception to this defense is that a rogue at least 4 levels higher than the dwarven defender can flank him (and thus sneak attack him).

At 10th level, the dwarven defender gains an intuitive sense that alerts him to danger from traps, giving him a +1 bonus to Reflex saves made to avoid traps.

Defensive awareness is cumulative with uncanny dodge. If the dwarven defender has another class that grants the uncanny dodge ability, add together all the class levels of the classes that grant these two abilities and determine the character's defensive awareness ability on that basis.

TABLE 2–13: THE DWARVEN DEFENDER

Class Level	Base Attack Bonus	Fort Save	Ref Save	Will Save	AC Bonus	Special
1st	+1	+2	+0	+2	+1	Defensive stance 1/day
2nd	+2	+3	+0	+3	+1	Defensive awareness (Dex bonus to AC)
3rd	+3	+3	+1	+3	+1	Defensive stance 2/day
4th	+4	+4	+1	+4	+2	
5th	+5	+4	+1	+4	+2	Defensive stance 3/day
6th	+6	+5	+2	+5	+2	Damage reduction (3), defensive awareness (can't be flanked)
7th	+7	+5	+2	+5	+3	Defensive stance 4/day
8th	+8	+6	+2	+6	+3	
9th	+9	+6	+3	+6	+3	Defensive stance 5/day
10th	+10	+7	+3	+7	+4	Damage reduction (6), defensive awareness (+1 vs. traps)

Damage Reduction: At 6th level, the dwarven defender gains the extraordinary ability to shrug off some amount of injury from each blow or attack. Subtract 3 from the damage the dwarven defender takes each time he is dealt damage. At 10th level, this damage reduction rises to 6. Damage reduction can reduce damage to 0 but not below 0. (That is, the defender cannot actually gain hit points in this manner.)

Loremaster

Loremasters are spellcasters who concentrate on knowledge, valuing lore and secrets over gold. They uncover secrets that they then use to better themselves mentally, physically, and spiritually.

Characters without at least one level of wizard, sorcerer, cleric, or druid gain little benefit to becoming a loremaster. Paladins, rangers, and bards might gain some benefit, but overall, it would be minor.

Loremasters sometimes gather in secluded cabals but are more likely to be located as an order attached to a university, a library, or some other source of information. They're likely to earn extra money as sages and information brokers, pouring their wages in their own research. A loremaster might also adopt a position as a wise one in a community, or even as its leader, drawing upon her knowledge to help others.

Hit Die: d4.

Requirements

To qualify to become a loremaster, a character must fulfill all the following criteria.

Spellcasting: Ability to cast seven different divinations, one of which must be 3rd level or higher.

Two Knowledge Skills (Any Type): 10 ranks in each.

Feats: Any three metamagic or item creation feats, plus Skill Focus (Knowledge [any individual Knowledge skill]).

Class Skills

The loremaster's class skills (and the key ability for each skill) are Alchemy (Int), Appraise (Int), Concentration (Con), Decipher Script (Int, exclusive skill), Gather Information (Cha), Handle Animals (Cha), Heal (Wis), Knowledge (all skills taken individually) (Int), Perform (Cha), Profession (Wis), Scry (Int), Speak Language, Spellcraft (Int), and Use Magic Device (Cha, exclusive skill). See Chapter 4: Skills in the *Player's Handbook* for skill descriptions.

Skill Points at Each Level: 4 + Int modifier.

A loremaster

Class Features

All of the following are class features of the loremaster prestige class.

Weapon and Armor Proficiency: Loremasters gain no proficiency in any weapon or armor. Note that armor check penalties for armor heavier than leather apply to the skills Balance, Climb, Escape Artist, Hide, Jump, Move Silently, Pick Pocket, and Tumble.

Spells per Day: A loremaster continues training in magic as well as her field of research. Thus, when a new loremaster level is gained, the character gains new spells per day as if she had also gained a level in a spellcasting class she belonged to before she added the prestige class. She does not, however, gain any other benefit a character of that class would have gained (improved chance of controlling or rebuking undead, metamagic or item creation feats, and so on). This essentially means that she adds the level of loremaster to the level of some other spellcasting class the character has, then determines spells per day and caster level accordingly. For example, if Gremda, an 8th-level wizard, gains a level in loremaster, she gains new spells as if she had risen to 9th level in wizard, but uses the other loremaster aspects of level progression such as attack bonus and save bonus. If she next gains a level of wizard, making her a 9th-level wizard/1st-level loremaster, she gains and casts spells as if she had risen to 10th-level wizard.

If a character had more than one spellcasting class before she became a loremaster, she must decide to which class she adds each level of loremaster for purposes of determining spells per day when she adds the new level.

Secret: In their studies, loremasters stumble upon all sorts of applicable knowledge and secrets. At 1st level and every two levels afterward (3rd, 5th, 7th, and 9th levels), the loremaster chooses one secret from Table 2–15: Loremaster Secrets. Her level plus Intelligence modifier determines which secrets she can choose. She can't choose the same secret twice.

Lore: Loremasters gather knowledge. At 2nd level, they gain the ability to know legends or information regarding various topics, just like a bard can with bardic knowledge. The loremaster adds her level and her Intelligence modifier to the Knowledge check. See page 29 in the *Player's Handbook* for more information on bardic knowledge.

Bonus Languages: Loremasters, in their laborious studies, learn new languages in order to access more knowledge. The loremaster can choose any new language at 4th and 8th level.

Greater Lore: At 6th level, a loremaster gains the ability to *identify* magic items, as the spell, as an extraordinary ability. She may do this once per item examined.

True Lore: At 10th level, once per day a loremaster can use her knowledge to gain the affects of a *legend lore* spell or an *analyze dweomer* spell. True lore is an extraordinary ability.

Shadowdancer

Operating in the border between light and darkness, shadow-dancers are nimble artists of deception. They are mysterious and

TABLE 2–14: THE LOREMASTER

Class Level	Base Attack Bonus	Fort Save	Ref Save	Will Save	Special	Spells per Day
1st	+0	+0	+0	+2	Secret	+1 level of existing class
2nd	+1	+0	+0	+3	Lore	+1 level of existing class
3rd	+1	+1	+1	+3	Secret	+1 level of existing class
4th	+2	+1	+1	+4	Bonus language	+1 level of existing class
5th	+2	+1	+1	+4	Secret	+1 level of existing class
6th	+3	+2	+2	+5	Greater lore	+1 level of existing class
7th	+3	+2	+2	+5	Secret	+1 level of existing class
8th	+4	+2	+2	+6	Bonus language	+1 level of existing class
9th	+4	+3	+3	+6	Secret	+1 level of existing class
10th	+5	+3	+3	+7	True lore	+1 level of existing class

TABLE 2–15: LOREMASTER SECRETS

Level + Int Modifier	Secret	Effect
1	Instant mastery	4 ranks of a skill in which the character has no ranks
2	Secret health	+3 hit points
3	Secrets of inner strength	+1 bonus to Will saves
4	The lore of true stamina	+1 bonus to Fortitude saves
5	Secret knowledge of avoidance	+1 bonus to Reflex saves
6	Weapon trick	+1 bonus to attack rolls
7	Dodge trick	+1 dodge bonus to AC
8	Applicable knowledge	Any one feat
9	Newfound arcana	1 bonus 1st-level spell*
10	More newfound arcana	1 bonus 2nd-level spell*

*As if gained through having a high ability score.

unknown, never completely trusted but always inducing wonder when met.

Rogues, bards, and monks make excellent shadowdancers, but fighters, barbarians, rangers, and paladins also find shadowdancer abilities allow them to strike at their opponents with surprise and skill. Wizard, sorcerer, cleric, and druid shadowdancers employ the defensive capabilities inherent in the prestige class to allow them to cast their spells from safety and move away quickly. Despite their link with shadows and trickery, shadowdancers are as often good as evil. They may use their incredible abilities as they wish.

Shadowdancers often work in troupes, never staying in one place too long. Some use their abilities to entertain. Others operate as thieves, using their abilities to infiltrate past defenses and dupe others. All shadowdancer troupes maintain an aura of mystery among the populace, who never know whether to think well or ill of them.

Hit Die: d8.

Requirements

To qualify to become a shadowdancer, a character must fulfill all the following criteria.

Move Silently: 8 ranks.

Hide: 10 ranks.

Perform: 5 ranks.

Feats: Dodge, Mobility, Combat Reflexes.

Class Skills

The shadowdancer's class skills (and the key ability for each skill) are Balance (Dex), Bluff (Cha), Decipher Script (Int, exclusive skill), Diplomacy (Cha), Disguise (Cha), Escape Artist (Dex), Hide (Dex), Jump (Str), Listen (Wis), Move Silently (Dex), Perform (Cha), Pick Pocket (Dex), Profession (Wis), Search (Int), Spot (Wis), Tumble (Dex), and Use Rope (Dex). See Chapter 4: Skills in the *Player's Handbook* for skill descriptions.

Skill Points at Each Level: 6 + Int modifier.

Class Features

All of the following are features of the shadowdancer prestige class.

Weapon and Armor Proficiency: Shadowdancers are proficient with the club, crossbow (hand, light, or heavy), dagger (any type), dart, mace, morningstar, quarterstaff, rapier, sap, shortbow (normal and composite), and short sword. Shadowdancers are proficient with light armor but not with shields. Note that armor check penalties for armor heavier than leather apply to the skills Balance, Climb, Escape Artist, Hide, Jump, Move Silently, Pick Pocket, and Tumble.

Hide in Plain Sight: Shadowdancers can use the Hide skill even while being observed. As long as they are within 10 feet of some sort of shadow, shadowdancers can hide themselves from view in the open without anything to actually hide behind. They cannot, however, hide in their own shadows. Hide in plain sight is a supernatural ability.

Evasion: At 2nd level, a shadowdancer gains evasion. If exposed to any effect that normally allows her to attempt a Reflex saving throw for half damage (such as a *fireball*), she takes no damage with a successful saving throw. The evasion ability can only be used if the shadowdancer is wearing light armor or no armor.

Darkvision: At 2nd level, a shadowdancer can see in the dark as though she were permanently under the affect of a *darkvision* spell. This is a supernatural ability.

Uncanny Dodge: Starting at 2nd level, the shadowdancer gains the extraordinary ability to react to danger before her senses would normally allow her to even be aware of it. At 2nd level and above, she retains her Dexterity bonus to AC (if any) regardless of being caught flat-footed or struck by an invisible attacker. (She still loses any Dexterity bonus to AC if immobilized.)

At 5th level, the shadowdancer can no longer be flanked, since she can react to opponents on opposite sides of her as easily as she can react to a single attacker. This defense denies rogues the ability to use flank attacks to sneak attack the shadowdancer. The exception to this defense is that a rogue at least 4 levels higher than the shadowdancer can flank her (and thus sneak attack her).

At 10th level, the shadowdancer gains an intuitive sense that alerts her to danger from traps, giving her a +1 bonus to Reflex saves made to avoid traps.

If the shadowdancer has another class that grants the uncanny dodge ability, add together all the class levels of the classes that grant the ability and determine the character's uncanny dodge ability on that basis.

Shadow Illusion: When a shadowdancer reaches 3rd level, she can create visual illusions from surrounding shadows. This spell-like ability is identical to the arcane spell *silent image* and may be employed once per day.

Summon Shadow: At 3rd level, a shadowdancer can summon a shadow, an undead shade. (See the *Monster Manual* for the shadow's statistics.) Unlike a normal shadow, this shadow's alignment matches that of the shadowdancer. The summoned shadow cannot be turned, rebuked, or commanded by any third

TABLE 2–16: THE SHADOWDANCER

Class Level	Base Attack Bonus	Fort Save	Ref Save	Will Save	Special
1st	+0	+0	+2	+0	Hide in plain sight
2nd	+1	+0	+3	+0	Evasion, darkvision, uncanny dodge (Dex bonus to AC)
3rd	+2	+1	+3	+1	Shadow illusion, summon shadow
4th	+3	+1	+4	+1	Shadow jump (20 ft.)
5th	+3	+1	+4	+1	Defensive roll, uncanny dodge (can't be flanked)
6th	+4	+2	+5	+2	Shadow jump (40 ft.), summon shadow
7th	+5	+2	+5	+2	Slippery mind
8th	+6	+2	+6	+2	Shadow jump (80 ft.)
9th	+6	+3	+6	+3	Summon shadow
10th	+7	+3	+7	+3	Shadow jump (160 ft.), improved evasion, uncanny dodge (+1 vs. traps)

party. This shadow serves as a companion to the shadowdancer and can communicate intelligibly with the shadowdancer. Every third level gained by the shadowdancer allows her to summon an additional shadow and adds +2 HD (and the requisite base attack and base save bonus increases) to all her shadow companions. For example, a 9th-level shadowdancer can have three shadow companions, each with 6 HD.

If a shadow companion is destroyed, or the shadowdancer chooses to dismiss it, the shadowdancer must attempt a Fortitude saving throw (DC 15). If the saving throw fails, the shadowdancer loses 200 experience points per shadowdancer level. A successful saving throw reduces the loss by half, to 100 XP per prestige class level. The shadowdancer's experience can never go below 0 as the result of a shadow's dismissal or destruction. A destroyed or dismissed shadow companion cannot be replaced for a year and a day.

A shadowdancer

Shadow Jump: At 4th level, the shadowdancer gains the ability to travel between shadows as if by means of a *dimension door* spell. The limitation is that the magical transport must begin and end in an area with at least some shadow. The shadowdancer can jump up to a total of 20 feet each day in this way, although this may be a single jump of 20 feet or two jumps of 10 feet each. Every two levels thereafter, the distance a shadowdancer can jump each day doubles (40 feet at 6th level, 80 feet at 8th level, and 160 feet at 10th level). This amount can be split up among many jumps, but each jump, no matter how small, counts as a 10-foot increment. (For instance, a 6th-level shadowdancer who jumps 32 feet cannot jump again until the next day.)

Defensive Roll: Starting at 5th level, the shadowdancer can roll with a potentially lethal blow to take less damage from it. Once per day, when a shadowdancer would be reduced to 0 hit points or less by damage in combat (from a weapon or other blow, not a spell or special ability), the shadowdancer can attempt to roll with the damage. She makes a Reflex saving throw (DC = damage dealt) and, if successful, takes only half damage from the blow. She must be aware of the attack and able to react to it in order to execute her defensive roll. If she is in a situation that would deny her

any Dexterity bonus to AC, she can't attempt the defensive roll.

Slippery Mind: This extraordinary ability, gained at 7th level, represents the shadowdancer's ability to wriggle free from magical effects that would otherwise control or compel her. If the shadowdancer is affected by an enchantment and fails her saving throw, 1 round later she can attempt her saving throw again. She only gets this one extra chance to succeed at her saving throw. If it fails as well, the spell's effects proceed normally.

Improved Evasion: This extraordinary ability, gained at 10th level, works like evasion (see above). The shadowdancer takes no damage at all on successful saving throws against attacks that allow a Reflex saving throw for half damage (breath weapon, *fireball*, and so on). What's more, she takes only half damage even if she fails her saving throw, since the shadowdancer's reflexes allow her to get out of harm's way with incredible speed.

NPC CLASSES

The *Player's Handbook* extensively describes adventurers. But what about the rest of the world? Surely not everyone's a fighter, rogue, or wizard. Presented below are NPC classes. None of them, with the possible exceptions of the expert and the aristocrat, stands up as a playable class for PCs. Instead, they represent the rest of the people in the world around the PCs who don't train to go on adventures and explore dungeons.

Treat these classes as you would any other. They get feats every three levels and ability score increases every four levels (see Table 3–2: Experience and Level-Dependent Benefits, page 22 in the *Player's Handbook*). Most NPCs take feats such as Endurance, Skill Focus, Track, and other noncombat-related abilities. It's possible for NPCs to multiclass, and even to obtain PC classes if you so desire.

The fact that each NPC class has differing levels provides the DM with a means to measure NPCs against each other. A typical blacksmith might only be a 3rd-level commoner, but the world's greatest blacksmith is probably a 20th-level expert. That 20th-level blacksmith is a capable person with great skill, but she can't fight as well as a fighter equal to her level (or even one much lower in level), nor can she cast spells or do the other things that characters with PC classes can do.

NPCs gain experience the same way that PCs do (see Chapter 7: Rewards for details). Not being adventurers, however, their oppor-

TABLE 2–17: THE ADEPT

NPC Level	Base Attack Bonus	Fort Save	Ref Save	Will Save	Special	Spells per Day					
						0	1st	2nd	3rd	4th	5th
1st	+0	+0	+0	+2		3	1	—	—	—	—
2nd	+1	+0	+0	+3	Summon familiar	3	1	—	—	—	—
3rd	+1	+1	+1	+3		3	2	—	—	—	—
4th	+2	+1	+1	+4		3	2	0	—	—	—
5th	+2	+1	+1	+4		3	2	1	—	—	—
6th	+3	+2	+2	+5		3	2	1	—	—	—
7th	+3	+2	+2	+5		3	3	2	—	—	—
8th	+4	+2	+2	+6		3	3	2	0	—	—
9th	+4	+3	+3	+6		3	3	2	1	—	—
10th	+5	+3	+3	+7		3	3	2	1	—	—
11th	+5	+3	+3	+7		3	3	3	2	—	—
12th	+6/+1	+4	+4	+8		3	3	3	2	0	—
13th	+6/+1	+4	+4	+8		3	3	3	2	1	—
14th	+7/+2	+4	+4	+9		3	3	3	2	1	—
15th	+7/+2	+5	+5	+9		3	3	3	3	2	—
16th	+8/+3	+5	+5	+10		3	3	3	3	2	0
17th	+8/+3	+5	+5	+10		3	3	3	3	2	1
18th	+9/+4	+6	+6	+11		3	3	3	3	2	1
19th	+9/+4	+6	+6	+11		3	3	3	3	3	2
20th	+10/+5	+6	+6	+12		3	3	3	3	3	2

tunities are more limited. Therefore, a commoner is likely to progress in levels very slowly. Most never reach more than 2nd or 3rd level in their whole lives. A warrior serving as a town guard is more likely to gain experience here and there and thus might gain a few levels, but this experience is still paltry compared to what an adventurer gains. Note, though, that dangerous areas are more likely to produce higher-level NPCs than peaceful, settled lands. A commoner who must regularly fight off gnolls from ransacking his farm or burning his crops is likely to be a high-level commoner.

You should find that these NPC classes provide enough distinction so that anyone the PCs meet who isn't an adventurer can be created using these classes. See the Generating Towns section (pages 137–140) in Chapter 4: Adventuring for information on how many characters belonging to each of these NPC classes are found in a typical town and their respective levels.

Adept

Some tribal societies or less sophisticated regions don't have the resources to train wizards and clerics. Reflecting a lesser knowledge of magic yet an intriguing combination of arcane and divine skills, the adept serves these cultures as both wise woman (or holy man) and mystical defender.

Adepts can be found in isolated human, elf, dwarf, gnome, and halfling communities but are most prevalent among more bestial humanoid and giant species such as orcs, goblins, gnolls, bugbears, and ogres.

Hit Die: d6.

Class Skills

The adept's class skills (and the key ability for each skill) are Alchemy (Int), Concentration (Con), Craft (Int), Handle Animal (Cha), Heal (Wis), Knowledge (all skills taken individually) (Int), Profession (Wis), Scry (Int, exclusive skill), Spellcraft (Int), and Wilderness Lore (Wis). See Chapter 4: Skills in the *Player's Handbook* for skill descriptions.

Skill Points at 1st Level: (2 + Int modifier) × 4.
Skill Points at Each Additional Level: 2 + Int modifier.

Class Features

All of the following are class features of the adept NPC class.

Weapon and Armor Proficiency: Adepts are skilled with all simple weapons. Adepts are not proficient with any type of armor nor with shields. Note that armor check penalties for armor heavier than leather apply to the skills Balance, Climb, Escape Artist, Hide, Jump, Move Silently, Pick Pocket, and Tumble.

Spells: An adept casts divine spells. She is limited to a certain number of spells of each spell level per day, according to her class level. Like a cleric, an adept may prepare and cast any spell on the adept list, provided she can cast spells of that level. Like a cleric, she prepares her spells ahead of time each day (see page 156 in Chapter 10: Magic in the *Player's Handbook*).

The DC for a saving throw against an adept's spell is 10 + spell level + the adept's Wisdom modifier.

Adepts, unlike wizards, do not acquire their spells from books or scrolls, nor prepare them through study. Instead, they meditate or pray for their spells, receiving them as divine inspiration or through their own strength of faith. Each adept must choose a time each day at which she must spend an hour in quiet contemplation or supplication to regain her daily allotment of spells. Time spent resting has no effect on whether an adept can prepare spells.

When the adept gets 0 spells of a given level (see Table 2–17: The Adept), she gets only bonus spells for that spell slot. An adept without a bonus spell for that level cannot yet cast a spell of that level. Bonus spells are based on Wisdom.

Each adept has a particular holy symbol (as a divine focus) depending on the adept's magical tradition.

Familiar: At 2nd level, an adept can call a familiar, just like a sorcerer or wizard can. See the section on familiars in the *Player's Handbook* (page 51) for more information.

Starting Gear

2d4 × 10 gp worth of equipment.

Adept Spell List

Adepts choose their spells from the following list:

0 level—*create water, cure minor wounds, detect magic, ghost sound, guidance, light, mending, purify food and drink, read magic.*

1st level—*bless, burning hands, cause fear, command, comprehend languages, cure light wounds, detect chaos, detect evil, detect good, detect law, endure elements, obscuring mist, protection from chaos, protection from evil, protection from good, protection from law, sleep.*

2nd level—*aid, animal trance, bull's strength, cat's grace, cure mod-*

erate wounds, darkness, delay poison, endurance, invisibility, mirror image, resist elements, see invisibility, web.

3rd level—animate dead, bestow curse, contagion, continual flame, cure serious wounds, daylight, deeper darkness, lightning bolt, neutralize poison, remove curse, remove disease, tongues.

4th level—cure critical wounds, minor creation, polymorph other, polymorph self, restoration, stoneskin, wall of fire.

5th level—break enchantment, commune, heal, major creation, raise dead, true seeing, wall of stone.

Aristocrat

Aristocrats are usually educated, wealthy individuals born into high position. Aristocrats are not only the well-born, but also the wealthy or politically influential people in the world. They are given the freedom to train in the fields of their choice, for the most part, and to travel widely. With access to all the best goods and opportunities, many aristocrats become formidable individuals. Some even go on adventures with fighters, wizards, and other classes, although usually such activities are nothing more than a lark.

The aristocrat might offer potential as a PC class. They have an impressive selection of skills and respectable combat training. Being a aristocrat, however, isn't so much a choice as a position you're born into. Characters cannot take aristocrat as a multiclass unless aristocrat is the class chosen first. Mostly, the DM should reserve the aristocrat class for rulers, their families, and their courtiers.

Hit Die: d8.

TABLE 2–18: THE ARISTOCRAT

NPC Level	Base Attack Bonus	Fort Save	Ref Save	Will Save
1st	+0	+0	+0	+2
2nd	+1	+0	+0	+3
3rd	+2	+1	+1	+3
4th	+3	+1	+1	+4
5th	+3	+1	+1	+4
6th	+4	+2	+2	+5
7th	+5	+2	+2	+5
8th	+6/+1	+2	+2	+6
9th	+6/+1	+3	+3	+6
10th	+7/+2	+3	+3	+7
11th	+8/+3	+3	+3	+7
12th	+9/+4	+4	+4	+8
13th	+9/+4	+4	+4	+8
14th	+10/+5	+4	+4	+9
15th	+11/+6/+1	+5	+5	+9
16th	+12/+7/+2	+5	+5	+10
17th	+12/+7/+2	+5	+5	+10
18th	+13/+8/+3	+6	+6	+11
19th	+14/+9/+4	+6	+6	+11
20th	+15/+10/+5	+6	+6	+12

Class Skills

The aristocrat's class skills (and the key ability for each skill) are Appraise (Int), Bluff (Cha), Diplomacy (Cha), Disguise (Cha), Forgery (Int), Gather Information (Cha), Handle Animal (Cha), Innuendo (Wis), Intimidate (Cha), Knowledge (all skills taken individually) (Int), Listen (Wis), Perform (Cha), Read Lips (Int, exclusive skill), Ride (Dex), Sense Motive (Wis), Speak Language, Spot (Wis), Swim (Str), and Wilderness Lore (Wis). See Chapter 4: Skills in the *Player's Handbook* for skill descriptions.

Skill Points at 1st Level: (4 + Int modifier) × 4.
Skill Points at Each Additional Level: 4 + Int modifier.

Class Features

The following is a class feature of the aristocrat NPC class.

Weapon and Armor Proficiency: The aristocrat is proficient in the use of all simple and martial weapons and with all types of armor and shields. Note that armor check penalties for armor heavier than leather apply to the skills Balance, Climb, Escape Artist, Hide, Jump, Move Silently, Pick Pocket, and Tumble.

Starting Gear

6d8 × 10 gp worth of equipment.

Commoner

The common folk farm the fields, staff the shops, build the homes, and produce (and transport) the goods in the world around the adventurers. Commoners usually have no desire to live the wandering, dangerous life of an adventurer and possess none of the skills needed to undertake the challenges adventurers must face. Commoners are skilled in their own vocations and make up the majority of the population.

Player characters should not be commoners, since commoners make poor adventurers. Instead, the commoner class should be reserved for everyone who does not qualify for any other class.

Hit Die: d4.

TABLE 2–19: THE COMMONER

NPC Level	Base Attack Bonus	Fort Save	Ref Save	Will Save
1st	+0	+0	+0	+0
2nd	+1	+0	+0	+0
3rd	+1	+1	+1	+1
4th	+2	+1	+1	+1
5th	+2	+1	+1	+1
6th	+3	+2	+2	+2
7th	+3	+2	+2	+2
8th	+4	+2	+2	+2
9th	+4	+3	+3	+3
10th	+5	+3	+3	+3
11th	+5	+3	+3	+3
12th	+6/+1	+4	+4	+4
13th	+6/+1	+4	+4	+4
14th	+7/+2	+4	+4	+4
15th	+7/+2	+5	+5	+5
16th	+8/+3	+5	+5	+5
17th	+8/+3	+5	+5	+5
18th	+9/+4	+6	+6	+6
19th	+9/+4	+6	+6	+6
20th	+10/+5	+6	+6	+6

Class Skills

The commoner's class skills (and the key ability for each skill) are Climb (Str), Craft (Int), Handle Animal (Cha), Jump (Str), Listen (Wis), Profession (Int), Ride (Dex), Spot (Wis), Swim (Str), and Use Rope (Dex). See Chapter 4: Skills in the *Player's Handbook* for skill descriptions.

Skill Points at 1st Level: (2 + Int modifier) × 4.
Skill Points at Each Additional Level: 2 + Int modifier.

Class Features

The following is a class feature of the commoner NPC class.

Weapon and Armor Proficiency: The commoner is proficient with one simple weapon. He is not proficient with weapons, armor, or shields. Note that armor check penalties for armor heavier than leather apply to the skills Balance, Climb, Escape Artist, Hide, Jump, Move Silently, Pick Pocket, and Tumble.

Starting Gear

5d4 gp worth of equipment.

TABLE 2–20: THE EXPERT

NPC Level	Base Attack Bonus	Fort Save	Ref Save	Will Save
1st	+0	+0	+0	+2
2nd	+1	+0	+0	+3
3rd	+2	+1	+1	+3
4th	+3	+1	+1	+4
5th	+3	+1	+1	+4
6th	+4	+2	+2	+5
7th	+5	+2	+2	+5
8th	+6/+1	+2	+2	+6
9th	+6/+1	+3	+3	+6
10th	+7/+2	+3	+3	+7
11th	+8/+3	+3	+3	+7
12th	+9/+4	+4	+4	+8
13th	+9/+4	+4	+4	+8
14th	+10/+5	+4	+4	+9
15th	+11/+6/+1	+5	+5	+9
16th	+12/+7/+2	+5	+5	+10
17th	+12/+7/+2	+5	+5	+10
18th	+13/+8/+3	+6	+6	+11
19th	+14/+9/+4	+6	+6	+11
20th	+15/+10/+5	+6	+6	+12

Expert

Experts operate as craftsfolk and professionals in the world. They normally do not have the inclination or training to be adventurers, but they are capable in their own field. The skilled blacksmith, the astute barrister, the canny merchant, the educated sage, and the master shipwright are all experts.

Potentially, the expert could make a PC-worthy class choice, but only for those players willing to create a character focused in something other than traditional adventuring careers. Experts have a vast number of skills. Most towns and communities have at least a few experts in various fields. DMs should use the expert class for NPCs such as elite craftsfolk, experienced merchants, seasoned guides, wily sailors, learned sages, and other highly skilled professions.

Hit Die: d6.

Class Skills

The expert can choose any ten skills to be class skills. One or two of these skills can be skills exclusive to some other class. See Chapter 4: Skills in the *Player's Handbook* for skill descriptions.

Skill Points at 1st Level: (6 + Int modifier) × 4.
Skill Points at Each Additional Level: 6 + Int modifier.

Class Features

The following is a class feature of the expert NPC class.

Weapon and Armor Proficiency: The expert is proficient in the use of all simple weapons and with light armor but not shields. Note that armor check penalties for armor heavier than leather apply to the skills Balance, Climb, Escape Artist, Hide, Jump, Move Silently, Pick Pocket, and Tumble.

Starting Gear

3d4 × 10 gp worth of equipment.

Warrior

The warrior is a strong, stout combatant without the specialized training and finesse of a fighter, the survival and outdoor skills of the barbarian or ranger, or the sophistication and religious focus of a paladin. The warrior is a straightforward and unsubtle opponent in a fight, but not an inconsiderable one.

Warriors are not as good as fighters, and thus PCs should be encouraged to avoid this class in favor of the standard combat-oriented ones given in the *Player's Handbook*. Representing experience in fighting and related areas but not sophisticated training, warriors are common among the humanoids and giants (orcs, ogres, and so forth). You should also use the warrior class for soldiers (although perhaps not for commanders or career soldiers), guards, local thugs, toughs, bullies, and even regular people who have learned to defend their homes with some ability.

Hit Die: d8.

A warrior, an expert, a commoner, an aristocrat, and an adept

TABLE 2–21: THE WARRIOR

NPC Level	Base Attack Bonus	Fort Save	Ref Save	Will Save
1st	+1	+2	+0	+0
2nd	+2	+3	+0	+0
3rd	+3	+3	+1	+1
4th	+4	+4	+1	+1
5th	+5	+4	+1	+1
6th	+6/+1	+5	+2	+2
7th	+7/+2	+5	+2	+2
8th	+8/+3	+6	+2	+2
9th	+9/+4	+6	+3	+3
10th	+10/+5	+7	+3	+3
11th	+11/+6/+1	+7	+3	+3
12th	+12/+7/+2	+8	+4	+4
13th	+13/+8/+3	+8	+4	+4
14th	+14/+9/+4	+9	+4	+4
15th	+15/+10/+5	+9	+5	+5
16th	+16/+11/+6/+1	+10	+5	+5
17th	+17/+12/+7/+2	+10	+5	+5
18th	+18/+13/+8/+3	+11	+6	+6
19th	+19/+14/+9/+4	+11	+6	+6
20th	+20/+15/+10/+5	+12	+6	+6

Class Skills

The warrior's class skills (and the key ability for each skill) are Climb (Str), Handle Animal (Cha), Intimidate (Cha), Jump (Str), Ride (Dex), and Swim (Str). See Chapter 4: Skills in the *Player's Handbook* for skill descriptions.

Skill Points at 1st Level: (2 + Int modifier) × 4.
Skill Points at Each Additional Level: 2 + Int modifier.

Class Features

The following is a class feature of the warrior NPC class.

Weapon and Armor Proficiency: The warrior is proficient in the use of all simple and martial weapons and all armor and shields. Note that armor check penalties for armor heavier than leather apply to the skills Balance, Climb, Escape Artist, Hide, Jump, Move Silently, Pick Pocket, and Tumble, and that carrying heavy gear imposes a check penalty on Swim checks.

Starting Gear

3d4 × 10 gp worth of equipment.

VARIANT: 1ST-LEVEL MULTICLASS CHARACTERS

At the DM's option, a character may be multiclass at 1st level. Such a character may only have two classes, and one of them must be favored by his race (see Chapter 2: Races in the *Player's Handbook*). Half-elves and humans favor no particular class and so can combine any two classes at 1st level.

Since a PC's character level is equal to the sum of all his class levels, a 1st-level multiclass character cannot have yet achieved 1st level in either of his classes. Instead, he is considered to be apprentice level in each class. An apprentice gets some but not all of the class benefits usually gained at 1st level. Once the character reaches 2nd level, each class becomes 1st level, and all benefits denied at apprentice level are gained.

At 1st Character Level

Find the two classes that the character starts with on Table 2–22: Apprentice-Level Characters. The character gets all benefits from both classes combined except when noted below.

In addition to the standard and special abilities shown here, the character gets all weapon and armor skills from both classes. (Overlapping weapon and armor skills are not cumulative.)

For hit points, choose one of the two classes to be primary and take standard 1st-level hit points for that class. The other class is the secondary class, and the character uses that class's Hit Die for hit points upon gaining 2nd level (see below).

The character has skill points as if he were a 1st-level member of his primary class. Skills purchased from the skill list (Table 4–2: Skills, page 59 in the *Player's Handbook*) are purchased as a member of the primary class. Maximum rank is calculated as if the character were 1st level: 4 for a class skill (for the primary class) and 2 for a cross-class skill (for the primary class).

The 1st-level multiclass character has starting gear as his primary class.

Example: Gersh is a 1st-level gnome wizard (illusionist)/rogue. He is considered apprentice-level in both his wizard and his rogue classes. As a 1st-level multiclass character, he consults the line for wizard and the line for rogue on Table 2–22: Apprentice-Level Characters. He comes up with the following statistics:

Attack Bonus: +0
Fortitude Save: +0
Reflex Save: +1
Will Save: +1
Special: None

TABLE 2–22: APPRENTICE-LEVEL CHARACTERS

Class	Base Attack Bonus	Fort Save	Ref Save	Will Save	Special	Spells* 0	Spells* 1st
Fighter	+0	+1	+0	+0	One bonus feat	—	—
Barbarian	+0	+1	+0	+0	Rage, fast movement	—	—
Paladin	+0	+1	+0	+0	*Detect evil, lay on hands*†	—	—
Ranger	+0	+1	+0	+0	One favored enemy	—	—
Wizard	+0	+0	+0	+1	—	2	0**
Sorcerer	+0	+0	+0	+1	—	4	2
Cleric	+0	+1	+0	+1	Turn undead†	2	1††
Druid	+0	+1	+0	+1	—	2	1
Rogue	+0	+0	+1	+0		—	—
Bard	+0	+0	+1	+0	—	1	—
Monk	+0	+1	+0	+1	Unarmed combat, Wis bonus to AC	—	—

*Apprentice-level spellcasters know as many spells as their 1st-level counterparts. They just can't cast as many per day. Apprentice-level spellcasters can cast more spells per day when they achieve 1st level, but they do not gain knowledge of more spells. Bonus spells do apply at apprentice level.

**A specialist gains an additional spell from her specialty school, as normal.

†This ability is level-based. Treat the apprentice-level character as level zero.

††The only 1st-level spell an apprentice cleric gets is his domain spell, which he selects each day from one of his two domains.

Spells: Two cantrips and zero 1st-level spells, plus the three cantrips he receives for being a gnome (see the *Player's Handbook,* page 17), the bonus 1st-level spell he receives for having a high Intelligence (see Table 1–1: Ability Modifiers and Bonus Spells, page 8 in the *Player's Handbook*), and the bonus 1st-level illusion spell he gets for being an illusionist (see School Specialization, page 54 in the *Player's Handbook*). His total per day is five cantrips and two 1st-level spells, one of which must be an illusion spell.

Hit Points: He elects to have rogue as his primary class. Thus, he begins with 6 hit points plus his Constitution modifier (again, see Table 1–1: Ability Modifiers and Bonus spells, page 8 in the *Player's Handbook*).

Skills: Gersh's primary class is rogue, and his Intelligence is 15 (+2 modifier), so he has 40 skill points ([8+2] × 4) to start with. He can buy skills from Table 4–2: Skills (page 59, *Player's Handbook*) at the rogue cost. Maximum rank is 4 for rogue class skills and 2 for rogue cross-class skills (even if they are illusionist class skills).

In addition, he has all the rogue weapon and armor skills. Unfortunately, the wizard weapon and armor skills add nothing to his selection, because as a rogue, he's already skilled in every weapon a wizard is skilled in, and wizards aren't skilled in armor.

Achieving 2nd Level

At 1,000 XP, the character becomes 2nd level. At this time, each class becomes 1st level. Make the following changes:

- Add a Hit Die (plus Constitution modifier) for the secondary class. (This secondary class did not contribute to hit points at 1st character level.)
- Increase base attack bonus, saving throw bonuses, special abilities, and spell abilities for each class so that they match 1st-level figures in each class. Add up these figures for the multiclass character's totals.
- Acquire and spend skill points as if the character were a member only of the secondary class. Skills purchased from the skill list (Table 4–2: Skills, page 59 in the *Player's Handbook*) are purchased as a member of the secondary class. Maximum rank is 5 for class skills and 2 1/2 for cross-class skills.

Example: At 2nd level, Gersh, no longer an apprentice, becomes a 1st-level rogue/1st-level wizard (illusionist). He gets the following benefits:

Base Attack Bonus & Fortitude Save: Still 0, that being the bonus for 1st-level rogues and wizards.

Reflex Save: Now +2 (for being a 1st-level rogue).

Will Save: Now +2 (for being a 1st-level wizard).

Special: As a rogue, Gersh picks up the sneak attack. As a wizard, he picks up the ability to summon a familiar and the Scribe Scroll item creation feat.

Spells: He now gets three cantrips and one 1st-level spell, plus the usual extras, for a total of six cantrips and three 1st-level spells per day (one of which must still be an illusion, from his school of specialization).

Hit Points: He rolls the d4 provided by his secondary class, wizard, and adds his Constitution modifier.

Skills: Gersh gains 4 more skill points (2 for gaining a level of wizard, plus 2 for the Intelligence modifier), which he must spend as a wizard. His maximum rank is 5 for wizard class skills and 2 1/2 for wizard cross-class skills

Gersh's statistics are now identical with what they would have been if he had started as a 1st-level rogue and picked up a level of wizard (illusionist) at 2nd level.

ADVANCING LEVELS

As characters gain levels, they gain new abilities, new skills, new feats, and generally get better at what they do. This section details a few things you need to keep in mind while all this is going on.

Access and Training

The rules in the *Player's Handbook* assume that characters have access to everything they need to advance in level—libraries where they can research new spells, trainers to guide their efforts, and places to practice new skills and abilities. Research and training aren't a part of the standard rules. They're assumed to be going on in the background. However, you control the background and can decide how you want to handle things such as this. Keep in mind, however, that leaving them unspoken in the background is a fine choice.

Variant: Learning Skills and Feats

According to the rules in the *Player's Handbook*, characters pick up a new skills and feats as they go up in levels. In your campaign, however, you can require that a character can't learn a new skill or feat that he hasn't been exposed to. For example, a character in the desert can't learn swimming unless he spends time at an oasis. You might even require that a character can't *improve* existing skills without the ability to practice.

One step further would be to require that a character have an instructor to teach him new skills and feats. Under this approach, a character can't learn to swim unless he has access to a body of water *and* someone who can swim willing to train him. Likewise, a character can't learn the Cleave feat unless he's got a trainer who knows how to do it and the time and place to practice by sparring with that trainer. A trainer can be another PC (which encourages interaction and cooperation among the players) or an NPC. Non-player character trainers who are friends of the PCs might train them for nothing; otherwise, professional trainers, who are usually found only in large cities, charge money.

Training Cost: 50 gp per week for a professional trainer (and related expenses).

Training Time: One week per rank gained for a skill, or two weeks for a feat. A character may work on two skills or feats at once, paying separately for each.

If you allow it, at the expense of a certain degree of realism, a character can obtain training ahead of time. A player whose character is at 2nd level, knowing that the character will get a new feat at 3rd level, might choose to have his character train for the feat now either because the opportunity is available or to just get it out of the way. (The realism problem is that, although the character completes his training, he still can't use the feat he has learned until he acquires enough XP to advance a level.)

Distinguishing Skills and Feats: You don't have to treat skills and feats the same in this context. For example, you can require training or exposure for skills but not feats, ruling that feats are something that develop on their own as a character adventures. Or you can set such requirements for feats but not skills, justifying this by the fact that feats are so much more potent than skills and thus require more investment on the PC's part to acquire.

Variant: Learning New Spells

Divine spellcasters just get new spells when they gain the ability to cast them. Their deity takes care of it all for them. You will not find a ranger in a library trying to learn a new spell. Arcane spellcasters don't have things quite so easy.

Wizards must learn new spells and add them to their spellbooks. This process is detailed in the *Player's Handbook* (page 154). They must either learn them from spellbooks and scrolls discovered while adventuring or wait until they gain a level, at which time it's assumed they gain two new spells. If you require wizards to actually spend game time on spell research to gain those new spells, assume that it takes one day per spell (but no roll is needed for spells that come with level advancement) and that such research costs twice what it would normally cost to have an NPC cast that spell for the character (see NPC Spellcasting, page 149).

It's perfectly all right for two PC wizards to share spells.

According to the standard rules, sorcerers and bards don't need to study books to get their spells but just automatically gain new spells when they gain levels. However, as a variant rule you could require that each sorcerer contact an intelligent supernatural entity (anything from a lammasu to a demon) to learn new spells. Such creatures usually don't want payment in gold but prefer to strike a bargain instead. These supernatural patrons teach their mortal friends spells in exchange for an occasional service (which could lead to an exciting adventure in its own right). Playing the patron is in the purview of the DM and, depending on the creature chosen, you should require whatever sort of bargain you see fit. The following are but a few examples:

- A lammasu only makes a bargain with a good-aligned sorcerer. In exchange for spells, once every other level the sorcerer must right a wrong or do some specific good deed, such as freeing a captive cleric unjustly placed in prison, building a shelter for diseased beggars, or destroying an evil temple.
- A dragon only makes a bargain with a sorcerer of the same alignment. In exchange for spells, the dragon requires payment either in magic treasure or in service. If treasure, the item must be of a value twice what it would normally cost to have an NPC cast that spell for the character (see NPC Spellcasting, page 149). If a service, every other level (typically) the sorcerer must perform some task appointed by the dragon. Usually, this service is to procure some specific object and bringing it to the dragon, slay a creature the dragon considers a threat or pest, or spy on one of the dragon's enemies and report what he learns.
- A devil only makes a bargain with a lawful or evil sorcerer. In exchange for spells, once every other level the sorcerer must perform a task for that devil. The task is always evil. For example, it might require the sorcerer to kill some good-aligned character, destroy a temple of a good-aligned deity, spread a vicious and destructive lie, or tempt a good character to do something evil.

Bards gain new spells by learning new songs. You can treat this just like a wizard learning new spells from books in a library, but the bard is studying with another bard and learning new music. Alternatively, you can rule that the bard must spend an equivalent period of time and money scouring the countryside for new songs, new rumors, and so on.

Researching Original Spells

A spellcaster of any type can create a new spell. This research requires access to a well-stocked library, typically in a large city or metropolis. Research requires an expenditure of 1,000 gp per week and takes one week per level of the spell. This money goes into fees, consultants, material component experimentation, and other miscellaneous expenditures. At the end of that time, the character makes a Spellcraft check (DC 10 + spell level). If that roll succeeds, the character learns the new spell if her research produced a viable spell. If the roll fails, the character must go through the research process again if she wants to keep trying.

A viable spell is one that you allow into the game. Don't tell the player whether or not you think the spell is viable when research begins. (That's the point of the research.) However, feel free to work with the player and give him guidance on the parameters under which such a spell might be acceptable in your game. You're perfectly justified in ruling ahead of time that some topics, such as time travel, are never viable, and thus spells associated with them cannot be successfully researched in your campaign.

Research to create new spells is always in addition to any other research involved for gaining spells (if you decide to require spell research for normal spell acquisition). Remember, however, that sorcerers and bards are strictly restricted in the number of spells they can know and can never exceed these limits even via the research of original spells.

Variant: Gaining Class Abilities

You can mandate that to gain any of the newfound abilities earned by advancing a level, a character needs to perform some overall training. This training requires one week per every two levels, rounded up. (In other words, to gain 3rd level, a character must train for two weeks.) Training requires a character to train with a character of the same class who is higher in level and costs 1,000 gp per week. If no such trainer can be found, the cost is the same, but the time required is doubled. The money goes into fees, consultants, material component experiments, and other miscellaneous expenditures. Without the training, a character cannot acquire more hit points, class abilities, saving throw and attack bonuses, spells per day, skills new spells, and so on.

Don't require characters to train for skills and feats or research their spells in addition to this. Use one or the other. The costs and time here assume skill advancement, gaining feats, and the acquiring of new spells.

Variant: General Downtime

If you dislike the idea of all this formalized training getting in the way of the heroic, epic campaign you have going, simply require that whenever a character gains a new level she must spend one day per level (or just 1d4 days) in downtime. During this period the character is busy training, focusing, or simply resting and cannot cast spells, go on adventures, and so on. This variant rule means that the characters take a breather now and again, which is certainly realistic. No one is willing to delve into danger every day of her life.

Variant: Gaining Fixed Hit Points

Instead of rolling for hit points when she gains a level, a player may (if you use this variant) take the average roll for the class, rounded down (see Table 2–23: Fixed Hit Points per Hit Die). A player may choose from one level to the next whether to roll or to take the fixed amount. (Constitution modifiers still apply to either option.) Since below-average hit points hurt a PC more than above-average hit points help, the increased certainty balances the slightly reduced average result.

TABLE 2–23: FIXED HIT POINTS PER HIT DIE

Class	Hit Die	Hit Points
Sorcerer, wizard	d4	2
Bard, rogue	d6	3
Cleric, druid, monk	d8	4
Fighter, paladin, ranger	d10	5
Barbarian	d12	6

CREATING CHARACTERS ABOVE 1ST LEVEL

Sometimes you're going to want to create characters that aren't 1st level. Perhaps you need an NPC foe capable of challenging your players' high-level characters. Perhaps you have purchased an adventure you're dying to play, but no one has characters of the appropriate level. Perhaps you just want to jump right to 5th level and start your campaign there. Whatever the reason, creating new characters at any given level isn't hard (and, in fact, many players find it fun).

If you tell players to create characters of higher than 1st level, assign an experience point total for them to use. This is better than just assigning a level because it balances characters who take multiclassing penalties against those who do not. Then they should follow these steps:

1. Determine abilities and race normally.
2. Determine character class. If the character is multiclass, determine how many levels of each class the character has, and in what order they were gained. (The order is important in step 3.)
3. Determine character statistics. This includes base attack bonus, save bonuses, spells, abilities, feats, hit points (maximum hp at first level and rolled hp for each level afterward). If the characters are 4th level or above, allow them to add to their ability scores at 4th level and every four levels beyond that (see Table 3–2: Experience and Level-Dependent Benefits, page 22 in the *Player's Handbook*). It is important to note if Intelligence gets modified, because a raised Intelligence score might gain the character more skill points, but only at each level thereafter. (That is, the extra skill points are not retroactive.)
4. Determine skills. The best way to do this is to buy them one level at a time. This allows a player to take into account increased skill points from Intelligence (if any) and changes due to multiclassing. However, if a character's skill points per level do not change (such as when she puts the extra ability point boost into some ability other than Intelligence) and no multiclassing is involved, the player can buy all the character's skills at once. In either case, keep in mind that maximum rank is level + 3 for class skills and (level + 3) ÷ 2 for cross-class skills.
5. Equip the character. When creating a 1st-level character, this meant buying normal equipment. At higher levels, it also means deciding which magic items a character has acquired so far. Refer to Chapter 8: Magic Items, where all magic items are listed along with their market price. Table 2–24: Starting Equipment for PCs above 1st Level shows the total value of a character's gear at a given level. This value includes mundane items described in Chapter 7: Equipment in the *Player's Handbook*, but the bulk of it (especially at higher levels) is composed of magic items. Note that these values apply only to PCs. NPCs use Table 2–44: NPC Gear Value (page 58) to find the total value of their equipment.

TABLE 2–24: STARTING EQUIPMENT FOR PCs ABOVE 1ST LEVEL

Character Level	—Wealth—	Character Level	—Wealth—
2nd	900 gp	12th	88,000 gp
3rd	2,700 gp	13th	110,000 gp
4th	5,400 gp	14th	150,000 gp
5th	9,000 gp	15th	200,000 gp
6th	13,000 gp	16th	260,000 gp
7th	19,000 gp	17th	340,000 gp
8th	27,000 gp	18th	440,000 gp
9th	36,000 gp	19th	580,000 gp
10th	49,000 gp	20th	760,000 gp
11th	66,000 gp		

Limitation on Magic Items: You're free to limit characters to what items they can choose, just as if you were assigning them to treasure hoards in the game. You're welcome to exercise an item-by-item veto, but an easier method is to limit them by maximum cost for a single item. For example, while an 8th-level character has 27,000 gp to spend, you can limit him to owning no single item worth more than 5,000 gp. This is a good way to prevent power imbalances such as an 8th-level fighter with hardly a copper piece to his name who is armed with a *nine lives stealer*.

You could also limit characters by the type of magic item found—minor, medium, or major. For example, a player creating a 3rd-level character has 2,700 gp to spend, but you could rule she can't equip the character with any item that could not be obtained by a minor treasure roll.

Regardless of their level, characters generated using this method cannot gain artifacts, since these are (literally) priceless.

Character-Created Magic Items: A PC spellcaster can spend as many of the XP and gp you have awarded toward making magic items as she wishes, provided that she has the proper item creation feats and prerequisites.

Charged Magic Items: A player may select a partially used magic item, such as a wand with only 25 charges left. Such an item should have half the full number of charges, and its value is proportional to the charges left (half price for a wand with 25 charges).

6. Work out the details. A paladin needs a warhorse, a druid or experienced ranger needs animal companions, a wizard might want a familiar, a character might belong to a guild or have a cohort, and so on.

CHARACTERS AND THE WORLD AROUND THEM

The PCs live in a living, breathing world. Although Chapter 6: World-Building provides guidance on creating that world (also look to Chapter 1: Dungeon Mastering), included here are specific details regarding character classes and their place in the world.

PCs and NPCs

The NPC classes presented above showcase the difference between PCs and the rest of the world: The PCs are among the most capable members of the populace, or at least among those with the greatest potential. The variance of ability scores (from 3 to 18 or higher) shows that not all people in the world are created equal, and not all have the same opportunities.

Having the same opportunities, in this case, means having training. Training is the difference between an adept and a wizard, a warrior and a fighter, a commoner and everyone else. An NPC with good ability scores might still be a warrior rather than a fighter because she's never had the opportunity to obtain the training assumed with the fighter class. She can swing a sword, but she does not have the finesse of a trained fighter. In theory, however, she could be trained as a fighter at some point after beginning her career as a warrior, gaining fighter levels through multiclassing.

Obviously, however, training isn't everything. Someone with an Intelligence of 6 is never going to be a wizard, since he is unable to cast spells. In theory, though, anyone with the Intelligence, the inclination, and the training can learn wizardry.

Class Roles in Society

Characters, particularly as they advance in level, need to know how they and those like them fit into the world. This section may be helpful in giving an idea of what classes particular NPCs might belong to, what sorts of NPCs one might find in a world where the classes are available, how PCs can fit in, and what PCs can potentially aspire to. Of course, PCs can form whatever goals they wish, but the following information might at least generate some ideas.

Barbarian: Barbarians have no place in civilized society—that's the point. In their own tribal society they are hunters, warriors, and war chiefs. But in a civilized community, the best they can hope for is to join fighters' organizations and fill a fighter's roles. Often, fighters from a civilized society will not follow a barbarian leader unless he's somehow proved himself worthy of their loyalty. Barbarians of legend often aspire to gather those like them and found their own tribe, or even their own kingdom.

Bard: Bards serve as entertainers, either on their own, singing for their supper, or in troupes. Some bards aspire to be an aristocrat's personal troubadour. Bards occasionally gather in colleges of learning and entertainment. Well-known, high-level bards often found bard colleges. These colleges serve as the standard educational system for a city as well as a kind of bards' guild where they can find training and support.

Cleric: Most clerics have an organizational structure built right into their class. Religions have hierarchies, and each cleric has his place within it. Clerics may find themselves assigned duties by their churches, or they might be free agents. Clerics can serve in the military of an aristocrat sanctioned by their religion, or within some autonomous church-based military order established for defense. A high-level cleric can hope to one day be the shepherd of his own congregation and temple, although some become religious advisors to aristocrats or the leaders of communities of their own, with its people looking to the cleric for religious and temporal guidance. Clerics often work with paladins, and virtually every knightly order has at least one cleric member.

Druid: Druids are often loners. They cloister themselves deep in the wilderness in sacred groves or other areas that they have claimed for themselves, sometimes working with a single ranger or a group of rangers. Druids sometimes organize themselves in loose affiliations. On rare occasions, druids sharing a particular focus may organize themselves as a tight-knit order. Sometimes creatures such as satyrs, centaurs, or other feys join these groups as well.

All druids are at least nominally members of druidic society, which spans the globe. The society is so loose, however, that it may have little influence on a particular druid.

Druids assist and sometimes even lead small, rural communities that benefit from their wisdom and power.

Fighter: These characters often serve as mercenaries or officers in the army. The sheriff in a small town might well be a fighter. Common soldiers and guards are usually warriors (see page 39).

Fighters may be loners or may gather to form martial societies for training, camaraderie, and employment (as mercenary companies, bodyguards, and so on). High-level fighters of great renown typically found such societies. A fighter of common birth can also hope to become an aristocrat's champion one day, but those with aspirations to true greatness plan on earning their own grants of land to become nobility in their own right.

Monk: The tradition of monk training started in distant lands but now has become common enough so that local people can go off to monasteries and learn the spiritual and martial arts. In large cities, monks learn their skills in special academies. Monks often serve the monastery or academy that trained them. Other times, however, they may join a different monastery or academy. A high-level monk with a good reputation can even found her own monastery or academy.

Only on rare occasions does a monk find a place in society outside her monastery. Such monks can become spiritual advisors, military commanders, or even law enforcers. A unit of monks in an army or in the local constabulary would be feared indeed.

Paladin: Paladins are knights, working for their church or within a knightly order. Qualifying for an order is often difficult, and membership always requires that the paladin follow a specific code of conduct. These orders sometimes allow nonpaladins as members, with good-aligned rangers and fighters being the most common sort of nonpaladin members. No paladin organization exists long without a cleric for support, advice, or leadership, however.

Paladins can serve in the military of an aristocrat sanctioned by their religion, or within some autonomous church-based military order established for defense. A high-level paladin might seek to rule her own domain (to bestow her just benevolence upon the masses), establish her own temple where none existed before, or to serve as the trusted lieutenant of a high priest or worthy aristocrat. Paladins in such service are often called justicars or something similar, implying that the paladin is in charge of dispensing church-sanctified justice.

Ranger: Rangers often seclude themselves, wandering into the wilderness for long stretches of time. If they aspire to leadership, it is often as the warden of a small, frontier community. Some rangers form loose-knit and often secretive organizations. These ranger groups watch over events in the land and gather to exchange information. They often have the best view of the grand picture of everything that occurs. High-level rangers aspire to found their own ranger societies or to establish and rule new communities, often those they have carved out of the wilderness itself.

Rangers and druids often work together, even sharing the same secretive network. Sometimes a ranger group includes a few druids, or vice versa.

Rogue: Rogues may serve in armies as spies or scouts. They can work as operatives of temples or as general troubleshooters for aristocrats, having attained these unique positions because of the versatility of their skills and abilities.

Frequently, however, rogues gather together in guilds devoted to their area of expertise: theft. Thieves' guilds are common. The larger a city is, the more likely it is to have a thieves' guild. The populace and the constabulary sometimes hate these guilds. At other times they are tolerated or even accepted, so long as they don't allow themselves to get out of hand in their work. Acceptance is often gained through bribery in politically corrupt areas.

Sorcerer: Sorcerers, to the general populace, are indistinguishable from wizards. They often fill the same roles in society, although they rarely join wizards' guilds, since they have no need to research and study. Sorcerers, more than wizards, keep to themselves. Sorcerers are more likely to hang about the fringes of society, among creatures that other people would consider monsters.

Conversely, some sorcerers find that military life suits them even better than wizards. Sorcerers focused on battle spells are more deadly than wizards, and they often are better with weapons. A high-level sorcerer might aspire to the same sorts of goals a wizard would. Despite their similarities, their differing approaches means wizards and sorcerers find themselves in conflict more often than they get along.

Wizard: Wizards can serve many roles in society. Wizards for hire are useful to the military as firepower (some armies employ entire units of wizards to blast the enemy, protect troops from danger, tear down castle walls, and so on). Or a wizard can serve the community as a well-paid troubleshooter—someone able to rid the town of vermin, stop the levee from bursting, or foretell the future. A wizard can open a shop and sell magic items she creates or cast needed spells for a fee. She can aspire to serve an aristocrat as an advisor and chief wizard, or to even rule over a community on her own. Sometimes, the public fears a wizard for her power, but more often than not the local wizard is a highly respected member of the community.

Wizards sometimes gather in guilds, societies, or cabals for mutual research, and to live among those who understand the endless fascination of magic. Only the most powerful and famous of wizards have the reputations necessary to found permanent establishments, such as a wizard's school. Where they exist, wizards' guilds control such issues as the price and availability of spells and magic items in a community.

Guilds and Organizations

As mentioned in many of the preceding descriptions, characters often gather in groups with characters of the same class. Sometimes this is simply the best way to keep one's place in society and to make friends with common interests. Sometimes it's required by law or outside pressure. For example, if you're a wizard in the town of Dyvers, you had better register with the local Wizards' Cabal. To do otherwise and use magic without its blessing results in swift retribution. Thieves' guilds are also notorious for the displeasure with which they view nonmember rogues operating in their area, and the vigor of their response. On the other hand, guilds can be simply beneficial to members of the appropriate class (see below). Or they can be a way of controlling characters of a specific class by some outside force. For example, a city might require all bards who perform within its city walls to be licensed by the local bards' guild, the better to suppress scandalous ballads that are overly critical of local figures.

Guilds often require dues, oaths of loyalty, or other requirements of their members. The extent of these requirements should be based on the number and quality of benefits a member gains. Tangible benefits include any or all of the following:

- Training
- Equipment availability (sometimes at a discount)
- Lodging
- Information
- Hiring opportunities
- Influential contacts
- Legal benefits (members are allowed to do things others can't)
- Safety

One good reason to join a guild is to get an assist in character training. If you use training requirements and/or costs in your game, guilds can offer training at reduced rates to their members. And guild members are always assured of having a trainer when the time comes. Guilds that offer training often do so for free, but then require yearly dues of at least 1,000 gp. Other groups offer training at half normal cost and only charge dues of 50 gp.

Not every organization need be based on class. The Defenders of Truth is an organization made up of members of almost every class (even rogues) based on upholding order and the rights of the people in a localized community. The Society of the Claw is a secretive, evil group of monks, fighters, rogues, and sorcerers who seek to overthrow the king and take control of the kingdom on their own.

LEADERSHIP

You are the sort of person others want to follow, and you have done some work attempting to recruit cohorts and followers.

Prerequisites: The character must be at least 6th level.

Benefits: Having this feat enables the character to attract loyal companions and devoted followers, subordinates who assist her. See Table 2–25: Leadership for what sort of cohort and how many followers the character can recruit.

TABLE 2–25: LEADERSHIP

Leadership Score	Cohort Level	1st	2nd	3rd	4th	5th	6th
1 or less	—	—	—	—	—	—	—
2	1st	—	—	—	—	—	—
3	2nd	—	—	—	—	—	—
4	3rd	—	—	—	—	—	—
5	3rd	—	—	—	—	—	—
6	4th	—	—	—	—	—	—
7	5th	—	—	—	—	—	—
8	5th	—	—	—	—	—	—
9	6th	—	—	—	—	—	—
10	7th	5	—	—	—	—	—
11	7th	6	—	—	—	—	—
12	8th	8	—	—	—	—	—
13	9th	10	1	—	—	—	—
14	10th	15	1	—	—	—	—
15	10th	20	2	1	—	—	—
16	11th	25	2	1	—	—	—
17	12th	30	3	1	1	—	—
18	12th	35	3	1	1	—	—
19	13th	40	4	2	1	1	—
20	14th	50	5	3	2	1	—
21	15th	60	6	3	2	1	1
22	15th	75	7	4	2	2	1
23	16th	90	9	5	3	2	1
24	17th	110	11	6	3	2	1
25+	17th	135	13	7	4	2	2

Leadership Score: A character's Leadership score equals his level plus any Charisma modifier. In order to take into account negative Charisma modifiers, Table 2–25: Leadership allows for very low Leadership scores, but the character must still be 6th level or higher in order to gain the Leadership feat and thus attract a cohort. Outside factors can affect a character's Leadership score, as detailed in Table 2–26: Leadership Modifiers.

Cohort Level: The character can attract a cohort of up to this level. Regardless of the character's Leadership score, he can't recruit a cohort of his level or higher. A 6th-level paladin with a +3 Charisma bonus, for example, can still only recruit a cohort of 5th level or lower.

Number of Followers by Level: The character can lead up to the indicated number of characters of each level. For example, a character with a Leadership score of 14 can lead up to fifteen 1st-level followers and one 2nd-level follower.

TABLE 2–26: LEADERSHIP MODIFIERS

General Leadership Modifiers

The Leader Has a Reputation of	Leadership Modifier
Great prestige	+2
Fairness and generosity	+1
Special power	+1
Failure	−1
Aloofness	−1
Cruelty	−2

Cohort-Only Leadership Modifiers

The Leader	Leadership Modifier
Has a familiar/paladin's warhorse/ animal companion	−2
Recruits a cohort of a different alignment	−1
Caused the death of a cohort	−2*
*Cumulative per cohort killed.	

Follower-Only Leadership Modifiers

The Leader	Leadership Modifier
Has a stronghold, base of operations, guildhouse, and so on	+2
Moves around a lot	−1
Caused the death of other followers	−1

TABLE 2–27: EXAMPLE SPECIAL COHORTS

Creature	Alignment	Level Equivalent
Werebear	Lawful good	9th
Pegasus	Chaotic good	6th
Unicorn*	Chaotic good	8th
Dire wolf	Neutral	6th
Owlbear	Neutral	6th
Griffon	Neutral	9th
Dragonne**	Neutral	10th
Hell hound	Lawful evil	6th
Displacer beast	Lawful evil	7th
Imp	Lawful evil	7th
Young green dragon†	Lawful evil	9th
Erinyes (devil)	Lawful evil	15th
Quasit	Chaotic evil	8th
Ettin	Chaotic evil	8th

*Leader must be a human, elven, or half-elven maiden.

**The leader is immune to the dragonne's roar.

†The dragon ages but does not gain XP.

Cohorts and Followers

When PCs gain levels, they also garner reputations. Those who show promise, great power, a path toward success, or perhaps just a friendly demeanor may find that NPCs want to follow them. These NPCs may wish for apprenticeships, employment, or a leader they can look up to.

Attracting Cohorts

A character of 6th level or higher can start attracting cohorts (elite companions) and followers (loyal underlings). To do so, the character must take the Leadership feat (see sidebar). Unlike other feats, this one depends heavily on the social setting of the campaign, the actual location of the PC, and the group dynamics. You're free to disallow this feat if it would disrupt the campaign. Be sure to consider the effect of a PC having a cohort. A cohort is effectively another PC in the party under that player's control, one whose share of XP, treasure, and spotlight time is bound to take something away from the other players' characters. If your group is small, cohorts may be a great idea. If it's big enough that a cohort would be a problem, don't let the PCs have cohorts.

Once the character has a cohort, the cohort earns XP at one-half the rate a PC would. She does not automatically gain levels as the leader's Leadership score improves, nor does the leader's Leadership score limit her level.

A character can try to attract a cohort of a particular race, class, and alignment. The cohort's alignment may not be opposed to the leader's alignment on either the law-vs.-chaos or good-vs.-evil axis, and the leader suffers a Leadership penalty if he recruits a cohort of an alignment different from his own. The DM determines the details of the cohort. The cohort has gear as an NPC (see Table 2–44: NPC Gear Value, page 58). For more on cohorts, see page 147 in Chapter 5: Campaigns.

Special Cohorts

With the DM's permission, a leader may seek out a special cohort who is not a member of the standard PC races (the common races). For creatures with classes, such as a lizardfolk cohort, calculate its level according to the rules for PCs of that kind of monster (see Monsters as Races, page 22). For example, a leader with a Leadership score of 8 could have a 5th-level human fighter as a cohort, or a lizardfolk with four fighter levels, or a bugbear with three fighter levels. For more unusual creatures, add at least +3 to a creature's Challenge Rating to determine its effective level. The more special abilities a creature has, the larger the number you should add. See Table 2–27: Example Special Cohorts. Note that evil special cohorts may have agendas of their own.

Followers

Followers can be warriors, experts, or commoners. The leader can generally choose their races and classes. A leader attracts followers whose alignments are within one step of his own. A neutral good leader, for example, attracts neutral good, lawful good, chaotic good, and neutral followers. These characters have gear appropriate to NPCs of their level (see Table 2–44: NPC Gear Value, page 58). As the leader's Leadership rises, he can attract more followers. If his Leadership goes down, followers may desert. For more on followers, see the Cohorts section on page 147 in Chapter 5: Campaigns.

Replacing Cohorts and Followers

If a leader loses a cohort or followers, he can generally replace them, according to his current Leadership score. It takes time (1d4 months) to recruit replacements. If the leader is to blame for the deaths of the cohort or followers, it takes extra time to replace

ANIMAL COMPANIONS

Druids and rangers can use the *animal friendship* spell to gain animal companions, which are something like cohorts. Use these rules of thumb when characters have animal companions.

While the spell allows a character to have animals whose Hit Dice total double the character's caster level, that maximum assumes optimal conditions. The typical adventurer should be able to maintain animal companions whose Hit Dice total half the maximum (caster level for a druid, half of caster level for a ranger). If the character spends most of her time in the animals' home territory and treats them well, she can approach and even achieve her maximum Hit Dice. If she spends most of her time at sea, in cities, or otherwise in places that the animals don't like, her animals desert, and she will not be able to retain even half her maximum. Remember, these creatures are loyal friends but not pets or servants. They won't remain loyal if being the character's friend becomes too onerous.

The animal is still an animal. It's not a magical beast, as a familiar or a paladin's mount is. While it may have learned some tricks, it's still no more intelligent than any other animal of its kind, and it retains all its bestial instincts. Unlike intelligent followers or cohorts, animals can't follow complex instructions, such as "Attack the gnoll with the wand." A character can give a simple verbal command, such as "Attack" or "Come," as a free action, provided such a command is among the tricks the animal has learned. A more complex instruction, such as telling an animal to attack and pointing out a specific target, is a standard action. Animals are ill-equipped to handle unusual situations, such as combats with invisible opponents, and they typically hesitate to attack weird and unnatural creatures, such as beholders and oozes.

Left to its own judgment, an animal follows a character and attacks creatures that attack her (or that attack the animal itself). To do more than that, it needs to learn tricks. An animal with an Intelligence of 2 can learn six tricks. Possible tricks include:

"Attack": The animal attacks apparent enemies. The character may point to a particular creature to direct the animal to attack that creature. Normally, an animal will not attack unnatural creatures (though it will defend people, guard places, and protect characters against them). Teaching an animal to be willing to attack unnatural creatures counts as two tricks.

"Come": The animal comes to the character, even if the animal normally would not do so (such as following the character onto a boat).

"Defend": The animal defends the character (or is ready to defend the character if no threat is present).

"Down": The animal breaks off from combat or otherwise backs down.

"Fetch": The animal goes and gets something. The character must point out a specific object or the animal fetches some random object.

"Guard": The animal stays in place and prevents others from approaching.

"Heel": The animal follows the character closely, even to places where it normally wouldn't go.

"Perform": The animal does a variety of simple tricks like sitting up, rolling over, roaring, and so on.

"Protect": The animal follows a specific other character and protects him from danger (like "Defend," but for another character).

"Seek": The animal moves into an area and looks around for anything unusual.

"Stay": The animal stays in place waiting for the character to return. It does not challenge other creatures that come by, though it still defends itself if it needs to.

"Track": The animal tracks the scent presented to it.

them, up to a full year. Note that the leader also picks up a reputation of failure, which decreases his Leadership score.

See page 149 for more on NPC attitudes. Remember that even fanatically loyal followers are not stupid.

NPC STATISTICS

This section provides baseline statistics for NPCs of every standard class at levels 1–20, with rules for how to adjust those statistics by race or kind of monster. Starting with just an NPC's level (or Challenge Rating, which is usually the same thing), you can generate an NPC randomly, or you can put the pieces together as you see fit. The rules cover everything from a typical dwarven fighter to a half-fiend minotaur sorcerer.

These statistics give you basic characters with minimum work. If you want to put more work into handcrafting NPCs, you can use these statistics as a place to start, or do it all from scratch.

To create an NPC, you can select options from the following tables, determine information from the table randomly, or create an NPC from scratch.

TABLE-BASED NPC
To create an NPC from these tables:

1. Decide the NPC's class, level, and race or kind of monster.
2. Find the class and level on the NPC tables (Table 2–33 to Table 2–43).
3. Modify the statistics listed there by the information pertaining to the NPC's race or kind on Table 2–44: NPC Adjustments by Race or Kind.

RANDOM NPC
To create an NPC randomly, start with the NPC's level (or Challenge Rating, which is usually the same thing). Then determine the following information randomly:

1. Roll the NPC's alignment on Table 2–28: Random NPC Alignment.
2. Roll class randomly on Table 2–29: Random NPC Class.
3. Roll the race or kind randomly on the appropriate column on Table 2–30: Good NPC Race or Kind, 2–31: Neutral NPC Race or Kind, or 2–32: Evil NPC Race or Kind.

4. Combine the class-based statistics from the appropriate NPC table from Table 2–33 to Table 2–43 with the race or kind information from NPC Adjustments by Race or Kind, page 57.

TABLE 2–28: RANDOM NPC ALIGNMENT

d%	Alignment
01–20	Good (LG, NG, or CG)
21–50	Neutral (LN, N, or CN)
51–100	Evil (LE, NE, or CE)

TABLE 2–29: RANDOM NPC CLASS

Good	Neutral	Evil	Class
01–05	01–05	01–10	Barbarian
06–10	06–10	11–15	Bard
11–30	11–15	16–35	Cleric
31–35	11–25	36–40	Druid
36–45	26–45	41–50	Fighter
46–50	46–50	51–55	Monk
51–55	—	—	Paladin
56–65	51–55	56–60	Ranger
66–75	56–75	61–80	Rogue
76–80	76–80	81–85	Sorcerer
81–100	81–100	86–100	Wizard

HANDCRAFTED NPC
To create an NPC from scratch, simply use the information from the *Player's Handbook*, the *Monster Manual*, and the earlier parts of this chapter.

The one additional piece of information you need is the value of an NPC's gear. See Table 2–44: NPC Gear Value to find the total value of the NPC's equipment. Select equipment whose total value is this amount or less and let the balance simply be money. You can use the other tables as guidelines and shortcuts.

Count a charged item as half its full value, and roll randomly for the number of charges it has just as you do for normal for a random magic item. (If the item is one of the few with value beyond its charges, however, halve only the part of its value that's based on its charges. Use your discretion.)

When selecting gear for a spellcaster, count magic items that she can make herself as 70% as expensive as normal. This rule effectively treats the XP cost as an extra gold piece cost. If the item is charged, then count it as half normal value (a net 35%) and determine charges left randomly.

READING THE NPC DESCRIPTIONS
The NPC descriptions summarize a lot of information about the NPCs. The material that is not self-explanatory is explained below.

Increased Ability Scores: Magically enhanced scores are in parentheses.

Lvl: Class level.

Init: Bonus to initiative checks. This and all other numbers are totals, with relevant modifiers already added in.

Spd: Speed.

Weapons: Each NPC is equipped with a melee weapon and a ranged weapon (the monk has an unarmed attack listing as well). The weapon columns list the total attack bonuses due to class and level and total damage bonuses (in parentheses). If an NPC has more than one kind of ammunition, attack and damage figures use the ammunition with the best bonuses.

F/R/W: Bonuses to Fortitude, Reflex, and Will saves.

Skills: Skill abbreviations are Alch (Alchemy), Ani Emp (Animal Empathy), Appr (Appraise), Ba (Balance), Cli (Climb), Con (Concentration), D Dev (Disable Device), Dipl (Diplomacy), Hi (Hide), Ju (Jump), Kno (Knowledge, one appropriate to the class), List (Listen), M Sil (Move Silently), O Lock (Open Lock), Perf (Performance), S Mot (Sense Motive), Spellc (Spellcraft), Srch (Search), Tum (Tumble), U M Dev (Use Magic Device), and Wild (Wilderness Lore). Skill modifiers include armor check penalties, where appropriate.

For every 2 points by which an NPC's Intelligence score goes up or down (because of race or creature kind), the creature gains or loses one skill. New skills have ranks of 3 + class level (or half that for cross-class skills).

Spells: The numbers of spells a spellcaster has are listed in order of level, from lowest to highest. The 4th-level sorcerer's "6/7/4" means six 0-level spells, seven 1st-level spells, and four 2nd-level spells.

Gear: Several paragraphs in each description list armor, weapons, and various types of equipment each NPC possesses. Parenthetical notations indicate at which level or levels the character has the item in question.

Spell-storing items store spells at the minimum caster level needed to cast those spells (unless otherwise specified). Roll randomly for the number of charges in a charged item as you do for a randomly generated charged magic item.

Daggers are listed under gear, not weapons, but NPCs can use them as weapons if they need to.

COMBINATION APPROACH

Of course, you can combine these approaches, using the material here as a starting point and then making different choices for the NPC: different skills, different feats, different gear, even different classes (for a multiclass character).

NOTES ON NPC DESIGN

Keep these notes in mind when working with these tables.

- Character statistics are average; hit points are elite (using maximum hit points at 1st level). The abilities use the standard array. You can roll these statistics, but be be sure to note how doing so affects other statistics. For example, a fighter with a lower Dexterity can't take Dodge.
- Adjustments for unusual creatures sometimes interact strangely with the class material. For example, a kobold fighter isn't big or strong enough to be proficient with a bastard sword, nor can

it take the Power Attack feat. Be prepared to adjust equipment and feats (mostly) as needed. (Of course, there are precious few kobold fighters.)

- These statistics are for exceptional characters (the same way that PCs are exceptional). That's why, for example, a gnoll ranger has a higher Strength score than the gnoll in the *Monster Manual*.

Elite and Average Characters

All PCs and all the NPCs described in this section are "elites," a cut above the average. Elites (whether they are PCs or not) roll above-average ability scores and automatically get maximum hit points from their first Hit Die. Average characters, on the other hand, roll average abilities (3d6) and don't get maximum hit points from their first Hit Die. The monsters described in the *Monster Manual* are average characters rather than elites (though elite monsters also exist). Likewise, some fighters, wizards, and so on are average people rather than elites; they

TABLE 2–30: GOOD NPC RACE OR KIND

Bbn	Brd	Clr	Drd	Ftr	Mnk	Pal	Rgr	Rog	Sor	Wiz	Race/Kind	Level**
—	01	01	—	0	01–02	01–10	—	—	01–02	01	Aasimar (planetouched)	Normal
—	—	02	—	01–03	—	—	—	—	03	—	Dwarf, deep	Normal
01–02	02–06	20–22	—	04–33	03	11–20	01–05	01–05	04–05	02	Dwarf, hill	Normal
—	—	23–24	—	34–41	—	21	—	06	06	—	Dwarf, mountain	Normal
—	07–11	25	01	42	—	—	—	—	07–08	03–07	Elf, gray	Normal
—	12–36	26–35	02–11	43–47	04–13	—	06–20	07–19	09–11	08–41	Elf, high	Normal
03–32	37	36–40	21–21	—	—	—	21	—	12–36	—	Elf, wild	Normal
33–34	38	41	22–31	—	—	—	22–36	—	37	42	Elf, wood	Normal
—	39	42	32–36	—	—	—	37–41	20	38	43	Gnome, forest	Normal
—	40–44	43–51	37	48	—	22	42	21–25	39–40	44–48	Gnome, rock	Normal
35	45–53	52–56	38–46	49–50	14–18	23–27	43–57	26–35	41–45	49–58	Half-elf	Normal
36	54	57–66	47	51	19	28	58	36–60	46–54	59–63	Halfling, lightfoot	Normal
—	55	67	—	52	20	29	—	61–66	55	64	Halfling, deep	Normal
—	56	68–69	48	—	—	—	59	67–72	56	65–67	Halfling, tallfellow	Normal
37–61	57	70	49	53–57	21–25	30	60–64	73–77	57–58	68	Half-orc	Normal
62–98	58–97	71–95	50–99	58–97	25–97	31–97	65–97	77–96	59–95	69–96	Human	Normal
—	98	96	—	—	—	—	—	97	96	97	Svirfneblin (gnome)	–1
99	99	97–98	100	98	98	98	98	98	97	98	Half-celestial*	–1
100	100	99	—	99	99	99	99	99	98–99	99	Half-dragon*	–2
—	—	100	100	100	100	100	100	100	100	100	Werebear (lycanthrope)*	–2

*Reroll to determine the NPC's base race or kind. (On the reroll, ignore rolls marked by asterisks.)
**If the creature is exceptionally powerful, reduce its class level to balance. If its class level is 0 or lower, reroll.

TABLE 2–31: NEUTRAL NPC RACE OR KIND

Bbn	Brd	Clr	Drd	Ftr	Mnk	Rgr	Rog	Sor	Wiz	Race/Kind	Level**
01	01	01–15	—	01–10	—	—	01	—	—	Dwarf, deep	Normal
02	02–03	16–25	—	11–29	—	01	02–04	01	—	Dwarf, hill	Normal
—	—	26	—	30–34	—	—	—	—	—	Dwarf, mountain	Normal
—	04–05	—	01	—	—	—	—	—	01	Elf, gray	Normal
—	06–15	27	02–06	35	01–02	02–06	05–08	02	02–26	Elf, high	Normal
03–13	16	28	07–11	—	—	07	—	03–12	—	Elf, wild	Normal
14	17–21	29–38	12–31	36–41	03	08–36	09	13–15	27–28	Elf, wood	Normal
—	—	—	32	—	—	37	—	—	—	Gnome, forest	Normal
—	22–23	39	—	—	—	38	10	16	29	Gnome, rock	Normal
15–16	24–33	40–48	33–37	42–46	04–13	39–55	11–25	17–31	30–44	Half-elf	Normal
17–18	34–36	49–58	38	47	14	56	26–53	32–41	45–47	Halfling, lightfoot	Normal
19	37	59	—	48	15	—	54–58	42	—	Halfling, deep	Normal
—	38	60	39	—	—	57	59–63	43	48–49	Halfling, tallfellow	Normal
20–58	39–40	61–62	40	49–58	16–25	58–67	64–73	44–48	50	Half-orc	Normal
59–87	41–98	63–90	41–88	59–96	26–100	68–96	74–97	49–95	51–97	Human	Normal
88–98	—	91–97	89–98	97	—	97–98	—	96–97	—	Lizardfolk	Normal
—	—	98	—	98	—	—	98	98	98	Svirfneblin (gnome)	–1
—	—	—	—	—	—	—	—	—	—	Doppelganger	–3
99	99	99	99	99	—	99	99	99	99	Wereboar (lycanthrope)*	–1
100	100	100	100	100	—	100	100	100	100	Weretiger (lycanthrope)*	–1

*Reroll to determine the NPC's base race or kind. (On the reroll, ignore rolls marked by asterisks.)
**If the creature is exceptionally powerful, reduce its class level to balance. If its class level is 0 or lower, reroll.

TABLE 2–32: EVIL NPC RACE OR KIND

Bbn	Brd	Clr	Drd	Ftr	Mnk	Rgr	Rog	Sor	Wiz	Race/Kind	Level
—	—	01–02	—	01–02	—	—	01	—	—	Dwarf, deep	Normal
—	—	03	—	03–04	—	—	—	—	—	Dwarf, hill	Normal
—	01	04	—	05	—	01	02	—	01–10	Elf, high	Normal
01	—	05	—	—	—	—	—	01	—	Elf, wild	Normal
02–03	02	06–08	01–02	06–07	—	02–11	03	—	11	Elf, wood	Normal
04	03–17	09–18	03	08–12	01–10	12–28	04–18	02–16	12–26	Half-elf	Normal
05	18	19–20	—	13	—	29	19–38	17–21	27	Halfling, lightfoot	Normal
06	19	21	—	14	—	—	39	22	—	Halfling, deep	Normal
—	20	22	04	—	—	30	40	23	28	Halfling, tallfellow	Normal
07–29	21–22	23–25	05–06	15–23	11–20	31–39	41–50	24–28	—	Half-orc	Normal
30–39	23–97	26–56	07–56	24–53	21–90	40–69	51–70	29–68	29–78	Human	Normal
40–44	—	57–63	57–71	54	—	70–71	—	—	—	Lizardfolk	Normal
45	98	64	72	55	—	—	71–85	70	—	Goblin	Normal
46	—	65	73	56–80	91–93	72	86	71	79–80	Hobgoblin	Normal
47	—	66	74	81	—	—	87	72–86	—	Kobold	Normal
48–77	—	67	75	82–86	—	—	—	—	—	Orc	Normal
78	99	68	—	—	94	—	88–89	—	81	Tiefling (planetouched)	Normal
—	—	69–71	87	—	—	—	—	—	—	Drow (elf) [female]	–1
—	—	—	88	—	—	—	—	—	82–91	Drow (elf) [male]	–1
—	—	72	89	—	—	—	—	—	—	Duergar (dwarf)	–1
—	—	—	90	—	—	—	—	—	—	Dwarf, derro	–1
79–83	—	73–74	76–100	91	—	73–92	—	87	92	Gnoll	–1
84	—	75–89	—	92	—	93	—	88–90	—	Troglodyte	–1
85–86	—	90–91	—	93	—	94	90–93	91	93	Bugbear	–2
87–90	—	92	—	94	—	95	—	92	—	Ogre	–2
91–94	—	93	—	—	—	—	—	93	—	Minotaur	–4
—	—	94	—	—	—	—	94	94	94	Mind flayer	–8
—	—	95	—	96	95–96	—	—	95	95–96	Ogre mage	–8
—	—	96	—	97	97–98	96	95–96	96	97	Wererat (lycanthrope)*	–1
95–96	100	97	—	98	—	97–98	97	97	98	Werewolf (lycanthrope)*	–1
97–98	—	98–99	—	99	99	99	98–99	98	99	Half-fiend*	–2
99–100	—	100	—	100	100	100	100	99–100	100	Half-dragon*	–2

*Reroll to determine the NPC's base race or kind. (On the reroll, ignore rolls marked by asterisks.)

**If the creature is exceptionally powerful, reduce its class level to balance. If its class level is 0 or lower, reroll.

have fewer hit points and lower ability scores than the NPCs described here.

NPC Barbarian

Starting Ability Scores: Str 15, Dex 14, Con 13, Int 10, Wis 12, Cha 8.

Increased Ability Scores: 4th, Str 16; 8th, Con 14; 12th, Str 17; 16th, Str 18; 17th, Str 18 (20); 19th, Str 18 (24), Dex 14 (16); 20th, Str 19 (25).

Feats: 1st, Weapon Focus (greataxe); 3rd, Dodge; 6th, Track; 9th, Blind-Fight; 12th, Improved Critical (greataxe); 15th, Power Attack; 18th, Improved Critical (composite longbow).

Class Features: 1st, rage 1/day; 2nd, uncanny dodge (AC bonus); 4th, rage 2/day; 5th, uncanny dodge (no flank); 8th, rage

TABLE 2–33: NPC BARBARIAN

Lvl	hp	AC	Init	Spd	Greataxe (1d12)	Composite Longbow (1d8)	F/R/W	Cli	Ju	List	Wild
1st	13	16	+2	30 ft.	+5 (+2 damage)	+3 (+2 damage)	+3/+2/+1	+3	+3	+5	+5
2nd	20	17	+2	30 ft.	+6 (+2)	+5 (+2)	+4/+2/+1	+4	+4	+6	+6
3rd	28	17	+2	30 ft.	+7 (+2)	+6 (+2)	+4/+3/+2	+5	+5	+7	+7
4th	35	17	+2	30 ft.	+9 (+3)	+7 (+3)	+5/+3/+2	+7	+6	+8	+8
5th	43	18	+2	30 ft.	+10 (+3)	+8 (+3)	+5/+3/+2	+8	+8	+9	+9
6th	50	18	+2	30 ft.	+11/6 (+3)	+9/4 (+3)	+6/+4/+3	+9	+9	+10	+10
7th	58	18	+2	30 ft.	+12/7 (+4)	+10/5 (+3)	+6/+4/+3	+10	+10	+11	+11
8th	73	19	+2	30 ft.	+13/8 (+4)	+11/6 (+3)	+8/+4/+3	+11	+11	+12	+12
9th	81	20	+2	30 ft.	+14/9 (+4)	+12/7 (+3)	+8/+5/+4	+12	+12	+13	+13
10th	90	20	+2	30 ft.	+15/10 (+4)	+14/9 (+4)	+9/+5/+4	+13	+13	+14	+14
11th	98	21	+2	30 ft.	+16/11/6 (+4)	+15/10/5 (+4)	+9/+5/+4	+14	+14	+15	+15
12th	107	22	+2	30 ft.	+17/12/7 (+4)	+16/11/6 (+4)	+10/+6/+5	+15	+15	+16	+16
13th	115	24	+2	30 ft.	+18/13/8 (+4)	+17/12/7 (+4)	+10/+6/+5	+16	+16	+17	+17
14th	124	24	+2	30 ft.	+20/15/10 (+5)	+18/13/8 (+4)	+11/+6/+5	+17	+17	+18	+18
15th	132	24	+2	60 ft.	+22/17/12 (+6)	+19/14/9 (+4)	+11/+7/+6	+18	+28	+19	+19
16th	141	24	+2	60 ft.	+25/20/15/10 (+9)	+23/18/13/8 (+8)	+12/+7/+6	+19	+29	+20	+20
17th	149	26	+2	60 ft.	+27/22/17/12 (+9)	+24/19/14/9 (+8)	+12/+7/+6	+21	+31	+21	+21
18th	158	28	+2	60 ft.	+28/23/18/13 (+9)	+26/21/16/11 (+9)	+13/+7/+6	+22	+32	+22	+22
19th	166	29	+3	60 ft.	+31/26/21/16 (+11)	+28/23/18/13 (+9)	+13/+8/+6	+25	+35	+23	+23
20th	175	29	+3	60 ft.	+32/27/22/17 (+11)	+29/24/19/14 (+9)	+19/+13/+11	+26	+36	+24	+24

TABLE 2–34: NPC BARD

Lvl	hp	AC	Init	Spd	Longsword (1d8)	Light Crossbow (1d8)	F/R/W	Bluff	Dipl	Perf	S Mot	Spellc	Tum
1st	7	14	+1	30 ft.	+1	+2	+1/+3/+1	+6	+6	+6	+3	+6	+5
2nd	11	14	+1	30 ft.	+2	+3	+1/+4/+2	+7	+7	+7	+4	+7	+6
3rd	16	14	+1	30 ft.	+4	+4	+2/+4/+2	+8	+8	+8	+5	+8	+7
4th	20	14	+1	30 ft.	+5	+5	+2/+5/+3	+10	+10	+10	+6	+9	+8
5th	25	15	+1	30 ft.	+5	+5	+2/+5/+3	+11	+11	+11	+7	+10	+9
6th	29	15	+5	30 ft.	+6	+6	+3/+6/+4	+12	+12	+12	+8	+11	+10
7th	34	15	+5	30 ft.	+7	+7	+3/+6/+4	+13	+13	+13	+9	+12	+11
8th	38	15	+5	30 ft.	+8/3	+8	+3/+7/+5	+15	+15	+15	+10	+13	+12
9th	43	15	+5	30 ft.	+8/3	+8	+4/+7/+5	+16	+16	+18	+11	+14	+13
10th	47	15	+5	30 ft.	+9/4	+9	+4/+8/+6	+17	+17	+19	+12	+15	+14
11th	52	16	+5	30 ft.	+10/5 (+1 damage)	+10	+4/+8/+6	+18	+18	+20	+13	+16	+15
12th	56	18	+5	30 ft.	+11/6 (+1)	+11	+5/+9/+7	+20	+20	+22	+14	+19	+16
13th	61	19	+5	30 ft.	+11/6 (+1)	+11	+5/+9/+7	+21	+21	+23	+15	+20	+17
14th	65	19	+5	30 ft.	+13/8 (+2)	+12	+5/+10/+8	+22	+22	+24	+16	+21	+18
15th	70	19	+5	30 ft.	+14/9/4 (+2)	+13	+6/+10/+8	+23	+25	+25	+17	+22	+19
16th	74	20	+5	30 ft.	+15/10/5 (+2)	+14	+6/+11/+9	+24	+26	+26	+18	+23	+20
17th	79	22	+5	30 ft.	+15/10/5 (+2)	+14	+6/+11/+9	+26	+28	+28	+19	+24	+21
18th	83	23	+5	30 ft.	+16/11/6 (+2)	+15	+7/+12/+10	+30	+30	+30	+20	+25	+22
19th	88	28	+5	30 ft.	+17/12/7 (+2)	+16	+7/+12/+10	+31	+31	+31	+21	+26	+23
20th	92	28	+5	30 ft.	+18/13/8 (+2)	+17	+7/+13/+11	+32	+32	+32	+22	+27	+24

SPELLS CAST/KNOWN

(15% chance of arcane spell failure at 1st–9th level)

Class Level	0	1st	2nd	3rd	4th	5th	6th
1st	2/4	—	—	—	—	—	—
2nd	3/5	1/2	—	—	—	—	—
3rd	3/6	2/3	—	—	—	—	—
4th	3/6	3/3	1/2	—	—	—	—
5th	3/6	4/4	2/3	—	—	—	—
6th	3/6	4/4	3/3	—	—	—	—
7th	3/6	4/4	3/4	1/2	—	—	—
8th	3/6	4/4	4/4	2/3	—	—	—
9th	3/6	4/4	4/4	3/3	—	—	—
10th	3/6	4/4	4/4	3/4	1/2	—	—
11th	3/6	4/4	4/4	4/4	2/3	—	—
12th	3/6	5/4	4/4	4/4	3/3	—	—
13th	3/6	5/4	4/4	4/4	3/4	1/2	—
14th	4/6	5/4	4/4	4/4	4/4	2/3	—
15th	4/6	6/4	4/4	4/4	4/4	3/3	—
16th	4/6	6/5	5/4	4/4	4/4	3/4	—
17th	4/6	6/5	6/5	5/4	4/4	4/4	2/3
18th	4/6	6/5	6/5	6/5	5/4	4/4	3/3
19th	4/6	6/5	6/5	6/5	5/5	5/4	4/4
20th	4/6	6/5	6/5	6/5	6/5	5/5	5/4

3/day; 10th, uncanny dodge (+1 vs. traps); 11th, damage reduction 1/—; 12th, rage 4/day; 13th, uncanny dodge (+2 vs. traps); 14th, damage reduction 2/—; 15th, greater rage; 16th, rage 5/day, uncanny dodge (+3 vs. traps); 18th, uncanny dodge (+4 vs. traps); 20th, rage 6/day, not winded after rage, damage reduction 4/—.

Armor: Masterwork scale mail (1st), masterwork breastplate (2nd–4th), *+1 breastplate* (5th–8th), *+2 breastplate* (9th–10th), *+3 breastplate* (11th–16th), *+4 breastplate* (17th), *+5 breastplate* (18th–20th).

Greataxe (Melee): Masterwork (1st–6th), +1 (7th–13th), +2 (14th), +3 (15th), +4 (16th–20th).

Composite Longbow (Ranged): Mighty [Str 14] (1st–3rd), mighty [Str 16] (4th–9th), *+1 mighty* [Str 16] (10th–15th), *+2 mighty* [Str 18] (16th–17th), *+3 mighty* [Str 18] (18th–20th).

Arrows: 20 normal (1st), 20 masterwork (2nd–15th), 20 +2 (16th–20th).

Potions: 1 *cure light wounds* (1st), 1 *cure moderate wounds* (2nd), 1 *delay poison* (2nd–3rd), 1 *lesser restoration* (2nd–3rd), 2 *cure moderate wounds* (3rd), 3 *cure moderate wounds* (4th–5th), 1 *neutralize poison* (4th–5th), 2 *lesser restoration* (4th–20th), 2 *cure serious wounds*

(6th–14th), 2 *neutralize poison* (6th–20th), 2 *haste* (10th–14th), 4 *cure serious wounds* (15th–20th), 4 *haste* (15th–20th), 4 *heroism* (16th–20th).

Other Magic Gear: *Amulet of natural armor +1* (8th–11th), *amulet of natural armor +2* (12th–16th), *ring of protection +2* (13th–17th), *boots of striding and springing* (15th–20th), *amulet of natural armor +3* (17th–20th), *gauntlets of ogre power +2* (17th–18th), *ring of protection +3* (18th–20th), *bag of holding 2* (19th–20th), *belt of giant strength +6* (19th–20th), *gloves of Dexterity +2* (19th–20th), *cloak of resistance +5* (20th), *rod of thunder and lightning* (20th).

Other Normal Gear: Climber's kit (1st–20th), dagger (1st), silver dagger (2nd–20th), 3 flasks alchemist's fire (3rd–20th).

NPC Bard

Starting Ability Scores: Str 10, Dex 13, Con 12, Int 14, Wis 8, Cha 15.

Increased Ability Scores: 4th, Cha 16; 8th, Cha 17 (19); 12th, Cha 18 (20); 16th, Cha 19 (21); 17th, Cha 19 (23); 18th, Cha 19 (25); 20th, Cha 20 (26).

Feats: 1st, Dodge; 3rd, Weapon Focus (longsword); 6th, Improved Initiative; 9th, Skill Focus (Perform); 12th, Skill Focus (Spellcraft); 15th, Skill Focus (Diplomacy); 18th, Skill Focus (Bluff).

Class Features: 1st, Bardic music, bardic knowledge.

Armor: Masterwork studded leather (1st–9th), none (10th–20th).

Longsword (Melee): Masterwork (1st–10th), +1 (11th–13th), +2 (14th–20th).

Light Crossbow (Ranged): Masterwork (1st–20th).

Bolts: 10 normal (1st–20th).

Potions: 1 *Charisma* (1st–5th), 3 *cure light wounds* (1st–2nd), 1 *tongues* (2nd–6th), 3 *cure moderate wounds* (3rd–7th), 1 *glibness* (3rd–6th), 1 *fly* (4th–8th), 2 *Charisma* (6th–20th), 2 *glibness* (7th–8th), 2 *tongues* (7th–20th), 3 *cure serious wounds* (8th–20th), 2 *fly* (9th–20th), 3 *glibness* (9th–20th).

Other Magic Gear: *Wand of summon monster I* (2nd–13th), *amulet of natural armor +1* (5th–9th), *mirror of vanity +2* (8th–16th), *bracers of armor +2* (10th), *amulet of natural armor +2* (10th–16th), *bracers of armor +3* (11th–15th), *ring of protection +2* (12th), *ring of protection +3* (13th–20th), *horn of blasting* (14th–20th), *wand of summon monster II* (14th–18th), *bracers of armor +4* (16th), *wand of polymorph self* (16th–20th), *bracers of armor +5* (17th–20th), *amulet of natural armor +3* (17th), *mirror of vanity +4* (17th), *amulet of natural armor +4* (18th–20th), *mirror of vanity +6* (18th–20th), *carpet of flying* [5 ft. × 7 ft.] (19th–20th), *eyes of charming* (20th).

TABLE 2–35: NPC CLERIC

Lvl	hp	AC	Init	Spd	Morningstar (1d8)	Light Crossbow (1d8)	F/R/W	Spellc	Con	Spells per Day
1st	10	17	–1	20 ft.	+2 (+1 damage)	–1	+4/–1/+4	+4	+6	3/3
2nd	16	18	–1	20 ft.	+3 (+1)	+0	+5/–1/+5	+5	+7	4/4
3rd	23	19	–1	20 ft.	+4 (+1)	+1	+5/+0/+5	+6	+8	4/4/3
4th	29	19	–1	20 ft.	+5 (+1)	+2	+6/+0/+7	+7	+9	5/5/4
5th	36	19	–1	20 ft.	+5 (+1)	+2	+7/+1/+8	+8	+10	5/5/4/3
6th	42	20	–1	20 ft.	+6 (+1)	+3	+8/+2/+9	+9	+11	5/5/5/4
7th	49	20	–1	20 ft.	+7 (+1)	+4	+8/+2/+9	+10	+12	6/6/5/4/2
8th	55	21	–1	20 ft.	+8/3 (+1)	+5	+9/+2/+10	+11	+13	6/6/5/5/3
9th	62	22	–1	20 ft.	+8/3 (+1)	+5	+9/+3/+10	+12	+14	6/6/6/5/3/2
10th	68	22	–1	20 ft.	+9/4 (+1)	+6	+10/+3/+12	+13	+15	6/6/6/5/3
11th	75	22	–1	20 ft.	+10/5 (+1)	+7	+10/+3/+12	+14	+16	6/7/6/6/5/3/2
12th	81	23	–1	20 ft.	+11/6 (+2)	+8	+11/+4/+14	+15	+17	6/8/6/6/5/5/3
13th	88	24	0	20 ft.	+11/5 (+2)	+10 (+1 damage)	+11/+5/+14	+16	+18	6/8/7/6/6/5/3/2
14th	94	24	0	20 ft.	+12/6 (+2)	+11 (+1)	+12/+5/+16	+17	+19	6/8/8/6/6/5/5/3
15th	101	24	0	20 ft.	+13/8/3 (+2)	+12 (+1)	+13/+7/+17	+18	+20	6/8/8/7/6/6/5/3/2
16th	107	26	0	20 ft.	+14/9/4 (+2)	+13 (+1)	+15/+8/+19	+19	+21	6/8/8/7/6/6/5/4/3
17th	114	26	0	20 ft.	+14/9/4 (+2)	+13 (+1)	+15/+8/+20	+20	+22	6/8/8/8/7/6/6/5/3/2
18th	120	26	0	20 ft.	+15/10/5 (+2)	+14 (+1)	+16/+9/+21	+21	+23	6/8/8/8/7/6/6/5/4/3
19th	126	26	0	20 ft.	+16/11/6 (+2)	+15 (+1)	+16/+9/+21	+22	+24	6/8/8/8/7/7/6/6/4/3
20th	133	26	0	20 ft.	+17/12/7 (+2)	+16 (+1)	+17/+9/+23	+23	+25	6/8/8/8/8/7/6/6/6/5

Note: You must choose one spell per spell level from the appropriate domains.

NPC Cleric

Starting Ability Scores: Str 13, Dex 8, Con 14, Int 10, Wis 15, Cha 12.

Increased Ability Scores: 4th, Wis 16; 8th, Wis 17; 10th, Wis 17 (19); 12th, Wis 18 (20); 13th, Dex 8 (10); 14th, Wis 18 (22); 16th, Wis 19 (23); 17th, Wis 19 (25); 20th, Wis 20 (26).

Feats: 1st, Scribe Scroll; 3rd, Brew Potion; 6th, Combat Casting; 9th, Forge Wand; 12th, Heighten Spell; 15th, Maximize Spell; 18th, Quicken Spell.

Class Features: 1st, Turn or rebuke undead.

Armor: Splint mail (1st), half-plate (2nd), full plate (3rd–5th), +1 full plate (6th–15th), +2 full plate (16th–20th), large metal shield (1st–7th), +1 large metal shield (8th–15th), +2 large metal shield (16th–20th).

Morningstar (Melee) [or Deity's Favored Weapon]: Masterwork (1st–11th), +1 (12th–20th).

Light Crossbow (Ranged): Normal (1st–20th).

Bolts: 10 normal bolts (1st–12th), 10 +1 (13th–20th).

Scrolls: *Protection from elements* (1st–2nd), 3 *cure light wounds* (2nd–3rd), 5 *cure light wounds* (4th–6th), *silence* (6th), *neutralize poison* (7th), *raise dead* (7th–13th), *ethereal jaunt* (9th–14th), *wind walk* (11th–13th), *resurrection* (12th–13th), *implosion* (13th–20th), 2 *resurrection* (14th–20th), *true resurrection* (15th), 2 *true resurrection* (16th–20th), *etherealness* (17th–20th), *antilife shell* (17th–20th), *mass heal* (17th–20th).

Potions: *Blur* (2nd–6th), *levitate* (2nd–6th), *fly* (4th–16th), *spider climb* (8th–10th), *heroism* (9th–12th).

Other Magic Gear: *Cloak of resistance +1* (5th–14th), *wand of cure light wounds* (7th–8th), *ring of protection +1* (9th–20th), *wand of hold person* (9th–13th), *pearl of Wisdom +2* (10th–13th), *wand of searing light* (11th–14th), *amulet of natural armor +1* (12th–20th), *gloves of Dexterity +2* (13th–20th), *pearl of Wisdom +4* (14th–16th), *cloak of resistance +2* (15th), *wand of searing light [10th level]* (15th–20th), *cloak of resistance +3* (16th–20th), *pearl of Wisdom +6* (17th–20th), *ring of blinking* (18th–20th), *gem of seeing* (19th–20th), *rod of absorption* (20th).

NPC Druid

Starting Ability Scores: Str 10, Dex 14, Con 13, Int 12, Wis 15, Cha 8.

Increased Ability Scores: 4th, Wis 16; 8th, Wis 17; 11th, Wis 17 (19); 12th, Wis 18 (20); 14th, Wis 18 (22); 16th, Wis 19 (23);

17th, Wis 19 (25); 20th, Wis 20 (26).

Feats: 1st, Scribe Scroll; 3rd, Track; 6th, Dodge; 9th, Combat Casting; 12th, Still Spell; 15th, Spell Focus (Enchantment); 18th, Maximize Spell.

Class Features: 1st, nature sense, animal companion; 2nd, woodland stride; 3rd, trackless step; 4th, resist nature's lure; 9th, venom immunity; 13th, a thousand faces; 15th, timeless body.

Armor: Hide armor (1st–5th), large wooden shield (1st–8th), +1 hide armor (6th–12th), +1 large wooden shield (9th–16th), +2 hide armor (13th–17th), +2 large wooden shield (17th), +3 hide armor (18th–20th), +4 large wooden shield (18th–20th).

Scimitar (Melee): Masterwork (1st–12th), +1 (13th–15th), +2 (16th–20th).

Sling (Ranged): Normal (1st–20th).

Bullets: 10 masterwork (1st–20th).

Scrolls: 3 *cure light wounds* (1st), 2 *endure elements* (1st–2nd), *heat metal* (2nd–4th), 2 *barkskin* (3rd–4th), 2 *flaming sphere* (3rd–4th), *warp wood* (3rd–4th), 2 *call lightning* (5th–6th), 2 *neutralize poison* (5th–6th), 2 *protection from elements* (5th–6th), 2 *speak with plants* (5th–6th), 2 *flame strike* (7th–8th), 2 *reincarnate* (7th–20th), 2 *sleet storm* (7th–8th), *ice storm* (9th–10th), *wall of fire* (9th–10th), *antilife shell* (11th–12th), *healing circle* (11th–12th), *summon nature's ally VI* (11th–12th), *control weather* (13th–14th), *fire storm* (13th–14th), *heal* (13th–16th), *true seeing* (13th–14th), *finger of death* (15th–16th), *repel metal or stone* (15th–16th), 2 *summon nature's ally VIII* (15th–16th), *earthquake* (17th–20th), 2 *elemental swarm* (17th–20th), 2 *mass heal* (17th–20th), *shapechange* (17th–20th).

Other Magic Gear: *Potion of blur* (2nd–4th), *wand of cure light wounds* (2nd–14th), 2 *Quaal's feather token—tree* (3rd–20th), *phylactery of faithfulness* (4th–8th), *bag of tricks [gray]* (6th–14th), 2 *potions of darkvision* (6th–8th), *ring of protection +1* (8th–15th), *wand of faerie fire* (9th–12th), *amulet of natural armor +1* (10th–14th), *pearl of Wisdom +2* (11th–13th), *druid's vestment* (12th–20th), *stone of good luck* (12th–20th), *pearl of Wisdom +4* (14th–16th), *amulet of natural armor +2* (15th–20th), *bag of tricks [rust]* (15th–17th), *wand of cure moderate wounds* (15th–20th), *ring of protection +2* (16th–20th), *cloak of resistance +2* (17th–20th), *pearl of Wisdom +6* (17th–20th), *bag of tricks [tan]* (18th–20th), *orb of storms* (19th–20th), *ring of shooting stars* (20th).

Animal Companions: 1st–2nd, wolf; 3rd, eagle, wolf; 4th, black bear, eagle; 5th, black bear, eagle, owl; 6th, eagle, 2 lions; 7th, brown bear, eagle; 8th, dire boar, eagle; 9th, dire lion, eagle; 10th, dire lion,

TABLE 2–36: NPC DRUID

Lvl	hp	AC	Init	Spd	Scimitar (1d6)	Sling (1d4)	F/R/W	Spellc/Con/Kno	Ani Emp	Wild	Wild Shape
1st	9	17	+2	30 ft.	+1	+3	+3/+2/+4	+5	+3	+6	
2nd	14	17	+2	30 ft.	+2	+4	+4/+2/+5	+6	+4	+7	
3rd	20	17	+2	30 ft.	+3	+5	+4/+3/+5	+7	+5	+8	
4th	25	17	+2	30 ft.	+4	+6	+5/+3/+7	+8	+6	+10	
5th	31	17	+2	30 ft.	+4	+6	+5/+3/+7	+9	+7	+11	1/day
6th	36	18	+2	30 ft.	+5	+7	+6/+4/+8	+10	+8	+12	2/day
7th	42	18	+2	30 ft.	+6	+8	+6/+4/+8	+11	+9	+13	3/day
8th	47	19	+2	30 ft.	+7/2	+9	+7/+4/+9	+12	+10	+14	Large
9th	53	20	+2	30 ft.	+7/2	+9	+7/+5/+9	+13	+11	+15	
10th	58	21	+2	30 ft.	+8/3	+10	+8/+5/+10	+14	+12	+16	4/day
11th	64	21	+2	30 ft.	+9/4	+11	+8/+5/+11	+15	+13	+18	Tiny
12th	69	21	+2	30 ft.	+10/5	+12	+9/+6/+12	+16	+14	+20	Dire
13th	75	22	+2	30 ft.	+10/5 (+1 damage)	+12	+9/+6/+12	+17	+15	+21	
14th	80	22	+2	30 ft.	+11/6 (+1)	+13	+11/+7/+15	+18	+16	+23	5/day
15th	86	23	+2	30 ft.	+12/7/2 (+1)	+14	+11/+8/+15	+19	+17	+24	Huge
16th	91	24	+2	30 ft.	+14/9/4 (+2)	+15	+12/+8/+17	+20	+18	+25	Elemental ×1
17th	97	25	+2	30 ft.	+14/9/4 (+2)	+15	+14/+10/+20	+21	+19	+27	
18th	102	27	+2	30 ft.	+15/10/5 (+2)	+16	+15/+11/+21	+22	+20	+28	6/day, elemental ×3
19th	108	27	+2	30 ft.	+16/11/6 (+2)	+17	+15/+11/+21	+23	+21	+29	
20th	113	27	+2	30 ft.	+17/12/7 (+2)	+18	+16/+11/+23	+24	+22	+31	

SPELLS PER DAY

Level	Spells	Level	Spells	Level	Spells	Level	Spells
1st	3/2	2nd	4/3	3rd	4/3/2	4th	5/4/3
5th	5/4/3/2	6th	5/4/4/3	7th	6/5/4/3/1	8th	6/5/4/4/2
9th	6/5/5/4/2/1	10th	6/5/5/4/3/2	11th	6/6/5/5/4/2/1	12th	6/7/5/5/4/3/2
13th	6/7/6/5/5/4/2/1	14th	6/7/7/5/5/4/4/2	15th	6/7/7/5/5/4/2/1	16th	6/7/7/6/5/4/3/2
17th	6/7/7/7/6/5/5/4/2/1	18th	6/7/7/7/6/5/5/4/3/2	19th	6/7/7/7/6/5/5/3/3	20th	6/7/7/7/7/6/5/5/4

eagle, owl; 11th, dire lion, 2 eagles, owl; 12th, dire bear; 13th, dire bear, eagle; 14th, dire bear, eagle, owl; 15th, dire bear, 2 eagles, owl; 16th, dire tiger; 17th, dire tiger, eagle; 18th, dire tiger, eagle, owl; 19th, dire tiger, 2 eagles, owl; 20th, dire bat, dire tiger.

NPC Fighter

Starting Ability Scores: Str 15, Dex 13, Con 14, Int 10, Wis 12, Cha 8.

Increased Ability Scores: 4th, Str 16; 8th, Str 17; 12th, Str 18; 16th, Str 19; 17th, Str 19 (21); 19th, Str 19 (25); 20th, Str 20 (26).

Feats: 1st, Exotic Weapon (bastard sword), Weapon Focus (bastard sword); 2nd, Improved Initiative; 3rd, Power Attack; 4th, Weapon Specialization (bastard sword); 6th, Cleave, Point-Blank Shot; 8th, Improved Critical (bastard sword); 9th, Great Cleave; 10th, Dodge, 12th, Precise Shot, Weapon Focus (composite longbow); 14th, Improved Critical (composite longbow), 15th, Mounted Combat; 16th, Blind-Fight; 18th, Mounted Archery, Far Shot; 20th, Combat Reflexes.

Armor: Splint mail (1st), large metal shield (1st–7th), half-plate (2nd), full plate (3rd–5th), +1 full plate (6th–9th), +1 large metal shield (8th–14th), +2 full plate (10th–16th), +2 large metal shield (15th), +3 large metal shield (16th–20th), +3 full plate (17th), +4 full plate (18th–20th).

Bastard Sword (Melee): Masterwork (1st–6th), +1 (7th–11th), +2 (12th–14th), +3 (15th–17th), +4 (18th–20th).

Composite Longbow (Ranged): Normal (1st), mighty [Str 14] masterwork (2nd–3rd), mighty [Str 16] masterwork (4th–8th), mighty [Str 16] +1 (9th–11th), +1 mighty [Str 18] (12th–15th), +2 mighty [Str 18] (16th–20th).

Arrows: 20 normal (1st–7th), 25 +1 arrows (8th–13th), 50 +1 arrows (14th–17th), 50 +2 arrows (18th–20th).

Magic Gear: Potion of cure moderate wounds (1st–20th), potion of endurance (2nd–20th), cloak of resistance +1 (5th–10th), cloak of resistance +2 (11th–17th), ring of protection +1 (11th–15th), boots of speed (13th–20th), amulet of natural armor +2 (14th–20th), potion of heroism (14th–16th), eyes of the eagle (15th–20th), ring of protection +2 (16th–19th), gauntlets of ogre power (17th–18th), rope of climbing (17th–20th), quiver of Ehlonna (18th–20th), cloak of resistance +3 (18th–20th), belt of giant strength +6 (19th–20th), pink Ioun stone (19th–20th), ring of protection +4 (20th), helm of teleportation (20th).

NPC Monk

Starting Ability Scores: Str 14, Dex 13, Con 12, Int 10, Wis 15, Cha 8.

Increased Ability Scores: 4th, Dex 14; 8th, Wis 16; 12th, Dex 15; 15th, Dex 15 (17), Wis 16 (18); 16th, Dex 16 (18); 19th, Str 14 (16), Con 12 (14), Dex 16 (20), Wis 16 (20); 20th, Dex 16 (22), Wis 17 (23).

Feats: 1st, Dodge; 3rd, Weapon Focus (kama); 6th, Mobility; 9th, Spring Attack; 12th, Improved Critical (unarmed); 15th, Combat Reflexes; 18th, Improved Initiative.

Class Features: 1st, Unarmed Strike, stunning attack, evasion; 2nd, Deflect Arrows; 3rd, still mind; 4th, slow fall (20 ft.); 5th, purity of body; 6th, slow fall (30 ft.), Improved Trip; 7th, wholeness of body, leap of the clouds; 8th, slow fall (50 ft.); 9th, improved evasion; 10th, ki strike (+1); 11th, diamond body; 12th, abundant step; 13th, diamond soul, ki strike (+2); 15th, quivering palm; 16th, ki strike (+3); 17th, timeless body, tongue of the sun and moon; 18th, slow fall (any distance); 19th, empty body; 20th, perfect self.

Kama (Melee): Masterwork (1st–2nd), +1 (3rd–9th), +2 (10th–13th), +3 (14th–16th), +4 (17th), +5 (18th–20th).

Sling (Ranged): normal (1st), masterwork (2nd–8th), +1 (9th–11th), +2 (12th–20th).

Bullets: 10 normal (1st–10th), 10 +1 (11th–20th).

Potions: 2 cure light wounds (1st–2nd), 1 cat's grace (1st–5th), 1 heroism (2nd, 9th, 12th–16th), 1 cure moderate wounds (4th–12th), 2 cat's grace (11th–12th), 3 heroism (17th–20th).

Table 2–37: NPC Fighter

Lvl	hp	AC	Init	Spd	Bastard Sword (1d10)	Composite Longbow (1d8)	F/R/W	Cli/Ju	Ride
1st	12	18	+1	20 ft.	+5 (+2 damage)	+2	+4/+1/+1	–3	—
2nd	19	19	+5	20 ft.	+6 (+2)	+4 (+2)	+5/+1/+1	–2	—
3rd	27	21	+5	20 ft.	+7 (+2)	+5 (+2)	+5/+2/+2	+0	—
4th	34	21	+5	20 ft.	+9 (+5)	+6 (+3)	+6/+2/+2	+2	—
5th	42	21	+5	20 ft.	+10 (+5)	+7 (+3)	+7/+3/+3	+3	—
6th	49	22	+5	20 ft.	+11/6 (+5)	+8/3 (+3)	+8/+4/+4	+5	—
7th	57	22	+5	20 ft.	+12/7 (+6)	+9/4 (+3)	+8/+4/+4	+6	—
8th	64	23	+5	20 ft.	+13/8 (+6)	+11/6 (+4)	+9/+4/+4	+8	—
9th	72	23	+5	20 ft.	+14/9 (+6)	+12/7 (+5)	+9/+5/+5	+9	—
10th	79	24	+5	20 ft.	+15/10 (+6)	+13/8 (+5)	+10/+5/+5	+10	—
11th	87	25	+5	20 ft.	+16/11/6 (+6)	+14/9/4 (+5)	+11/+6/+6	+11	—
12th	94	25	+5	20 ft.	+19/14/9 (+8)	+16/11/6 (+6)	+12/+7/+7	+13	—
13th	102	25	+5	20 ft.	+20/15/10 (+8)	+17/12/7 (+6)	+12/+7/+7	+14	—
14th	109	27	+5	20 ft.	+21/16/11 (+8)	+18/13/8 (+6)	+13/+7/+7	+15	—
15th	117	28	+5	20 ft.	+23/18/13 (+9)	+19/14/9 (+6)	+13/+8/+8	+15	+2
16th	124	30	+5	20 ft.	+24/19/14/9 (+9)	+21/16/11/6 (+7)	+14/+8/+8	+15	+4
17th	132	31	+5	20 ft.	+27/22/17/12 (+11)	+22/17/12/7 (+7)	+14/+8/+8	+16	+6
18th	139	32	+5	20 ft.	+28/23/18/13 (+11)	+24/19/14/9 (+8)	+16/+10/+10	+16	+8
19th	166	32	+5	20 ft.	+31/26/21/16 (+13)	+25/20/15/10 (+8)	+17/+10/+10	+18	+10
20th	175	34	+5	20 ft.	+33/28/23/18 (+14)	+26/21/16/11 (+8)	+18/+10/+10	+18	+12

Table 2–38: NPC Monk

Lvl	hp	AC	Init	Spd	Unarmed	Kama (1d6)	Sling (1d4)	F/R/W	Jum	Ba/Hi/Tum
1st	9	13	+1	30 ft.	+2 (1d6+2)	+3 (+2 damage)	+1 (1d4)	+3/+3/+4	+6	+5
2nd	14	13	+1	30 ft.	+3 (1d6+2	+4 (+2)	+3 (1d4)	+4/+4/+5	+7	+6
3rd	20	13	+1	40 ft.	+4 (1d6+2)	+6 (+3)	+4 (1d4)	+4/+4/+5	+8	+7
4th	25	14	+2	40 ft.	+5 (1d8+2)	+7 (+3)	+6 (1d4)	+5/+6/+6	+9	+9
5th	31	16	+2	40 ft.	+5 (1d8+2)	+7 (+3)	+6 (1d4)	+5/+6/+6	+10	+10
6th	36	16	+2	50 ft.	+6/3 (1d8+2)	+8/5 (+3)	+7/2 (1d4)	+7/+8/+8	+11	+11
7th	42	17	+2	50 ft.	+7/4 (1d8+2)	+9/6 (+3)	+8/3 (1d4)	+7/+8/+8	+12	+12
8th	47	19	+2	50 ft.	+8/5 (1d10+2)	+10/7 (+3)	+9/4 (1d4)	+8/+9/+10	+13	+13
9th	53	19	+2	60 ft.	+8/5 (1d10+2)	+10/7 (+3)	+9/4 (1d4+1)	+8/+9/+10	+14	+14
10th	58	20	+2	60 ft.	+9/6/3 (1d10+2)	+12/9/6 (+4)	+10/5 (1d4+1)	+8/+9/+10	+15	+15
11th	64	21	+2	60 ft.	+10/7/4 (1d10+2)	+13/10/7 (+4)	+12/7 (1d4+2)	+8/+9/+10	+16	+16
12th	69	21	+2	70 ft.	+11/8/5 (1d12+2)	+14/11/8 (+4)	+14/9 (1d4+3)	+9/+10/+11	+17	+17
13th	75	21	+2	70 ft.	+11/8/5 (1d12+2)	+14/11/8 (+4)	+14/9 (1d4+3)	+9/+10/+11	+18	+18
14th	80	21	+2	70 ft.	+12/9/6/3 (1d12+2)	+16/13/10/7 (+5)	+15/10 (1d4+3)	+10/+11/+12	+19	+19
15th	86	25	+3	80 ft.	+13/10/7/4 (1d12+2)	+17/14/11/8 (+5)	+17/12/7(1d4+3)	+10/+12/+13	+20	+21
16th	91	26	+3	80 ft.	+14/11/8/5 (1d20+2)	+18/15/12/9 (+5)	+19/14/9 (1d4+3)	+11/+14/+14	+21	+23
17th	97	27	+3	80 ft.	+14/11/8/5 (1d20+2)	+19/16/13/10 (+6)	+19/14/9 (1d4+3)	+11/+14/+14	+22	+24
18th	102	28	+7	90 ft.	+15/12/9/6/3 (1d20+2)	+21/18/15/12/9 (+7)	+20/15/10 (1d4+3)	+12/+15/+15	+23	+25
19th	127	30	+8	90 ft.	+17/14/11/8/5 (1d20+3)	+23/20/17/14/11 (+8)	+22/17/12 (1d4+3)	+13/+16/+16	+25	+27
20th	133	34	+9	90 ft.	+18/15/12/9/6 (1d20+3)	+24/21/18/15/12 (+8)	+24/19/14 (1d4+3)	+14/+17/+17	+26	+29

Other Magic Gear: *Bracers of armor +1* (5th–10th), *cloak of resistance +1* (6th–9th), *ring of protection +1* (7th–16th), *amulet of natural armor +1* (8th–17th), *bracers of armor +2* (11th–14th), *monk's belt* (13th–20th), *bracers of armor +3* (15th–19th), *pearl of Wisdom +2* (15th–18th), *gloves of Dexterity +2* (15th–18th), *cloak of displacement* (16th–20th), *slippers of spider climbing* (17th–20th), *ring of protection +2* (17th–20th), *amulet of natural armor +2* (18th–20th), *circlet of blasting* [minor] (18th–20th), *pearl of Wisdom +4* (19th), *gloves of Dexterity +4* (19th), *pink Ioun stone* (19th–20th), *pale blue Ioun stone* (19th–20th), *bracers of armor +4* (20th), *pearl of Wisdom +6* (20th), *gloves of Dexterity +6* (20th).

NPC Paladin

Starting Ability Scores: Str 14, Dex 8, Con 12, Int 10, Wis 13, Cha 15.

Increased Ability Scores: 4th, Wis 14; 8th, Cha 16; 12th, Cha 17 (19); 16th, Cha 18 (20); 19th, Cha 18 (24); 20th, Cha 19 (25).

Feats: 1st, Weapon Focus (longsword); 3rd, Mounted Combat; 6th, Lightning Reflexes; 9th, Improved Critical (longsword); 12th, Extra Turning; 15th, Iron Will; 18th, Spell Penetration.

Class Features: 1st, *detect evil*, divine grace, *lay on hands*, divine health; 2nd, aura of courage, smite evil; 3rd, *remove disease*, turn undead; 5th, special mount; 6th, *remove disease* 2/week; 9th, *remove disease* 3/week; 12th, *remove disease* 4/week; 15th, *remove disease* 5/week; 18th, *remove disease* 6/week.

Armor: Splint mail (1st), large metal shield (1st–3rd), half-plate (2nd), masterwork half-plate (3rd), full plate (4th–6th), masterwork large metal shield (4th–7th), +1 full plate (7th–11th), +1 large metal shield (8th–12th), +2 full plate (12th–14th), +2 large metal shield (13th–14th), +3 full plate (15th–16th), +3 large metal shield (15th–17th), +4 full plate (17th–20th), +4 large metal shield (18th–20th).

Longsword (Melee): Masterwork (1st–5th), +1 (6th–10th), +2 (11th–13th), +3 (14th–16th), +4 (17th), +5 (18th–20th).

Composite Longbow (Ranged): Normal (1st), mighty [Str 14] masterwork (2nd–12th), +1 mighty [Str 14] (13th–18th), +2 mighty [Str 14] (19th–20th).

Arrows: 20 normal (1st–12th), 5 +1 arrows (3rd–12th), 20 +1 arrows (13th–20th).

Potions: 4 *cure light wounds* (1st–7th), 2 *cure light wounds* (8th–14th), 2 *cure moderate wounds* (8th–9th, 15th–20th), 2 *cure se-*

TABLE 2–39: NPC PALADIN

Lvl	hp	AC	Init	Spd	Longsword (1d8)	Composite Longbow (1d8)	F/R/W	Heal	Ride	Con	Spells per day
1st	11	17	–1	20 ft.	+5 (+2 damage)	+0	+5/+1/+3	+5	+3	—	—
2nd	17	18	–1	20 ft.	+6 (+2	+2 (+2 damage)	+6/+1/+3	+6	+4	—	—
3rd	24	18	–1	20 ft.	+7 (+2)	+4 (+3)	+6/+2/+4	+7	+5	—	—
4th	30	19	–1	20 ft.	+8 (+2)	+5 (+3)	+7/+2/+5	+8	+5	+3	1
5th	37	19	–1	20 ft.	+9 (+2)	+6 (+3)	+7/+2/+5	+9	+6	+3	1
6th	43	19	–1	20 ft.	+10/5 (+3)	+7/2 (+3)	+8/+5/+6	+9	+7	+4	2
7th	50	20	–1	20 ft.	+11/6 (+3)	+8/3 (+3)	+8/+5/+6	+10	+7	+5	2
8th	56	21	–1	20 ft.	+12/7 (+3)	+9/4 (+3)	+10/+6/+7	+11	+8	+5	2/1
9th	63	22	–1	20 ft.	+13/8 (+3)	+10/5 (+3)	+10/+7/+8	+11	+9	+6	2/1
10th	69	22	–1	20 ft.	+14/9 (+3)	+11/6 (+3)	+11/+7/+8	+12	+9	+7	2/2
11th	76	22	–1	20 ft.	+16/11/6 (+4)	+12/7/2 (+3)	+11/+7/+8	+13	+10	+7	2/2
12th	82	23	–1	20 ft.	+17/12/7 (+4)	+13/8/3 (+3)	+13/+9/+10	+13	+11	+8	2/2/1
13th	89	24	–1	20 ft.	+18/13/8 (+4)	+14/9/4 (+4)	+14/+10/+11	+14	+11	+9	2/2/1
14th	95	24	–1	20 ft.	+20/15/10 (+5)	+15/10/5 (+4)	+15/+10/+11	+15	+12	+9	3/2/1
15th	102	26	–1	20 ft.	+21/16/11 (+5)	+16/11/6 (+4)	+16/+12/+15	+15	+13	+10	3/2/1/1
16th	108	28	–1	20 ft.	+22/17/12/7 (+5)	+17/12/7/2 (+4)	+18/+13/+16	+16	+13	+11	3/3/1/1
17th	115	29	–1	20 ft.	+24/19/14/9 (+6)	+18/13/8/3 (+4)	+18/+13/+16	+17	+14	+11	3/3/2/1
18th	121	30	–1	20 ft.	+26/21/16/11 (+7)	+19/14/9/4 (+4)	+20/+15/+18	+17	+15	+12	4/3/2/1
19th	128	30	–1	20 ft.	+27/22/17/12 (+7)	+21/16/11/6 (+5)	+20/+15/+18	+18	+15	+13	4/4/3/2
20th	134	30	–1	20 ft.	+28/23/18/13 (+7)	+22/17/12/7 (+5)	+21/+15/+18	+19	+16	+13	4/4/3/3

rious wounds (10th–20th), flying (10th–20th), tongues (10th–20th), wisdom (10th–20th).

Scrolls: *2 magic weapon (4th–20th), 2 protection from evil (4th–14th), remove paralysis (11th–20th), detect poison (12th–14th), 3 delay poison (12th–20th), 2 resist elements—fire (13th–20th), death ward (13th–20th).*

Other Magic Gear: *2 javelins of lightning (7th–11th), ring of protection +1 (9th–15th), mirror of vanity +2 (12th–18th), cloak of resistance +1 (13th–14th), cloak of resistance +2 (15th–17th), amulet of natural armor +1 (16th–20th), horn of goodness (16th–20th),*

Keoghtom's ointment (16th–20th), ring of protection +2 (16th–20th), phylactery of faithfulness (17th–20th), cloak of resistance +3 (18th–20th), mirror of vanity +6 (19th–20th), circlet of blasting [major] (20th).

Horse and Gear: Bit and bridle (2nd–20th), heavy warhorse (2nd–4th), military saddle (2nd–20th), saddlebags (2nd–20th), studded leather barding (3rd), masterwork studded leather barding (4th–5th), paladin's mount (5th–20th), masterwork scale mail barding (6th–9th), banded mail barding (10th–11th), masterwork banded mail barding (12th–15th), masterwork half-plate barding (16th–20th).

TABLE 2–40: NPC RANGER

Lvl	hp	AC	Init	Spd	Longsword (1d8)	Composite longbow (1d8)	F/R/W	Wild	Spot	M Sil	Hide
1st	11	15	+2	30 ft.	+3 (+2 damage)	+3 (+2 damage)	+3/+2/+1	+5	+5	+5	+5
2nd	17	15	+2	30 ft.	+4 (+2)	+4 (+2)	+4/+2/+1	+6	+6	+7	+7
3rd	24	15	+2	30 ft.	+5 (+2)	+5 (+2)	+4/+3/+2	+7	+12	+8	+8
4th	30	17	+3	30 ft.	+6 (+2)	+7 (+2)	+5/+4/+2	+8	+13	+10	+10
5th	37	17	+3	30 ft.	+7 (+2)	+8 (+2)	+5/+4/+2	+9	+14	+11	+11
6th	43	17	+7	30 ft.	+8/3 (+2)	+10/5 (+2)	+6/+5/+3	+10	+15	+12	+22
7th	50	17	+7	30 ft.	+9/4 (+2)	+11/6 (+3)	+6/+5/+3	+11	+16	+13	+23
8th	56	17	+7	30 ft.	+10/5 (+3)	+12/7 (+3)	+7/+5/+3	+12	+17	+14	+24
9th	63	17	+7	30 ft.	+11/6 (+3)	+13/8 (+3)	+7/+6/+4	+13	+18	+15	+25
10th	69	19	+8	30 ft.	+12/7 (+3)	+15/10 (+3)	+8/+7/+4	+14	+19	+17	+27
11th	76	20	+8	30 ft.	+13/8/3 (+3)	+16/11/6 (+3)	+8/+7/+4	+15	+20	+18	+28
12th	82	21	+9	30 ft.	+14/9/4 (+3)	+19/14/9 (+4)	+9/+9/+5	+16	+21	+20	+30
13th	89	23	+9	30 ft.	+15/10/5 (+3)	+22/17/12 (+5)	+9/+9/+5	+17	+22	+21	+31
14th	95	23	+9	30 ft.	+17/12/7 (+4)	+23/18/13 (+5)	+10/+9/+6	+19	+24	+22	+32
15th	102	24	+9	60 ft.	+18/13/8 (+4)	+25/20/15 (+6)	+10/+10/+7	+20	+25	+23	+33
16th	108	24	+9	60 ft.	+21/16/11/6 (+6)	+26/21/16/11 (+8)	+11/+10/+7	+21	+26	+24	+34
17th	115	24	+10	60 ft.	+23/18/13/8 (+6)	+29/24/19/14 (+8)	+12/+12/+8	+23	+28	+27	+37
18th	121	25	+10	60 ft.	+25/20/15/10 (+7)	+31/26/21/16 (+9)	+13/+13/+9	+24	+29	+28	+38
19th	128	25	+10	60 ft.	+27/22/17/12 (+7)	+32/27/22/17 (+9)	+13/+13/+9	+25	+30	+29	+54
20th	134	25	+11	60 ft.	+29/24/19/14 (+8)	+34/29/24/19 (+10)	+14/+14/+9	+26	+32	+31	+56

Note: As a full attack action, you can use longsword and short sword in combat. Doing so allows an extra attack with the short sword at the highest attack value, but all attacks that round suffer a –2 penalty. From 18th–20th level, doing so allows two extra attacks with the short sword, once at the highest attack value and once at a –5 penalty. (There's still a –2 penalty on all attacks.)

SPELLS PER DAY

Level	Spells	Level	Spells	Level	Spells	Level	Spells
1st	—	2nd	—	3rd	—	4th	1
5th	1	6th	2	7th	2	8th	2
9th	2	10th	2/1	11th	2/1	12th	2/1
13th	2/1	14th	3/2/1	15th	3/2/1	16th	3/3/1
17th	3/3/2	18th	4/3/2	19th	4/4/3	20th	4/4/3

Normal Gear: Dagger (1st–20th), healer's kit (1st–5th), holy water (1st–2nd), wooden holy symbol (1st), silver holy symbol (2nd–20th), 3 holy water (3rd–10th), masterwork healer's kit (6th–20th), 4 holy water (11th–20th).

NPC Ranger

Starting Ability Scores: Str 14, Dex 15, Con 13, Int 10, Wis 12, Cha 8.

Increased Ability Scores: 4th, Dex 16; 8th, Dex 17; 10th, Dex 17 (19); 12th, Dex 18 (20); 14th, Wis 12 (14); 16th, Str 14 (18); Dex 19 (21); 17th, Dex 19 (23); 20th, Dex 20 (24).

Feats: 1st, Point-Blank Shot; 3rd, Precise Shot; 6th, Weapon Focus (composite longbow); 9th, Rapid Shot; 12th, Improved Critical (composite longbow); 15th, Improved Critical (longsword); 18th, Improved Two-Weapon Fighting.

Class Features: 1st, track, favored enemy (goblinoid); 5th, favored enemy (undead); 10th, favored enemy (giant); 15th, favored enemy (dragon); 20th, favored enemy (devil).

Armor: Studded leather (1st), masterwork studded leather (2nd–3rd), +1 studded leather (4th–10th), +2 studded leather (11th–14th), +3 studded leather (15th–17th), +4 studded leather (18th–20th).

Longsword (Melee): Normal (1st), masterwork (2nd–7th), +1 (8th–13th), +2 (14th–17th), +3 (18th–19th), +4 (20th).

Short Sword (Melee, Off-Hand): Normal (1st), masterwork (2nd–8th), +1 (9th–20th).

Composite Longbow (Ranged): Mighty [Str 14] masterwork (1st–6th), +1 mighty [Str 14] (7th–12th), +2 mighty [Str 14] (13th–15th), +2 mighty [Str 18] (16th–17th), +3 mighty [Str 18] (18th–19th), +4 mighty [Str 18] (20th).

Arrows: 20 normal (1st–14th), 12 +1 arrows (15th–17th), 8 slaying arrows (15th), 8 greater slaying arrows (16th–17th), 10 +1 arrows (18th–20th), 10 greater slaying arrows (18th–20th).

Other Magic Gear: 2 potions of cure light wounds (1st), 1 potion of hide (1st), 3 potions of cure light wounds (2nd–8th), eyes of the eagle (3rd–20th), cloak of elvenkind (6th–20th), potion of endurance (9th–10th), gloves of Dexterity +2 (10th–16th), Heward's handy haversack (11th–20th), potion of heroism (11th–12th), amulet of natural armor +1 (13th–20th), bracers of archery (13th–20th), ring of protection +1 (13th–20th), pearl of Wisdom +2 (14th–20th), boots of striding and springing (15th–20th), belt of giant strength +4 (16th–20th), gloves of Dexterity +4 (17th–20th), pale green Ioun stone (17th–20th), ring of sustenance (17th–20th), robe of blending (19th–20th), scabbard of keen edges (19th–20th), wand of cure serious wounds (19th–20th), figurine of wondrous power [obsidian steed] (20th).

NPC Rogue

Starting Ability Scores: Str 12, Dex 15, Con 13, Int 14, Wis 10, Cha 8.

Increased Ability Scores: 4th, Dex 16; 8th, Dex 17; 12th, Dex 18 (20); 16th, Dex 19 (21); 17th, Dex 19 (23); 19th, Dex 19 (25); 20th, Dex 20 (26).

Feats: 1st, Improved Initiative; 3rd, Shield Proficiency; 6th, Alertness; 9th, Lightning Reflexes; 12th, Weapon Finesse (rapier); 15th, Improved Critical (rapier); 18th, Combat Reflexes.

Class Features: 1st, sneak attack +1d6; 2nd, evasion; 3rd, uncanny dodge (Dex bonus to AC), sneak attack +2d6, 5th, sneak attack +3d6; 6th, uncanny dodge (can't be flanked); 7th, sneak attack +4d6; 9th, sneak attack +5d6; 10th, improved evasion; uncanny dodge (+1 vs. traps), sneak attack +6d6; 13th, defensive roll, sneak attack +7d6; 14th, uncanny dodge (+2 vs. traps); 15th, sneak attack +8d6; 16th, slippery mind; 17th, uncanny dodge (+3 vs. traps), sneak attack +9d6; 19th, opportunist, sneak attack +10d6; 20th, uncanny dodge (+4 vs. traps).

Armor: Masterwork studded leather (1st–6th), masterwork buckler (3rd–6th), +1 buckler (7th–9th), +1 studded leather (7th–9th), +2 buckler (10th–14th).

Rapier (Melee): Masterwork (1st–8th), +1 (9th–12th), +2 (13th–18th), +3 (19th–20th).

Composite Shortbow (Ranged): Mighty [Str 12] masterwork (1st–8th), +1 mighty [Str 12] (9th–16th), +2 mighty [Str 12] (17th–19th), +3 mighty [Str 12] (20th).

Arrows: 20 masterwork (1st–9th), 10 +1 arrows (10th–20th), 10 masterwork arrows (10th–20th).

Potions: 2 cure light wounds (1st), hiding (1st), sneak (1st), 2 spider climb (1st), 4 cure light wounds (2nd–4th), darkvision (2nd–8th), neutralize poison (2nd–4th), 6 cure light wounds (5th), 2 neutralize poison (5th–20th), cure serious wounds (6th–11th), haste (6th–20th), alter self (12th–20th), 2 cure serious wounds (12th–20th), invisibility (12th–15th), gaseous form (18th–20th).

Other Magic Gear: Cloak of resistance +1 (4th–11th), bag of holding 1 (8th–12th), bracers of armor +2 (10th–14th), ring of protection +1 (10th–14th), amulet of natural armor +1 (12th–16th), cloak of resistance +2 (12th–13th), gloves of Dexterity +2 (12th–16th), bag of holding 2 (13th–17th), cloak of resistance +3 (14th–15th), bracers of armor +4 (15th–16h), ring of protection +2 (15th–20th), cloak of resistance +4 (16th–20th), ring of invisibility (16th–20th), amulet of protection against detection and location (17th–20th), bracers of armor +5 (17th–20th), gloves of Dexterity +4 (17th–18th), bag of holding 3 (18th–20th), gloves of Dexterity +6 (19th–20th), winged boots

TABLE 2–41: NPC ROGUE

Lvl	hp	AC	Init	Spd	Rapier (1d6)	Composite Shortbow (1d6)	F/R/W	Hi/M Sil/ Tum	O Lock	List/ Spot	Srch/ Appr	D Dev	U M Dev
1st	7	15	+6	30 ft.	+2 (+1 damage)	+4 (+1 damage)	+1/+4/+0	+6	+6	+4	+6	+6	+3
2nd	11	15	+6	30 ft.	+3 (+1)	+5 (+1)	+1/+5/+0	+7	+9	+5	+7	+9	+4
3rd	16	16	+6	30 ft.	+4 (+1)	+6 (+1)	+2/+5/+1	+8	+10	+6	+8	+10	+5
4th	20	17	+7	30 ft.	+5 (+1)	+8 (+1)	+3/+8/+2	+10	+12	+7	+9	+11	+6
5th	25	17	+7	30 ft.	+5 (+1)	+8 (+1)	+3/+8/+2	+11	+13	+8	+10	+12	+7
6th	29	17	+7	30 ft.	+6 (+1)	+9 (+1)	+4/+9/+3	+12	+14	+11	+11	+13	+8
7th	34	19	+7	30 ft.	+7 (+1)	+10 (+1)	+4/+9/+3	+13	+15	+12	+12	+14	+9
8th	38	19	+7	30 ft.	+8/3 (+1)	+11/6 (+1)	+4/+10/+3	+14	+16	+13	+13	+15	+10
9th	43	19	+7	30 ft.	+8/3 (+2)	+11/6 (+2)	+5/+12/+4	+15	+17	+14	+14	+16	+11
10th	47	19	+7	30 ft.	+9/4 (+2)	+12/7 (+3)	+5/+13/+4	+16	+18	+15	+15	+17	+12
11th	52	19	+7	30 ft.	+10/5 (+2)	+13/8 (+3)	+5/+13/+4	+17	+19	+16	+16	+18	+13
12th	56	22	+9	30 ft.	+15/10 (+2)	+16/11 (+3)	+7/+17/+6	+20	+22	+17	+17	+19	+14
13th	61	22	+9	30 ft.	+16/11 (+3)	+16/11 (+3)	+7/+17/+6	+21	+23	+18	+18	+20	+15
14th	65	22	+9	30 ft.	+17/12 (+3)	+17/12 (+3)	+8/+19/+7	+22	+24	+19	+19	+21	+16
15th	70	22	+9	30 ft.	+18/13/8 (+3)	+18/13/8 (+3)	+9/+19/+8	+23	+25	+20	+20	+22	+17
16th	74	22	+9	30 ft.	+19/14/9 (+3)	+19/14/9 (+3)	+10/+21/+9	+24	+26	+21	+21	+23	+18
17th	79	23	+10	30 ft.	+20/15/10 (+3)	+21/16/11 (+4)	+10/+22/+9	+26	+28	+22	+22	+24	+19
18th	83	27	+10	30 ft.	+21/16/11 (+3)	+22/17/12 (+4)	+11/+23/+10	+27	+29	+23	+23	+25	+20
19th	88	28	+11	30 ft.	+24/19/14 (+4)	+24/19/14 (+4)	+11/+24/+10	+29	+31	+24	+24	+26	+21
20th	92	29	+12	30 ft.	+26/21/16 (+4)	+26/21/16 (+5)	+11/+26/+10	+31	+33	+25	+25	+27	+22

TABLE 2–42: NPC SORCERER

Lvl	hp	AC	Init	Spd	Shortspear (1d8)	Crossbow (1d8)	F/R/W	Spellc	Con	Spells per day
1st	8	12	+2	30 ft.	−1 (−1 damage)	+3	+1/+2/+3	+4	+5	5/4
2nd	11	12	+2	30 ft.	+0 (−1)	+4	+1/+2/+4	+5	+6	6/5
3rd	15	12	+6	30 ft.	+0 (−1)	+4	+2/+3/+4	+6	+7	6/6
4th	18	13	+6	30 ft.	+1 (−1)	+6	+2/+3/+5	+7	+8	6/7/4
5th	22	13	+6	30 ft.	+2 (−1)	+6	+3/+4/+6	+8	+9	6/7/5
6th	25	13	+6	30 ft.	+3 (−1)	+7	+4/+5/+7	+9	+10	6/7/6/4
7th	29	14	+6	30 ft.	+3 (−1)	+7	+4/+5/+7	+10	+11	6/7/7/5
8th	34	14	+6	30 ft.	+4 (−1)	+8	+4/+5/+8	+11	+12	6/7/7/6/3
9th	38	15	+6	30 ft.	+4 (−1)	+8	+5/+6/+8	+12	+13	6/7/7/7/4
10th	41	15	+6	30 ft.	+5 (−1)	+9	+5/+6/+9	+13	+14	6/7/7/7/5/3
11th	45	16	+6	30 ft.	+5 (−1)	+9	+5/+6/+9	+14	+15	6/7/7/7/6/4
12th	48	17	+6	30 ft.	+6/1 (−1)	+10	+6/+7/+10	+15	+16	6/8/7/7/6/3
13th	52	18	+6	30 ft.	+6 /1	+10	+6/+7/+10	+16	+17	6/8/7/7/7/4
14th	55	19	+7	30 ft.	+7/2	+12	+6/+8/+11	+17	+18	6/8/7/7/7/5/3
15th	59	19	+7	30 ft.	+7/2	+12	+7/+10/+11	+18	+19	6/8/8/7/7/7/4
16th	62	19	+7	30 ft.	+8/3	+13	+7/+10/+12	+19	+20	6/8/8/7/7/7/5/3
17th	66	21	+7	30 ft.	+8/3	+13	+7/+10/+12	+20	+21	6/16/8/7/7/7/6/4
18th	69	22	+7	30 ft.	+9/4	+14	+8/+11/+13	+21	+22	6/16/8/8/7/7/5/3
19th	73	22	+7	30 ft.	+9/4	+14	+7/+10/+12	+22	+23	8/16/8/7/7/7/6/4
20th	76	22	+7	30 ft.	+10/5	+15	+7/+10/+13	+23	+24	6/8/8/16/8/7/7/7/6

SPELLS KNOWN PER LEVEL

Level	Spells	Level	Spells	Level	Spells	Level	Spells
1st	4/2	2nd	5/2	3rd	5/3	4th	6/3/1
5th	6/4/2	6th	7/4/2/1	7th	7/5/3/2	8th	8/5/3/2/1
9th	8/5/4/3/2	10th	9/5/4/3/2/1	11th	9/5/5/4/3/2	12th	9/5/5/4/3/2/1
13th	9/5/5/4/4/3/2	14th	9/5/5/4/4/3/2/1	15th	9/5/5/4/4/4/3/2	16th	9/5/5/4/4/4/3/2/1
17th	9/5/5/4/4/4/3/3/2	18th	9/5/5/4/4/4/3/3/2/1	19th	9/5/5/4/4/4/3/3/3/2	20th	9/5/5/4/4/4/3/3/3/3

(19th–20th), *lavender and green Ioun stone* (20th).

Other Gear: 50-ft. silk rope (1st–20th), thieves' tools (1st), masterwork thieves' tools (2nd–20th).

NPC Sorcerer

Starting Ability Scores: Str 8, Dex 14, Con 13, Int 10, Wis 12, Cha 15.

Increased Ability Scores: 4th, Cha 16; 8th, Cha 17; 12th, Cha 18 (20); 14th, Dex 14 (16); 15th, Cha 18 (22); 16th, Cha 19 (23); 18th, Cha 19 (25); 20th, Cha 20 (26).

Feats: 1st, Toughness; 3rd, Improved Initiative; 6th, Combat Casting; 9th, Dodge; 12th, Maximize Spell; 15th, Craft Wand; 18th, Spell Penetration.

Class Features: 1st, Summon familiar.

Shortspear (Melee): Normal (1st–12th), +1 (13th–20th).

Light Crossbow (Ranged): Masterwork (1st–20th).

Bolts: 10 normal bolts (1st–3rd), 10 masterwork (4th–20th).

Potions: *Blur* (1st–2nd), *invisibility* (1st–3rd), *cat's grace* (2nd–4th), *cure moderate wounds* (3rd–6th, 9th–20th), *cure serious wounds* (5th, 8th), *detect thoughts* (11th).

Scrolls: 2 *magic missile* (1st–2nd), 2 *shield* (1st–3rd), 2 *sleep* (1st), 2 *color spray* (2nd–3rd), *invisibility* (4th), 2 *invisibility* (5th), 2 *Melf's acid arrow* (5th), 2 *web* (5th), *hold person* (6th–7th), *charm monster* (8th), *summon monster IV [8th-level caster]* (9th), *teleport* (11th), *fear* (12th), *power word stun* (14th), *domination* (15th), *prismatic spray* (15th), *Bigby's clenched fist* (17th), *horrid wilting* (17th), *maze* (18th–20th), *meteor swarm* (18th–20th), *summon monster IX* (18th–20th).

Other Magic Gear: *Wand of sleep* (2nd), *wand of burning hands* (3rd), *bracers of armor +1* (4th–8th), *wand of magic missile* (4th), *cloak of resistance +1* (5th–18th), *wand of Melf's acid arrow* (6th–7th), *ring of protection +1* (7th–11th), *wand of magic missile [9th-level caster]* (8th), *bracers of armor +2* (9th–12th), *bead of force* (10th, 18th–20th), *wand of lightning bolt* (10th), *amulet of natural armor +1* (11th–16th), *Keoghtom's ointment* (11th), *wand of fireball [6th-level caster]* (11th), *mirror of vanity +2* (12th–14th), *ring of protection +2* (12th–20th), *wand of lightning bolt [7th-level caster]* (12th), *bracers of armor +3* (13th–16th), *wand of fireball*

[10th-level caster] (13th), *gloves of Dexterity +2* (14th–20th), *wand of magic missile [9th-level caster, maximized]* (14th–15th, 18th), *mirror of vanity +4* (15th–17th), *ring of fire resistance [minor]* (16th), *wand of stoneskin* (16th–17th), *amulet of natural armor +2* (17th–20th), *bracers of armor +4* (17th), *ring of wizardry I* (17th–18th), *bracers of armor +5* (18th–20th), *mirror of vanity +6* (18th–20th), *cloak of displacement* (19th–20th), *ring of wizardry II* (19th), *ring of wizardry III* (20th).

Other Gear: Thunderstone (1st), dagger (1st–20th), 2 tanglefoot bags (2nd), smokestick (3rd), alchemist's fire (3rd).

NPC Wizard

Starting Ability Scores: Str 10, Dex 14, Con 13, Int 15, Wis 12, Cha 8.

Increased Ability Scores: 4th, Int 16; 8th, Int 17; 12th, Int 18 (20); 14th, Dex 14 (16); 15th, Int 18 (22); 16th, Int 19 (23); 18th, Int 19 (25); 20th, Int 20 (26).

Feats: 1st, Scribe Scroll, Toughness; 3rd, Combat Casting; 5th, Brew Potion; 6th, Improved Initiative; 9th, Lightning Reflexes; 10th, Quicken Spell; 12th, Heighten Spell; 15th, Craft Wondrous Item, Heighten Spell; 18th, Spell Penetration; 20th, Craft Staff.

Class Features: 1st, Summon familiar.

Quarterstaff (Melee): Normal (1st–12th), +1 (13th–17th), *staff of frost* (18th–20th).

Light Crossbow (Ranged): Normal (1st), masterwork (2nd–20th).

Bolts: 10 normal (1st–7th), 10 masterwork (8th–20th).

Scrolls: *Dispel magic* (1st–3rd), *fly* (1st–4th), 2 *summon monster I* (1st), *web* (2nd, 5th), *lightning bolt* (4th), *confusion* (5th), 2 *fireball* (5th), *improved invisibility* (6th), 2 *hold person* (7th), *lightning bolt [7th-level caster]* (7th), 2 *charm monster* (8th), *fireball [7th–level caster]* (8th), *summon monster IV [8th-level caster]* (9th), *fireball [10th-level caster]* (10th), *flesh to stone* (10th), *teleport* (10th–12th), *cloudkill* (11th), *acid fog* (12th), *incendiary cloud* (14th), *power word stun* (14th), *solid fog* (14th), *domination* (15th), *shapechange* (16th), *wail of the banshee* (16th), *Bigby's clenched fist* (17th), *horrid wilting* (17th), *maze* (18th–20th), *summon monster IX* (18th–20th).

Table 2–43: NPC Wizard

| | | | | | | Crossbow | | Spllc/Kno | | | | |
Lvl	hp	AC	Init	Spd	Quarterstaff (1d6)	(1d8)	F/R/W	(Any 2)	Con	Alch	Scry	Spells/Day
1st	8	12	+2	30 ft.	+0	+2	+0/+2/+3	+6	+5	—	—	3/2
2nd	11	12	+2	30 ft.	+1	+4	+0/+2/+4	+7	+6	—	—	4/3
3rd	15	12	+2	30 ft.	+1	+4	+1/+3/+4	+8	+7	—	—	4/3/2
4th	18	13	+2	30 ft.	+2	+5	+1/+3/+5	+10	+8	—	—	4/4/3
5th	22	13	+2	30 ft.	+2	+5	+2/+4/+6	+11	+9	+4	—	4/4/3/2
6th	25	13	+6	30 ft.	+3	+6	+3/+5/+7	+12	+10	+5	—	4/4/4/3
7th	29	14	+6	30 ft.	+3	+6	+3/+5/+7	+13	+11	+6	—	4/5/4/3/1
8th	34	14	+6	30 ft.	+4	+8	+3/+5/+8	+14	+12	+7	—	4/5/4/4/2
9th	38	15	+6	30 ft.	+4	+8	+4/+6/+8	+15	+13	+8	—	4/5/5/4/2/1
10th	41	15	+6	30 ft.	+5	+9	+4/+6/+9	+16	+14	+9	—	4/5/5/4/3/2
11th	45	16	+6	30 ft.	+5	+9	+4/+6/+9	+17	+15	+10	—	4/5/5/5/3/2/1
12th	48	17	+7	30 ft.	+6/1	+10/5	+5/+7/+10	+19	+16	+13	—	4/5/5/5/4/3/2
13th	52	18	+7	30 ft.	+7/2 (+1 damage)	+10/5	+6/+8/+11	+20	+17	+15	—	4/5/5/5/3/2/1
14th	55	19	+7	30 ft.	+8/3 (+1)	+12/7	+6/+9/+12	+22	+18	+18	—	4/6/5/5/4/3/2
15th	59	20	+7	30 ft.	+8/3 (+1)	+12/7	+8/+11/+13	+23	+19	+21	—	4/6/5/5/5/3/2/1
16th	62	20	+7	30 ft.	+9/4 (+1)	+13/8	+8/+11/+14	+24	+20	+24	+7	4/6/5/5/5/3/3/2
17th	66	22	+7	30 ft.	+9/4 (+1)	+13/8	+8/+11/+14	+26	+21	+26	+10	4/12/6/5/5/5/3/2/1
18th	69	23	+7	30 ft.	+10/5	+14/9	+9/+12/+15	+27	+22	+27	+13	4/12/6/5/5/5/3/3/2
19th	73	23	+7	30 ft.	+10/5	+14/9	+9/+12/+15	+28	+23	+28	+16	4/12/6/5/5/5/5/4/3/3
20th	76	23	+7	30 ft.	+11/6	+15/10	+9/+12/+16	+31	+24	+31	+20	4/12/6/6/6/5/5/5/4

Potions: Cat's grace (1st), cure light wounds (2nd), invisibility (2nd–3rd), cure moderate wounds (3rd–6th), cure serious wounds (5th, 8th–9th, 14th–20th), alter self (6th), haste (10th), detect thoughts (11th).

Other Magic Gear: Wand of burning hands (2nd), wand of ray of enfeeblement (3rd), bracers of armor +1 (4th–8th), wand of magic missile (4th), cloak of resistance (5th–12th), wand of summon monster II (6th), ring of protection +1 (7th–12th), wand of Melf's acid arrow (7th), wand of magic missile [9th-level caster] (8th–9th), bracers of armor +2 (9th–11th), wand of lightning bolt (10th), amulet of natural armor +1 (11th–14th), wand of fireball [9th-level caster] (11th), bracers of armor +3 (12th–16th), headband of intellect +2 (12th–14th), wand of lightning bolt [9th-level caster] (12th), cloak of resistance +2 (13th–14th), ring of protection +2 (13th–20th), wand of fireball [10th-level caster] (13th), gloves of Dexterity +2 (14th–20th), wand of magic missile [9th-level caster, maximized] (14th–15th), amulet of natural armor +2 (15th–20th), cloak of resistance +3 (15th), headband of intellect +4 (15th–17th), pearl of power [3rd-level spell] (16th), wand of stoneskin (16th–17th), bracers of armor +5 (17th), ring of wizardry I (17th–20th), bracers of armor +6 (18th–20th), headband of intellect +6 (18th–20th), staff of frost (18th–20th), rod of absorption (20th).

Other Gear: Dagger (1st–20th), 2 tanglefoot bags (2nd).

NPC Adjustments by Race or Kind

Add the adjustments below to the class-based statistics. Add and apply all adjustments, such as ability score adjustments. For example, a halfling gains a racial modifier of +2 to Dexterity (and thus a +1 Dex bonus) and a +1 to Reflex saves, which means that the finished character has a +2 Reflex save bonus. If a feat is duplicated, select a new one.

See the *Player's Handbook* or *Dungeon Master's Guide* for other traits by race or kind. (Racial traits that always affect a skill check are already included in the adjustments to total skill bonuses.)

Explanations/Definitions

The following notes explain or define certain terms used in the adjustments list.

–3 ranks/skill: Subtract 3 from each skill the NPC is listed as having at 1st level. (The NPC gained the class by multiclassing and therefore doesn't get four times his per-level skill ranks at 1st level.)

Large: The character's AC and attack bonuses are 1 lower, and it suffers a –4 penalty on Hide checks. The character's weapon is larger, increasing its damage. See the *Monster Manual* introduction to see how damage increases. The creature has 10-foot reach.

Slow: The character's base speed is 20 feet instead of 30 feet.

Small: The character's AC and attack bonuses are 1 higher, and it gains a +4 bonus on Hide checks. The character's weapon is smaller. Choose a smaller weapon.

Weapon Proficiency: Regardless of class, the NPC is proficient at least with simple weapons and weapons listed for its kind in the *Monster Manual*.

NPC Adjustments

Aasimar (Planetouched): +2 Wis, +2 Cha. +2 Listen, +2 Spot.

Bugbear: +2 CR. +4 Str, +2 Dex, +2 Con, –2 Cha. +3d8 HD. +2 base attack. +1 Fort, +3 Ref, +1 Will. +3 natural armor. –3 ranks/skill, +2 Climb, +2 Hide, +1 Listen, +2 Move Silently, +1 Spot. Alertness. Weapon proficiency.

Derro (Dwarf): +1 CR. –2 Str, +4 Dex, +2 Con, –4 Cha. Blind-Fight. Slow.

Doppelganger: +3 CR. +2 Str, +2 Dex, +2 Con, +2 Int +4, Wis, +2 Cha. +4d8 HD. +3 base attack. +4 Fort, +4 Ref, +4 Will. +4 natural armor. –3 ranks/skill, +11 Bluff, +11 Disguise, +7 Listen, +4 Sense Motive, +4 Spot. Alertness, Dodge. Weapon proficiency.

Drow, Female (Elf): +1 CR. +2 Dex, –2 Con, +2 Int, +2 Cha. +2 Listen, +2 Search, +2 Spot.

Drow, Male (Elf): +1 CR. +2 Dex, –2 Con, +2 Int, –2 Cha. +2 Listen, +2 Search, +2 Spot.

Duergar (Dwarf): +1 CR. +2 Con, –4 Cha. +1 Listen, +4 Move Silently, +1 Spot. Alertness. Slow.

Dwarf, Deep: +2 Con, –4 Cha. Slow.

Dwarf, Hill [Standard]: +2 Con, –2 Cha. Slow.

Dwarf, Mountain: +2 Con, –2 Cha. Slow.

Elf, Gray: –2 Str, +2 Dex, –2 Con, +2 Int. +2 Listen, +2 Search, +2 Spot.

Elf, High [Standard]: +2 Dex, –2 Con. +2 Listen, +2 Search, +2 Spot.

Elf, Wild: +2 Dex, –2 Int. +2 Listen, +2 Search, +2 Spot.

Elf, Wood: +2 Str, +2 Dex, –2 Con, –2 Int, –2 Cha. +2 Listen, +2 Search, +2 Spot.

Gnoll: +1 CR. +4 Str, +2 Con, –2 Int, –2 Cha. +2d8 HD. +1 base attack. +3 Fort. +1 natural armor. –3 ranks/skill, +3 Listen, +3 Spot. Power Attack. Weapon proficiency.

Gnome, Forest: –2 Str, +2 Con. Small. +4 Hide. Slow.

Gnome, Rock [Standard]: –2 Str, +2 Con. Small. Slow.

Goblin: –2 Str, +2 Dex, –2 Cha. Small. +4 Move Silently.

Half-Celestial: +1 CR. +4 Str, +2 Dex, +4 Con, +2 Int, +4 Wis, +4 Cha. +1 natural armor. 75% wings (double speed).

Half-Dragon: +2 CR. +8 Str, +2 Con, +2 Int, +2 Cha. Hit Die increases one type to max of d12 (for all but the barbarian, add +1 hp/level +1 additional hit point). If Large, it has wings and can fly at normal speed.

Half-Elf: +1 Listen, +1 Search, +1 Spot.

Half-Fiend: +2 CR. +1 natural armor. +4 Str, +4 Dex, +2 Con, +4 Int, +2 Cha. 50% wings, fly at normal speed.

Halfling, Deep: –2 Str, +2 Dex. +1 Fort, +1 Ref, +1 Will. +1 attack with thrown weapon (if any). Small. +2 Listen. Slow.

Halfling, Lightfoot [Standard]: –2 Str, +2 Dex. +1 Fort, +1 Ref, +1 Will. +1 attack with thrown weapon (if any). Small. +2 Climb, +2 Jump, +2 Listen. +2 Move Silently. Slow.

Halfling, Tallfellow: –2 Str, +2 Dex. +1 Fort, +1 Ref, +1 Will. +1 attack with thrown weapon (if any). Small. +2 Listen, +2 Search, +2 Spot. Slow.

Half-Orc: +2 Str, –2 Int, –2 Cha.

Hobgoblin: +2 Dex, +2 Con. +4 Move Silently.

Human: 1 extra feat. +1 skill (ranks = level +3).

Kobold: –4 Str, +2 Dex. Small. +2 Craft (trapmaking), +2 Profession (miner), +2 Search.

Lizardfolk: +1 CR. +2 Str, +2 Con, –2 Int. +2d8 HD. +1 base attack. +3 Ref. +5 natural armor. –3 ranks/skill, +6 Jump, +8 Swim, +4 Balance. Multiattack. Weapon proficiency.

Mind Flayer: +8 CR. +2 Str, +4 Dex, +2 Con, +8 Int, +6 Wis, +6 Cha. +8d8 HD. +6 base attack. +2 Fort, +2 Ref, +6 Will. +3 natural armor. –3 ranks/skill, +6 Bluff, +11 Concentration, +11 Hide, +11 Intimidate, +4 Knowledge (any two), +11 Listen, +11 Move Silently, +11 Spot. Alertness, Combat Casting, Dodge, Improved Initiative, Weapon Finesse (Tentacle). Weapon proficiency.

Minotaur: +4 CR. +8 Str, +4 Con, –4 Int, –2 Cha. +6d8 HD. +6 base attack. +2 Fort, +5 Ref, +5 Will. Large. +5 natural armor. –3 ranks/skill, +6 Intimidate, +4 Jump, +8 Listen, +8 Search, +8 Spot. Power Attack. Weapon proficiency.

Ogre: +2 CR. +10 Str, –2 Dex, +4 Con, –4 Int, –4 Cha. +4d8 HD. +3 base attack. +4 Fort, +1 Ref, +1 Will. Large. +5 natural armor. –3 ranks/skill, +3 Climb, +3 Listen, +3 Spot. Weapon Focus (greatclub). Weapon proficiency.

Ogre Mage: +8 CR. +10 Str, +6 Con, +4 Int, +4 Wis, +6 Cha. +5d8 HD. +3 base attack. +4 Fort, +1 Ref, +1 Will. Large. +5 natural armor. –3 ranks/skill, +3 Concentration, +3 Listen, +2 Spellcraft, +3 Spot. Improved Initiative. Weapon proficiency.

Orc: +4 Str, –2 Int, –2 Wis, –2 Cha.

Svirfneblin (Gnome): +1 CR. +2 Dex, +2 Wis, –4 Cha. +2 Fort, +2 Ref, +2 Will. Small. +4 dodge bonus to AC. +2 Hide. Slow.

Tiefling (Planetouched): +2 Dex, +2 Int, –2 Cha. +2 Bluff, +2 Hide.

Troglodyte: +1 CR. –2 Dex, +4 Con, –2 Int. +2d8 HD. +3 Fort. +1 base attack. +6 natural armor. –3 ranks/skill, +7 Hide, +3 Listen. Multiattack, Weapon Focus (javelin). Weapon proficiency.

Werebear (Lycanthrope): +2 CR. +2 Fort, +2 Will. +2 natural armor. +2 Listen, +2 Search, +2 Spot. See *Monster Manual* for bear form. NPC loses gear in animal form.

Wereboar (Lycanthrope): +1 CR. +2 natural armor. +2 Fort, +2 Will. +2 Listen, +2 Search, +2 Spot. See *Monster Manual* for boar form. NPC loses gear in animal form.

Wererat (Lycanthrope): +1 CR. +2 natural armor. +2 Fort, +2 Will. +2 Listen, +2 Search, +2 Spot. See *Monster Manual* for rat or hybrid form. NPC loses gear in animal form.

Weretiger (Lycanthrope): +1 CR. +2 natural armor. +2 Fort, +2 Will. +2 Listen, +2 Search, +2 Spot. See *Monster Manual* for tiger or hybrid form. NPC loses gear in animal form.

Werewolf (Lycanthrope): +1 CR. +2 natural armor. +2 Fort, +2 Will. +2 Listen, +2 Search, +2 Spot. See *Monster Manual* for wolf or hybrid form. NPC loses gear in animal form.

TABLE 2–44: NPC GEAR VALUE

NPC Level	Value of Gear
1st	900 gp
2nd	2,000 gp
3rd	2,500 gp
4th	3,300 gp
5th	4,300 gp
6th	5,600 gp
7th	7,200 gp
8th	9,400 gp
9th	12,000 gp
10th	16,000 gp
11th	21,000 gp
12th	27,000 gp
13th	35,000 gp
14th	45,000 gp
15th	59,000 gp
16th	77,000 gp
17th	100,000 gp
18th	130,000 gp
19th	170,000 gp
20th	220,000 gp

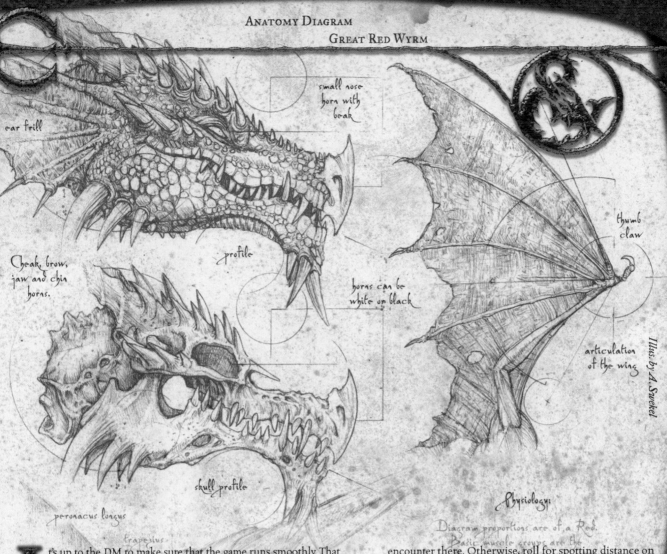

ANATOMY DIAGRAM
GREAT RED WYRM

small nose
horn with
beak

ear frill

profile

Cheek, brow,
jaw and chin
horns.

horns can be
white or black

thumb
claw

skull profile

articulation
of the wing

peronacus longus

Illus. by A. Swekel

trapezius

Physiology:

Diagram proportions are of a Red.
Basic muscle groups are the
same within the species.

latissimus

deltoid

biceps

I t's up to the DM to make sure that the game runs smoothly. That responsibility includes handling combat, but it also means knowing how the characters fare when they're caught in a snowstorm, what happens to a character who is turned into gaseous form, and how much damage the monk takes when she gets pushed off the top of a 70-foot-high tower.

ENCOUNTER DISTANCE

While riding across the plains, the adventurers see a giant bombardier beetle lumbering along in the distance. When they're hiking through the mountains, displacer beasts suddenly appear on a rocky shelf above them just a dozen yards away. And when they're camped for the night in the woods, they can hear something stalking through the shadows beyond the light of the campfire, but they can't see it. Determining the distance at which an encounter begins sets the stage for combat, or any other type of encounter. The following rules are especially important for wilderness encounters. Encounter distance indoors, on the other hand, usually depends on the amount of illumination available and whether the opposing sides have a line of sight to each other.

Once you've established that the PCs are about to have an encounter, determine the distance at which they see the creatures (or vice versa). The PCs and monsters have a chance to spot each other at a distance, but even if they notice each other at first, they're certain to spot each other once they get closer together. Follow these steps:

1. Determine vision conditions and terrain. Choose from the choices on Table 3–1: Spotting Distance.
2. If line of sight or illumination defines the distance at which the encounter occurs (as often happens indoors), start the

encounter there. Otherwise, roll for spotting distance on Table 3–1: Spotting Distance.
3. All creatures involved make Spot checks. Success means that creature sees the other creature or group. See Table 3–2: Spotting Difficulty for modifiers on these checks.
4. If neither side succeeds, all creatures spot each other at one-half the rolled range.

The circumstances that can affect the DC of a Spot check (see Table 3–2) are as follows:

Size: Add +4 to the base DC of 20 for each size category the creature being spotted is smaller than Medium-size or –4 for each size category larger. You can make exceptions for creatures with unusual shapes, such as a Large snake that's low to the ground and thus as hard to see as a Small creature.

Contrast: How starkly the creature's coloring stands out against the surroundings. It's easy to spot a brightly colored couatl in a dark jungle and hard to see winter wolves in the snow.

Stillness: It's harder to see creatures that are not moving.

Six or More Creatures: Groups of creatures are easier to spot, even if the creatures are smaller than Medium-size.

Moonlight: Nighttime, but with moonlight (or similar light).

Starlight: Nighttime with no moon but a clear, starry sky (or similar light).

Total Darkness: Overcast at night, or otherwise lightless.

Example: Four adventurers are trekking through a light forest when the DM determines that they encounter eight trolls out on patrol. The DM rolls 3d6 ∞ 10 and gets a result of 120 feet, the distance at which each group has the chance to see the other.

The DC to spot the trolls is 20 – 4 (they are Large) – 2 (six or more creatures) = 14.

The DC for the trolls to spot the PCs is 20. Their Spot skill modifier is +5, so it's likely that at least one troll will spot the party.

Any group that fails to spot the other group will do so automatically at 60 feet.

HIDING AND SPOTTING

If creatures are trying not to be seen, it's usually harder to spot them, but creatures that are keeping low to avoid being spotted also are less likely to notice other creatures.

If creatures are hiding, they can only move at half their normal overland speed. They also suffer a –2 penalty on their own Spot checks to notice other creatures because they are staying low and using cover.

Instead of a base DC of 20 for others to spot them at the standard spotting distance, the DC is 25 + the hider's Hide skill modifier. The circumstance modifiers from Table 3–2: Spotting Difficulty still apply, except for the size modifier (which is already part of the character's skill modifier). A character whose Hide ranks, Dexterity modifier, and armor check penalty total –6 or lower is actually has a lower DC than if he or she weren't hiding. In such cases, simply calculate the Spot DC as if the character weren't hiding (according to Table 3–2: Spotting Difficulty). If a creature gets a special bonus to Hide because of camouflage, special coloring, and so on, use that bonus rather than the contrast bonus from Table 3–2: Spotting Difficulty.

Additionally, the other creatures do not automatically spot hiding creatures at one-half the encounter distance. Instead, that is the distance at which the other creatures can make Spot checks to notice the hiding creatures. These are normal Spot checks opposed by the hiders' Hide checks.

MISSED ENCOUNTERS

The rules for spotting creatures assume that both sides will eventually notice each other, and they simply establish the distance at which they do so. But sometimes you want to take into account the possibility that the two groups will miss each other entirely. For example, the adventurers might spot a roaming behir at a distance and hide, hoping it misses them. They might also try to sneak past patrols when they are trying to infiltrate an enemy camp. Conceivably, two groups could even pass each other with neither ever knowing that the other was there.

To handle these possibilities, simply let there be a 50% chance that the other creatures encountered and the PCs don't get any closer but rather pass by each other, such as when one group is moving north and the other east. (Creatures following the PCs' trail, of course, always close with them.)

If you use this rule regularly, increase the chance for random encounters (since some of the encounters won't actually lead to confrontations).

TABLE 3–1: SPOTTING DISTANCE

Terrain	Distance
Smoke or heavy fog	2d4 × 5 ft. (avg. 25 ft.)
Jungle or dense forest	2d4 × 10 ft. (50 ft.)
Light forest	3d6 × 10 ft. (105 ft.)
Scrub, brush or bush	6d6 × 10 ft. (210 ft.)
Grassland, little cover	6d6 × 20 ft. (420 ft.)
Total darkness	Limit of sight
Indoors (lit)	Line of sight

TABLE 3–2: SPOTTING DIFFICULTY

Circumstances	DC
Base	20
Size	+/–4 per size category
Contrast	+/–5 or more
Stillness (not moving)	+5
Six or more creatures	–2
Moonlight*	+5
Starlight**	+10
Total darkness	Impossible†

*+5 bonus on Spot check if the spotter has low-light vision or if he or she has darkvision that extends far enough.

**+5 bonus on Spot check if the spotter has low-light vision or +10 if he or she has darkvision that extends far enough.

†Unless the spotter has darkvision that extends far enough.

COMBAT

The brave party of adventurers smashes through the wooden door and into an ambush of bloodthirsty hobgoblins with spears and rusted blades. The trio of knights charges through the forest on their gallant mounts, their lances plunging into the scaly flesh of the horrible hydra that waits near the river's edge. The dragon takes to the air and chases the elven lord and his retinue, jaws snapping behind them as they run in terror.

Combat is a big part of what makes the D&D game exciting. There are few better ways to test your mettle against your foes than in pitched battle. Your most important job as DM is running combats—making things move quickly and smoothly, and adjudicating what happens during each round of the action.

STARTING AN ENCOUNTER

An encounter can begin in one of three situations:

- One side becomes aware of the other side and thus can act first.
- Both sides become aware of each other at the same time.

- Some, but not all, creatures on one or both sides become aware of the other side.

When you decide that it is possible for either side to become aware of the other, use Spot checks, Listen checks, sight ranges, and so on to determine which of the three above cases comes into play. Although it's good to give characters some chance to detect a coming encounter, ultimately it's you who decides when the first round begins and where each side is when it does.

One Side Aware First: In this case, you determine how much time the aware side has before the unaware side can react. Sometimes, there is no time for the unaware side to do anything before the aware side gets a chance to interact. If so, the character or party that is aware gets to take a partial action before initiative is rolled, while the unaware character or party does nothing, caught flat-footed. During this time, the unaware character or party gains no Dexterity bonus to AC. After this partial action, both sides make initiative checks to determine the order in which the participants act.

Other times, the aware side has a few rounds to prepare. (If its members see the other side off in the distance, heading their way, for example.) The DM should track time in rounds at this point to determine how much the aware characters can accomplish. Once the two sides come into contact, the aware characters can take a partial action while the unaware characters do nothing. Keep in mind that if the aware characters alert the attention of the unaware side before actual contact is made, then both sides are treated as aware and no one gets partial actions to begin the encounter.

Example (Sudden Awareness): A kobold sorcerer with darkvision sees a party of adventurers coming down a long hallway. He can see the adventurers, since they've got light, but they can't see him since he's out of the range of their illumination. The sorcerer gets a partial action and casts *lightning bolt* at the party. Caught unaware, the party can do nothing but roll saving throws. Once the damage from the spell is assessed, both sides roll initiative.

Example (Time to Prepare): Jozan the cleric hears the sounds of creatures moving beyond a door in a dungeon. He also hears some voices, and determines that the creatures are speaking Orc. He figures that they don't know he's there. He takes the time to cast *bless* and *armor of faith* on himself before opening the door and using a partial action to cast *hold person* on the first foes he sees. He can cast the *hold person* spell before anyone makes an initiative check, unless the orcs heard him casting *bless* or *armor of faith* in the previous 2 rounds, in which case they become aware, Jozan doesn't get the partial action that enabled him to cast *hold person*, and he'd better hope he gets the higher result on his initiative check.

Both Sides Aware at the Same Time: If both sides are aware at the same time and can interact, both should roll initiative and resolve actions normally.

If both sides become aware of the other but they cannot interact immediately, track time in rounds, giving both sides the same amount of time in full rounds, until the two sides can begin to interact.

Example (Both Aware and Can Interact Immediately): A party of adventurers burst into a dungeon room full of orcs, and neither knew of the other ahead of time. All are equally surprised and equally flat-footed. Initiative is rolled, reflecting that those characters with better reflexes act quicker in such situations.

Example (Both Aware, But Cannot Interact Immediately): A party of adventurers comes along a dungeon corridor and hears the laughter of orcs beyond the door ahead. Meanwhile, the orc lookout sees the adventures through a peephole in the door and warns his comrades. The door is closed, so no direct interaction is possible yet. Jozan casts *bless*. Lidda drinks a potion. Tordek and Mialee move up to the door. At the same time, the orcs move into position, and one uses a *ring of invisibility* to hide. The DM records the passage of 1 round. The adventurers arrange themselves around the door and make a quick plan. The orcs turn over tables and nock arrows in their shortbows. The DM tracks another round. The fighter opens the door, and the DM calls for an initiative check from all. The third round begins, this time with the order of actions being important (and dictated by the initiative check results).

Some Creatures (But Not All) on One or Both Sides: In this case, only the creatures that are aware can act. These creatures can take partial actions before the main action starts.

Example: Lidda is scouting ahead. She and a gargoyle spot each other simultaneously, but the rest of Lidda's party doesn't see the monster (through they are close enough to hear any fighting that erupts). Lidda and the gargoyle each get partial actions, and then normal combat starts. Lidda and the gargoyle roll initiative before taking their partial actions, and everyone else rolls initiative after those partial actions are concluded.

Variant: The Surprise Round

Whether one side is aware of the other or not, the DM can run the first round of combat as a surprise round. In this round, only partial actions are allowed. Only those on a side aware of the other side can take any action at all. This reflects that even when a combatant is prepared, some amount of time is spent assessing the situation, and thus only partial actions are allowed to begin with.

This variant rule makes initiative carry less of an impact, since it is in the first round when initiative matters most. Even if a warrior gets the jump on an opponent, he can at best make a single attack against a foe before that foe can react. Using the standard rule, some players will be bothered by the fact that a high-level archer who gains the advantage in initiative can fire four or five arrows at his foes before they get to act. This variant takes care of that potential problem.

NEW COMBATANTS ENTER THE FRAY

The adventurers in the dungeon are fighting for their lives against a group of trolls intent on throwing them into a dank pit to feed to the dragon that controls this level. Suddenly, in the middle of the fight, a strike team of dwarves wanders into the room where the battle rages. If, in the course of a battle between two sides, some third group enters the battle, they should come into the action in between rounds. The following rules apply to this situation, whether the new group is allied or not allied with one or more existing side involved in the encounter.

Newcomers Are Aware: If any (or all) of the newcomers are aware of one or both of the sides in the battle, they take their actions before anyone else. In effect, they go first in the initiative sequence. Their initiative check result is considered to be 1 higher than the highest initiative check result among the other participants in the encounter. If differentiation is needed for the actions of the newcomers, they act in order of their Dexterity scores, highest to lowest. The reason for this rule is twofold:

- Since they're aware, but there's no way to get a partial action ahead of everyone else (because the encounter has already started), they go first to simulate their advantage. This happens whether the other sides are aware of the new side or not.
- Placing them at the beginning of the round means that those who had the highest initiative scores prior to their arrival are the first characters to have an opportunity to react to them. This is an important advantage for the characters with high initiative scores.

Newcomers Not Aware: If any (or all) of the newcomers are not aware of the other sides when they enter the encounter (for example, the PCs stumble unaware into a fight between two monsters in a dungeon), they still come into play at the beginning of the round, but they roll initiative normally. If one of the other characters involved in the encounter has a higher initiative score than one or more of the newcomers, that character can react to those newcomers before they get a chance to act (the newcomers are caught flat-footed).

If more than one new group enters an existing encounter at the same time, you must first decide if they are aware of the encounter or not. Those that are unaware, "stumbling in," roll initiative. Those that are aware act first in the round, in the order of their Dexterity scores, even if they are not in the same group.

Example: A group of powerful adventurers fights a naga in a dungeon room. The naga rolled badly for initiative, and all the adventurers act before it. Between rounds three and four of that battle, three orcs on a random patrol stumble in. At the same time, two more nagas arrive, having been alerted by the sounds of the battle. At the beginning of round three, the two new nagas act in the order of their Dexterity scores. Then the orcs roll for initiative, and the results of their rolls are placed within the normal initiative order for the battle. In this case, poor rolls place them dead last, even after the original naga.

Then the adventurers act, able to react to either the flat-footed orcs or the new naga reinforcements. Then the original naga acts,

followed by the orcs (who probably flee from this battle, which is clearly out of their league). This same sequence is used for subsequent rounds of the battle.

KEEPING THINGS MOVING

Initiative dictates the flow of who goes when. It is the tool that the game uses to keep things moving, but ultimately it's you who needs to make sure that happens. Encourage the players to be ready with their action when it comes to their turn. Players have less fun if they spend a lot of time sitting at the table waiting for someone else to decide what to do.

Some resourceful players will learn tricks to help you move things along. When attacking, they roll attack and damage dice at once, so that if successful, they can tell you the damage that they deal immediately. If they know that their next action will require a die roll, they'll roll it ahead of time, so that when you ask them what they're going to do, they can tell you immediately ("I attack with my battleaxe, and hit AC 14. If that's good enough, I deal 9 points of damage.") Some DMs like to see each roll made by the players, so you'll have to decide for yourself whether you allow prerolling.

One useful thing that a DM can do is to write down the initiative sequence once it's determined for a given encounter. If you place this where all the players can see it, each will remember when his character's turn is coming and hopefully will be ready to tell you his action when it comes time for him to act. Don't write down the NPCs' places in the initiative sequence, at least not until they have acted once—the players shouldn't know who's going to act before the enemies and who will act after. It's too easy to plan actions around when their opponents act.

Simultaneity

Sometimes it's important for you to impose ad hoc simultaneity. For instance, suppose Tordek hustles 15 feet ahead of his friends down a corridor, turns a corner, and hustles another 10 feet down a branching corridor, only to trigger a trap at the end of his round. You're within your rights to rule that Tordek won't trigger the trap until the end of the round. After all, it takes him some time to get down the corridor. You have three options.

- Play by standard initiative and let the other characters know about the trap at the start of their actions.
- Before resolving the trap's effect on Tordek, get some commitment from the other players about what their characters are doing, so they can't use the information about the trap to help determine their characters' actions.
- Don't tell Tordek about the trap until the end of the round, when everyone else has already acted.

Variant: Roll Each Round

Some players find combat more fun if they get to roll initiative every round rather than rolling once at the beginning of the encounter. Rather than determining a sequence of actions for each round at the beginning of an encounter, the players and DM reroll for all combatants determining a different sequence at the start of each new round. The goal is to give the combat a feeling of shifting variability.

Ultimately, this variant rule doesn't change things much. You'll find that it slows down play, because a new sequence of activity will need to be determined each round—more die rolling, more calculation, more organizing time. It doesn't change spell durations, or how various combat actions work. Effects that last until the character's next action still operate that way. The difference is that it's possible for someone to take an action at the end of one round (such as a charge attack) that puts him at a penalty until his next action, and then to roll well the next round so that he goes first and the penalty has no effect. This means that sometimes it can be beneficial to roll low for initiative in a round.

And consider this case: A wizard wants to cast a spell unhindered by the oncoming monk who rushes toward him. He knows that if the monk reaches him, it will be difficult to cast a spell without drawing attacks of opportunity from her. He thinks to himself that his actions will depend on whether he wins initiative in this round (you need to keep this sort of change in approach in mind if you use this variant). Meanwhile, the monk wants to reach the wizard and use her stun attack to keep him from casting spells. They roll initiative, and the wizard wins, casting a spell on the monk (but the monk saves and isn't affected). The monk runs forward and stuns the wizard, a condition that lasts until the monk's next action. In the next round, the monk wins again, and attacks, but misses. Now the wizard casts another spell—but because he lost the initiative in this round, and acted after the monk's action, the fact that he was stunned hardly hindered him at all.

If you roll initiative each round, taking a readied action later in the same round or delaying an action until later in the same round gives you a cumulative –2 penalty on later initiative rolls. (The first time you do this causes a –2 penalty. If you take a readied action later in the same round or delay an action until later in the same round again during the current combat, the penalty becomes –4, and so on.) Taking a readied action in the next round or delaying until the next round carries no penalty, but you get no other action that round. The refocus action eliminates all accumulated penalties from readying or delaying.

Even if you normally use a single set of initiative rolls for the whole combat, some turn of events could make it worthwhile to reroll initiative. For example, the PCs are fighting a drow wizard using *improved invisibility*. It's a climactic encounter with the survival of the party hinging on it. The drow, on his turn, walks within 30 feet of Jozan, who has cast *invisibility purge*. Suddenly, the drow is visible. Under normal initiative rules, whoever just happens to act next would be able to attack the newly visible drow. Outside of game mechanics, there's no good reason to let that character act first. Additionally, everyone else will get one turn before the drow gets to act again. Instead of following the previous order, you can call for everyone—the drow included—to roll initiative again to see how fast each character reacts to the new condition (the drow becoming visible).

COMBAT ACTIONS

A troll mounted on a purple worm with a long spear can reach opponents two squares away. Surrounded by enemies, it can guide its mount's attacks against the same foe that it attacks, hoping to take him out of the combat entirely, or it can attack one foe and encourage the worm to bite (and try to swallow) another while it stings another with its venomous tail. Combat can be a tactical game in and of itself, filled with good and bad decisions.

You need to play each NPC appropriately. A combat-savvy fighter with a fair Intelligence isn't going to allow his opponents to get opportunity attacks unless he has to, but a stupid goblin might. A phase spider with an Intelligence of 7 might figure that phasing in behind the dexterous wizard he's fighting is the best course of action (since the wizard blasted him with a *magic missile* spell last round), but an ankheg (Intelligence 1) might not know which character is the biggest threat.

Adjudicating Actions Not Covered

While the combat actions defined in the *Player's Handbook* are numerous and fairly comprehensive, they cannot begin to cover every possible action that a character might want to take. Your job is to make up rules on the spot to handle such things. In general, use the rules for combat actions as guidelines, and apply ability checks, skill checks and (rarely) saving throws when they are appropriate. (For more information on ad hoc adjudication, see Chapter 1: Dungeon Mastering.)

The following are a few examples of ad hoc rules decisions.

- Reinforcements show up to help the bugbears that the adventurers are fighting. Tordek can hear these newcomers attempting to open the door to get in. He races to the door and tries to hold it shut while the others finish off the foes in the room. If it were a normal door, you might call for an opposed Strength check between Tordek and the bugbears pushing on the door. Since the door is already stuck, however, you decide that the bugbears must first push it open and then (if they succeed) make an opposed check against Tordek.
- A monk wants to jump up, grab a chandelier, and swing on it into an enemy. You rule that a successful Dexterity check (DC 13) allows the monk to grab the chandelier and swing. The player asks if the monk can use his Tumble skill, and you let him. Ruling that the swing is somewhat like a charge, you give the monk a +2 attack bonus with his dramatic swinging attack.
- A sorcerer readies an attack spell so that he casts it as soon as he sees a beholder's small eyes shoot rays. (He decides this is the best way for him to determine whether the beholder's antimagic ray is currently active.) That means, however, that the rays need to have actually fired before the spell is cast (the spell can't go before the rays in this case). Still, the sorcerer needs to know if he gets his spell cast before he's struck by the dangerous rays. You rule that if the sorcerer can beat the beholder in an opposed roll, he can get the spell off. The sorcerer makes a Wisdom check, and the beholder makes a Dexterity check.

Combat Actions Outside of Combat

As a general rule, combat actions should only be performed in combat. That means that only when you're keeping track of rounds and the players are acting in initiative order. You'll find obvious exceptions to this. For example, a cleric doesn't need to roll initiative to cast *cure light wounds* on a friend after the battle's over. Spellcasting and skill use are often used outside of combat, and that's fine. Attacks, readied actions, charges, and other actions are meant to simulate combat, however, and are best used within the round structure.

Consider the following situation: Outside of combat, Lidda decides to pull a mysterious lever that she's found in a dungeon room. Mialee, standing right next to her, thinks that Lidda's sudden plan is a bad one. Mialee tries to stop Lidda. The best way to handle this is using the combat rules as presented. Lidda and Mialee roll initiative. If Lidda wins, she pulls the lever. If Mialee wins, she grabs Lidda, requiring a melee touch attack (as if starting a grapple). If Mialee hits, Lidda needs to determine whether or not she resists. (Since Mialee is a good friend, grabbing Lidda's arm might be enough to make her stop.) If Lidda keeps trying to pull the lever, use the grapple rules to determine whether or not Mialee can hold Lidda back.

Adjudicating the Ready Action

The ready action is particularly open-ended and requires that you make the players using it be as specific as possible about what their characters are doing. If a character readies a spell so that it will be cast when a foe comes at him or her, the player needs to specify the exact spell—and you're justified in making the player identify a specific foe, either one that the character is currently aware of or one that might come from a certain direction.

If a character specifies a readied action and then decides not to perform the action when the conditions are met, the standard rule is that the character can keep his action ready. Given that combat is often confusing and fast, however, you're within your rights to make it a little harder on the character who readies an action and doesn't take that action when the opportunity presents itself. You have two options:

- Allow the character to forgo the action at the expense of losing the readied action.
- Allow the character to make a Wisdom check (DC 15) to avoid taking the readied action. Thus, if a character covers a door with a crossbow, he can make a Wisdom check to not fire the crossbow when his friend comes through the door. A successful roll means that he doesn't fire at his friend, and is still ready to shoot the ghoul chasing the friend. A failure means he completes the action he readied and shoots the first creature through the door—his friend.

Smart players are going to learn that often being specific is better than making a general statement. If a character is covering a door with a crossbow, he might say, "I shoot the first enemy that comes through the door." Although players can benefit from being specific, you should decide if a certain set of conditions is too specific. "I cover the door with my crossbow so that I shoot the first unwounded ghoul that comes through" might be too specific, since it's not necessarily easy to tell an unwounded ghoul from a wounded one, especially when the judgment must be made in an instant. Ultimately, it's your call.

Don't allow players to use the ready action outside of combat. While the above examples are all acceptable in the middle of an encounter, a player cannot use the ready action to cover a door with his crossbow outside of combat. It's okay for a player to state that he's covering the door, but what that means is that if something comes through the door he's unlikely to be caught unaware. If the character coming through the door wasn't aware of him, he gets a free partial action because he surprised the other character, and so he can shoot the weapon. Otherwise, he still needs to roll initiative for his character normally.

ATTACK ROLLS

Rolling a d20 to see if an attack hits is the bread and butter of combat encounters. It's almost certainly the most common die roll in any campaign. Because of that, these rolls run the risk of becoming boring. When a roll as exciting and important as one that determines success or failure in combat becomes dull, you've got to do something about it.

Attack rolls can be boring if a player feels like hitting is a foregone conclusion or that his character has no chance to hit. One way that the rules address this potential problem is with the decreasing attack bonuses for multiple attacks. Even if a character's primary attack always hits everything he fights, that's not true of his secondary or tertiary attacks.

One thing that can keep attack rolls from becoming humdrum is good visual description. It's not just "a hit," it's a slice across the dragon's neck, bringing forth a gout of foul, draconic ichor. See below for more descriptive advice.

Variant: Automatic Hits and Misses

The *Player's Handbook* says that an attack roll of natural 1 (the d20 comes up 1) is always a miss. A natural 20 (the d20 comes up 20) is always a hit.

This rule means that the lowliest kobold can strike the most magically protected, armored, dexterous character on a roll of a 20. It also means that regardless of a warrior's training, experience, and magical assistance, he still misses a given foe at least 5% of the time.

A different way to handle this is to say that a natural 1 is treated as a roll of –10. Someone with an attack bonus of +6 nets a –4 result, which can't hit anything. Someone with a +23 attack bonus rolling a 1 would hit AC 13 or lower. At the other extreme, a natural 20 is treated as a roll of 30. Even someone with a –2 attack penalty would hit AC 28 with such a roll.

Variant: Defense Roll

More randomness can sometimes eliminate the foregone conclusion of a high-level character who always hits or a lowly one who never has a chance. A good way to introduce this randomness is to allow (or force) characters to make defense rolls. Every time a character is attacked, rather than just using his never-changing, static AC, he makes a d20 roll and adds it to all his AC modifiers. Every attack becomes an opposed roll, with attacker and defender matching their modified rolls against one another. (One way to look at it is that without the defense roll, characters are "taking 10" on the roll each round, and thus are using a base of 10 for Armor Class.)

The defense roll can be expressed like this:

$$1d20 + (AC - 10)$$

For example, a paladin attacks an evil fighter. The paladin rolls a 13 and adds his attack bonus of +10 for a total of 23. The fighter makes his defense roll and gets a 9. He adds his defensive bonuses (all the things that modify AC, including armor), which come to +11. The fighter's total is 20, less than 23, so the paladin hits.

This variant rule really comes in handy at high levels, where high-level fighters always hit with their primary attacks, and other characters rarely do. Unfortunately, it can slow down play, almost doubling the number of rolls in any given combat. A compromise might be to have each defender make a defense roll once in a round, using that same total against all attacks made against him that round.

Critical Hits

When someone gets a 20 on an attack roll, you should be sure to point out that this is a threat, not a critical hit. Calling it a crit raises expectations that might be dashed by the actual critical roll. When a critical hit is achieved, a vital spot on the creature was hit. This is an opportunity for you to give the players some vivid description to keep the excitement level high: "The mace blow hits the orc squarely on the side of the head. He lets out a groan, and his knees buckle from the impact."

Certain creatures are immune to critical hits because they do not have vital organs, points of weakness, or differentiation from one portion of the body to another. A stone golem is a solid, human-shaped mass of rock. A ghost is all insubstantial vapor. A gray ooze has no front, no back, and no middle.

Variant: Instant Kill

When you or a player rolls a natural 20 on an attack roll, a critical roll is made to see if a critical hit is scored. If that critical roll is also a 20, that's considered a threat for an instant kill. Now a third roll, an instant kill roll, is made. If that roll scores a hit on the target in question (just like a normal critical roll after a threat), the target is instantly slain. Creatures immune to critical hits are also immune to instant kills.

The instant kill only applies to natural 20s, regardless of the threat range for a combatant or weapon. (Otherwise weapons, feats, and magical powers that improve threat ranges would be much more powerful than they are intended to be.)

The instant kill variant makes a game more lethal and combat more random. In any contest, an increase in randomness improves the odds for the underdog. Since the PCs win most fights, a rule that makes combat more random hurts the PCs more than it hurts their enemies.

Variant: Softer Critical Hits

Instead of making critical hits more lethal, you can make them less lethal. Do so by reducing each weapon's critical capacity one step. Weapons with a threat range of 20 and ×2 damage deal no critical hits at all. Those with expanded threat ranges see those ranges go down, and those with extra damage multiples see those multiples go down as well.

Standard Threat Range	Softer Threat Range
19–20	20
18–20	19–20

Standard Damage Multiple	Softer Damage Multiple
×3	×2
×4	×3

With softer critical hits, most weapons don't deal critical damage at all, and those that still deal critical hits do so less often or for less damage. This variant makes feats and magical powers that improve threat ranges less valuable, it slightly decreases the value of a monster's immunity to critical hits, and it reduces randomness in combat.

Variant: Critical Misses (Fumbles)

If you want to model the chance that in combat a character could fumble his weapon, then when a player rolls a 1 on his attack roll, make him roll a Dexterity check (DC 10). If he fails, his character fumbles. You need decide what it means to fumble, but in general, that character should probably lose a turn of activity as he regains his balance, picks up a dropped weapon, clears his head, steadies himself, or whatever.

Fumbles are not appropriate to all games. They can add excitement or interest to combat, but they can also detract from the fun. They certainly add more randomness to combat. Add this variant rule only after careful consideration.

Variant: Firing into a Crowd

Normally, if you fire a ranged weapon at a foe engaged in combat with someone you don't want to hit, you suffer a –4 attack penalty (see the *Player's Handbook*, page 124). Sometimes, however, a player wants to know exactly where an arrow went if she missed her target. For groups that want to simulate reality in a very detailed way, the following guidelines answer that question. Be warned, however, this is an example of how D&D rules, in the interest of simulating reality, can become fairly complex—there's a lot of work here for very little payoff.

The attacker makes the attack roll normally. If it's a miss, check to see whether the thrown weapon or projectile at least connects. If the attack roll would have been good enough for a ranged touch attack, then the thrown weapon or projectile has flown true but failed to damage the target. If the roll isn't good enough for a ranged touch hit, then the thrown weapon or projectile is errant.

Now determine the path of the errant thrown weapon or projectile. For direct fire shots, an errant thrown weapon or projectile is most likely to veer to the right or the left. For indirect fire, a projectile is most likely to go too far or fall short of its target. The range out to which a projectile weapon or a thrown weapon makes a direct fire attack is summarized on Table 3–3, below. If the weapon is fired at a target farther away than the listed distance, then the attack is indirect fire.

TABLE 3–3: DIRECT FIRE RANGE

Weapon	Direct Fire Range
Shortbow	Up to 60 ft.
Longbow	Up to 100 ft.
Short composite bow	Up to 80 ft.
Long composite bow	Up to 120 ft.
Hand crossbow	Up to 120 ft.
Light crossbow	Up to 200 ft.
Heavy crossbow	Up to 250 ft.
Sling	Up to 50 ft.
Any thrown weapon	Up to 20 ft.

TABLE 3–4: DIRECT FIRE PATH

1d20	Fire Path
1–8	Left
9–16	Right
17–19	Long
20	Short

TABLE 3–5: DIRECT FIRE DEVIATION

1d20	Deviation
1–12	One-tenth of the distance between attacker and target (round to nearest square)
13–17	One-fifth of the distance between attacker and target (round to nearest square)
18–19	One-third of the distance between attacker and target (round to nearest square)
20	Half of the distance between attacker and target (round to nearest square)

Once the direction and the amount of deviation is determined, trace a path starting at the firer. If characters are in the path, starting with the character nearest the firer, determine if the thrown weapon or projectile has a chance to attack each character. A ranged touch attack roll is made for the thrown weapon or

---

BEHIND THE CURTAIN: CRITICAL HITS

Critical hits are in the game to add moments of particular excitement. Critical hits, however, are deadly. The PCs, over the course of a single game session, let alone a campaign, are subject to many more attack rolls than any given NPC. That makes sense, since the PCs are in every battle, and most NPCs are in just one (the one in which the PCs defeat them, usually). Thus more critical hits are going to be dealt upon any single PC than any single NPC (and the NPC was probably not going to survive the encounter anyway). Any given PC is more likely to survive an encounter—but a critical hit against the character can change all that. Be aware of this potential, and decide how you want to deal with it ahead of time (see Chapter 1 for information on DM cheating).

The reason that critical hits multiply all damage, rather than just the die roll, is so that they remain significant at high levels. When a fighter at high level adds +5 to his damage from magic and +10 from his magically enhanced strength, the result of the 1d8 from his longsword becomes trivial, even if doubled by a critical hit. Multiplying all damage, the roll and the bonuses, makes critical hits particularly dangerous. In fact, they can completely determine the course of a battle if one or two are dealt. That's

why they make the game both more interesting and more uncontrollable.

Remember, a critical hit feels like a lot of damage, but the difference between a double-damage critical hit and a normal hit is no greater than the difference between a miss and a hit. Taking a triple-damage critical hit, however, is like getting hit an extra two times, and taking a quadruple-damage critical hit is like getting hit an extra three times.

The weapons in the *Player's Handbook* are balanced with the following idea in mind: Good weapons that deal triple-damage critical hits do so only on a 20. Good weapons that deal double-damage critical hits do so on a 19–20. Axes are big and heavy. They're somewhat difficult to use efficiently, but when one does, the effect is devastating. An executioner uses an axe for this reason. Swords, on the other hand, are more precise—sword wielders get in decisive strikes more often, but they're not as crushing as those dealt by axes. A few other factors are considered as well (reach, the ability to use a weapon as a ranged weapon, and more), but for the most part, this is the basic rule of thumb. Thus, it would be a mistake to add to the weapon list some new weapon that dealt triple-damage critical hits on a 19–20. (Results such as this might be possible through magic or feats, but should not be a basic quality of any weapon.)

projectile with no modifications for the skill of the firer but using magical adjustments and modifications for cover. If the roll is a hit, then apply the same attack result against the target's full AC (not as a touch attack). If that's successful, roll damage. If it's not, the thrown weapon or projectile stops.

If the touch attack was unsuccessful, the thrown weapon or projectile keeps traveling along its path, with each new target in that path using the same procedure. No modification is made for range, but direct fire thrown weapons or projectiles effectively travel no farther than the distances given above, at which time the thrown weapon or projectile drops to the ground.

TABLE 3–6: INDIRECT FIRE TARGET AREA

1d20	Target Area
1–4	Left
5–8	Right
9–14	Long
15–20	Short

TABLE 3–7: INDIRECT FIRE DEVIATION

1d20	Deviation
1–12	One-tenth of the distance between attacker and target (round to nearest square)
13–17	One-fifth of the distance between attacker and target (round to nearest square)
18–19	One-third of the distance between attacker and target (round to nearest square)
20	Half of the distance between attacker and target (round to nearest square)

Once the direction and the amount of deviation is determined, determine if there is a character in the given square. If so, make an attack roll for the ranged weapon with no modifications from the skill of the firer but using magical adjustments and modifications for cover. If this is successful, roll damage. If it's not, the projectile goes no farther.

DAMAGE

Since combat is a big part of the game, handling damage is a big part of being the DM.

Subdual Damage

When running a combat, make sure that you describe subdual and normal damage differently. The distinction should be clear—both in the players' imaginations and on their character sheets.

Use subdual damage to your advantage. It is an invaluable tool if your adventure plans involve the PCs' capture or defeat, but you don't want to risk killing them. However, if the PCs' opponents are dealing subdual damage more often than not, the players begin to lose any feeling of their characters being threatened. Use subdual damage sparingly, but to good effect.

Players, in general, hate for their characters to be captured. When your NPCs start dealing subdual damage on the characters, the players may actually get more worried than if they were taking normal damage! This is occasionally an effective way to frighten players in an otherwise average encounter.

You can rule that certain damaging effects deal subdual damage when it seems appropriate. For example, a variant rule in Chapter 4: Adventures states that you can make the first 1d6 of falling damage subdual damage. You can do so on a case-by-case basis if you wish. If a villager throws a rock at a knight, that also might be subdual damage. Certain types of damage, however, should never be subdual damage—puncturing wounds and most energy attacks, such as fire.

Variant: Clobbered

Ultimately, damage doesn't matter until a character is unconscious or dead. It has no effect while she's up and fighting. It's easy to imagine, however, that she could be hit so hard that she's clobbered, but not knocked unconscious or dead.

Using this variant, if a character takes half her current hit points in damage from a single blow, she is clobbered. On her next turn, she can only take a partial action, and after that turn she is no longer clobbered.

If you choose to use this variant, it will often lead to slightly faster fights, since taking damage would somewhat reduce the ability to deal damage. It would also increase randomness by increasing the significance of dealing substantial but less than lethal damage. It would also make hit points more important; clerics would want to cure fighters long before fighters are at risk of dying, because they might be at risk of being clobbered. Finally, it may be easier for the superior combatant to get unlucky. That fact could hurt PCs more than NPCs in the long run.

Variant: Death from Massive Damage Based on Size

If a creature takes 50 points of damage or more from a single attack, she must make a Fortitude save or die. This rule exists primarily so there is at least a nod toward realism in the abstract system of hit point loss. As an extra touch of realism, you can vary the massive damage threshold by size, so that each size category larger or smaller than Medium-size raises or lowers the threshold by 10 hp. This variant hurts halfling and gnome PCs, familiars, and some animal companions. It generally favors monsters.

Variant: Damage to Specific Areas

Sometimes, despite the abstract nature of combat, you're going to want to apply damage to specific parts of the body, such as when a character's hands are thrust into flames, when he steps on caltrops, or when he peeks through a hole in the wall and someone shoots an arrow into the hole from the other side. (This situation comes up most frequently with devious traps meant to chop at feet, smash fingers, etc.)

When a specific body part takes damage, you can apply a –2 penalty to any action that the character undertakes using that portion of his

A ranger and his griffon mount face off against wyverns high in the air.

TABLE 3–8: MASSIVE DAMAGE BASED ON SIZE

Size	F	D	T	S	M	L	H	G	C
Damage	10	20	30	40	50	60	70	80	90

TABLE 3–9: EFFECTS OF DAMAGING SPECIFIC AREAS

Location	Damage Affects:
Hand	Climb, Craft, Disable Device, Escape Artist, Forgery, Alchemy, Heal, Open Lock, Pick Pocket, and Use Rope checks; attack rolls.
Arm	Climb and Swim checks; attack rolls; Strength checks.
Head	All attack rolls, saves, and checks.
One eye	Spot, Search, Appraise, Alchemy, Forgery, Decipher Script, Open Lock, Disable Device, Craft, Read Lips, Scry, Sense Motive, and Spellcraft checks; Wilderness Lore checks (for tracking); initiative checks; Dexterity checks; Reflex saving throws. Severe damage to both eyes blinds a character. (See Blinded in the Condition Summary, page 83.)
One ear	Listen checks; initiative checks. Severe damage to both ears deafens a character. (See Deafened in the Condition Summary, page 84.)
Foot/Leg	Climb, Swim, Jump, Ride, Tumble, Balance, and Move Silently checks; Reflex saving throws; Dexterity checks.

TABLE 3–10: CREATURE SIZE AND SCALE ON GRIDS

Creature Size	Example Creature	Natural Reach	Face*
Fine	Fly	0**	100/square
Diminutive	Toad	0**	25/square
Tiny	Cat	0**	4/square
Small	Halfling	1 square	1 square
Medium-size	Human	1 square	1 square
Large (tall)	Hill giant	2 squares	1 square
Large (long)	Horse	1 square	1 × 2 squares
Huge (tall)	Cloud giant	3 squares	2 × 2 squares
Huge (long)	Bulette	2 squares	2 × 4 squares
	Retriever	2 squares	3 × 3 squares
Gargantuan (tall)	50-foot animated statue	4 squares	4 × 4 squares
Gargantuan (long) (coiled)	Kraken	2 squares†	4 × 8 squares
	Purple worm	3 squares	6 × 6 squares
Colossal (tall)	The tarrasque	5 squares	8 × 8 squares
Colossal (long)	Great red wyrm	3 squares	8 × 16 squares

*Face is width by length.

**Creatures with 0 reach must be in the same square as an opponent to attack.

†Bite attack.

body. For example, if a character's fingers get slashed, he makes attacks rolls with a weapon in that hand at –2, he takes a –2 check penalty on Climb, Open Lock, Disable Device, Forgery, etc. If a character steps on a caltrop, he suffers a –2 penalty to Climb, Jump, and Balance checks, and so on (in addition to the effects described on page 107 of the *Player's Handbook*).

The Condition Summary (page 83) defines some effects of damage to specific body parts, such as what happens when a character is blinded or deafened. In addition to that information, use the following table as a guide for what rolls are modified by injuries to what body parts. Impose other penalties as you see fit.

This penalty lasts until the character heals, either magically or by resting. For a minor wound, such as stepping on a caltrop, a Heal check (DC 15), 1 point of magical healing, or a day of rest removes the penalties.

You can also allow a character to make a Fortitude saving throw (DC 10 + damage taken) to "tough it out" and ignore the penalty.

Also, these penalties shouldn't stack. Two hand injuries shouldn't impose a –4 penalty.

This sort of rule puts a lot of pressure on the DM to create ad hoc rulings. If that's acceptable to you, use this rule freely. If not, ignore it.

USING MINIATURES AND GRIDS

While this is a game of imagination, props and visual aids can help everyone imagine the same thing, avoid confusion, and enhance the entire game play experience. If you use miniatures or counters as described in Chapter 1: Dungeon Mastering, use the following guidelines to assist tactical-level play.

Movement and Position

Few characters in a fight are likely to stand still for long. Enemies appear and charge the party; the adventurers reply, advancing to take on new foes after they down their first opponents. Wizards circle the fight, looking for the best place to use their magic; rogues quietly skirt the fracas, seeking a straggler or an unwary opponent to strike with a sneak attack. Finally, if the fight is lost, most characters find it to their advantage to remove themselves from the vicinity. With all this tactical maneuvering going on, something to represent character location within a defined scale can really aid the game.

Movement and position can be handled by using miniature figures (representing the characters and monsters) on a grid (representing the battlefield, wherever that happens to be). Miniatures show where a figure is in relation to any others, and the grid makes it clear how far the characters and monsters can move.

Standard Scale

1-inch square = 5 feet
30mm figure = human-size creature

Scale and Squares

The standard unit for tactical maps is the 5-foot square. This unit is useful for miniatures and for drawing dungeon maps, which are usually created on graph paper.

In a fight, each Small or Medium-size character occupies a single 5-foot square. Larger creatures may take up more squares, and several smaller creatures fit in a square. See Table 3–10: Creature Size and Scale on Grids.

Creature Size: The size category of the creature in question. "Tall" creatures, such as bipeds, are mostly upright. "Long" creatures, such as most quadrupeds, are long or wide but not upright.

Example Creature: An example creature of this size.

Number of Squares: The number of squares that a typical creature of this size occupies. Huge or larger long creatures have several possible configurations, depending on the creature's shape. In any case, these are only typical configurations, and certain creatures have different configurations.

Natural Reach: How many squares away the typical creature of this type can reach with a normal attack. Creatures that use especially long weapons can reach farther.

Line of Sight

Line of sight establishes whether a particular character can see something else represented on the grid. When using a grid, draw imaginary lines (or use a ruler or a piece of string) from the center of the square the character is in to the object in question. If nothing blocks this line, the character has line of sight (and can thus see it to cast a spell on it, target it with a bow, etc.). If the object in question is actually another creature, measure line of sight from the center of the square the character is in to the center of the square that the creature occupies. If a character can see a portion of a large creature that occupies more than one square, she can target that creature for a spell or any other attack.

Deviation
(1 Ft. to 5 Ft.)

4 1
⊕
3 2

Roll 1d4

Deviation
(6 Ft. to 10 Ft.)

8 1
7 2
⊕
6 3
5 4

Roll 1d8

Deviation
(10 Ft. to 16 Ft.)

12 1
11 2
10 3
⊕
9 4
8 5
7 6

Roll 1d12

If line of sight is completely blocked, a character can't cast spells or use ranged weapons against the target. If it's partially blocked, such as by the corner of a building, spells work normally but ranged attacks suffer penalties for the target's cover.

Grenadelike Weapons

A grenadelike weapon is one that "splashes" when it impacts with a solid surface, having a broad enough effect to hurt characters just by landing close to them. Grenadelike weapons include vials of acid and flasks of alchemist's fire. Attacks with grenadelike weapons are ranged touch attack rolls. If you miss your target, roll 1d6 to see how many feet away from the target the grenadelike weapon lands. Add +1 foot for every range increment of distance that you threw the weapon. Unlike a spell, a grenadelike weapon's splash is centered on a square on the battle grid. Once you know the distance, find the right Deviation Diagram and roll 1d4, 1d8, or 1d12 (as called for) to see where the grenadelike weapon's splash is centered relative to your target.

Refer to pages 114 and 138 in the *Player's Handbook* for specifics on damage dealt and splash damage.

Area Spells

These spells are not targeted on a single creature, but on a volume of space, and thus must fit into the grid in order for you to adjudicate

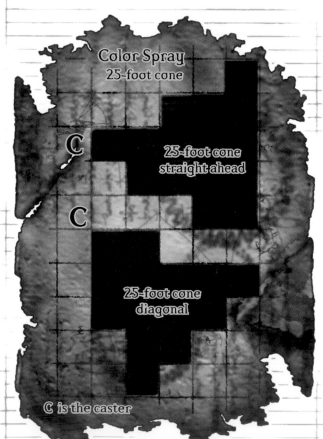

Color Spray
25-foot cone

C

25-foot cone
straight ahead

C

25-foot cone
diagonal

C is the caster

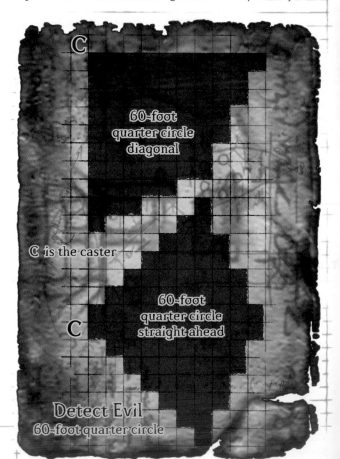

C

60-foot
quarter circle
diagonal

C is the caster

60-foot
quarter circle
straight ahead

C

Detect Evil
60-foot quarter circle

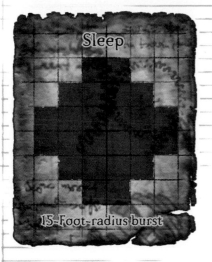

Sleep

15-Foot-radius burst

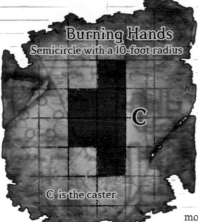

Burning Hands
Semicircle with a 10-foot radius

C

C is the caster

MOVEMENT

In a round-by-round simulation, particularly when using miniatures, movement will often feel choppy, even though in reality it's continuous. If a character runs across a room so large that it takes him 2 rounds to do so, it might seem as though he runs halfway, stops, and then runs the rest of the way a little later. Although there's no way to avoid representing movement in a start-stop-start-stop fashion, try to keep in mind—and try to stress to the players—that actually all movement throughout an encounter is fluid and continuous.

Unconventional Movement

Not every kind of creature gets around by walking and running. A shark, even though it moves by swimming, can take a "run" action to swim faster. A character under the influence of a *fly* spell can make a flying charge. A climbing thief can use part of his speed to climb down a short wall and then use the remainder to hustle toward a foe. Use the movement rules to apply to any sort of movement, not just traveling across a flat surface.

Tactical Aerial Movement

The elven barbarian mounted on the giant eagle swoops over the group of mind flayers, launching arrows from his bow. One of the mind flayers wears *boots of flying* and takes to the air to better confront the elf. Once movement becomes three-dimensional and involves turning in midair and maintaining a minimum velocity to stay aloft, it gets more complicated.

Most flying creatures have to slow down at least a little to make a turn, and many are limited to fairly wide turns and must maintain a minimum forward speed. Each flying creature has a maneuverability, as shown on Table 3–11: Flight Maneuverability.

Minimum Forward Speed: If a flying creature fails to maintain its minimum forward speed, it must land at the end of its movement. If it is too high above the ground to land, it falls straight down, descending 150 feet in the first round of falling. If this distance brings it to the ground, it takes falling damage. If the fall doesn't bring the creature to the ground, it must spend its next turn recovering from the stall. It must succeed at a Reflex saving throw (DC 20) to recover. Otherwise it falls another 300 feet. If it hits the ground, it takes falling damage. Otherwise, it has another chance to recover on its next turn.

Hover: The ability to stay in one place while airborne.

Fly Backward: The ability to fly backward.

Reverse: A creature with good maneuverability uses up 5 feet of its speed to start flying backward.

Turn: How much the creature can turn after covering the stated distance.

who is affected and who is not. Realize ahead of time that you will have to make ad hoc rulings when applying areas onto the grid. Use the following as guidelines.

Bursts and Emanations: To employ the spell using a grid, the caster needs to designate an intersection of lines on the grid as the center of the effect. From that intersection, it's easy to measure a radius using the scale on the grid. If you were to draw a circle using the measurements on the grid, with the chosen intersection at the center, then if the majority of a grid square lies within that circle, the square is a part of the spell's area. Refer to the diagram of the *sleep* spell's area to see which squares are covered by the burst. The diagram of the *burning hands* spell's area shows a burst that covers a semicircle instead of a circle. Also see the diagram of the *detect evil* spell's area; this is the way an emanation spreads out from the caster.

Cones: Determining the area of a cone spell requires that the caster declare whether she's casting it straight ahead or on the diagonal. In either case, the caster must pick an intersection where the cone starts. From there, the cone expands so that it is as wide as it is long at its far end. For a cone extending straight ahead, the width increases by one square for each extra square of distance from the caster. A cone cast on the diagonal is trickier to describe on the grid because diagonal lengths and distances are harder to measure. The same general rule applies, however: The width of the cone at any point equals that point's distance from the caster. Refer to the diagram of the *color spray* spell's area to see which squares are within the cone.

Miscellaneous: Using the rules given above, apply areas to the grid as well as you can. Remember to maintain a consistent number of affected squares in areas that differ on the diagonal.

TABLE 3–11: FLIGHT MANEUVERABILITY

	Maneuverability and Example Creature				
	Perfect (Will-o'-wisp)	Good (Beholder)	Average (Gargoyle)	Poor (Wyvern)	Clumsy (Manticore)
Minimum Forward Speed	None	None	Half	Half	Half
Hover	Yes	Yes	No	No	No
Fly Backward	Yes	Yes	No	No	No
Reverse	Free	−5 ft.	—	—	—
Turn	Any	90°/5 ft.	45°/5 ft.	45°/5 ft.	45°/10 ft.
Turn in Place	Any	+90°/−5 ft.	+45°/−5 ft.	No	No
Maximum Turn	Any	Any	90°	45°	45°
Up Angle	Any	Any	60°	45°	45°
Up Speed	Full	Half	Half	Half	Half
Down Angle	Any	Any	Any	45°	45°
Down Speed	Double	Double	Double	Double	Double
Between Down and Up	0	0	5 ft.	10 ft.	20 ft.

Turn in Place: A creature with good or average maneuverability can "spend" some of its speed to turn in place.

Maximum Turn: How much the creature can turn in any one space.

Up Angle: The angle at which the creature can climb.

Up Speed: How fast the creature can climb.

Down Angle: The angle at which the creature can descend.

Down Speed: A flying creature can fly down at twice its normal flying speed.

Between Down & Up: An average, poor, or clumsy flier must fly level for a minimum distance after descending and before climbing. Any flier can begin descending after a climb without an intervening distance.

Evasion and Pursuit

In round-by-round movement, simply counting off squares, it's impossible for a slow character to get away from a determined fast character without some sort of mitigating circumstances. Likewise, it's no problem for a fast character to get away from a slower one.

When the speeds of the two concerned characters are equal, there's a simple way to resolve a chase: If one creature is pursuing another, both are moving at the same speed, and the chase continues for at least a few rounds, have them make opposed Dexterity checks to see who is the faster over those rounds. If the creature being chased wins, it escapes. If the pursuer wins, it catches the fleeing creature.

Sometimes a chase occurs overland and could last all day, with the two sides only occasionally getting glimpses of each other at a distance. In the case of a long chase, an opposed Constitution check made by all parties determines which can keep pace the longest. If the creature being chased rolls the highest, it gets away. If not, the chaser runs down its prey, outlasting it with endurance.

Moving Around in Squares

The characters are all within a corridor only 5 feet wide. A fighter stands at the end of the corridor, at a dead end. He's been poisoned and is dying. The cleric wants to get at the fighter to help, but two other characters are between them. Thus, there's no way for the cleric to get next to the fighter and cast *neutralize poison*. You can rule that it's okay for the cleric to squeeze past the characters who are in the way, cast the spell, and then move back to where she previously stood.

In general, when the characters aren't engaged in round-by-round combat, they should be able to move anywhere and in any manner that you can imagine real people could. A 5-foot square,

for instance, can hold several characters; they just can't all fight effectively in that small space. The rules for movement of miniatures are important for combat, but outside of combat they can impose unnecessary hindrances upon character activities.

DESCRIBING THE ACTION

The players take all their cues from you. If you describe something incompletely or poorly, the players have no chance of understanding what's going on in the game world. While this is important all the time that you're running a game, it's crucial that you do it well during combats.

Your descriptions of each action that occurs, the locations of all important objects and participants, and the general environment are all crucial to the players' abilities to make intelligent decisions for their characters. Thus, you need to be clear about everything. Allow the players to ask questions and answer them as concisely as you can. Refer to each character distinctly. If you call each NPC "that guy," the players will never know what you mean. If a monster attacks, describe its horns, bite, or claws so that the players understand what the beast is doing.

If the players do not seem to have understood something you said, say it again. Sometimes important points are lost among lots of new description. Don't be afraid to repeat that a great deal of heat comes up from the grate, or each time the dragonne moves, the ceiling rumbles and dust shakes down onto the floor. The worst that can happen is that players are reminded how important the statement is, and they will act accordingly.

When a character moves, add background. Say "The manticore moves away from the opening in the far wall, where the foul smell seems to originate," or "The barbarian steps even closer to the pit," or "The roper slides slowly across the uneven floor." When a character uses an object, describe the object. "The warrior slashes you with his wavy-bladed dagger" is much better than "He hits you for 3 points of damage."

The tone of your descriptions controls the flow of an encounter and the mood that the encounter projects over the entire group. If you speak quickly and intently, this lends intensity to the action. If your words are frantic, they will make the mood of the scene seem urgent and desperate.

Sometimes it's effective to add a little pantomime to your descriptions. If a PC's opponent raises his huge, two-handed sword above his head to attack the character, raise your hands as if you are grasping the sword's hilt. When someone takes a terrible hit in battle, flinch or recoil with a momentary look of mock pain. If the PCs are fighting a giant, stand up when the giant takes his actions, looking down at the seated players.

Sometimes it's hard to avoid "You miss. He hits. You take 12 points of damage." And sometimes, that's okay

Long verbal descriptions can get tedious to give and to hear, and the game effects are the important thing. However, that's the exception, not the rule. Most of the time, at the very least, make that "He ducks, and slashes with his longsword for 12 points of damage." It is usually better in a descriptive way to talk about dealing damage rather than taking damage. "Its claws rake for 8 points" is at least somewhat interesting, but "You take 8 points" describes nothing.

Remember, too, that an attack that does not deal damage is not always a miss. Heavily armored characters may be frequently hit, but their armor protects them. If you say "His short sword glances off your plate armor," this not only describes the action, but makes the player feel good about his choice to spend extra gold on the good armor.

NPC Actions

When an NPC takes a combat action, the players sometimes need to have a clue what's going on—both in the fictional reality of the game and in terms of the game's mechanics as well. This means that when a lizardfolk with a crossbow is taking a ready action to cover the area in front of a door, the players should have a pretty good idea that if they move in front of that door, the lizardfolk is going to shoot them.

You need to think about what various actions look like while they're happening. If you were all watching the combat in a movie, what would you see when a character refocuses, casts a spell, or does something else that none of you have ever seen a real person do? Be dramatic, and describe the action fully, but avoid over-explaining, because that will slow down the flow of the action. Be consistent as well, because your words are not just description, they're cues by which the players make game decisions. If the last time someone used the aid another action, you described it as "distracting" and "harrying," use those words again. If that means that pretty soon your players listen to your description and then say "Ooh, the wizard must be casting a spell," you have accomplished something good—the players have learned your verbal cues to spellcasting. Not only does that allow them to make good decisions based on your descriptions, but it lends believability to the fictional world you are creating.

Some actions, along with a sample, short, verbal description, follow:

Action	Description
Charge	"He lunges forward at full speed, eyes full of violence."
Full defense	"She raises her weapon and watches your attacks closely, attempting to parry each one."
Aiding another	"While his ally attacks, he darts in and out of the fight, distracting his foe."
Readying a ranged weapon	"He's got his weapon trained on that area, and he's obviously waiting for something."
Casting a spell	"He motions with his hands in a deliberate manner and speaks words that sound more like an invocation than a sentence."
Casting a stilled spell	"She speaks a few short words, staring intently."
Casting a quickened spell	"With a single word and a flick of his hand . . ."
Casting a silenced spell	"She does nothing but make a powerful gesture."
Using a special ability	"Without using words or gestures, she calls upon some power within herself, using her great will and inner strength."
Activating a magic item	"He focuses intently on his item, drawing power from it."
Delaying	"She's looking around, sizing up the situation, and waiting to react."

Interesting Combats

The spiral pathway rose up to the circular platform where the seventeen magical gems were held in stasis. Below the path, a seething pit of raw, explosive magical energy waited like an open maw. The four adventurers climbed up the path, eager to reach their goal, but suddenly a quasit swooped down from some hidden recess. Tordek drew his axe, knowing that fighting on this narrow path would be difficult and dangerous. He wasn't sure what would happen if one of them fell into that magical energy, but he didn't want to find out.

While any combat can be exciting, you should occasionally have the PCs face opponents in a nontraditional setting. Sometimes mounted combat, or aerial mounted combat, can provide a change of pace, and underwater settings can be interesting as well. A short list of other suggestions is below.

Factor	Game Effect
Pits, chasms, bridges, and ledges	Characters can attempt to push opponents with a bull rush (see *Player's Handbook*, page 136).
Fog	One-half concealment (20% miss chance) for everyone involved.
Whirling blades or giant, spinning gears	Characters must make Dex checks (DC 13) each round or take 6d6 points of slashing or crushing damage.
Steam vents	One random character must make a Dex check (DC 15) each round or take 3d6 points of heat damage.
Rising or lowering platforms	Characters can only melee opponents on the same level; platforms change level every other round.
Ice or other slippery surfaces	Characters must make Balance checks (DC 10) each round or fall prone, and then spend a move action to stand.

For yet more ideas, look to Chapter 4: Adventures or The Environment, below, or take inspiration from an exciting action movie or book.

SPECIAL ABILITIES

Throughout the game, you'll find references to special abilities of all kinds—rays of energy, life-numbing touches, and the ability to become insubstantial, to name a few. This section identifies the most significant abilities and provides details on how to use them and what they look like.

Following this section you can find a comprehensive listing of conditions, such as *held*, panicked, and helpless. If a character falls victim to any sort of debilitation or strange effect, refer to that condition's listing for how to handle the situation.

Special abilities are extraordinary, spell-like, or supernatural.

Extraordinary Abilities (Ex): Extraordinary abilities are nonmagical. They are however, not something that just anyone can do or even learn to do without extensive training (which, in game terms, means to take a new character class). A monk's ability to evade attacks and a barbarian's uncanny dodge are extraordinary. Effects or areas that negate or disrupt magic have no effect on extraordinary abilities.

Spell-Like Abilities (Sp): Spell-like abilities, as the name implies, are spells and magical abilities that are very much like spells. Spell-like abilities are subject to spell resistance and *dispel magic*. They do not function in areas where magic is suppressed or negated (such as an *antimagic field*).

Supernatural Abilities (Su): Supernatural abilities are magical but not spell-like. This far-reaching category includes the basilisk's petrifying stare, the monk's *ki* strike, and the ghoul's paralytic touch. Supernatural abilities are not subject to spell resistance or *dispel magic*. However, supernatural abilities still do not function in areas where magic is suppressed or negated (such as an *antimagic field*).

TABLE 3–12: SPECIAL ABILITY TYPES

	Extraordinary	Supernatural	Spell-Like
Dispel	No	No	Yes
Spell Resistance	No	No	Yes
Antimagic Field	No	Yes	Yes
Attack of Opportunity	No	No	Yes

Dispel: Can dispel magic and similar spells dispel the effects of abilities of that type?

Spell Resistance: Does spell resistance protect a creature from these abilities?

Antimagic Field: Does an antimagic field or similar magic suppress the ability?

Attack of Opportunity: Does using the ability provoke attacks of opportunity the way that casting a spell does?

ABILITY SCORE LOSS

An undead shadow touches Tordek, and his axe immediately feels heavier in his hand. A giant wasp stings Mialee, and her normally graceful movements become halting and stiff. A wraith touches Lidda, and she feels woozy and tired.

Various attacks cause ability score loss, either temporary ability damage or permanent ability drain. Points lost to temporary damage return at the rate of 1 point per day (or double that if the character gets total rest) to each damaged ability, and the spells *lesser restoration* and *restoration* offset temporary damage as well. Drains, however, are permanent, though *restoration* can restore even those lost ability score points.

While any loss is debilitating, losing all points in an ability score can be devastating.

- Strength 0 means that the character cannot move at all. He lies helpless on the ground.
- Dexterity 0 means that the character cannot move at all. He stands motionless, rigid, and helpless.
- Constitution 0 means that the character is dead.
- Intelligence 0 means that the character cannot think and is unconscious in a comalike stupor, helpless.
- Wisdom 0 means that the character is withdrawn into a deep sleep filled with nightmares, helpless.
- Charisma 0 means that the character is withdrawn into a catatonic, comalike stupor, helpless.

Keeping track of negative ability score points is never necessary. A character's ability score can't drop below 0.

Having a 0 score in an ability is different from having no ability score whatsoever. A wraith has no Strength score, not a Strength score of 0. A clay golem has no Intelligence, not an Intelligence score of 0. The wraith can move, it just can't act physically on other objects. The golem is not in a stupor or helpless, but it has no thoughts or memory.

Some spells or abilities impose an effective ability score reduction, which is different from ability score loss. Any such reduction disappears at the end of the spell's or ability's duration, and the ability score immediately returns to its former value.

If a character's Constitution score drops, then he loses 1 hit point per Hit Die for every point by which his Constitution modifier drops. For example, at 7th level, Tordek is hit by poison that causes his Constitution to drop from 16 to 13. His bonus falls from +3 to +1, so he loses 14 hit points (2 per level). A minute later, the poison deals another 8 points of temporary Constitution damage, dropping his score to 5 and his modifier from +1 to −3. He loses another 28 hit points—for a total of 42 hit points lost because of an overall 6-point drop in his Constitution modifier.

A full hit point score, however, can't drop to less than 1 hit point per Hit Die. At 7th level, Mialee has 22 hit points. Even if her Constitution score drops to 5 or below, she will still have at least 7 hit points (less any damage she's taken).

The ability that some creatures have to drain ability scores (such as shadows draining Strength or lamias draining Wisdom) is a supernatural one, requiring some sort of attack. Such creatures do not drain abilities from enemies when the enemies strike them, even with unarmed attacks or natural weapons.

Variant: Separate Ability Loss

Some players don't like keeping track of ability scores that go down because they find it hard to recalculate their statistics based on their new ability modifiers. These players may find it easier to track ability loss separately, sort of the way subdual damage works. In this variant, for each 2 points of ability damage, the character suffers a −1 penalty to checks related to that ability. If the ability loss equals or exceeds the ability score, then the character suffers the effects of having a 0 score in that ability. Temporary ability damage goes away at the rate of 1 point per day.

This variant leads to very nearly the same results as standard ability loss does.

ANTIMAGIC

The beholder opens its large, central eye, and suddenly Lidda (who had been invisible) becomes visible, and Tordek, who had been flying, drops unceremoniously to the floor. The adventurers' magic weapons are now no better than masterworks, and their layers of magical protections are gone. The fire giant working with the beholder hefts her axe, grins, and charges.

An *antimagic field* spell or the main eye ray of a beholder cancels magic altogether. This spell-like effect is extremely powerful—the ultimate defense against magic.

- No supernatural ability, spell-like ability, or spell works in an area of antimagic (but extraordinary abilities still work).
- Antimagic does not dispel magic; it suppresses it. Once a magical effect is no longer affected by the antimagic (the antimagic fades, the center of the effect moves away, etc.), the magic returns. Spells that still have part of their duration left begin functioning again, magic items are once again useful, and so forth.
- Spell areas that include both an antimagic area and a normal area, but are not centered in the antimagic area, still function in the normal area. If the spell's center is in the antimagic area, then the spell is suppressed.
- Some artifacts are not hampered by antimagic. See the individual artifact descriptions in Chapter 8: Magic Items.
- Golems and other magic constructs, elementals, outsiders, and corporeal undead, still function in an antimagic area (though the antimagic area suppresses their supernatural, spell-like, and spell abilities normally). If such creatures are summoned or conjured, however, see below.
- Summoned or conjured creatures of any type and incorporeal undead wink out if they enter an antimagic field. They reappear in the same spot once the field goes away.
- Magic items with continuous effects, such as a *bag of holding*, do not function in the antimagic area, but their effects are not canceled (so the contents of the bag are unavailable, but do not spill out in an antimagic area, nor do they disappear forever).
- Two antimagic fields in the same place do not cancel each other out, nor do they stack.
- *Wall of force*, *prismatic wall*, and *prismatic sphere* are not affected by antimagic. *Break enchantment*, *dispel magic*, and *greater dispelling* spells do not dispel antimagic. *Mordenkainen's disjunction* has a 1% chance per caster level of destroying an *antimagic field*. If the *antimagic field* survives the disjunction, no items within it are disjoined.

BLINDSIGHT

The juvenile black dragon evokes darkness around the adventurers, and then they hear it bound among them. While they struggle in the blackness, the dragon strikes them unerringly, relying on other senses besides sight.

Some creatures have the extraordinary ability to use a nonvisual sense (or a combination of such senses) to operate effectively without vision. Such sense may include sensitivity to vibrations, acute scent, keen hearing, or echolocation. This ability makes invisibility and darkness (even magical darkness) irrelevant to the creature (though it still can't see ethereal creatures). This ability operates out to a range specified in the creature description.

- Blindsight never allows a creature to distinguish color or visual contrast. A creature cannot read with blindsight.
- Blindsight does not subject a creature to gaze attacks (even though darkvision does).
- Blinding attacks do not affect creatures using blindsight.
- Deafening attacks thwart blindsight if it relies on hearing (as a bat's "sonar" does).
- Blindsight works underwater but not in a vacuum.

BREATH WEAPON

A red dragon opens its mouth and exhales a gout of flame. The adventurers caught in the flame try to take cover behind corners and under tables, while one caught in the open ducks and covers her face with her arms.

While dragon fire is the classic example, a breath weapon may also be a cloud of poisonous gas, a bolt of lightning, or a stream of acid. The creature is actually expelling something from its mouth (rather than conjuring it by means of a spell or some other magical effect). Most creatures with breath weapons are limited to a number of uses per day or by a minimum length of time that must pass between uses. Such creatures are usually smart enough to save their breath weapon until they really need it.

- Using a breath weapon is typically a standard action.
- No attack roll is necessary. The breath simply fills its stated area. For example, a Medium-size black dragon breathes an acid spray 60 feet long, 5 feet high, and 5 feet wide.
- Any character caught in the area must make the appropriate saving throw or suffer the breath weapon's full effects. In many cases, a character who succeeds at his saving throw still takes half damage or some other reduced effect.
- Breath weapons are supernatural abilities except where noted (such as a *potion of fire breath*, which is spell-like, or nonmagical spittle, which is extraordinary).
- Creatures are immune to their own breath weapons.
- Creatures unable to breathe can still use breath weapons. (The name is something of a misnomer.)

CHARM AND COMPULSION

As the strange, wolflike creature loped toward Tordek, he realized that it was a good friend that meant him no harm. But why was Mialee casting a *fireball* at it? He needed to stop her from doing that again. Later, it was even worse when Lidda didn't know that the noble she was chatting up was actually a vampire. After one look into his eyes, she heard his voice in her mind, giving her orders that she obeyed without hesitation. She felt like a mere observer, trapped behind her own eyes, watching as "she" sought out her companions and invited them to a private party at the noble's estate.

Many abilities and spells can cloud the minds of characters and monsters, leaving them unable to tell friend from foe—or worse yet, deceiving them into thinking that their former friends are now their worst enemies. Two general types of enchantments affect characters and creatures: *charm* and *compulsion*.

Charming another creature gives the charming character the ability to befriend and suggest courses of actions to his minion, but the servitude is not absolute or mindless. Charms of this type include the various *charm* spells. Essentially, a charmed character retains free will but makes choices according to a skewed view of the world.

- The charmed creature doesn't gain any magical ability to understand his new friend.
- The charmed character retains his original alignment and allegiances, generally with the exception that he now regards the charming creature as a dear friend and will give great weight to his suggestions and directions.
- A charmed character fights his former allies only if they threaten his new friend, and even then he uses the least lethal means at his disposal as long as these tactics show any possibility of success (just as he would in a fight between two actual friends).
- A charmed character is entitled to an opposed Charisma check against his master in order to resist instructions or commands that would make him do something he wouldn't normally do even for a close friend. If he succeeds, he decides not to go along with that order but remains charmed.
- A charmed character never obeys a command that is obviously suicidal or immediately and grievously harmful to her.
- If the charming creature commands his minion to do something that the influenced character would be violently opposed to, the subject may attempt a new saving throw to break free of the influence altogether.
- Any charmed character who is openly attacked by the creature who charmed him or the charmer's apparent allies is automatically freed of the spell or effect.

Compulsion is a different matter altogether. A compulsion overrides the subject's free will in some way or simply changes the way the subject's mind works. A charm makes the subject a friend of the caster; a compulsion makes the subject obey the caster.

Regardless whether a character is charmed or compelled, he won't volunteer information or tactics that his master doesn't ask for. If a 1st-level wizard happens to have a *wand of fire* tucked into his boot, the vampire that is compelling him doesn't know that the wand is there and can't tell the wizard to give him the wand or use the wand on his former friends. The vampire, however, can say, "Hand over your most powerful magic item."

COLD

The frost giant strides out of the blizzard, oblivious to the freezing cold.

A "cold" creature, such as a frost giant, is immune to cold damage. It takes double damage from fire unless the fire attack allows a saving throw for half damage, in which case it takes half damage on a successful save and double damage on a failed save.

DAMAGE REDUCTION

The arrow sticks into the vampire, but she just pulls it out and laughs as the wound instantly heals. "You'll need to do better than that," she hisses.

Some magic creatures have the supernatural ability to instantly heal damage from weapons or to ignore blows altogether as though they were invulnerable.

- The number in a creature's damage reduction is the amount of hit points the creature ignores from normal attacks. Thus, a creature with a damage reduction number of 5 struck for 8 points of damage ignores 5 points and takes only 3.
- Usually, a certain type of weapon—usually a magic weapon—can overcome this reduction. This information is separated from the damage reduction number by a slash. For example, a

werewolf's damage reduction is 15/silver, meaning the werewolf ignores the first 15 points of damage from every normal attack unless the weapon is made of silver. If a dash follows the slash (as with the damage reduction that is a class feature of the barbarian), then the damage reduction is effective against any attack that does not ignore damage reduction.

- Any weapon more powerful than the type given after the slash also negates the ability, so a +1 *longsword* damages a werewolf normally, but a longsword made of some other special material won't work. For purposes of damage reduction, the power rankings are listed on Table 3–13: Damage Reduction Rankings.
- Whenever damage reduction completely negates the damage from an attack, it also negates most special effects that accompany the attack, such as injury type poison, a monk's stunning, and injury type disease. Damage reduction does not negate touch attacks, energy damage dealt along with an attack (such as fire damage from a fire elemental), or energy drains. Nor does it affect poisons or diseases delivered by inhalation, ingestion, or contact. Attacks that deal no damage because of the target's damage reduction do not disrupt spells.

A mind flayer in the light.

- Magical attacks and energy attacks (even mundane fire) ignore damage reduction.
- For purposes of harming other creatures with damage reduction, a creature's natural weapons count as weapons of the type that can ignore its own innate damage reduction. The amount of damage reduction is irrelevant. For example, a Large air elemental (damage reduction 10/+1) deals full damage to a werewolf, as if the elemental's attack were with a +1 weapon. However, damage reduction from spells, such as *stoneskin*, does not confer this ability.
- Sometimes damage reduction is instant healing. A sword slash across a demon's hide slices it open, but the open wound seals as fast as it's made. Sometimes damage reduction represents the creature's tough hide or body, such as with a gargoyle or iron golem. In either case, characters can see that conventional attacks don't work.

TABLE 3–13: DAMAGE REDUCTION RANKINGS

Power Rank	Weapon Type
Best	+5 enhancement bonus
2nd best	+4 enhancement bonus
3rd best	+3 enhancement bonus
4th best	+2 enhancement bonus
5th best	+1 enhancement bonus
Weakest	Silver, mithral, or other special material

DARKVISION

Tordek looks around a lightless cavern. He sees the chamber as a shadowless scene in black and white, fading into an indistinct gray 60 feet away.

Darkvision is the extraordinary ability to see with no light source at all, to a range specified for the creature.

- Darkvision is black and white only.
- Darkvision does not allow characters to see anything that they could not see otherwise—invisible objects are still invisible, and illusions are still visible as what they seem to be. Likewise, darkvision subjects a creature to gaze attacks normally.
- The presence of light does not spoil darkvision. If a character has darkvision with a 60-foot range, and he stands within a 30-foot radius of light, the character can see normally in the light, and 30 feet beyond the light because of his darkvision.

DEATH ATTACKS

Lidda, scouting ahead of her party, meets the gaze of the figure she discovers in the shadows. It's a bodak, whose eyes are death. She feels a sudden vertigo, as her spark of life itself is attacked by the undead creature's supernatural power.

The bodak's abyssal eyes kill with a glance. The dreaded *power word, kill* spell can slay without even allowing the victim a saving throw. A single *arrow of slaying* can fell a dragon. Even a fighter with 100 hit points can be killed by a single death attack. In most cases, death attacks allow the victim to make a Fortitude save to avoid the affect, but if the save fails the character dies instantly.

- *Raise dead* doesn't work on someone killed by a death attack.
- Death attacks slay instantly. There is no chance for a character to stabilize and thus stay alive.
- In case it matters, a dead character, no matter how she died, has –10 hit points.
- The spell *death ward* protects a character against these attacks.

DISEASE

A dirty, foul otyugh bites Tordek, but he survives the encounter. Two days later, however, a fever strikes, and he becomes shaky and tired. The fever lasts a few more days until he can throw it off. Then, gradually, his body recovers. Tordek counts himself lucky because some diseases weaken their victims permanently.

When a character is injured by a contaminated attack, touches an item smeared with diseased matter, or consumes disease-tainted food or drink, he must make an immediate Fortitude saving throw. If he succeeds, the disease has no effect—his immune system fought off the infection. If he fails, he takes damage after an incubation period. Once per day afterward he must make a successful Fortitude saving throw to avoid repeated damage. Two successful saving throws in a row indicate that he has fought off the disease and recovers, taking no more damage.

You can roll these Fortitude saving throws for the player so that he doesn't know whether the disease has taken hold.

Disease Descriptions

Diseases have various symptoms and are spread through a number of vectors. The characteristics of several typical diseases are summarized on Table 3–14: Diseases.

Disease: Diseases in *italic* are supernatural in nature. The rest are extraordinary.

Infection: The disease's method of delivery—ingested, inhaled, via injury, or contact. Keep in mind that some injury diseases may be transmitted by as small an injury as a flea bite and that most inhaled diseases can also be ingested (and vice versa).

DC: The DC for the saving throws to prevent infection (if the character has been infected), to prevent each instance of repeated damage, and to recover from the disease.

Incubation Period: The time before damage begins.

Damage: The damage the character takes after incubation and each day afterward. Ability score damage is temporary unless otherwise noted.

Types of Diseases: Typical diseases include the following:

Blinding Sickness: Spread in tainted water.

Cackle Fever: Symptoms include high fever, disorientation, and frequent bouts of hideous laughter. Also known as "the shrieks."

Demon Fever: Night hags spread it.

Devil Chills: Barbazu and pit fiends spread it. It takes three, not two, successful saves in a row to recover from devil chills.

Filth Fever: Dire rats and otyughs spread it. Those injured while in filthy surrounding might also catch it.

Mindfire: Feels like your brain is burning. Causes stupor.

Mummy Rot: Spread by mummies. Successful saving throws do not allow the character to recover (though they do prevent damage normally).

The same mind flayer seen with darkvision.

Red Ache: Skin turns red, bloated, and warm to the touch.

The Shakes: Causes involuntary twitches, tremors, and fits.

Slimy Doom: Victim turns into infectious goo from the inside out.

Healing Diseases

Use of the Heal skill can help a diseased character. Every time the diseased character makes a saving throw against disease effects, the healer makes a check. The diseased character can use the healer's result in place of his saving throw if the Heal result is higher. The diseased character must be in the healer's care and must spend most of each day resting.

Characters recover points lost to ability score damage at a rate of 1 per day, and this rule applies even while a disease is in progress. That means that a lucky character with a minor disease might be able to withstand it without accumulating any damage.

TABLE 3–14: DISEASES

Disease	Infection	DC	Incubation	Damage
Blinding sickness	Ingested	16	1d3 days	1d4 Str††
Cackle fever	Inhaled	16	1 day	1d6 Wis
Demon fever	Injury	18	1 day	1d6 Con**
Devil chills†	Injury	14	1d4 days	1d4 Str
Filth fever	Injury	12	1d3 days	1d3 Dex, 1d3 Con
Mindfire	Inhaled	12	1 day	1d4 Int
*Mummy rot**	Contact	20	1 day	1d6 Con
Red ache	Injury	15	1d3 days	1d6 Str
Shakes	Contact	13	1 day	1d8 Dex
Slimy doom	Contact	14	1 day	1d4 Con**

*Successful saves do not allow the character to recover. Only magical healing can save the character.

**When damaged, character must succeed at another saving throw or 1 point of temporary damage is permanent drain instead.

†The victim must make three successful Fortitude saving throws in a row to recover from devil chills.

††Each time the victim takes 2 or more damage from the disease, he must make another Fortitude save or be permanently blinded.

ENERGY DRAIN

An undead wight bashes an adventurer, and she feels cold and weak, while the wight moves with greater vigor than before. When the wight strikes her again, she grows weaker, as if her life force were slipping away. Her friends see her face drain of color and her flesh shrivel slightly. With the third strike, the adventurer falls to the ground, a desiccated husk. A fellow adventurer, also struck by the wight, survives the encounter. Over the next day his spirit rallies, and he throws off the hungry force that clawed at his very soul.

Some horrible creatures, especially undead monsters, possess a fearsome supernatural ability to drain levels from those they strike in combat. The creature making an energy drain attack draws a portion of its victim's life force from her.

- Most energy drains require a successful melee attack—mere physical contact is not enough. Monks, for instance, can pound such creatures with their fists without risking their life energy.
- Each successful energy draining attack bestows one or more negative levels on the opponent. A creature suffers the following penalties for each negative level it has gained:

  –1 to all skill and ability checks
  –1 to attacks
  –1 to saving throws
  –1 effective level (whenever the creature's level is used in a die roll or calculation, reduce it by one for each negative level)

- If the victim casts spells, she loses access to one spell as if she had cast her highest-level, currently available spell. (If she has more than one spell at her highest level, she chooses which she loses.) In addition, when she next prepares spells or regains spell slots, she gets one less spell slot at her highest spell level.

- Negative levels remain for 24 hours or until removed with a spell, such as *restoration*. After 24 hours, the afflicted creature must attempt a Fortitude save. The DC is 10 + one-half the attacker's Hit Dice + the attackers' Charisma modifier. (The DC is provided in the attacker's description.) If the saving throw succeeds, the negative level goes away with no harm to the creature. If the save fails, the negative level goes away, but the creature's level is also reduced by 1. The afflicted creature makes a separate saving throw for each negative level it has gained.
- A character who loses a level to an energy drain instantly loses one Hit Die. The character's base attack bonus, base saving throw bonuses, and special class abilities are now reduced to the new, lower level. A 2nd-level rogue, for example, normally has the evasion ability, but when she is drained to 1st level, she loses that ability. Likewise, the character loses any ability score gain, skill ranks, and any feat associated with the level (if any). If the exact ability score or skill ranks increased from a level now lost is unknown (or the player has forgotten), lose a point from the highest ability score or ranks from the highest-ranked skills. If a familiar or companion creature (such as a paladin's mount) has abilities tied to a character who has lost a level, the creature's abilities are adjusted to fit the character's new level.
- The victim's experience point total is immediately set to the midpoint of the previous level. For example, a character drained from 2nd to 1st level would drop to 500 experience points.
- A character with negative levels at least equal to her current level, or drained below 1st level, is instantly slain. Depending on the creature that killed her, she may rise the next night as a monster of that kind. If not, she rises as a wight.
- A creature gains 5 temporary hit points for each negative level it inflicts (though not if the negative level is caused by a spell or similar effect).

ETHEREALNESS

Out of nowhere, a spider the size of a horse appears and bites Mialee. Lidda wheels to stab it, but it's gone. The adventurers know the phase spider is somewhere nearby, lurking on the Ethereal Plane, watching them and waiting.

Phase spiders and certain other creatures can exist on the Ethereal Plane, which lies parallel to the Material Plane (the normal world). While on the Ethereal Plane, a creature is called ethereal.

- Ethereal creatures are invisible, inaudible, insubstantial, and scentless to creatures on the Material Plane (the normal world). Even most magical attacks have no effect on them. *See invisibility* and *true seeing* reveal ethereal creatures.
- An ethereal creature can see and hear into the Material Plane in a 60-foot radius, though material objects still block sight and sound. (An ethereal creature can't see through a material wall, for instance.) Things on the Material Plane, however, look gray, indistinct, and ghostly. An ethereal creature can't affect the Material Plane, not even magically. An ethereal creature, however, interacts with other ethereal creatures and objects the way material creatures interact with material creatures and objects.
- Ethereal creatures move in any direction (including up or down) at will. They do not need to walk on the ground, and material objects don't block them (though they can't see while their eyes are within solid material).
- Force effects are a special exception. A material force effect extends onto the Ethereal Plane, so that a *wall of force* blocks an ethereal creature, and a *magic missile* can strike one (provided the spellcaster can see the ethereal target). Gaze effects and abjurations also extend from the Material Plane to the Ethereal Plane. None of these effects extend from the Ethereal Plane to the Material Plane.

- Ghosts have a power called manifestation that allows them to appear on the Material Plane as incorporeal creatures. Still, they are on the Ethereal Plane, and another ethereal creature can interact normally with a manifesting ghost.
- Ethereal creatures pass through and operate in water as easily as air.
- Ethereal creatures do not fall or suffer falling damage.

EVASION AND IMPROVED EVASION

The blue dragon's lightning breath blasts Tordek, Mialee, and Lidda. They all twist and duck to escape the worst of the attack, but Tordek and Mialee are still burned. Lidda is merely sweaty.

These extraordinary abilities allow the target of an area attack to leap or twist out of the way. Rogues and monks have evasion and improved evasion as class features, but certain other creatures have these abilities, too.

- If subjected to an attack that allows a Reflex save for half damage, a character with evasion takes no damage on a successful save.
- As with a Reflex save for any creature, a character must have room to move in order to evade. A bound character or one in a completely restrictive area (crawling through a 2 1/2-foot-wide shaft, for example) cannot use evasion.
- As with a Reflex save for any creature, evasion is a reflexive ability. The character need not know that the attack is coming to use evasion.
- Rogues and monks cannot use evasion in medium or heavy armor. Some creatures with the innate evasion ability do not face this limitation.
- Improved evasion is like evasion, except that even on a failed saving throw the character takes only half damage.

FAST HEALING

As Tordek fights the red slaad, the wounds he has already given it heal before his eyes.

The creature has the extraordinary ability to regain hit points at an exceptional rate. Except for what is noted here, fast healing is just like natural healing (see page 129 in the *Player's Handbook*).

- At the beginning of each of the creature's turns, it heals a certain number of hit points (defined in its description, usually 1 or 2).
- Unlike regeneration (see below), fast healing does not allow a creature to regrow or reattach lost body parts.
- A creature that has taken both subdual and normal damage heals the subdual damage first.
- Fast healing does not restore hit points lost from starvation, thirst, or suffocation.
- Fast healing does not increase the number of hit points regained when a creature *polymorphs*.

FEAR

A young adult green dragon charges the adventurers. Tordek feels a twinge of fear but grits his teeth and ignores it. Lidda doesn't stand up as well to the charge. She holds her ground, but fear takes the edge off her skill. The cohort who had recently joined them, however, drops her sword and flees recklessly, her screams fading in the distance.

Spells, magic items, and certain monsters can affect characters with fear. In most cases, the character makes a Will saving throw to resist this effect, and a failed roll means that the character is shaken, frightened, or panicked.

Shaken: Characters who are shaken suffer a –2 morale penalty to attack rolls, saves, and checks.

Frightened: Characters who are frightened are shaken, and in addition they flee from the source of their fear as quickly as they can, although they can choose the path of their flight. Other than that stipulation, once they are out of sight (or hearing) of the source of their fear, they can act as they want. However, if the duration of their fear continues, characters can be forced to flee once more if the source of their fear presents itself again. Characters unable to flee can fight (though they are still shaken).

Panicked: Characters who are panicked are shaken, and in addition they have a 50% chance to drop what they're holding, and they run away from the source of their fear as quickly as they can. Other than running away from the source, their path is random. They flee from all other dangers that confront them rather than facing those dangers. Panicked characters cower if they are prevented from fleeing.

Becoming Even More Fearful: Fear effects are cumulative. A shaken character who is made shaken again becomes frightened, and a shaken character who is made frightened becomes panicked instead. A frightened character who is made shaken or frightened becomes panicked instead.

FIRE

Red-hot boulders fly out of an inferno, striking the unexpecting adventurers. Looking closely, they can see the figure of a fire giant in the roaring flames, laughing.

A "fire" creature is immune to fire damage. It takes double damage from cold unless the cold attack allows a saving throw for half damage, in which case it takes half damage on a successful save and double damage on a failed save.

GASEOUS FORM

The characters have the vampire cornered, when suddenly her form gets blurry. In an instant, she and her gear, including the signet ring that the adventurers need, have turned into a mist, which floats out through an arrow slit in the stone wall.

Some creatures have the supernatural or spell-like ability to take the form of a cloud of vapor or gas.

- Gaseous creatures can't run but can fly. A gaseous creature can move about and do the things that a cloud of gas can conceivably do, such as issue under the crack of a door. It can't, however, pass through solid matter.
- Gaseous creatures can't attack physically or cast spells with verbal, somatic, material, or focus components. They lose their supernatural abilities (except for the supernatural ability to assume gaseous form, of course).
- Creatures in gaseous form have damage reduction 20/+1. Spells, spell-like abilities, and supernatural abilities affect them normally. Creatures in gaseous form lose all benefit of material armor (including natural armor), though size, Dexterity, deflection bonuses, and armor bonuses from force armor (for example, from the *mage armor* spell) still apply.
- Gaseous creatures do not need to breathe and are immune to attacks involving breathing (troglodyte stench, poison gas, etc.).
- Gaseous creatures can't enter water or other liquid.
- Gaseous creatures are not ethereal or incorporeal.
- Gaseous creatures are affected by winds or other forms of moving air to the extent that the wind pushes them in the direction the wind is moving. However, even the strongest wind can't disperse or damage a creature in gaseous form.
- Discerning a creature in gaseous form from natural mist requires a Spot check (DC 15). Creatures in gaseous form attempting to hide in an area with mist, smoke, or other gas gain a +20 bonus.

GAZE ATTACKS

The medusa looks around, throwing dangerous glances everywhere, and focusing its eyes on specific victims. Lidda closes her eyes and tries to aim her arrows by ear. Jozan averts his eyes but tries to watch the creature with peripheral vision so he knows where to project his *searing light* spell. Tordek trusts fate and looks the thing in the eye as he swings his mighty axe. Magic washes through him, and he shrugs it off. Jozan, however, accidentally catches the thing's eye, and he's not strong enough to resist. His body hardens and turns to stone.

While the medusa's gaze is well known, gaze attacks can also charm, curse, or even kill. Gaze attacks not produced by a spell (such as *eyebite*) are supernatural.

- Each character within range of a gaze attack must attempt a saving throw (usually Fortitude or Will) each round at the beginning of his turn.
- An opponent can avert his eyes from the creature's face, looking at the creature's body, watching its shadow, or tracking the creature in a reflective surface. Each round, the opponent has a 50% chance of not having to make a saving throw. The creature with the gaze attack gains one-half concealment against the opponent (so any attack the opponent makes against the creature has a 20% miss chance).
- An opponent can shut his eyes, turn his back on the creature, or wear a blindfold. In these cases, the opponent does not need to make a saving throw. The creature with the gaze attack gains total concealment against the opponent as if the creature were invisible. Thus, any attack the opponent makes against the creature has a 50% miss chance, and the opponent can't use sight to target attacks.
- A creature with a gaze attack can actively attempt to use its gaze as an attack action. The creature simply chooses a target within range, and that opponent must attempt a saving throw. If the target has chosen to defend against the gaze as discussed above, the opponent gets a chance to avoid the saving throw (either 50% chance for averting or 100% chance for shutting eyes). It is possible for an opponent to save against a creature's gaze twice during the same round, once before its own action and once during the creature's action.
- Looking at the creature's image (such as in a mirror or as part of an illusion) does not subject the viewer to a gaze attack.
- A creature is immune to its own gaze attack.
- If visibility is limited (by dim lighting, a fog, etc.) so that it results in concealment, there is a percentage chance equal to the normal miss chance for that amount of concealment that a character won't need to make a saving throw in a given round. This chance is not cumulative with chances to avoid the gaze, but instead is rolled separately.
- Invisible creatures cannot use gaze attacks.
- Characters using darkvision in complete darkness are affected by a gaze attack normally.
- Unless specified otherwise, an intelligent creature with a gaze attack can control its gaze attack and "turn it off" when so desired.

INCORPOREALITY

Lidda spots a translucent face poking forth from a wall, but it's gone by the time she alerts her companions. The party starts to back out of the ruined throne room they're exploring, when suddenly several ghostly figures fly out of the walls toward them. Tordek raises his magic shield to fend off a spectre's attack, but the incorporeal hand passes through the shield and through his magic plate armor. It touches his heart, which grows suddenly cold.

Spectres, wraiths, and a few other creatures lack physical bodies. Such creatures are insubstantial and can't be touched by nonmagical matter or energy. Likewise, they cannot manipulate objects or exert physical force on objects. However, incorporeal beings have a tangible presence that sometimes seems like a physical attack (such as the touch of a spectre) against a corporeal creature.

- Incorporeal creatures can only be harmed by other incorporeal creatures, by +1 or better weapons, or by spells, spell-like

effects, or supernatural effects. They are immune to all non-magical attack forms. They are not burned by normal fires, affected by natural cold, or harmed by mundane acids.

- Even when struck by magic or magic weapons, an incorporeal creature has a 50% chance to ignore any damage from a corporeal source—except for a force effect, such as *magic missile*, or damage inflicted by a ghost touch weapon (page 186).
- Incorporeal creatures move in any direction (including up or down) at will. They do not need to walk on the ground.
- Incorporeal creatures can pass through solid objects at will, although they cannot see when their eyes are within solid matter.
- Incorporeal creatures are inaudible unless they decide to make noise.
- The physical attacks of incorporeal creatures ignore material armor, even magic armor, unless it is made of force (such as *mage armor* or *bracers of defense*) or has the ghost touch ability.
- Incorporeal creatures pass through and operate in water as easily as they do in air.
- Incorporeal creatures cannot fall or suffer falling damage.
- Corporeal creatures cannot trip or grapple incorporeal creatures.
- Incorporeal creatures have no weight and do not set off traps that are triggered by weight.
- Incorporeal creatures do not leave footprints, have no scent, and make no noise unless they manifest, and even then they only make noise intentionally.

INVISIBILITY

An invisible quasit is spying on the adventurers when Lidda gets a strange feeling. "There's something here," she whispers, and signals for silence as she tries to locate it by ear.

The ability to move about unseen is wonderful, but it's not foolproof. While they can't be seen, invisible creatures can be heard, smelled, or felt.

- Invisibility makes a creature undetectable by vision, including darkvision.
- A creature can generally notice the presence of an active invisible creature within 30 feet with a Spot check (DC 20). The observer gains a hunch that "something's there" but can't see it or target it accurately with an attack. A creature who is holding still is practically impossible to

Incorporeal wraiths lunge toward an adventurer.

notice (DC 30). An inanimate object, or an unliving creature holding still, or a completely immobile creature, is even harder to spot (DC 40). It's practically impossible (+20 DC) to pinpoint an invisible creature's location with a Spot check, and even if a character succeeds at such a check, the invisible creature still benefits from full concealment (50% miss chance).

- A creature can use hearing to find an invisible creature. A character can make a Listen check for this purpose as a free action each round. A Listen check result at least equal to the invisible creature's Move Silently check result reveals its presence. (A creature with no ranks in Move Silently makes a Move Silently check as a Dexterity check to which an armor check penalty applies.)

A successful check lets a character hear an invisible creature "over there somewhere." It's practically impossible to pinpoint the exact location of an invisible creature. A Listen check that beats the DC by 20 reveals the invisible creature's location.

TABLE 3–15: LISTEN CHECK DCs TO DETECT INVISIBLE CREATURES

Invisible Creature Is:	DC
In combat or speaking	0
Moving at half speed	Move Silently check
Moving at full speed	Move Silently check at –4
Running or charging	Move Silently check at –20
Some distance away	+1 per 10 feet
Behind an obstacle (door)	+5
Behind an obstacle (stone wall)	+15

- A creature can grope about to find an invisible creature. A character can make a touch attack with his hands or a weapon into two adjacent 5-foot areas using a standard action. If an invisible target is in the designated area, there is a 50% miss chance on the touch attack. If successful, the groping character inflicts no damage but has successfully pinpointed the invisible creature's current location. (If the invisible creature moves, its location, obviously, is once again unknown.)
- If an invisible creature strikes a character, the character struck still knows the location of the creature that struck him (until, of course, the invisible creature moves). The only exception is if the invisible creature has a reach greater than 5 feet. In this case, the struck character knows the general location of the creature but has not pinpointed the exact location.
- If a character tries to attack an invisible creature whose location he has pinpointed, he attacks normally, but the invisible creature still benefits from full concealment (and thus a 50% miss chance). At your option, a particularly large and slow creature might get a smaller miss chance. If a wizard projects a disintegration ray into the center of an invisible Huge black pudding, you could reduce or ignore the miss chance; it's pretty hard to miss something that big.
- If a character tries to attack an invisible creature whose location he has not pinpointed, have the player choose the space where the character will direct the attack. If the invisible creature is there, conduct the attack normally. If the enemy's not there, roll the miss chance as if it were there, don't let the player see

the result, and tell him that the character has missed. That way the player doesn't know whether the attack missed because the enemy's not there or because you successfully rolled the miss chance.

- If an invisible character picks up a visible object, the object remains visible. One could coat an invisible object with flour to at least keep track of its position (until the flour fell off or blew away). An invisible creature can pick up a small visible item and hide it on his person (tucked in a pocket or behind a cloak) and render it effectively invisible.
- Invisible creatures leave tracks. They can be tracked normally. Footprints in sand, mud, or other soft surfaces can give enemies clues to an invisible creature's location.
- An invisible creature in the water displaces water, revealing its location. The invisible creature, however, is still hard to see and benefits from one-half concealment (20% miss chance).
- A creature with the scent ability can detect invisible creatures as it would a visible one (see Scent, below).
- A creature with the Blind-Fight feat has a better chance to hit an invisible creature. Roll the miss chance twice, and he misses only if both rolls indicate a miss. (Alternatively, make one 25% miss roll rather than two 50% miss rolls.)
- A creature with blindsight can attack (and otherwise interact with) creatures regardless of invisibility.
- An invisible burning torch still gives off light, as does an invisible object with a *light* spell (or similar spell) cast upon it.
- Ethereal creatures are invisible. Since ethereal creatures are not materially present, Spot checks, Listen checks, Scent, Blind-Fight, and Blindsight don't help locate them. Incorporeal creatures are often invisible. Scent, Blind-Fight, and blindsight don't help creatures find or attack invisible, incorporeal creatures, but Spot checks and possibly Listen checks can help.
- Invisible creatures cannot use gaze attacks.
- Invisibility does not thwart *detect* spells.
- Since some creatures can detect or even see invisible creatures, it is helpful to be able to hide even when invisible.

LOW-LIGHT VISION

Lidda hears something stalking through the trees beyond the circle of light thrown up by the campfire, but she can't see it. She nudges Mialee and points. Mialee looks into the darkness and says, "Displacer beasts."

Characters with low-light vision have eyes that are so sensitive to light that they can see twice as far as normal in dim light. Thus, if a group of adventurers passes down a dark passage with a torch illuminating a 20-foot radius, an elf with low-light vision can see everything within 40 feet of the torch. Low-light vision is color vision. A spellcaster with low-light vision can read a scroll as long as even the tiniest candle flame is next to her as a source of light.

Characters with low-light vision can see outdoors on a moonlit night as well as they can during the day.

PARALYSIS AND *HOLD*

A cleric of Hextor brandishes his unholy symbol at Tordek, gestures with it, and speaks unintelligible words. Suddenly Tordek feels his body freeze up, and he can't will his limbs to obey. He stands rigid and helpless. He hears a fight raging around him and sees whatever passes in front of his eyes, but he can't turn to see how his friends are faring. The sound of his own breath and the beating of his heart fill his ears. Then he hears someone behind him, and all he can do is hope it's a friend.

Some monsters and spells have the supernatural or spell-like ability to paralyze or *hold* their victims, immobilizing them through magical means. (Paralysis from toxins is discussed in the Poison section below.)

- A paralyzed or *held* character cannot move, speak, or take any physical action. He is rooted to the spot, frozen and helpless. Not even friends can move his limbs. He may take purely mental actions, such as casting a spell with no components.
- Paralysis works on the body, and a character can usually resist it with a Fortitude saving throw. *Hold* is an enchantment, a mind-affecting compulsion. A character usually resists it with a Will save.
- A winged creature flying in the air at the time that it is *held* or paralyzed cannot flap its wings and falls. A swimmer can't swim and may drown.

POISON

A giant scorpion grabs Jozan in its pincers and stings him. The wound burns like fire, and pain spreads through his body, bringing a strange weakness with it. Jozan struggles to free himself from the pincers, but his arms have become weak, and the scorpion just stings him again. Mialee uses *polymorph other* to turn the scorpion into a carp, so Jozan is safe from further harm, but the poison still courses through his veins. Soon it overcomes him, and he falls helpless to the ground.

When a character takes damage from an attack with a poisoned weapon, touches an item smeared with contact poison, consumes poisoned food or drink, or is otherwise poisoned, he must make a Fortitude saving throw. If he fails, he suffers the poison's initial damage (usually ability damage). Even if he succeeds, he typically faces more damage 1 minute later, which he can also avoid with a successful Fortitude saving throw.

One dose of poison smeared on a weapon or some other object affects just a single target. A poisoned weapon or object retains its venom until the weapon scores a hit or the object is touched (unless the poison is wiped off before a target comes in contact with it). Any poison smeared on an object or exposed to the elements in any way—if the vial containing it is left unstoppered, for instance—remains potent until it is touched or used.

Although supernatural and spell-like poisons are possible, poisonous effects are almost always extraordinary.

Poisons are described on Table 3–16: Poisons (see the next page).

Perils of Using Poison

A character has a 5% chance to expose himself to a poison whenever he applies it to a weapon or otherwise readies it for use. Additionally, a character who rolls a 1 on an attack roll with a poisoned weapon must make a Reflex saving throw (DC 15) or accidentally poison himself with the weapon.

Poison Immunities

Wyverns, medusas, and other creatures with natural poison attacks are immune to their own poison. Nonliving creatures (constructs and undead) and creatures without metabolisms (such as elementals) are always immune to poison. Oozes, plants, and certain kinds of creatures (such as tanar'ri) are also immune to poison, although conceivably a special poison could be concocted specifically to harm them.

POLYMORPH

Lidda thought that the captain of the guard was acting a little strangely, but she put it down to stress. When she turned away, however, she heard a strange squishing sound behind her. She spun around to see that the man had turned into a 10-foot-tall blue-skinned monster, complete with a greatsword—an ogre mage.

Magic can cause creatures and characters to change their shapes—sometimes against their will, but usually to gain an advantage. Polymorphed creatures retain their own minds but have new physical forms.

- The *polymorph other* spell (see the *Player's Handbook*) defines the general polymorph effect.

- Creatures that polymorph themselves with an ability (not a spell) do not suffer disorientation (as described in *polymorph other*).
- Since creatures do not change types, a slaying or bane weapon designed to kill or harm creatures of a specific type affects those creatures even if they are *polymorphed*. Likewise, a creature *polymorphed* into the form of a creature of a different type is not subject to slaying and bane effects directed at that type of creature.
- A ranger's favored enemy bonus is based on knowing what the foe is, so if a creature that is a ranger's favored enemy polymorphs into another form, the ranger is denied his bonus.
- A dwarf's bonus for fighting giants is based on shape and size, so he does not gain a bonus against a giant *polymorphed* into something else, but does gain the bonus against any creature *polymorphed* into a giant.

PSIONICS

The mind flayer turns its alien visage toward the adventurers, and the air seems to ripple as a wave of psychic force cascades toward them. Mialee resists the attack, but her friends are stunned. She casts *hold monster* on the thing, and it becomes rigid. Nevertheless, she feels the creature's mind enter her own as it tries to win her allegiance by psychic force.

Telepathy, mental combat and psychic powers—psionics is a catchall word that describes special mental abilities possessed by various creatures. These are spell-like abilities that a creature generates from the power of its mind alone—no other outside magical force or ritual is needed. The most well known of the psionic creatures is the dreaded mind flayer, which blasts its prey's mind and then devours the brain of the prey while it lies stunned. Each creature's description in the *Monster Manual* contains details on its psionic abilities (if it has any).

Psionic attacks almost always allow Will saving throws to resist them. However, not all psionic attacks are mental attacks. Some psionic abilities allow the psionic creature to reshape its own body, heal its wounds, or teleport great distances. Some psionic creatures can see into the future, the past, and the present (in far-off locales) as well as read the minds of others.

Variant: Nonmagical Psionics

Psionics aren't magical at all, but a different sort of extraordinary power altogether. Antimagic fields have no power over psionics (and likewise, most psionic abilities cannot interfere with magic). A creature's special immunities or resistances to magic do not protect it from psionic abilities.

The danger of this variant is that, without the traditional checks that exist for magic, psionic abilities quickly threaten to become overwhelmingly powerful. Since conventional magical defenses don't work, psionic defenses need to be added to the treasure tables and spells.

RAYS

A thin, green beam leaps from one of the beholder's eyes and streaks across the chamber at Mialee. She twists to avoid it (as she

TABLE 3–16: POISONS

Poison	Type	Initial Damage	Secondary Damage	Price
Small centipede poison	Injury DC 11	1d2 Dex	1d2 Dex	90 gp
Greenblood oil	Injury DC 13	1 Con	1d2 Con	100 gp
Medium-size spider venom	Injury DC 14	1d4 Str	1d6 Str	150 gp
Bloodroot	Injury DC 12	0	1d4 Con + 1d3 Wis	100 gp
Purple worm poison	Injury DC 24	1d6 Str	1d6 Str	700 gp
Large scorpion venom	Injury DC 18	1d6 Str	1d6 Str	200 gp
Wyvern poison	Injury DC 17	2d6 Con	2d6 Con	3,000 gp
Blue whinnis	Injury DC 14	1 Con	Unconsciousness	120 gp
Giant wasp poison	Injury DC 18	1d6 Dex	1d6 Dex	210 gp
Shadow essence	Injury DC 17	1 Str*	2d6 Str	250 gp
Black adder venom	Injury DC 12	0	1d6 Str	120 gp
Deathblade	Injury DC 20	1d6 Con	2d6 Con	1,800 gp
Malyss root paste	Contact DC 16	1 Dex	2d4 Dex	500 gp
Nitharit	Contact DC 13	0	3d6 Con	650 gp
Dragon bile	Contact DC 26	3d6 Str	0	1,500 gp
Sassone leaf residue	Contact DC 16	2d12 hp	1d6 Con	300 gp
Terinav root	Contact DC 16	1d6 Dex	2d6 Dex	750 gp
Carrion crawler brain juice	Contact DC 13	Paralysis	0	200 gp
Black lotus extract	Contact DC 20	3d6 Con	3d6 Con	2,500 gp
Oil of taggit	Ingested DC 15	0	Unconsciousness	90 gp
Id moss	Ingested DC 14	1d4 Int	2d6 Int	125 gp
Striped toadstool	Ingested DC 11	1 Wis	2d6 Wis + 1d4 Int	180 gp
Arsenic	Ingested DC 13	1 Con	1d8 Con	120 gp
Lich dust	Ingested DC 17	2d6 Str	1d6 Str	250 gp
Dark reaver powder	Ingested DC 18	2d6 Con	1d6 Con + 1d6 Str	300 gp
Ungol dust	Inhaled DC 15	1 Cha	1d6 Cha + 1 Cha*	1,000 gp
Burnt othur fumes	Inhaled DC 18	1 Con*	3d6 Con	2,100 gp
Insanity mist	Inhaled DC 15	1d4 Wis	2d6 Wis	1,500 gp

Type: The poison's method of delivery—ingested, inhaled, via an injury, or contact—and the DC needed to save.

Initial Damage: The damage the character takes immediately upon failing his saving throw against this type of poison. Ability score damage is temporary unless marked with an asterisk (*), in which case the loss is a permanent drain. Paralysis lasts for 2d6 minutes.

Secondary Damage: The amount of damage the character takes 1 minute after exposure as a result of the poisoning, if he fails a second saving throw. Unconsciousness lasts for 1d3 hours. Loss marked with an asterisk is permanent drain instead of temporary damage.

Price: The cost of one dose (one vial) of the poison. It is not possible to use or apply poison in any quantity smaller than one dose. The purchase and possession of poison is always illegal, and even in big cities it can only be obtained from specialized, less than reputable sources.

would move to avoid an arrow or a sword), but the beam flies true and connects. Green energy encompasses her in a flash, trying to disintegrate her. Her face contorts as she struggles to resist the spell. In an instant, the green energy is gone, and Mialee is safe. The beholder then projects a second eye beam at her.

All ray attacks, whether from a *ray of enfeeblement* spell or a beholder's eye ray, require the attacker to make a successful ranged touch attack against the target. Rays have varying ranges, which are simple maximums. A ray's attack roll never suffers a range penalty. Even if a ray hits, it usually allows the target to make a saving throw (Fortitude or Will). Rays never require a Reflex saving throw, but if a character's Dexterity bonus to AC is high, it might be hard to hit her with the ray in the first place.

REGENERATION

The trolls' wounds kept healing up as Tordek fought them, until Mialee dropped a *fireball* on all of them (and hoped that Tordek could take the heat).

Creatures with this extraordinary ability recover from wounds quickly and can even regrow or reattach severed body parts.

- Damage dealt to the creature is treated as subdual damage, and the creature automatically cures itself of subdual damage at a fixed rate (for example, 3 points per round for a troll).
- Certain attack forms, typically fire and acid, deal damage to the creature normally; that sort of damage doesn't convert to subdual damage and so doesn't go away. The creature's description includes the details.
- These creatures can regrow lost portions of their bodies and can reattach severed limbs or body parts. Severed parts die if they are not reattached.
- Regeneration does not restore hit points lost from starvation, thirst, or suffocation.
- Attack forms that don't deal hit point damage (for example, disintegration and most poisons) ignore regeneration.
- An attack that can cause instant death, such as a coup de grace, massive damage, or an assassin's death attack, only threatens the creature with death if it is delivered by weapons that deal it normal damage.

RESISTANCE TO ENERGY

Mialee's *fireball* singed the janni, but mostly the spell just made it angrier.

A creature with resistance to energy has the ability (usually extraordinary) to ignore some damage of a certain type (such as cold, electricity, or fire) each round, but it does not have total immunity.

- Each ability is defined by what energy type it resists and how many points of damage are resisted. For example, a janni has fire resistance 30. A janni can ignore the first 30 points of fire damage it takes each round. It doesn't matter whether the damage has a mundane or magical source.
- The creature still makes saving throws normally. A janni, for example, makes a Reflex save against a 5d6 fireball even though the fireball can't hurt it; if the janni succeeds at the save and takes half damage, only that amount of damage counts toward its resistance that round.
- Count the creature's resistance from the start of its turn to the start of its turn the next round. Its resistance "resets" on its turn.
- When resistance completely negates the damage from an energy attack, the attack does not disrupt a spell.
- This resistance does not stack with the resistance that a spell, such as *endure elements*, might provide.

SCENT

Tordek is dragging Jozan's wounded, unconscious form out of the dungeon when he hears the sound of pursuit. Behind them is a carrion crawler, following the scent of blood. Lidda waits to ambush it while Tordek keeps going, but the aberration smells her and is ready for her when she comes out of hiding.

This extraordinary ability lets a creature detect approaching enemies, sniff out hidden foes, and track by sense of smell.

- The creature can detect opponents by sense of smell, generally within 30 feet. If the opponent is upwind, the range is 60 feet. If it is downwind, the range is 15 feet. Strong scents, such as smoke or rotting garbage, can be detected at twice the ranges noted above. Overpowering scents, such as skunk musk or troglodyte stench, can be detected at three times these ranges.
- The creature detects another creature's presence but not its specific location. Noting the direction of the scent is a standard action. If it moves within 5 feet of the scent's source, the creature can pinpoint that source.
- The creature can follow tracks by smell, making a Wisdom check to find or follow a track. The typical DC for a fresh trail is 10. The DC increases or decreases depending on how strong the quarry's odor is, the number of creatures, and the age of the trail. For each hour that the trail is cold, the DC increases by 2. The ability otherwise follows the rules for the Track feat. Creatures tracking by scent ignore the effects of surface conditions and poor visibility.
- Creatures with the scent ability can identify familiar odors just as humans do familiar sights.
- Water, particularly running water, ruins a trail for air-breathing creatures. Water-breathing creatures such as sharks, however, have the scent ability and can use it in the water easily.
- False, powerful odors (such as red herring) can easily mask other scents. The presence of such an odor completely spoils the ability to properly detect or identify creatures, and the base Wilderness Lore DC to track becomes 20 rather than 10.

Variant Rule: Characters with Scent

Half-orcs and gnomes, as well as many types of NPC humanoids such as orcs and gnolls, can take Scent as a feat. The feat's prerequisite is Wisdom 11+. Scent is more powerful than many feats, however, and this option may make these characters and creatures too good.

SPELL RESISTANCE (SR)

Mialee's fireball engulfs the ogre mage. It flinches reflexively, but it doesn't try to avoid the blast. When the flames dissipate, the ogre mage is untouched.

Spell resistance is the extraordinary ability to avoid being affected by spells. (Some spells also grant spell resistance.)

- To affect a creature that has spell resistance, a spellcaster must make a caster level check (1d20 + caster level) at least equal to the creature's spell resistance rating. (The defender's spell resistance rating is like a magical AC.) If the caster fails the check, the spell doesn't affect the creature. The possessor does not have to do anything special to use spell resistance. The creature need not even be aware of the threat for its spell resistance to operate.
- Only spells and spell-like abilities are subject to spell resistance. Extraordinary and supernatural abilities (including enhancement bonuses on magic weapons) are not. For example, the *fear* effect from a *rod of lordly might* is subject to spell resistance because it is a spell-like effect. The rod's combat bonuses (such as the +2 bonus from the rod's mace form) are not. A creature can have some abilities that are subject to spell resistance and some that are not. For example, an androsphinx's divine spells are subject to spell resistance, but its roar is not. (The roar is a supernatural ability.) A cleric's spells are subject to spell resistance, but his

use of positive or negative energy is not. Even some spells ignore spell resistance; see When Spell Resistance Applies, below.

- A creature can voluntarily lower its spell resistance. Doing so is a standard action that does not provoke an attack of opportunity. Once a creature lowers its resistance, it remains down until the creature's next turn. At the beginning of the creature's next turn, the creature's spell resistance automatically returns unless the creature intentionally keeps it down (also a standard action that does not provoke an attack of opportunity).

- A creature's spell resistance never interferes with its own spells, items, or abilities.

- A creature with spell resistance cannot impart this power to others by touching them or standing in their midst. Only the rarest of creatures and a few magic items have the ability to bestow spell resistance upon another.

- Spell resistance does not stack. It overlaps. If a cleric wearing +1 *chainmail* that grants him SR 15 casts *holy aura*, which grants SR 25 against evil spells and spells cast by evil creatures, he has SR 25 against the aforementioned spells and SR 15 against other spells and spell-like abilities.

by the spell. For example, if an ogre mage flies within 10 feet of a *wall of fire*, the caster must make a caster level check against the ogre mage's SR of 18. If the caster fails, the wall does not damage the ogre mage.

Check spell resistance only

Mialee fails to overcome the spell resistance of a marilith.

When Spell Resistance Applies

Each spell described in the *Player's Handbook* includes an entry that indicates whether spell resistance applies to the spell. In general, whether spell resistance applies depends on what the spell does:

- *Targeted Spells:* Spell resistance applies if the spell is targeted at the creature. Some individually targeted spells, such as *magic missile* when cast by a 3rd-level caster, can be directed at several creatures simultaneously. In such cases, a creature's spell resistance applies only to the portion of the spell actually targeted at that creature. If several different resistant creatures are subjected to such a spell, each checks its spell resistance separately.

- *Area Spells:* Spell resistance applies if the resistant creature is within the spell's area. It protects the resistant creature without affecting the spell itself.

- *Effect Spells:* Most effect spells summon or create something and are not subject to spell resistance. For instance, *summon monster I* summons a monster that can attack a creature with spell resistance normally. Sometimes, however, spell resistance applies to effect spells, usually to effect spells that affect a creature more or less directly, such as *web*.

Spell resistance can protect a creature from a spell that's already been cast. Check spell resistance when the creature is first affected

once for any particular casting of a spell or use of a spell-like ability. If spell resistance fails the first time, it fails each time the creature encounters that same casting of the spell. Likewise, if the spell resistance succeeds the first time, it always succeeds. For example, a succubus encounters Jozan's *blade barrier* spell. If the cleric makes a successful roll to overcome the spell resistance of the succubus, the creature takes damage from the spell. If the succubus survives and enters that particular *blade barrier* a second time, the creature will be damaged again. No second roll is needed. If the creature has voluntarily lowered its spell resistance and is then subjected to a spell, the creature still has a single chance to resist that spell later, when its spell resistance is up.

Spell resistance has no effect unless the energy created or released by the spell actually goes to work on the resistant creature's mind or body. If the spell acts on anything else (the air, the ground, the room's light), and the creature is affected as a consequence, no roll is required. Creatures can be harmed by a spell without being directly affected. For example, a *daylight* spell harms a drow elf because drow are sensitive to light. *Daylight*, however, usually is cast on the area containing the drow, making it bright, not on the drow itself, so the effect is indirect. Spell resistance would only apply if someone tried to cast *daylight* on an object the drow was holding.

Spell resistance does not apply if an effect fools the creature's senses or reveals something about the creature, such as *minor illusion* or *detect thoughts* does.

Magic actually has to be working for spell resistance to apply. Spells that have instantaneous durations but lasting results aren't subject to spell resistance unless the resistant creature is exposed to the spell the instant it is cast. For example, a creature with spell resistance can't undo a *wall of stone* that has already been cast.

When in doubt about whether a spell's effect is direct or indirect, consider the spell's school.

Abjuration: The target creature must be harmed, changed, or restricted in some manner for spell resistance to apply. Perception changes, such as *nondetection*, aren't subject to spell resistance. Abjurations that block or negate attacks are not subject to an attacker's spell resistance—it is the protected creature that is affected by the spell (becoming immune or resistant to the attack).

Conjuration: These spells are usually not subject to spell resistance unless the spell conjures some form of energy, such as *Melf's acid arrow* or *power word, stun*. Spells that summon creatures or produce effects that function like creatures are not subject to spell resistance.

Divination: These spells do not affect creatures directly and are not subject to spell resistance, even though what they reveal about a creature might be very damaging.

Enchantment: Since enchantment spells affect creatures' minds, they are typically subject to spell resistance.

Evocation: If an evocation spell deals damage to the creature, it has a direct effect. If the spell damages something else, it has an indirect effect. For example, a *lightning bolt* cast at a resistant creature is subject to spell resistance (which would protect only the creature but would not affect the spell itself). If the *lightning bolt* is cast at a chamber's ceiling, bringing down a rain of debris, it is not subject to spell resistance.

Illusion: These spells are almost never subject to spell resistance. Illusions that inflict a direct attack, such as *phantasmal killer* or *shadow evocation*, are exceptions.

Necromancy: Most of these spells alter the target creature's life force and are subject to spell resistance. Unusual necromancy spells, such as *spectral hand*, don't affect other creatures directly and are not subject to spell resistance.

Transmutation: These spells are subject to spell resistance if they transform the target creature. Transmutation spells are not subject to spell resistance if they are targeted on a point in space instead of on a creature. *Transmute rock to mud* and *entangle* change a creature's surroundings, not the creature itself, and are not subject to spell resistance. Some transmutations make objects harmful (or more harmful), such as *magic stone*. Even these spells are not generally subject to spell resistance because they affect the objects, not the creatures against which the objects are used. Spell resistance works against *magic stone* only if the creature with spell resistance is holding the stones when the cleric casts *magic stone* on them.

Successful Spell Resistance

Spell resistance prevents a spell or a spell-like ability from affecting or harming the resistant creature, but it never removes a magical effect from another creature or negates a spell's effect on another creature. Spell resistance prevents a spell from disrupting another spell.

Against an ongoing spell that has already been cast, a failed check against spell resistance allows the resistant creature to ignore any effect the spell might have. The magic continues to affect others normally.

TREMORSENSE

The red-hot thoqqua lunges unexpectedly from hiding, closing in unerringly on Tordek even though it couldn't see him before it attacked.

A creature with tremorsense locates other creatures by sensing vibrations in the ground.

- The creature automatically senses the location of anything that is in contact with the ground and within range (such as 60 feet for the thoqqua).
- If no straight path exists through the ground from the creature to those that it's sensing, then the range defines the maximum distance of the shortest indirect path. It must itself be in contact with the ground, and the creatures must be moving.
- As long as the other creatures are taking physical actions, including casting spells with somatic components, they're considered moving; they don't have to move from place to place for a creature with tremorsense to detect them.

TURN RESISTANCE

The cleric brandishes his holy symbol and commands a vampire to begone, but the creature merely sneers and closes in for the kill.

By virtue of superior strength of will or just plain unholy power, some creatures (usually undead) are less easily affected by clerics or paladins (see Turn and Rebuke Undead, page 139 in the *Player's Handbook*).

Turn resistance is an extraordinary ability.

- When resolving a turn, rebuke, command, or bolster attempt, added the listed bonus to the creature's Hit Dice total. For example, a shadow has +2 turn resistance and 3 HD. Attempts to turn, rebuke, command, or bolster treated the shadow as though it had 5 HD, though it is a 3 HD creature for any other purpose.

CONDITION SUMMARY

This section describes the adverse conditions that weaken, slow, or even kill characters. If more than one condition affects a character, apply them all. If certain effects can't combine, apply the most severe effect. For example, a character who is dazed and confused takes no actions whatsoever (dazed is more severe than confused). The confused character might want to attack a random character, but he can't because he's dazed.

Ability Damaged: The character has temporarily lost 1 or more ability score points. These points return at a rate of 1 per day. Ability damage is different from effective ability loss, which is an effect that goes away when the condition causing it (fatigue, entanglement, etc.) goes away. A character with Strength 0 falls to the ground and is helpless. A character with Dexterity 0 is paralyzed. A character with Constitution 0 is dead. A character with Intelligence, Wisdom, or Charisma 0 is unconscious. (See Ability Score Loss, page 72.)

Ability Drained: The character has permanently lost 1 or more ability score points. The character can only regain these points through magical means. A character with Strength 0 falls to the ground and is helpless. A character with Dexterity 0 is paralyzed. A character with Constitution 0 is dead. A character with Intelligence, Wisdom, or Charisma 0 is unconscious. (See Ability Score Loss, page 72.)

Blinded: The character cannot see at all, and thus everything has full concealment to him. He has a 50% chance to miss in combat, loses his positive Dexterity bonus to AC (if any), and grants a +2 bonus on attack rolls to enemies that attack him, just as if all his enemies were invisible. He moves at half speed and suffers a –4 penalty on most Strength and Dexterity-based skills. He cannot make Spot skill checks or perform any other activity (such as reading) that requires vision. Characters who remain blinded for a long time grow accustomed to these drawbacks and can overcome some of them (DM's discretion).

Blown Away: Depending on their size, creatures can be blown away by winds of high velocity (see Table 3–17: Wind Effects). Creatures on the ground that are blown away are knocked down and rolled 1d4×10 feet, sustaining 1d4 points of subdual damage per 10 feet. Flying creatures that are blown away are blown back 2d6×10 feet and sustain 2d6 points of subdual damage due to battering and buffering.

Checked: Prevented from achieving forward motion by an applied force, such as wind. Checked creatures on the ground merely stop. Checked flying creatures move back a distance specified in the description of the specific effect.

Confused: A confused character's actions are determined by a 1d10 roll, rerolled each round: 1: wander away (unless prevented) for 1 minute (and don't roll for another random action until the minute is up); 2–6: do nothing for 1 round; 7–9: attack the nearest creature for 1 round; 10: act normally for 1 round. Any confused creature who is attacked automatically attacks her attackers on her next turn.

Cowering: The character is frozen in fear, loses her Dexterity bonus to AC (if any), and can take no actions. Foes gain a +2 bonus to hit cowering characters.

Dazed: A dazed creature can take no actions (but defends itself normally). A dazed condition typically lasts 1 round.

Dazzled: Unable to see well because of overstimulation of the eyes. A dazzled creature suffers a –1 penalty on attack rolls until the effect ends.

Dead: The character's soul leaves his body permanently, or until he is *raised* or *resurrected*. A dead body decays, but magic that allows a dead character to come back to life restores the body either to full health or to its condition at the time of death (depending on the spell or device). Either way, resurrected characters need not worry about rigor mortis, decomposition, and other similar sorts of unpleasantness. A dead character cannot regain hit points.

Deafened: A deafened character cannot hear, suffers a –4 penalty to initiative checks, and has a 20% chance of spell failure when casting spells with verbal components. He cannot make Listen skill checks. Characters who remain deafened for a long time grow accustomed to these drawbacks and can overcome some of them (DM's discretion).

Disabled: A character with 0 hit points, or one who has negative hit points but has stabilized and then improved, is disabled. He is conscious and able to act but horribly wounded. He can take only a partial action each round, and if he performs any strenuous action, he takes 1 point of damage after the completing the act. Strenuous actions include running, attacking, casting a spell, or using any ability that requires physical exertion or mental concentration. Unless the strenuous action increased the character's hit points, he is now dying.

A disabled character with negative hit points recovers hit points naturally if he is being helped. Otherwise, each day he has a 10% chance to start recovering hit points naturally (starting with that day); otherwise, he loses 1 hit point. Once an unaided character starts recovering hit points naturally, he is no longer in danger of losing hit points (even if his current hit points are negative).

Dying: A dying character has negative hit points. She is unconscious and near death. At the end of each round (starting with the round in which the character dropped below 0 hit points), her player rolls d% to see whether she stabilizes. She has a 10% chance to become stable. If she doesn't stabilize, she loses 1 hit point.

Energy Drained: The character gains one or more negative levels. If the subject has at least as many negative levels as Hit Dice, he dies. Each negative level gives a creature the following penalties: –1 competence penalty on attack rolls, saving throws, skill checks, ability checks, and effective level (for determining the power, duration, DC, and other details of spells or special abilities). Additionally, a spellcaster loses one spell or spell slot from her highest available level. Negative levels stack.

Entangled: An entangled creature suffers a –2 penalty to attack rolls and a –4 penalty to effective Dexterity. If the bonds are anchored to an immobile object, the entangled character cannot move. Otherwise, he can move at half speed, but can't run or charge. An entangled character who attempts to cast a spell must make a Concentration check (DC usually 15) or lose the spell.

Exhausted: Characters who are exhausted move at half normal speed and suffer an effective penalty of –6 to Strength and Dexterity. A fatigued character becomes exhausted by doing something else that would normally cause fatigue. After 1 hour of complete rest, exhausted characters become fatigued.

Fatigued: Characters who are fatigued cannot run or charge and suffer an effective penalty of –2 to Strength and Dexterity. A fatigued character becomes exhausted by doing something else that would normally cause fatigue. After 8 hours of complete rest, fatigued characters are no longer fatigued.

Flat-Footed: A character who has not yet acted during a combat is flat-footed, not yet reacting normally to the situation. A flat-footed character loses his Dexterity bonus to AC (if any).

Frightened: A creature that is frightened flees as well as it can. If unable to flee, the creature may fight. It suffers a –2 morale penalty on attack rolls, weapon damage rolls, and saving throws. A frightened creature can use special abilities, including spells, to flee; indeed, the creature must use such means if they are the only way to escape.

Frightened is like shaken, except that the creature must flee, if possible. Panicked is a more extreme condition of fear.

Grappled: Engaged in wrestling or some other form of hand-to-hand struggle with one or more attackers. A grappled character cannot move, cast a spell, fire a missile, or undertake any action more complicated than making a barehanded attack, attacking with a Small weapon, or attempting to break free from the opponent. In addition, grappled characters do not threaten any area and lose any Dexterity bonuses to AC against opponents they aren't grappling.

Held: *Held* characters are subject to enchantments that make them unable to move. They are helpless. They can perform no physical actions (but they continue to breathe and can take purely mental actions).

Helpless: Bound, *held*, sleeping, paralyzed, or unconscious characters are helpless. Enemies can make advantageous attacks against helpless characters, or even deliver a usually lethal coup de grace.

A melee attack against a helpless character is at a +4 bonus on the attack roll (equivalent to attacking a prone target). A ranged attack gets no special bonus. A helpless defender can't use any Dexterity bonus to AC. In fact, his Dexterity score is treated as if it were 0 and his Dexterity modifier to AC were –5 (and a rogue can sneak attack him).

As a full-round action (allowing no move other than a 5-foot step), an enemy can use a melee weapon to deliver a coup de grace to a helpless foe. An enemy can also use a bow or crossbow, provided he is adjacent to the target. The attacker automatically hits and scores a critical hit. If the defender survives, he must make a Fortitude save (DC 10 + damage dealt) or die.

It's overkill, but a rogue also gets her sneak attack damage bonus against a helpless foe when delivering a coup de grace.

Delivering a coup de grace provokes attacks of opportunity from threatening foes because it involves focused concentration and methodical action.

Creatures that are immune to critical hits do not take critical damage, nor do they need to make Fortitude saves to avoid being killed by a coup de grace.

Incapacitated: Characters who are incapacitated are treated as helpless.

Incorporeal: Having no physical body. Incorporeal creatures are immune to all nonmagical attack forms. They can be harmed only by other incorporeal creatures, +1 or better magical weapons, spells, spell-like effects, or supernatural effects. (See Incorporeality, page 77.)

Invisible: Visually undetectable. Invisible creatures gain a +2 bonus to attack rolls and negate Dexterity bonuses to their opponents' AC. (See Invisibility, page 78.)

Knocked Down: Depending on their size, creatures can be knocked down by winds of high velocity (see Table 3–17: Wind

Effects). Creatures on the ground are knocked prone by the force of the wind. Flying creatures are instead blown back 1d6×10 feet.

Nauseated: Experiencing stomach distress. Nauseated creatures are unable to attack, cast spells, concentrate on spells, or do anything else requiring attention. The only action such a character can take is a single move (or move-equivalent action) per turn.

Normal: The character is unharmed (except, possibly, for hit points that have been lost) and unafflicted. She acts normally.

Panicked: A panicked creature suffers a −2 morale penalty on saving throws and must flee. A panicked creature has a 50% chance to drop what he's holding, chooses his path randomly (as long as he is getting away from immediate danger), and flees any other dangers that confront him. If cornered, a panicked creature cowers. A creature may use a special ability or spell to escape; being panicked, for example, doesn't prevent a wizard from *teleporting* away.

Panicked is a more extreme state of fear than shaken or frightened.

Paralyzed: A paralyzed character stands rigid and helpless, unable to move or act physically. He has effective Strength and Dexterity scores of 0 but may take purely mental actions.

Petrified: A petrified character is not dead as long as a majority of his body remains intact. He cannot move or take actions of any kind, not even purely mental ones. His Strength and Dexterity scores are effectively (but not actually) 0. He is unaware of what occurs around him, since all of his senses have ceased operating. If a petrified character cracks or breaks but the broken pieces are joined with him as he returns to flesh, he is unharmed. If the character's petrified body is incomplete when it returns to flesh, the body is likewise incomplete.

Pinned: Held immobile (but not helpless) in a grapple.

Prone: The character is on the ground. He suffers a −4 penalty on melee attack rolls, and the only ranged weapon he can effectively use is a crossbow, which he may use without penalty. Opponents receive +4 bonuses on melee attack against him but −4 penalties on ranged attacks. Standing up is a move-equivalent action.

Shaken: A shaken character suffers a −2 morale penalty on attack rolls, weapon damage rolls, and saving throws.

Shaken is a less severe fear condition than frightened or panicked.

Stable: A character who was dying but who has stabilized and still has negative hit points is stable. The character is no longer dying, but is still unconscious. If the character has become stable because of aid from another character (such as the Heal skill or magical healing), then the character no longer loses hit points. He has a 10% chance each hour to become conscious and be disabled (even though his hit points are still negative).

If the character stabilized on his own and hasn't had help, he is still at risk of losing hit points. Each hour, he has a 10% chance to become conscious and be disabled. Otherwise he loses 1 hit point.

Staggered: A character whose subdual damage exactly equals his current hit points is staggered. He so badly weakened or roughed up that he can only take a partial action when he would normally be able to take a standard action.

Stunned: The character loses her Dexterity bonus to AC (if any) and can take no actions. Foes gain a +2 bonus to hit stunned characters.

Turned: Affected by a turn undead attempt. Turned undead flee for 10 rounds (1 minute) by the best and fastest means available to them. If they cannot flee, they cower.

Unconscious: Knocked out and helpless. Unconsciousness can result from having current hit points between −1 and −9, or from subdual damage in excess of current hit points.

THE ENVIRONMENT

Characters crossing the burning desert face heatstroke and dehydration. Plunging into the murky depths raises the risk of drowning and even decompression. Adventurers spend a lot of time in the most dismal, dangerous, and generally unpleasant places imaginable. If the monsters and the villains don't kill them, the environment itself might. This section details hazards the player characters face from the physical world around them.

LANDSLIDES AND AVALANCHES

A landslide or avalanche consists of two distinct areas: the bury zone (in the direct path of the falling debris) and the slide zone (the area the debris spreads out to encompass). Characters in the bury zone always take damage from the avalanche; characters in the slide zone may be able to get out of the way.

Characters in the bury zone sustain 8d6 points of damage, or half that amount if they make a successful Reflex saving throw (DC 15). They are subsequently pinned (see below).

Characters in the slide zone sustain 3d6 points of damage, or no damage if they make a successful Reflex saving throw (DC 15). Those who fail their saves are pinned.

Pinned characters take 1d6 points of subdual damage per minute while pinned. If a pinned character falls unconscious, he or she must make a Constitution check (DC 15) or take 1d6 points of normal damage each minute thereafter until freed or dead.

WATER DANGERS

Historically, waterways were one of the most important modes of travel and communication within and between countries. On the other hand, characters on foot will find that lakes, rivers, and streams often block their travels in the wilderness. What's more, underground streams, cisterns, sewers, and moats are all part of the dungeon environment.

Water presents adventurers with five general problems. First, it's an obstacle that can block their movement. Second, characters in the water face the danger of drowning or losing gear. Third, a character caught in fast-moving water can be swept away from the rest of his party and battered or killed by rapids and waterfalls. Fourth, really deep water deals damage from the great pressure it exerts. Finally, exposure to cold water can be dangerous, afflicting characters with hypothermia.

The skills most commonly used in dealing with water as an obstacle are Swim and Profession (sailor). Unfortunately, not every character who gets into the water has these skills.

Any character can wade in relatively calm water that isn't over his head, no check required (hence the importance of fords). Similarly, swimming in calm water only requires skill checks with a DC of 10. Trained swimmers can just take 10. (Remember, however, that armor or heavy gear makes any attempt at swimming much more difficult. See Chapter 4: Skills and Chapter 7: Equipment in the *Player's Handbook*.)

By contrast, fast-moving water is much more dangerous. On a successful Swim or Strength check (DC 15), it deals 1d3 points of subdual damage per round (1d6 points of normal damage if flowing over rocks and cascades). On a failed check, the character must make another check that round to avoid going under.

THE DROWNING RULE

Any character can hold her breath for a number of rounds equal to twice her Constitution score. After this period of time, the character must make a Constitution check (DC 10) every round in order to continue holding her breath. Each round, the DC increases by 1.

When the character finally fails her Constitution check, she begins to drown. In the first round, she falls unconscious (0 hp). In the following round, she drops to −1 hit points and is dying. In the third round, she drowns.

It is possible to drown in substances other than water, such as sand, quicksand, fine dust, and silos full of grain.

Very deep water is not only generally pitch black, posing a navigational hazard, but worse, it deals water pressure damage of 1d6 points per minute for every 100 feet the character is below the surface. A successful Fortitude saving throw (DC 15, +1 for each previous check) means the diver takes no damage in that minute.

Very cold water deals 1d6 points of subdual damage from hypothermia per minute of exposure.

STARVATION AND THIRST DANGERS

Characters might find themselves without food or water and no means to obtain them. In normal climates, Medium-size characters need at least a gallon of fluids and about a pound of decent food to avoid starvation. (Small characters need half as much.) In very hot climates, characters need two or three times as much water to avoid dehydration.

A character can go without water for 1 day plus a number of hours equal to his Constitution score. After this time, the character must make a Constitution check each hour (DC 10, +1 for each previous check) or sustain 1d6 points of subdual damage.

A character can go without food for 3 days, in growing discomfort. After this time, the character must make a Constitution check each day (DC 10, +1 for each previous check) or sustain 1d6 points of subdual damage.

Characters who have taken subdual damage from lack of food or water are fatigued (see page 84). Subdual damage from thirst or starvation cannot be recovered until the character gets food or water, as needed—not even magic that restores hit points (such as *cure light wounds*) heals this damage.

HEAT DANGERS

The hot desert sun is as deadly an enemy as a hostile tribe of orcs. Prolonged exposure to hot temperatures can quickly wear down a character, and heatstroke can be deadly.

Heat deals subdual damage that cannot be recovered until the character gets cooled off (reaches shade, survives until nightfall, gets doused in water, is targeted by *endure elements*, etc.). Once rendered unconscious through the accumulation of subdual damage, the character begins to take normal damage at the same rate.

A character in very hot conditions (above 90° F) must make a Fortitude saving throw each hour (DC 15, +1 for each previous check) or sustain 1d4 points of subdual damage. Characters wearing heavy clothing or armor of any sort have a –4 penalty to their saves. A character with the Wilderness Lore skill may receive a bonus to this saving throw and may be able to apply this bonus to other characters as well (see the skill description on page 76 in the *Player's Handbook*). Characters reduced to unconsciousness begin taking normal damage (1d4 points per hour).

In extreme heat (above 110° F), a character must make a Fortitude save once every 10 minutes (DC 15, +1 for each previous check) or sustain 1d4 points of subdual damage. Characters wearing heavy clothing or armor of any sort have a –4 penalty to their saving throws. A character with the Wilderness Lore skill may

receive a bonus to this saving throw and may be able to apply this bonus to other characters as well. Characters reduced to unconsciousness begin taking normal damage (1d4 points per each 10-minute period).

A character who sustains any subdual damage from heat exposure now suffers from heatstroke and is fatigued (see page 84). These penalties end when the character recovers the subdual damage she took from the heat.

Abysmal heat (air temperature over 140° F, fire, boiling water, lava) deals normal damage. Breathing air in these temperatures deals 1d6 points of damage per minute (no save). In addition, a character must make a Fortitude save every 5 minutes (DC 15, +1 per previous check) or sustain 1d4 points of subdual damage. Those wearing heavy clothing or any sort of armor have a –4 penalty to their saving throws. In addition, those wearing metal armor or coming into contact with very hot metal are affected as if by a *heat metal* spell (see the *Player's Handbook* for the spell description).

Boiling water deals 1d6 points of scalding damage, unless the character is fully immersed, in which case it deals 10d6 points of damage per round of exposure. See Catching on Fire, below, for fire damage and the entry on page 89 for lava damage.

COLD DANGERS

The prickly fingers of icy death have robbed many an adventurer of her life. Prolonged exposure to cold temperatures and harsh weather can wear down a character who isn't protected against the climate. Hypothermia, frostbite, and exhaustion can quickly kill in bad weather. The best defense against cold and exposure is to get under cover and keep warm.

Cold and exposure deal subdual damage to the victim. This subdual damage cannot be recovered until the character gets out of the cold and warms up again. Once a character is rendered unconscious through the accumulation of subdual damage, the cold and exposure begins to deal normal damage at the same rate.

An unprotected character in cold weather (below 40° F) must make a Fortitude saving throw each hour (DC 15, + 1 per previous check) or sustain 1d6 points of subdual damage. A character who has the Wilderness Lore skill may receive a bonus to this saving throw and may be able to apply this bonus to other characters as well (see the skill description on page 76 in the *Player's Handbook*).

In conditions of extreme cold or exposure (below 0° F), an unprotected character must make a Fortitude save once every 10 minutes (DC 15, +1 per previous check), taking 1d6 points of subdual damage on each failed save. A character who has the Wilderness Lore skill may receive a bonus to this saving throw and may be able to apply this bonus to other characters as well (see the skill description in Chapter 4: Skills in the *Player's Handbook*). Characters wearing winter clothing only need check once per hour for cold and exposure damage.

A character who sustains any subdual damage from cold or exposure suffers from frostbite or hypothermia (treat her as

---

CATCHING ON FIRE

Characters exposed to burning oil, bonfires, and noninstantaneous magic fires such as a *wall of fire* might find their clothes, hair, or equipment on fire. Spells such as *fireball* or *flame strike* don't normally set a character on fire, since the heat and flame from these come and go in a flash.

Characters at risk of catching fire are allowed a Reflex saving throw (DC 15) to avoid this fate. If a character's clothes or hair catch fire, he takes 1d6 points of damage immediately. In each subsequent round, the burning character must make another Reflex saving throw. Failure means he takes another 1d6 points of damage that round. Success

means that the fire has gone out. (That is, once he succeeds at his saving throw, he's no longer on fire.)

A character on fire may automatically extinguish the flames by jumping into enough water to douse himself. If no body of water is at hand, rolling on the ground or smothering the fire with cloaks or the like permits the character another save with a +4 bonus.

Those unlucky enough to have their clothes or equipment catch fire must make Reflex saving throws (DC 15) for each item. Flammable items that fail sustain the same amount of damage as the character. (See alchemist's fire, page 113 in the *Player's Handbook*.)

fatigued; see page 84). These penalties end when the character recovers the subdual damage she took from the cold and exposure.

WEATHER HAZARDS

Aside from heat and cold, the weather itself can present dangers and obstacles to characters.

Winds: Winds can create a stinging spray of sand or dust, fan a large fire, heel over a small boat, and blow gases or vapors away. If powerful enough, they can even knock characters down (see Table 3–17: Wind Effects), interfere with ranged attacks, or impose penalties on some skill checks.

Light Wind: A gentle breeze, having little or no game effect.

Moderate Wind: A steady wind with a 50% chance of extinguishing small unprotected flames, such as candles.

Strong Wind: Gusts that automatically extinguish unprotected flames (candles, torches, and the like). Such gusts impose a –2 penalty to ranged attacks and to Listen checks.

Severe Wind: In addition to automatically extinguishing any unprotected flames, winds of this magnitude cause protected flames (such as those of lanterns) to dance wildly and have a 50% chance of extinguishing these lights. Ranged weapon attacks and Listen checks are at a –4 penalty. This is the velocity of wind produced by the *gust of wind* spell.

Windstorm: Powerful enough to bring down branches if not whole trees, windstorms automatically extinguish unprotected flames and have a 75% chance of blowing out protected flames, such as those of lanterns. Ranged weapon attacks are impossible, and even siege weapons have a –4 penalty to attack. Listen checks are at a –8 penalty due to the howling of the wind.

Hurricane-Force Wind: All flames are extinguished. Ranged attacks are impossible (except with siege weapons, which have a –8 penalty to attack). Listen checks are impossible: All characters can hear is the roaring of the wind. Hurricane-force winds often fell trees.

Tornado: All flames are extinguished. All ranged attacks are impossible (even with siege weapons), as are Listen checks. Instead of being blown away (see Table 3–17: Wind Effects), characters in close proximity to a tornado who fail their Fortitude saves are sucked toward the tornado. Those who come in contact with the actual funnel cloud are picked up and whirled around for 1d10 rounds, taking 6d6 points of damage per round, before being violently expelled (falling damage may apply). While a tornado's rotational speed can be as great as 300 mph, the funnel itself moves forward at an average of 30 mph. A tornado uproots trees, destroys buildings, and causes other similar forms of major destruction.

Precipitation: Most precipitation is in the form of rain, but in cold conditions it can manifest as snow, sleet, or hail. Precipitation of any kind followed by a cold snap in which the temperature dips from above freezing to 30° F or below may produce ice (see page 88).

Rain: Rain reduces visibility ranges by half, resulting in a –4 penalty to Spot and Search checks. It has the same effect on flames, ranged weapon attacks, and Listen checks as severe wind (see above).

Snow: While falling, snow reduces visibility as rain (–4 penalty to ranged weapon attacks, Spot checks, and Search checks). Once on the ground, it reduces movement by half. Snow has the same effect on flames as moderate wind (see above).

Sleet: Essentially frozen rain, sleet has the same effect as rain while falling (except that its chance to extinguish protected flames is 75%) and the same effect as snow once on the ground.

Hail: Hail does not reduce visibility, but the sound of falling hail makes Listen checks more difficult (–4 penalty). Sometimes (5% chance) hail can become large enough to deal 1 point of damage (per storm) to anything in the open. Once on the ground, hail has the same effect on movement as snow.

Storms: The combined effects of precipitation (or dust) and wind that accompany all storms reduce visibility ranges by three quarters, imposing a –8 penalty to all Spot, Search, and Listen checks. Storms make ranged weapon attacks impossible, except for with siege weapons, which have a –4 penalty to attack. They automatically extinguish candles, torches, and similar unprotected flames. They cause protected flames, such as those of lanterns, to dance wildly and have a 50% chance to extinguish these lights. See

TABLE 3–17: WIND EFFECTS

Wind Force	Wind Speed	Ranged Attacks Normal/Siege Weapons*	Creature Size**	Wind Effect on Creatures	Fort Save DC
Light	0–10 mph	—/—	Any	None	—
Moderate	11–20 mph	—/—	Any	None	—
Strong	21–30 mph	–2/—	Tiny or smaller	Knocked down	10
			Small or larger	None	
Severe	31–50 mph	–4/—	Tiny	Blown away	15
			Small	Knocked down	
			Medium-size	Checked	
			Large or larger	None	
Windstorm	51–74 mph	Impossible/–4	Small or smaller	Blown away	18
			Medium-size	Knocked down	
			Large or Huge	Checked	
			Gargantuan or Colossal	None	
Hurricane	75–174 mph	Impossible/–8	Medium-size or smaller	Blown away	20
			Large	Knocked down	
			Huge	Checked	
			Gargantuan or Colossal	None	
Tornado	175–300 mph	Impossible/impossible	Large or smaller	Blown away	30
			Huge	Knocked down	
			Gargantuan or Colossal	Checked	

*The siege weapon category includes ballista and catapult attacks as well as boulders tossed by giants.

**Flying or airborne creatures are treated as one size class smaller than their actual size, so an airborne Gargantuan dragon is treated as Huge for purposes of wind effects.

Checked: Creatures are unable to move forward against the force of the wind. Flying creatures are blown back 1d6×5 feet.

Knocked Down: Creatures are knocked prone by the force of the wind. Flying creatures are instead blown back 1d6×10 feet.

Blown Away: Creatures on the ground are knocked prone and rolled 1d4×10 feet, sustaining 1d4 points of subdual damage per 10 feet. Flying creatures are blown back 2d6×10 feet and sustain 2d6 points of subdual damage due to battering and buffering.

Table 3–17: Wind Effects for possible consequences to creatures caught outside without shelter during such a storm. Storms are divided into the following three types:

Duststorm: These desert storms differ from other storms in that they have no precipitation. Instead, a duststorm blows fine grains of sand that obscure vision, smother unprotected flames, and can even choke protected flames (50% chance). Most duststorms are accompanied by severe winds (see above) and leave behind a deposit of 1d6 inches of sand. However, there is a 10% chance of a greater duststorm accompanied by windstorm-magnitude winds (see above and Table 3–17: Wind Effects). These greater duststorms deal 1d3 points of subdual damage each round on anyone caught out in the open without shelter and also pose a choking hazard (see The Drowning Rule, page 85—except that a character with a scarf or similar protection across her mouth and nose does not begin to choke until after a number of rounds equal to ten times her Constitution score). Greater duststorms leave 2d3–1 feet of fine sand in their wake.

Snowstorm: In addition to the wind and precipitation common to other storms, snowstorms leave 1d6 inches of snow on the ground afterward.

Thunderstorm: In addition to wind and precipitation (usually rain, but sometimes also hail), thunderstorms are accompanied by lightning that can pose a hazard to characters without proper shelter (especially those in metal armor). As a rule of thumb, assume one bolt per minute for a 1-hour period at the center of the storm (see page 89). Each bolt causes electrical damage equal to 1d10 eight-sided dice. One in ten thunderstorms is accompanied by a tornado (see below).

Powerful Storms: Very high winds and torrential precipitation reduce visibility to zero, making Spot and Search rolls, Listen checks, and all ranged weapon attacks impossible. Unprotected flames are automatically extinguished, and even protected flames have a 75% chance of being doused. Creatures caught in the area can make a Fortitude saving throw (DC 20) or face the following effects based on the size of the creature. Powerful storms are divided into the following four types:

Windstorm: While accompanied by little or no precipitation, windstorms can cause considerable damage simply through the force of their wind (see Table 3–17: Wind Effects).

Blizzard: The combination of high winds (see Table 3–17: Wind Effects), heavy snow (typically 1d3 feet), and bitter cold (see Cold Dangers, page 86) make blizzards deadly for all who are unprepared for them.

Hurricane: In addition to very high winds (see Table 3–17: Wind Effects) and heavy rain, hurricanes are accompanied by flash floods (see below). Most adventuring activity is impossible under such conditions.

Tornado: One in ten thunderstorms is accompanied by a tornado (see Table 3–17: Wind Effects).

Fog: Whether in the form of a low-lying cloud or a mist rising from the ground, fog obscures all sight, including darkvision,

beyond 5 feet. Creatures within 5 feet have one-half concealment (attacks by or against them have a 20% miss chance).

Flash Floods: Runoff from heavy rain forces creatures in its path to make a Fortitude save (DC 15). Large or smaller creatures who fail the save are swept away by the rushing water, taking 1d6 points of subdual damage per round (1d3 points on a successful Swim check). Huge creatures who fail are knocked down and face potential drowning (see The Drowning Rule, page 85). Gargantuan and Colossal creatures are checked, but they only drown if the waters rise above their heads.

OTHER DANGERS

Use the following guidelines to cover the other sorts of dangers a character can face.

Acid

Corrosive acids deals 1d6 points of damage per round of exposure except in the case of total immersion (such as into a vat of acid), which deals 10d6 points of damage per round. An attack with acid, such as from a hurled vial or a monster's spittle, counts as a round of exposure.

The fumes from most acids are inhalant poisons. Those who come close enough to a large body of acid to dunk a creature in it must make a Fortitude save (DC 13) or take 1 point of temporary Constitution damage. All such characters must make a second save 1 minute later or take another 1d4 points of temporary Constitution damage.

Creatures immune to acid's caustic properties might still drown in it if they are totally immersed (see The Drowning Rule, page 85).

Ice

Characters walking on ice must make Balance checks (DC 15) to avoid slipping and falling. Over long distances, a character must make a check each minute. Characters in prolonged contact with ice may run the risk of cold damage (see above).

Lack of Air/High Altitude

Characters in conditions of low oxygen, such as on top of a mountain, must roll a Fortitude saving throw each hour (DC 15, +1 per previous check), taking 1d6 points of subdual damage each time they fail.

A character who sustains any subdual damage from lack of oxygen is automatically fatigued (see page 84). These penalties end when the character recovers the subdual damage he took from low oxygen.

Altitude Sickness: Long-term oxygen deprivation due to high altitude affects mental and physical ability scores. After each 6-hour period a character spends at an altitude of over 20,000 feet, he must make a Fortitude save (DC 15, +1 per previous check) or take 1 point of temporary damage to all ability scores.

SUFFOCATION

A character who has no air to breathe can hold her breath for 2 rounds per point of Constitution. After this period of time, the character must make a Constitution check (DC 10) in order to continue holding her breath. The save must be repeated each round, with the DC increasing by +1 for each previous success.

When the character fails one of these Constitution checks, she begins to suffocate. In the first round, she falls unconscious (0 hp). In the following round, she drops to –1 hit points and is dying. In the third round, she suffocates.

Slow Suffocation: A Medium-size character can breathe easily for 6 hours in a sealed chamber measuring 10 feet on a side. After that time,

the character takes 1d6 points of subdual damage every 15 minutes. Each additional Medium-size character or significant fire source (a torch, for example) proportionally reduces the time the air will last. Thus, two people can last for 3 hours, after which they each take 1d6 points per 15 minutes. If they have a torch (equivalent to another Medium-size character in terms of the air it uses), the air runs out in only 2 hours.

Small characters consume half as much air as Medium-size characters. A larger volume of air, of course, lasts for a longer time. So, for instance, if two humans and a gnome are in a sealed chamber measuring 20 feet by 20 feet by 10 feet, and they have a torch, the air will last almost 7 hours (6 hours/3.5 people and torches × 4 10-ft. cubes = 6.86 hours).

Lava

Lava or magma deals 2d6 points of damage per round of exposure, except in the case of total immersion (such as when a character falls into the crater of an active volcano), which deals 20d6 points of damage per round. Damage from magma continues for 1d3 rounds after exposure ceases, but this additional damage is only half of that dealt during actual contact (that is, 1d6 or 10d6 points per round).

An immunity or resistance to heat or fire serves as an immunity to lava or magma. However, a creature immune to heat might still drown if completely immersed in lava (see The Drowning Rule, page 85).

Smoke

A character who breathes heavy smoke must make a Fortitude saving throw each round (DC 15, +1 per previous check) or spend that round choking and coughing. A character who chokes for two consecutive rounds takes 1d6 points of subdual damage.

Smoke obscures vision, giving one-half concealment (20% miss chance) to characters within it.

Falling Objects

Just as characters take damage when they fall more than 10 feet, so too do they take damage when they are hit by falling objects. Objects that fall upon characters deal damage based on their weight and the distance they have fallen.

For each 200 pounds of an object's weight, the object deals 1d6 points of damage, provided it falls at least 10 feet. Distance also comes into play, adding an additional 1d6 points of damage for every 10-foot increment it falls beyond the first (to a maximum of 20d6 points of damage).

Objects smaller than 200 pounds also deal damage when dropped, but they must fall farther to deal the same damage. Use Table 3–18: Damage from Falling Objects to see how far an object of a given weight must drop to deal 1d6 points of damage.

Example: A magic flying ship tilts to one side and drops a 400-pound stone statue (a petrified comrade) overboard. The statue deals 2d6 points of damage to anything it strikes by virtue of its weight alone. If the ship were 100 feet in the air at the time, the falling statue would deal an additional 9d6 points of damage, for a total of 11d6.

TABLE 3–18: DAMAGE FROM FALLING OBJECTS

Object Weight	Falling Distance
200–101 lb.	20 ft.
100–51 lb.	30 ft.
50–31 lb.	40 ft.
30–11 lb.	50 ft.
10–6 lb.	60 ft.
5–1 lb.	70 ft.

For each additional increment an object falls, it deals an additional 1d6 points of damage. For example, since a 30-pound metal sphere must fall 50 feet to deal damage (1d6 points of damage), such a sphere that fell 150 feet would deal 3d6 points of damage. Objects weighing less than 1 pound do not deal damage to those they land upon, no matter how far they have fallen.

WEATHER

Player characters have a tendency to ignore the weather, but sometimes it can play an important role in an adventure—rain can wash away tracks, a thunderstorm can force the adventurers to seek shelter, or a gale can delay their ship from sailing. Roll once per day on Table 3–19: Random Weather to determine the weather for that day. Terms on that table are defined as follows:

Calm: Wind speeds are light (0 to 10 mph).

Cold: Between 0° and 40° Fahrenheit during the day, 10 to 20 degrees colder at night.

Cold Snap: Lowers temperature by −10° F.

Downpour: Treat as rain (see Precipitation, below), but conceals as fog. Creates flash floods (see page 88). A downpour lasts for 2d4 hours.

Heat Wave: Raises temperature by +10° F.

Hot: Between 85° and 110° Fahrenheit during the day, 10 to 20 degrees colder at night.

Moderate: Between 40° and 60° Fahrenheit during the day, 10 to 20 degrees colder at night.

Powerful Storm: (*Windstorm/Blizzard/Hurricane/Tornado*): Wind speeds are over 50 mph (see Table 3–17: Wind Effects). In addition, blizzards are accompanied by heavy snow (1d3 feet), and hurricanes are accompanied by downpours (see above). Windstorms last for 1d6 hours. Blizzards last for 1d3 days. Hurricanes can last for up to a week, but their major impact on characters will come in a 24-to-48-hour period when the center of the storm moves through their area. Tornadoes are very short-lived (1d6×10 minutes), typically forming as part of a thunderstorm system (see Storm, below). See page 88 for more details.

Precipitation: Roll d% to determine whether the precipitation is Fog (01–30), Rain/Snow (31–90), or Sleet/Hail (91–00). Snow and sleet occur only when the temperature is 30° Fahrenheit or below. Most precipitation lasts for 2d4 hours. By contrast, hail lasts for only 1d20 minutes but usually accompanies 1d4 hours of rain. See page 87.

Storm: (*Duststorm/Snowstorm/Thunderstorm*): Wind speeds are severe (30 to 50 mph) and visibility is cut by half; see page 87. Storms last for 2d4−1 hours.

Warm: Between 60° and 85° Fahrenheit during the day, 10 to 20 degrees colder at night.

Windy: Wind speeds are moderate to strong (10 to 30 mph); see page 87.

SKILL AND ABILITY CHECKS

The whole game can be boiled down to the characters trying to accomplish various tasks, the DM determining how difficult the tasks are to accomplish, and the dice determining success or failure. While combat and spellcasting have their own rules for how difficult tasks are, skill checks and ability checks handle just about everything else.

TABLE 3–19: RANDOM WEATHER

d%	Weather	Cold Climate	Temperate Climate*	Desert
01–70	Normal weather	Cold, calm	Normal for season**	Hot, calm
71–80	Abnormal weather	Heat wave (01–30) or cold snap (31–100)	Heat wave (01–50) or cold snap (51–100)	Hot, windy
81–90	Inclement weather	Precipitation (snow)	Precipitation (normal for season)	Hot, windy
91–99	Storm	Snowstorm	Thunderstorm, snowstorm†	Duststorm
100	Powerful storm	Blizzard	Windstorm, blizzard††, hurricane, tornado	Downpour

*Temperate includes forest, hills, marsh, mountains, plains, and warm aquatic.
**Winter is cold, summer is warm, spring and autumn are moderate. Warm or marshy regions are always slightly warmer in winter.
†Only in wintertime; otherwise, treat as thunderstorm (01–75) or windstorm (76–00).
††Only in wintertime; otherwise, treat as hurricane (01–50) or tornado (51–00).

MODIFYING THE ROLL OR THE DC

Circumstances can modify a character's die roll, and they can modify the Difficulty Class needed to succeed.

- Circumstances that improve performance, such as having the perfect tools for the job, getting help from another character, and having unusually accurate information, provide a bonus to the die roll.
- Circumstances that hamper performance, such as being forced to use improvised tools or having misleading information, provide a penalty to the die roll.
- Circumstances that make the task easier, such as a friendly audience or helpful environmental conditions, make the DC lower.
- Circumstances that make the task harder, such as a hostile audience or doing work that must be flawless, make the DC higher.

In general, what a character does, has, or knows modifies her roll, but what the surrounding conditions are like or how difficult the task is modifies the DC. However, the truth of the matter is, even if you forget this distinction, you'll be okay. Adding to the roll and subtracting from the DC accomplish the same thing.

When modifying either the roll or the DC, you don't need to tell the player that you are doing so. In fact, in many cases, you should not tell them. See Chapter 1: Dungeon Mastering for more information.

THE DM'S BEST FRIEND

A favorable circumstance gives a character a +2 bonus on a skill check (or a –2 modifier to the DC) and an unfavorable one gives a –2 penalty on the skill check (or a +2 modifier to the DC). Take special note of this rule, for it may be the only one you'll need.

Mialee runs down a dungeon corridor, running from a beholder. Around the corner ahead wait two ogres. Does Mialee hear the ogres getting ready to make their ambush? The DM calls for a Listen check and rules that her running from the beholder makes it less likely that she's being careful: –2 to the check. But one of the ogres is readying a portcullis trap, and the cranking winch of the device makes a lot of noise: –2 to the DC. Mialee heard from another adventurer that the ogres in this dungeon like to ambush adventurers: +2 to the check. Her ears are still ringing from the *lightning bolt* that she cast at the beholder: –2 to the check. The dungeon is already noisy because of the sound of the roaring dragon on the level below: +2 to the DC.

You can add modifiers endlessly (and doing that is not really a good thing, since it slows down play), but the point is, other than the PC's Listen check total bonus, the only numbers that the DM and the player need to remember when calculating all the situational modifiers are +2 and –2. Multiple conditions add up to give the check a total modifier and the DC a final result.

Going beyond the Rule: It's certainly acceptable for you to modify this rule. For extremely favorable or unfavorable circumstances, you can use modifiers larger than +/–2. For example, you can decide that a task is practically impossible and modify the roll or the DC by 20. Feel free to modify these numbers as you see fit, using modifiers from 2 to 20.

You can also make things a little easier on yourself by applying all the modifiers either to the roll or to the DC. Sometimes it's worthwhile to make a fine distinction between a modifier to a roll and the opposite modifier to the DC, but usually it doesn't matter.

DELINEATING TASKS

A task is anything that requires a roll. Climbing half your speed is a task, as is making a pot, despite the fact that one takes seconds and the other hours (or even days).

A single task can be any of the following:

- Moving a set distance (covered in skill description)
- Making one item
- Influencing one person, creature or group (DM decides if NPCs are acting as individuals or as a group)
- Dealing with one object (opening a door, breaking a board, tying a rope, slipping out of a manacle, picking a lock)
- Determining one piece of information
- Searching or tracking over one area (described in description)
- Perceive one sound or sight (DM decides if NPCs are acting as individuals or as a group)

Different skills handle task delineation in different ways. In fact, the same skill may handle tasks in different ways depending on what the character is doing. For example, Heal allows the healer to stabilize one character or assist in a group's overall healing rate over a night's rest. Both of these are single tasks, requiring only one roll.

Sometimes, however, a task requires multiple rolls. The DM must decide, for example, if a character attempting to use Sense Motive on a group of ogres must treat them as a group (one roll) or as individuals (a different roll for each ogre).

If two different groups approach a character from a distance, he has to make two different Spot checks to see them if the DM has decided that they are indeed different groups. If a character searches one wall using the Search skill, he might find several objects of importance—but each such object requires a separate roll. In such a case, the DM should make the second (and third, etc.) roll in secret. Asking the player to make three rolls gives him information that he shouldn't have. See Chapter 1: Dungeon Mastering for more information on controlling what information the players pick up.

A few examples of long-term duties (and how many tasks they comprise) follow.

Character on Watch: The rest of the party is asleep while Mialee takes the watch. The DM asks for a Listen check (it's dark, so the PC can't use Spot as well as Listen at this point), and Mialee succeeds—but the DM says nothing about what she's listening for (it's an opposed roll with a goblin that will sneak up on the party during her watch). He tells her that about a half hour into her watch, she hears some rustling in the nearby bushes (the goblin). She investigates, but discovers nothing (the goblin sneaks off, quieter this time—she fails the opposed roll, using Spot this time), so she goes back to where she was keeping watch. The DM asks for another Listen roll, and she succeeds again. This time she catches the goblin, and the rest of the party wakes up to deal with the foe. Eventually they go back to sleep, and she goes back on watch. The DM requires another Listen roll, even though he knows there's nothing to hear this time.

The "task" of going on watch required three Listen rolls, mostly because the watch was broken into three segments—the beginning, after checking for the goblin the second time, and after the goblin was dealt with.

Riding: Soveliss rides his horse along rocky terrain, making no roll for this mundane task. He guides it down into a steep gully—the DM calls for a Ride check (DC 10) to do so. At the bottom of the gully, an owlbear menaces a wounded centaur. The ranger spurs his mount into the fray, making no roll to do so. Once in battle, the owlbear slashes at the ranger with a powerful claw. The DM requires a Ride check to stay on the horse, and another one to keep the now-panicking horse from running off. The ranger succeeds at both checks, and then decides to leap out of the saddle and fight the beast. The DM requires another roll. Soveliss succeeds again, meaning that he dismounts without falling and moves to engage the owlbear.

Riding a mount doesn't normally require rolls. Only riding into difficult terrain or specific tasks involving riding require rolls.

Tracking: Soveliss is following a giant scorpion across the desert. He follows the vermin for three miles, making a Wilderness Lore check each mile, but tracking in the soft sand is easy. Shortly after the third mile, a windstorm comes up. Soveliss waits it out, and it passes after an hour, mercifully short. Now he must make a fourth check to see if he can pick up the trail in the wind-tossed sand. This check is of course more difficult, as are all subsequent checks until the tracker gets to the point where the scorpion was when the storm passed.

Normally, tracking requires a Wilderness Lore check each mile, but a sudden change in situation can require an additional roll.

Sneaking: Lidda is sneaking through a dungeon filled with hobgoblins. She must pass by an open doorway beyond which is a room where the brutes are drinking from a keg of ale. She makes a Move Silently check and the hobgoblins make opposed Listen checks, but they're not paying much attention, so the halfling sneaks by easily. The hobgoblins aren't even looking at the door, so the DM requires no Hide check. To get out, however, she must pass right through a guard room. She must make a Hide check to keep to the dark shadows near the walls, and a new Move Silently check (new because the listeners are different individuals, plus they're more alert) to get past the guards and through the room.

A new Move Silently check is needed for each different group that the sneaker is trying to avoid. Sometimes both a Move Silently check and a Hide check are needed when sneaking around. Sometimes they're not.

THE GENERAL VERSUS THE SPECIFIC

Sometimes a player will say, "I look around the room. Do I see anything?" and sometimes she'll say, "I look into the room, knowing that I just saw a kobold dart inside. I look behind the chair and the table, and in all the dark corners. Do I see it?" In both cases, the DM replies, "Make a Spot check." However, in the second example, the character has specialized knowledge of the situation. She's asking specific questions. In such cases, always award the character a +2 bonus for favorable conditions. It's good to reward a character who has knowledge that allows her to ask specific questions.

If the kobold's actually not in the room, but a cloaker waits in ambush on the ceiling, the character has no special knowledge and gains no bonus. She doesn't get a penalty, either—don't penalize specific questions. If both the kobold and the cloaker are in the room, unless they're working together as a group (see above—but it's unlikely), two Spot checks are required. The character gets a +2 bonus to the roll to spot the kobold and no bonus to the roll to spot the cloaker.

DEGREES OF SUCCESS

Sometimes determining success isn't enough, and the degree of success is important to a task. For example, an invisible assassin sneaks up on a cleric. The cleric makes a Listen check opposed to the assassin's Move Silently check, and the cleric is successful. You could describe this success to the player of the cleric in many different ways, including:

- "You heard a noise and you know something's out there, but you don't see anything."
- "You heard a noise. It sounded like a person moving, and it came from 'over there.' "
- "You heard a noise. You know there's an invisible creature about 15 feet northeast of you, and you can target that creature's square with an attack."

To determine how much information to give out, compare the opposed rolls (or for a nonopposed roll, the roll and the DC). In the example above, success means that the DM gives the first answer. If the cleric beats the assassin's roll by 10 or more, he gets the second answer. If he exceeds the assassin's roll by 20, he gets all the information—the third answer.

In general, this means:

TABLE 3–20: VARYING DEGREES OF SUCCESS

Roll	Degree of Success
DC or above	Success
DC +10 or above	Greater success
DC +20 or above	Perfect success

Degrees of success usually only apply when the amount of information you have to give out can be different depending on how well the character succeeds. Most of the time, the only outcome that matters is whether the character succeeds or fails. (See below for information on critical success.)

TAKING 10

Encourage players to use the take 10 rule. When a character is swimming or climbing a long distance, for example, this rule can really speed up play. Normally, you make a check each round with these movement-related skills, but if there's no pressure, taking 10 allows them to avoid making a lot of rolls just to get from point A to point B.

ABILITY CHECKS

There are no rules for trying to stay awake through the night, writing down every word someone says without a mistake, or opening a stuck, heavy metal jug without spilling a single drop of its contents. However, in the course of a game any of these situations could potentially make or break an adventure. You're going to have to be ready to make up checks for nonstandard activities.

Using the example situations above, staying awake might be a Constitution check (DC 12, +4 for every previous night without sleep), with an elf character gaining a +2 bonus to her check because an elf is only giving up 4 hours of trance instead of 8 hours of sleep. Writing down every word that someone says would be an Intelligence check (DC 15), and a successful Dexterity check (DC 10) prior to the Intelligence check would add +2 to the roll. Opening the metal jug would normally be a Strength check (DC about 17), and once that's accomplished, a Dexterity check with (DC 13) is required to keep from spilling the contents.

The three types of ability checks you could call for to handle a nonstandard situation are these:

- A single roll using an appropriate ability (as in staying awake)
- One ability check that, depending on the result, might provide a modifier to another check involving a different ability (as in writing down every word)
- Two or more separate ability checks, usually involving different abilities, to accomplish a multipart task (such as opening the jug without spilling)

You can also use a combination of an ability check and a skill check in an appropriate situation. For example, in heavy gravity, Lidda might have to make a Strength check (DC 15) to avoid a –2 penalty on her Open Lock check.

Decisions on how to handle nonstandard situations are left to your best judgment. For more tips on winging it, see Chapter 1: Dungeon Mastering.

Variant: Skills with Different Abilities

Sometimes a check involves a character's training (skill ranks) plus an innate talent (ability) not usually associated with that training. A skill check always includes skill ranks plus an ability modifier, but you can use a different ability modifier from normal if the character is in a situation where the normal key ability does not apply.

For example:

- A character is floating in a null-gravity area and tries to maneuver by pulling himself along some improvised handholds.

Since he's weightless, the DM rules that the player should make a Climb check keyed to Dexterity rather than to Strength.

- A character is trying to pick the best horse from several that a merchant is selling. Normally this would be an Appraise check, but familiarity with horses ought to count for something. The DM lets the player use the character's Ride ranks instead of Appraise ranks and applies the character's Wisdom modifier (as normal for an Appraise check).

- A character needs to use main force to restrain a panicked horse. Normally this would call for a Strength check, but a character skilled at handling animals ought to be able to use his knowledge to restrain the horse more easily. The DM lets the player add the character's Handle Animal ranks (but not his Charisma modifier) to the Strength check.

- A character has created a masterwork dagger as a gift for a visiting noble. He attempts to inscribe it with intricate designs. The DM rules that this is a Dexterity check to which the character's Craft (weaponsmithing) ranks apply.

- A character is trying to climb a ladder to the bottom of a very deep chute. Normally, the DM would call for a Constitution check to see if the character can keep going, but he can also allow the player to add the character's Climb ranks to the roll.

These sorts of unusual situations are always handled on a case-by-case basis, and only as exceptions. The vast majority of the time, use the normal key ability.

Remember that when you change the way a skill works in this fashion, you should dictate when the change comes into play—it's not up to a player to make this sort of decision. Players may try to rationalize why they should get to use their best ability score modifier with a skill that doesn't normally use that ability, but you shouldn't allow this sort of rule change unless you happen to agree with it.

Adventurers learn how deadly a dragon's breath weapon can be.

VARIANT: CRITICAL SUCCESS OR FAILURE

If a player rolls a natural (unmodified) 20 on a check, allow him or her to make another check. If the second check is successful, the character has achieved a critical success with the use of that skill or ability, and something particularly good happens. Likewise, if a player rolls a natural 1, he rolls again. If the second check is a failure, the character has achieved a critical failure (made a critical blunder), and something really bad happens.

It's up to you to determine the specific result of a critical success or failure. Some examples follow.

Critical Successes

- When climbing or swimming, the character moves twice as far as she would on a normal success.
- When using Diplomacy, the character makes a good, trusted friend for long-term play.
- When using a Knowledge skill, the character comes to an important conclusion related to the task at hand.
- When searching, the character discovers something that she otherwise never could have found (if there is anything to be found).
- When tracking, the character determines some amazing minutiae about her prey. For instance, she realizes that the three subjects she's tracking aren't happy with one another because they occasionally stop and apparently argue, based on where they stand in relation to each other.
- When using Heal to give first aid, the character heals 1 point of damage dealt to the subject.

Critical Failures

- When performing, the character displeases his audience so greatly that they wish to do him harm.
- When climbing, the character falls so badly that he takes an additional 1d6 points of damage, or he falls and tears away a few good handholds,

TABLE 3–21: DIFFICULTY CLASS EXAMPLES

DC	Example	Roll (Key Ability)	Who Could Do It
–10	Hear the sounds of a pitched battle	Listen (Wis)	A commoner on the other side of a stone wall
0	Track ten hill giants across a muddy field	Search (Int)	The village fool hustling at full speed at night
5	Climb a knotted rope	Climb (Str)	An average human carrying a 75-pound pack
5	Hear people talking on the other side of a door	Listen (Wis)	An absent-minded sage who is being distracted by allies
10	Follow tracks of fifteen orcs across firm ground	Search (Int)	A peasant
10	Ransack a chest full of junk to find a map	Search (Int)	A peasant
10	Tie a firm knot	Rope Use (Dex)	A peasant
10	Find out the current gossip	Gather Information (Cha)	A peasant
11*	Avoid being tripped by a wolf	— (Str or Dex)	A peasant
13**	Resist the *command* spell	Will save (Wis)	A 1st-level wizard or a low-level fighter
13	Bash open a simple wooden door	— (Str)	A fighter
15	Stabilize a dying friend	Heal (Wis)	A 1st-level cleric
15	Make indifferent people friendly	Diplomacy (Cha)	A 1st-level paladin
15	Jump 10 feet (with a running start)	Jump (Str)	A 1st-level fighter
15*	Get a minor lie past a canny guard	Bluff (Cha)	A 1st-level rogue
16	Identify a 1st-level spell as it is being cast	Spellcraft (Int)	A wizard (but not anyone untrained in spells)
17**	Resist a 10th-level vampire's dominating gaze	Will save (Wis)	A low-level monk or a high-level fighter
18	Bash open a strong wooden door	— (Str)	An enraged half-orc barbarian
18	Cast *fireball* while being shot with an arrow	Concentration (Con)	A low-level wizard
20	Notice a typical secret door	Search (Int)	A smart, 1st-level half-elf rogue
20	Notice a scry sensor	Scry (Int)	A low-level wizard (and only someone with an Int of 12+)
20	Notice that there's an invisible creature moving nearby	Spot (Wis)	A low-level ranger
20	Pick a very simple lock	Open Lock (Dex)	A dexterous, 1st-level halfling rogue (but not anyone untrained at picking locks)
20	Find out what sorts of crimes the baron's daughter has gotten away with	Gather Information (Cha)	A low-level bard
20	Avoid falling into a pit trap	Reflex save (Dex)	An mid-level rogue or a high-level paladin
20	Walk a tightrope	Balance (Dex)	A low-level rogue
21*	Sneak quietly past a hellcat 50 feet away	Move Silently (Dex)	A low-level rogue
22*	Escape from an owlbear's clutches	Escape Artist (Dex)	A low-level rogue
23*	Grab a guard's spear and wrest it out of his hands	Melee attack (Str)	A mid-level fighter
24	Resist the *wail of the banshee* spell	Fortitude save (Con)	A high-level fighter
24†	Shoot an armored guard through an arrow slit	Ranged attack (Dex)	A high-level fighter
25	Notice that something's wrong with a friend who's under a vampire's control	Sense Motive (Wis)	A mid-level rogue
25	Persuade the dragon that's captured you that it would be a good idea to let you go	Diplomacy (Cha)	A high-level bard
25	Find out from a city's inhabitants who the power behind the throne is	Gather Information (Cha)	A high-level bard
26	Jump over an orc's head (with a running start)	Jump (Str)	A 20th-level ranger wearing light armor or a mid-level barbarian wearing light armor (who really only needs a 22 because his speed is higher)
28	Disable a *glyph of warding*	Disable Device (Int)	A high-level rogue (but not anyone of another class)
30	Notice a well-hidden secret door	Search (Int)	A high-level rogue
28	Bash open an iron door	— (Str)	A fire giant
29	Calm a hostile owlbear	Animal Empathy (Cha)	A high-level druid (and only a druid or ranger)
30	Hurriedly climb a slick brick wall	Climb (Str)	A high-level barbarian
30	Pick a good lock	Open Lock (Dex)	A high-level rogue
43	Track a goblin that passed over hard rocks a week ago, and it snowed yesterday	Wilderness Lore (Wis)	A 20th-level ranger who has maxed out his Wilderness Lore skill and has been fighting goblinoids as his favored enemy since 1st level

DC: The number a character needs to roll to succeed.

*This number is actually the average roll on the opponent's opposed check rather than a fixed number.

**Actual DC may be higher or lower depending on the caster or ability user.

†This is the target's adjusted Armor Class.

Example: An example of a task with that DC.

Roll (Key Ability): The roll the character makes, usually a skill check, but sometimes a saving throw, an ability check, or even an attack roll. The ability that modifies the roll is in parentheses. A "—" means that the check is an ability check and no skill ranks, base save bonuses, or base attack bonuses apply.

Who Could Do It: An example of a character that would have about a 50% chance to succeed. When this entry names a character by class, it assumes that the character has the skill in question. (Other characters might have a better or worse chance to succeed.)

making it a more difficult climb (+5 DC) on the next try.

- When using Disguise, the character not only doesn't look like what he intended, but actually looks like something offensive or hateful to the viewers.
- When using Escape Artist, the character actually gets himself more entangled or pinned, adding +5 to the DC on the next try.
- When using a rope, the character breaks it.
- When trying to open a lock, the character breaks off his pick in the lock, making it impossible to open.
- When using any kind of tool, the character destroys the tool.

Sometimes, there's nothing more that can be achieved with a critical success, or there's nothing worse than a normal failure. In such a case, ignore this variant rule.

You should also ignore this variant whenever a character takes 10 or takes 20. It's not possible to attain a critical success when all you're trying to do is complete a task without worrying about completing it as well as possible, and it's not possible to suffer a critical failure if you're not under pressure when you're making the check.

SAVING THROWS

Adjudicating and varying saving throws works a lot like adjudicating and varying skill and ability checks.

ASSIGNING SAVING THROWS

There are many issues to consider when you're assigning saving throws.

Which One?

Fortitude, Reflex or Will? When assigning something a saving throw, use these guidelines:

Fortitude: Fortitude saves reflect physical toughness. They incorporate stamina, ruggedness, physique, bulk, metabolism, resistance, immunity, and other similar physical qualities. If it seems like something that a "tough guy" would be good at, it's a Fortitude save.

Reflex: Reflex saves reflect physical (and sometimes mental) agility. They incorporate quickness, nimbleness, hand-eye coordination, overall coordination, speed, and reaction time. If it seems like something that an agile person would be good at, it's a Reflex save.

Will: Will saves reflect inner strength. They incorporate willpower, mental stability, the power of the mind, level-headedness, determination, self-confidence, self-awareness, the superego, and resistance to temptation. If it seems like something that a confident or determined person would be good at, it's a Will save.

Save or Check?

A character slips and falls. He tries to catch himself on a ledge, while another character reaching forward, attempting to catch him. Are these Reflex saves or Dexterity checks?

The answer to the above question is "both." The character attempting to save himself makes a Reflex save. The character trying to grab him makes a Dexterity check.

Key Concept 1: Checks are used to accomplish something, while saves are used to avoid something.

Key Concept 2: Checks don't always reflect level. Saves always do. This is a subtler point. If a task seems like it should be easier for a high-level character, use a saving throw. If it seems like the task should be equally difficult for any two characters with the same score in the relevant ability, use a check. For example, opening a door is merely a reflection of strength, not experience. Thus, it's a Strength check. The middle ground is a skill check, such as a

Balance check to avoid falling while running over broken ground. A Balance check reflects level only if the character has ranks in the skill.

DIFFICULTY CLASSES

Assigning DCs is your job, but usually the rules are straightforward. There is a standard rule for the DC of a saving throw against a spell, and creatures and magic items with abilities that force others to make saves always have that saving throw clearly detailed (or else they function just like spells, and you use the spell rule). The general rules are:

Spells: 10 + Spell Level + Caster Ability Modifier.
Monster Abilities: 10 + 1/2 hit dice + Ability Modifier.
Miscellaneous: 10 to 20. Use 15 when in doubt.

As with checks, saving throw die rolls can be modified, or the DC can be modified. See The DM's Best Friend, page 90.

Variant: Saves with Different Abilities

To model unusual situations, you can change the ability score that modifies a save, just like you can do with a skill (see above). This is purely a variant, however, since not all DMs want to go to this level of complication.

- Fortitude saves against mental attacks (such as *phantasmal killer*) could be based on Wisdom, making it a cross between a Fortitude and a Will save. (Apply the character's Fortitude save bonus from class and level, and then add his Will ability modifier instead of his Constitution modifier.)
- The DM may allow a character to cast a quickened *dimension door* spell in response to falling into a pit trap. Reacting quickly to a trap requires a Reflex save, but in this case the DM might make this a Reflex save based on Wisdom rather than Dexterity, since casting the spell is mainly a mental action.
- Will saves against enchantments could use Charisma instead of Will, since Charisma reflects force of personality.
- Will saves against illusions could be keyed to Intelligence, the ability that best represents discernment.

As with skills, changes to a saving throw's key ability are always handled on a case-by-case basis. Unless you institute changes to saving throws as a house rule, these changes are very rare.

Remember that when you change the way a saving throw works in this fashion, you should dictate when the change comes into play—it's not up to a player to make this sort of decision. Players may try to rationalize why they should get to use their best ability score modifier on a saving throw that doesn't normally use that ability, but you shouldn't allow this sort of rule change unles you happen to agree with it.

ADJUDICATING MAGIC

At the middle range of levels, most characters cast spells, and they all use magic items, many of which produce strange magical effects. Handling spells and effects well is often the difference between a good game and a really good one.

DESCRIBING SPELL EFFECTS

Magic is flashy. When characters (PCs or NPCs) cast spells or use magic items, you should describe what the spell looks, sounds, smells, or feels like as well as its game effects.

A *magic missile* could be a dagger-shaped burst of energy that flies through the air. It also could be a fistlike creation of energy that bashes into its target or the sudden appearance of a demonic head that spits a blast of energy. When someone becomes invisible, he or she fades away. A summoned fiend appears with a flash of blood-red energy and a smell of brimstone. Other spells have more obvious visual effects. A *fireball* and a *lightning bolt*, for example, appear pretty much the way they are described in the *Player's Handbook*. For dramatic flair, however, you could describe the *lightning bolt* as being a thin arc of blue lightning and the *fireball* as a blast of green fire with red twinkling bursts within it.

You can let players describe the spells that their characters cast. Don't, however, allow a player to use an original description that makes a spell seem more powerful than it is. A *fireball* spell that creates an illusion of a dragon breathing flames goes too far.

Spells without obvious visual effects can be described as well. Since a target who makes his saving throw against a spell knows that something happened to him (the effect of the spell's being targeted on him), you could describe a charm or a compulsion as a cold claw threatening to enclose his mind that he manages to shake off. (If the spell worked, the target would not be aware of such an effect, for his mind would not be entirely his own.)

Sound can be a powerful descriptive force. You could say that a *lightning bolt* is accompanied by a clap of thunder. A *cone of cold* sounds like a rush of wind followed by a tinkling of crystalline ice.

HANDLING DIVINATIONS

Spells such as *augury*, *divination*, and *legend lore* require you to come up with information on the spot. Two problems can arise when dealing with such divinations.

The Player Could Learn Too Much: The strategic use of a divination spell could put too much information into the hands of the players, ruining a mystery or revealing a surprise too soon. The way to avoid this problem is to keep in mind the capabilities of the PCs when you create adventures. Don't forget that the cleric might be able to use her *commune* spell to learn the identity of the king's murderer. While you shouldn't allow a divination to give a player more information than you want her to have, you shouldn't cheat a player out of the effects of her spells just for the sake of the plot. Remember also that certain spells can protect someone from divinations such as *detect evil* and *discern lies*—but that's not really the point. Don't design situations that make the PCs' divinations worthless—design situations to take divinations into account. Assume that the cleric learns the identity of the king's murderer. That's fine, but the adventure is about apprehending him, not just identifying him, and it's especially important to stop him before he kills the queen as well.

In short, you should control information, but don't deny it to the character who has earned it.

Needing Answers on the Fly: Most likely you won't know that a character is going to use a divination spell until the spell is cast, and so you often need to come up with an answer on the fly.

One of the ways to get around this problem is obvious. To answer a question about what lies at the bottom of the dark staircase, you have to know what's there. Chances are you already do know what's there, or the character using the divination wouldn't consider the question worth asking. If you don't know, then you need to make something up in a hurry.

More difficult is coming up with a way to convey the information. For example, the description of the *divination* spell notes that "The advice can be as simple as a short phrase, or it might take the form of a cryptic rhyme or omen." Cryptic rhymes are often difficult to come up with in the middle of the game. One trick is to create a rhyme ahead of time that can fit just about any question, such as "If X is the seed you sow, reap you will Y and know," where X is an action and Y is the result. Or "If into X fate doth thee send, thou wilt find Y in the end," where X is a place and Y is a result or consequence such as "danger" or "treasure."

CREATING NEW SPELLS

Introducing an unbalanced spell does more damage to your game than handing out an unbalanced magic item. A magic item can get stolen, destroyed, sold, or otherwise taken away—but once a character knows a spell, she's going to want to keep using it.

When creating a new spell, use the existing spells as benchmarks, and use common sense. Creating a spell is actually fairly easy—it's assigning a level to the new spell that's hard. If the "best" 2nd-level spell is *invisibility*, and the "best" 1st-level spell is *charm person* or *sleep*, and the new spell seems to fall between those spells in power, it's probably a 2nd-level spell. (*Sleep*, however, is a strange example, because it's a spell that gets less useful as the caster gains levels—as opposed to a spell such as *magic missile* or *fireball*, which gets better, up to a point, for higher-level casters. Make sure spells that only affect low-level creatures are low-level spells.)

- If a spell is so good that you can't imagine a caster *not* wanting it all the time, it's either too powerful or too low in level.
- An experience point (XP) cost is a good balancing force. An expensive material component is only a moderately good balancing force. (Money can be easy to come by; an XP loss almost always hurts.)
- When determining level, compare range, duration, and target (or area) to other spells to balance. A long duration or large area can make up for a lesser effect, depending on the spell.
- A spell with a very limited use (only works against red dragons) could conceivably be one level lower than it would be if it had a more general application. Even at a low level, this is the sort of spell a sorcerer or bard never takes and other casters would prepare only if they knew in advance it would be worthwhile.
- Wizards and sorcerers should not cast healing spells, but they should have the best offensive spells. If the spell is flashy or dramatic, it should probably be a wizard/sorcerer spell.
- Clerics are best at spells that deal with alignment and have the best selection of curative and repair spells. They also have the best selection of information-gathering spells such as *commune* and *divination*.
- Druids are best at spells that deal with plants and animals.
- Rangers and paladins should not have flashy attack spells such as *magic missile* and *fireball*.
- Bard spells are enchantments, information-gathering spells, and include a mixture of other types of spells, but do not include large, offensive spells such as *cone of cold*.

Damage Caps for Spells

For spells that deal damage, use Table 3–22: Maximum Damage for Arcane Spells and Table 3–23: Maximum Damage for Divine Spells to determine approximately how much damage a spell should deal. Remember that some spells (such as *burning hands*) use a d4 for damage, but a *fireball* uses a d6. For clerics, a d8 counts as two dice for determining the damage cap. This table also reflects the spells of wizards, sorcerers, clerics, and druids more accurately than those for bards, rangers, and paladins.

TABLE 3–22: MAXIMUM DAMAGE FOR ARCANE SPELLS

Arcane Spell Level	Max Damage (Single Creature)	Max Damage (Multiple Creatures)
1st	5 dice	—
2nd	10 dice	5 dice
3rd	10 dice	10 dice
4th	15 dice	10 dice
5th	15 dice	15 dice
6th	20 dice	15 dice
7th	20 dice	20 dice
8th	25 dice	20 dice
9th	25 dice	25 dice

TABLE 3-23: MAXIMUM DAMAGE FOR DIVINE SPELLS

Divine Spell Level	Max Damage (Single Creature)	Max Damage (Multiple Creatures)
1st	1 die	—
2nd	5 dice	5 dice
3rd	10 dice	5 dice
4th	10 dice	10 dice
5th	15 dice	10 dice
6th	15 dice	15 dice
7th	20 dice	15 dice
8th	20 dice	20 dice
9th	25 dice	20 dice

The damage cap depends on whether a spell affects a single creature or multiple creatures. A single-creature spell affects only one creature or has its total damage divided among several creatures. For example, a *magic missile* spell can deliver 5 dice of damage to one target. If it strikes more than one target, its damage dice must be divided among them. A multiple-creature spell inflicts full damage on two or more creatures simultaneously. For example, a *fireball* damages everything within its 20-foot spread.

VARIANT: SPELL ROLL

Substitute this variant for the standard method of determining saving throw DCs for spells. Every time a character casts a spell that requires a target to make a saving throw, the caster rolls 1d20 and adds the spell level and the appropriate spellcasting ability modifier. The result is the DC for the saving throw. Roll once even for a spell that affects many creatures.

This variant introduces a great deal more randomness into spellcasting—sometimes low-level spells cast by mediocre casters will have difficult DCs, and sometimes high-level spells cast by powerful casters are easy to resist. It downplays the level of the spell and the ability score modifier. As with variant combat rules, any change that increases chance in a battle favors the underdog, and that's usually the enemies of the PCs.

The advantage to this variant is that it gives the player the fun of casting "good spells" and "bad spells," just like the player running the fighter can have good swings and bad.

VARIANT: POWER COMPONENTS

The horn of the rare red minotaur can be combined with a potent mixture of herbs that can aid in restoring wholeness to the afflicted. So potent is the energy contained in the concoction that a cleric who uses it while casting *greater restoration* (and uses it up) need not devote any personal power (XP) in order to cast the spell.

This variant allows for special rare ingredients ("power components") to be added to material spell components in place of XP. You're free to allow this only on a case-by-case basis. Perhaps these components exist only for certain spells. They're certainly rare, and certainly expensive—ten to twenty times the XP loss in gold pieces is a good baseline price. Further, characters may need to consult sages or cast divinations in order to find out what the proper ingredients are.

Consider not allowing characters to buy power components at all. Make them the object of an adventure. The hunt for the red minotaur can be a challenging and entertaining adventure by itself, but if the defeat of the minotaur is the first step toward the goal of bringing back a fallen comrade, the scenario takes on a larger importance.

In the same way, special ingredients can substitute for the XP that a character otherwise has to spend to create magic items.

This variant works if it makes powerful magic more colorful and if it fits the way you want to portray magic in your campaign. It fails if it means that the only hard control on casting powerful spells and creating magic items (the XP cost) slips away, so that such action become commonplace.

VARIANT: SUMMONING INDIVIDUAL MONSTERS

When a character casts a *summon monster* or *summon nature's ally* spell, she gets a typical, random creature of the type she chooses. As a variant for your campaign, you can rule that each spellcaster gets specific, individual creatures rather than just some random one. This variant lets players feel more ownership over the creatures that their characters summon, but it entails some special problems, so don't allow it without considering it carefully.

Specific Creatures: Whenever a spellcaster summons a single creature of a given type, it's always the same creature. A player can roll the ability scores and hit points for each creature that his character can summon. His specific creatures may be above or below average. Allow the player to take average statistics instead of rolling if he wants to avoid the risk of getting stuck with a bad creature thanks to bad dice rolls. (There's no "hopeless creature reroll" for bad ability scores.) The player can also name each creature and define its distinguishing characteristics.

Multiple Creatures: Whenever the spellcaster summons more creatures, the first one is always the same, and each successive creature is likewise always the same. Thus, if Mialee can summon up to three formian workers named Kulik, Skitky, and Kliss, then she always gets Kulik when she summons one formian worker, Kulik and Skitky when she summons two, and all three when she summons three. The player can roll ability scores and hit points for all three.

The summoner gets the same creatures no matter which version of a spell she uses. Mialee gets Kulik with *summon monster II* and she gets Kulik plus possibly Skitky and Kliss with *summon monster III*.

Summoning Limits: Getting the same intelligent summoned creature over and over again gives a summoner certain advantages. She can, for instance, send a creature to scout out an area for the duration of the spell and then summon it up again to get a report. If the creature is killed (and thus sent back to its home) or dispelled, however, that individual creature is not available for summoning for 24 hours. The summoner summons one fewer creature of that type because the unavailable creature still takes up its normal "slot." Thus, if Kulik is killed and later that day Mialee summons two formian workers, she only gets Skitky (instead of Kulik and Skitky).

If a creature that a character summons is actually, truly killed (not just "killed" while summoned), it is no longer available, and the summoner gets one fewer creature of that type than normal. On achieving a new level, however, the summoner may replace the slain creature (see below).

Replacing Creatures: Each time a summoner gains a level in a spellcasting class, she can drop out one of her creatures and roll up a new one to fill its "slot." For example, at 5th level, Mialee can summon Kulik, Skitky, and Kliss with *summon monster III*. When she reaches 6th level, she can drop any one of her summonable creatures and replace it with a new one. If Kulik has low ability scores or if it has permanently died, she can drop it in favor of a new, randomly rolled creature, which then occupies her "first formian worker" slot.

Improving Creatures: Summoners can improve their creatures. Typically, they do so by giving them magic items or other special objects. The trick is, a summoned creature can't take things back home with it. When a summoned creature disappears, it leaves all the things that it gained while on the Material Plane. Mialee can't just summon up Kulik and give it a *cloak of resistance*. She has to go to its plane or bring it really on the Material Plane before she can give it anything it can keep. The way to get a creature to really come to the Material Plane is to use a *lesser planar ally*, *planar ally*, *greater planar ally*, *lesser planar binding*, *planar binding*, *greater planar binding*, or *gate* spell, since these are all calling spells and really bring the creature completely to the caster.

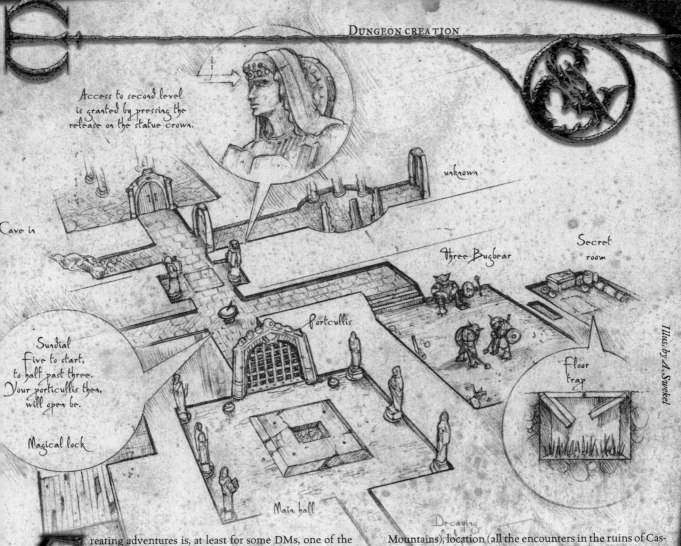

Access to second level is granted by pressing the release on the statue crown.

unknown

Cave in

Three Bugbear

Secret room

Portcullis

Sundial Five to start, to half past three. Your porticullis then, will open be.

Magical lock

Floor trap

Main hall

Decaying

Illus. by A. Swekel

Creating adventures is, at least for some DMs, one of the great benefits of being a Dungeon Master. It's a way to express yourself creatively, designing fantastic places and events filled with monsters and imaginative elements of all kinds. When you design an adventure, you call the shots. You do things exactly the way you want to. Designing an adventure can be a lot of work, but the rewards are great. Your players will thrill at the challenges and mysteries you have created for them. Experienced DMs pride themselves on masterful adventures, creative new situations and locales, and intriguing NPCs. A well-honed encounter—whether it's a monster, a trap, or an NPC who must be reasoned with—can be a thing of beauty.

"What is an adventure?" isn't as easy a question to answer as you might think. While a campaign is made up of adventures, it's not always clear where one adventure ends and another begins. Adventures can be so varied that it's tough to pin down the basics. This chapter is going to try to help you do that.

An adventure starts with some sort of hook, whether it's a rumor of treasure in an old, abandoned monastery or a plea for help from the queen. The hook is what draws the PCs into the action and gets them to the point where the story of the adventure truly begins. This point might be a location (such as the monastery or the queen's palace) or an event (the theft of the queen's scepter, which the PCs are tasked with recovering).

Adventures are broken down into encounters. Encounters are typically keyed to areas on a map that you have prepared. Encounters can also be designed in the form of if/then statements: "If the PCs wait outside the druid's grove for more than an hour, then his three trained owlbears attack." The encounters of an adventure are all linked in some way, whether in theme (all the encounters that occur as they travel from the City of Greyhawk to the Crystalmist Mountains), location (all the encounters in the ruins of Castle Temerity) or events (all the encounters that occur as the PCs attempt to rescue the mayor's son from Rahurg the ogre king).

Adventures can be classified as site-based or event-based.

SITE-BASED ADVENTURES

The Tomb of Horrors, the Temple of Elemental Evil, the Ghost Tower of Inverness—these are places of legend, mystery, and adventure. If you create an adventure based around some place—a dungeon, a ruin, a mountain, a valley, a cave complex, a wilderness, a town—then you have created a site-based adventure. Site-based adventures revolve around a map with a key, detailing important spots on that map. Encounters in the adventure are triggered when the PCs enter a new location at the site. The implication is that each encounter describes what occurs at that site when the PCs arrive (or first arrive).

Creating a site-based adventure involves two steps: drawing the map and keying the encounters.

Draw a Map: Graph paper is useful for mapping out dungeons, because you can assign a scale for the squares, such as 5 feet or 10 feet per square. The lines also aid in drawing straight lines (particularly useful when drawing building interiors or dungeons). Mark important areas with numbers or letters that reference the map key. Make notes on the map describing anything of importance, including room contents (statues, pools, furniture, pillars, steps, pits, curtains, etc.). Plan out which areas are linked by similar or allied inhabitants. Place traps, taking care to note particularly the location of trap triggers. Consider spell ranges—if an NPC wizard is in a particular area and you know that she might cast a particular spell, save yourself time during the playing of the adventure by noting now how far the effect can stretch.

Remember that the player characters are catalysts for change. While you play, note changes caused by the PCs' presence—possibly even writing them directly on the map. That way it's easier to remember, the second time they pass through an area, which doors they have knocked down, which traps they have triggered, which treasures they have looted, which guardians they have defeated, and so forth.

Create a Key: The key is nothing more than a set of notes (as detailed or brief as you need them to be) detailing each area's contents, NPCs (description, statistics, possible actions), and whatever else makes that place special. For example, in an outdoor map you might mark an area that triggers a landslide if crossed, a bridge over the river guarded by lizardfolk, and the lair of a basilisk—complete with details about the interior of the lair and the treasure formerly in the possession of the half-eaten, petrified victims in the back. Each entry should include the game information needed to run that encounter. If an area has nothing to write about, don't bother marking it on the key.

Most dungeon adventures are site-based. See the Dungeon section, page 105, as well as the sample dungeon adventure that begins on page 126.

A site-based adventure allows the PCs to drive the action. If they come to a fork in the path, they're free to choose whichever way they want. It doesn't matter which they choose, which order they choose them in, or if they never go down one path at all. The characters can leave the location and come back, often starting the adventure back up again exactly where they left off (although some aspects of the site may have changed, depending on how static the site is; see below).

A site-based adventure is easy for the DM to run. All the information is right there in front of you on the map and in the key. Between the two of them, the map and the key should cover any potential action the PCs may take during the adventure.

Site-based adventures usually lure PCs to them based on their reputation alone, but sometimes an event triggers the adventure, drawing the PCs to the site. Once at the site, the map channels where they go—if a hallway leads straight ahead or back the way the PCs came, and there's a door on the right, the PCs have only three basic courses of action: ahead, back, or through the door.

STATIC OR DYNAMIC

Sometimes a site-based adventure takes place at a completely static location. The map shows an old ruin filled with monsters that live there, where the ancient treasures are located within the ruin, where the traps or danger spots are located, and so on. The PCs can arrive at this location at any time, stay as long as they desire, leave whenever they want, and come back later to find the site pretty much the same as they left it (although more monsters may have taken up residence, or a few may have wandered off; maybe a trap has been triggered by the monsters and no longer threatens the PCs, or a trap the PCs previously triggered has been reset).

Designing a static site-based adventure is fairly easy. You don't have to think much about how the residents of the various encounter areas interact, and each encounter area need only be designed with the most immediate implications in mind—namely, what happens when the PCs arrive?

By contrast, a good example of a dynamic site is a drow fortress-temple. A dynamic site usually involves some sort of intelligent organization. As the PCs move around the site, they discover that actions in certain areas affect the encounters in other areas. For example, if the PCs kill two of the drow priestesses in the fortress-temple but allow a third one to escape, the fortress-temple mobilizes its

populace—now, defenders are moving around from location to location and are much more likely to attack any unknown intruders rather than ask questions.

Designing a dynamic site is a little more complicated than designing a static one. You must take into account elements such as the following:

- Formulate defensive plans for the inhabitants. "If attacked, the guards use the gong to raise the alarm. The sound of the gong can be heard in areas A, B, and D. The inhabitants in those areas don armor and overturn the tables for cover. The sorcerer in area B casts *invisibility* on himself and the barbarian."
- Develop conditional requirements for various areas. "If anyone disturbs the three unholy gems upon the altar, the Infernal Gates in area 5 open, allowing access to the City of Dis but also summoning 3d4 barbazu devils, who occupy the entire dungeon and come out at night to raid the countryside in a 5-mile radius."
- Determine the inhabitants' long-term plans. "In a month's time, the goblins will have completed the wall in area 39. With that defense to fall back on, they begin the assault on the kobold caves in areas 32–37. If no one intervenes, the goblins will clear out the kobolds in three weeks and the goblin adept will gain the *wand of lightning bolt* stored in the secret vault in area 35."

EVENT-BASED ADVENTURES

The death of the king. The Rain of Colorless Fire. The carnival's arrival in town. Unexplained disappearances. Merchants of Druus looking for caravan guards. Events can lead to adventures, drawing the PCs in and getting them involved in amazing predicaments. Event-based adventures can be thought of being structured as "This happens, and then if the PCs do *this*, then *that* happens. . . ." They involve a series of events influenced by the PCs' actions. The PCs' reactions change the events that occur, or the order in which they occur, or both.

In an event-based adventure, the PCs usually have a goal or a mission beyond "Kill all the monsters" or "Get as much treasure as possible" or even "Explore this area." The adventure instead focuses on the adventurers trying to accomplish something specific. The encounters come as a result of that effort—either as a consequence of their actions, or as opposing forces attempt to stop them, or both.

This type of adventure is often described as more story-based, because it's more like a book or a movie and less like exploration of a passive site. Event-based adventures usually don't involve a room-by-room key but instead notes on what happens when. Here are a few ideas for organizing these notes:

Flowchart: By drawing connected boxes or circles with event descriptions in them, it's easy to visually track the flow of events. "As the PCs investigate the murder, if they question the innkeeper. She tells them that she saw someone suspicious hanging around the back of the livery last night. If they ask specifically about Gregory, she tells them where he lives." In this example, the flowchart has two lines drawn away from the innkeeper. One goes to the livery and the other goes to Gregory's house, since those are the two likely paths the PCs will take next. Of course, the party is free to ignore these clues and follow up on some other lead.

Timeline: Another way to organize an event-based adventure is by time. A timeline starts when the PCs get involved in the story (sometime even before then). It marks what happens when. "One day after the PCs arrive in town, Joham comes to them pleading for help. The next day, Joham is found dead in his room at the inn. That evening, Gregory comes to the inn, poking around for information to see if the body's been found." Often, however, events on the timeline need to be conditional: "If it's apparent that the PCs are on to him, Gregory tries to slip out of town that night."

Don't fall into the trap of leading the PCs by the nose with an event-based adventure. See the section on Structure, below.

MOTIVATION

Motivation is what drives the adventure—it's what gets the PCs involved in whatever you have designed for them to do. If the PCs aren't motivated, they won't do what you want them to, and all your work will be wasted. Greed, fear, revenge, need, morality, anger, and curiosity are all powerful motivators. So, of course, is fun. Never forget that last one.

TAILORED VS. STATUS QUO

Tailored motivations are ones that you have specifically designed with your group's PCs in mind. Here are just a few of many possible examples.

- The PCs are a hardened group of mercenaries, not interested in the pleas of innocents or stories of evil that threatens some good kingdom. However, they are quite interested in gold. . . .
- Mialee the wizard has been slain by the gargoyles in the Caverns of Dread. Now, the other PCs seek a means to *raise* her. Knowing this, you mention that they have heard of a good-hearted cleric of Pelor to the south, in the city of Dyvers. When they arrive, the cleric is willing to raise Mialee, but only if the PCs help him by ridding the temple's lower level of wererats. . . .
- You know that the party has just finished clearing out a wizard's tower and has lots of treasure. Therefore, you don't lure them to the next adventure using the promise of gold, but instead with the rumor that the wizard isn't dead, but has risen as a vampire and has sworn revenge. . . .
- Tordek's brother Ralcoss comes to the PCs, explains that a terrible tragedy has beset the dwarven city of Dumadan, and asks for their help . . .

A status quo motivation isn't really a motivation in the strict sense of the word. It's the fact that (for instance) adventure awaits in the Lost Valley for anyone who dares brave the wyvern-haunted cliffs that surround the place. The PCs can go there or not, depending on how they feel. While a tailored motivation is good for ensuring that the PCs end up in the adventure you have designed and for letting the players feel like their characters have a real place in the world, a status quo motivation allows you to set up situations unrelated to the PCs specifically. This creates a sense of perspective, the feeling that the campaign world is a real place that extends beyond the PCs.

STRUCTURE

Whether site-based or event-based, an adventure always runs its course from the beginning to an ending. Some adventures are completed in an hour. Others take months of playing sessions. Length is up to you, although it's smart to plan ahead and know about how many sessions an adventure will last (and make sure that the current group of players can commit to that length). Here are some guidelines that you should keep in mind for structuring good adventures and avoiding bad ones.

Tordek is unprepared for an ogre's ambush.

GOOD STRUCTURE

Good adventures are fun. That's an easy generalization, but it's also true. Whatever you and your players find fun adds to your game. An adventure that everyone enjoys likely includes these features:

Choices: Every good adventure has at least a few crux points where the players need to make important decisions. What they decide should have significant impact on what happens next. This can be as simple as the players deciding not to go down the corridor to the left (where the pyrohydra waits for them) and instead going to the right (toward the magic fountain), or as complex as the PCs deciding not to help the queen against the grand vizier (so that she ends up being assassinated and the vizier's puppet gains the throne).

Difficult Choices: On the topic of choices with consequence, the choices should sometimes be difficult ones to make. Should the PCs help the church of Heironeous wage war on the goblins, even though the conflict will almost certainly keep them from reaching the Fortress of Nast before the evil duke summons the slaadi assassins? Should the PCs trust the words of a dragon, or ignore her warning?

Different Sorts of Encounters: A good adventure should provide a number of different experiences—attack, defense, problem-solving, roleplaying, and investigation. Make sure you vary the types of encounters the adventure provides (see Encounters, page 100).

Exciting Events: Like the pacing of a story, a good adventure should have rising and falling tension—and an exciting climax is always a good thing. This sort of pacing is easier to accomplish with an event-based adventure (since you have more control over when each encounter takes place), but it's possible in a site-based adventure to design a locale where the encounters are likely to occur in a desired fashion. Make sure to pace things well. Start slowly and have the action build. A climactic encounter always makes for a good ending.

Encounters that Make Use of PC Abilities: If the party's wizard or sorcerer can cast *fly*, incorporate aerial encounters into the adventure. When there's a cleric along, occasionally include undead that she can use her turning ability upon. If the party has a ranger or a druid, include encounters with animals (dire animals can make challenging encounters for even mid- to high-level PCs—see the *Monster Manual* for more information). The advice to remember is "Everyone gets his or her chance to shine." All abilities available to PCs were designed to make the characters better, but an ability (or a spell) that a character never gets to use is a waste.

BAD STRUCTURE

Try to avoid these pitfalls.

Leading the PCs by the Nose: A bad event-based adventure is marked by mandates restricting PC actions or is based on events that occur no matter what the PCs do. For example, a plot that hinges on the PCs finding a mysterious heirloom, only to have it stolen by NPCs, is dangerous—if the players invent a good way to protect the heirloom, they won't like having it stolen anyway just because that's what you planned beforehand. The players end up feeling powerless and frustrated. No matter what, all adventures should depend upon player choices. Players should always feel as though what they choose to do matters. The results should affect the campaign setting (albeit perhaps in minor ways), and they should have consequences (good or bad) for the PCs.

PCs as Spectators: In this type of bad adventure, NPCs accomplish all the important tasks. There might be an interesting story going on, but it's going on around the PCs, and they have very little to do with it. As much as you might like one of your NPCs, resist the urge to have him or her accomplish everything instead of letting the PCs do the work. As great as it might be to have your big NPC hero fight the evil wizard (also an NPC) threatening the land, this is not much fun for the players if all they get to do is watch.

Deus ex Machina: Similar to the "PCs as Spectators" problem is the potential pitfall of the *deus ex machina*, a term used to describe the ending to a story in which the action is resolved by an intervention of some outside divine agency rather than by the characters' own actions. Don't put the PCs in situations in which they can only survive through the intervention of others. Sometimes it's interesting to be rescued, but using this sort of "escape hatch" gets frustrating quickly. Players would rather defeat a young dragon on their own than face an ancient wyrm and only defeat it because a high-level NPC teleports in to help them.

Preempting the Characters' Abilities: It's good to know the PCs' capabilities, but you shouldn't design adventures that continually countermand or foil what they can do. If the wizard just learned *fireball*, don't continually throw fire-resistant foes at him. Don't create dungeons where *fly* and *teleport* spells don't work just because it's more difficult to design challenging encounters for characters with those capabilities. Use the PCs' abilities to allow them to have more interesting encounters—don't arbitrarily rule that their powers suddenly don't work.

THE FLOW OF INFORMATION

Much of the structure of an adventure depends on what the PCs know and when. If they know that there's a dragon at the bottom of the dungeon, they will conserve their strength for that encounter and have proper spells and strategies prepared. When they learn the identity of the traitor, they will probably act on this information immediately. If they learn too late that their actions will cause the cavern complex to collapse, they won't be able to keep it from happening.

Don't give away the whole plot in one go, but do give the players some new bit of knowledge every so often. For example, if the drow elves are the secret masters behind the uprising of giants, slowly reveal clues to that fact. Information gained while fighting the hill giants leads the PCs to the frost giants, which in turn garners them clues that take them to the fire giants. Only among the fire giants do the PCs encounter information that leads them to understand that the drow are involved. And thus the final encounter with those drow masters is made all the more dramatic.

In some situations, the PCs know everything they need to know before the adventure begins. That's okay. Occasionally, there is no mystery. For example, the adventurers learn that a haunted tower in the woods is inhabited by a vampire and her minions. They go in with stakes and holy water, slay a bunch of undead, and finally meet up with the vampire and take her out. That's a fine adventure. Sometimes, however, a surprise that the PCs never could have seen coming makes it all the more interesting—the vampire turns out to be a good-aligned undead resisting her bloodlust but slowly succumbing to the temptation of an erinyes devil who lives under the church back in town. Both the "no surprises" and the "unexpected twist" structures work well, so long as you avoid overusing either.

Finally, keep in mind divination spells when predetermining how you're going to control the flow of information. Don't deny the spells their potency. Instead, learn what they can and cannot do, and plan for the PCs to use them. (See Handling Divinations, page 95.) After all, if you have assumed that they would cast the proper spells and they don't use what's available to them, they deserve to fail!

ENCOUNTERS

As interesting as it is to talk about adventures (and the stories behind them), the game is really composed of encounters. Each individual encounter is like its own game—with a beginning, a middle, an end, and victory conditions to determine a winner and a loser.

TAILORED OR STATUS QUO

Just as with motivations, encounters can be tailored specifically to the PCs, or not. A tailored encounter is one in which you take into consideration that the wizard PC has a *wand of invisibility* and the fighter's AC is 23. In a tailored encounter, you design things to fit the PCs and the players. In fact, you can specifically design something for each PC to do—the skeletal minotaur is a challenge for the barbarian, another skeleton with a crossbow is on a ledge that only the rogue can reach, only the monk can leap across the chasm to pull the lever to raise the portcullis in front of the treasure, and the cleric's *invisibility to undead* allows her to get to the treasure the skeletons are guarding while the battle rages.

A status quo encounter forces the PCs to adapt to the encounter rather than the other way around. Bugbears live on Clover Hill, and if the PCs go there, they encounter bugbears, whether bugbears are an appropriate encounter for them or not. This type of encounter gives the world a certain verisimilitude, and so it's good to mix a few in with the other sorts of encounters.

If you decide to use only status quo encounters, you should probably let your players know about this. Some of the encounters you place in your adventure setting will be of an appropriate level for the PCs, but others might not be. For instance, you could decide where the dragon's lair is long before the characters are experienced enough to survive a fight against the dragon. If players know ahead of time that the setting includes status quo encounters that their characters might not be able to handle, they will be more likely to make the right decision if they stumble upon a tough encounter. That decision, of course, is to run away and fight again another day (after the party is better equipped to meet the challenge).

CHALLENGE RATINGS AND ENCOUNTER LEVELS

A monster's Challenge Rating (CR) tells you the level of the party for which that monster is a good challenge. A monster of CR 5 is an appropriate challenge for a group of four 5th-level characters. If the characters are higher level than the monster, they get fewer XP because the monster should be easy to defeat. Likewise, if the party level (the average of the character levels of every member of the party) is lower than a monster's Challenge Rating, the PCs get a greater award.

Parties with five or more members can often take on monsters with higher CRs, and parties of three or fewer are challenged by monsters with lower CRs. Nevertheless, XP awards depend on the group's average level. See Chapter 7: Rewards.

Multiple Monsters and Encounter Levels

Obviously, if one monster is a given Challenge Rating, more than one monster is a greater challenge than that. You can use Table 4–1: Encounter Numbers to determine the Encounter Level of a group of monsters, as well as to determine how many monsters equate to a given Encounter Level (useful in balancing an encounter with a PC party).

To balance an encounter to a party, determine the party's effective level (the average of all their character levels). You want the party's level to match the level of the encounter, so find that number in the "Encounter Level" column. Then look across that line to find the CR of the creature type that you want to use in the encounter. Once you have found it, look at the top of that column to find the number of creatures that makes a balanced encounter for the party.

For example, suppose you want to send ogres against a 6th-level party. The *Monster Manual* entry on ogres shows that they are CR 2. Looking at the "6" row in the "Encounter Level" column, you read across to the "2" entry and then check the top of that column to find that four CR 2 monsters make a good 6th-level encounter.

To determine the Encounter Level of a group of monsters, reverse these steps (begin with the number of creatures, read down to find the CR for the creature type, then look left to find the appropriate EL).

Matched Pair: In general, if a creature's Challenge Rating is two lower than a given Encounter Level, then two creatures of that type equal an encounter of that Encounter Level. Thus, a pair of frost giants (CR 9 each) make an EL 11 encounter. The progression holds of doubling the number of creatures for each drop of two places in their individual CR, so that four CR 7 creatures (say, four hill giants) are an EL 11 encounter, as are eight CR 5 creatures (such as ettins). This calculation does not work, however, with creatures whose CR is 1 or less, so be sure to use Table 4–1: Encounter Numbers for such encounters.

Mixed Pair: When dealing with a creature whose Challenge Rating is only 1 lower than the intended EL, you can raise the EL by 1 by adding a second creature whose CR is three less than the desired EL. For example, a DM wants to set up an encounter with an aboleth (CR 7) for an 8th-level party. Two aboleths would be EL 9, and she wants an encounter of EL 8, so she decides to give the aboleth a companion or pet to raise the encounter to EL 8. Checking Table 4–1: Encounter Numbers, she finds that the entry for 8th-level encounters in the "Mixed Pair" column is "7+5." This means that a CR 7 monster and a CR 5 monster together are an EL 8 encounter.

In general, you can treat a group of creatures as a single creature whose CR equals the group's EL. For example, instead of having

TABLE 4–1: ENCOUNTER NUMBERS

| Encounter Level | Number of Creatures | | | | | | | | |
	One	Two	Three	Four	Five or Six	Seven to Nine	Ten to Twelve	Matched Pair	Mixed Pair
1	1 or 2	1/2	1/3	1/4	1/6	1/8	1/8	1/2	1/2 + 1/3
2	2 or 3	1	1/2 or 1	1/2	1/3	1/4	1/6	1	1 + 1/2
3	3 or 4	1 or 2	1	1/2 or 1	1/2	1/3	1/4	1	2 + 1
4	3, 4, 5	2	1 or 2	1	1/2 or 1	1/2	1/3	2	3 + 1
5	4, 5, 6	3	2	1 or 2	1	1/2	1/2	3	4 + 2
6	5, 6, 7	4	3	2	1 or 2	1	1/2	4	5 + 3
7	6, 7, 8	5	4	3	2	1	1/2	5	6 + 4
8	7, 8, 9	6	5	4	3	2	1	6	7 + 5
9	8, 9, 10	7	6	5	4	3	2	7	8 + 6
10	9, 10, 11	8	7	6	5	4	3	8	9 + 7
11	10, 11, 12	9	8	7	6	5	4	9	10 + 8
12	11, 12, 13	10	9	8	7	6	5	10	11 + 9
13	12, 13, 14	11	10	9	8	7	6	11	12 + 10
14	13, 14, 15	12	11	10	9	8	7	12	13 + 11
15	14, 15, 16	13	12	11	10	9	8	13	14 + 12
16	15, 16, 17	14	13	12	11	10	9	14	15 + 13
17	16, 17, 18	15	14	13	12	11	10	15	16 + 14
18	17, 18, 19	16	15	14	13	12	11	16	17 + 15
19	18, 19, 20	17	16	15	14	13	12	17	18 + 16
20	19+	18	17	16	15	14	13	18	19 + 17

WHAT'S CHALLENGING?

So, what counts as a "challenge"? Since a game session probably includes many encounters, you don't want to make every encounter one that taxes the PCs to their limits. They would have to stop the adventure and rest for an extensive period after every fight, and that slows down the game. An encounter with an Encounter Level (EL) equal to the PCs' level is one that should expend about 20% of their resources—hit points, spells, magic item uses, etc. This means, on average, that after about four encounters of the party's level the PCs need to rest, heal, and regain spells. A fifth encounter would probably wipe them out.

The PCs should be able to take on many more encounters lower than their level but fewer encounters with Encounter Levels higher than their party level. As a general rule, if the EL is two lower than the party's level, the PCs should be able to take on twice as many encounters before having to stop and rest. Two levels below that, and the number of encounters they can cope with doubles again, and so on. By contrast, an encounter even one or two levels above the party level might tax the PCs to their limit, although with luck they might be able to take on two such encounters before needing to recover. Remember that when the EL is higher than the party level, the chance for PC fatality raises dramatically.

the PCs encounter one CR 4 creature (say, a brown bear), you could substitute two CR 2 creatures (a pair of black bears), whose EL together is 4.

Some monsters' CRs are fractions. For instance, an orc (CR 1/2) is not a good challenge even for a 1st-level party. This means either calculate XP as if the orc were Challenge Rating 1, then divide by 2, or treat each pair of orcs encountered as a Challenge Rating 1 monster.

Encounters with more than a dozen creatures are difficult to judge. If you need thirteen or more creatures to provide enough XP for a standard encounter, then those individual monsters are probably so weak that they don't make for a good encounter. That's why Table 4–1: Encounter Numbers doesn't have an entry larger than twelve for "Number of Creatures."

DIFFICULTY

Sometimes, the PCs encounter something that's a pushover for them. At other times, an encounter is too difficult and they have to run away. A well-constructed adventure has a variety of encounters at several different levels of difficulty. Table 4–2: Encounter Difficulty shows (in percentage terms) how many encounters of a certain difficulty an adventure should have.

TABLE 4–2: ENCOUNTER DIFFICULTY

% of Total	Encounter	Description
10%	Easy	EL lower than party level
20%	Easy if handled properly	Special (see below)
50%	Challenging	EL equals that of party
15%	Very difficult	EL 1 to 4 higher than party level
5%	Overpowering	EL 5+ higher than party level

Easy: The PCs win handily with little threat to themselves. The Encounter Level for the encounter is lower than the party level. The group should be able to handle an almost limitless number of these encounters.

Easy if Handled Properly: There's a trick to this type of encounter—a trick the PCs must discover to have a good chance of victory. Find and eliminate the cleric with *improved invisibility* first so she stops healing the ogres, and everything else about the encounter becomes much easier. If not handled properly, this type of encounter becomes challenging or even very difficult.

Challenging: Most encounters seriously threaten at least one member of the group in some way. These are challenging encounters, about equal in Encounter Level to the party level. The average adventuring group should be able to handle four or more challenging encounters before they run low on spells, hit points, and other resources. If an encounter doesn't cost the PCs some significant portion of their resources, it's not challenging.

Very Difficult: One PC might very well die. The Encounter Level is higher than the average party level. This sort of encounter may be more dangerous than an overpowering one, because it's not immediately obvious to the players that the PCs should flee.

Overpowering: The PCs should run. If they don't, they will probably lose. The Encounter Level is five or more levels higher than the party level.

Difficulty Notes

- Tight quarters make things more difficult for rogues, since it's harder to skulk about and gain a sneak attack.
- A spread-out force makes things more difficult for spellcasters, since the area affected by most spells is small.
- Many lesser foes are harder for a character to engage in melee than one powerful foe.
- Undead are much more difficult to fight without a cleric.
- Encounters involving animals or plants are much more difficult without a druid or a ranger.
- Encounters involving evil outsiders are much more difficult without a paladin or cleric (and perhaps a wizard or sorcerer).
- A large force is much more difficult to fight without a wizard or sorcerer.
- Locked doors and traps are much more difficult to overcome without a rogue.
- Multiple combat encounters are more difficult to win without a fighter, a barbarian, a ranger, or a paladin.
- Multiple combat encounters are more difficult to survive without a cleric.
- The bard and the cleric make good group support characters. Their presence makes practically every encounter easier.

None of the above notes should necessarily be taken into account when assigning or modifying Challenge Ratings, but you should keep them in mind when designing encounters.

TOUGHER MONSTERS

A really big basilisk with more hit points and a higher attack bonus than a normal basilisk is a greater challenge. If you use the rules found in the *Monster Manual* for increasing the Hit Dice of monsters, you should also increase the experience point (XP) award for the monster appropriately. If you increase the HD by 50%, increase the XP award by 50%. If you double the HD, double the XP award. For determining the CR, figure that a 50% increase in HD raises the CR of the monster by 1, and doubling the HD raises the CR by 2.

If you give monsters levels in PC or NPC classes, add the original CR to the class level to get the CR of this special individual. Subtract one from this total if the class is an NPC class rather than a PC class (see Chapter 2: Classes), although the minimum result is still one greater than the original monster CR.

Monster CR + PC class levels = adjusted CR
(Monster CR + NPC class levels) –1 = adjusted CR
Minimum adjusted CR = Monster CR +1

LOCATION

A fight between characters perched on a bridge made of skulls over a pool of bubbling lava is more exciting and more dangerous than that same fight in a nice, safe dungeon room. Location serves two purposes, both equally important. It can make a humdrum encounter more interesting, and it can make an encounter easier or much more difficult.

Making Things Interesting

Arguably, the dungeon itself is a fairly exotic locale, but eventually the same old 20-foot-by-20-foot room starts to grow stale. Likewise, a trip through the dark woods can be interesting and frightening, but the tenth trip through is less so. Since this is a fantasy game, allow yourself the freedom to consider all sorts of strange locations for encounters. Imagine an encounter inside a volcano, along a narrow ledge on the side of a cliff, atop a flying whale, or deep underwater. Think of the exciting location first, and then worry about how and why the PCs would get there.

Situations within a location can have as much impact as the location itself. If a rogue has to pick the lock on the only door out of the top room of a tower that's collapsing, it's suddenly a much more exciting situation than just another locked door in a dungeon corridor. Create an encounter in which the PCs must be diplomatic while all around them a battle rages. Fill an underground cave complex with water for a different sort of dungeon adventure. Set a series of encounters in a large wooden fort—on fire.

See Interesting Combats, page 71 in Chapter 3: Running the Game, for a short discussion that deals with this same issue.

Modifying Difficulty

Orcs with crossbows, behind cover, firing down at the PCs while the characters cross a narrow ledge over a pit full of spikes are much more dangerous than the same orcs being engaged in hand-to-hand combat in some tunnel. Likewise, if the PCs find themselves on a balcony, looking down at oblivious orcs who are carrying barrels of flammable oil, the encounter is likely to be much easier than if the orcs were aware of the PCs.

Consider the sorts of factors, related to location or situation, that make an encounter more difficult, such as:

- Enemy has cover (for example, behind a wall with arrow slits)
- Enemy is at higher elevation or is hard to get at (on a ledge or atop a defensible wall)
- Enemy has guaranteed surprise (PCs are asleep)
- Conditions make it difficult to see or hear (mist, darkness, rumbling machinery all around)
- Conditions make movement difficult (underwater, heavy gravity, very narrow passage)
- Conditions require delicate maneuvering (climbing down a sheer cliff, hanging from the ceiling)
- Conditions deal damage (in the icy cold, in a burning building, over a pit of acid)

Conversely, the first three conditions given above make encounters easier from the PCs' point of view if they are the ones benefiting from the cover, elevation, or surprise.

REWARDS AND BEHAVIOR

Encounters, either individually or strung together, reward certain types of behavior whether you, as the DM, are conscious of it or not. Encounters that can or must be won by killing the opponents reward aggression and fighting prowess. If you set up your encounters like this, expect wizards and priests to soon go into every adventure with only combat spells prepared. The PCs will learn to use tactics to find the best way to kill the enemy quickly. By contrast, encounters that can be won by diplomacy encourage the PCs to talk to everyone and everything they meet. Encounters that reward subterfuge and sneaking encourage sneakiness. Encounters that reward boldness speed up the game, while those that reward caution slow it down.

Always be aware of the sorts of actions you're rewarding your players for taking. Reward, in this case, doesn't just mean experience points and treasure. More generally, it means anything that consistently leads to success. An adventure should contain encounters that reward different types of behavior. This not only adds variety, but it tends to please all the players. Not everyone prefers the same kind of encounter, and even those with a favorite enjoy a change of pace. Remember, then, that you can offer many different types of encounters, including all of the following:

Combat: Combat encounters can be divided into two groups: attack and defense. Most of the time, PCs are on the attack, invading monsters' lairs and exploring dungeons. A defense encounter, in which the PCs must keep an area, an object, or a person safe from the enemy, can be a nice change of pace.

Negotiation: Although threats can often be involved, a negotiation encounter involves less swordplay and more wordplay. Convincing NPCs to do what the PCs want them to is challenging for both players and DM—quick thinking and good roleplaying are the keys here. Don't be afraid to play an NPC appropriately (stupid or intelligent, generous or selfish), as long as it fits. But don't make an NPC so predictable that the PCs can always tell exactly what he or she will do in any given circumstance. Consistent, yes; one-dimensional, no.

Environmental: Weather, earthquakes, landslides, fast-moving rivers, and fires are just some of the environmental conditions that can challenge even mid- to high-level PCs.

Problem-Solving: Mysteries, puzzles, riddles, or anything that requires the players to use logic and reason to try to overcome the challenge counts as a problem-solving encounter.

Judgment Calls: "Do we help the prisoner here in the dungeon, even though it might be a trap?" Rather than depending on logic, these encounters usually involve inclination and gut instinct.

Investigation: This is a long-term sort of encounter involving some negotiation and some problem-solving. An investigation may be called for to solve a mystery or to learn something new.

Ugh, a spider!

THE END (?)

Eventually, each adventure comes to an end. A climactic encounter places a nice capstone on an adventure, particularly if it's one that the players have seen coming. (If the ogres they have been fighting have been referring to a dragon, then an encounter with the dragon is a perfect ending.)

Many adventures require a denouement—some wrap-up to deal with the aftermath of the final encounter. This can be the time when they discover what treasure is in the dragon's hoard, a dramatic scene in the king's court in which he thanks the adventurers for slaying the dragon and passes out knighthoods all round, or a time to mourn those comrades who did not survive the battle. Generally, the denouement should not take nearly as long as the climax itself.

As with movies and books, adventures sometimes deserve sequels. Many adventures suggest further adventures for the PCs, relating to what they have accomplished or discovered. If the characters just destroyed the fortress of the evil overlord, they may find clues within the fortress that betray the identity of a traitor allied with the overlord operating in the town council. Perhaps the overlord's orc minions fled the site—where did they go? (Orcs, no matter where they go, are sure to cause trouble!) Suppose bandits attacked the adventurers while they were on their way to the overlord's fortress—going back now and finding the bandits' lair is an adventure of both justice and vengeance.

BRINGING ADVENTURES TOGETHER

Taking different adventures and tying them together makes a campaign. While creating a campaign is discussed elsewhere (see Chapter 5: Campaigns), here are some ideas for designing adventures that fit together.

EPISODIC OR CONTINUING

Episodic adventures are those that stand alone, with no relation to the one that came before or the one that follows. These sorts of adventures are fun, stand-alone scenarios that can be inserted anytime they're needed. They often provide interesting diversions from a continuing campaign. For example, in the middle of a series of adventures dealing with an evil prince, his minions, and the plague he unleashes on the land, the PCs might have a short episode dealing with recovering a lost lammasu cub.

A continuing adventure has links that connect the individual adventures. A link may be something such as a recurring NPC or related starting points. A sorcerer who sends the PCs on three different adventures, all to recover lost relics, forms the link that transforms those three adventures into a continuing adventure. Another example might be three adventures dealing with defeating an evil monk, coping with his evil cronies who come to avenge his death, and fending off the evil bard who seeks the powerful magic gem the monk once owned. Each part of a continuing adventure builds on what has come before, with the ramifications of one series of events causing another series of events and thus producing another adventure.

Most campaigns need a blend of episodic and continuing adventures to be successful and fun. To get the best of both worlds, it's possible to string together a number of unrelated episodic adventures with hints of a continuing plot in the background that eventually comes to fruition. For example, as the PCs progress from dungeon to dungeon and ruin to ruin, they hear rumors and find clues that some Underdark race is preparing to launch a strike against the surface world. Perhaps, as they delve into dungeons, they learn that some of the monsters they face work for the masterminds, whom they eventually discover to be the mind flayers.

Finally, the mind flayers make their move and the PCs are there to stop it. Thus, a series of unrelated adventures suddenly feels like a coherent whole. This is the beginning of plot weaving.

PLOT WEAVING

Plot weaving is the art of taking multiple adventures and running them at the same time. Consider these two adventures: In the first, the identity of a murderer leads the PCs into conflict with a powerful guild of assassins. In the second, the PCs seek a magic staff rumored to be in the hands of a troglodyte priest. Here's an example of how they can be interwoven into a single sequence.

1. The PCs, in town seeking the staff, witness a murder. When they look into it, they discover the culprit and track him down. He fights to the death, and on his body they discover a mysterious tattoo.
2. They learn that the *staff of curing* they seek was stolen by troglodytes years ago.
3. While they attempt to learn more about the trogs and their lair, an assassin with the same mysterious tattoo attacks the PCs.
4. They head to the caves where the troglodytes live. They encounter heavy resistance and withdraw.
5. Returning to town again, the PCs find themselves under surveillance and even attack from the guild.
6. They go back to the caves and obtain the staff.
7. They return to town and, after learning the location of the assassins' guild, confront the assassins directly.

Plot weaving can make your campaign seem less like a series of adventures and more like . . . well, like real life. It can be difficult to manage, however, and once you begin to weave more than two or three plots together, players may feel somewhat dissatisfied with the number of "loose ends" that seem to always be left behind them relating to one adventure while they find their characters embroiled in another. Some players don't want plots to be woven. They stick with one goal if possible and don't start anything new until they feel they have achieved closure on what has come before. In the above example, the PCs might ignore the troglodytes and the staff until they have completely dealt with the assassins. Ultimately, a good DM runs the adventures that players want to play by paying attention to the way they want to play them.

END OF AN ADVENTURE CHECKLIST

When an adventure is finished, you should always do a few things.

AWARD EXPERIENCE

If you do not award experience at the end of each session, award experience points at the end of each adventure. See Chapter 7: Rewards for more information.

MAKE A RECORD

Make notes of what happened in the adventure. Record new NPCs encountered, monsters defeated, secrets learned, magic discovered, and so forth. Make notes to yourself about opportunities for further adventures based on what has happened. Note what the players seemed to like and dislike.

Update your original adventure notes or map keys to reflect the changes wrought by the PCs.

UPDATE PC INFORMATION

Record new magic items gained by the PCs, new levels they earned (and accompanying improvements), enemies they have angered, friends they have made, and anything else that's pertinent.

THE DUNGEON

Dungeons are deep, dark pits filled with subterranean horrors and lost, ancient treasures. Dungeons are labyrinths where evil villains and carnivorous beasts hide from the light, waiting for a time to strike into the sunlit lands of good. Dungeons contain pits of seething acid and magic traps that blast intruders with fire, as well as dragons guarding their hoards and magic artifacts waiting to be discovered.

In short, dungeons mean adventure.

THE DUNGEON AS ADVENTURE SETTING

The term "dungeon" is a loose one. A dungeon is usually underground, but an aboveground site can be a dungeon as well. Some DMs apply the term to virtually any adventure site. For this discussion, a dungeon is an enclosed, defined space of encounter areas connected in some fashion.

The most common form of dungeon is the underground complex built by intelligent creatures for some purpose. Physically, such a place has rooms joined by corridors, stairs connecting it with the surface, and doors and traps to keep out intruders. The archetypal dungeon is abandoned, with creatures other than the builders now occupying areas within it. Adventurers explore such places with the hope of finding treasure either left behind by the original inhabitants or in the hoards of such squatters.

TYPES OF DUNGEONS

There are four basic dungeon types, defined by their current status. Many dungeons are variations on these basic types or combinations of more than one of them. Sometimes old dungeons are used again and again by different inhabitants for different purposes.

Ruined Structure: Once occupied, this place is now abandoned (completely or in part) by its original creator or creators, and other creatures have wandered in. Many subterranean creatures look for abandoned underground constructions in which to make their lairs. Any traps that might exist have probably been set off, but wandering beasts might very well be common.

Areas within the ruined structure usually contain clues as to their original intended use. What is now the lair of a family of rust monsters might once have been an old barracks, the rotting remains of the beds and other furnishings now arranged to make nests for the creatures. An ancient throne room, adorned with the tatters of once-beautiful tapestries, might be empty and quiet—the ancient curse that struck down the queen still hanging in the air before the verdigris-encrusted bronze throne.

The ruined structure dungeon is a place that cries out to be explored. Adventurers might hear tales of treasure still lingering in the abandoned labyrinth, leading them to brave the dangers to uncover it. This is the simplest and most straightforward of the dungeon types, and it usually balances danger (the inhabitants) with reward (the treasure). The creatures dwelling in a ruined structure aren't necessarily organized, so adventurers can usually come and go as they please, making it easy to start and stop adventures.

Occupied Structure: This dungeon is still in use. Creatures (usually intelligent) live there, although they may not be the dungeon's creators. An occupied structure might be a home, a fortress, a temple, an active mine, a prison, or a headquarters. This type of dungeon is less likely to have traps or wandering beasts, and more likely to have organized guards—both on watch and on patrol. Traps or wandering beasts that might be encountered are usually under the control of the occupants. Occupied structures have furnishings to suit the inhabitants, as well as decorations, supplies, and the ability for occupants to move

Gnolls attempt to use a pit to their advantage in a fight.

around (doors they can open, hallways large enough for them to pass through, etc.). The inhabitants might have a communication system, and they almost certainly control an access to the outside.

Some dungeons are partially occupied and partially empty or in ruins. In such cases, the occupants are typically not the original builders but instead a group of intelligent creatures that have set up their base, lair, or fortification within an abandoned dungeon.

Use the occupied structure dungeon for the lair of a goblin tribe, a secret underground fortress, or an occupied castle. This is one of the most challenging types of dungeons for adventurers to enter and explore if the occupants are hostile. The challenge comes from the organized nature of the inhabitants. It's always harder to fight a foe on his own terms in an area he knows well and is prepared to defend.

Safe Storage: When people want to protect something, they might bury it underground. Whether the item they want to protect is a fabulous treasure, a forbidden artifact, or the dead body of an important figure, these valuable objects are placed within the dungeon and surrounded by barriers, traps, and guardians.

The safe storage type of dungeon is the most likely to have traps but the least likely to have wandering beasts. The crypt of an ancient lich may be filled with all manner of magic traps and guardians, but it's unlikely that any subterranean monster has moved in and made a part of the dungeon its lair—the traps and guardians will have held them at bay. This type of dungeon normally is built for function rather than appearance, but sometimes it has ornamentation in the form of statuary or painted walls. This is particularly true of the tombs of important people.

Sometimes, however, a vault or a crypt is constructed in such a way as to house living guardians. The problem with this strategy is that something must be done to keep the creatures alive between intrusion attempts. Magic is usually the best solution to provide food and water for these creatures.

Even if there's no way anything living can survive in a safe storage dungeon, certain monsters can still serve as guardians. Builders of vaults or tombs often place undead and constructs, with no need for sustenance or rest, to guard their dungeons. Magic traps can summon monsters into the dungeon to attack intruders without ever having to worry about sustaining the guardians, who disappear after they're needed.

Natural Cavern Complex: Caves underground provide homes to all sorts of subterranean monsters. Created naturally and connected by a labyrinthine tunnel system, these caverns lack any sort of pattern, order, or decoration. With no intelligent force behind its construction, this type of dungeon is the least likely to have traps or even doors.

Fungi of all sorts thrive in caves, sometimes growing up like a huge forest of mushrooms and puffballs. Subterranean predators prowl these forests, looking for those feeding upon the fungi itself. Sometimes, fungus gives off an eerie phosphorescence, providing natural cavern complexes with their own limited light source. In other areas, *continual flame* or other magical effects can provide enough light for green plants to grow.

Often, natural cavern complexes connect with other sorts of dungeons, having been discovered when the artificial dungeon was delved. They can connect two unrelated dungeons, sometimes creating a strange mixed environment. Natural cavern complexes joined with other dungeons often provide a route by which subterranean creatures find their way into created dungeons and populate them. Rumors tell of the Underdark, a subterranean world that is one big natural cavern complex dungeon running under the surface of entire continents.

Natural cavern complexes can be quite beautiful, with stalactites, stalagmites, flowstone, columns, and other limestone formations. However, from an adventuring point of view they have a serious shortcoming: less treasure. Since the dungeon was not created for a specific purpose, there's little chance of happening upon a secret room filled with gold left behind by the previous occupants.

DUNGEON FEATURES

Practically all dungeons have walls, floors, doors, and other types of basic features. Many are quite elaborate. Dungeon adventurers learn the common features quickly. Use this fact to your advantage. Common features create consistency (which helps suspend disbelief) and allow you to create interesting surprises by changing the features—sometimes only slightly.

Walls

Masonry walls—stones piled on top of each other (usually but not always held in place with mortar)—divide dungeons into corridors and chambers. Dungeon walls can also be hewn from solid rock, leaving them with a rough, chiseled look. Or, dungeon walls can be the smooth, unblemished stone of a

Hewn stone wall

naturally occurring cave. Dungeon walls are difficult to break down or through, but they're generally easy to climb.

Masonry Walls: These are usually at least 1 foot thick. Often these ancient walls sport cracks and crevices, and sometimes dangerous slimes or small monsters live in these areas and wait for prey. Masonry walls stop all but the loudest noises.

Superior Masonry Walls: Sometimes masonry walls are better built (smoother, with tighter-fitting stones and less cracking), and occasionally these superior walls are covered with plaster or stucco. Covered walls often bear paintings, carved reliefs, or other decoration. Such walls are no more difficult to destroy than regular masonry walls but are more difficult to climb.

BEHIND THE CURTAIN: WHY DUNGEONS?

Dungeons facilitate game play. Dungeons, being underground, set apart the "adventure" from the rest of the world in a clean way. The idea of walking down a corridor, opening a door, and entering an encounter—while a gross oversimplification and generalization—facilitates the flow of the game by reducing things down to easily grasped and digestible concepts.

You have an easy way to control the adventure in a dungeon without leading the characters by the nose. In a dungeon, the parameters are clearly defined for the PCs—they can't walk through walls (not at first, anyway) or go into rooms that aren't there. Yet aside from those limits, they can go wherever they like in whatever order they like. The limited environment of the dungeon grants players a feeling of control over their own destiny.

A dungeon is really nothing but an adventure flowchart. The rooms are encounters, and the corridors are connections between the encounters, showing which should follow which. You could design a dungeon-like flowchart for an adventure that didn't take place in a dungeon and accomplish the same thing. One encounter leads to two more, which in turn lead to others, some of which double back on previous encounters. The dungeon becomes a model, in this way, for all adventures.

Academic analysis aside, dungeons are fun. Deep, dark underground places are mysterious and frightening. Dungeons have many encounters crammed into one small space. Nothing is more exciting than anticipating what's on the other side of the next dungeon door. Dungeons often many different kinds of challenges—combat, tactics, navigation, overcoming obstacles, traps, and more. They encourage players to pay close attention to their environment, since everything in a dungeon is a potential danger.

In the DUNGEONS & DRAGONS game, the classes, spells, magic items, and many other facets of the game have been designed with dungeons in mind. That's not to say that the dungeon is the only possible adventuring environment, but it is the default setting. Many of the tasks that characters can do well, such as a rogue's Open Lock skill or an elf's ability to notice secret doors, are centered around dungeon adventuring.

When in doubt while creating the setting for an adventure, use a dungeon. However, despite the opportunities for exploration and combat-intensive nature of dungeons, don't neglect to include chances for PCs to interact with NPCs such as dwarven strike teams, other adventuring parties, or weird denizens that are happier to talk than to fight.

TABLE 4–3: WALLS

Wall Type	Typical Thickness	Break DC	Hardness	Hit Points*	Climb DC
Masonry	1 ft.	35	8	90 hp	15
Superior masonry	1 ft.	35	8	90 hp	20
Reinforced masonry	1 ft.	45	8	180 hp	15
Hewn stone	3 ft.	50	8	540 hp	22
Unworked stone	5 ft.	65	8	900 hp	20
Iron	3 in.	30	10	90 hp	25
Paper	Paper-thin	1	—	1 hp	30
Wood	6 in.	20	5	60 hp	21
Magically treated**	—	+20	×2	×2†	—

*Per 10-ft.-by-10-ft. section.

**These modifiers can be applied to any of the other categories and types.

†Or 50, whichever is greater.

Hewn Stone Walls: Such walls usually result when a chamber or passage is tunneled out from solid rock. The rough surface of a hewn wall frequently provides small ledges where fungus grows and small creatures live (often vermin, bats, or coiled subterranean snakes). When there is an "other side" (that is, this wall separates two chambers in the dungeon), these walls are usually at least 3 feet thick; anything thinner risks collapsing from the weight of all that stone overhead.

Unworked Stone Walls: These surfaces are uneven and rarely flat. They are smooth to the touch but filled with tiny holes, hidden alcoves, and ledges at various heights. They're also usually wet or at least damp, since it's water that most frequently creates natural caves. When there is an "other side," these walls are usually at least 5 feet thick.

Special Walls: Sometimes you can place special walls in a dungeon. Expect players to react with curiosity and suspicion when their characters encounter these exceptional walls.

Reinforced Walls: These are masonry walls with iron bars on one or both sides of the wall, or placed within the wall itself to strengthen it. The hardness of the reinforced wall remains the same, but the hit points are doubled and the DC to break through is increased by 10.

Magically Treated Walls: These walls are stronger than average, with a greater hardness, more hit points, and a higher break DC. Magic can usually double the hardness and hit points and can add up to +20 to the break DC. A magically treated wall also gains a saving throw against spells that could affect it, with the save bonus equaling 2 + half the caster level of the magic reinforcing the wall. Creating a magic wall is just like creating a wondrous Item (see Chapter 8: Magic Items).

Iron Walls: These walls are placed within dungeons around important places such as vaults.

Paper Walls: Paper walls are the opposite of iron walls, placed as screens to prevent sight but nothing more.

Masonry wall

Wooden Walls: Wooden walls often exist as recent additions to older dungeons, used to create animal pens, storage bins, or just to make a number of smaller rooms out of a larger one.

Walls with Arrow Slits: Walls with arrow slits can be made of any durable material but are most commonly masonry, hewn stone, or wood. They allow defenders to fire arrows or crossbow bolts at intruders from behind the safety of the wall. Such archers have nine-tenths cover, gaining them a +10 bonus to Armor Class.

Floors

As with walls, dungeon floors come in many types.

Flagstone Floors: Like masonry walls, flagstone floors are made of fitted stones. They are usually cracked and only somewhat level. Slime and mold grows in these cracks. Sometimes water runs in rivulets between the stones or sits in stagnant puddles. Over time, these floors can become so uneven that a Dexterity check (DC 13) is required if someone attempts to run across the surface. Those failing the check fall, halting their movement and requiring a move-equivalent action to stand again. Floors this treacherous should be the exception, not the rule.

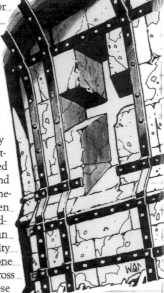

Reinforced wall

Unworked stone wall

Hewn Stone Floors: Rough and uneven, hewn floors are usually covered with loose stones, gravel, dirt, or other debris. The floors of older dungeons may be worn fairly smooth by the passage of many feet over the years, but newer hewn floors can be as dangerous to run across as an older flagstone construction (see above).

Smooth Stone Floors: Finished and sometimes even polished, smooth floors are found only in dungeons with capable and careful builders. (They are a hallmark of dwarf-delved dungeons.) Sometimes mosaics are set in the floor, some depicting interesting images and others just smooth marble. Smooth dungeon floors may have wooden planks laid over the top of them, greatly increasing the comfort of the dungeon as a dwelling, but such floorings rot in just a few years, so they are rare.

Natural Stone Floors: The floors of natural caves are as uneven as the walls. Caves rarely have large flat surfaces. Rather, their floors have many levels. Some adjacent floor surfaces might vary in elevation by only a foot, so that moving from one to the other is no more difficult than negotiating a stair, but in other places the floor might suddenly drop off or rise up several feet or more, requiring Climb checks to get from one surface to the other. Unless a path has been worn and well marked in the floor of a natural cave, running and charging in this environment are usually impossible.

Special Floors: A number of strange floorings and floor features exist to make a dungeon more interesting.

Grates: Grates cover pits or areas lower than the main floor. They are usually made from iron, but large grates can also be made from iron-bound timbers. Many grates have hinges to allow access to what lies below (such grates can be locked like any door), while others are permanent and unmoving. A typical 1-inch-thick iron grate has 25 hit points, a hardness of 10, and a DC of 27 to break through or tear away.

Ledges: Ledges allow creatures to walk above some lower area. They often circle around pits, run along underground streams, form balconies around large rooms, or provide a place for archers to stand while firing upon enemies below. Narrow ledges (less than 1 foot wide) require those moving along them to make Balance checks (see the skill description. page 63 in the *Player's Handbook*). Ledges covered in water, slime, or some other slippery substance are dangerous. Slipperiness adds +5 to the DC determined above. A Balance check (DC 17) is needed to traverse even wide ledges (more than 1 foot wide, but less than 2 1/2 feet) at normal speed (DC 15 if the character is willing to walk at half speed). Failure results in the moving character falling off the ledge.

Bridges: Brides are like ledges, but they connect to higher areas separated by a lower area. Bridges stretch across chasms, over rivers, or above pits. A simple bridge might be a single wooden plank, while an elaborate one could be made of mortared stone with iron supports and side rails. Narrow bridges are treated just like ledges.

Transparent Floors: Transparent floors, made of reinforced glass or magic materials (even a *wall of force*), allow a dangerous setting to be viewed safely from above. Transparent floors are sometimes placed over lava pools, arenas, monster dens, and torture chambers. They can be used by defenders to watch key areas for intruders.

Trick Floors: Trick floors are designed to become suddenly dangerous. With the application of just the right amount of weight, or the pull of a lever somewhere nearby, spikes protrude from the floor, gouts of steam or flame shoot up from hidden holes, or the entire floor tilts. These strange floors are usually found in an arena area and are designed to make combats more exciting and deadly.

Sliding Floors: Sliding floors are really more of a type of trapdoor, since they normally reveal something underneath. Sliding floors generally move so slowly that anyone standing on one can avoid falling into the gap it creates, assuming there's somewhere else to go. However, some can be constructed so that a Balance check (DC 15) is required to keep from falling into whatever lies below the sliding floor—a spiked pit, a vat of burning oil, or a pool filled with sharks (or perhaps just mutant sea bass).

Doors

Doors in dungeons are much more than mere entrances and exits. Often they can be encounters all by themselves. After all, anything that can trigger a nasty trap, offer you a clue, zap you with a spell, or simply block your way deserves serious attention from the dungeon explorer. The doorways they are set in may be plain arches and lintels, or may be festooned with carvings—often gargoyles or leering faces but sometimes carved words that might reveal a clue to what lies beyond. Dungeon doors come in three basic types: wooden, stone, and iron.

Wooden Doors: Constructed of thick planks nailed together, sometimes bound with iron for strength (and to reduce swelling from dungeon dampness), wooden doors are the most common type. Wooden doors come in varying strengths: simple, good, and strong doors. Simple doors (break DC 13) are not meant to keep out motivated attackers. Good doors (break DC 18), while sturdy and long-lasting, are still not meant to take much punishment. Strong doors (break DC 23) are bound in iron and are a fairly good barrier to those attempting to get past them.

Iron hinges fasten the door to its frame, and typically a circular pull-ring in the center is there to help open it. Since most doors only open in one direction, the pull-ring is located only on the side toward which the door opens (the side with the hinges). Sometimes, instead of a pull-ring, a door has an iron pull-bar on one or both sides of the door to serve as a handle. In inhabited dungeons, these doors are usually well maintained (not stuck) and unlocked, although important areas are locked up if possible.

Stone: Carved from solid blocks of stone, these heavy, unwieldy doors are often built so that they pivot when they are opened, although dwarves and other skilled craftsfolk are able to fashion hinges strong enough to hold up a stone door. Secret doors concealed within a stone wall are usually stone doors. Otherwise, such doors stand as tough barriers protecting something important beyond. Thus, they are often locked or barred.

Iron: Rusted but sturdy, iron doors in a dungeon are hinged like wooden doors. These doors are the toughest form of nonmagical door. They are usually locked or barred.

Door Locks, Bars, Seals, and Traps

Dungeon doors may be locked, trapped, enchanted, reinforced, barred, magically sealed, or sometimes just stuck. All but the weakest characters can eventually knock down a door with a heavy tool such as a sledgehammer, and a number of spells and magic items give characters an easy way around a locked door. Attempts to literally chop a door down with an axe use the hardness and hit points given in Table 4–4: Doors. Often the easiest way to overcome a recalcitrant door is not by demolishing it but by breaking its lock, bar, or hinges. When assigning DCs to attempts to knock a door down, use the following as guidelines:

- DC 10 or lower: a door just about anyone can break open.
- DC 11–15: a door that a strong person could break with one try and an average person might be able to break with one try.
- DC 16–20: a door that almost anyone could break, given time.
- DC 21–25: a door that only a strong or very strong person has a hope of breaking, probably not on the first try.
- DC 26+: a door that only an exceptionally strong person has a hope of breaking.

For specific examples in applying these guidelines, see Table 4–9: Door Types, page 119.

Locks: Dungeon doors are often locked, and thus the Open Lock skill comes in very handy. Locks are usually built into the door, either on the edge opposite the hinges or right in the middle of the door. Built-in locks either control an iron bar that juts out of the door and into the wall of its frame, or else a sliding iron bar or heavy wooden bar that rests behind the entire door. By contrast, padlocks are not built-in but usually run through two rings, one on the door and the other on the wall. More complex locks, such as combination locks and puzzle locks, are usually built into the door itself. Since such keyless locks are expensive, they are typically only found in sturdy doors (iron-bound wooden, stone, or iron doors).

The DC to pick a lock with an Open Lock check often falls into the range of DC 20 to DC 30, although locks with lower or higher DCs can exist. A door can have more than one lock, each of which must be unlocked separately. Locks often are trapped, usually with poison needles that extend out to prick a rogue's finger.

Breaking a lock is sometimes quicker than breaking the whole door. If a PC wants to whack at a lock with a weapon, treat the typical lock as having a hardness of 15 and 30 hit points. A lock can only be broken if it can be attacked separately from the door, which means that a built-in lock is immune to this sort of treatment.

TABLE 4–4: DOORS

Door Type	Typical Thickness	Hardness	Hit Points	Break DC Stuck	Break DC Locked
Simple wooden	1 in.	5	10 hp	13	15
Good wooden	1 1/2 in.	5	15 hp	16	18
Strong wooden	2 in.	5	20 hp	23	25
Stone	4 in.	8	60 hp	28	28
Iron	2 in.	10	60 hp	28	28
Portcullis, wooden	3 in	5	30 hp	25*	25*
Portcullis, iron	2 in.	10	60 hp	25*	25*
Lock	—	15	30 hp		
Hinge	—	15	30 hp		

*DC to lift. Use appropriate door figure for breaking.

Keep in mind that in an occupied dungeon, every locked door has a key somewhere. If the adventurers are unable to pick a lock or break down the door, finding whoever has the key and getting it away from its possessor can be an interesting part of the adventure.

A special door (see below for examples) might have a lock with no key, instead requiring that the right combination of nearby levers must be manipulated or the right symbols must be pressed on a keypad in the correct sequence to open the door. You're perfectly justified in ruling that some puzzle doors must be solved by the players rather than being bypassed by an Open Lock check—for example, if a door only unlocks when the riddle carved on it is correctly answered, then it's up to the players to solve the riddle.

Stuck Doors: Dungeons are often damp, and sometimes doors get stuck, particularly wooden doors. Assume that about 10% of wooden doors and 5% of nonwooden doors are stuck. These numbers can be doubled (to 20% and 10%, respectively) for long-abandoned or neglected dungeons.

Wooden door

Hinges: Most doors have hinges. Obviously, sliding doors do not. (They usually have tracks or grooves instead, allowing them to slide easily to one side.)

Standard Hinges: These hinges are metal, joining one edge of the door to the doorframe or wall. Remember that the door swings open toward the side with the hinges. (So if the hinges are on the PCs' side, the door opens toward them; otherwise it opens away from them.) Adventurers can take the hinges apart one at a time with successful Disable Device checks (assuming the hinges are on their side of the door, of course). Such a task has a DC of 20, since most hinges are rusted and stuck. Breaking a hinge is difficult. Most have a hardness of 15 and 30 hit points. The break DC for a hinge is the same as for breaking down the door (see Table 4–9: Door Types).

Nested Hinges: These hinges are much more complex, and are found only in areas of excellent construction, such as an underground dwarven citadel. These hinges are built into the wall and allow the door to swing open in either direction. PCs can't get at the hinges to fool with them unless they break through the doorframe or wall. Nested hinges are typically found on stone doors but sometimes occur on wooden or iron doors.

Pivots: Pivots aren't really hinges at all, but simple knobs jutting from the top and bottom of the door that fit into holes in the doorframe, allowing the door to spin. The advantages of pivots are that they can't be dismantled like hinges and they're simple to make. The disadvantage is that since the door pivots on its center of gravity (typically in the middle), nothing larger than half the door's width can fit through. Doors with pivots are usually stone and are often quite wide to overcome this disadvantage. Another solution is to place the pivot toward one side and have the door be thicker at that end and thinner toward the other end so that it opens more like a normal door. Secret doors in walls often pivot,

Stone door

since the lack of hinges makes it easier to hide the door's presence. Pivots also allow objects such as bookcases to be used as secret doors.

Door Traps: More than just about any other facet of a dungeon, doors are protected by traps. The reason is pretty obvious—an open door means an intruder. A mechanical trap can be connected to a door by wires or springs so that it activates when the door is opened—firing an arrow, releasing a cloud of gas, opening a trap door, letting loose a monster, dropping a heavy block on intruders, or whatever. Magic traps such as *glyphs of warding* typically are cast directly on the door, blasting intruders with flame or some other magical attack.

Example: A magic door is trapped with a sequence of spells (*programmed image* and *teleport* or *dimension door*). When the door is opened, an illusion of a dragon's head reaches forth out of the darkness beyond and appears to swallow the opener whole, receding back into the darkness and no doubt leaving the rest of the adventurers with mouths agape. In reality, the opener was teleported into a nearby prison cell filled with the bones of previous explorers who fell victim to the same trap. Only if the rest of the PCs are brave enough to press onward can they find their comrade and free him. (Of course, for all they know, he's been killed and eaten. . . .)

Special Doors: An interesting facet of a dungeon might be a sealed door too strong to break down. Such a door might be opened only by operating secret switches, or hidden (and distant) levers. Crafty builders make using the switches or levers more difficult by requiring that they be used in a special way. For example, a particular door might only open if a series of four levers is moved into a specific configuration—two pushed up, and two pushed down. If a lever in the series is put in the wrong position, it springs a trap. Now imagine how much more difficult it would be if there were a dozen or more levers, with multiple settings, spread out through the entire dungeon. Finding the method to open a special door (perhaps leading into the vault, the vampire's lair, or the dragon's secret temple) can be an adventure in itself.

Sometimes a door is special because of its construction. A lead-lined door, for example, provides a barrier against many detection spells. A heavy iron door might be built in a circular design, rolling to one side on a track once it is opened. A mechanical door linked with levers or winches might not open unless the proper mechanism is activated. Such doors often sink into the floor, rise up into the ceiling, lower like a drawbridge, or slide into the wall rather than merely swinging open like a normal door.

Magic Doors: Enchanted by the original builders, a door might speak to explorers, warning them away. It might be protected from harm, increasing its hardness or giving it more hit points as well as an improved saving throw bonus against *disintegrate* and other similar spells.

A magic door might not lead into the space revealed beyond, but

Iron door

Illustration by W. Reynolds

instead it might be a portal to a faraway place or even another plane of existence. A door magically shaped from a *wall of force* would resist spells as well as any attempt to break it down (short of a *disintegrate* spell). Other magic doors might require passwords or special keys (ranging from the tail feather of an evil eagle, to a note played upon a lute, to a certain frame of mind) to open them. Effectively, the range and variety of magic doors is limited only by your imagination.

Portcullises: These special doors consist of iron or ironbound, thick, wooden shafts that descend from a recess in the ceiling above an archway. Sometimes they have crossbars that create a grid, sometimes not. Typically raised by means of a winch or a capstan, a portcullis can be dropped quickly, and the shafts end in spikes to discourage anyone from standing underneath (or from attempting to dive under as it drops). Once it is dropped, a portcullis locks, unless it is so large that no normal person could lift it anyway. In any event, lifting a typical portcullis requires a Strength check (DC 25).

Rooms

Rooms in dungeons vary in shape and size. Although many are simple in construction and appearance, particularly interesting rooms have multiple levels joined by stairs, ramps, or ladders as well as statuary, altars, pits, chasms, bridges, and more.

Keep three things in mind when designing a dungeon room:

- Underground chambers are prone to collapse, so many rooms—particularly large ones—have arched ceilings or columns to support the weight of the rock overhead.
- Most types of intelligent creatures have a tendency to decorate their lairs. It should be fairly commonplace to find carvings or paintings on the walls of dungeon rooms. Exploring adventurers also often encounter statues and bas reliefs, as well as scrawled messages, marks, and maps left behind by others who have come this way before. Some of these marks amount to little more than graffiti ("Robilar was here"), while others may be useful to adventurers who examine them closely.
- Pay close attention to the exits. Creatures that can't open doors can't lair in a sealed room without some sort of external assistance. Strong creatures without the ability to open doors smash them down if necessary. Burrowing creatures might dig their own exits.

Corridors

Stretching into the darkness, a mysterious cobweb-filled passage deeper into the dungeon can be intriguing and a little frightening. All dungeons have rooms, and most have corridors. While most corridors simply connect rooms, sometimes they can be encounter areas in their own right due to traps, guard patrols, and wandering monsters out on the hunt.

When designing a dungeon, make sure that the corridors are large enough for the dungeon residents to use. (For example, a dragon needs a pretty big tunnel to get in and out of its lair.) Wealthy, powerful, or talented dungeon builders may favor wide corridors to give a grand appearance to their residence. Otherwise, passages are no larger than they need to be. (Tunneling through solid rock is expensive, back-breaking, time-consuming work.) Corridors narrower than 10 feet can make it difficult for all the members of the PC party to get involved in any fights that occur, so make them the exception rather than the rule.

Corridor Traps: Because passageways in dungeons tend to be narrow, offering few movement options, dungeon builders like to place traps in them. In a cramped passageway, there's no way for intruders to move around concealed pits, falling stones, arrow traps, tilting floors, and sliding or rolling rocks that fill the entire passage. For the same reason, magic traps such as *glyphs of warding* are effective in hallways as well.

Mazes: Usually, passages connect chambers in the simplest and straightest manner possible. Some dungeon builders, however,

design a maze or a labyrinth within the dungeon. These are difficult to navigate (or at least to navigate quickly) and, when filled with monsters or traps, can be an effective barrier. Mazes cut off one area of the dungeon, deflecting intruders away from a protected spot. Generally, though, the far side of a maze holds an important crypt or vault—someplace that the dungeon's intended inhabitants rarely need to get to.

Miscellaneous Features

Any dungeon is made more interesting by the inclusion of some or all of these features.

Stairs: The usual way to connect different levels of a dungeon is with stairs. Straight stairways, spiral staircases, or stairwells with multiple landings between flights of stairs are all common in dungeons, as are ramps (sometimes with an incline so slight that it can be difficult to notice—DC 15 Spot check). Stairs are important accessways, and are sometimes guarded or trapped. Traps on stairs often cause intruders to slide or fall down to the bottom, where a pit, spikes, a pool of acid, or some other dangers await.

Statue of a warrior

Chutes and Chimneys: Stairs aren't the only way to move up and down in the dungeon. Sometimes a vertical shaft connects levels or links the dungeon with the surface. Chutes are usually traps that dump characters into a lower area—often a place with some dangerous situation with which they must contend.

Pillars: A common sight in any dungeon, pillars and columns give support to ceilings. The larger the room, the more likely it has pillars. Pillars can be anywhere from 1 foot to 5 feet in diameter—as a rule of thumb, the deeper in the dungeon, the thicker the pillars need to be to support the overhead weight. Some pillars are large enough for characters (and some monsters) to hide behind, creating some interesting tactical possibilities. Pillars tend to be polished and often have carvings, paintings, or inscriptions upon them.

Statues: Reflections of bygone days, statues found in dungeons can be realistic depictions of persons, creatures, or scenes, or they can be less lifelike in their imagery. Statues often serve as commemorative representations of people from the past as well as idols of gods. Statues may be either painted or left bare. Some have inscriptions. Adventurers wisely distrust statues in dungeons for fear that they may animate and attack, as a stone golem can do. Statues in a dungeon could also be a sign indicating the presence of a monster with a petrifying power (medusa, cockatrice, etc.). Feel free to utilize both of these ideas, but don't forget that sometimes a statue is just a statue.

Tapestries: Elaborately embroidered patterns or scenes on cloth, tapestries hang from the walls of well-appointed dungeon rooms or corridors. They not only make chambers more comfortable as a residence but can add a ceremonial touch to shrines and throne rooms.

WALLS, DOORS, AND *DETECT* SPELLS

Stone walls, iron walls, and iron doors are usually thick enough to block most *detect* spells, such as *detect thoughts*. Wooden walls, wooden doors, and stone doors are usually not thick enough to do so. However, a secret stone door built into a wall and as thick as the wall itself (at least 1 foot) does block most *detect* spells.

Crafty builders take advantage of tapestries to place alcoves, concealed doors, or secret switches behind them. Sometimes the images in a tapestry contain clues to the nature of the builders, the inhabitants, or the dungeon itself.

Secret Doors: Disguised as a bare patch of wall (or floor, or ceiling), a bookcase, a fireplace, or a fountain, a secret door leads to a secret passage or room. Someone examining the area finds a secret door, if any, on a successful Search roll (DC 20 for a typical secret door to DC 30 for a well-hidden secret door). Remember that elves have a chance to detect a secret door just by casually looking at the area. Many secret doors require a special method of opening, such as a hidden button or pressure plate. Secret doors can open like normal doors, or they may pivot, slide, sink, rise, or even lower like a drawbridge to permit access. Builders might put a secret door down low near the floor or high up in a wall, making it difficult to find or reach. Wizards

Spiral staircase made of iron

have a spell, *phase door*, that allows them to create a magic secret door that only they can use.

Daises and Pedestals: Anything important on display in a dungeon, from a fabulous treasure to a coffin, tends to rest atop a dais or a pedestal. Raising the object off the floor focuses attention on it (and, in practical terms, keeps it safe from any water that might seep onto the floor). A dais or a pedestal is often trapped to protect whatever sits atop it. It can conceal a secret trap door beneath itself or provide a way to reach a door in the ceiling above itself.

Vaults: Well protected, often by a locked iron door, a vault is a special room that contains treasure. There's usually only one entrance—an appropriate place for a trap.

Crypts: Although sometimes constructed like a vault, a crypt can also be a series of individual rooms, each with its own sarcophagus, or a long hall with recesses on either side—shelves to hold coffins or bodies. Wise adventurers expect to encounter undead in a crypt, but are often willing to risk it to look for the treasure that's often buried with the dead. Crypts of most cultures are well appointed and highly decorated, since the fact that the crypt was created at all shows great reverence for the dead entombed within.

People worried about undead rising from the grave take the precaution of locking and trapping a crypt from the outside—making the crypt easy to get into but difficult to leave. Those worried about tomb robbers make their crypts difficult to get into. Some builders do both, just to be on the safe side.

Pools: Pools of water collect naturally in low spots in dungeons (a dry dungeon is rare). Pools can also be wells or natural underground springs. Or they can be intentionally created basins, cisterns, and fountains. In any event, water is fairly common in dungeons. Deep pools harbor sightless fish and sometimes worse—aquatic monsters. Pools provide water for dungeon

denizens, and thus are as important an area for a predator to control as a watering hole aboveground in the wild.

Through accident or design, pools can become polluted or even enchanted. While this usually just makes the water foul or tainted, rarely a pool or a fountain gains the ability to bestow enchantments on those who drink from it—healing, ability score modification, transmutation magic, or even something as amazing as a *wish* spell. However, enchanted pools are just as likely to curse the drinker, causing a loss of health, an unwanted polymorph, or some even greater affliction. Typically, water from a magic pool loses its potency if removed from the pool for more than an hour or so.

Some pools have fountains. Occasionally these are merely decorative, but they often serve as the focus of a trap or the enchanted functioning of a magic pool.

Elevators: In place of or in addition to stairs, elevators (essentially oversized dumbwaiters) can take inhabitants from one dungeon level to the next. Such elevators may be mechanical (using gears, pulleys, and winches) or magical (*Tenser's floating disk*, etc.). A mechanical elevator might be as small as a platform that holds one character at a time, or as large as an entire room that raises and lowers. A clever builder might design an elevator room that moves up or down without the occupants' knowledge to catch them in a trap, or one that appears to have moved when it actually remained still.

Shifting Stones or Walls: These features can cut off access to a passage or room, trapping adventurers in a dead end or preventing escape out of the dungeon. Shifting walls can force explorers to go down a dangerous path or prevent them from entering a special area. Not all shifting walls need be traps. For example, stones controlled by pressure plates, counterweights, or a secret lever can shift out of a wall to become a staircase leading to a hidden upper room or secret ledge.

Teleporters: Sometimes useful, sometimes devious, places in dungeons rigged with a teleportation effect (such as a *teleportation circle*) transport characters to some other location in the dungeon or someplace far away. They can be traps, teleporting the unwary into dangerous situations, or they can be an easy mode of transport for those who built or live in the dungeon, good for bypassing barriers and traps or simply to get around more quickly. Devious dungeon designers might place a teleporter in a room that transports characters to another seemingly identical room so that they don't even know they've been teleported.

Altars: Temples—particularly to dark gods—often exist underground. Usually taking the form of a simple stone block, the altar is the main fixture and central focus of such a temple. Sometimes all the trappings of the temple are long gone, lost to theft, age, and decay, but the altar itself survives. Surely there's some divine power or connection there still. . . .

Pillar

Illustration by W. Reynolds

Tapestry

Major Furnishings and Features

Table 4–5: Dungeon Dressing—Major Features and Furnishings is a list of large or predominant features commonly found in dungeons. Use this as a random generator when creating a random dungeon or to round out one you are creating.

III

Minor Furnishings and Features

Adventures can come across small bits and contents of dungeon rooms while exploring. Use Table 4–6: Dungeon Dressing—Minor Features and Furnishings as an idea generator when creating a random dungeon or to round out one you are creating.

OBSTACLES, HAZARDS, AND TRAPS

In a dungeon, adventurers can fall to their deaths, be burned alive, or find themselves peppered with poisoned darts—all without ever having encountered a single monster. Dungeons tend to be filled with barriers or life-threatening traps of one kind or another. The following sections lay down some basic rules for handling common obstacles and traps. Remember that you are always free to modify the DC or other details to reflect specific conditions in your dungeon.

A pedestal displaying a grand gem

Falling

One of the most common hazards to adventurers is a fall from some great height.

Falling Damage: The basic rule is simple: 1d6 points of damage per 10 feet fallen, to a maximum of 20d6.

If a character deliberately jumps instead of merely slipping or falling, the damage is the same but the first 1d6 is subdual damage. A successful Jump check (DC 15) allows the character to avoid any damage from the first 10 feet fallen and converts any damage from the second 10 feet to subdual damage. Thus, a character who slips from a ledge 30 feet up takes 3d6 damage. If the same character deliberately jumped, he takes 1d6 points of subdual damage and 2d6 points of normal damage. And if the character leaps down with a successful Jump check, he takes only 1d6 subdual damage and 1d6 normal damage from the plunge.

Falls onto yielding surfaces (soft ground, mud) also convert the first 1d6 to subdual damage. This reduction is cumulative with reduced damage due to deliberate jumps and the Jump skill.

Falling into Water: Falls into water are handled somewhat

A pool with a grim fountain

Table 4–5: Dungeon Dressing—Major Features and Furnishings

d%	Feature/Furnishing	d%	Feature/Furnishing	d%	Feature/Furnishing
1	Alcove	34	Fallen stones	67	Platform
2	Altar	35	Firepit	68	Pool
3	Arch	36	Fireplace	69	Portcullis
4	Arrow slit (wall)/murder hole (ceiling)	37	Font	70	Rack
5	Balcony	38	Forge	71	Ramp
6	Barrel	39	Fountain	72	Recess
7	Bed	40	Furniture (broken)	73	Relief
8	Bench	41	Gong	74	Sconce
9	Bookcase	42	Hay (pile)	75	Screen
10	Brazier	43	Hole	76	Shaft
11	Cage	44	Hole (blasted)	77	Shelf
12	Caldron	45	Idol	78	Shrine
13	Carpet	46	Iron bars	79	Spinning wheel
14	Carving	47	Iron maiden	80	Stall or pen
15	Casket	48	Kiln	81	Statue
16	Catwalk	49	Ladder	82	Statue (toppled)
17	Chair	50	Ledge	83	Steps
18	Chandelier	51	Loom	84	Stool
19	Charcoal bin	52	Loose masonry	85	Stuffed beast
20	Chasm	53	Manacles	86	Sunken area
21	Chest	54	Manger	87	Table (large)
22	Chest of drawers	55	Mirror	88	Table (small)
23	Chute	56	Mosaic	89	Tapestry
24	Coat rack	57	Mound of rubble	90	Throne
25	Collapsed wall	58	Oven	91	Trash (pile)
26	Crate	59	Overhang	92	Tripod
27	Cupboard	60	Painting	93	Trough
28	Curtain	61	Partially collapsed ceiling	94	Tub
29	Divan	62	Pedestal	95	Wall basin
30	Dome	63	Peephole	96	Wardrobe
31	Door (broken)	64	Pillar	97	Weapon rack
32	Dung heap	65	Pillory	98	Well
33	Evil symbol	66	Pit (shallow)	99	Winch and pulley
				100	Workbench

Illustration by W. Reynolds

differently. So long as the water is at least 10 feet deep, the first 20 feet of falling do no damage. The next 20 feet do subdual damage (1d3 per 10-foot increment). Beyond that, falling damage is normal damage (1d6 per additional 10-foot increment).

Characters who deliberately dive into water take no damage on a successful Swim or Tumble check (DC 15), so long as the water is at least 10 feet deep for every 30 feet fallen. However, the DC of the check increases by 5 for every 50 feet of the dive.

Variant: Generous DMs who feel that falling is too lethal can make the first 1d6 of falling damage always subdual damage, no matter what the circumstances.

Pits and Chasms

Pits in dungeons come in three basic varieties: uncovered, covered, and chasms. Like a cliff or a wall, a pit or a chasm forces characters to either detour around it or go through the time and trouble of figuring out a way across. Pits and chasms can be defeated by judicious application of the Climb skill, the Jump skill, or various magical means.

Uncovered pits serve mainly to discourage intruders from going a certain way, although they cause much grief to characters who stumble into them in the dark, and they can greatly complicate a melee taking place nearby.

Covered pits are much more dangerous. They can be detected with a Search check (DC 20), but only if the character is taking the time to carefully examine the area before walking across it. A char-

An altar dedicated to an evil deity

acter who fails to detect a covered pit is still entitled to a Reflex save (DC 20) to avoid falling into it. However, if she was running or moving recklessly at the time, she gets no saving throw and falls automatically.

Trap coverings can be as simple as piled refuse (straw, leaves, sticks, garbage), a large rug, or an actual trapdoor concealed to appear as a normal part of the floor. Trapdoors usually swing open when enough weight (usually about 50 to 80 pounds) is placed upon them. Devious trap builders sometimes design trapdoors so that they swing back shut after they open, ready for the next victim. A variant of this is to have the trapdoor lock once it's back in place, leaving the stranded character well and truly trapped. Opening such a trapdoor is just as difficult as opening a regular door (assuming the character can reach it at all), and a Strength check (DC 13) is needed to keep a spring-loaded door open.

Pit traps often have something nastier than just a hard floor at the bottom. Trap designers may put spikes, monsters, or a pool of acid, lava, or even water at the bottom (since even a victim proficient in swimming eventually will tire and drown if trapped long enough).

Spikes at the bottom of a pit may impale unlucky characters. Such spikes deal damage as daggers with a +10 attack bonus and a +1 damage bonus for every 10 feet of the fall (to a maximum damage bonus of +5). If there are multiple spikes, the falling victim is attacked by 1d4 of them. Naturally, all this damage is in addition to any damage from the fall itself.

TABLE 4–6: DUNGEON DRESSING—MINOR FEATURES AND FURNISHINGS

d%	Feature/Furnishing	d%	Feature/Furnishing	d%	Feature/Furnishing
1	Anvil	34	Dripping water	67	Pillows
2	Ash	35	Drum	68	Pipe (smoking pipe)
3	Backpack	36	Dust	69	Pole
4	Bale (straw)	37	Engraving	70	Pot
5	Bellows	38	Equipment (broken)	71	Pottery shard
6	Belt	39	Equipment (usable)	72	Pouch
7	Bits of Fur	40	Flask	73	Puddle (water)
8	Blanket	41	Flint and Tinder	74	Rags
9	Bloodstain	42	Foodstuffs (spoiled)	75	Razor
10	Bones (humanoid)	43	Foodstuffs (edible)	76	Rivulet
11	Bones (nonhumanoid)	44	Fungus	77	Ropes
12	Books	45	Grinder	78	Runes
13	Boots	46	Hook	79	Sack
14	Bottle	47	Horn	80	Scattered stones
15	Box	48	Hourglass	81	Scorch marks
16	Branding iron	49	Insects	82	Scroll (nonmagical)
17	Broken glass	50	Jar	83	Scroll case (empty)
18	Bucket	51	Keg	84	Skull
19	Candle	52	Key	85	Slime
20	Candelabra	53	Lamp	86	Sound (unexplained)
21	Cards (playing cards)	54	Lantern	87	Spices
22	Chains	55	Markings	88	Spike
23	Claw marks	56	Mold	89	Teeth
24	Cleaver	57	Mud	90	Tongs
25	Clothing	58	Mug	91	Tools
26	Cobwebs	59	Musical instrument	92	Torch (stub)
27	Cold spot	60	Mysterious stain	93	Tray
28	Corpse (adventurer)	61	Nest (animal)	94	Trophy
29	Corpse (monster)	62	Odor (unidentifiable)	95	Twine
30	Cracks	63	Oil (fuel)	96	Urn
31	Dice	64	Oil (scented)	97	Utensils
32	Discarded weapons	65	Paint	98	Whetstone
33	Dishes	66	Paper	99	Wood (scraps)
				100	Words (scrawled)

Illustration by W. Reynolds

Monsters sometimes live in pits—oozes and jellies find that plenty of food comes to them if the trapped area is well traveled. Any monster that can fit into the pit might have been placed there by the dungeon's designer, or might simply have fallen in and not been able to climb back out. In the latter case, either it hasn't been there long, or something has been feeding it. If the pit has water, the builder may have stocked it with piranhas or other carnivorous fish. When all is said and done, though, monsters that need no upkeep—such as undead and constructs—make the best choices for creatures to inhabit a pit.

A secondary trap, mechanical or magical, at the bottom of a pit can be particularly deadly. Activated by the falling victim, the secondary trap attacks the already injured character when she's least ready for it. Arrow traps, blasts of flame, sprays of acid, magic *symbols* or *glyphs of warding*, or even magic *monster summoning* devices can all be found at the bottoms of pits.

Cave-Ins and Collapses

Cave-ins and collapsing tunnels are extremely dangerous. Not only do dungeon explorers face the danger of being crushed by tons of falling rock, even if they survive they may be pinned beneath a pile of rubble or cut off from the only known exit. A cave-in buries anyone in the middle of the collapsing area, and then sliding debris damages anyone in the periphery of the collapse. A typical corridor subject to a cave-in might have a bury zone 30 feet long and a slide zone of 10 feet at either end of the bury zone.

A weakened ceiling can be spotted by a successful Knowledge (architecture and engineering) or Craft (stonemasonry) check (DC 20). Remember that Craft checks can be made untrained as Wisdom checks. A dwarf can make such a check if he simply passes within 10 feet of a weakened ceiling.

A weakened ceiling may collapse under the impact of a major impact or concussion. A character can cause a cave-in by dealing 20 points of damage to the weakened ceiling or by breaking it with a successful Strength check (DC 24). A weakened ceiling also collapses if this damage is done to the columns or pillars supporting it rather than directly to the ceiling itself.

Characters in the bury zone of a cave-in sustain 8d6 points of damage, or half that amount if they make a successful Reflex saving throw (DC 15). They are subsequently pinned. Characters in the slide zone sustain 3d6 points of damage, or no damage at all if

A water trap threatens to quench Alhandra's life.

they make a successful Reflex saving throw (DC 15). Characters in the slide zone who fail their saves are pinned.

Pinned characters take 1d6 points of subdual damage per minute while pinned. If such a character falls unconscious, he must make a Constitution check (DC 15). If the character fails, he takes 1d6 points of normal damage each minute thereafter until freed or dead.

Characters who aren't buried can dig out their friends. In 1 minute, using only her hands, a character can clear rocks and debris equal to five times her heavy load rating (see Table 9–1: Carrying Capacity, page 142 in the *Player's Handbook*). The amount of loose stone that fills a 5-foot-by-5-foot area weighs one ton (2,000 pounds). Therefore, the average adventurer (Str 10, heavy load 100 lb.) takes 4 minutes to clear a 5-foot cube filled with stone (100 lb. × 5 = 500 lb., 500 lb. × 4 = 2,000 lb.). A half-orc with 20 Strength (heavy load 400 lb.) can accomplish the same feat in 1 minute (400 lb. × 5 = 2,000 lb.). Armed with an appropriate tool, such as a pick, crowbar, or shovel, a digger can clear loose stone twice as quickly as by hand. You may allow a pinned character to free himself with a successful Strength check (DC 25).

Mechanical Traps

Dungeons are frequently equipped with fiendish mechanical (nonmagical) traps, such as hidden crossbows that fire when the victim unwittingly steps on a trigger plate on the floor, or hallways rigged to collapse in a deadly cave-in. A trap typically is defined by its location and triggering conditions, how hard it is to spot before it goes off, how much damage it deals, and whether or not the heroes receive a saving throw to mitigate its effects. Traps that attack with arrows, sweeping blades, and other types of weaponry make normal attack rolls, with an attack bonus as determined by the Dungeon Master.

Creatures who succeed at a Search check (DC 20) detect a simple mechanical trap before it is triggered. (A simple trap is a snare, a trap triggered by a tripwire, or a large trap such as a pit.)

A rogue (and only a rogue) who succeeds at a Search check (DC 21) detects a well-hidden or complex mechanical trap before it is triggered. Complex traps are denoted by their triggering mechanisms and involve pressure plates, mechanisms linked to doors, changes in weight, disturbances in the air, vibrations, and other sorts of unusual triggers.

Building Mechanical Traps

Like any other form of crafting, the building of mechanical traps requires the proper materials, time, and the appropriate Craft skill (in this case, Craft [trapmaking]). As a rough estimate, assume that a trap costs 1,000 gp and requires one week to construct per point of Challenge Rating. Thus a typical portcullis trap (CR 2) costs 2,000 gp and requires two weeks to construct. See Chapter 7: Rewards for rules on assigning Challenge Ratings to traps.

Sample Mechanical Traps

The following are common mechanical traps, found in dungeons the world over. Provided for each trap is its Challenge Rating (CR), its attack bonus (when applicable), the amount of damage it inflicts (in parentheses), and the DCs for saving throws or skill checks to find, avoid, and/or disable the trap.

Arrow Trap: CR 1; +10 ranged (1d6/×3 crit); Search (DC 20); Disable Device (DC 20). *Note:* 200-ft. max range, target determined randomly from those in its path.

Spear Trap: CR 2; +12 ranged (1d8/×3 crit); Search (DC 20); Disable Device (DC 20). *Note:* 200-ft. max range, target determined randomly from those in its path.

Pit Trap (20 Ft. Deep): CR 1; no attack roll necessary (2d6); Reflex save (DC 20) avoids; Search (DC 20); Disable Device (DC 20).

Spiked Pit Trap (20 Ft. Deep): CR 2; no attack roll necessary (2d6), +10 melee (1d4 spikes for 1d4+2 points of damage per successful hit); Reflex save (DC 20) avoids; Search (DC 20); Disable Device (DC 20).

Pit Trap (40 Ft. Deep): CR 2; no attack roll necessary (4d6); Reflex save (DC 20) avoids; Search (DC 20); Disable Device (DC 20).

Spiked Pit Trap (40 Ft. Deep): CR 3; no attack roll necessary (4d6), +10 melee (1d4 spikes for 1d4+4 points of damage per successful hit); Reflex save (DC 20) avoids; Search (DC 20); Disable Device (DC 20).

Pit Trap (60 Ft. Deep): CR 3; no attack roll necessary (6d6); Reflex save (DC 20) avoids; Search (DC 20); Disable Device (DC 20).

Spiked Pit Trap (60 Ft. Deep): CR 4; no attack roll necessary (6d6), +10 melee (1d4 spikes for 1d4+5 points of damage per successful hit); Reflex save (DC 20) avoids; Search (DC 20); Disable Device (DC 20).

Pit Trap (80 Ft. Deep): CR 4; no attack roll necessary (8d6); Reflex save (DC 20) avoids; Search (DC 20); Disable Device (DC 20).

Spiked Pit Trap (80 Ft. Deep): CR 5; no attack roll necessary (8d6), +10 melee (1d4 spikes for 1d4+5 points of damage per successful hit); Reflex save (DC 20) avoids; Search (DC 20); Disable Device (DC 20).

Pit Trap (100 Ft. Deep): CR 5; no attack roll necessary (10d6); Reflex save (DC 20) avoids; Search (DC 20); Disable Device (DC 20).

Spiked Pit Trap (100 Ft. Deep): CR 6; no attack roll necessary (10d6), +10 melee (1d4 spikes for 1d4+5 points of damage per successful hit); Reflex save (DC 20) avoids; Search (DC 20); Disable Device (DC 20).

Poison Needle Trap: CR 2; +8 ranged (1, plus greenblood oil poison); Search (DC 22); Disable Device (DC 20). *Note:* See page 80 for a description of greenblood oil poison and its effects.

Hail of Needles: CR 1; +20 ranged (2d4); Search (DC 22); Disable Device (DC 22).

Crushing Wall Trap: CR 10; no attack roll required (20d6); Search (DC 20); Disable Device (DC 25).

Scything Blade Trap: CR 1; +8 melee (1d8/×3 crit); Search (DC 21); Disable Device (DC 20).

Falling Block Trap: CR 5; +15 melee (6d6); Search (DC 20); Disable Device (DC 25). *Note:* Can strike all characters in two adjacent specified squares (see Falling Objects, page 89).

Large Net Trap: CR 1; +5 melee (see note); Search (DC 20); Disable Device (DC 25). *Note:* Characters in 10-ft. square are grappled by net (Str 18) if they fail a Reflex save (DC 14).

Poison Gas Trap: CR 10; no attack roll necessary (see note below); Search (DC 21); Disable Device (DC 25). *Note:* Trap releases burnt othur fumes (see Poison, pages 79–80).

Flooding Room Trap: CR 5; no attack roll necessary (see note below); Search (DC 20); Disable Device (DC 25). *Note:* Room floods in 4 rounds (see The Drowning Rule, page 85).

Portcullis Trap: CR 2; +10 melee (3d6/×2 crit); Search (DC 20); Disable Device (DC 20). *Note:* Damage applies only to those underneath the portcullis. Portcullis blocks passageway.

Magic Traps

Many spells can be used to create dangerous traps. For example, high-level clerics can create *glyphs of warding* or *symbols* to prevent intruders from entering a particular area, while high-level wizards can create *fire traps* or *permanent images* to conceal dangers or confuse invaders. Unless the spell or item description states otherwise, assume the following to be true:

- A successful Search check (DC 25 + spell level) made by a rogue (and only a rogue) detects a magic trap before it goes off. Other characters have no chance to find a magic trap with a Search check.
- Magic traps permit a saving throw in order to avoid the effect (DC 10 + spell level × 1.5).
- Magic traps may be disarmed by a rogue (and only a rogue) with a successful Disable Device check (DC 25 + spell level).

Creating Magic Traps

Creating a magic trap costs experience points and gold, just like creating magic items. If a trap is a one-use device, the cost for creation is 50 gp and 2 XP, both multiplied by the caster level. If a trap has multiple uses (or functions continually), the cost for creation is 500 gp and 20 XP, both multiplied by the caster level. Devising and placing a magic trap not covered by existing spell effects is just like creating a magic item (see Chapter 8: Magic Items). Building a trap-filled dungeon filled with magical dangers is thus a costly process.

The spells listed in Table 4–7: Spells for Magic Traps can create interesting magic traps. Use the list to pick from, get ideas, or generate traps randomly. Keep in mind that this list does not respect power level, and some effects may be clearly underpowered or overpowered for a given encounter.

Sample Magic Traps

Magic traps come in all shapes and forms. Only the power and deviousness of their creators limit them. The following are merely a few examples of the simpler magic traps. Provided for each trap is its Challenge Rating (CR), the area the trap affects or its attack bonus (whichever applies), the amount of damage it inflicts (in parentheses), and the DCs for saving throws or skill checks to find, avoid, and/or disable the trap.

Flame Jet: CR 2; 1-ft.-wide, 50-ft.-long stream of flame (3d6); Reflex save (DC 13) avoids; Search (DC 25); Disable Device (DC 26).

BEHIND THE CURTAIN: TRAPS

Why use traps? Traps change the play of the game. If the adventurers suspect traps or have encountered them frequently in the past, they're much more likely to be cautious on adventures and particularly in dungeons. While instilling a little fear and paranoia in players can be fun, you should be aware that this also tends to slow down play, and searching every square foot of a corridor can get tedious for players and DM alike.

The solution is to place traps only when appropriate. People trap tombs and vaults to keep out intruders, but traps can be annoying and inappropriate in well-traveled areas. An intelligent creature is never going to build a trap that it might fall victim to itself.

Lightning Blast: CR 3; 5-ft.-wide, 50-ft.-long blast (3d6); Reflex save (DC 13) avoids; Search (DC 26); Disable Device (DC 25).

Globe of Cold: CR 4; 20-ft.-radius sphere or hemisphere (5d6); Reflex save (DC 15) avoids; Search (DC 27); Disable Device (DC 25).

Electrified Floor: CR 4; section of floor (3d10); Reflex save (DC 14) for half damage; Search (DC 25); Disable Device (DC 25).

Floor Transforms into Acid: CR 6; section of floor (10d6); Reflex save (DC 16) negates; Search (DC 28); Disable Device (DC 30). *Note:* Successful save means character dives to safety in time.

Illusion over Spiked Pit (20 Ft. deep): CR 3; no attack roll required (2d6), +10 melee (1d4 spike attacks for 1d4+2 points of damage per successful hit); Reflex save (DC 15) negates; Search (DC 20); Disable Device (DC 20).

Air Sucked out of Room: CR 5; one room (see note below); Search (DC 28); Disable Device (DC 30). *Note:* Deals suffocation damage (see Suffocation, page 88).

DUNGEON ECOLOGY

The inhabited dungeon is an environment in and of itself. The creatures that live there need to eat, drink, breathe, and sleep just like the creatures of the forest or the plains. Predators need prey.

Tordek falls victim to a magic lightning trap.

Creatures living in the dungeon need to be able to get around. Locked doors, or even doors that require hands to open, can prevent creatures from getting to food or water.

Consider these factors when designing a dungeon you want the players to believe in. If the environment doesn't have some logic behind it, the PCs can't make decisions based on reasoning while adventuring there. For example, upon finding a pool of fresh water in the dungeon, a character

should be able to make the assumption that many of the creatures inhabiting the place come to that spot often. Thus, the PCs could wait in ambush for a particular creature that they're after. Bits of faulty dungeon logic, such as all the doors in a dungeon being locked when the dungeon is home to many creatures, destroy any chance of verisimilitude.

Dungeon Animals

Not everything that lives in a dungeon is a monster. Other creatures inhabit these unlit labyrinths as well.

Creepy Crawlers: Insects, spiders, grubs, and worms of all types live in the dark recesses of dungeons. They don't present a real threat, but they do provide food for predators and scavengers in the dungeon—who in turn pose a threat to adventurers.

Rats: Rats make up an important part of any dungeon ecology. These omnipresent vermin serve as the staple for most dungeon predators and scavengers. In huge packs, they become a threat themselves.

Bats: Like rats, bats are found throughout any dungeon with access to outside air. Although never truly dangerous, a swarm of bats can obscure vision and hamper the actions of dungeon delvers—particularly spellcasting.

Other Animals: Strange as it may sound, other animals ranging from small creatures such as badgers and ferrets to large omnivores such as bears and apes may take to a full-time (or almost full-time) subterranean existence in a world filled with dungeons and caverns. Predatory animals such as tigers, wolves, and snakes follow their prey down into the dungeons and remain, becoming a part of the ecology. Deep dungeon delvers have brought back stories of colossal caverns far underground with flocks of birds flying about. And of course underground streams, lakes, and even seas teem with all sorts of fish, water mammals, and aquatic reptiles.

Over the generations, dungeon animals have developed darkvision in order to survive. They adapted to their environment, and now they thrive in the dark confines of caves and passages. They feed on mold, fungi, or each other. Because of the lack of sunlight, many species have become entirely white, while others have evolved a black coloration to hide in the darkness.

Dungeon Slimes, Molds, and Fungi

In a dungeon's damp, dark recesses, molds and fungi thrive. While some plants and fungi are monsters (see the *Monster Manual*), and other slime, mold, and fungus is just normal, innocuous stuff, a few varieties are dangerous dungeon encounters. For purposes of spells and other special effects, all slimes, molds, and fungi are treated as plants. Like traps, dangerous slimes and molds have CRs, and characters earn XP for encountering them.

Green Slime (CR 4)

Glistening organic sludge coats almost anything that remains in the damp and dark for too long, but green slime is a dangerous variety of this normal slime. Green slime devours flesh and organic materials on contact, and is even capable of dissolving metal. Bright green, wet, and sticky, it clings to walls, floors, and ceilings in patches, reproducing as it consumes organic matter. It drops from walls and ceilings when it detects movement (and possible food) below.

A single patch of green slime deals 1d6 points of temporary Constitution damage per round while it devours flesh. On the first round of contact, the slime can be scraped off a creature (most likely destroying the scraping device), but after that it must be frozen, burned, or cut away (applying damage to the victim as well). Extreme cold or heat, sunlight, or a *cure disease* spell destroys a patch of green slime. Against wood or metal, green slime deals 2d6 points of damage per round, ignoring metal's hardness but not that of wood. It does not harm stone.

Dwarves consider green slime to be one of the worst hazards of mining and underground construction. They have their own ways of burning it out of infested areas, methods that they say are thorough. "If you don't do it right, the stuff comes right back," they claim.

Mold and Fungus

Molds and fungi flourish in dark, cool, damp places. While some are as inoffensive as the normal dungeon slime, others are quite dangerous. Mushrooms, puffballs, yeasts, mildew, and other sorts of bulbous, fibrous, or flat patches of fungi can be found throughout most dungeons. They are usually inoffensive and some are even edible (though most are unappealing or odd-tasting).

Yellow Mold (CR 6): If disturbed, a patch of this mold bursts forth with a cloud of poisonous spores. All within 10 feet of the mold must make a Fortitude save (DC 15) or take 1d6 points of temporary Constitution damage. Another Fortitude save (DC 15) is required 1 minute later—even by those who succeeded at the first save—to avoid taking 2d6 points of temporary Constitution damage. Fire destroys yellow mold, and sunlight renders it dormant.

Brown Mold (CR 2): Brown mold feeds on warmth, drawing heat from anything around it. It normally comes in patches 2 to 3 feet in diameter, and the temperature is always cold in the area surrounding it. Living creatures within 5 feet of it take 3d6 points of cold subdual damage. Fire brought within 5 feet of the mold causes it to instantly double in size. Cold damage, such as from a *cone of cold*, instantly destroys it.

Phosphorescent Fungus (No CR): This strange underground fungus grows in patches that look almost like stunted shrubbery. It gives off a soft violet glow that illuminates underground caverns and passages. Drow cultivate it for food and light.

WANDERING MONSTERS

While the adventurers are exploring the dungeon, the light of their lanterns attracts the attention of hungry dire weasels, who come to see if they can catch some soft and juicy things to eat. On another delve, a carrion crawler finds them and follows behind

TABLE 4–7: SPELLS FOR MAGIC TRAPS

d%	Spell	d%	Spell	d%	Spell
1	Acid fog	36	Geas/quest	69	Screen
2	Alarm*	37	Giant vermin	70	Sepia snake sigil
3	Animate object	38	Glyph of warding	71	Shatter
4	Antimagic field (keeps spellcasters from foiling another trap)*	39	Grease (particularly useful for making victims slide into a dangerous area)*	72	Silence (keeps spellcasters from foiling another trap)
5	Bigby's clenched fist	40	Harm	73	Slay living
6	Bigby's forceful hand	41	Hold monster*	74	Slow
7	Bigby's grasping hand	42	Hold person*	75	Spell turning*
8	Binding	43	Imprisonment	76	Suggestion*
9	Blade barrier	44	Inflict critical wounds	77	Summon monster I
10	Blindness (or deafness)	45	Inflict light wounds	78	Summon monster II
11	Circle of death	46	Inflict moderate wounds	79	Summon monster III
12	Color spray	47	Inflict serious wounds	80	Summon monster IV
13	Confusion	48	Invisibility (cast upon a dangerous object such as a pendulum blade)*	81	Summon monster IX
14	Contagion			82	Summon monster V
15	Darkness*	49	Levitate	83	Summon monster VI
16	Disintegration	50	Lightning bolt	84	Summon monster VII
17	Dispel good	51	Magic jar*	85	Summon monster VIII
18	Dispel magic	52	Magic missile	86	Summon monster IX
19	Dominate person	53	Mass suggestion	87	Symbol
20	Doom	54	Melf's acid arrow	88	Tasha's hideous laughter
21	Energy drain	55	Mind fog	89	Telekinesis*
22	Enervation	56	Mordenkainen's disjunction	90	Teleport
23	Enlarge*	57	Nightmare	91	Temporal stasis
24	Explosive runes	58	Otiluke's telekinetic sphere	92	Trap the soul
25	Eyebite	59	Permanency (works with other spells to make long-lasting traps)*	93	Vanish
26	False vision			94	Wall of fire
27	Fear	60	Permanent image*	95	Wall of force (to seal off an area)*
28	Feeblemind	61	Plane shift	96	Wall of iron (to seal off an area)*
29	Fireball	62	Polymorph other	97	Wall of stone (to seal off an area)*
30	Fire trap	63	Power word, kill	98	Web*
31	Flaming sphere	64	Prismatic spray	99	Weird
32	Flesh to stone	65	Programmed image*	100	Word of chaos
33	Forbiddance	66	Reduce		
34	Forcecage	67	Repulsion*		
35	Gate	68	Reverse gravity*		

*Best when used in conjunction with another spell, another trap, a dangerous area, or a guardian creature.

them, out of sight. When it hears a fight, it scrambles up from behind and tries to make off with a character who has fallen in combat. On yet another expedition, the party meets another party of adventurers. If the two groups can work together, they can exchange vital information, trade valuable items, and possibly even work together. The meeting, however, could just as easily turn into a nasty fight. Wandering monsters such as these add unpredictability and action to dungeon adventures.

Wandering Monster Rolls

As the adventurers explore a dungeon, make wandering monster rolls to see if they encounter wandering monsters. Use wandering monster rolls to add an unpredictable element to a dungeon delve, to encourage characters to keep moving, and to put a price on being noisy. The exact formula for when you roll for wandering monsters is up to you. Generally, there is a 10% chance for a wandering monster to show up in certain conditions.

TABLE 4–8: WANDERING MONSTER SUMMARY

Wandering Monster Chance = 10%
Make a wandering monster roll on d% in the following circumstances:

- Every hour the characters are in the dungeon.
- When the characters make noise.
- In high-traffic areas.

You may decide to add or omit rolls in the following circumstances:

- In cleared-out areas of the dungeon.
- While the characters are leaving the dungeon.

When a Certain Amount of Time Has Passed: Making one roll per hour is typical. You can roll more often in heavily populated areas, up to as often as once per every 10 minutes. If you're not already tracking time in the dungeon and you don't want to start, roll for wandering monsters when the characters are doing anything that takes a long time (such as taking 20 while searching a room for secret doors) instead of by the clock.

When Characters Make Noise: Breaking a door or having a typical fight counts as making noise. Breaking a door and then having a fight right away counts as one instance of noise, so it's one roll. Getting into a loud argument, knocking over a statue, and running up and down stairs in full kit at top speed are other actions that might call for a wandering monster roll.

In High-Traffic Areas: Deciding what constitutes a high-traffic area is up to you. You can roll every time the characters enter a new large corridor, provided those corridors make it easy for creatures to get to and fro and thus have a lot of traffic. Other areas, such as pools of fresh water, might also attract many creatures.

In Cleared-Out Areas: If the PCs have cleared out part of the dungeon, then you can roll for wandering monsters as they travel through a cleared area to an uncleared area. After all, creatures spread out to fill a vacuum, claiming abandoned territory as their own. These rolls reward players for staying in the dungeon longer at a stretch rather than returning to the surface frequently to heal up. (The more often they leave and return, the more wandering monsters they face.)

When Leaving the Dungeon: While you have every right to roll for wandering monsters as the party is leaving the dungeon, you might decide not to. The characters generally make good time as they head for the surface, and they're usually taking a route they have just used on their way in, so it's reasonable for the chance for wandering monsters to go down. Also, if the players know that the characters might face an extra encounter on the way home, they tend to break off their exploration when they feel they can still handle another encounter, causing them to act more cautiously than they want to or than you may want them to.

Monsters Encountered

In a sprawling, random dungeon, you can simply use the random monster tables (Table 4–15: 1st-Level Dungeon Encounters through Table 4–35: Random Dragons) to determine which monsters wander by. Reroll if the result would be a stationary creature or one unlikely to wander. In a smaller or special dungeon, make your own random encounter tables.

The entries on a customized wandering monster list can indicate individual monsters or groups of monsters rather than kinds of monsters. For example, the entry "Large monstrous scorpion" could mean a particular scorpion that lives in this dungeon rather than a random scorpion from an indefinitely large population of similar scorpions. That way, once the characters have killed that scorpion, they can't encounter it again. Creatures on a customized chart could also have lairs keyed on the dungeon map, so that adventurers who kill a creature while it's wandering would later find its lair empty. Similarly, those who kill it in its lair would never encounter it wandering.

In the same way that you can invent the denizens of specific dungeon rooms rather than determining them randomly, you can invent specific wandering monsters. These could include monsters that escaped from the PCs before (or that the PCs escaped from). Indeed, you can replace the idea of the wandering monster with a random event instead. The characters could hear fighting in the distance, stumble across random clues to the dungeon's past, or become subject to strange, fluctuating magical auras in place of encountering a wandering monster.

Wandering Monsters' Treasure

Overall, wandering monsters don't have as much treasure as monsters encountered in their lairs. When NPCs are encountered as "wandering monsters," their gear is their treasure. Intelligent wandering monsters might (50% chance) have a treasure whose level is equal to the dungeon level. Unintelligent monsters don't have treasure. A dire weasel's den might be littered with the valuables of creatures it has killed, but it doesn't carry that stuff around with it.

Since wandering monsters have less treasure than monsters in their lairs or homes, characters typically try to minimize their encounters with wandering monsters.

RANDOM DUNGEONS

This section shows you how to generate dungeons randomly, from the first door to the great red wyrm and its massive treasure hoard on the lowest, most dangerous level.

DUNGEON LEVEL

The dungeon level measures how dangerous the dungeon (or any other adventure area) is at that location. Generally, a party of adventurers should adventure in areas whose level matches their own party level (though large groups can handle tougher areas and small groups might need to stay in easier areas).

Some dungeons are a series of levels or floors, each beneath the one above, with more dangerous levels found lower down and safer ones nearer the surface. For such dungeons, the floor nearest the surface can be 1st level (EL 1) and each successively lower level can be one dungeon level higher. (The second one down would be 2nd level, the third one 3rd level, and so forth.)

THE MAP AND THE KEY

Once you have decided the level of your dungeon, draw a map on graph paper (or regular paper, if that's easier). Determine the general wall and floor types—masonry, hewn stone, natural caves, and so on, as you draw the map. The map should show rooms, corridors, and doors. If you plan to make a sprawling dungeon of nearly endless size, you don't need to map it all first.

TABLE 4–9: DOOR TYPES

d%	Type (DC to break)
01–08	Wooden, simple, free
09	Wooden, simple, free and trapped
10–23	Wooden, simple, stuck (13)
24	Wooden, simple, stuck (13) and trapped
25–29	Wooden, simple, locked (13)
30	Wooden, simple, locked (13) and trapped
31–35	Wooden, good, free
36	Wooden, good, free and trapped
37–44	Wooden, good, stuck (18)
45	Wooden, good, stuck (18) and trapped
46–49	Wooden, good, locked (18)
50	Wooden, good, locked (18) and trapped
51–55	Wooden, strong, free
56	Wooden, strong, free and trapped
57–64	Wooden, strong, stuck (23)
65	Wooden, strong, stuck (23) and trapped
66–69	Wooden, strong, locked (23)
70	Wooden, strong, locked (23) and trapped
71	Stone, free
72	Stone, free and trapped
73–75	Stone, stuck (28)
76	Stone, stuck (28) and trapped
77–79	Stone, locked (28)
80	Stone, locked (28) and trapped
81	Iron, free
82	Iron, free and trapped
83–85	Iron, stuck (28)
86	Iron, stuck (28) and trapped
87–89	Iron, locked (28)
90	Iron, locked (28) and trapped
91–93	Door slides to one side rather than opening normally. Reroll type (ignoring rolls of 91+). Add +1 to break DC.
94–96	Door slides down rather than opening normally. Reroll type (ignoring rolls of 91+). Add +1 to break DC.
97–99	Door slides up rather than opening normally. Reroll type (ignoring rolls of 91+). Add +2 to break DC.
100	Door magically reinforced. Reroll type (ignoring rolls of 91+). Break DC is 30 for wooden and 40 for stone or iron doors.

Trapped: Roll on Table 4–11: Traps CR 1–3 or Table 4–12: Traps CR 4+ to determine the nature of the trap.

You also want a separate sheet of paper for the dungeon's key. The key describes the dungeon.

First, create the special parts of your dungeon. These could be rooms with your favorite monsters and treasures, devious traps, strange rooms with magic pools or enchanted statues, mysteries and enigmas, or anything unusual you want to include. When you invent the contents of a room, describe it in the key, give it a number, and then put that number on the map to indicate where those features are found. To determine what sort of door (or doors) a room will have, you can roll d% and refer to Table 4–9: Door Types or simply select a type from that list.

Next, you can fill out the rest of the dungeon, either by deciding what goes in each room or determining it randomly. If you determine it randomly, roll on Table 4–10: Room Contents for each room. The results you get will lead you to other random tables here and in other chapters.

You can roll for each door ahead of time and record the results on your key, or just roll for each door randomly as you play. If you like, you can even start with a blank map and roll door features and room contents as the player characters explore, one room at a time.

RANDOM DUNGEON ENCOUNTERS

This section shows you how to generate encounters randomly, especially for encounters in dungeons. You can also use these

TABLE 4–10: ROOM CONTENTS

d%	Room Contents
01–18	Monster only
19–44	Monster and features
45	Monster and hidden treasure
46	Monster and trap
47	Monster, features, and hidden treasure
48	Monster, features, and trap
49	Monster, hidden treasure, and trap
50	Monster, features, hidden treasure, trap
51–76	Features only
77	Features and hidden treasure
78	Features and trap
79	Features, hidden treasure, and trap
80	Hidden treasure only
81	Hidden treasure and trap
82	Trap only
83–100	Nothing

Features: Roll 1d4 minor features on Table 4–6: Minor Features and Furnishings (01–40), 1d4 major features on Table 4–5: Major Features and Furnishings (41–80), or both (81–100).

Hidden Treasure: Roll a random treasure of the dungeon's level on Table 7–4: Treasure. Typically, the treasure is hidden in such a way that it takes a Search check (DC 20 + the dungeon level) to find it.

Monster: Roll starting on Table 4–13: Random Encounter Master Table. Creatures in rooms with traps or hidden treasures may or may not know about them.

Trap: Roll on Table 4–11: Traps CR 1–3 or Table 4–12: Traps CR 4+, or invent one that suits the other contents of the room.

TABLE 4–11: TRAPS CR 1–3

d%	Trap	CR
01–10	Arrow trap	1
11–15	Spear trap	2
16–25	Pit trap (20 ft. deep)	1
26–35	Spiked pit trap (20 ft. deep)	2
36–45	Pit trap (40 ft. deep)	2
46–50	Spiked pit trap (40 ft. deep)	3
51–55	Pit trap (60 ft. deep)	3
56–65	Poison needle trap	2
66–70	Hail of needles	1
71–75	Scything blade trap	1
76–80	Large net trap	1
81–85	Portcullis trap	2
86–90	Flame Jet	2
91–95	Lightning blast	3
96–100	Illusion over spiked pit	3

DC to find a trap or to disable it is generally 20 + the dungeon level.

TABLE 4–12: TRAPS CR 4+

d%	Trap	CR
01–10	Spiked pit trap (60 ft. deep)	4
11–20	Pit trap (80 ft. deep)	4
21–25	Spiked pit trap (80 ft. deep)	5
26–30	Pit trap (100 ft. deep)	5
31–35	Spiked pit trap (100 ft. deep)	6
36–38	Crushing wall trap	10
39–43	Falling block trap	5
44–45	Poison gas trap	10
46–50	Flooding room trap	5
51–55	Globe of cold	4
56–60	Electrified floor	4
61–65	Air sucked out of room	5
66–70	Floor transforms into acid	6
71–100	Spell-related trap*	Varies

DC to find a trap or to disable it is generally 20 + the dungeon level.

*Roll on Table 4–7: Spells for Magic Traps for spell.

tables simply as lists from which you choose the encounters you want to put in your dungeon.

Rolling the Encounter

To generate a random dungeon encounter, follow these steps:

1. Determine the dungeon level (see above).
2. Roll d% and look at Table 4–13: Random Encounter Master Table to see which Dungeon Encounters table to roll on for the encounter.
3. Roll on the appropriate Dungeon Encounters table (Table 4–15: 1st-Level Dungeon Encounters through Table 4–34: 20th-Level Dungeon Encounters) to see what creatures are in the encounter. If the result is a dragon, roll on Table 4–35: Random Dragons. If the result is one or more NPCs, see the NPC tables at the end of Chapter 2: Characters.
4. Where applicable, roll the indicated die to see how many creatures are in the encounter. If you rolled on an encounter table that's lower than the dungeon level, increase the number of creatures encountered. If you rolled on an encounter table that's higher than the dungeon level, decrease the number of creatures encountered (see Number of Creatures, below).
5. Refer to the "Treasure" column on the Dungeon Encounters table you are using and roll d% to see if the encounter includes treasure. If it does, roll on Table 7–4: Treasure. Usually, you roll on the line that corresponds to the dungeon level, but sometimes you roll on a higher-level line (according to the bonus listed in the "Treasure" column). Base the treasure level on the dungeon level, not the level of the Dungeon Encounters table.

Exception: If you can't reduce the number of creatures encountered far enough, you can base the treasure on the encounter's actual level. For example, if on the 4th level of the dungeon a roll of 93 on Table 4–13: Random Encounter Master Table sends you to Table 4–21: 7th-Level Dungeon

TABLE 4–13: RANDOM ENCOUNTER MASTER TABLE

	Dungeon Level									
d%	1st	2nd	3rd	4th	5th	6th	7th	8th	9th	10th
01–05	1st	1st	1st	1st	2nd	2nd	3rd	4th	5th	6th
	—	×2	×3	×4	×4	×4	×4	×4	×4	×4
06–10	1st	1st	1st	1st	2nd	3rd	4th	5th	6th	7th
	—	×2	×3	×4	×3	×3	×3	×3	×3	×3
11–20	1st	1st	2nd	2nd	3rd	4th	5th	6th	7th	8th
	—	×2	×3/2	×2	×2	×2	×2	×2	×2	×2
21–30	1st	2nd	2nd	3rd	4th	5th	6th	7th	8th	9th
	—	—	×3/2	×3/2	×3/2	×3/2	×3/2	×3/2	×3/2	×3/2
31–70	1st	2nd	3rd	4th	5th	6th	7th	8th	9th	10th
	—	—	—	—	—	—	—	—	—	—
71–80	2nd	3rd	4th	5th	6th	7th	8th	9th	10th	11th
	×1/2	×2/3	×2/3	×2/3	×2/3	×2/3	×2/3	×2/3	×2/3	×2/3
81–90	2nd	4th	5th	6th	7th	8th	9th	10th	11th	12th
	×1/2	×1/2	×1/2	×1/2	×1/2	×1/2	×1/2	×1/2	×1/2	×1/2
91–100	3rd	5th	6th	7th	8th	9th	10th	11th	12th	13th
	×1/3	×1/3	×1/3	×1/3	×1/3	×1/3	×1/3	×1/3	×1/3	×1/3

d%	11th	12th	13th	14th	15th	16th	17th	18th	19th	20th
01–05	7th	8th	9th	10th	11th	12th	13th	14th	15th	16th
	×4	×4	×4	×4	×4	×4	×4	×4	×4	×4
06–10	8th	9th	10th	11th	12th	13th	14th	15th	16th	17th
	×3	×3	×3	×3	×3	×3	×3	×3	×3	×3
11–20	9th	10th	11th	12th	13th	14th	15th	16th	17th	18th
	×2	×2	×2	×2	×2	×2	×2	×2	×2	×2
21–30	10th	11th	12th	13th	14th	15th	16th	17th	18th	19th
	×3/2	×3/2	×3/2	×3/2	×3/2	×3/2	×3/2	×3/2	×3/2	×3/2
31–70	11th	12th	13th	14th	15th	16th	17th	18th	19th	20th
	—	—	—	—	—	—	—	—	—	—
71–80	12th	13th	14th	15th	16th	17th	18th	19th	19th	20th
	×2/3	×2/3	×2/3	×2/3	×2/3	×2/3	×2/3	×2/3	—	—
81–90	13th	14th	15th	16th	17th	18th	19th	20th	20th	20th
	×1/2	×1/2	×1/2	×1/2	×1/2	×1/2	×1/2	×1/2	×2/3	—
91–100	14th	15th	16th	17th	18th	19th	20th	20th	20th	20th
	×1/3	×1/3	×1/3	×1/3	×1/3	×1/3	×1/3	×1/2	×2/3	—

1st to 20th: Roll the encounter on the appropriate table below (Table 4–15: 1st-Level Random Encounters through Table 4–34: 20th-Level Random Encounters).

—: Don't modify the number of creatures encountered.

×3/2: Increase the number of creatures encountered by 1/2 (or multiply by 3 and divide by 2). Round up fractions 50% of the time.

×2: Double the number of creatures.

×3: Triple the number of creatures.

×4: Quadruple the number of creatures.

×2/3: Decrease the number of creatures encountered by 1/3 (or multiply by 2 and divide by 3). Round off fractions (1/3 down and 2/3 up).

×1/2: Divide the number of creatures by 2. Round up fractions 50% of the time.

×1/3: Divide the number of creatures by 3. Round off fractions (1/3 down and 2/3 up).

Encounters, where a subsequent roll of 02 indicates a black pudding, there's no way to reduce the number encountered to 1/3 normal (as indicated in the entry rolled on Table 4–13). The encounter is thus with a single full-size black pudding. And if the pudding has treasure, make it a 7th-level treasure, not a 4th-level one.

6. Roll hit points for each monster. If any of the creatures are using item treasures as weapons, as armor, or in other ways, adjust their statistics accordingly.

Number of Creatures

Each entry on the Dungeon Encounters tables tells you how many creatures are in that encounter. Table 4–13: Random Encounter Master Table tells you how to increase or decrease the number of creatures encountered, depending on the dungeon level and the Dungeon Encounters table's level. For instance, if on the 2nd level of the dungeon you roll an encounter with 1d4+2 goblins on Table 4–15: 1st-Level Dungeon Encounters, then the corresponding entries on the Master Table (01–20 on the 2nd-level column) show that you should double the number of goblins to make it a good 2nd-level encounter.

If you get more than twelve creatures, you might want to reroll the encounter. Combats with that many creatures can be hard to play and take a long time to resolve, and the creatures are probably too weak to be a good fight.

TABLE 4–14: MODIFIED DIE ROLL

Die Roll	×1/3	×1/2	×2/3	×3/2	×2	×3	×4
1	1	1	1	1d2	1d3	1d3+1	1d4+2
1d2	1	1	1	1d3	1d3+1	1d4+2	1d6+3
1d3	1	1	1d2	1d3+1	1d4+2	1d6+3	1d6+5
1d3+1	1	1d2	1d3	1d4+2	1d6+3	1d6+5	1d4+10
1d4+2	1d2	1d3	1d3+1	1d6+3	1d6+5	1d4+10	*
1d6+3	1d3	1d3+1	1d4+2	1d6+5	1d4+10	*	*
1d6+5	1d3+1	1d4+2	1d6+3	1d4+10	*	*	*

*Reroll the encounter. The creatures are too weak for this dungeon level.

Instead of rolling normally and multiplying, you can instead choose to go to Table 4–14: Modified Die Roll, which tells you the appropriate larger or smaller die to substitute.

Role

Each encounter has a role: critter, dragon, fiend, friend, NPC, terror, tough, or undead. The encounter's role helps you think about how the creatures might act, especially how they might interact with other dungeon denizens. As used here, most of these terms are strictly convenient labels for those roles (note that undead, NPC, and dragon are game terms in their own right).

Critter: Creatures of limited (usually bestial) intelligence whose main strength lies in good combat abilities rather than special powers. A critter is different from a tough in that the critter is unintelligent and less likely to work in a group (or with other creatures). However, critters can be pets or companions of fiends or toughs. Dire animals, gelatinous cubes, and purple worms are good examples of critters.

Dragon: So powerful they deserve a category all to themselves. Good-aligned dragons effectively count as friends. Evil ones count as fiends. The less intelligent ones might simply act as terrors.

Fiend: Intelligent, usually hostile creatures, more likely to defeat the characters with special abilities than in a stand-up fight. (When such a creature is good, it's a friend instead of a fiend. If it has special powers but isn't the sort of creature that could be the brains in an operation, it's a terror.) Fiends can have critters or terrors as pets or companions, toughs as guards, undead as guards or companions, or other fiends as partners. Mind flayers and ogre mages are good examples of fiends.

Friend: A good-aligned creature. (Some dragons and NPCs are good, too.) They can have critters as pets. Note that not all friends automatically ally themselves with the PCs, although they are inclined to be friendly to nonevil parties (see Table 5–3: Initial NPC Attitude). Couatls and celestials are good examples of friends.

NPCs: Fellow adventurers. NPCs come in all varieties of alignment, race, and class. An individual NPC may function as a tough, a terror, a fiend, or a friend, depending on his or her personality,

STRENGTHENING ENCOUNTERS

Instead of (or in addition to) increasing the number of creatures in a lower-level encounter in order to balance it for use as a higher-level encounter, you can add a second group of creatures, make the creatures stronger, or give the creatures some unusual advantage.

To add a second group of creatures, roll another encounter on Table 4–13: Random Encounter Master Table and have all the creatures you roll work together as a group. You might get ogres with zombies (probably given to the ogres by an evil ogre cleric) or mephits with bugbears (probably working together as brains and brawn, respectively). If you get something crazy, such as a gold dragon and a vampire, reroll the second encounter (or just increase the numbers in the first one). Alternatively, instead of rolling the second encounter, you can just choose a logical companion group from the appropriate Dungeon Encounters table.

The extra encounter you roll depends on the multiplier you got from Table 4–13: Random Encounter Master Table:

- ×3/2: Roll once on the indicated level and once more on the Dungeon Encounters table two levels lower (with a minimum of at least 1st-level).
- ×2: Roll twice on the indicated level.
- ×3: Roll twice on the indicated level and double one of the encounters.
- ×4: Roll twice on the indicated level and double both encounters.

Generate treasure according to the more generous treasure entry found for the two encounters.

To make creatures stronger, you can increase the creatures' Hit Dice rather than their numbers (see the rules for creature advancement in the *Monster Manual*). For instance, a black pudding might have 15 Hit Dice instead of the usual 10 HD (and instead of there being 1d2 black puddings). Adding Hit Dice is an especially good idea for strengthening a creature that is usually solitary or found in small numbers.

For creatures that advance by adding class levels rather than Hit Dice, add 1, 2, 3, or 4 levels of an appropriate class or appropriate classes. All the creatures can be the same class, or they can be a mix, like an adventuring party. The number of class levels you add depends on the multiplier:

- ×3/2: +1 level
- ×2: +2 levels
- ×3: +3 levels
- ×4: +4 levels

Give the creatures the gear appropriate for NPCs of their class and class levels. See the NPC section at the end of Chapter 2: Characters, especially the sample NPCs.

Finally, you can strengthen an encounter by giving the creature or creatures special advantages. For example, a black pudding is normally balanced for a 7th-level encounter, but a black pudding in a room filled with fog would be a fine 8th-level encounter. (Oozes have blindsight, so the fog wouldn't hinder the pudding in any way.)

goals, and ability. See the section on NPCs at the end of Chapter 2: Characters, as well as the section on NPC Attitudes in Chapter 5: Campaigns (page 149).

Terror: A creature with special combat powers. A terror is different from a fiend in that a fiend is capable of being the brains in a group of monsters and a terror is not. A terror can be the pet or companion of a fiend or a tough. Displacer beasts and hell hounds are good examples of terrors.

Tough: A reasonably intelligent creature whose main feature is strong combat ability. They often work in groups. Alone, a tough might be the boss of a group of lower-level toughs or the bodyguard of a fiend. As a group, toughs could be guards or troops for a higher-level tough or for a fiend. Toughs can have critters or terrors as pets or companions. Hobgoblins and trolls are good examples of toughs.

Undead: Undead creatures. Some of them, such as vampires, might also effectively qualify as fiends.

TABLE 4–15: 1ST-LEVEL DUNGEON ENCOUNTERS

d%	Role	Number of Creatures and Kind	Treasure
01–04	Critter	1d3 centipedes, Medium-size monstrous (vermin)	20%
05–09	Critter	1d3+1 dire rats	20%
10–14	Critter	1d3+1 fire beetles, giant (vermin)	20%
15–17	Critter	1d3 scorpions, Small monstrous (vermin)	20%
18–20	Critter	1d3 spiders, Small monstrous (vermin)	20%
21–25	Dragon	1 dragon [see Table 4–35: Random Dragons]	80% +2
26–30	Friend	1d3 dwarven warriors	80% +1
31–35	Friend	1d3 elven warriors	80% +1
36–40	NPC	1 1st-level NPC	Gear
41–45	Terror	1 darkmantle	50% +1
46–55	Terror	1 krenshar	50% +1
56–60	Terror	1 lemure (devil)	50% +1
61–65	Tough	1d4+2 goblins	80% +1
66–70	Tough	1 hobgoblin + 1d3 goblins	80% +1
71–80	Tough	1d6+3 kobolds	80% +1
81–90	Undead	1d3+1 skeletons, Medium-size [human]	50%
91–100	Undead	1d3 zombies, Medium-size [human]	50%

TABLE 4–16: 2ND-LEVEL DUNGEON ENCOUNTERS

d%	Role	Number of Creatures and Kind	Treasure
01–05	Critter	1d3 centipedes, Large monstrous (vermin)	20%
06–10	Critter	1d3 giant ants (vermin)	20%
11–15	Critter	1d3 scorpions, Medium-size monstrous (vermin)	20%
16–20	Critter	1d3 spiders, Medium-size monstrous (vermin)	20%
21–25	Dragon	1 dragon [see Table 4–35: Random Dragons]	80% +4
26–30	Friend	1d4+2 elven warriors	80% +2
31–35	NPC	1d3 1st-level NPCs	Gear
36–37	Terror	1 choker	20%
38–42	Terror	1 ethereal marauder	20%
43–45	Terror	1d3 shriekers	20%
46–50	Terror	1d4+2 formian workers	80% +2
51–55	Tough	1d4+2 hobgoblins	80% +2
56–60	Tough	1d3 hobgoblins + 1d4+2 goblins	80% +2
61–70	Tough	1d3 lizardfolk	80% +2
71–80	Tough	1d4+2 orcs	80% +2
81–90	Undead	1d4+2 zombies, Medium-size [human]	50%
91–100	Undead	1d3 ghouls	50%

TABLE 4–17: 3RD-LEVEL DUNGEON ENCOUNTERS

d%	Role	Number of Creatures and Kind	Treasure
01–02	Critter	1d2 bombardier beetles, giant (vermin)	20%
03–04	Critter	1d2 centipedes, Huge monstrous (vermin)	20%
05–06	Critter	1d2 dire badgers	20%
07–08	Critter	1d2 dire bats	20%
09–11	Critter	1 gelatinous cube (ooze)	20%
12–13	Critter	1d2 praying mantises, giant (vermin)	20%
14	Critter	1d2 scorpions, Large monstrous (vermin)	20%
15	Critter	1d2 spiders, Large monstrous (vermin)	20%
16–20	Dragon	1 dragon [see Table 4–35: Random Dragons]	80% +4
21–25	Fiend	1d2 imps (devil)	80% +3
26–30	Fiend	1 wererat (lycanthrope) and 1d3+1 dire rats	80% +3
31–35	Friend	1d6+3 dwarven warriors	80% +3
36–40	NPC	1d3+1 1st-level NPCs	Gear
41–44	Terror	1d2 dretches (demon)	50%
45–48	Terror	1 ethereal filcher	50%
49–52	Terror	1 phantom fungus	20%
53–56	Terror	1d2 thoqquas	20%
57–60	Terror	1d2 vargouilles	50%
61–62	Tough	1 bugbear and 1d4+2 goblins	80% +3
63–67	Tough	1d3+1 gnolls	80% +3
68–69	Tough	1d4+2 goblins and 1d3 wolves	80% +3
70–71	Tough	1d3 hobgoblins and 1d3 wolves	80% +3
72–75	Tough	1d6+3 kobolds and 1 dire weasel	80% +3
76–80	Tough	1d3+1 troglodytes	80% +3
81–90	Undead	1 shadow	50%
91–100	Undead	1d3+1 skeletons, large [ogre]	50%

TABLE 4–18: 4TH-LEVEL DUNGEON ENCOUNTERS

d%	Role	Number of Creatures and Kind	Treasure
01–04	Critter	1d2 ankhegs	20%
05–08	Critter	1d3 dire weasels	20%
09–12	Critter	1 ooze, gray	20%
13–15	Critter	1d2 snakes, Huge viper (animal)	20%
16–20	Dragon	1 dragon [see Table 4–35: Random Dragons]	80% +4
21–23	Fiend	1 formian warrior and 1d3 formian workers	80% +3
24–26	Fiend	1 imp (devil) and 1d3 lemures (devil)	80% +3
27–30	Fiend	1d2 quasits (demon)	80% +3
31–35	Friend	1d3 lantern archons (celestial)	50% +2
36–40	NPC	1d3 2nd-level NPCs	Gear
41–45	Terror	1 carrion crawler	20%
46–50	Terror	1 mimic	50%
51–55	Terror	1d2 rust monsters	20%
56–60	Terror	1d2 violet fungi	20%
61–62	Tough	1 bugbear and 1d6+3 hobgoblins	80% +3
63–65	Tough	1 ettercap	80% +3
66–67	Tough	1d3 gnolls and 1d3 hyenas [treat as wolf (animal)]	80% +3
68–70	Tough	1d3 lizardfolk and 1 giant lizard (animal)	80% +3
71–73	Tough	1d2 magmins	80% +3
74–76	Tough	1 ogre and 1d4+2 orcs	80% +3
77–78	Tough	1d3 orcs and 1d2 dire boars	80% +3
79–80	Tough	1d2 worgs and 1d4+2 goblins	80% +3
81–85	Undead	1d2 allips	50%
86–90	Undead	1 ghost [NPC level 1d3]	50%
91–95	Undead	1 vampire spawn	50%
96–100	Undead	1d2 wights	50%

TABLE 4–19: 5TH-LEVEL DUNGEON ENCOUNTERS

d%	Role	Number of Creatures and Kind	Treasure
01–02	Critter	1 ant, giant soldier and 1d4+2 giant worker ants (vermin)	20%
03–05	Critter	1d2 dire wolverines	20%
06–09	Critter	1 ochre jelly (ooze)	20%
10–11	Critter	1 snake, giant constrictor (animal)	20%
12	Critter	1d2 spiders, Huge monstrous (vermin)	20%
13–15	Critter	1 spider eater	20%
16–20	Dragon	1 dragon [see Table 4–35: Random Dragons]	80% +4
21–23	Fiend	1d3 doppelgangers	80% +3
24–25	Fiend	1 greenhag (hag)	80% +3
26–27	Fiend	1d3 mephits	80% +3
28–30	Fiend	1d3+1 wererats (lycanthrope)	80% +3
31–35	Friend	1d3+1 blink dogs	50% +2
36–40	NPC	1d3+1 2nd-level NPCs	Gear
41–43	Terror	1d3 cockatrices	20%
44–47	Terror	1 gibbering mouther	20%
48–50	Terror	1d3 gricks	20%
51–52	Terror	1 hydra, 1d3+4 heads	20%
53–55	Terror	1 nightmare	20%
56–58	Terror	1d3+1 shocker lizards	20%
59–60	Terror	1 violet fungus and 1d3+1 shriekers	20%
61–64	Tough	1d3+1 azers	80% +3
65–67	Tough	1d3+1 bugbears	80% +3
68–69	Tough	1 ettercap and 1d3 Medium-size monstrous spiders	80% +3
70–72	Tough	1d3+1 ogres	80% +3
73–75	Tough	1d3+1 salamanders, Small	80% +3
76–77	Tough	1d3+1 troglodytes and 1d2 giant lizards (animal) [immune to stench]	80% +3
78–80	Tough	1d3+1 worgs	80% +3
81–85	Undead	1 ghast and 1d3+1 ghouls	50%
86–90	Undead	1d3 mummies	50%
91–95	Undead	1d3+1 skeletons, Huge [giant]	50%
96–100	Undead	1 wraith	50%

TABLE 4–20: 6TH-LEVEL DUNGEON ENCOUNTERS

d%	Role	Number of Creatures and Kind	Treasure
01–02	Critter	1 digester	20%
03–04	Critter	1d3+1 dire apes	20%
05–06	Critter	1d3+1 dire wolves	20%
07	Critter	1d3 giant stag beetle (vermin)	20%
08–09	Critter	1d3+1 giant wasp (vermin)	20%
10–12	Critter	1d3 owlbears	20%
13–15	Critter	1 shambling mound	20%
16–20	Dragon	1 dragon [see Table 4–35: Random Dragons]	80% +4
21–22	Fiend	1 annis (hag)	80% +3
23–25	Fiend	1d3 harpies	80% +3
26	Fiend	1 quasit (demon) and 1d2 dretches (demon)	80% +3
27–28	Fiend	1d3+1 wereboars (lycanthropes)	80% +3
29–30	Fiend	1d3+1 werewolves (lycanthrope)	80% +3
31–35	Friend	1d2 werebears (lycanthrope)	80% +3
36–40	NPC	1d3+1 3rd-level NPCs	Gear
41–43	Terror	1d3+1 arrowhawks, Small	20%
44–46	Terror	1d2 basilisks	20%
47–50	Terror	1d3 displacer beasts	20%
51–53	Terror	1d3 gargoyles	50%
54–56	Terror	1d3+1 hell hounds	20%
57–59	Terror	1d3+1 howlers	20%
60–62	Terror	1d3 otyughs	20%
63–65	Terror	1 ravid and 1 animated object, Large	20%
66–67	Terror	1d3+1 xorns, Small	20%
			1d6 gems each

TABLE 4–21: 7TH-LEVEL DUNGEON ENCOUNTERS

d%	Role	Number of Creatures and Kind	Treasure
68–70	Terror	1d3+1 yeth hounds	20%
71–77	Tough	1 ettin and 1d6+3 orcs	80% +3
78–82	Tough	1d3 ogres and 1d3 boars (animal)	80% +3
83–90	Tough	1d2 weretigers (lycanthrope)	80% +3
91–100	Undead	1d3+1 zombies, Huge [giants]	50%

(Table 4–21 continued)

d%	Role	Number of Creatures and Kind	Treasure
01–04	Critter	1 black pudding (ooze)	20%
05	Critter	1d2 centipedes, Gargantuan monstrous (vermin)	20%
06–08	Critter	1 criosphinx (sphinx)	20%
09–10	Critter	1d3+1 dire boars	20%
11–14	Critter	1 remorhaz	20%
15	Critter	1d2 scorpions, Huge monstrous (vermin)	20%
16–20	Dragon	1 dragon [see Table 4–35: Random Dragons]	80% +4
21–22	Fiend	1d3+1 araneas	80% +3
23–24	Fiend	1d3+1 barghests, Medium-size	80% +3
25–26	Fiend	1d3 djinn	80% +3
27–28	Fiend	1 formian taskmaster and 1 minotaur [or other CR 4 creature]	80% +3
29–30	Fiend	1d3+1 jann (genie)	80% +3
31–35	Friend	1d3+1 hound archon (celestial)	80% +3
36–40	NPC	1d3+1 4th-level NPCs	Gear
41–45	Terror	1d3 cloakers	20%
46–48	Terror	1 cryohydra, 1d3+4 heads (hydra)	20%
49–52	Terror	1d4+2 formian warriors	80% +3
53–57	Terror	1 invisible stalker	20%
58–60	Terror	1 pyrohydra, 1d3+4 heads (hydra)	20%
61–65	Tough	1d3+1 bugbears and 1d3+1 wolves	80% +3
66–70	Tough	1 ettin and 1d2 brown bears (animal)	80% +3
71–75	Tough	1d3+1 minotaurs	50%
76–80	Tough	1 salamander, Medium-size and 1d3+1 salamanders, Small	80% +3
81–90	Undead	1 ghost [NPC level 1d3+3]	50%
91–100	Undead	1 vampire [NPC level 1d2+4]	Gear

TABLE 4–22: 8TH-LEVEL DUNGEON ENCOUNTERS

d%	Role	Number of Creatures and Kind	Treasure
01–03	Critter	1d6+5 ants, giant soldier (vermin)	20%
04–08	Critter	1d6+5 dire bats	20%
09–10	Critter	1d2 spiders, Gargantuan monstrous (vermin)	20%
11–20	Dragon	1 dragon [see Table 4–35: Random Dragons]	80% +4
21–22	Fiend	1 aboleth and 1d3+1 skums	80% +3
23–24	Fiend	1d3+1 barghests, Large	80% +3
25–26	Fiend	1d2 erinyes (devil)	80% +3
27–28	Fiend	1 medusa and 1d6+3 grimlocks	80% +3
29–30	Fiend	1 mind flayer	80% +3
31–33	Fiend	1 ogre mage	80% +3
34–35	Fiend	1 yuan-ti halfblood and 1d3 yuan-ti purebloods	80% +3
36–40	Friend	1 lammasu	80% +3
41–45	NPC	1d3+1 5th-level NPCs	Gear
46–47	Terror	1d3+1 achaierais	20%
48	Terror	1d3+1 arrowhawks, Medium-size	20%
49–50	Terror	1d3+1 girallons	20%
51–52	Terror	1d2 golems, flesh	20%
53–54	Terror	1 gray render	20%
55–56	Terror	1d3+1 hieracosphinxes (sphinx)	20%
57–59	Terror	1 hydra, 1d3+7 heads	20%
60	Terror	1 hydra, Lernaean, 1d3+4 heads	20%
61–62	Terror	1d3+1 phase spiders	20%
63–64	Terror	1d3+1 rasts	20%

d%	Role	Number of Creatures and Kind	Treasure
65–66	Terror	1d3+1 shadow mastiffs	20%
67–68	Terror	1d3+1 winter wolves	20%
69–70	Terror	1d3 xorns, Medium-size	20%
			2d6 gems each
71–74	Tough	1 drider and 1d3+1 Large monstrous spiders (vermin)	80% +2
75–78	Tough	1d3+1 ettins	80% +2
79–82	Tough	1d3+1 manticores	80% +2
83–86	Tough	1d3+1 salamanders, Medium-size	80% +2
87–90	Tough	1d3+1 trolls	80% +2
91–100	Undead	1d2 spectres	50%

Table 4–23: 9th-Level Dungeon Encounters

d%	Role	Number of Creatures and Kind	Treasure
01–05	Critter	1d3 bulettes	20%
06–10	Critter	1d4+2 dire lions	20%
11–20	Dragon	1 dragon [see Table 4–35: Random Dragons]	80% +3
21	Fiend	1 bebilith (demon)	80% +2
22	Fiend	1d3+1 lamias	80% +2
23–24	Fiend	1 mind flayer and charmed creatures (roll on Table 4–20: 6th-Level Dungeon Encounters)	80% +2
25–26	Fiend	1 night hag	80% +2
27–28	Fiend	1 ogre mage and 1d4+2 ogres	80% +2
29–30	Fiend	1 rakshasa	80% +2
31–32	Fiend	1 succubus	80% +2
33–34	Fiend	1d3+1 xill, barbaric [01–50] or civilized [51–100]	80% +2
35	Fiend	1 yuan-ti abomination and 1d3 yuan-ti purebloods [01–50] or halfbloods [51–100]	80% +2
36–40	Friend	1 androsphinx (sphinx)	80% +2
41–45	NPC	1d3+1 6th-level NPCs	Gear
46–47	Terror	1d2 behirs	20%
48–49	Terror	1d3+1 belkers	20%
50	Terror	1 cryohydra, 1d3+6 heads (hydra)	20%
51–52	Terror	1 delver	20%
53–54	Terror	1 dragon turtle	20%
55	Terror	1 pyrohydra, 1d3+6 heads (hydra)	20%
56–57	Terror	1d3+1 will-o'-wisps	20%
58–60	Terror	1d3+1 wyverns	20%
61–64	Tough	1 barbazu (devil) and 1d2 osyluths (devil)	80% +2
65–68	Tough	1 giant, hill and 1d3 dire wolves	80% +2
69–72	Tough	1d3+1 kytons (devil)	80% +2
73–76	Tough	1d3+1 osyluths (devil)	80% +2
77–80	Tough	1d3+1 trolls and 1d3 dire boars	80% +2
81–90	Undead	1d2 bodaks	50%
91–100	Undead	1 vampire [NPC level 1d2+6]	Gear

Table 4–24: 10th-Level Dungeon Encounters

d%	Role	Number of Creatures and Kind	Treasure
01–05	Critter	1d3+1 dire bears	20%
06–15	Dragon	1 dragon [see Table 4–35: Random Dragons]	80% +3
16–17	Fiend	1d3+1 aboleths	80% +2
18–19	Fiend	1d3+1 athachs	80% +2
20–21	Fiend	1 formian myrmarch	80% +2
22–24	Fiend	1d3+1 medusas	80% +2
25–26	Fiend	1d3+1 nagas, water	80% +2
27–28	Fiend	1 night hag + 1 nightmare	80% +2
29–30	Fiend	1 salamander, Large and 1d3 salamanders, Medium-size	80% +2
31–32	Fiend	1d3+1 yuan-ti abominations	80% +2
33–37	Friend	1d3+1 lillends	80% +2
38–47	NPC	1d3+1 7th-level NPCs	Gear
48–49	Terror	1d3+1 chaos beasts	20%
50–51	Terror	1d3+1 chimeras	20%
52–53	Terror	1d3+1 chuuls	20%
54	Terror	1 cryohydra, Lernaean, 1d4+4 heads (hydra)	20%
55–56	Terror	1d3+1 dragonnes	20%
57–58	Terror	1d3+1 hellcats (devil)	20%
59	Terror	1 hydra, 1d3+9 heads	20%
60	Terror	1 phasm	50%
61	Terror	1 pyrohydra, Lernaean, 1d4+4 heads (hydra)	20%
62–63	Terror	1 retriever (demon)	20%
64–65	Terror	1d3+1 slaadi, red	80% +2
66–67	Terror	1d3+1 umber hulks	20%
68–71	Tough	1d3+1 barbazu (devil)	80% +2
72–75	Tough	1d3+1 driders	80% +2
76–79	Tough	1 giant, frost and 1d3 winter wolves	80% +2
80–83	Tough	1 giant, stone and 1d2 dire bears	80% +2
84–87	Tough	1d3+1 giants, hill	80% +2
88–90	Tough	1 hamatula (devil) and 1d2 barbazu (devil)	80% +2
91–100	Undead	1 ghost [NPC level 1d3+6]	50%

Table 4–25: 11th-Level Dungeon Encounters

d%	Role	Number of Creatures and Kind	Treasure
01–05	Critter	1d3 dire tigers	20%
06–15	Dragon	1 dragon [see Table 4–35: Random Dragons]	80% +3 / 80% +1
16–18	Fiend	1 covey of hags (hag): 1 green hag, 1 annis, 1 sea hag, 1d4+2 ogres and 1d3 giants, hill	
19–21	Fiend	1d3+1 efreet	80% +1
22–24	Fiend	1 formian myrmarch and 1d6+3 formian warriors	80% +1
25–27	Fiend	1d3+1 gynosphinxes	80% +1
28–30	Fiend	1d3+1 nagas, dark	80% +1
31–35	Friend	1d3 avoral guardinal (celestial)	80% +1
36–45	NPC	1d3+1 8th-level NPCs	Gear
46–48	Terror	1d3+1 arrowhawks, Large	20%
49–51	Terror	1d3+1 destrachans	20%
52–54	Terror	1d2 golems, clay	20%
55–57	Terror	1d3+1 gorgons	20%
58–59	Terror	1 hydra, Lernaean, 1d3+7 heads	20%
60–62	Terror	1d3+1 slaadi, blue	80% +1
63–65	Terror	1d3+1 xorn, Large 4d6 gems	20%
66–70	Tough	1 giant, fire and 1d6+3 hell hounds	80% +1
71–75	Tough	1d3+1 giants, stone	80% +1
76–80	Tough	1d3+1 hamatulas (devil)	80% +1
81–90	Undead	1 devourer	50%
91–100	Undead	1d3+1 mohrgs	50%

Table 4–26: 12th-Level Dungeon Encounters

d%	Role	Number of Creatures and Kind	Treasure
01–04	Critter	1 purple worm	20%
05	Critter	1d2 scorpions, Colossal monstrous (vermin)	20%
06–15	Dragon	1 dragon [see Table 4–35: Random Dragons]	80% +3
16–20	Fiend	1d4+2 mind flayers [an inquisition]	50% +1
21–25	Fiend	1d3+1 nagas, spirit	50% +1
26–30	Fiend	1d3+1 slaadi, green	50% +1
31–35	Friend	1 giant, cloud [good] and 1d4+2 dire lions	50% +1
36–50	NPC	1d3+1 9th-level NPCs	Gear
51–55	Terror	1 cryohydra, 1d3+9 heads (hydra)	20%

56–60	Terror	1d2 golems, stone	20%
61–65	Terror	1 pyrohydra, 1d3+9 heads (hydra)	20%
66–70	Terror	1d3+1 yrthaks	20%
71–75	Tough	1 cornugon (devil) and 1d3 hamatulas (devil)	50% +1
76–80	Tough	1 giant, cloud [evil] and 1d4+2 dire lions	50% +1
81–85	Tough	1d3+1 giants, frost	50% +1
86–90	Tough	1d3+1 salamanders, Large	50% +1
91–100	Undead	1 vampire [NPC level 1d3+8]	Gear

TABLE 4–27: 13TH-LEVEL DUNGEON ENCOUNTERS

d%	Role	Number of Creatures and Kind	Treasure
01–15	Dragon	1 dragon [see Table 4–35: Random Dragons]	80% +3
16–20	Fiend	1 beholder	50% +1
21–30	Fiend	3 night hags and 3 nightmares	50% +1
31–35	Fiend	1d3+1 slaadi, gray	50% +1
36–40	Friend	1d3+1 couatls	50% +1
41–45	Friend	1d3+1 nagas, guardian	50% +1
46–60	NPC	1d3+1 10th-level NPCs	Gear
61–67	Terror	1d2 frost worms	20%
68–73	Terror	1 hydra, Lernaean, 1d3+9 heads	20%
74–80	Terror	1d3+1 ropers	20%
81–90	Tough	1d3+1 cornugons (devil)	50% +1
91–100	Undead	1 ghost [NPC level 1d3+9]	50%

TABLE 4–28: 14TH-LEVEL DUNGEON ENCOUNTERS

d%	Role	Number of Creatures and Kind	Treasure
01–15	Dragon	1 dragon [see Table 4–35: Random Dragons]	80% +2
16–25	Fiend	1 beholder and charmed monster(s) [roll on 11th-level table]	50% +1
26–35	Fiend	1d2 slaadi, death	50% +1
36–40	Friend	1d3+1 giant, cloud [good]	50% +1
41–55	NPC	1d3+1 11th-level NPCs	Gear
56–60	Terror	1 cryohydra, Lernaean, 1d4+8 heads (hydra)	20%
61–65	Terror	1d2 golems, iron	50%
66–70	Terror	1 pyrohydra, Lernaean, 1d4+8 heads (hydra)	20%
71–80	Tough	1d3+1 giant, cloud [evil]	50% +1
81–90	Tough	1 giant, storm and d4+2 griffons	50% +1
91–100	Undead	1 lich [cleric (01–10), sorcerer (11–40), wizard (41–100), NPC level 1d3+10]	Gear

TABLE 4–29: 15TH-LEVEL DUNGEON ENCOUNTERS

d%	Role	Number of Creatures and Kind	Treasure
01–20	Dragon	1 dragon [see Table 4–35: Random Dragons]	80% +1
21–30	Fiend	1d3 beholders	50%
31–40	Fiend	1d2 slaadi, death and 1d3+1 slaadi, green	50%
41–45	Friend	1d3 ghaeles (celestial)	80%
46–70	NPC	1d3+1 12th-level NPCs	Gear
71–80	Tough	1d2 hezrous (demon)	50%
81–90	Tough	1 gelugon (devil) and 1d3+1 cornugons (devil)	50%
91–100	Undead	1 vampire [NPC level 1d3+11]	Gear

TABLE 4–30: 16TH-LEVEL DUNGEON ENCOUNTERS

d%	Role	Number of Creatures and Kind	Treasure
01–20	Dragon	1 dragon [see Table 4–35: Random Dragons]	80% +1
21–30	Fiend	1 pit fiend (devil)	50% +1
31–35	Friend	1d3 astral devas (celestial)	50% +1
36–60	NPC	1d3+1 13th-level NPCs	Gear
61–70	Tough	1d3+1 gelugons (devil)	50%
71–80	Tough	1d3+1 giants, storm	50%
81–90	Tough	1d3+1 vrocks (demon)	50%
91–100	Undead	1 ghost [NPC level 1d3+12]	20%

TABLE 4–31: 17TH-LEVEL DUNGEON ENCOUNTERS

d%	Role	Number of Creatures and Kind	Treasure
01–20	Dragon	1 dragon [see Table 4–35: Random Dragons]	80% +1
21–30	Fiend	1 marilith (demon)	50%
31–35	Friend	1d3+1 trumpet archons (celestial)	50%
36–60	NPC	1d3+1 14th-level NPCs	Gear
61–70	Tough	1d3 glabrezu (demon)	50%
71–80	Tough	1d3+1 hezrous (demon)	50%
81–90	Undead	1 lich [cleric (01–10), sorcerer (11–40), wizard (41–100), NPC level 1d3+13]	Gear
91–100	Undead	1d3+1 nightwings (nightshade)	20%

TABLE 4–32: 18TH-LEVEL DUNGEON ENCOUNTERS

d%	Role	Number of Creatures and Kind	Treasure
01–20	Dragon	1 dragon [see Table 4–35: Random Dragons]	80% +1
21–30	Fiend	1d3 balors (demon)	50%
31–40	Fiend	1 pit fiend (devil) and 1d3+1 gelugons (devil)	50%
41–45	Friend	1d3 planetars (celestial)	50%
46–70	NPC	1d3+1 15th-level NPCs	Gear
71–80	Tough	1d3+1 glabrezu (demon)	50%
81–90	Undead	1 vampire [NPC level 1d3+14]	Gear
91–100	Undead	1d3+1 nightwalkers (nightshade)	20%

TABLE 4–33: 19TH-LEVEL DUNGEON ENCOUNTERS

d%	Role	Number of Creatures and Kind	Treasure
01–20	Dragon	1 dragon [see Table 4–35: Random Dragons]	80% +1
21–30	Fiend	1 marilith (demon) and 1d3 glabrezu (demon)	50% +1
31–40	Fiend	1d3+1 pit fiends (devil)	50% +1
41–45	Friend	1 solar (celestial)	50% +1
46–70	NPC	1d3+1 16th-level NPCs	Gear
71–80	Tough	1d3+1 nalfeshnees (demon)	50% +1
81–90	Undead	1 ghost [NPC level 1d3+15]	20%
91–100	Undead	1d3 nightcrawlers (nightshade)	20%

TABLE 4–34: 20TH-LEVEL DUNGEON ENCOUNTERS

d%	Role	Number of Creatures and Kind	Treasure
01–20	Dragon	1 dragon [see Table 4–35: Random Dragons]	80% +1
21–30	Fiend	1d3 balors (demon)	50%
31–40	Fiend	1d3+1 mariliths (demon)	50%
41–45	Friend	1 solar (celestial) and 1d2 planetars (celestial)	50%
46–55	NPC	1d3+1 17th-level NPCs	Gear
56–60	NPC	1d3 18th-level NPCs	Gear
61–65	NPC	1d2 19th-level NPCs	Gear
66–70	NPC	1 20th-level NPC	Gear
71–80	Tough	1d3+1 nalfeshnees (demons) and 1d3+1 hezrous (demon)	20%
81–85	Undead	1 ghost [NPC level 1d2+18]	20%
86–90	Undead	1 lich [cleric (01–10), sorcerer (11–40), wizard (41–100), NPC level 1d4+16]	Gear
91–95	Undead	1d3 nightcrawlers (nightshade)	20%
96–100	Undead	1 vampire [NPC level 1d3+17]	Gear

TABLE 4–35: RANDOM DRAGONS

Enc.	d% 01–16	d% 17–32	d% 33–48	d% 49–64	d% 65–80	d% 81–84	d% 85–88	d% 89–91	d% 92–96	d% 97–100
Table*	White	Black	Green	Blue	Red	Brass	Copper	Bronze	Silver	Gold
1st	*Wyrmling*	Wyrmling	Wyrmling	Wyrmling	Wyrmling	Wyrmling	Wyrmling	Wyrmling	Wyrmling	Wyrmling
2nd	Very young	*Wyrmling*	*Wyrmling*	Wyrmling	Wyrmling	Wyrmling	*Wyrmling*	Wyrmling	Wyrmling	Wyrmling
3rd	Young	*Very young*	Very young	Very young	Wyrmling	Very young	Very young	Very young	*Wyrmling*	Wyrmling
4th	Juvenile	*Young*	Young	Young	Very young	Young	*Very young*	*Very young*	*Very young*	Wyrmling
5th	*Juvenile*	Juvenile	*Young*	*Young*	Young	Young	Young	Young	Young	Very young
6th	Yng. adult	*Juvenile*	Juvenile	Juvenile	*Young*	Juvenile	*Young*	*Young*	Young	Very young
7th	*Yng. adult*	Yng. adult	*Juvenile*	*Juvenile*	Juvenile	*Juvenile*	Juvenile	Juvenile	Juvenile	Young
8th	Adult	*Yng. adult*	Yng. adult	Yng. adult	Juvenile	Yng. adult	*Juvenile*	*Juvenile*	Juvenile	*Young*
9th	*Adult*	Adult	Yng. adult	Yng. adult	*Juvenile*	*Yng. adult*	Yng. adult	Yng. adult	*Juvenile*	Juvenile
10th	Mat. adult	*Adult*	*Yng. adult*	*Yng. adult*	Yng. adult	Adult	*Yng. adult*	Yng. adult	Yng. adult	*Juvenile*
11th	*Mat. adult*	Mat. adult	Adult	Adult	*Yng. adult*	*Adult*	Adult	*Yng. adult*	*Yng. adult*	Yng. adult
12th	Old	*Mat. adult*	*Adult*	Adult	*Yng. adult*	Mat. adult	Adult	Adult	*Yng. adult*	Yng. adult
13th	Old	*Mat. adult*	Mat. adult	*Adult*	Adult	Mat. adult	*Adult*	Adult	Adult	*Yng. adult*
14th	*Old*	Old	Mat. adult	Mat. adult	*Adult*	*Mat. adult*	Mat. adult	*Adult*	*Adult*	Adult
15th	Very old	*Old*	*Mat. adult*	*Mat. adult*	Mat. adult	Old	*Mat. adult*	Mat. adult	Mat. adult	*Adult*
16th	*Very old*	Very old	Old	Old	Mat. adult	*Old*	Old	*Mat. adult*	*Mat. adult*	Mat. adult
17th	Ancient	*Very old*	Old	Old	*Mat. adult*	Very old	Old	Old	*Mat. adult*	Mat. adult
18th	Wyrm	Ancient	*Very old*	Very old	Old	*Very old*	Old	Old	Old	Mat. adult
19th	Great wyrm	Wyrm	Ancient	Ancient	*Old*	Ancient	Very old	Very old	Old	Old
20th	*Great wyrm*	Great wyrm	Ancient+	Ancient+	Very old+	Wyrm+	Ancient+	Ancient+	Very old+	Old+

The dragons are arranged from least powerful chromatic (white) to most powerful chromatic (red), followed by least powerful metallic (brass) to most powerful metallic (gold). The terms are age categories (see the *Monster Manual*). *Italicized* terms indicate where the dragon's CR matches the Encounter Table's level. If the age category listed is not in *italic*, then the dragon's CR is higher than the Encounter Table's level. A plus sign (+) means if you use a dragon of older than this age of the respective type, it is at least a 20th-level encounter.

*Enc. Table: Dungeon Encounters table (4–15 to 4–34).

A SAMPLE DUNGEON

Here are a few room descriptions to match the map on page 127. The dungeon's not fully described, because these sample descriptions are here primarily to show what your own adventure notes might look like. These may be more (or less) detailed than the notes you use, but they give you an idea of what you need recorded in order to have a ready-to-play adventure planned out. The notes in *italics* explain why certain things are the way they are. They include reminders for what you will want to do in your own notes.

Shaded Text: The following sample entries include shaded text meant to be paraphrased or read aloud to your players. Shaded text is found in most published D&D adventures. Shaded text represents those features that would be apparent to the PCs upon first entering that area (and is thus very helpful to the mapper). It does not include hidden features such as traps, nor monsters and items out of the PCs' immediate line of sight.

You don't have to literally make shaded text for your own notes, but be sure to highlight material in your notes that you want to use to quickly describe the area in an interesting way. Be sure not to include information that could not be known to the characters, and avoid describing PC actions or emotions (such as "As you cower in fear . . ."). Be fair about providing the players with clues, such as the webs in the shaded text for area 1 below, but don't draw attention to them. The best way to write shaded text or note what the characters entering a location would sense is to imagine what you could see, hear, smell, or feel if you were entering that area, then set down the pertinent information as succinctly as possible.

MONASTERY CELLARS AND SECRET CRYPTS

The abandoned monastery on the surface is a burned-out ruin, destroyed when the place was attacked years ago by gnolls. The interesting part lies belowground, in the cellars and crypts underneath the ruins. A successful bardic knowledge or Gather Information check (DC 10 for both) lets the PCs know rumors about the legendary jewel lost somewhere within.

1. Entry Chamber

This damp chamber has an arched, vaulted ceiling 20 feet high in the center. The walls are masonry (cut stone blocks), the floor rough flagstones. Thick webs hide the ceiling.

A litter of husks, skin, bones, spider castings, and filth lies in a disgusting pile in the middle of the room (at the point marked A on the map). A Spot check (DC 22) is required to notice the **Creatures** (a spider and its young; see below) hiding in the webs above. The refuse pile in the middle of the room contains the **Treasure**.

Special areas are called out in the notes and on the map by giving them designations such as "A" and "B," making it easier to remember that they're there. The Spot DC for the lurking spider is intentionally difficult, but not out of the reach of the intended PCs (in this case, all 1st-level characters). The gem inside the skull is odd and intended to get PCs wondering about what's going on. (It's actually a relatively meaningless detail, other than for the value of the gem.)

Ten moldy sacks of flour and grain are stacked in the southwest corner (marked B on the map). The cloth tears easily, revealing the ruined contents. One of the sacks contains the **Trap**.

The solid oak door to the west (marked C on the map) is stuck (DC 16 to open). Anyone listening at it who makes a successful Listen check (DC 12) hears a moaning sound, rising and then fading. This is merely a strong breeze that blows in area 2. As soon as the door opens, the breeze rushes out the new opening in a gust, extinguishing torches and possibly (50% chance) blowing out lanterns as well. Torches can't be relit in the corridor while the door is open.

The low DC for the Listen check is intentional—you want the PCs to hear the moaning and get spooked, thinking it's a ghost or something similarly horrible. Also, always remember to make a note of the DC to open a stuck or locked door.

A Sample Dungeon

Key

- ▨ Stairs
- ▣ Door
- ☒ Trap Door
- ▨ Secret Door
- Ⓢ Secret Trap Door
- ▨ Stream

Scale: One Square Equals 10 Feet

Some 20 feet down the east passage, on the right side, a secret door awaits discovery. Locating it requires a successful Search check (DC 18). If detected, the secret door pivots open with a simple push, the scraping when it does revealing years of disuse.

It's necessary to always note the DC needed to find a secret door. It's also good to note how it's opened.

Creatures: A Small monstrous spider and nine Tiny young hide in the upper part of the webs in the center of the room. If the characters fail to spot the Small spider, it drops down on any character in the center of the room (a partial action). A successful touch attack roll indicates that the spider lands on a character. The Tiny spiders remain in the web and eat small meals trapped by the web. They only move down from the web when all is still to eat a meal pacified by the larger spider.

If the PCs burn the webs, the nine young spiders are killed and the adult spider (if still in the web) takes 1d6 points of damage. The webs burn for 8 rounds.

- **Small Monstrous Spider** (1): hp 7.
- **Tiny Monstrous Spiders** (9): hp 2 each.
- **Treasure:** Scattered amid the pile in the middle of the room are 19 sp and a goblin skull with a 50 gp garnet inside. Characters only notice the gem with a successful Search check (DC 15).
- **Trap:** One of the sacks in the southwest corner has yellow mold inside it. If disturbed, it bursts—all within 10 feet must make a Fortitude save (DC 15) or take 1d6 points of temporary Constitution damage. One minute later, everyone exposed to the initial burst must save again (same DC) or take 2d6 points of temporary Constitution damage, whether or not they took damage in the initial exposure.

It's not always necessary to write out complete rules, as has been done here for yellow mold. You can add this level of description to your notes if you need it, or you can simply jot down the page number and book where it's found.

2. Water Room

A fast-flowing stream 3 to 5 feet deep enters this rough-hewn chamber at the north from a passage that it fills entirely, and exits to the south in the same manner. Toward the south, it forms a pool some 4 feet deep at its edge and about 7 feet deep at the center. The pool is home to a group of blind, white fish, and you can see a few blind, white crayfish crawling among the rocks on the bottom.

A good example of what not to include in shaded text is the fact that the water is icy cold—there's no way the characters could know this just by looking at the water from the doorway. Characters who simply turn around and leave after a glance inside may never discover the sunken skeleton, much less the helpful items beside it.

The monks who once lived here worked this natural cavern in order to enlarge it. A strong, damp breeze makes it impossible to keep torches lit here. Eight rotting barrels remain (at the location marked A) from when the room was used to gather water for the monastery. A few buckets also lie scattered about.

In a ruin, it's always handy to know what a room or area was formerly used for, even if it now serves a different purpose (or no purpose at all). Your descriptions can often convey that former purpose, reminding the players that this place has its own history—it's not just a backdrop for adventures.

Lying at the bottom of the pool (at the point marked B) is the limed-over skeleton of the abbot. Without a successful Spot check (DC 15), this appears to be just an unusual mineral formation. In its bony fingers, the skeleton still holds a special key that allows

the secret door in area 28 to open to the treasury (area 29) rather than the steps leading down into the caverns (area 30). If the remains are disturbed, the act dislodges a tube next to the skeleton. The stream's current carries away the tube unless a character dives into the icy water immediately to get it. This requires a Swim check (DC 13) and an attack roll against the tube's AC of 14 (modified for size and, in this special case, speed). If the players do not act quickly, the tube is swept away and lost in a single round. The tube contains the **Treasure**.

The rules for hitting small objects are presented in Chapter 8: Combat in the Player's Handbook (page 135), but the DM here decided to modify them slightly for a specific situation. Getting the map will be hard for characters unless they act fast and roll well. However, the reward is great, because they are shown a secret passage that they probably would otherwise miss.

- **Treasure:** Inside this not-quite-watertight ivory tube is a vellum map, smeared due to water seepage. The map shows the underground levels of the monastery. Areas 1, 2, and the passage to area 3 still show clearly. Area 3 itself has been reduced to a smudge, but just beyond it can be made out most of the secret passage to the south. Several tiny sarcophagi have been carefully drawn around the southernmost terminus of the passage. The rest of the map is illegible.

3. Empty Ceremonial Chamber

This large, square room appears to be a dead end. Its domed ceiling arches up to 25 feet high in the center.

The monks brought the faithful here after death, consecrated each corpse, and then carried it to its final resting place in area 24. A wooden platform placed against the south wall served as both a dais upon which to hold the ceremony and as a means to reach the secret door leading into the crypts to the south. The platform rose 9 feet off the ground, with the bottom of the secret door being 1 foot above that. Some knobs just above the level of the vanished platform look like mere bumps in the wall, but one of them when pushed in causes a 10-foot-by-10-foot portion of the wall to swing inward with a grinding noise.

Now only four socket holes in the south wall bear testimony that the platform was ever here. Two are parallel to each other, 10 feet apart and 3 feet from the floor. The other two are 3 feet higher up and directly above the first two. These square holes are 6 inches wide and about 6 inches deep. One still has a few wooden splinters in it. Behind the secret door is a 10-foot-wide passage inhabited by **Creatures** (ghouls).

Creatures: Unknown to the PCs, four ghouls from area 25 lurk at the south end of the secret passage. If they make a successful Listen check (DC 25, but ghouls have a +7 bonus on Listen checks, so they succeed on a roll of 18, 19, or 20), the ghouls come up the secret passage and wait behind the secret door in ambush.

- **Ghouls** (4): hp 10, 13, 13, 18.

Monster Statistics

Here are the statistics blocks (a form of condensed creature statistics) for the creatures briefly mentioned above. These sample statistics blocks present all the information needed to run an encounter with the spider and one with the ghouls, should they detect the PCs (or vice versa). For your own notes, you can write out this information in as much or as little detail as you like. It's best to include all the information you may need at first, then gradually make the entries more abbreviated (for example: ghouls, hp 13 [×4], Listen +7, paralysis, undead immunities) as you become familiar with various creatures' abilities through repeated encounters. Also be sure to note any ways in which these ghouls may differ from others of their kind (dressed in tattered vestments, constantly finger prayer beads when not in combat, refer to themselves in the third person, and so on).

Small Monstrous Spider (1): CR 1/2; Small vermin; HD 1d8; hp 7; Init +3 (Dex); Spd 30 ft., climb 20 ft.; AC 14; Atk +4 melee (1d2 and poison, bite); SA Poison, web; SQ Vermin, 60-ft. darkvision; AL N; SV Fort +2, Ref +3, Will +0; Str 7, Dex 17, Con 10, Int —, Wis 10, Cha 2, 3 1/2 ft. diameter.

Skills and Feats: Climb +10, Hide +14*, Spot +7*; Weapon Finesse (bite).

Special Attack: Poison (Ex): Bite, Fortitude save (DC 11); initial and secondary damage of 1d3 points of temporary Strength damage. Web (Ex): This spider produces silk. Spiders can wait in their webs, then lower themselves silently on silk strands and leap onto prey passing beneath. A single strand is strong enough to support the spider and one creature of the same size. *Monstrous spiders gain a +8 competence bonus to Hide and Move Silently checks when using their webs.

Web-spinning spiders can cast a web (8/day). This is similar to an attack with a net but maximum range of 50 feet, range increment 10 feet, and effective against targets up to one size smaller than the spider. The web anchors the target in place, allowing no movement. An entangled creature can escape with a successful Escape Artist check (DC 18) or burst it with a Strength check (DC 24). Both are standard actions.

Web-spinning spiders often create sheets of sticky webbing. Approaching creatures must succeed at a Spot check (DC 20) to notice a web; otherwise, they stumble into it and become trapped as though by a successful web attack. Attempts to escape or burst the webbing gain a +5 bonus if the trapped creature has something to walk on or grab while pulling free. Each 5-foot section has 4 hit points, and sheet webs have damage reduction 5/fire.

A monstrous spider can move across its own sheet web at its climb speed and can determine the exact location of any creature touching the web.

Special Qualities: Vermin: No Intelligence score, and thus immune to all mind-influencing effects (charms, compulsions, patterns, phantasms, and morale effects).

Tiny Monstrous Spiders (9): CR 1/4; Medium-size vermin; HD 1/2 d8; hp 2 each; Init +3 (Dex); Spd 20 ft., climb 10 ft.; AC 15; Atk +5 melee (bite poison); Face/Reach 2 1/2 ft. by 2 1/2 ft./0 ft.; SA Poison, web; SQ Vermin, 60-ft. darkvision; AL N; SV Fort +2, Ref +3, Will +0; Str 3, Dex 17, Con 10, Int —, Wis 10, Cha 2, 1 ft. diameter.

Skills and Feats: Climb +8, Hide +18*, Spot +7*; Weapon Finesse (bite).

Special Attack: Poison: Bite, Fortitude save (DC 11); initial and secondary damage of 1d2 points of temporary Strength damage.

Web (Ex): This spider produces silk. Spiders can wait in their webs, then lower themselves silently on silk strands and leap onto prey passing beneath. A single strand is strong enough to support the spider and one creature of the same size. *Monstrous spiders gain a +8 competence bonus to Hide and Move Silently checks when using their webs.

The webs near here were all produced by the mother spider (see the Small monstrous spider entry). These spiders do not fling webs yet because they are not yet mature.

These monstrous spiders can move across their mother's sheet web at their climb speed and can determine the exact location of any creature touching the web.

Special Qualities: Vermin: No Intelligence score, and thus immune to all mind-influencing effects (charms, compulsions, patterns, phantasms, and morale effects).

STATISTICS BLOCKS

In the adventures you run, you probably won't need to note monster statistics in a format as detailed as this. After all, you can refer to the *Monster Manual*. However, most published adventures, whether standalone products or adventures in DUNGEON® magazine, use statistics blocks for monsters and for NPCs. When a commoner or other unimportant NPC is noted who is not in any way vital, a particularly short statistical notation is often used. The shortened statistics block provides gender, template, class, and any relevant skills or feats bearing on the encounter. While the following format will evolve to meet the needs of the D&D game, here is information on how to read a standard nonclassed creature statistics block and an NPC (or classed creature) statistics block. The number signs (#) represent numerical values that would be filled in appropriately. If no information needs to go under a certain heading, that heading is omitted. (For instance, if a creature has no spell resistance, that heading is omitted. If an NPC is not a spellcaster, the entire spells section is omitted.)

Nonclassed Creature's Name: CR #; Size and type (subtype); HD #d#; hp #; Init # (Init modifiers); Spd #ft.; AC #; Atk +# melee (damage, attack type), +# ranged (damage, attack type); Face/Reach if other than 5 ft. by 5 ft./5 ft.; SA Short descriptions of special attacks (if necessary, explained below under Special Attacks); SQ Short descriptions of special qualities (if necessary, explained below under Special Qualities); SR spell resistance; AL alignment abbreviation; SV Fort +#, Ref +#, Will +#; Str #, Dex #, Con #, Int #, Wis #, Cha #. Height or length # ft., weight # lb.

Skills and Feats: List skills and modifiers; list feats.
Special Abilities: Type: Type explained. Type: Type explained.
Special Qualities: Type: Type explained. Type: Type explained.
Possessions: List possessions worn or carried.

NPC's Name: Gender and kind or class; CR #; Size and type (subtype); HD #d#; hp #; Init # (Init modifiers); Spd #ft.; AC #; Atk =# melee (damage, attack type), +# ranged (damage, attack type); Face/Reach if other than 5 ft. by 5 ft./5 ft.; SA Short descriptions of special attacks (if necessary, explained below under Special Attacks); SQ Short descriptions of special qualities (if necessary, explained below under Special Qualities); SR spell resistance; AL alignment abbreviation; SV Fort +#, Ref +#, Will +#; Str #, Dex #, Con #, Int #, Wis #, Cha #. Height or length # ft., weight # lb.

Skills and Feats: List skills and modifiers; list feats.
Special Attacks: Type: Type explained. Type: Type explained.
Special Qualities: Type: Type explained. Type: Type explained.
Possessions: List possessions carried on person.
Spells Prepared (#/#/#): 0—0-level spell, 0-level spell (3); 1st—1st-level spell, 1st-level spell (2); 2nd—2nd-level spell. [For spellcasters who prepare spells. Use "(3)," "(2)," etc. to indicate multiples of same spell prepared.]

OR

Spells Known (cast #/#/#): 0—0-level spell, 0-level spell; 1st—1st-level spell, 1st-level spell. [For spellcasters who do not prepare spells or have spellbooks.]

(Optional:)

Spellbook (#/#/#/#): 0—0-level spell, 0-level spell, 0-level spell, 0-level spell, 0-level spell; 1st—first, first, first, first; 2nd—second, second, second; 3rd—third, third, third.

🗡 **Ghouls (4):** CR 1; Medium-size undead; HD 2d12; hp 10, 13, 13, 18; Init +2 (Dex); Spd 30 ft.; AC 14; Atk +3/+0/+0 melee (1d6+1 and paralysis, bite; 1d3 and paralysis [×2], claws); SA Paralysis; SQ Undead, 60-ft. darkvision; AL CE; SV Fort +0, Ref +2, Will +5; Str 13, Dex 15, Con —, Int 13, Wis 14, Cha 16. Height 6ft. tall.

Skills and Feats: Climb +6, Escape Artist +7, Hide +7, Intuit Direction +3, Jump +6, Listen +7, Move Silently +7, Search +6, Spot +7; Multiattack (see *Monster Manual* for details), Weapon Finesse (bite).

Special Attack: Paralysis: Those hit by a ghoul's claws or bite must succeed at a Fortitude save (DC 14) or be paralyzed for 1d6+2 minutes. (Elves are immune to this paralysis.)

Special Qualities: Undead: Immune to poison, sleep, paralysis, stunning, disease, death effects, and necromantic effects. Ignore mind-influencing effects (charms, compulsions, patterns, phantasms, and morale effects); not subject to critical hits, subdual damage, ability damage, ability drain, or energy drain. No Constitution score, and thus immune to anything requiring a Fortitude save (unless it affects objects). Cannot die from massive damage, but immediately destroyed if reduced to 0 hit points or less.

EXAMPLE OF PLAY

Using the previously detailed sample dungeon rooms, a DM guides four players through their first adventure. The players are playing Tordek (a dwarf fighter), Mialee (an elven wizard), Jozan (a human cleric), and Lidda (a halfling rogue). These four adventurers seek the ruins of the abandoned monastery, drawn by rumors telling of a fabulous fire opal, supposedly hidden there by the abbot when the place was attacked.

After passing through the lifeless aboveground ruins of the monastery, the adventurers find a rubble-strewn staircase leading down.

PC (Tordek): Let's give these upper ruins one more quick examination.

DM: *[Making some rolls in secret, but knowing there's nothing to find in the burned-out shell of the monastery.]* You don't find anything. What are you going to do now?

PC (Jozan): Let's go down!

PC (Lidda): We'll light a torch first.

DM: Fine, but I'll need the marching order that you'll be in.

At this point, the players arrange their miniature figures, each representing one character, in the order in which they will march down the stairs (and walk down corridors, and enter rooms). Tordek goes first, followed by Jozan (with the torch), then Mialee. Lidda brings up the rear, her player noting that she will be watching behind them occasionally.

If the players didn't have miniatures, writing down the marching order on a piece of paper would suffice.

PC (Tordek): Fortunately, the torchlight won't spoil my darkvision—that'll help us navigate in the dark down there.

PC (Jozan): Okay, we go down the stairs.

DM: You descend southward, possibly 30 feet laterally, and at the end of the stairway you see an open space.

PC (Tordek): I enter and look around.

PC (Jozan): I come in behind with the torch.

DM: You are in a chamber about 30 feet across to the south and 30 feet wide east and west. There are 10-foot-wide passages to the left and right as well as straight ahead, each in the center of its respective wall. Looking back, you see the stairway entered the chamber in the center of the north wall.

PC (Lidda): What else do we see?

DM: The floor is rough and damp. The ceiling is supported by arches that probably rise to meet in the center, about 20 feet above you—it's hard to tell because of all the webs. There are some moldering old sacks in the southwest corner and some rubbish jumbled in the center of the floor—dirt, old leather, scraps of cloth, and some sticks or maybe bones.

After a short discussion and the formation of a plan, each player announces an action for his or her character. Tordek looks down the south passage, Mialee investigates the rubbish in the middle, Jozan looks at the old sacks, and Lidda looks down the west passage. The players position their figures on a floorplan the DM has sketched out on paper.

Since no one paid the webs any attention, the DM doesn't worry about Spot checks to see the spider.

DM: Okay. As two of you are looking down the passages and Jozan starts looking at the sacks . . . [*The DM rolls a touch attack for the monstrous spider in the webs. He knows a 14 indicates success because he wrote down everyone's ACs ahead of time and knows Mialee's AC is 13.*] . . . Mialee, you feel something land on your shoulder—it feels hairy and moves toward your neck!

PC (Mialee): Yikes! What is it?

PC (Tordek): If I hear her call out, I'll turn around. What do I see?

DM: Wait, just a minute. First, Mialee, roll for initiative.

PC (Mialee): [*Rolls*] I got a 19!

DM: [*Rolls initiative for the spider, and gets a 14.*] Everyone else should roll for initiative as well. Tordek, you heard Mialee gasp, and you turn to see a large, hairy spider on her neck.

Jozan rolls a 10, Lidda an 8, and Tordek a 4.

DM: Mialee, you go first. What do you do?

PC (Mialee): I grab it from my shoulder and throw it to the ground, where I can stomp on it with my boot.

DM: Okay, but your unarmed attack provokes an attack of opportunity for the spider, so it bites as you grab at it. [*He rolls an attack roll for the spider, and gets a 16.*] Yug! Mialee, you feel a sharp prick on your neck. Make a Fortitude saving throw.

The group all gasp in fear. Mialee rolls a die and would add her Fortitude bonus, except that she has none.

PC (Mialee): Fortitude, my worst save! Let's see—15 plus 0 is, well, 15. Is that good enough?

DM: You feel okay. But the bite still delivers 1 hit point of damage.

PC (Mialee): Ouch. Okay, then I roll a 14 to grab it and throw it to the ground. Do I succeed?

DM: Yes. The spider lands on the ground but looks like it's going to scuttle away. Perhaps back up the wall to the webs above.

PC (Jozan): My turn? I run up to it and smash it with my mace! I roll a natural 20! With my bonus, that's 22 in all.

DM: Good roll! You can move that far and attack, so roll a confirmation roll to see if that's a critical hit.

PC (Jozan): [*Excitedly rolling again*] Is a 15 good enough?

DM: Yep. Roll damage—twice. Add them together.

PC (Jozan): [*Rolling*] Sweet! 12 points altogether once I add my Strength bonus—which also doubled with the crit!

DM: That mighty blow smashes the creature to bits.

PC (Mialee): Cool. Well, now that all the excitement's over, I'm going to search through this refuse on the floor like I said I would.

DM: Okay. First, make another Fort save to see if there are any lingering effects from that spider bite.

PC (Mialee):   Uh-oh, that doesn't sound good . . . [rolls] . . . a 17!

DM: No problems, then. You feel fine. Looking at the pile of debris, you'd guess it's probably refuse from the spider—leftovers of its victims and its own castings. Amid bits of bone and tatters of clothing, you find 19 silver pieces. And make a Search roll.

Mialee rolls a 9 and adds her +6 bonus for a result of 15—just enough to notice the hidden gem!

DM: You also see something sparkle inside a small skull. Looking closer, you see it's a gem—a garnet.

PC (Mialee):   Great. I get it out and put it in my pouch. We can try to appraise it later. You know, I'm getting a little nervous about that web.

PC (Lidda):   Good point. Jozan, why not light the webs on fire with your torch?

PC (Jozan):   Okay, I do. What happens? [*Looks at the DM.*]

DM: The webs burn quickly. As they do, tiny burning husks of smaller spiders fall from the ceiling, but nothing the size of the creature that attacked.

PC (Tordek):   [*On lookout*] What do we see down the passages?

DM: The south tunnel runs straight as far as you can see. The west corridor ends in a door at about 20 feet.

PC (Tordek):   Okay, I'll also glance down the east passage.

DM: You see the east corridor goes straight for about 20 feet and then turns a corner to head north.

PC (Lidda):   Let's check out that door. [*Everyone agrees.*]

DM: Okay. You walk down the west passage. The door is a great, heavy thing with a huge ring of corroded bronze in the center.

PC (Tordek):   Mialee, your Listen skill is better than mine. Why don't you listen at this door?

PC (Mialee):   Okay. I move forward to do so. [*Rolls*] I roll a 13. Do I hear anything?

DM: You hear a faint moaning sound—you can't really tell what it is—that rises and then fades away. The door is hinged on the left and looks like it pulls inward toward you.

PC (Mialee):   I hear moaning on the other side. Let's get ready for action! And, by the way, I move to my position toward the back. . . .

PC (Tordek):   [*Laughs*] All right, I'll open the door while the elf scrambles to the back of the line.

DM: Make a Strength check.

PC (Tordek):   [*Rolls*] I only got a 10. If that's not good enough, can I try again?

DM: That's not good enough, but if you're willing to spend more time on it, you can keep trying.

PC (Tordek):   [*To the other players*] Look, we really want to get through this door, right? [*They agree, so the player turns back to the DM.*] I'm willing to spend enough time to take 20 on my roll. With my Strength bonus, that gives me a 22.

DM: Ah, easily good enough. After a couple of minutes, Tordek forces open the stuck door. Immediately a blast of cold, damp air gusts into the passage where you are, blowing out Jozan's torch!

PC (Tordek):   Do I see anything with my darkvision?

DM: Beyond the door is a chamber with rough walls—not blocks of stone like the room behind you. It's 25 feet wide and extends about 40 feet to the south. A small stream spills through the room into a pool, carrying with it a cold, damp breeze. You don't see anything moving around, but there are some old barrels and buckets about.

PC (Jozan):   I cast *light* on a rock, since we'll never get a torch lit in this wind.

DM: Okay, now everyone can see.

PC (Tordek):   I look at the ceiling and the floor for any more nasty surprises.

PC (Mialee):   I'll look in the barrels and buckets.

PC (Lidda):   Jozan, bring your light over and we'll check out the pool.

DM: Tordek and Mialee, make Search checks. Lidda and Jozan, give me Spot checks, since you can't "search" the pool without getting into it, but you can look into the water to spot anything that might be there. [*The players comply and tell the DM their results, although the DM knows that there's nothing for Tordek or Mialee to find.*] There's nothing alarming about the ceiling and floor, and the buckets are empty. The pool has some small white fish that look harmless—they also don't react at all to your light. The pool itself looks to be about 4 to 6 feet deep with a rough and rocky bottom. Jozan, with your roll of 17 you see that what had at first looked to be a rock formation near the center of the pool looks somewhat like a skeleton, but still . . .

PC (Jozan):   Cool! Mialee, will you cast your own *light* spell so I can toss this one down into the pool to get a better look at this skeleton? It might be something interesting.

PC (Mialee):   Okay, I do.

PC (Jozan):   I toss the rock that I've cast *light* upon into the water, toward the center.

DM: Your stone falls to the bottom of the pool, illuminating the center. The formation is clearly a limed-over skeleton—it must have been there for many years. Your stone impacts with it, stirring up dirt and muck, and dislodges what appears to be a cylinder about a foot long. The current quickly begins to carry it away. . . .

PC (Lidda):   Oh, no! I leap into the water and get it—at least I'll be able to see down there. Better, in fact, because of my low-light vision.

DM: Hmm. Make a Swim check.

PC (Lidda):   Uh-oh. I don't have that skill. Untrained, I use my Strength bonus, right? Uhh . . . don't have one of those either. [*Rolls*] Hey! I still got a 17!

DM: You guys are rolling great tonight. Even with a penalty for the weight of the gear you're carrying, you succeed. Lidda, you manage to jump in and swim up to the tube just as the current is going to sweep it out of the room and down the underground stream. You have no idea if there'd be air to breathe if you swam down the dark, narrow passage, which seems to be completely filled with water.

PC (Lidda):   Okay, then I try to grab the tube now.

DM: Make an attack roll.

Lidda rolls high enough to grab the tube. The DM relays this information, and Lidda swims up to the surface and climbs out of the pool with the help of the others—all of whom announce that their characters crowd around her to see what she's found. The DM describes the sealed tube.

PC (Lidda):   I dry it off a little, and then open it!

DM: Inside is a roll of vellum.

PC (Tordek):   Let's get out of this room and back into that entry chamber where we can light torches again. It's probably not going to be easy to read a scroll or whatever with this air current. [*The other PCs agree, and they return to the first room, closing the door behind them.*]

DM: The tube must have allowed a bit of water to seep in slowly, because parts of the scroll are smudged and obliterated, but you can see what looks like a map of the passages under the monastery. You recognize the stairs down and the room with the pool and barrels. The eastern portion is smeared beyond recognition, but you see that the south passage runs out of the room you're in now to a blurred area, and beyond that you see a large area with coffinlike shapes drawn along the perimeter. That's all you can make out.

PC (Tordek): Let's head south and see what the map is leading toward. [*Everyone agrees.*]

DM: You pass down a long passage of stone blocks with an arched ceiling about 15 feet overhead. It stretches for about 80 paces, then opens into the northern portion of a chamber that looks to be about 50 feet by 50 feet to those of you with darkvision or low-light vision. It's completely empty and looks to be a dead end. What do you do?

PC (Lidda): Does this room look like the one with the coffin shapes on the map?

DM: No. You think that this might be the blotched area on the map.

PC (Mialee): I bet there's a secret door here. Let's check the south wall.

The DM now decides to make the Search checks himself, hidden from the players so that they won't know the results. He knows that they can't find anything—the secret door is 10 feet above the floor—but he doesn't want them to know that. Finding the holes requires no roll, so the DM randomly determines who finds them. He also makes a Listen check for the ghouls at the far end of the secret corridor—an 18 means they have heard the party tapping on the walls looking for a hollow spot.

DM: The wall seems solid. However . . . Tordek, you noticed some strange holes in the wall. Square places cut into the stone, each about half a foot on a side and about that deep. There are four all together—two pairs, 10 feet apart, with two about 3 feet from the floor, and two about 6 feet up. You find some wooden splinters in one.

PC (Jozan): Let's look at that map again.

PC (Tordek): While you do that, I'll feel around to find if the holes have any levers or catches or anything.

DM: [*Making some meaningless rolls, knowing there are no levers to find*] You don't find anything like that, Tordek.

PC (Mialee): The only thing I can think of is that the holes are sockets for some sort of wooden construction. . . .

PC (Lidda): Sure! How about a ramp or stairs? How high is the ceiling in this place?

DM: Oh, about 25 feet.

PC (Lidda): How about hoisting me up and letting me search up high?

PC (Jozan): Good idea. Tordek, will you help me hold her steady?

PC (Tordek): Sure.

PC (Mialee): While they do that, I'll keep a lookout to make sure nothing sneaks up behind us from the way we came.

DM: Looks clear, Mialee. Lidda's not heavy, so you guys don't have to make Strength checks to lift her. You do have to make them to hold her steady so that she can . . . What is it you're going to do once you're hoisted up, Lidda?

PC (Lidda): I'll scan the stone first to see if there are marks or some operating device evident.

DM: Okay, how about those Strength checks? Tordek, you're stronger, so Jozan is helping you rather than the other way around. If the cleric can succeed at a check with a DC of 10, he'll add +2 to Tordek's attempt.

The check results are good enough that Tordek and Jozan are able to hold Lidda steady, so the DM makes a Search check for Lidda. She finds something.

DM: Lidda, you find some stone projections that seem rather smooth, as if worn by use.

PC (Lidda): Then I'll see if I can move any of the knobs. Maybe they'll open a secret door. I'll pull, push, twist, turn, slide . . .

DM: Okay. One of the fist-sized projections moves inward, and there's a grinding sound. A 10-foot-by-10-foot section of the wall, 10 feet above the floor in the center of the south wall, swings inward and to the right.

PC (Lidda): I'll pull myself up into the doorway, and then I'll see if I can use my tools to somehow anchor a rope up here to help the others climb.

DM: You get up there, and you're looking around for a crack or something to wedge a spike into, right? Make a Spot check.

The Spot check is actually to see if Lidda sees the ghouls waiting in the darkness, but Lidda doesn't know that (although the fact that the DM didn't ask for a Search roll might have tipped off a more experienced player).

PC (Lidda): Oops. A 7.

Now the DM begins rolling attacks for the ghouls. The players ask what's going on, and why he's rolling dice, but his silence adds to the tension and suspense. The ghouls hit Lidda with their paralyzing touch.

DM: Lidda, make a Fortitude save.

PC (Lidda): Oh, no! Why? A trap? [*Rolls*] 1? Arrgh. This is where our luck runs out.

DM: [*To the others*] You see a sickly gray arm strike the halfling as she's looking around at the floor where she stands, 10 feet above you. She utters a muffled cry, and then a shadowy form drags her out of sight. What do you do?

WILDERNESS ENCOUNTERS

In the great outdoors, dragons cross the sky, looking for prey on the ground, while tribes of hobgoblins stalk their own victims. An ankheg bursts forth from the earth, and monstrous spiders drop from the trees.

Encounters and adventures outdoors can be as interesting as those underground, but they're different in many ways. See Chapter 3: Running the Game for how to handle the environmental hazards of the wilderness. This section discusses outdoor encounters.

The first thing you need to do is determine the chance for an encounter to happen in a given area. This is not a set chance, but rather a variable based on the area. Desolate areas have a smaller chance for encounters than a well-traveled road.

TABLE 4–36: CHANCE OF WILDERNESS ENCOUNTER

Terrain	d% Chance
Desolate/wasteland	5% chance per hour
Frontier/wilderness	8% chance per hour
Verdant/civilized area	10% chance per hour
Heavily traveled	12% chance per hour

The chance for an encounter assumes a significant encounter—not an encounter with a bluejay or a squirrel. (The DM is free to ad lib these as desired.) A significant encounter is one that is worthy of your and the players' attention—a monster, a threat, or a challenge of some sort (even if the challenge is to get valuable information out of the traveling pilgrims about the lands that lie ahead).

BUILDING WILDERNESS ENCOUNTER TABLES

Below you can find all the tools that you need to build encounter tables suited to various regions of your campaign world. These tools include Table 4–38: Wilderness Encounter Lists. The table orclassifies all the creatures found in the *Monster Manual* according to the climate and terrain where they can be encountered. It also includes two special lists—Civilized Area and Haunted/Magical—that can be used to fill in special areas regardless of terrain.

To create an encounter list, choose as many or as few of the creatures listed for the appropriate terrain as you want, assigning each an encounter chance (a detailed example is presented on page 136). Note that some of the climate/terrain lists include other categories (which are printed in *italic*). This means that all the creatures on the other list or lists are also available for you to choose from. For example, the list for Temperate Forest also includes all the creatures on the lists for Any Land, Any Forest, and Temperate Land.

Make sure the encounter chances for all the creatures you choose add up to 100 so you can use d% to determine which encounter occurs. These encounter chances can vary as much as you want. In the Hills of Longing, the chance to encounter bugbears is only 2%, but in the Blue Hills the chance is 10%, indicating that bugbears are much more common in the Blue Hills.

Only interesting encounters are listed. Toads, ponies, and a few other creatures found in the *Monster Manual* are not on these lists. Otherwise, they are entirely comprehensive. So comprehensive, in fact, that you shouldn't use the entire list to create encounters for a given location. No one area of mountains, for example, should have all the creatures listed under Any Mountains. (There could be either dire lions or dire tigers but not both.) These lists don't presume to present a workable ecosystem. They're merely here for your convenience.

Some areas probably exist in your campaign world that are both wooded and mountainous, or both magical and a desert. In these cases, you can choose some creatures from each appropriate list.

Choosing creatures can simply be a matter of selecting what you think is appropriate and interesting. However, you may want to use the opportunity to exert more control than that. Everyone knows that the Dark Mountains are dangerous, and only the brave or foolhardy travel there. The Greenacre Hills, however, are thought by most to be relatively safe. The area is dotted with villages and homesteads. To reflect this, you can assign each area an approximate Encounter Level, or Encounter Level range. When devising the encounter tables for the Dark Mountains, the DM picks EL 8 to be the average level of encounters found there. By contrast, the Greenacre Hills are EL 2. This allows you to choose appropriate creatures from the lists to fit that Encounter Level or to gauge the number of creatures found in a given encounter.

Table 4-37: Terrain Modifiers to Encounter Levels gives a basic range for Encounter Levels in each type of terrain. As a general, rule, average Encounter Levels should fit into these ranges, although a magical forest could be higher than EL 9, and (Text continues on page 136)

TABLE 4–37: TERRAIN MODIFIERS TO ENCOUNTER LEVELS

Terrain	EL	NPC Level*
Plains	1–6	+0
Hills	2–7	+0
Forest	4–9	+1
Desert	5–10	+2
Mountains	7–12	+3
Aquatic	8–13	+4
Swamp	10–15	+5

*This modifier can be applied to the highest-level NPC, using the town generation system found later in this chapter. This reflects that more dangerous areas make for tougher inhabitants, overall.

TABLE 4–38: WILDERNESS ENCOUNTER LISTS

Any Aquatic
Gargoyle
Gibbering mouther
Sea hag
Kraken
Kuo-toa
Lacedon
Merrow
Orca (animals)
Porpoise (animals)
Purple worm
Shark (animals)
Dire shark (dire animals)
Squid (animals)
Giant squid (animals)
Tojanida
Triton
Baleen whale (animals)
Cachalot whale (animals)

Temperate Aquatic
Bronze dragon
Dragon turtle
Aquatic elf
Storm giant
Merfolk
Nixie
Octopus (animals)
Giant octopus (animals)
Sea lion
Skum
Viper snake (animals)
Toad (animals)
Any Aquatic

Warm Aquatic
Crocodile (animals)
Giant crocodile (animals)
Bronze dragon
Elasmosaurus (dinosaur)
Storm giant
Hippopotamus
Shocker lizard
Locathah
Octopus (animals)
Giant octopus (animals)
Sahuagin
Sea lion
Skum
Constrictor snake (animals)
Giant constrictor snake (animals)
Viper snake (animals)

Any Desert
Lamia
Mummy

Temperate Desert
Giant ant (vermin)
Bat (animals)
Dire bat (dire animals)
Blue dragon
Brass dragon
Copper dragon

Dragonne
Any Land
Any Desert
Temperate Land

Warm Desert
Giant ant (vermin)
Baboon (animals)
Bat (animals)
Dire bat (dire animals)
Blue dragon
Brass dragon
Copper dragon
Dragonne
Any Land
Any Desert
Warm Land

Any Forest
Brown bear (animals)
Dire bear (dire animals)
Giant eagle
Gnome (rock gnome)
Forest gnome
Kobold
Dire lion (dire animals)
Giant owl
Sprite
Stirge
Tiger (animals)
Dire tiger (dire animals)
Treant
Werebear (lycanthrope)
Weretiger (lycanthrope)
Werewolf (lycanthrope)
Wolf (animals)
Worg
Dire wolf (dire animals)

Cold Forest
Any Land
Any Forest
Cold Land

Temperate Forest
Ankheg
Giant ant (vermin)
Aranea
Assassin vine
Dire badger (dire animals)
Bat (animals)
Dire bat (dire animals)
Black bear (animals)
Giant stag beetle (vermin)
Boar (animals)
Dire boar (dire animals)
Centaur
Chuul
Displacer beast
Green dragon
Dryad
Elf (high elf)
Gray elf
Wild elf
Wood elf
Ettercap
Grig

TABLE 4–38: WILDERNESS ENCOUNTER LISTS (CONT.)

Green hag
Tallfellow halfling
Krenshar
Owlbear
Pegasus
Pixie
Giant praying mantis (vermin)
Pseudodragon
Satyr
Shambling mound
Tendriculos
Unicorn
Dire weasel (dire animals)
Wereboar (lycanthrope)
Dire wolverine (dire animals)
Wyvern
Any Land
Any Forest
Temperate Land

Warm Forest
Giant ant (vermin)
Dire ape (dire animals)
Aranea
Assassin vine
Bat (animals)
Dire bat (dire animals)
Black bear (animals)
Giant stag beetle (vermin)
Boar (animals)
Dire boar (dire animals)
Chuul
Couatl
Deinonychus (dinosaur)
Green dragon
Pseudodragon
Dryad
Elephant (animals)
Wild elf
Ettercap
Gorilla
Girallon
Grig
Green hag
Krenshar
Leopard (animals)
Megaraptor (dinosaur)
Monkey (animals)
Pegasus
Giant praying mantis (vermin)
Rakshasa
Shambling mound
Constrictor snake (animals)
Giant constrictor snake (animals)
Criosphinx
Tendriculos
Triceratops (dinosaur)
Tyrannosaurus (dinosaur)
Wereboar (lycanthrope)
Wyvern
Any Land
Any Forest
Warm Land

Any Hills
Brown bear (animals)
Dire bear (dire animals)
Dwarf (hill dwarf)
Eagle (animals)
Giant eagle
Hill giant
Gnome (rock gnome)
Deep halfling
Lamia
Dire lion (dire animals)
Giant owl
Tiger (animals)
Dire tiger (dire animals)
Werebear (lycanthrope)
Weretiger (lycanthrope)
Werewolf (lycanthrope)
Wolf (animals)
Worg
Dire wolf (dire animals)
Yrthak

Cold Hills
Ettin
Wolverine (animals)
Any Land
Any Hills
Cold Land

Temperate Hills
Giant ant (vermin)
Athach
Dire badger (dire animals)
Bat (animals)
Dire bat (dire animals)
Black bear (animals)
Displacer beast
Red dragon
Copper dragon
Dragonne
Ettin
Griffon
Hippogriff
Giant praying mantis (vermin)
Tendriculos
Dire weasel (dire animals)
Wolverine (animals)
Dire wolverine (dire animals)
Wyvern
Any Land
Any Hills
Temperate Land

Warm Hills
Giant ant (vermin)
Athach
Bat (animals)
Dire bat (dire animals)
Black bear (animals)
Deinonychus (dinosaur)
Red dragon
Copper dragon
Dragonne
Griffon
Hippogriff
Megaraptor (dinosaur)
Giant praying mantis (vermin)

Hieracosphinx
Tendriculos
Triceratops (dinosaur)
Tyrannosaurus (dinosaur)
Wyvern
Any Land
Any Hills
Warm Land

Any Land
Annis
Basilisk
Behir
Beholder
Chimera
Doppelganger
Gold dragon
Gargoyle
Fire giant
Gibbering mouther
Gray render
Halfling (lightfoot)
Medusa
Mimic
Nymph
Ogre
Ogre mage
Orc
Half-orc
Phasm
Rat (animals)
Dire rat (dire animals)
Tarrasque
Titan
Troll
Vargouille
Wererat (lycanthrope)

Cold Land
Polar bear (animals)
White dragon
Frost worm
Frost giant
Remorhaz
Winter wolf

Temperate Land
Giant bee (vermin)
Giant bombadier beetle (vermin)
Giant fire beetle (vermin)
Bulette
Monstrous centipede (vermin)
Cockatrice
Digester
Wild dog (animals; treat as dog)
Gnoll
Goblin
Gorgon
Harpy
Hobgoblin
Manticore
Dark naga
Guardian naga
Spirit naga
Monstrous scorpion (vermin)
Viper snake (animals)
Monstrous spider (vermin)

Spider eater
Giant wasp (vermin)

Warm Land
Giant bee (vermin)
Giant bombardier beetle (vermin)
Giant fire beetle (vermin)
Monstrous centipede (vermin)
Cockatrice
Digester
Wild dog (animals; treat as dog)
Gnoll
Goblin
Gorgon
Harpy
Hobgoblin
Lammasu
Giant lizard (animals)
Manticore
Dark naga
Guardian naga
Spirit naga
Monstrous scorpion (vermin)
Viper snake (animals)
Androsphinx
Gynosphinx
Monstrous spider (vermin)
Spider eater
Giant wasp (vermin)

Any Mountains
Brown bear (animals)
Dire bear (dire animals)
Dwarf (hill dwarf)
Mountain dwarf
Eagle (animals)
Giant eagle
Hill giant
Stone giant
Grimlock
Deep halfling
Dire lion (dire animals)
Giant owl
Tiger (animals)
Dire tiger (dire animals)
Troglodyte
Werebear (lycanthrope)
Weretiger (lycanthrope)
Werewolf (lycanthrope)
Wolf (animals)
Worg
Dire wolf (dire animals)
Yrthak

Cold Mountains
Ettin
Any Land
Any Mountains
Cold Land

Temperate Mountains
Athach
Black bear (animals)
Displacer beast
Red dragon
Copper dragon
Silver dragon

TABLE 4–38: WILDERNESS ENCOUNTER LISTS (CONT.)

Gray elf
Ettin
Cloud giant
Storm giant
Griffon
Roc
Dire weasel (dire animals)
Wyvern
Any Land
Any Mountains
Temperate Land

Warm Mountains

Dire ape (dire animals)
Athach
Black bear (animals)
Red dragon
Copper dragon
Silver dragon
Cloud giant
Storm giant
Gorilla
Girallon
Griffon
Roc
Wyvern
Any Land
Any Mountains
Warm Land

Any Plains

Dire bear (dire animals)
Eagle (animals)
Giant eagle
Dire lion (dire animals)
Giant owl
Tiger (animals)
Dire tiger (dire animals)
Weretiger (lycanthrope)
Werewolf (lycanthrope)
Wolf (animals)
Worg
Dire wolf (dire animals)

Temperate Plains

Ankheg
Giant ant (vermin)
Dire badger (dire animals)
Bat (animals)
Dire bat (dire animals)
Blink dog
Brass dragon
Hippogriff
Krenshar
Giant praying mantis (vermin)
Dire weasel (dire animals)
Dire wolverine (dire animals)
Any Land
Any Plains
Temperate Land

Warm Plains

Ankheg
Giant ant (vermin)

Bat (animals)
Dire bat (dire animals)
Cheetah (animals)
Deinonychus (dinosaur)
Brass dragon
Elephant (animals)
Hippogriff
Hippopotamus
Krenshar
Leopard (animals)
Lion (animals)
Megaraptor (dinosaur)
Giant praying mantis (vermin)
Rhinoceros (animals)
Triceratops (dinosaur)
Tyrannosaurus (dinosaur)
Any Land
Any Plains
Warm Land

Any Swamp

Black pudding
Black dragon
Gray ooze
Hydra
Ochre jelly
Will-o'-wisp

Temperate Swamp

Chuul
Green hag
Lizardfolk
Giant praying mantis (vermin)
Shambling mound
Tendriculos
Any Land
Any Swamp
Temperate Land

Warm Swamp

Chuul
Crocodile (animals)
Giant crocodile (animals)
Deinonychus (dinosaur)
Green hag
Shocker lizard
Lizardfolk
Megaraptor (dinosaur)
Giant praying mantis (vermin)
Rakshasa
Shambling mound
Tendriculos
Tyrannosaurus (dinosaur)
Any Land
Any Swamp
Warm Land

Civilized Area

Bandits*
Cat (animals)
Dog (animals)
Wild dog (animals; treat as dog)
Farmers*
Ghost
Herders*
Hunters*
Merchants*

Minstrels/Actors*
Patrol*
Pilgrims*
Travelers*
Vampire

*NPCs encountered are treated as monsters—that is, their level should be the average CR you have assigned for the region or lower if encountered in numbers.

Bandits: 3d4+2 warriors and 1 higher-level warrior leader. 10% chance that the leader is a fighter.

Farmers: 1d4 commoners.

Herders: 1d4 commoners with 5d6 livestock.

Hunters: 1d4 commoners. 10% chance 1 is a warrior.

Merchants: 1d4 commoners, 1d4 warriors (guards), and 1 expert (leader). Usually with mounts or wagons laden with goods.

Minstrels/Actors: 2d4 commoners and 1 expert (leader). 10% chance that the leader is a bard. They usually have a wagon full of props and costumes that can also double as a stage.

Patrol: 2d4+1 warriors and 1 higher level warrior leader. 10% chance that the leader is a fighter.

Pilgrims: 3d4+4 commoners, 1d6−1 warriors (guards), and 1 cleric (leader).

Travelers: 1d4 individuals of any class.

Haunted/Magical

Allip
Animated object
Hound archon (celestial)
Lantern archon (celestial)
Trumpet archon (celestial)
Arrowhawk
Azer
Balor (demon)
Barbazu (devil)
Barghest
Bebilith (demon)
Belker
Bodak
Celestial creature
Chaos beast
Cornugon (devil)
Astral deva (celestial)
Devourer
Djinni
Dretch (demon)
Ghaele eladrin (celestial)
Air elemental
Earth elemental
Fire elemental
Water elemental
Efreeti
Erinyes (devil)
Ethereal filcher

Fiendish creature
Formian
Gelugon (devil)
Glabrezu (demon)
Clay golem
Flesh golem
Iron golem
Stone golem
Avoral guardinal (celestial)
Night hag
Hamatula (devil)
Hellcat (devil)
Hell hound
Hezrou (demon)
Homunculus
Howler
Imp (devil)
Janni
Kyton (devil)
Lillend
Magmin
Marilith (demon)
Air mephit
Dust mephit
Earth mephit
Fire mephit
Ice mephit
Magma mephit
Ooze mephit
Salt mephit
Steam mephit
Water mephit
Mohrg
Nalfeshnee (demon)
Nightcrawler
Nightmare
Nightwalker
Nightwing
Osyluth (devil)
Phase spider
Pit fiend (devil)
Planetar (celestial)
Quasit (demon)
Ravid
Salamander
Shadow
Shadow mastiff
Skeleton
Blue slaad
Death slaad
Gray slaad
Green slaad
Red slaad
Solar (celestial)
Spectre
Succubus (demon)
Thoqqua
Tiefling
Vampire spawn
Vargouille
Vrock (demon)
Wight
Wraith
Xill
Xorn
Yeth hound
Zombie

TABLE 4–39: DARK MOUNTAINS WILDERNESS ENCOUNTERS

d% Day	d% Night	Encounter	Number Encountered	CR	At EL		d% Day	d% Night	Encounter	Number Encountered	CR	At EL
01	01	Athach	1	7	7		—	37	Gibbering mouther	1	5	5
02	02	Bandits	*	*	11		51–52	38–40	Gnoll	2d8	1	7
03	03	Basilisk	1d4	5	7		53	41–42	Goblin	4d6+2	1/4	4
04–07	—	Black bear	1d4+1	2	5		—	43	Gorgon	1	8	8
08–09	—	Brown bear	1d4	4	6		54–56	44–46	Gray render	1	8	8
10–11	—	Dire bear	1	7	7		57–61	—	Griffon	1d4	4	6
—	04	Behir	1	8	8		—	47–48	Grimlock	2d8	1	7
—	05–06	Beholder	1	13	13		—	49	Hag, annis	1d3	6	8
—	07–08	Chimera	1	7	7		62–65	—	Deep halfling	3d6	1/2	5
12	—	Cockatrice	2d4	3	7		—	50	Harpy	1d4	4	6
13	09	Digester	1	6	6		66–67	51–53	Hobgoblin	3d6	1/2	5
14–15	10	Displacer beast	1d4	4	6		68–69	—	Dire lion	1d4	5	7
16	—	Doppelganger	1d4	3	5		70–72	54–57	Manticore	1d3	5	7
17	—	Red dragon, young	1	6	6		73	58–59	Medusa	1d3	7	9
18	11	Red dragon, juvenile	1	9	9		—	60–61	Dark naga	1	8	8
19	12	Red dragon, young adult	1	12	12		74–76	62–64	Ogre	2d6	2	8
20	13	Red dragon, adult	1	14	14		—	65	Ogre	3d6	2	8
21	14	Red dragon, mature adult	1	17	17		77–79	66–69	Orc	3d6	1/2	5
22	15	Red dragon, old	1	19	19		—	70–71	Giant owl	1d4	3	5
—	16	Red dragon, very old	1	20	20		—	72	Phasm	1	10	10
—	17	Red dragon, ancient	1	22	22		80	—	Roc	1	9	9
23	—	Gold dragon, young	1	7	7		81–83	—	Huge viper snake	1d4	3	5
24	—	Gold dragon, juvenile	1	10	10		—	73	Spectre	1	7	7
25	—	Gold dragon, young adult	1	13	13		84–85	74–75	Large monstrous spider	2d6	2	8
26	—	Gold dragon, adult	1	15	15		86–87	76–77	Huge monstrous spider	1d4	4	6
27	—	Gold dragon, mature adult	1	18	18		—	78	Huge monstrous spider	2d4	4	8
28	—	Gold dragon, old	1	20	20		88–89	79–80	Gargantuan monstrous spider	1	7	7
29	—	Gold dragon, very old	1	21	21		—	81	Gargantuan monstrous spider	1d3	7	9
30	—	Gold dragon, ancient	1	23	23		90	—	Spider eater	1d4	5	7
31–36	—	Mountain dwarf	3d6	1/2	5		—	82	Troglodyte	2d8	1	7
37	—	Giant eagle	1d4	3	5		—	83–86	Troll	1d4	5	7
38–41	—	Gray elf	3d6	1/2	5		—	87	Vampire	1	7	7
—	18	Ettin	1d3	5	7		91–92	—	Dire weasel	2d6	2	8
—	19	Ettin	2d4	5	9		93–94	—	Werebear	1d4	5	7
—	20	Gargoyle	1d4	4	6		—	88	Wererat	2d6	2	8
—	21	Gargoyle	2d4	4	8		—	89–91	Werewolf	1d4	3	5
—	22–23	Ghast	2d4	3	7		—	92	Wight	2d4	3	7
—	24–25	Ghoul	2d8	1	7		95–97	—	Wolf	2d8	1	8
—	26	Ghost**	1	7	7		—	93–95	Worg	2d6	2	8
42–43	—	Cloud giant	1	11	11		98–99	96–98	Dire wolf	2d4	3	7
44–45	27	Fire giant	1	10	10		—	99	Wraith	1d4	5	7
—	28–29	Fire giant	1d3	10	12		100	—	Wyvern	1	6	6
46	30–31	Hill giant	1d3	7	9		—	100	Yrthak	1	9	9
47–49	32–34	Stone giant	1d3	8	10							
50	35–36	Storm giant	1	13	13							

*Bandits: One 5th-level warrior leader (CR 5) and 3d4+2 1st-level warriors (CR 1 each) who raid the intelligent races in the mountains. Roll d% to determine the race or kind of bandits: 01–75, human; 76–85, half-orc; 86–90, gray elf; 91–95, deep halfling; or 96–100 mountain dwarf.

**Use the sample ghost found in the *Monster Manual*.

† Use the sample vampire found in the *Monster Manual*.

a somewhat civilized swamp might be lower—even drastically lower—than EL 10.

At your option, you can set up encounter tables so that creatures encountered by day are different from the ones encountered at night. Having two d% columns to roll on for the same area allows nighttime encounters that are both appropriate (undead, more nocturnal beasts, etc.) and more dangerous. (Everyone knows that an area is more dangerous at night—tougher monsters or simply more of them in nighttime encounters reinforce that fact.) It also increases the plausible variety of encounters in a given area.

EXAMPLE: THE DARK MOUNTAINS

Table 4–39: Dark Mountains Wilderness Encounters is an example of how to construct a wilderness encounter table from the lists given above. The DM has assigned an approximate average Encounter Level for the Dark Mountains of 8. He chose the following encounters mainly from the Temperate Mountains list, although a few creatures from the Haunted/Magical list are used for night encounters.

GENERATING TOWNS

When the PCs come into a town and you need to generate facts about that town quickly, you can use the following material.

TABLE 4–40: RANDOM TOWN GENERATION

d%	Town Size	Population*	GP Limit
01–10	Thorp	20–80	40 gp
11–30	Hamlet	81–400	100 gp
31–50	Village	401–900	200 gp
51–70	Small town	901–2,000	800 gp
71–85	Large town	2,001–5,000	3,000 gp
86–95	Small city	5,001–12,000	15,000 gp
96–99	Large city	12,001–25,000	40,000 gp
100	Metropolis	25,001+	100,000 gp

*Adult population. Depending on the dominant race of the community, the number of nonadults will range from 10% to 40% of this figure.

COMMUNITY WEALTH AND POPULATION

Every community has a gold piece limit based on its size and population. The gold piece limit (see Table 4–40) is an indicator of the price of the most expensive item available in that community. Nothing that costs more than a community's gp limit is available for purchase there. Anything having a price under that limit is most likely available, whether it be mundane or magical. While exceptions are certainly possible (a boomtown near a newly discovered mine, a farming community impoverished after a prolonged drought), these exceptions are temporary; all communities will conform to the norm over time.

To determine the amount of ready cash in a community, or the total value of any given item of equipment for sale at any given time, multiply half the gp limit by one-tenth of the community's population. For example, suppose a band of adventurers brings a bagful of loot (one hundred gems, each worth 50 gp) into a hamlet of 90 people. Half the hamlet's gp limit times one-tenth its population equals 450 (100 ÷ 2 = 50, 90 ÷ 10 = 9, 50 × 9 = 450). Therefore, the PCs can only convert nine of their recently acquired gems to coins on the spot before exhausting the local cash reserves. The coins will not be all bright, shiny gold pieces. They should include a large number of battered and well-worn silver pieces and copper pieces as well, especially in a small or poor community.

If those same adventurers hope to equip their one hundred newly recruited followers with new longswords (price 15 gp each), they can find a longsword in even the smallest community, but a community of at least 300 people is necessary in order to have the resources to construct that many weapons (100 ÷ 2 = 50, 300 ÷ 10 = 30, 50 × 30 = 1,500).

POWER CENTER FOR THE COMMUNITY

Sometimes all the DM needs to know about a community is who holds the real power. If this is the case, use Table 4–41: Power Centers, modified by the size of the community as follows:

TABLE 4–41: POWER CENTERS

1d20	Power Center Type
13 or less	Conventional*
14–18	Nonstandard
19+	Magical

*5% of these have a monstrous power center in addition to the conventional.

Community Size	Modifier to 1d20 roll
Thorp	–1
Hamlet	0
Village	+1
Small town	+2
Large town	+3
Small city	+4 (roll twice)
Large city	+5 (roll three times)
Metropolis	+6 (roll four times)

Conventional: The community has a traditional form of government—a mayor, a town council, a noble ruling over the surrounding area under a greater liege, a noble ruling the community as a city-state. Choose whichever form of government seems most appropriate to the area.

Nonstandard: While the community may have a mayor or a town council, the real power lies in other hands. It may center on a guild—a formal organization of merchants, craftsmen, professionals, thieves, assassins, or warriors who collectively wield great influence. Wealthy aristocracy, in the form of one or more rich individuals with no political office, may exert influence through their wealth. Prestigious aristocracy, such as a group of accomplished adventurers, may exert influence through their reputation and experience. Wise elders may exert influence through those who respect their age, reputation, and perceived wisdom.

Magical: From a powerful temple full of priests to a single sorcerer cloistered in a tower, a cleric or a wizard might be the actual, official ruler of the town, or she may just be someone with a great deal of influence.

Monstrous: Consider the impact on a community of a dragon who occasionally makes nonnegotiable demands and must be consulted in major decisions, or a nearby ogre tribe that must be paid a monthly tribute, or a secret mind flayer controlling the minds of many of the townsfolk. A monstrous power center represents any influence (beyond just a simple nearby danger) held by a monstrous being or beings not native to the community.

TABLE 4–42: POWER CENTER ALIGNMENT

d%	Alignment
01–35	Lawful good
36–39	Neutral good
40–41	Chaotic good
42–61	Lawful neutral
62–63	True neutral
64	Chaotic neutral
65–90	Lawful evil
91–98	Neutral evil
99–100	Chaotic evil

Alignment of the Power Centers

The alignment of the ruler or rulers of a community need not conform to the alignment of all or even the majority of the residents, although this is usually the case. In any case, the alignment of the power center strongly shapes the residents' daily lives. Due to their generally organized and organizing nature, most power centers are lawful.

Lawful Good: A community with a lawful good power center usually has a codified set of laws, and most people willingly obey those laws.

Neutral Good: A neutral good power center rarely influences the residents of the community other than to help them when they are in need.

Chaotic Good: This sort of power center influences the community by helping the needy and opposing restrictions on freedom.

Lawful Neutral: A community with a lawful neutral power center has a codified set of laws that are followed to the letter. Those in power usually insist that visitors (as well as residents) obey all local rules and regulations.

True Neutral: This sort of power center rarely influences the community. Those in power prefer to pursue their private goals.

Chaotic Neutral: This sort of power center is unpredictable, influencing the community in different ways at different times.

Lawful Evil: A community with a lawful evil power center usually has a codified set of laws, which most people obey out of fear of harsh punishment.

Neutral Evil: The residents of a community with a neutral evil power center are usually oppressed and subjugated, facing a dire future.

Chaotic Evil: The residents of a community with a chaotic evil power center live in abject fear because of the unpredictable and horrific situations continually placed upon them.

Conflicting Power Centers

As shown on Table 4–41: Power Centers, any community at least as large as a small city has more than one power center. If a community has more than one power center, and two or more of the power centers have opposing alignments (either good vs. evil or law vs. chaos), they conflict in some way. Such conflict is not always open, and sometimes the conflicting power centers begrudgingly get along.

For example, a small city contains a powerful chaotic good wizards' guild but is ruled by a lawful good aristocrat. The wizards are sometimes exasperated by the strict laws imposed by the aristocrat ruler and occasionally break or circumvent them when it serves their (well-intentioned) purposes. Most of the time,

though, a representative from the guild takes their concerns and disagreements to the aristocrat, who attempts to fairly resolve any problems.

Another example: A large city contains a lawful evil fighter, a lawful good temple, and a chaotic evil aristocrat. The selfish aristocrat is concerned only with his own gain and his debauched desires. The powerful fighter gathers a small legion of warriors, hoping to oust the aristocrat and take control of the city herself. Meanwhile, the clergy of the powerful temple helps the citizenry as best as they can, never directly confronting the aristocrat but aiding and abetting those who suffer at his hands.

COMMUNITY AUTHORITIES

It's often important to know who makes up the community's authority structure. The authority structure does not necessarily indicate who's in charge, but instead who keeps order and enforces the authority that exists.

Constable/Captain of the Guard/Sheriff

This position generally devolves upon the highest-level warrior in a community, or one of the highest-level fighters:

ONE HUNDRED ADVENTURE IDEAS

Use the following for spur-of-the-moment adventure seeds or for generating ideas.

d%	Adventure Idea
1	Thieves steal the crown jewels.
2	A dragon flies into a town and demands tribute.
3	The tomb of an old wizard has been discovered.
4	Wealthy merchants are being killed in their homes.
5	The statue in the town square is found to be a petrified paladin.
6	A caravan of important goods is about to leave for a trip through a dangerous area.
7	Cultists are kidnapping potential sacrifices.
8	Goblins riding spider eaters have been attacking the outskirts of a town.
9	Local bandits have joined forces with a tribe of bugbears.
10	A blackguard is organizing monsters in an area.
11	A gate to the Lower Planes threatens to bring more demons to the world.
12	Miners have accidentally released something awful that once was buried deep.
13	A wizard's guild challenges the ruling council.
14	Racial tensions rise between humans and elves.
15	A mysterious fog brings ghosts into town.
16	The holy symbol of a high priest is missing.
17	An evil wizard has developed a new type of golem.
18	Someone in town is a werewolf.
19	Slavers continue to raid a local community.
20	A fire elemental escapes from a wizard's lab.
21	Bugbears are demanding a toll on a well-traveled bridge.
22	A *mirror of opposition* has created an evil duplicate of a hero.
23	Two orc tribes wage a bloody war.
24	New construction reveals a previously unknown underground tomb.
25	A nearby kingdom launches an invasion.
26	Two well-known heroes fight a duel.
27	An ancient sword must be recovered to defeat a ravaging monster.
28	A prophecy foretells of coming doom unless an artifact is recovered.
29	Ogres kidnap the mayor's daughter.
30	A wizard is buried in a trap-filled tomb with her powerful magic items.
31	An enchanter is compelling others to steal for him.
32	A shapechanged mind flayer is gathering mentally controlled servitors.
33	A plague brought by wererats threatens a community.
34	The keys to disarming all the magic traps in a wizard's tower have gone missing.
35	Sahuagin are being driven out of the sea to attack coastal villages.
36	Gravediggers discover a huge, ghoul-filled catacomb under the cemetery.
37	A wizard needs a particularly rare spell component found only in the deep jungle.
38	A map showing the location of an ancient magic forge is discovered.
39	Various monsters have long preyed upon people from within the sewers of a major city.
40	An emissary going into a hostile kingdom needs an escort.
41	Vampires are preying upon a small town.
42	A haunted tower is reputed to be filled with treasure.
43	Barbarians begin tearing up a village in a violent rage.
44	Giants steal cattle from local farmers.
45	Unexplained snowstorms bring winter wolves into an otherwise peaceful area.
46	A lonely mountain pass is guarded by a powerful sphinx denying all passage.
47	Evil mercenaries begin constructing a fortress not far from a community.
48	An antidote to a magic poison must be found before the duke dies.
49	A druid needs help defending her grove against goblins.
50	An ancient curse is turning innocent people into evil murderers.
51	Gargoyles are killing giant eagles in the mountains.
52	Mysterious merchants sell faulty magic items in town and then attempt to slink away.
53	A recently recovered artifact causes arcane spellcasters' powers to go awry.
54	An evil noble puts a price on a good noble's head.

d%	Rank
01–60	Highest-level warrior
61–80	Second highest-level fighter
81–100	Highest-level fighter

Use Table 4–43: Highest-Level Locals (PC Classes) or Table 4–44: Highest-Level Locals (NPC Classes), modified by Table 4–45: Community Modifiers, to determine the constable's level.

Guards/Soldiers

For every one hundred people in the community (round down), the community has one full-time guard or soldier. In addition, for every twenty people in the community, an able-bodied member of the local militia or a conscript soldier can be brought into service within just a few hours.

NPCS IN THE COMMUNITY

For detailed city play, knowing exactly who lives in the community becomes important. The following guidelines allow you to determine the levels of the most powerful locals and then extrapolate from that to determine the rest of the classed characters living there.

Highest-Level NPC in the Community for Each Class

Use the following tables to determine the highest-level character in a given class for a given community. Roll the dice indicated for the class (Table 4–43, Table 4–44) and apply the modifier based on the size of the community (Table 4–45).

A result of 0 or lower for character level means that no characters of that type can be found in the community. The maximum level for any class is 20th.

TABLE 4–43: HIGHEST-LEVEL LOCALS (PC CLASSES)

PC Classes	Character Level
Barbarian	1d4 + community modifier*
Bard	1d6 + community modifier
Cleric	1d6 + community modifier
Druid	1d6 + community modifier
Fighter	1d8 + community modifier
Monk	1d4 + community modifier*
Paladin	1d3 + community modifier
Ranger	1d3 + community modifier
Rogue	1d8 + community modifier
Sorcerer	1d4 + community modifier
Wizard	1d4 + community modifier

*Where these classes are more common, level is 1d8 + modifier.

---

55 Adventurers exploring a dungeon have not returned in a week.

56 The funeral for a good fighter is disrupted by enemies he made while alive.

57 Colossal vermin are straying out of the desert to attack settlements.

58 An evil tyrant outlaws nonofficially sanctioned magic use.

59 A huge dire wolf, apparently immune to magic, is organizing the wolves in the wood.

60 A community of gnomes builds a flying ship.

61 An island at the center of the lake is actually the top of a strange, submerged fortress.

62 Buried below the Tree of the World lies the Master Clock of Time.

63 A child wanders into a vast necropolis, and dusk approaches quickly.

64 All the dwarves in an underground city have disappeared.

65 A strange green smoke billows out of a cave near a mysterious ruin.

66 Mysterious groaning sounds come from a haunted wood at night.

67 Thieves steal a great treasure and flee into *Mordenkainen's magnificent mansion*.

68 A sorcerer attempts to travel ethereally but disappears completely in the process.

69 A paladin's quest for atonement leads her to a troll lair too well defended for her to tackle alone.

70 A kingdom known for its wizards prepares for war.

71 The high priest is an illusion.

72 A new noble seeks to clear a patch of wilderness of all monsters.

73 A bulette is tearing apart viable farmland.

74 A infestation of stirges drives yuan-ti closer to civilized lands.

75 Treants in the woods are threatened by a huge fire of mysterious origin.

76 Clerics who have resurrected a long-dead hero discover she's not what they thought.

77 A sorrowful bard tells a tavern tale of his imprisoned companions.

78 Evil nobles create an adventurers' guild to monitor and control adventurers.

79 A halfling caravan must pass through an ankheg-infested wilderness.

80 All the doors in the king's castle are suddenly *arcane locked* and *fire trapped*.

81 An innocent man, about to be hanged, pleads for someone to help him.

82 The tomb of a powerful wizard, filled with magic items, has sunk into the swamp.

83 Someone is sabotaging wagons and carts to come apart when they travel at high speed.

84 A certain type of frogs, found only in an isolated valley, fall like rain on a major city.

85 A jealous rival threatens to stop a well-attended wedding.

86 A woman who mysteriously vanished years ago is seen walking on the surface of a lake.

87 An earthquake uncovers a previously unknown dungeon.

88 A wronged half-elf needs a champion to fight for her in a gladiatorial trial.

89 At the eye of the storm that tears across the land lies a floating citadel.

90 People grow suspicious of half-orc merchants peddling gold dragon parts in the market.

91 An absentminded wizard lets her *rod of wonder* fall into the wrong hands.

92 Undead shadows vex a large library, especially an old storeroom long left undisturbed.

93 The door into an abandoned house in the middle of town turns out to be a magic portal.

94 Barge pirates make a deal with a covey of hags and exact a high toll to use the river.

95 Two parts of a magic item are in the hands of bitter enemies; the third piece is lost.

96 A clutch of wyverns is preying upon sheep as well as shepherds.

97 Evil clerics gather in secret to summon a monstrous god to the world.

98 A major city faces a siege by a force of humans, duergar, and gnolls.

99 A huge gemstone supposedly lies within an ancient ruined monastery.

100 Lizardfolk riding dragon turtles sell their services as mercenaries to the highest bidder.

TABLE 4–44: HIGHEST-LEVEL LOCALS (NPC CLASSES)

NPC Classes	Character Level
Adept	1d6 + community modifier
Aristocrat	1d4 + community modifier
Commoner	4d4 + community modifier
Expert	3d4 + community modifier
Warrior	2d4 + community modifier

TABLE 4–45: COMMUNITY MODIFIERS

Community Size	Community Modifier
Thorp	–3*
Hamlet	–2*
Village	–1
Small town	0
Large town	+3
Small city	+6 (roll twice)**
Large city	+9 (roll three times)**
Metropolis	+12 (roll four times)**

*A thorp or a hamlet has a 5% chance to add +10 to the modifier of a ranger or druid level.

**Cities this large can have more than one high-level NPC per class, each of whom generates lower-level characters of the same class, as described below.

Total Characters of Each Class

Use the following method for determining the levels of all the characters in a community of any given class.

For PC classes, if the highest-level character indicated in the method is 2nd level or above, assume there are twice that number of characters half that level. If those characters are above 1st level, assume that for each such character, there are two of half that level. Continue until the number of 1st-level characters is generated. For example, if the highest-level fighter is 5th level, then there are also two 3rd-level fighters and four 1st-level fighters.

Do the same for NPC classes, but leave out the final stage that would generate the number of 1st-level individuals. Instead, take the remaining population after all character types are generated and divide it up so that 91% are commoners, 5% are warriors, 3% are experts, and the remaining 1% is equally divided between aristocrats and adepts (0.5% each). All these characters are 1st level.

Using these guidelines and Tables 4–43: Highest-Level Locals (PC Classes), 4–44: Highest-Level Locals (NPC Classes), and 4–45: Community Modifiers, the character class breakdown for the population of a typical hamlet of two hundred people looks like this:

- One 1st-level aristocrat (mayor)
- One 3rd-level warrior (constable)
- Nine 1st-level warriors (two guards and seven militia members)
- One 3rd-level expert smith (militia member)

- Seven 1st-level expert crafters and professionals of various sorts
- One 1st-level adept
- One 3rd-level commoner barkeep (militia member)
- One hundred sixty-six 1st-level commoners (one is a militia member)
- One 3rd-level fighter
- Two 1st-level fighters
- One 1st-level wizard
- One 3rd-level cleric
- Two 1st-level clerics
- One 1st-level druid
- One 3rd-level rogue
- Two 1st-level rogues
- One 1st-level bard
- One 1st-level monk

In addition to the residents you generate using the system described above, you might decide that a community also has some sort of special resident, such as the single, out-of-place 15th-level sorcerer who lives just outside a thorp of fifty people, or the secret assassins' guild brimming with leveled characters hidden in a small town. Residents such as these that you create "on the fly" do not count against the highest-level characters who are actually part of the community.

RACIAL DEMOGRAPHICS

The racial mix of a community depends on whether the community is isolated (little traffic and interaction with other races and places), mixed (moderate traffic and interaction with other races and places), or integrated (lots of interaction with other races and places).

TABLE 4–46: RACIAL MIX OF COMMUNITIES

Isolated	Mixed	Integrated
96% human	79% human	37% human
2% halfling	9% halfling	20% halfling
1% elf	5% elf	18% elf
1% other races	3% dwarf	10% dwarf
	2% gnome	7% gnome
	1% half-elf	5% half-elf
	1% half-orc	3% half-orc

If the area's dominant race is other than human, place that race in the top spot, put humans in the #2 rank, and push each other race down one rank. For example, in a dwarven town, the population is 96% dwarf, 2% human, 1% halfling, and 1% other races. (All dwarven communities are isolated.) You may also change the figures slightly for various racial preferences. For example, a mixed elven village is 79% elf, 9% human, 5% halfling, 3% dwarf, 2% gnome and 2% half-elf (with no half orcs). You might even switch the percentages of gnomes and dwarves in an elven town.

Mangonel

Watchtower

Guard room

Walls 8' thick

rear tower

Main tower

Gate house B

Illus. by A. Swekel

Encounters are to adventures what adventures are to campaigns. Good adventures make up good campaigns. Creating a campaign of your own is the most difficult, but most rewarding, task a DM faces.

It's important to distinguish between a campaign and a world, since the terms often seem to be used interchangeably. A campaign is a series of adventures, the nonplayer characters (NPCs) involved in those adventures, and the events surrounding everything that happens in those adventures. When you guide players through adventures you have designed and the players choose the paths for their characters within those adventures, you are running a campaign. A world is a fictional place in which the campaign is set. It's also often called a campaign setting. A campaign requires a world in which the action takes place, but whether you create your own world or use an already established setting, the campaign you run is always your own.

ESTABLISHING A CAMPAIGN

A campaign first requires a world. You have two options when it comes to making a world for your campaign:

- **Use a Published Campaign Setting:** The advantage of using a published setting is that you don't have to do so much work. A lot of the creation is done for you, often from the basics down to the details. Of course, you are always free to pick and choose from the published material and use only what you like. One drawback to using a published world is that your players might read the same products that you do and might therefore know as much (or more) about the world as you do. If this happens, don't let the players dictate the world to you.

("No, I think Ravensburg is on this side of the river. . . .") Above all, even if it's a published product, it's *your* world.

- **Create Your Own World:** For more information on how to do this, see Chapter 6: World-Building.

Once you have a fictional game world and an adventure for the characters to start with, the campaign can begin. The most important purpose of a campaign is to make the players feel that their characters live in a real world. This appearance of realism, also called verisimilitude, is important because it allows the players to stop feeling like they're playing a game and start feeling more like they're playing roles. When immersed in their roles, they are more likely to react to evil Lord Erimbar than they are to you playing Lord Erimbar.

You will know you have succeeded when the players ask you increasingly probing questions, questions not just of the depth of "What's beyond those woods?" but such as "If the rangers around the wood keep such a close watch on the edges of the forest, how can the orc raiders keep attacking the nearby villages without warning?" When the players ask questions of that sort, they're thinking in character. Don't ever answer such a question with "Because I said so" or "Because I'm the DM." Doing that encourages metagame thinking (see Chapter 1: Dungeon Mastering). Either provide an answer, or ask how the character is going to go about finding out.

Occasionally, a player will see a loophole or inconsistency in what you have created. Use such an observation to your advantage rather than admitting that you've made a mistake. Make the quest for the answer a part of the adventure. When the players discover that the leader of the rangers is taking bribes from the orcs to look the other way, they will feel rewarded for asking the right questions, and they will trust the verisimilitude of your world that much more.

THE ADVENTURING PARTY

Bringing the group of adventurers (the party) together can be a challenge. Not for the players—they are all sitting around the table—but for the characters. What brings such a disparate group of races and professions together and makes them a team that goes on adventures together? The objective when answering this question is to avoid the dissatisfaction players feel when they sense that they are adventuring with their comrades only because these folks are the other PCs. One way to prevent this feeling is to have the players create their characters together and put the burden of determining how they have come together on them before the first adventure ever starts. Here are a few other suggestions:

Happenstance: The first adventure is set up so that someone is putting out a call for mercenaries or adventurers to do some task, and the characters are the men and women who happened to answer the call. Alternatively, all the characters meet and discover that they are headed to the same place.

History: The characters are lifelong friends who have met in the past. Despite their different backgrounds and training, they are already good friends.

Mutual Acquaintances: The characters don't start as friends but are introduced as trusted friends of mutual friends.

Outside Intervention: The characters are called together by an outside force—someone with authority enough to get them to do as she says—and are commanded to work together, at least on the first adventure.

The Cliché: The characters all meet in a tavern over mugs of ale and decide to work together.

BEGINNING THE CAMPAIGN

Start small. Set the first adventure in whatever locale you desire, give the players the information they need for that adventure, and let them know just a little about the surrounding area. Later, you can expand on this information, or the PCs can explore and find out more firsthand. With each successive playing session, give the players a little more information about the campaign setting. Slowly, it will blossom before them into what seems to be a real world.

Another great moment in any DM's career is when the players begin to refer to places and people you have created in the campaign as if they were real: "They'd never let you get away with that in the City of Greyhawk!" "I wonder what Lord Nosh is up to these days? He was looking for an apprentice when we saw him last." When those sorts of comments start to flow, you can bask in the glow of a successful campaign.

MAINTAINING A CAMPAIGN

Once it's going, maintaining the campaign becomes as much work as preparing adventures. Keep track of everything that happens, everything that you tell the players about the setting, and work to make it all into a fully actualized world. Build each adventure upon those that came before. Learn from what's happened—both the good and the bad.

CONTEXT

The most important facet of a campaign is a context in which you can set adventures and players can place their characters.

Consistency: The way to make your campaign consistent is to keep accurate notes. If the Inn of the Blue Boar had a creaky door when the players visit the place, make sure it has a creaky door when they (unless you have a reason for why it doesn't creak anymore). Once the players notice consistent details (minor ones, such as the creaking door, or major ones, such as a high priestess's name), they begin to feel that the world you have created is a real place. Keep a notebook or binder with all your notes for the campaign, so that everything is at your fingertips during a game session. If a player asks for the name of the place that someone her character met said was under siege, you should have the answer for her.

Calendars and Timekeeping: Keep close track of time. Track the passing of each season so you can describe the weather. Mark the coming and going of holy days and other dates of importance. This practice helps you organizationally, as well as encouraging you to establish a calendar for your setting. It is another way to give your world verisimilitude.

VARIANT: UPKEEP

Instead of worrying about meal prices, lodging, replacing torn clothing, and other miscellaneous costs, as well as to represent the kinds of costs that turn up in daily life that aren't reflected on the equipment tables in Chapter 7: Equipment in the *Player's Handbook*, you can require each player to pay a monthly upkeep cost based on the lifestyle of the character.

The upkeep can be assumed to take into consideration every expense except the cost of specific adventuring equipment—even taxes. Ultimately, each player should choose the level of upkeep she's willing to pay. You might want consequences to be attached to each lifestyle. For example, someone living a meager existence might have to contend with thieves, while a wealthy character living an extravagant lifestyle might be required to deal with the troubles that come from hobnobbing with aristocrats—betrayals, infidelities, and expensive responsibilities.

From most modest to priciest, the levels of upkeep include self-sufficient, meager, poor, common, good, and extravagant.

Self-Sufficient: Cost 2 gp per month. Even if you own your home (or live with someone else), raise your own food, make your own clothes, and so on, you occasionally need to purchase a new pair of shoes, pay a road toll, or buy staples such as salt. Common laborers earn about 3 gp per month, so they usually have to live self-sufficiently just to survive.

Meager: Cost 5 gp per month. A meager upkeep assumes that you eat little (or hunt and gather a fair amount of your food in the wild) and sleep in flophouses and occasionally in the street or in the wild.

Poor: Cost 12 gp per month. Poor upkeep means providing for yourself from the most basic of travelers' accommodations, which are nevertheless better than living on the street or in the woods.

Common: Cost 45 gp per month. You live in inns and eat tavern meals every day, a practice that quickly grows to be moderately expensive. This level of upkeep assumes the occasional night drinking in the tavern or a nice glass of wine with dinner.

Good: Cost 100 gp per month. You always stay in your own room at inns, and you eat healthy, solid meals with a glass of wine. You maintain a jaunty style with your clothing and try to keep yourself supplied with the good things in life.

Extravagant: Cost 200 gp per month. You buy and use only the best. You take the finest rooms in the finest inns, eat lavish meals with the best wines, attend and throw stunning parties, have regal clothing, and make flamboyant gestures through large expenditures. You may even own your own impressive home with servants.

Events: Stagnation is unrealistic. Change encourages a feeling of realism. Droughts ruin crops, kingdoms go to war, the queen gives birth to a daughter, the price of steel rises as the iron mines close up, and new taxation policies raise an uproar among the common folk. In the campaign world, just as in the real world, new events happen every day. Unlike in our world, the campaign world might not have the technology to disseminate information quickly, but eventually word of change does reach the characters. Not all events need to be catalysts for adventures. Some serve well just providing background.

A Reactive Environment: Actions that the PCs take should affect the campaign. If the PCs burn down a tavern in the middle of town, the authorities will be after them at least for questioning, if not for punishment or restitution. (See Player Characters out of Control, page 145.) When the PCs accomplish something great, people in the campaign world hear about it. Common folk begin to recognize the characters' names and

Relaxing after a harrowing adventure.

perhaps even their faces. If the characters free a town from a tyrant, the next time they come to that town, conditions should be better—or at least different.

BUILDING ON THE PAST

Another key to maintaining a campaign is building on the past to heighten drama, establish motivation, and flesh out the world. Set the characters up for a hard fall. Establish a place in the campaign world as a wonderful, free, and peaceful area. Then, later on in the campaign, have that place invaded and ravaged by an evil force. Having already established in the characters' (and players') minds that it was a great place, you won't need to provide any sort of exposition to explain why the villains are so evil or give the characters motivation to get involved in stopping them.

Use what has come before and prepare for what is still to come. That approach is what makes a campaign different from a series of unrelated adventures. Some strategies for building on the past to

maintain a campaign include using recurring characters, having the PCs form relationships beyond the immediate adventure, changing what the PCs know, hitting the PCs where it hurts, preparing the PCs for the future, and foreshadowing coming events.

Recurring Characters: While this group includes Johanna the innkeeper, who's at the inn each time the PCs return from the dungeon, it also extends to other characters as well. The mysterious stranger that they saw in a back alley of the City of Greyhawk reappears on the road to the Duchy of Urnst, revealing his identity and original intentions. The villain responsible for inciting the goblins to attack the village returns, this time in possession of a powerful magic item. The other adventuring party the PCs encountered in the dungeons below Castle Reglis shows up just in time to help fight off the black dragon Irrkuth. Over-used recurring characters can make a setting seem artificial, but reusing existing characters judiciously not only lends realism but reminds PCs of their own past, thus reaffirming their place in the campaign.

Relationships Beyond the Adventure: The PCs make friends with the innkeeper's son and visit him every time they are in town just to hear another of his jokes. A PC falls in love with an azer princess, and eventually they marry. Old Kragar, a retired fighter, looks upon the PCs as the children he never had. Every year, the centaurs of Chalice Wood deliver a present to the PC who slew the green dragon on the anniversary of his heroic deed. Relationships such as these flesh out the campaign world.

Change What the PCs Know: The king of the elves is replaced by a usurper. The once dangerous roads near the Winding River are now safe, thanks to increased patrols and a powerful group of NPC adventurers who slew most of the monsters in the area. Change a few facts, and you intrigue the players by making them want to know why or how things changed.

Hit Them Where It Hurts: If a PC makes friends with the blacksmith in town, you can make things interesting by having the

Illus. by K. Walker

blacksmith tell the PC that his son was among those kidnapped when the slavers attacked. If the PCs really enjoy visiting the village of Shady Grove, put Shady Grove in the path of the evil cleric's advancing army. Don't overdo revelations of this sort, or else the PCs will never grow attached to anything, for fear of putting that thing in danger. However, this strategy works as a powerful motivator when used in moderation.

Prepare the PCs for the Future: If you know that later in the campaign you want to have trolls rise up from their lairs and begin raiding the Deep Cities of the dwarves, have the PCs hear about the Deep Cities or even visit them on an adventure long before this happens. Doing this will make the troll adventure much more meaningful when it occurs. Threading information into early adventures that informs the PCs of elements of future adventures helps weave a campaign into a whole.

Foreshadow Coming Events: If the kobold that the characters captured speaks about a new troll king, and the PCs hear from dwarves and gnomes the occasional tale of a battle with a troll, they will be better prepared for the time when they must try to stop the trolls from destroying the Deep Cities. They might even follow up on the leads you plant without your ever having to initiate the adventure at all.

OTHER CAMPAIGN ISSUES

Other factors in dealing with campaigns include introducing new players to an ongoing campaign, fostering player goals, changing alignments, managing the transition of PCs from low to high levels, and coping with increasing character power.

Introducing New Players

Players come and go. When a new player joins the group, take the average of the levels of the existing PCs and allow the new player to create a character of that level. The only exception to this guideline is when the new player is completely unfamiliar with the D&D game. Starting as anything but a 1st-level character might be difficult for the player in this case.

Working a new character into the group is similar to establishing why the group got together in the first place, but can be more difficult if the party is in the middle of an adventure. A few ideas include:

- The new PC is a friend or relative of one of the existing PCs and finally caught up with the group to join in.
- The new PC is a prisoner of the foes the existing PCs fight. When they rescue him, he joins their group.
- The new PC was a part of another adventuring group that was wiped out except for her.
- The new PC was sent to the site for reasons unrelated to the party's adventure (which might lead later to another adventure that the new PC can initiate) and joins with the existing PCs because there's strength in numbers.

Fostering Player Goals

Players should eventually develop goals for their characters. Goals might include joining a particular guild, starting their own church, building a fortress, starting a business, obtaining a particular magic item, getting powerful enough to defeat the enemies threatening their home town, finding a lost brother, or tracking down the villain who escaped them long ago. You should not only encourage goals for characters, but you should be willing to design adventures based around them. Goals shouldn't be easy to attain, but a player should always at least have the opportunity to realize the goals he developed for his character (assuming they are at all realistic).

Changing Alignment

A character can have a change of heart. Alignments aren't commitments, except in specific cases (such as for paladins and clerics). Player characters have free will, and their actions often dictate a change of alignment. Here are two examples of how a change of alignment can be handled:

- A player creates a new character—a rogue named Garrett. The player decides he wants Garrett to be neutral good and writes that on Garrett's character sheet. By the second playing session of Garrett's career, however, it's clear that the player isn't playing Garrett as a good-aligned character at all. Garrett likes to steal minor valuables from others (although not his friends) and does not care about helping people or stopping evil. Garrett is a neutral character, and the player made a mistake when declaring Garrett's alignment because he hadn't yet really decided how he wanted to play him. The DM tells the player to erase "good" on Garrett's character sheet, making his alignment simply "neutral." No big deal.
- An NPC traveling with the PCs is chaotic evil and is pretending to be otherwise because he was sent to spy on them and foil their plans. He's been evil all his life, and he has lived among others who acted as he did. As he fights alongside the good-aligned PC adventurers, however, he sees how they work together and help each other. He begins to envy them their camaraderie. Finally, he watches as the paladin PC gives his life to save not only his friends, but an entire town that was poised on the brink of destruction at the hands of an evil sorcerer. Everyone is deeply moved, including the evil NPC, and the town celebrates and honors the paladin's self-sacrifice. The townfolk hail the adventurers as heroes. The NPC is so moved that he repents, casting aside his own evil ways (and his mission). He becomes chaotic neutral, but he is well on his way to becoming chaotic good, particularly if he remains in the company of the PCs.

If the PCs had not acted so gallantly, he might not have changed his ways. If they turn on the NPC when they learn of his past, he may turn back to evil.

Most characters suffer no game penalty for changing alignment, but you should keep a few points in mind.

You're in Control: You control alignment changes, not the player. If a player says, "My neutral good character becomes chaotic good," the appropriate response from you is "Prove it." Actions dictate alignment, not statements of intent by players.

Alignment Change Is Gradual: Changes in alignment shouldn't be drastic. Usually, a character changes alignment only one step at a time—from lawful evil to lawful neutral, for example, and not directly to neutral good. A character on her way to another alignment might have a number of other alignments during the transition to the final alignment.

Time Requirements: Changing alignment takes time. Changes of heart are rarely sudden (although they can be). What you want to avoid is a player changing her character's alignment to evil to use an evil artifact properly and then changing it right back when she's done. Alignments aren't garments you can take off and put on casually. Require an interval of at least a week of game time between alignment changes.

Indecisiveness Indicates Neutrality: Wishy-washy characters should just be neutral. If a character changes alignment over and over again during a campaign, what's really happened is that the character hasn't made a choice, and thus she is neutral.

Exceptions: There are exceptions to all of the above. For instance, it's possible (although unlikely) that the most horrible neutral evil villain has a sudden and dramatic change of heart and immediately becomes neutral good.

The Transition from Low to High Level

One of the most rewarding and fun aspects of a campaign, for players and DMs alike, is the slow but steady transition from 1st level through the low levels (2–5) to the middle levels (6–11) into the high levels (12–15) and finally to the very high levels (16–20). You should be aware that low-level play and high-level play are very different experiences. At low levels, it's difficult to keep the characters alive. At high levels, it's difficult to cause them a lot of harm. Although you should be impartial overall, at low levels make sure that the challenges the PCs face aren't far too tough for them. There's plenty of time at the higher levels when you can feel free to take the kid gloves off and throw whatever you want at them. High-level characters have the power and resources to survive and overcome just about anything.

Low Level

As characters start out and even after they gain a few levels, the following points apply:

- Characters are fragile. Save bonuses, AC, and hit points are all low.
- Characters can face only a few encounters before resting.
- Characters shouldn't stray far from civilization.
- Characters can't count on having a specific capability. Even if the cleric prepares a spell, for example, there's no guarantee that he will still have it when he really needs it. Spell durations are short, and resources are few.

High Level

As the characters gain more levels, the following points become increasingly true:

- Characters are very tough. Save bonuses, AC, and hit points are all high.
- Characters can survive many encounters before resting. At very high levels, the need for rest is rarely an issue.
- Characters can provide their own food, their own magic items, and their own healing. They can even raise each other from the dead.
- Given time, characters can do almost anything. Even if the wizard in the group doesn't know the spell *disintegrate*, you can place a barrier that can only be bypassed by *disintegrate* and count on the party getting past it. (They can obtain access to the spell in some other way, or use their other resources to achieve the same goal.) At very high levels, don't be afraid to throw just about any challenge the way of the characters. All aspects of character action—movement, durability, dealing damage, influencing

As she gains levels, Mialee becomes very powerful.

others, accumulating information, and adaptation to circumstances and environments—increase with level.

Character Power Levels

As the campaign progresses, the PCs get more powerful through level advancement, the acquisition of money and magic items, and the establishment of their reputations. You have to carefully match this advancement with increasing challenges, both in foes who must be overcome and in the deeds that must be performed.

In addition, however, you need to watch the PCs closely and make sure that they neither get out of control in their increased power nor fail to use what's put before them. While it's up to them to make decisions regarding their characters' advancement and what they do with their newfound abilities, it's up to you to keep control of the campaign, maintain balance (see Chapter 1: Dungeon Mastering), and keep things running smoothly.

Character Wealth

One of the ways in which you can maintain measurable control on PC power levels is by strictly monitoring their wealth, including their magic items. Table 5–1: Character Wealth by Level is based on average treasures found in average encounters compared with the experience points earned in those encounters. Using that information, you can determine how much wealth a character should have based on her level.

All published adventures for this edition of the D&D game use this "wealth by level" guideline as a basis for balance in adventures. No adventure meant for 7th-level characters, for example, will require or assume that the party possesses a magic item that costs 20,000 gp.

Player Characters Out of Control

Power can get out of hand. Power corrupts. PCs may do things that show their arrogance as they advance in power—or their contempt for those below them. A 10th-level fighter may feel that he no longer has to treat the duke with respect since he can single-handedly defeat all the duke's soldiers. A powerful wizard

Illus. by K. Walker

TABLE 5–1: CHARACTER WEALTH BY LEVEL

Character Level	Wealth	Character Level	Wealth
2nd	900 gp	12th	88,000 gp
3rd	2,700 gp	13th	110,000 gp
4th	5,400 gp	14th	150,000 gp
5th	9,000 gp	15th	200,000 gp
6th	13,000 gp	16th	260,000 gp
7th	19,000 gp	17th	340,000 gp
8th	27,000 gp	18th	440,000 gp
9th	36,000 gp	19th	580,000 gp
10th	49,000 gp	20th	760,000 gp
11th	66,000 gp		

might feel so unstoppable that she wantonly tosses around fireballs in the middle of town. While it's fine for PCs to enjoy their abilities as they advance in level (that's the whole point), they shouldn't be allowed to do whatever they wish. Even high-level characters shouldn't run about completely unchecked.

Players should always remember one fact: There's always someone more powerful. You should set up your world with the idea that the PCs, while special, are not unique. Other characters, many of them quite powerful, have come along before the PCs. Institutions of influence have had to deal with individuals of great power long before the PCs. The duke may have some powerful warrior or fighter on retainer as a champion for when someone gets out of line. The city constabulary probably has a *rod of negation* or a scroll of *antimagic field* to deal with out-of-control wizards. The point is that NPCs with resources will be prepared for great danger. The sooner the PCs realize this, the less likely they will run amok in your campaign world.

HANDLING NPCS

As you run your campaign, you need to portray all sorts of characters. Use the following tips for creating and controlling NPCs.

EVERYONE IN THE WORLD

It's your job to portray everyone in the world who isn't a player character. These creatures are all your characters. NPCs run the gamut from the old woman who operates the livery to the foul necromancer out to destroy the kingdom to the dragon in its lair, counting gold. The vast majority of folk don't care about the PCs unless the PCs have reached the point where they are saving the world. Even then, most people probably don't know about them.

Most people and creatures go about their own lives, oblivious to the actions of the PCs and the events in their adventures. Common people whom they meet in a town won't see them as being different from anyone else unless the PCs do something in particular to draw attention to themselves. In short, the rest of the world doesn't know that the PCs are in fact, player characters. It treats them no differently from anyone else, gives them no special breaks (or

special penalties), and gives them no special attention whatsoever. The PCs have to rely on their own actions. If they are wise and kind, they make friends and garner respect. If they are foolish or unruly, they make enemies and earn the enmity of all.

ENEMIES

Villains and enemies provide an outlet for play that is unique to being a DM. Running the foes of the PCs is one of your main tasks, and one of the most fun. When creating enemies for the PCs, keep the following points in mind:

Fully Rounded Characters: Flesh out enemies. Give a fair amount of thought to why NPCs are doing what they do, why they are where they are, and how they interact with all that's around them. Don't think of them as just bad guys for the PCs to kill, and the players won't either.

Intelligence: Play enemies as smart as they are—no more, no less. Ogres might not be the best strategists, but mind flayers are incredibly intelligent and always have schemes and contingency plans.

Don't Be Afraid to Make Them Evil: Evil is evil. Don't hesitate to make the villains truly evil. Betrayal, devious lies, and hideous acts all make them more rewarding to defeat.

Evil Is Not Everywhere: An NPC opponent doesn't have to be evil. Sometimes neutral and even good characters might oppose whatever the PCs are doing, since not all good people agree on everything. Sometimes it's interesting to face an opponent whom you don't want to just kill outright.

Monolithic Evil Is Unrealistic: Avoid monolithic evil. Even if all the PCs' foes are evil, that doesn't mean that they work together. In fact, evil rarely gets along with evil (particularly in the case of chaotic evil creatures), for the goals of one selfish, destructive creature by definition conflict with the goals of other selfish, destructive creatures.

The Prisoner Dilemma: What should the PCs do with enemy prisoners? If an NPC foe surrenders, the characters immediately face a quandary. Do they spare the lives of their evil foes, or put them to the sword? What's the greater wrong, killing something evil or letting it live to commit more evil acts? In some campaigns

---

BEHIND THE CURTAIN:
COOL WAYS TO BREAK THE RULES

As you create your own campaign, you want the characters to fit into that setting. While Chapter 2: Characters gives plenty of advice on creating new classes and races, you will find that your own campaign requires its own special tweaks. Accommodating the needs of your campaign might not mean changing classes or races, but you may need to bend or break the established rules now and again to allow a player to play the character she wants.

A few examples might include the following:

- Allowing a paladin to have a hippogriff mount or a wizard to have a pseudodragon familiar, instead of the usual animals designated for those duties.
- Allowing a player to create a character of one race raised by members of another race, so as to have a character with an amalgam of racial abilities (some from each race).
- Allowing a player to play a child of a wealthy family or even a member of the nobility and starting the character out with five or even ten times the normal starting money.
- Allowing a player to play a character with divine blood who has special powers that manifest after certain deeds or certain levels are achieved.
- Providing a special tattoo artist in a traveling caravan passing through town that can grant characters body designs that hold

magical powers. These tattoos would essentially be permanent magic items that can't be lost or stolen, take up no space, and weigh nothing, but cost twice the price of an item of similar power.
- Deciding that a character inherits a special magic item that's also a family heirloom.

Likewise, you might want to break a rule now and again for NPCs. Such rule-breaking touches include the following:

- Giving them unusual spells or giving their spells an unusual touch (cold balls instead of fireballs, or magic missiles that fly through the air in the form of gloves of energy to slap their target).
- Creating magic traps or special effects that can't be duplicated by existing spells or items, such as permanent antimagic zones, places where undead can't be turned, or places where time runs backward.
- Granting monsters special abilities, such as skeletons that tear off their own bones and use them as weapons, or that reassemble after being destroyed.
- Changing monster ecologies so that goblins are immature bugbears or dragons can change color.

These sorts of changes personalize your campaign without changing the game in any radical way.

or some locales in a campaign world, bounties are paid for living prisoners. The prisoners' friends can also offer ransoms to get them back alive. These two facts can help PCs decide what to do with prisoners, as can some indication from you through other allied NPCs as to what the accepted course of action is for the land the characters are adventuring in. Although you should play the NPCs as appropriately as you can, don't make the PCs face a prisoner dilemma unless you are sure you want to.

Villains

A diabolical sorcerer, an evil high priest, a master assassin, a lich, an ancient red dragon—the possibilities for intelligent villains are endless, and they make for some of the most memorable and hated foes. A well-played villain can become a recurring character who is a constant thorn in the side of the PCs. You can create a villain whom the players love to hate.

Here are some tips for well-played villains:

Use Lackeys: Don't have the villain confront the PCs herself unless you have to. Eventually, they will want to take the fight to her, but she should use underlings, cohorts, and summoned creatures to fight them for her whenever possible. But don't deny the PCs the satisfaction of eventually having the opportunity to defeat her.

Be Sneaky and Resourceful: Use all available options to foil the PCs. Don't forget to have a sneaky villain use *undetectable alignment* or *nondetection* to foil attempts to find him. *Detect scrying* spells or—even better—*screen* spells can keep scrying from revealing his actions. *Mind blank* foils *detect thoughts*, and *spell resistance* potentially foils most everything. The basic idea to keep in mind is that for every ability the PCs might have, an NPC villain can counter it with the right spell, item, or ability.

Have an Escape Plan: Once the PCs have confronted the villain and foiled his plans, it can be hard for him to get away without a plan that was prepared beforehand. PCs are notorious for dogging the heels of a villain who tries to escape. Use secret passages, *invisibility*, *dimension door*, *teleport*, *contingency*, and swarms of underlings to aid the villain's escape.

Take Hostages: Put the PCs in a moral dilemma. Are they willing to attack the villain if her servants are prepared to slay on her command a number of townsfolk she captured?

Use Magic: Even a high-level fighter or rogue should have a great deal of magic to fall back on, perhaps by means of spellcasting servants or magic items. The PCs have plenty of magic to bring to bear against the villain, so she should have a fair number of tricks and surprises for them as well.

Fight on the Villain's Terms: Don't fight on the PCs' terms. A smart villain fights the PCs only when he has to and only when he's prepared. Preferably, he engages them after they have fought their way through his guardian- and trap-filled lair and are weakened.

Animals and Beasts

Animals, vermin, beasts, and low-intelligence monsters comprise a special category of NPC. They don't act the way more intelligent creatures do. Instead, they are driven by instinct and need. Hunger and fear, for example, motivate animals. They are occasionally curious, but usually they are looking for food. When setting up encounters with animals and low-intelligence creatures, remember to develop some sort of ecology. A hundred orcs might all organize themselves together in one area, but a hundred displacer beasts never would unless an intelligent, outside force was compelling them to do so. In a dungeon, for example, predators need something to eat and probably would not lair to close to each other to avoid competition for food. The logical demands of ecologies can sometimes make dungeons difficult to rationalize or to design so that they are at least somewhat believable. An intelligent, organizing force often helps to explain the presence of creatures in amounts or locations that their natural inclinations would tend to counterindicate.

Animals and low-intelligence monsters want to eat, want to be safe, and want to protect their young. They are not thrilled about competition for food, but only the most belligerent attack for no other reason than that. They don't collect treasure, but the possessions of the characters they have slain can probably be found in their lairs, untouched by the beasts.

These creatures make great foes for PCs, since few moral issues are brought to bear by slaying a dire wolf or even an umber hulk or a wyvern. Thus, even though humans are a poor choice of prey for most animals in the real world, assume that most predators in the campaign don't mind or even prefer hunting and eating intelligent creatures, so as to provide opportunities for PCs to fight them.

FRIENDS

Not everyone hates the PCs. If the characters are smart, as the campaign progresses, they will make as many friends as enemies.

Allies

Markiov Thenuril is a rugged ranger who patrols the wilderness to the west. Ever since the PCs helped him fight off the gnoll incursion two years ago, he's been willing to provide them with information about his territory whenever they need it. He also introduced them to Viran Rainsong, an elven wizard/bard who gives them great deals on potions and scrolls that she manufactures. Viran's half-brother Ethin traveled with the PCs when they went to the Forgotten Mountain and the Lichlair.

Allies come in two types: those who help the PCs with information, equipment, or a place to stay the night, and those who actually travel with them on adventures. The former make useful contacts and resources. The latter function as party members and earn a full share of experience points and treasure just as any other character does. Essentially, these latter allies are adventurers who just happen not to be controlled by players. They differ from cohorts or hirelings who work directly for the PCs.

Cohorts

Cohorts are loyal servants who follow a particular character or sometimes a group of characters, (NPC adventurers can have cohorts, too.) They are hired by or seek out a PC or PCs, and they work out a deal agreeable to both parties so that the NPC works for the characters. A cohort serves as a general helper, a bodyguard, a sidekick, or just someone to watch a character's back. Although technically subservient, cohorts are usually too valuable to require them to perform menial tasks.

There are no limitations to the class, race, or gender of a character's cohorts, nor are there limits to the number of cohorts who can be employed by a character. Mistreated cohorts become disloyal and eventually leave or even seek revenge against their employers. Loyal cohorts become trusted friends and long-time helpers.

So, what's really the difference between allies who come along and use their abilities to face dangers alongside the PCs, and cohorts who do the same thing? Cohorts are people who take on a subservient role. Cohorts are followers, not leaders. They might voice an opinion now and again, but for the most part, they do as they're told. Because they're not making a lot of decisions or helping much on the strategic level, they get only a half share of experience. Although the PCs can work out their own deals with their cohorts, they usually get only a half share of the treasure, too. Sometimes a cohort is a fanatic follower who seeks no pay, only the opportunity to serve alongside the PCs. Such cohorts require only living costs as pay. However, such cohorts are not common.

The easiest way to calculate a half share is to treat the cohort as getting a full share, but award him or her only half, and then divide out the remainder to the group. For instance, if a party of four PCs and one cohort earns 1,000 XP, divide the XP by 5 (which is 200 apiece), but award the cohort only 100, and divide the leftover 100 among the four PCs (25 each).

If a cohort is well treated and loyal, you can even allow the player controlling the employer to play the cohort as a character alongside the player's regular character instead of your having to control the cohort on top of all your other duties. In such a case, the cohort usually becomes a clearly secondary character. Be forewarned that playing more than one character, even with one being secondary, is difficult. Not all players can do it well or enjoy it. One nice benefit of handling cohorts this way (and having them around at all) is if a PC with a cohort is killed or incapacitated, the player can control the cohort and still remain active in the current adventure.

Hirelings

When the PCs need to hire someone to perform a task—make items, speak with sages, care for their horses, or help build a castle, the NPCs they employ are called hirelings. Characters can use hirelings to carry torches, tote their treasure, and fight for them. Hirelings differ from cohorts in that they have no investment in what's going on. They just do their jobs.

Hirelings do not make decisions. They do as they're told (at least in theory). Thus, even if they go on an adventure with the PCs, they gain no experience and do not affect any calculations involving the average character level of the party. Like cohorts, hirelings must be treated fairly well or they will leave and might even turn against their former employers. Some hirelings might require hazard pay if placed in particularly dangerous situations. Hazard pay might be as high as double normal pay. In addition to demanding hazard pay, hirelings placed in great danger can be considered unfriendly on Table 5–3: Initial NPC Attitude and Table 5–4: Influencing NPC Attitude, but characters potentially can influence them to a better attitude and perhaps even talk them out of hazard pay.

Hirelings are helpful to have around, particularly for specific tasks. If the PCs wipe out a nest of wererats but have to leave treasure behind, they can hire porters to come back down with them into the lair to help carry out the goods. An animal tender or two to watch the PCs' horses while they're down in a dungeon can be useful. Mercenary warriors can provide vital additional strength to the party's ability to combat foes. Wealthy PCs might find that having their own armorer, sage, alchemist, or smith is very useful. Having a valet or a cook

"We don't serve your kind here."

along on an adventure is a luxury, but it's useful to employ someone of a similar nature who remains behind to watch over a PC's home while she's gone.

High-level PCs should be aware that taking a 1st-level commoner with them on an adventure so that she can carry equipment or fight as a mercenary probably places her at great risk. Hirelings who are expected to fight are best used to deal with foes of their level: goblin warriors, for instance, or an evil cleric's skeleton army.

Some hirelings characters might employ include the following:

Alchemist: One who works with chemicals. Also includes apothecaries (those who deal with drugs and medicines).

Animal Tender/Groom: Someone to care for animals. Also includes shepherds, shearers, and swineherds.

Architect/Engineer: A skilled, educated planner, essential for large building projects. Also includes shipwrights.

Barrister: A lawyer.

Clerk: A scribe specializing in accounting. Also includes translators and interpreters.

Cook: Someone who can prepare meals, often large ones.

Entertainer/Performer: A minstrel, actor, singer, dancer, or poet.

Laborer: Anyone performing unskilled or relatively unskilled labor. Includes ditch-diggers, gravediggers, bloomers (forge-workers), plowers, quarriers, and many other types.

Limner: A painter. Includes all types of artisans.

Maid: A household servant who cleans.

Mason/Craftsperson: A mason is a stoneworker, but this category also covers carpenters, tanners (leatherworkers), haberdashers, brewers, coopers, cordwainers (shoemakers), bookbinders, fletchers, fullers (feltmakers), bowyers, cobblers, drapers, joiners, parchmentmakers, plasterers, chandlers (candlemakers), dyers, skinners, soapmakers, jewelers, tinkers, vintners, weavers, gemcutters, wheelwrights, cartwrights, horners, mercers, hosiers, and so on.

Mercenary: A 1st-level warrior.

Mercenary Horseman: A 1st-level warrior who can ride and fight on horseback.

Mercenary Leader: A 2nd-level warrior. If higher level than 2nd, add 3 sp per day per level more than is shown on Table 5–2: Price for Hireling Services.

Porter: Someone who carries heavy loads.

Sage: A researcher, a scholar, or a wise, educated person who provides information. You should assign a time period required to research the answer to a question that ranges in length from 1 day to a month or more. More renowned sages demand higher fees, particularly for difficult areas of research.

Scribe: Someone who can write. Also includes scriveners (manuscript copiers).

Smith: A metalworker. Includes blacksmiths, goldsmiths, silversmiths, coppersmiths, pewterers, minters (coinmakers), latoners (bronzeworkers), braziers (brassworkers), locksmiths, weaponsmiths, and armorers.

Teamster: Cart or wagon driver.

Valet/Lackey: A general servant required to perform many and varied duties.

TABLE 5–2: PRICES FOR HIRELING SERVICES

Hireling	Per Day	Hireling	Per Day
Alchemist	1 gp*	Mason/craftsman	3 sp*
Animal tender/groom	15 cp	Mercenary	2 sp
Architect/engineer	5 sp	Mercenary horseman	4 sp
Barrister	1 gp	Mercenary leader	6 sp
Clerk	4 sp	Porter	1 sp
Cook	1 sp	Sage	2 gp+
Entertainer/performer	4 sp	Scribe	3 sp
Laborer	1 sp	Smith	4 sp*
Limner	6 sp	Teamster	3 sp
Maid	1 sp	Valet/lackey	2 sp

*If paid to create a specific item, use item prices and working times instead. Price listed is for long-term retention of services. Prices do not include materials, tools, or weapons.

NPC SPELLCASTING

Characters need healing. They need curses removed. They need to be teleported. They need to be raised from the dead. At various points during the campaign, the PCs will need to find NPCs to cast spells for them, either because they don't want to do it themselves or, more often, because a particular spell is beyond them. Refer to page 139 in Chapter 4: Adventures for information on the highest-level spellcaster available in a given community.

- Assuming that the PCs can find a caster of the needed level and that she's amenable to helping them out, the NPC charges them 10 gp per spell level multiplied by her own level (or 5 gp multiplied by her own level for a 0-level spell). If she's a cleric, she might require the amount as a donation to her faith. If she's a wizard, she might call the price a magical research fee. Whatever the case, the higher the caster level, the more she can charge for spells.
- If a spell has an expensive material component, the NPC makes her client pay for those expenses in addition to the base cost.
- Further, if the spell requires a focus component (other than a divine focus), the NPC makes her client pay 10% of the cost of the focus.
- Finally, if the spell has an experience point cost, the NPC charges an additional 5 gp for each experience point lost.

NPC ATTITUDES

In general, you run an NPC just as a player would run a PC: You take whatever actions the character would take, assuming the action is possible. That's why it's important to determine an NPC's general outlook and characteristics ahead of time if possible, so you know how to play the character properly.

When a PC is dealing with NPCs, you determine the NPCs' attitude, and a character may try to use Charisma to influence this attitude as described below.

Choose the attitude of an NPC or NPCs based on circumstances. Most people met in a neutral city are indifferent. Most guards are indifferent but suspicious, because that's what's expected of them.

Charisma Checks to Alter Attitude: It is possible to alter another's attitude with a Charisma check (1d20 + Charisma modifier). Roll the check and consult the appropriate initial attitude line on Table 5–4: Influencing NPC Attitude to see what the result of the roll is. For instance, an NPC who is initially unfriendly has his

TABLE 5–3: INITIAL NPC ATTITUDE

Attitude	Means	Possible Actions
Hostile	Will take risks to hurt you.	Attack, interfere, berate, flee.
Unfriendly	Wishes you ill.	Mislead, gossip, avoid, watch suspiciously, insult.
Indifferent	Doesn't much care.	Socially expected interaction.
Friendly	Wishes you well.	Chat, advise, offer limited help, advocate.
Helpful	Will take risks to help you.	Protect, back up, heal, aid.

attitude improved to indifferent if the PC's Charisma check result is 15 or higher—and on a check result of 25, the NPC's attitude would improve all the way to friendly.

As the table illustrates, the more friendly that someone is initially toward the PCs, the easier it is to improve that NPC's attitude. It doesn't take a roll, just the right words and deeds, to turn someone more hostile. Note that a low result on the Charisma check can make an NPC less favorably inclined toward a character. In general, a character cannot repeat attempts to influence someone.

NPC Charisma Checks to Alter Other NPCs' Attitudes: Note also that should it come up, an NPC can use a Charisma check to influence another NPC. However, NPCs can never use a Charisma check to influence PC attitudes. The players always decide their characters' attitudes.

TABLE 5–4: INFLUENCING NPC ATTITUDE

Initial Attitude	New Attitude				
	Hostile	Unfriendly	Indifferent	Friendly	Helpful
Hostile	Less than 20	20	25	35	50
Unfriendly	Less than 5	5	15	25	40
Indifferent	—	Less than 1	1	15	30
Friendly	—	—	Less than 1	1	20

FLESHING OUT NPCS

An NPC with a hacking cough and strong opinions about the king is always more interesting than one you portray only as Kiale, the 2nd-level commoner. Remember that NPCs aren't just game statistics, they are individuals with personalities, quirks, and opinions. You should strive to make many of the NPCs you use in your game memorable characters whom the PCs will either like or dislike depending on how you play them. (Sometimes an NPC is not memorable or just leaves the characters flat. That's okay; not everyone is memorable in real life, either.)

This doesn't mean that you need to write every NPC's life story beforehand. As a rule of thumb, give an NPC one or two distinctive traits. Think of these traits as what the characters will remember the NPC by. ("Let's go back and see that guy with the bad breath. He seemed to know what he was talking about, even if talking to him was unpleasant.")

Don't feel you need to make every NPC a caricature based on his or her traits. Instead, just use them as much as needed to make the NPC a memorable character.

Table 5–5: One Hundred Traits (page 150) lists traits that you can choose from when creating NPCs (or you can roll them randomly from the list if you desire). This table is only the beginning. Many more traits could be added to the list. None of the ones listed here have any effect on ability scores, skills, or game mechanics of any kind. Some may seem to interact with game statistics (such as strong body odor and Charisma). In such a case, don't modify the Charisma score, but play the NPC so that the trait fits. For example, a character with body odor and a medium or high Charisma score is particularly charismatic to overcome the trait. A lawful good character with the cruel trait has no patience or compassion for evil. A character with a high Dexterity score that has the trait of walking with a limp is agile and sprightly despite the drawback.

You can also use game statistics to create traits. If a character has a low Constitution score, he tires easily, so he might be overweight. If a character is highly intelligent, he might be quick with a joke or a snappy comeback. If a character has a lot of physical skills and feats, she's probably athletic and muscular. Alignments also lend themselves to distinctive traits, such as altruism, sadism, or a love for freedom.

EXPANDED EQUIPMENT LIST

Over the course of the campaign, prices for items and services not found in the *Player's Handbook* may be required. The items found below are particularly expensive or not common enough to be included in the *Player's Handbook* lists. Use them when needed in the campaign, or use them to extrapolate items not found on any list in either book.

SHIPS

Characters may own ships as traders, ship captains, or smugglers, or they may simply need to travel on them.

Rowboat: An 8- to 12-foot-long boat for two or three people. It moves about 1-1/2 miles per hour.

Galley: A three-masted ship with seventy oars on either side and a total crew of two hundred. This ship is 130 feet long and 20 feet wide, and it can carry up to 150 tons of cargo or 250 soldiers. For 8,000 gp more, it can be fitted with a ram and castles with firing platforms fore, aft, and amidships. This ship cannot make sea voyages and sticks to the coast. It moves about 4 miles per hour when being rowed or under sail.

Longship: A 75-foot-long ship with forty oars and a total crew of fifty. It has a single mast and a square sail. It can carry fifty tons of cargo or one hundred twenty soldiers. A longship can make sea voyages. It moves about 3 miles per hour when being rowed or under sail.

Keelboat: A 50- to 75-foot-long ship that is 15 to 20 feet wide and has a few oars to supplement its single mast with a square sail. It has a crew of eight to fifteen and can carry forty to fifty tons of cargo or one hundred soldiers. It can make sea voyages as well as sail down rivers. (It has a flat bottom.) It moves about 1 mile per hour.

Sailing Ship: This larger, more seaworthy version of the coaster (a kind of sailing ship) is 75 to 90 feet long and 20 feet wide. It has a crew of twenty. It can carry cargo up to 150 tons. It has square sails on its two masts and can make sea voyages. It moves about 2 miles per hour.

Warship: This 100-foot-long ship has a single mast, although oars can also propel it. It has a crew of sixty to eighty rowers. This ship can carry up to 160 soldiers, but not for long distances, since there isn't room for supplies for that many. The warship cannot make sea voyages and sticks to the coast. It is not used for cargo. It moves about 2 1/2 miles per hour when rowed or under sail.

TRANSPORTATION

The most common methods to get from one place to another in a campaign are by foot or on horseback. But other methods may be more expedient.

Ship's Passage: Most ships do not specialize in passengers, but many have the capability to take a few along when transporting cargo.

TABLE 5–5: ONE HUNDRED TRAITS

d%	Trait	d%	Trait	d%	Trait
01	Distinctive scar	37	Flips a coin	69	Loquacious
02	Missing tooth	38	Fiddles and fidgets nervously	70	Friendly
03	Missing finger	39	Nervous eye twitch	71	Overbearing
04	Bad breath	40	Passionate hobbyist (fishing, hunting, gaming, animals, etc.)	72	Aloof
05	Strong body odor			73	Proud
06	Pleasant smelling (perfumed)	41	Collector (books, trophies, coins, weapons, etc.)	74	Individualist
07	Sweaty			75	Conformist
08	Hands shake	42	Wears flamboyant or outlandish clothes	76	Hot tempered
09	Strange eyes			77	Even tempered
10	Hacking cough	43	Distinctive jewelry	78	Easy going
11	Nearsighted	44	Skinflint	79	Jealous
12	Particularly low voice	45	Spendthrift	80	Brave
13	Particularly high voice	46	Pessimist	81	Cowardly
14	Slurs words	47	Optimist	82	Uncommitted
15	Lisps	48	Drunkard	83	Fanatic
16	Stutters	49	Teetotaler	84	Truthful
17	Enunciates very clearly	50	Forgiving	85	Liar
18	Hard of hearing	51	Well mannered	86	Lazy
19	Distinctive nose	52	Rude	87	Energetic
20	Birthmark	53	Doesn't like to be touched	88	Reverent or pious
21	Tattoo	54	Jumpy	89	Irreverent or irreligious
22	Stooped back	55	Suspicious	90	Strong opinions on politics
23	Walks with a limp	56	Trusting	91	Strong opinions on morals
24	Bald	57	Dirty and unkempt	92	Strong opinions on culture
25	Particularly long hair	58	Clean	93	Uses flowery speech or long words
27	Disloyal spouse/parent	59	Foppish	94	Uses the same phrases over and over
28	Gambler	60	Neurotic		
29	Passionate artist or art lover	61	Helpful	95	Sexist, racist, or otherwise prejudiced
30	Overly critical	62	Careless		
31	Not very observant	63	Capricious	96	Fascinated by magic
32	Observant	64	Sober	97	Distrustful of magic
33	Bookish	65	Curious	98	Prefers members of one class over all others
34	Very physical	66	Moody		
35	Whistles a lot	67	Cruel	99	Jokester
36	Sings a lot	68	Obsequious	100	No sense of humor

Keelboat

Warship

Longship

Rowboat

Sailing Ship

Galley

Illus. by W Reynolds

Coach Cab: The price listed is for a ride in a coach that transports people (and light cargo) between towns. For a ride in a cab that transports passengers within a city, 1 cp usually takes you anywhere you need to go.

Messenger: This entry includes horse-riding messengers and runners. Those willing to carry a message to a place they were going anyway (a crew member on a ship, for example) may ask for half the listed amount.

Teleportation: The cost to be teleported is based on caster level (see NPC Spellcasting, page 149), although the customer will have to pay double because the caster will need to teleport herself back. Further, some casters will charge as much as double to teleport into a dangerous area.

Road or Gate Toll: A toll is sometimes charged to cross a well-trodden, well-kept, and well-guarded road to pay for patrols on it and its upkeep. Occasionally, large, walled cities charge a toll to enter or exit the city (sometimes just to enter the city).

TABLE 5–6: ADDITIONAL GOODS AND SERVICES

Ships

Item	Cost
Rowboat	50 gp
Oar	2 gp
Galley	30,000 gp
Longship	10,000 gp
Keelboat	3,000 gp
Sailing ship	10,000 gp
Warship	25,000 gp

Transportation

Item	Cost
Ship's passage	1 sp per mile
Coach cab	3 cp per mile
Messenger	2 cp per mile
Teleportation	Varies*
Road or gate toll	1 cp

*See "NPC Spellcasting," above.

Buildings

Item	Cost
Simple house	1,000 gp
Grand house	5,000 gp
Mansion	100,000 gp
Tower	50,000 gp
Keep	150,000 gp
Castle	500,000 gp
Huge castle	1,000,000 gp
Moat with bridge	50,000 gp

Siege Engines

Item	Cost	Damage	Critical	Range Increment	Crew
Catapult, heavy	800 gp	5d6	—	200 ft.	5
				(100 ft. minimum)	
Catapult, light	550 gp	3d6	—	150 ft.	2
				(100 ft. minimum)	
Ballista	500 gp	3d6	×3	120	1
Ram	2,000 gp	4d6	×3	—	10
Siege tower	1,000 gp				

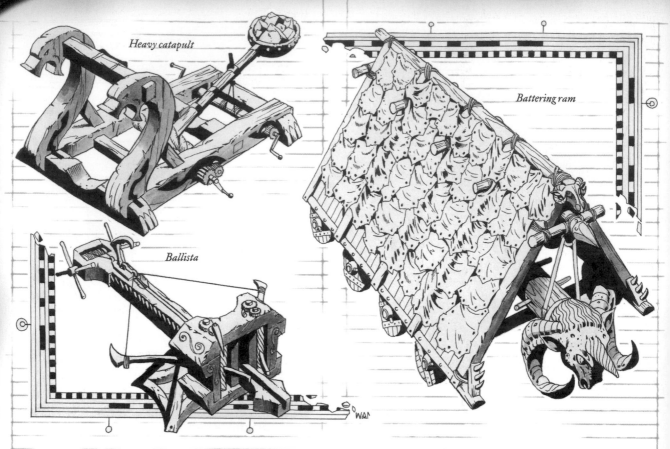

Heavy catapult

Battering ram

Ballista

BUILDINGS

These buildings and structures provide a baseline for those of their type. Heavily customized structures will doubtlessly cost more.

Simple House: This one- to three-room house is made of wood and has a thatched roof.

Grand House: This four- to ten-room room grand house is made of wood and has a thatched roof.

Mansion: This ten- to twenty-room mansion has two to three levels and is made of wood and brick. It has a slate roof.

Tower: This round or square, three-level tower is made of stone.

Keep: This fortified stone building has fifteen to twenty-five rooms.

Castle: The castle is a keep surrounded by a 15-foot stone wall with four towers. The wall is 10-feet thick.

Huge Castle: A particularly large keep with numerous associated buildings (stables, forge, granaries, etc.) and an elaborate 20-foot-high wall creating bailey and courtyard areas. The wall has six towers and is 10 feet thick.

Moat with Bridge: This moat is 15 feet deep and 30 feet wide. The bridge across it may be a wooden drawbridge or a permanent stone structure.

SIEGE ENGINES

Siege engines are large weapons, temporary structures, or pieces of equipment traditionally used in besieging a castle or fortress.

Catapult, Heavy: A heavy catapult is a large engine capable of throwing rocks or heavy objects with great force. When fired, one of the crew makes a Profession (siege engineer) check (DC 20). If successful, where the object actually lands is determined by rolling 1d12 and consulting the Deviation (10 Ft. to 16 Ft.) Diagram (found in Chapter 3: Running the Game). The center is the desired target. If the check is failed, the DM secretly rolls and consults the same deviation diagram. The result is now where the catapult is actually aimed. This new result is used as the center to determine the actual deviation of the attack. For example, a catapult is used to

attack a stone tower. The Profession (siege engineer) check fails, the DM rolls an 11. By consulting the diagram, she determines that the actual target is 10 feet from the desired target, behind and to the left. Now, a crew member rolls 1d12 and gets an 8. After consulting the Deviation (10 Ft. to 16 Ft.) Diagram to see where the object goes, the DM ascertains that it falls 10 feet short and to the left of the actual target, which is 20 feet to the left of the desired target.

Loading the catapult and preparing it to fire takes the full crew 8 full rounds. Initially aiming (or reaiming) takes 10 minutes in addition to loading and preparation time. Three to four crew members can operate the device in three times this time. Fewer than three crew members cannot operate the device.

Catapult, Light: This is a smaller, lighter version of the heavy catapult (see that entry for how to operate it). Two crew members can load and prepare this device in 5 full rounds and aim (or reaim) in 5 minutes. One person can crew the engine, but it takes three times the time to aim and prepare.

Ballista: The ballista is essentially a very large crossbow. It makes attacks with a straight attack roll (1d20) with no modifications (no character base attack bonuses, ability modifiers, etc.) except for range. Loading and cocking a ballista is 3 full-round actions.

Ram: This heavy pole is suspended from a movable scaffold that allows the crew to swing it back and forth against construction. Make an unmodified attack roll against the AC of the construction, with failed attempts dealing no significant damage. (See Strike an Object, page 135 in the *Player's Handbook*, to determine the AC.) The ram can be used to make an attack every 3 rounds if fully crewed. With five to nine people, it can be used every 6 rounds. Fewer than five people cannot operate it.

Siege Tower: This is a large wooden tower on wheels or rollers that can be rolled up against a wall to allow attackers to scale the tower and thus to get to the top of the wall with cover. The wooden walls are usually 1 foot thick.

The D&D game draws examples and source material from the GREYHAWK setting, a fictional world available for your use as a basis for your campaign. However, you may wish to build your own world. It's a challenging and rewarding task, but be aware that it can also be a time-consuming one.

CREATION METHODOLOGY

Once you have decided to create your own world, you face a number of choices. Do you make it like the real world, drawing from history and real-world knowledge, or do you create something completely different? Do you draw from your favorite fictional setting or create it all on your own? Do the laws of physics work as we know them, or is the world flat with a dome of stars overhead? Do you use the standard races, classes, and equipment in the *Player's Handbook*, or do you create new ones? The questions alone are daunting, but for those who love world-building, they are also exciting.

So where do you start? There are two approaches to creating a campaign world:

Inside Out: Start with a small area and build outward. Don't even worry about what the world looks like, or even the kingdom. Concentrate first on a single village or town, preferably with a dungeon or other adventure site nearby. Expand slowly and only as needed. When the PCs are ready to leave the initial area (which might not be for ten or more playing sessions, depending on your first adventures), expand outward in all directions so you're ready no matter which way they go. Eventually, you will have an entire kingdom developed, with the whole derived from what would fit with the initial starting point. Proceed to other neighboring lands, determining the political situations. Keep accurate notes as you play, for you may develop rumors of hostilities with a neighboring kingdom before you ever develop the kingdom itself!

The advantage to this method is that you don't need to do a lot of work to get started. Whip up a small area—probably with a small community—design an adventure, and go. This method also ensures that you won't develop areas of the campaign that are never visited by the PCs and that you can develop things (and change your mind) as you go.

Outside In: Start with the big picture—draw a map of an entire continent or a portion thereof. Alternatively, you could start with a grand design for how a number of kingdoms and nations interact or the outline of a vast empire. You could even start with a cosmology, deciding how the deities interact with the world, where the world is positioned in relation with other worlds, and what the world as a whole looks like. Only after you have this level of concept design worked out should you focus on a particular area. When you begin more detailed work, start with large-scale basics and work down to small-scale details. For example, after you have constructed your continent map, pick a single kingdom and create the ruler or rulers and the general conditions. From there, focus on some substate or region within the kingdom, develop who and what lives there (and why), and pepper the region with a few hooks and secrets for later development. Finally, once you get down to the small scale—a single community, a particular patch of forest or valley, or wherever you choose to start the campaign—develop the area in great detail. The specifics of the small area should reflect and tie back to the basics you have set up for the larger areas.

This method ensures that once you have started the campaign, you're already well on your way to having a complete setting. When things are moving along quickly in the campaign, you can focus on the characters and individual adventures, because the world is mostly done. This method also allows you to use foreshadowing of larger events, faraway places, and grander adventures early on in the campaign.

GEOGRAPHY

Campaigns need worlds. Worlds have geography. This means that when creating your world you need to place the mountains, the oceans, the rivers, the towns, the secret fortresses, the haunted forests, the enchanted places, and all the other locales and features.

If you want a realistic world, use encyclopedias and atlases to learn more about topography, climate, and geography (natural and political). You only need the basics to create a fantasy world, unless you or your players are sticklers for accuracy. Research and learn as much as you need to create a world that will please your players. In general, however, if you know a little about how terrain affects climate, how different types of terrain interact (mountains usually follow coastlines, for example), and how both climate and terrain determine where people usually live, that should be enough.

When you're done, you can create the map or maps you need for your campaign.

CLIMATE/TERRAIN TYPES

There are eleven different climate and terrain types that you need to be concerned with in the D&D game, although you could create additional types for your own world. These eleven types are those referenced in monster descriptions in the *Monster Manual* and in the wilderness encounter charts found in Chapter 4: Adventures.

You should assign each region of your world a climate/terrain type to designate what sort of landscape it has, what seasons and weather conditions prevail there, and what creatures inhabit the area.

Some of these types are incompatible. For example, without some sort of magical event, you won't find a tropical rain forest (a warm climate zone) next to an arctic plain (a cold climate zone). Some terrain types are much more habitable to the common races from which PCs are derived than others, although all have monsters, animals, and intelligent creatures native to them.

Cold: This climate type describes arctic and subarctic areas. Any area that has winter conditions for a larger portion of the year than any other seasonal variation is cold. See Cold Dangers, page 86.

Temperate: This climate type describes areas that have alternating warm and cold seasons of approximately equal length.

Warm: This climate type describes tropical and subtropical areas. Any area that has summer conditions for a larger portion of the year than any other seasonal variation is warm.

Aquatic: This terrain type is composed of fresh or salt water. See Water Dangers, page 85.

Desert: This terrain type describes any dry area with sparse vegetation. See Heat Dangers, page 86.

Plains: Any fairly flat area that is not a desert, marsh, or forest is considered plains.

Forest: Any area covered with trees is forest terrain.

Hill: Any area with rugged but not mountainous terrain is hill.

Mountains: Rugged terrain that is higher in elevation than hills is considered mountains.

Marsh: Low, flat, waterlogged areas are marsh terrain.

Underground: Subterranean areas are designated as underground terrain. See The Dungeon, page 105.

ECOLOGY

Once you have determined the lay of the land, you can develop what lives where.

The *Monster Manual* gives a climate/terrain type for each kind of creature. With that information to work with, decide exactly which creatures live where within each region of your world. If you have room on your map to mark such information, do so. It will help you keep track of things later on, both when determining random encounters and when developing adventure plots. For example, if you know that the PCs are on their way to the village of Thorris, you can see that living in the swamps around are trolls, harpies, and a black dragon that the travelers might encounter. You can also use this information to create an adventure involving Thorris and the black dragon in which the dragon coerces the trolls to attack the people living there.

Considering the ecology issues of the swamp helps you explain the creatures' existences. What do the trolls eat? What about the harpies? They must compete for resources, so do they avoid each other, or do they fight? The world is a predator-heavy one, based on the creatures described in the *Monster Manual*. Designing your world's ecology means coming up with a way to make sense of how it all works together. Perhaps there's bountiful prey in most areas that an overall abundance of vibrant, energy-rich plant life might help explain. Perhaps the predators prey upon each other. You don't have to design a complete food chain, but giving a moment's thought to some ecology issues will help you answer player questions later—and that will help make your world seem real to them.

BEHIND THE CURTAIN:
HOW REAL IS YOUR FANTASY?

This chapter assumes that your campaign is set in a fairly realistic world. That is to say that while wizards cast spells, deities channel power to clerics, and dragons raze villages, the world is round, the laws of physics are applicable, and most people act like real people. The reason for this assumption is that unless it's explained to them to be otherwise, this situation is what your players expect.

That said, you could create a world that is very different from even these basic premises. Your campaign could be set within a hollow world, on a flat world, or on the inside of a tube that spins around the sun.

You could change the laws of physics to produce a world with objects or materials so light that they float, areas where time flows at a different rate, or the very real threat that the ocean might wash seafarers off the side of the world so that they fall forever in an eternal waterfall. One point to keep in mind if you're going to change premises that we all take for granted, however, is that you should try to maintain some consistency. If time passes more slowly as you move away from the central Mountain of the Earth's Heart, then this fact should always be true. Further, the people of the world should understand and accept this reality. If that's the way the world works, it wouldn't seem odd to them.

You could establish a land where people are so truly good that no government or organization is needed to maintain order or peace. Or, you could create a land where everyone is born evil, the scions of an evil progenitor god, and they all work together for the downfall of goodness. Such people are not realistic, but they're certainly interesting.

DEMOGRAPHICS

Once the geography is determined, you can populate your world. This step is more important than monster placement and general ecology, not only because the PCs will spend more time in civilized areas, but also because the players have real-world experiences to measure their game experiences against when they're among other people.

People, in general, live in the most convenient places possible. They try to place their communities near sources of water and food, in comfortable climates, and close to sources of transportation (seas, rivers, flat land to build roads on, and so on). Of course, there are always exceptions, such as towns in the desert, isolated communities in the mountains, and secret cities in the middle of the swamp or at the top of a mesa. But there is also always a reason for those exceptions: The city at the top of the mesa is placed there for defense, and the isolated community in the mountains exists because the people there want to cut themselves off from the rest of the world.

TABLE 6–1: COMMUNITY SIZES

Community	Population
Thorp	20–80
Hamlet	81–400
Village	401–900
Small town	901–2,000
Large town	2,001–5,000
Small city	5,001–12,000
Large city	12,001–25,000
Metropolis	25,001+

Table 6–1: Community Sizes shows a breakdown of different city sizes (refer to Chapter 4: Adventures for more information on typical inhabitants of various sizes and types of communities). Small communities are much more common than larger ones. In general, the number of people living in small towns and larger communities should be about 1/10 to 1/15 the number living in villages, hamlets, thorps, or outside a community at all. You might create a metropolis at the civilized center of the world with 100,000 people, but such a community should be the exception, not the rule. The more closely a city matches the ideal parameters of a city location (near food and water, in a comfortable climate, close to sources of transportation), the larger it can become. A secret city in the swamp might exist, but it's unlikely to be a metropolis. People living in cities need food, so if there are not nearby sources of food (farms, plenty of wild animals, herds of livestock, etc.), the community needs efficient transportation sources to ship food in. Further, it needs some other renewable resource, such as nearby forests to harvest for timber or minerals to mine, to produce something to exchange for the imported food.

Small, agricultural-based communities are likely to surround a larger city and help to supply the city population with food. In such cases, the larger community is probably a source of defense (a walled town, a castle, a community fielding a large number of deployable troops) that inhabitants of surrounding communities can seek refuge in or rely on to defend them in times of need.

Sometimes, a number of nearby small communities clump together with no large community at the center. The small villages and hamlets form a support network, and the local lord often boasts a centrally located castle or fortress used as a defensible place to which the villagers can flee when threatened.

On a larger scale, the borders of kingdoms and countries usually coincide with physical, geographical barriers. Countries that draw boundaries through plains, farms, and undulating hills usually fight a lot of battles over such borders and have to redraw the borders frequently until they coincide with natural barriers. Therefore, mountain ranges, rivers, or abrupt landscape changes should mark the edges of the lands in your world.

ECONOMICS

Although treasure is what's important to PCs, you should have a fair grasp of the economic system that surrounds the treasure that they earn as well as the prices charged for services, equipment, and magic items. Economics in your campaign doesn't have to be convoluted or tedious, but it should at least be internally consistent. If the price of a broadsword in Thorris is 20 gp one day, it shouldn't be 200 gp the next without some explanation, such as the flow of metal or ore being suddenly cut off, the only smiths in a hundred miles having all been killed in a terrible accident, or something equally bizarre.

COINAGE

The economic system in the D&D game is based on the silver piece (sp). A common laborer earns 1 sp a day. That's just enough to allow his family to survive, assuming that this income is supplemented with food his family grows to eat, homemade clothing, and a reliance on self-sufficiency for most tasks (personal grooming, health, animal tending, and so on).

In your campaign, however, the PCs will deal primarily with gold pieces. The gold piece (gp) is a larger, more substantial unit of currency. That PCs mainly interact with the economy in gold pieces represents the fact that they, as adventurers, take much larger risks than common folk and thus earn much larger rewards if they survive.

Many of the people with whom adventurers interact also deal primarily in gold. Weaponsmiths, armorsmiths, and spellcasters all make more money (sometimes far more money) than common people. Spellcasters willing to make magic items or cast spells for hire can make a lot of money, although there are often expenditures of personal power (experience points) involved, and the demand for such expensive items is unsteady at best and can only be depended on in large cities. Nobles with whom the PCs might interact also deal mostly in gold, since they purchase whole ships and buildings and finance caravans and even armies using such currency.

Some economies have other forms of currency, such as trade bars or letters of credit representing various amount of gold that are backed by powerful governments, guilds, or other organizations to insure their worth. Some economies even use coins of different metals: electrum, iron, or even tin. In some lands, it's even permissible to cut a gold coin in half to make a separate unit of currency out of a half gold piece.

TAXES AND TITHES

Taxes paid to the queen, the emperor, or the local baroness might consume as much as one-fifth of a character's wealth (although these expenses can vary considerably from land to land). Well-guarded representatives of the government usually collect taxes yearly, biannually, or quarterly. Of course, as travelers, adventurers might avoid most collection periods (and so you can ignore taxes for the PCs if you want). Those who own land or a residence may find themselves assessed and taxed, however.

Tithes are paid to the church by those who are faithful participants in a religion. Tithes often amount to as much as one-tenth of a character's adventuring earnings, but collection is voluntary except in strict, oppressive religions that have their own tithe collectors. Such onerous religious taxation requires the support of the government.

MONEYCHANGERS

Characters who find their saddlebags full of ancient coin or foreign money probably need to exchange their wealth for the local currency before they can spend any of it. In a setting in which dozens of small nations and kingdoms are crowded close together, the moneychanger is the person at the hub of the economic system. Typically, a moneychanger charges a fee of one-tenth of the starting sum in order to convert currency. For example, if a character has a pouch full of 100 platinum pieces (pp) that she needs to convert to the local gold standard, the moneychanger charges 10 pp for the conversion. The character receives 900 gp, and the moneychanger keeps the rest.

SUPPLY AND DEMAND

The law of supply and demand can drastically affect the value of any currency. If characters start flashing around a lot of gold and pumping it into the local economy, merchants may quickly raise prices. This isn't a matter of gouging the rich—it's just the way a small economy works. A tavernkeeper who makes 100 gp from boarding a group of successful adventurers spends his newfound wealth just as the heroes did, and in a small town, *everyone* starts spending more in a short time. More spending means higher consumption, so goods and services become harder to come by, and prices increase.

Supply and demand can also affect the campaign in ways that don't have anything directly to do with gold. For instance, if the local lord commandeered most of the region's horses for his knights, then when the PCs decide to purchase half a dozen fine steeds, they find that there just aren't any to be had at any reasonable price. They have to settle for second-rate nags or spend much more than they had planned to in order to convince someone to part with a horse.

POLITICS

Intrigue between kingdoms, city-states at war, and political maneuvering are all fun aspects of many campaigns. For your own campaign, you at least need to determine who is in charge where. If there's any chance that rulers, nobility, and politics in general will become more involved than that, use the following material as a starting point. As always, research into real-world political systems and structures (particularly historical examples) can enrich your fictional setting. At the same time, don't be afraid to make up something wholly new and completely unhistorical.

POLITICAL SYSTEMS

The number of political systems possible is legion. Feel free to use more than one type for different lands. Such mixing and matching accentuates the differences in place and culture.

Note that any of the political systems listed below might be matriarchies (ruled only by women) or patriarchies (ruled only by men), but most make no such distinctions.

Monarchy

Monarchy is rule by a single leader. The monarch wields supreme power, sometimes even by divine right. Monarchs belong to royal bloodlines, and successors to the throne are almost always drawn from blood relatives. Rarely, a monarch rules with power granted by a mandate of the populace, usually established through representatives chosen by noble houses. The monarchy is likely to be the most common political system in your campaign.

Monarchs often have advisors and a court of nobles who work with them to administer the land. This arrangement creates a class system of nobles and nonnobles. Common people in such a land often do not have many of the rights and privileges of the nobility.

Tribal or Clan Structure

A tribe or clan usually has a single leader who wields great—almost absolute—power like the monarch in a monarchy. Although rulership is often drawn from a single bloodline, rulers are chosen based on their fitness to govern. They are also continually judged on this criterion and replaced if found wanting. Usually a council of elders exists to choose and judge the leader. In fact, it is often convened only for this purpose. Sometimes the council also advises the chief or leader.

Tribes exist as a social structure by grouping together otherwise disparate family units and uniting them for strength and the advantages of working together. Clans are similar in function but carry the added distinction of being extended family units. In both cases,

the group usually interacts with other tribes and clans, and often has particular laws and customs about how certain clans within a tribe must interact or how the tribe must interact with other tribes.

Feudalism

Feudalism is a complicated class-based system with successive layers of lieges and lackeys. It often exists under a monarchy. Serfs (peasants) work for a landed lord, who in turn owes fealty to a higher lord, who in turn owes fealty to an even higher lord, and so on, until the line reaches the supreme liege lord, who is usually a monarch.

The common people in a feudal state are always lowly and without rights. They are virtually owned by their immediate liege. Lords are generally free to abuse their power and exploit those under them as they see fit.

Republic

A republic is a system of government headed by politicians representing the people. The representatives of a republic rule as a single body, usually some sort of council or senate, which votes on issues and policies. Sometimes the representatives are appointed, and sometimes they are elected. The welfare of the people depends solely on the level of corruption among the representatives. In a mainly good-aligned republic, conditions can be quite good. An evil republic is as terrible a place to live as a land under the grip of a tyrant.

In an advanced republic, the people directly elect the representatives. This type of republic is often called a democracy. In such lands, the right to vote becomes a class-based privilege. Citizenship might be a status that can be bought or earned, it might be granted automatically through being born in the location governed by the republic, or it might only transfer via bloodline. Because having the entire populace vote on representatives is cumbersome, this political system usually works only in small areas, such as a city-state.

Magocracy

Magocracy is rule by mages. The ruler is usually the most powerful wizard or sorcerer in the land, although sometimes the ruler is merely a member of a royal bloodline who must be an arcane spellcaster. Thus, such a system could be a monarchy, and the viable heir to the throne would be the oldest member of the bloodline capable of casting spells. In a true magocracy in which the ruler is the most powerful spellcaster, the monarch may be challenged at certain specific times each year by contenders who believe themselves to be more powerful than she is.

In a magocracy, arcane spellcasters usually have the greatest rights and freedoms, and nonspellcasters are looked down upon. Divine spellcasters sometimes are outlawed, but usually they are treated as secondary to arcane spellcasters (although still higher in station than those who cast no spells).

Such societies are probably magic-rich. They are likely to have colleges that teach the intricacies of spellcasting, and magic-using units in their military organizations. They may use magic for even mundane tasks. Very rarely, a magocracy treats magic in the opposite way, as a closely guarded secret. Nonnoble arcane spellcasters would then be forbidden.

Theocracy

A theocracy is a political system in which clerics (or druids) rule. The ruler is the direct representative of the deity or deities that the theocracy is based upon. Most are similar to monarchies, but once a ruler is chosen, he normally remains in the position for life. The people cannot question the word of a deity or his representative.

Some theocracies see their leaders as ascending to divinity or semidivinity in and of themselves. Past (and sometimes present) rulers are worshiped as deities. Such rulers wield absolute power, and their bloodline carries the divine right to rule, so their successors are chosen from their descendants. A ruler doesn't need to be a cleric in such a case (although he often is), since he is not a divine representative, but a deity. In such a theocracy, it's possible that even an infant can be chosen as a ruler if he has divine blood.

Others

It's not too difficult to imagine a political system based on rule by other classes, by the oldest, the strongest, or the wealthiest. For your world, use whatever criteria you wish to determine the political structure of a group. Most of the time, however, the stranger the criterion, the smaller the group. For example, while a kingdom where the queen is chosen by taking a test of skill, intelligence, and stamina might be expansive, a land where the ruler is the most talented bard would probably be small. Being able to play the lute well is impressive, but it doesn't necessarily ensure fitness to rule.

CULTURAL TENDENCIES

Human societies run the gamut of different political structures. Other races seem to favor one or a few over the others.

Dwarves: Dwarves usually form monarchies, although a few theocracies dedicated to dwarven gods are possible. Dwarves are extremely lawful and rigid in their politics, fearing lawlessness and anarchy. They value order and security over personal freedom, and thus are inclined to judge political matters on what's best for the greatest number concerned. Dwarven societies usually have a strict and exacting code of laws.

Elves: Elves are likely to live within monarchies as well. Of all races, however, elves are the most likely to adopt a magocracy. Elves prize individual freedom and fear tyrants. Elven rulers judge each situation and case individually rather than according to a strict, codified set of laws.

Halflings: Since they are usually nomadic and most often live in small groups, halflings prefer a sort of tribal or clan system. Rulership is often bestowed upon the eldest member of a group, although most halflings rule with a light touch. True halfling leadership is based around the family unit, with parents giving direction to children. Halflings, more than any other race, seem to naturally work well with each other. They have little need for a strong ruling hand or a codified set of laws to maintain order and peace.

Gnomes: Gnomes favor small monarchies, although democracies, gnome republics, and gnome clans exist as well. Like halflings, gnomes have less need for a strong government and enjoy personal freedom. Gnome kings and queens usually have only a small impact on the daily life of their subjects, and they usually do not carry as elevated a status above the common gnome as a human regent might over her human subjects.

Orcs and Other Chaotic Evil Cultures: Orcs are usually too wild and corrupt to value a strict system of government other than rule by the strong. Orc leaders rule by intimidation and threats and thus usually command only a small populace. (Orc nations are rare.) If an orc leader fails to rule, it is because he was weak. If not gripped by complete anarchy, most chaotic evil cultures are likely to live in similar systems and tend to have similarly small populations unless many individuals are cowed by a single powerful master.

Goblins and Other Lawful Evil Cultures: Goblins live in tribal communities that bear the trappings of monarchy. The truth, however, is that their government is rulership of the strong. If a goblin ruler can be killed, his killer usually takes his place. Lawful evil humanoids often use a similar system, although kobolds often establish magocracies, and more sophisticated cultures frequently develop codified laws and rules of succession. Such complex societies are rife with backstabbing and betrayals, though, exemplifying the very definition of Byzantine politics.

HIGH-LEVEL CHARACTERS

Sometimes high-level characters build their own castles and establish their own territories. This usually occurs either on land granted to them by a ruler or in an area of relatively unclaimed wilderness that they have cleared. A just or generous character is likely to draw people toward her stronghold or cleared area. Before she knows it, she's a ruler.

How the character governs is completely up to her. However, the NPCs involved react appropriately to character actions and decrees. In exchange for protection, plots of land, and fair rulership, a character can expect to collect taxes or tithes from those she rules. Neglect, mistreatment, or overtaxation of the populace can lead to a revolt, which might come as an appeal to another more powerful or influential lord to depose or conquer the character, hired assassins making attempts against the character's life, or an outright uprising in which the peasants wield their pitchforks against their ruler.

In reality, however, such events are rare. More often than not, people live with the ruler that they have—for good or ill—for a long time. Those under a poor or unjust ruler will suffer for months and years before they feel compelled to act. If you want to reward good treatment of the people in a character's domain, do so by having well-treated people prosper and mistreated people languish as their lands decline and fail.

LEGAL ISSUES

You don't have to develop a legal code for each country you invent. Assume common-sense laws are in place. Murder, assault, theft, and treason are illegal and are punishable by imprisonment or even death. As long the laws make sense and the authorities are fairly consistent in enforcing them (or it's clear why they're not), the players won't think twice about the law. Develop a few exceptional laws as points of interest, such as:

- In one barony in the Shield Lands, lying is illegal, punishable by three days in the pillory.
- In the city of Highfolk, it is against the law to mistreat an animal.
- Anyone wearing red in the sight of the emperor is imprisoned for one month.

Some places might have laws directly affecting adventurers. These laws might restrict weapons that can be owned or carried by non-nobles or sanction the use of some weapons even by nobles, restricting their use to the royal guard. These laws might restrict or prohibit magic use. They might limit the number of well-armed people who can gather publicly without a permit or sanction. All of these laws would be put in place if the ruler or rulers of the area were concerned about powerful people roaming around uncontrolled—a legitimate worry to those in power. No king, duke, or mayor is going to want independent adventurers to be more powerful than his own guards, lackeys, or troops (and thus, himself) unless he trusts them absolutely or has some way to control them.

SOCIAL CLASSES

Most societies are, to one degree or another, class-based. Use these easy definitions for the typical society.

Upper Class: Nobles, the wealthiest of merchants, and the most important leaders (guildmasters, for example) make up the upper class. Lawmakers, administrators, and other officials are drawn from this class. Nobility and being a member of a wealthy merchant family allows entrance into the class by birth, while attaining wealth or significant position can raise one to this status.

By virtue of their wealth, adventurers are likely to rise to the upper class quickly. However, they may be rejected by other members of the upper class based on how society around them views sword-wielding, spell-slinging, self-governing mercenaries. Other members of the upper class might look upon adventurers as heroes, but they are just as likely to look upon them as dangerous threats to public safety (as well as their own personal safety) and to the existing sociopolitical structure.

Middle Class: Merchants, master artisans, educated professionals, and most significant guild members comprise the middle class. Lesser officials are sometimes drawn from the middle class. This status is normally based on one's occupation and education. Its primary determinant for membership is not birth, but wealth.

Lower Class: Tradesfolk, journeymen, laborers, hardscrabble farmers, poor freeholders, personal servants, and virtually everyone else comprise the lower class. The lower class is typically made up of the poor and the uneducated. While sometimes a council of elders or similar body exists to watch over the interests of and argue for the lower class, most of the time no officials or lawmakers come from these ranks.

Slaves: Some cultures (usually evil ones) practice slavery. Slaves are lower in station than even lower-class free people. Though they need not be uneducated or even unskilled, most slaves are laborers or servants.

Titles, Offices, and Positions

Here are some titles, offices, and positions common to a (primarily Western European) medieval society that you can make use of in your world.

Ale Conner: Official who tests and approves all ales and ciders.

Anchorite: A religious hermit.

Bailiff: A sergeant or commander of the guard.

Beadle: A messenger of the law courts.

Burgomaster: A town or city official.

Catchpoll: A commander of the guard.

Chamberlain: Overseer of a household, office, or court.

Common Weigher: Town official who checks merchants' weights and measures.

Constable: A commander of the local guard.

Councilor: A town or city official or an advisor of the court.

Customs Agent: One responsible for collecting the taxes on all imports and exports.

Elector or Solon: A town or city official who is a member of (but not necessarily the leader of) a governing or advisory body.

Magistrate: A judge.

Page: A servant to a noble.

Pardoner: A member of the clergy or a monk who sells pardons for the church.

Provost: A magistrate or keeper of a prison.

Provost-Marshal: Military magistrate.

Purveyor: An official responsible for obtaining supplies for an army or a noble's retinue.

Reeve: The leader of a village.

Regent: The ruler until a royal heir (princess or prince) reaches the age of majority.

Sergeant: The commander of a unit of soldiers or guards.

Sheriff: The ruler's representative for a given area.

Steward: Custodian of an appointed duty, such as a household.

Tax Collector: One who collects taxes.

Tronager: Supervisor of the scales at a town's port.

Umpire: An official who arbitrates disputes between neighbors.

Warden: The keeper of a noble's woodlands and parks.

Warder: A sergeant or a guard.

WAR AND OTHER CALAMITIES

As a campaign progresses, the land, the world, or even the plane of existence will eventually be shaken by drastic events. The most common of these is the outbreak of war. War can provide a backdrop for the campaign, existing mainly in the background of the action. It can also help generate adventures, because people and places will develop needs based on the conflict, such as when a city cut off from all supplies needs help, a plague started by the war ravages the land, or a shipment of arms needs guards. It can even involve the PCs directly as they join one side or the other, acting as spies, a small strike force, or even commanders in the army.

During wartime, authorities may restrict or even confiscate

materials and supplies—horses, food, weapons, vital ores, and other equipment. Able-bodied people may be conscripted into the ranks of the army. The PCs may find themselves unable to get the equipment they require for an adventure or even find their equipment— or themselves—confiscated by the authorities for the war effort.

INVASION IN THE D&D GAME

A war staged in a fantasy world is similar to one fought in the real world, but the fantastic elements of the setting—magic, heroes, and monsters—create some obvious differences in tactics that are reflected in the composition of the armies. In a war in the D&D game, an invasion force usually has several components: the army, monsters, and the strike team.

The Army: If a major invasion takes place, the invading army is composed mainly of conscripts. These serve as skirmishers and infantry. More extensively trained professional soldiers with better equipment support the conscripts as infantry and archers. Knights, cavalry, and units composed of wizards, sorcerers, and/or clerics fill specialized roles in the army.

Typical Conscript: A typical conscript is a 1st-level commoner wearing padded armor and carrying a wooden shield and a halfspear. After the conscript has suffered even one wound, even if he's still above 0 hp, he most likely drops to the ground and pretends to be dead. Conscripts don't follow orders well, and they are prone to breaking ranks and fleeing when the fight goes against them.

Typical Soldier: Most soldiers are 1st-level warriors who wear studded leather armor and carry either a Small or Medium-size martial weapon (default to a longsword) and a wooden shield or a longbow. These soldiers are professionals or experienced conscripts from harsh lands where conflict is common. They're better trained and more likely to hold their ground and follow orders than typical conscripts.

Typical Mounted Soldier: A typical mounted soldier is a 1st-level warrior wearing scale mail and bearing a light lance, a wooden shield, and a Medium-size martial weapon (default to a longsword). These soldiers are always professionals, and they are among the best trained typical warriors on the field.

Knights and Spellcasters: Actual members of the fighter class are rare on the battlefield. Typically, they wear chainmail or a breastplate and serve as armed knights (though they may not hold a title) and commanders. Just as rare as actual fighters are wizards, sorcerers, or clerics present to provide magical support and firepower. Wellfunded and well-organized armies have small units of low-level spellcasters armed with wands or other magic items that allow them to execute multiple magical attacks. Other armies elect to have a single spellcaster with each unit of soldiers to cast protective spells or supplement the soldiers' attacks with an offensive spell. Clerics are particularly welcome additions to any army, since they wear armor without hampering their spellcasting and wield weapons effectively in addition to casting spells. They can also help heal the fallen. In fact, a small unit of clerics with *wands of cure light wounds* is an effective second wave that can be assigned to follow the main force into battle and heal the fallen, providing a wave of reinforcements.

Monsters: Aerial cavalry on griffons or hippogriffs, *charmed* monsters and animals, and summoned creatures frequent the battlefield. Mounted lancers on elephants and triceratopses clash with goblins riding worgs and orcs riding dire tigers. Dragons circle the combat, their breath weapons decimating entire units of soldiers at once.

The Strike Team: Exceptional characters of above 1st level serve their side in a special way. They assist the main army in a battle, as mentioned above, as knights or magical support, or they work in a mixed-class unit (similar to an adventuring party) that confronts special threats such as enemy commanders, a defender's strong points, *charmed* monsters, or their counterparts on the opposite side. They can also form small strike teams that go into enemy territory to take out commanders, destroy supply storehouses,

Illus. by W. Reynolds

A unit of sorcerers and wizards supplements an army of warriors in combat.

steal plans, weaken defenses, or perform any number of other special missions. Having a party serve as a strike team is a great way to get PCs involved in a war without having to run endless huge battles at the forefront of the game session. (Although such battles can be entertaining, they're just as useful to the campaign in general if they remain in the background.)

OTHER CALAMITIES

Other major threats beyond war include earthquakes, large-scale storms (such as hurricanes), plagues, and famine. Like war, they drain the resources of the common folk. They also create dangerous and horrible situations that spark adventures for PCs who seek to solve the problems or alleviate the suffering of others.

RELIGION

No force affects society more strongly than religion. You need to match the religions in your world with the societies you present. How does the priesthood interact with the populace? What do most people think of the religion, the deity, or the clerics? Most of the time, in addition to serving a deity, a religion is geared toward filling some niche in society: recordkeeping, officiating at ceremonies, judging disputes, tending the poor or sick, defending the community, educating the young, keeping knowledge, preserving customs, and so on.

Sometimes a religious hierarchy is not unified. You can create interesting political intrigues by placing different factions of clerics of the same deity in opposition based on doctrine or approach (or even alignment). Different orders within the priesthood might be distinguished by different choices of domains chosen. A deity that offers the Good, Knowledge, Law, and War domains might have clerics of law and war (the justifiers) opposing those of good and knowledge (the prophets).

THE PANTHEON
AND THE CAMPAIGN SETTING

As an example, here's how the religions of the deities presented in the *Player's Handbook* fit into society.

Boccob: Boccob's priesthood is usually a somber group that takes its pursuit of knowledge and arcana very seriously. The clerics of the Archmage of the Deities wear purple robes with gold trim. Rather than meddle in public affairs and politics, they keep to themselves and their own agendas.

Corellon Larethian: Clergy members who serve the Creator of the Elves operate as defenders and champions of their race. They often serve as leaders and settle disputes in elven communities.

Ehlonna: The clergy of Ehlonna are hearty woodsfolk. Her clerics wear pale green robes and are quick to protect the woodlands against all threats.

Erythnul: The priesthood of Erythnul maintains a low profile in most civilized lands. In savage areas, members of the priesthood are known as bullies and murderous tyrants. Many evil humanoids worship Erythnul, but their priests do not cooperate with each other to advance the overall goals of the religion. Clerics of Erythnul favor rust-red garments or blood-stained robes.

Fharlanghn: Fharlanghn's clerics are wanderers who seek to help fellow travelers. A traveler who comes to one of Fharlanghn's wayside shrines, which are common on most well-used roads, won't find the same cleric watching over it twice. Fharlanghn's clerics move around frequently. They dress in nondescript brown or green clothing.

Garl Glittergold: Clerics of Garl Glittergold serve gnome communities as educators and protectors. They teach the young valuable gnome lore and skills using a light-handed humor. They also protect their fellow gnomes, ever watchful of the forces of evil humanoids that might threaten their community.

Gruumsh: Gruumsh, the evil god of the orcs, maintains a religion based on intimidation and fear. His clerics strive to become chieftains of orc tribes or advisors to the chief. Many pluck out one of their own eyes to emulate their deity.

Heironeous: The religious hierarchy of Heironeous is organized like a military order. It has a clear chain of command, lines of supply, and well-stocked armories. Clerics of Heironeous fight against worshipers of Hextor whenever they can and spend the rest of their time protecting the civilized lands from the threats of evil.

Hextor: Strength and power govern Hextor's priesthood. Although evil, it is not as secretive as other dark religions. Temples of Hextor operate openly in many cities. Clerics of Hextor wear black clothing adorned with skulls or gray faces.

Kord: Kord's clerics value strength, but not domination. Kord's temples sometimes resemble warrior feasthalls, and his clerics, who favor red and white garb, often seem more like fighters.

Moradin: Moradin's clerics preside over most formal ceremonies in dwarven culture, keep genealogical records, educate the young, and serve as part of the defense force of a community.

Nerull: The Reaper is feared across the lands. His rust-red garbed clerics are murderous psychopaths who work in secret, plotting against all that is good. They have no overall hierarchy, and they even work against each other at times.

Obad-Hai: Clerics of Obad-Hai have no hierarchy. They treat all those of their order as equals. They wear russet-colored clothing and maintain hidden woodland shrines that are usually located far from civilization. They keep to the wilderness and to themselves, rarely getting involved in society.

Olidammara: Olidammara's religion is loosely organized at best, and few temples are dedicated solely to him. That said, his clerics are numerous. They usually work among urban folk or wander the countryside. Olidammara's clerics often work at some other profession, such as minstrels, brewers, or jacks-of-all-trades, in addition to operating as clerics, and thus can be found almost anywhere doing or wearing anything.

Pelor: The clerics of the Shining One work to aid the poor and the sick, and thus most common folk look upon them with great favor. Pelor's temples are sanctuaries for the impoverished and diseased, and his yellow-robed clerics are usually kind, quiet folk, roused only in their opposition against evil.

St. Cuthbert: The no-nonsense order of St. Cuthbert does not suffer fools gladly or abide evil in any way. His clerics concern themselves with the needs of the common people over nobles or the well educated. They are zealous in their desire to convert others to their faith and quick to destroy their opponents.

Vecna: Vecna's priesthood is made up of isolated cells of cultists who seek dark, arcane secrets to further their evil schemes. Black and red are their favored colors.

Wee Jas: Wee Jas's priesthood has a strict hierarchy. Her clerics are known for their discipline and obedience to their superiors. They work as officiators at funerals, maintain graveyards, or operate libraries of arcane lore. They wear black or gray robes.

Yondalla: Yondalla's clerics help other halflings lead safe, prosperous lives by following her guidance. They often serve as community leaders.

CREATING NEW DEITIES

You can create your own deities and religions. You're free to set them up however you please. Deities can exist as individuals or as a unified pantheon that interacts all the time.

Each deity should have a portfolio or a sphere or spheres of influence. Elements of a portfolio can be concepts such as peace or death, events such as war or famine, elements such as fire or water, activities such as travel or entertainment, types of people or professions such as wizards or smiths, as well as races, alignments, places, or outlooks. Deities with similar areas of influence may work together or may be in conflict, depending on their alignments and respective power levels.

The domains that a cleric of a deity can choose from should always be based on the deity's sphere of influence. In general, four domains are appropriate to any deity. However, some deities might need more domains to represent the breadth of their dominion, while others might need just three, if they are very focused.

Polytheism is the assumption in the DUNGEONS & DRAGONS setting. You could create a monotheistic world, but a strong, singular religion probably wields great political and sociological power (as it did in Dark Ages Europe), which is a change with serious implications that might ripple throughout your entire campaign setting.

MAGIC

It's common for DMs to create cities in their campaigns that function just like medieval historical towns. They are populated by people who are not accustomed to (or who do not believe in) magic, who don't know anything about magical or mythical monsters, or who have never seen a magic item. This sort of creative work is a mistake. It will cause your players serious strain in their belief in reality of your world for them to see that they wield spells and magic items, and the lands and dungeons surrounding the city are filled with magic and monsters, but yet in the middle of the city everything looks and acts like Europe during the Middle Ages.

Magic forces you to deviate from a truly historical setting. When you create anything for your world, the idea that magic could possibly alter it should be in the back of your mind. Would the king simply surround his castle with a wall when *levitate* and *fly* spells are common? How do the guards of the treasury make sure that someone doesn't just teleport in or slip through the walls while ethereal?

Unless you are going to run a divergent game (see Differing Magic, page 164), magic is prevalent enough in the world that it will always be taken into account by smart individuals. A merchant wouldn't be flabbergasted by the idea that someone might try to steal from her while invisible. A swindler would be aware that someone might be able to detect his thoughts or his lies.

Magic shouldn't be something that common people are unaware of. Spellcasters may be fairly rare in the big picture, but they're common enough that people know that when Uncle Rufus falls off the back of the wagon, they could take him to the temple to have the priests heal the wound (although the average peasant probably couldn't afford the price). Only the most isolated farmer might not see magic or the results of magic regularly. A few things to consider including when fitting magic into your world:

- A tavern frequented by adventures might have a "No detections" sign above the bar to allow the patrons to relax in an atmosphere where they don't need to worry about someone discerning their alignments, reading their thoughts, figuring which of their items are magical, and so on.
- Merchants might jointly employ small squad of wizards that wander about the marketplace invisibly while watching for thieves, casting *detect thoughts* on suspicious characters, and using *see invisibility* to look for magic-using robbers.
- The town guard might employ a spellcaster or two (or more) to supplement its defensive strength, deal with unruly spellcasters, and help facilitate interrogations.
- A court might use *detect thoughts* or *discern lies* to help make accurate judgments in important cases.
- A town might use simple spells to make life easier, such as using *continual flame* to make a sort of street light. Very sophisticated or wealthy cities might use permanent *gates* to dispose of sewage and *carpets of flying* to deliver urgent messages. (However, don't let magic become boring or trite by overusing commonplace magic such as this.)

MAGIC ITEMS

The magic items described in Chapter 8: Magic Items all have prices. The assumption is that, while they are rare, magic items can be bought and sold like any other commodity. The prices listed are far beyond the reach of almost everyone, but the very rich, including mid- to high-level PCs, can buy and sell these items or even have spellcasters make them to order. In very large cities, some shops might specialize in magic items if they have a very wealthy or adventurer-based clientele (and lots of magical protections to ward away thieves). Magic items might even be sold in normal markets and shops occasionally. For example, a weaponsmith might have a few magic weapons for sale along with her normal wares.

SUPERSTITION

Just because magic works and most people are aware of it doesn't mean that they know exactly *how* it works. Superstition (magiclike ritual behaviors that don't produce actual results) is still likely to be common. Cheap nonfunctional charms and trinkets sold by vendors to common folk, special hand signs or spoken words required in certain situations (such as "Gesundheit!" after a sneeze), seeing omens in the movements of birds, and so forth, can add a lot of flavor to a campaign and provide details that portray both the quirks and underlying fears and concerns of a society.

RESTRICTIONS PLACED ON MAGIC

In some civilized areas, the use of magic might be restricted or prohibited. A license might be required, or perhaps official permission from the local ruler would enable a spellcaster to use his powers, but without such permission, magic use is forbidden. In such a place, magic items and in-place magical effects are rare, but protections against magic might not be. Whether there are many protections would depend on if the authorities are confident in their laws or if the laws were put in place because the authorities are paranoid about magic.

Some localities might prohibit specific spells. It could be a crime to cast any spells used to steal or swindle, such as those that bestow invisibility and many illusion spells. Enchantments (particularly charm spells, compulsion spells, *suggestions*, and domination effects) tend to be readily forbidden since they rob their subjects of free will. Destructive spells are likewise prohibited, for obvious reason. A local ruler could have a phobia about a specific effect or spell (such as polymorphing effects if she were afraid of being impersonated) and restrict that type of magic as well.

BUILDING A DIFFERENT WORLD

The rules leave a lot of room for flexibility when it comes to creating your world. However, they assume a few basic aspects: a medieval level of technology, a Western European flavor, and a moderately historical basis. You might want to reach beyond these boundaries and create a very different sort of world.

SOCIETY/CULTURE

You can deviate from the typical campaign simply by changing the cultural basis of the real-world history upon which it is modeled. Establishing an African, Indian, Mesoamerican, or Arabic campaign can be rewarding and entertaining. Don't, however, feel limited by the culture you have chosen. If you don't like the fact that most historical African warriors didn't wear metal armor, ignore that fact and change it. Though the default cultural assumption for most D&D game worlds is medieval Europe, most of those worlds deviate widely from history, too. Don't forget all the other basic factors of setting design mentioned earlier, either. Lots of magic that actually works will change an Arabian campaign as much as a European one.

Asian Culture

As an extended example, assume a DM decides that she wants to create a campaign setting based not on Western culture, but Asian.

Specifically, she wants to tailor her creation (in tone and look) to feudal Japan and ancient China. She decides not to change the PC race selections but disallows anyone from taking bard as a class, ruling that it's strictly Western. She changes the name of the paladin class to samurai, and she adjusts the powers of the class to have a nonreligious basis by basing the class's special abilities instead on inner *ki* power. She designs new prestige classes for ninjas, wu gen, and kensai.

Taking a look at the equipment section, she finds that most of it fits her needs, but she adds a number of weapons that she finds in her research (detailed on Table 6–2: Asian Weapons).

Asian Weapons

All other weapons on the *Player's Handbook* weapon charts (Table 7–4: Weapons, page 98, and Table 7–10: Grenadelike Weapons, page 114) work with an Asian campaign. In particular, the dagger, trident, shuriken, kama, nunchaku, siangham, kukri, halfspear, shortspear, longspear, handaxe, shortbow, composite shortbow, composite longbow, quarterstaff, light flail, light crossbow, sickle, scythe, club, and battleaxe are appropriate.

Blowgun: This is used to fire small needles a long distance. It is silent, and its needles most often are used to poison foes.

Needles, Blowgun: These 2-inch-long iron needles are sold in small wooden cases of 20. A full case is so light that its weight is negligible. The tips of the needles are often coated with poison such as greenblood oil, bloodroot, blue whinnis, shadow essence, or even deathblade.

Kusari-Gama: This small sickle is attached to a length of chain. A kusari-gama is an exotic weapon that has reach. It can strike opponents 10 feet away. In addition, unlike other weapons with reach, it can be used against an adjacent foe. It can be used in all respects like a spiked chain (see page 99 in the *Player's Handbook*) for trip attacks, disarming other foes, and using its wielder's Dexterity modifier instead of her Strength modifier in attack rolls.

Wakizashi: This small, slightly curved short sword is made with a skill only masterful weaponsmiths possess. It counts as a masterwork weapon and grants its wielder a +1 bonus to attack rolls. A masterwork weapon's bonus to attack does not stack with an enhancement bonus to attack.

Katana: While functionally a bastard sword, this sword is the most masterfully made nonmagical weapon in existence. It counts as a masterwork weapon and grants its wielder a +1 bonus to attack rolls. A katana is too large to use in one hand without special training; thus, it is an exotic weapon. A Medium-size creature can use a katana two-handed as a martial weapon, or a Large creature can use

TABLE 6–2: ASIAN WEAPONS

	Cost	Damage	Critical	Range Increment	Weight	Type
Simple Weapons—Ranged						
Small						
Blowgun	1 gp	1	×2	10 ft.	2 lb.	Piercing
Needles, blowgun (20)	1 gp	—	—	—	*	
Martial Weapons—Melee						
Small						
Wakizashi**	300 gp	1d6	19–20/×2	—	3 lb.	Slashing
Medium-size						
Kusari-gama	10 gp	1d6	×2	—	3 lb.	Slashing
Exotic Weapons—Melee						
Large						
Katana†	400 gp	1d10	19–20/×2	—	6 lb.	Slashing

*No weight worth noting.

**Except as indicated, same as masterwork short sword.

†Except as indicated, same as masterwork bastard sword.

it one-handed in the same way. With Exotic Weapon Proficiency (katana), a Medium-size creature can use it in one hand. A masterwork weapon's bonus to attack does not stack with an enhancement bonus to attack.

Other Asian Elements

The DM designs her world, filling it with feudal lords who each serve a more powerful lord above them and rule over the people below them in station. Monasteries are common, with monks serving alongside clerics as representatives of spiritual enlightenment. Certain arts, such as poetry, theater, and fine art, take on a greater importance in society (which is ironic, since she has done away with the bard), and so entertainment becomes a skill that almost every character needs to succeed in this campaign.

TECHNOLOGY

Technology defines a setting as much as culture does. If gunpowder is available, the world changes. Suddenly, a commoner with a rifle is a serious threat to an armored soldier, and high castle walls are no longer proof against invasion, which makes people, in turn, less elitist and isolationist.

Weapon Size and Damage

Some opponents you encounter might be wielding weapons that are of different sizes than the standard ones. As a weapon gets larger or smaller, the damage it deals changes according to the following progression:

One Size Smaller	Original Damage	One Size Larger
1	1d2	1d3
1d2	1d3	1d4
1d3	1d4	1d6
1d4	1d6	1d8
1d6	1d8	2d6
1d6	1d10	2d6
1d8	1d12	2d8

For an even larger version of a weapon that does 2 or more dice of damage, convert each die to the next larger category. For instance, a Large version of a longsword does 2d6 points of damage (up from 1d8), and a Huge version of a longsword does 2d8 points of damage (increasing each d6 to a d8).

A weapon reduced in size so that it does less than 1 point of damage is useless.

Extremely Low Tech

A campaign set in a Bronze Age world where weapons are more crude and armor is less advanced, or even an Ice Age/Stone Age

Illus. by A. Swekel

Arnie

In some campaigns, a firearm makes for a deadly weapon.

world where metal is barely available (if at all), can be very interesting. In such a campaign, survival often becomes a central focus, since finding food and keeping warm are suddenly much more difficult. There might not be shops in which to buy goods (particularly in an Ice Age/Stone Age campaign) or even safe places to spend the night. Killing a huge beast means not only victory, it also means meat to eat, fur or skin to wear, and bones to fashion into weapons and tools.

Low-Tech Weapons

Weapons in a Bronze Age or Ice Age/Stone Age worlds do not use iron or steel. Weapons made of inferior materials, such as bone or stone, have a −2 attack and damage penalty (with a minimum damage of 1).

Advancing the Technology Level

Conversely, a DM could advance the pseudohistorical basis for the game a few hundred years and set his campaign in a Renaissance-style setting. This would allow him to incorporate weapons and maybe a few more bits of equipment from a little later in history. Clocks, hot air balloons, printing presses, and even crude steam engines might be available. Most important to PCs, however, would be the new weapons—*gunpowder* weapons.

TABLE 6–3: RENAISSANCE WEAPONS

	Cost	Damage	Critical	Range Increment	Weight	Type
Exotic Weapons (Firearms)—Ranged						
Small						
Pistol	250 gp	1d10	×3	50 ft.	3 lb.	Piercing
Bullets, pistol (10)	3 gp	—		—	2 lb.	—
Medium-size						
Musket	500 gp	1d12	×3	150 ft.	10 lb.	Piercing
Bullets, rifle (10)	3 gp	—		—	2 lb.	—

TABLE 6–4: RENAISSANCE GRENADELIKE WEAPONS

Weapon*	Cost	Damage	Blast Radius	Range Increment	Weight
Bomb	150 gp	2d6	5 ft.	10 ft.	1 lb.
Smokebomb	70 gp	Smoke	**	10 ft.	1 lb.

*Grenadelike weapons require no proficiency to use.
**See description.

Renaissance Firearms

Firearms should be treated like other ranged projectile weapons. Exotic Weapon Proficiency (firearms) gains a creature proficiency with all firearms; otherwise, a –4 penalty is assessed against all attack rolls. A firearm cannot be constructed to take advantage of a user's exceptional Strength as part of the damage it deals (no mighty pistols, for instance).

Bullets: These large, round, lead bullets are sold in bags of 10. The bag has negligible weight.

Gunpowder: While gunpowder burns (with an ounce consuming itself in 1 round and illuminating as much as a sunrod) or even explodes in the right conditions, it is chiefly used to propel a bullet out of the barrel of a pistol or a rifle, or it is formed into a bomb (see below). An ounce of gunpowder is needed to propel a bullet. Gunpowder is sold in small kegs (15-pound capacity and 20 pounds total weight, 250 gp each) and in water-resistant powder horns (2-pound capacity and total weight, 35 gp for a full powder horn). If gunpowder gets wet, it cannot be used to fire a bullet.

Pistol: This pistol holds a single shot and requires a standard action to reload.

Musket: The musket holds a single shot and requires a standard action to reload.

Renaissance Grenadelike Weapons

These explosive grenadelike weapons require no proficiency to use, like other grenadelike weapons, and are ranged touch attacks. A direct hit with an explosive grenadelike weapons means that the weapon has hit the creature it was aimed at and everyone within the blast radius, including that creature, takes the indicated damage. A miss requires a roll for deviation as for regular grenadelike weapons, but rather than dealing splash damage to all creatures within 5 feet, the weapon deals the same damage to all creatures within the blast radius of where it actually lands.

Bomb: This round gunpowder bomb must be lit before it is thrown. Lighting the bomb is a standard action. The explosive deals 2d6 points of fire damage. Those caught within the blast radius can make a Reflex save (DC 20) to take half damage.

Smokebomb: This cylindrical bomb must be lit before it is thrown. Lighting it is a standard action. One round after it is lit, this nondamaging explosive emits a cloud of smoke in a 20-foot radius that persists in still conditions for 1d3+6 rounds and in windy conditions for 1d3+1 rounds. Visibility within the smoke is limited to 2 feet. Everything within the cloud has 90% concealment.

Very High Tech

You could create a setting with very high technology. Perhaps a starship from a much more highly advanced civilization landed or crashed in the campaign world. The crash might have happened long ago, so that now the starship is a mysterious, specialized dungeon setting in its own right, with a special sort of magic (advanced technology) and monsters (surviving aliens and robots). Or perhaps the advanced civilization was native to the campaign world but is now long gone, leaving behind remnants of its ancient cities filled with strange secrets, which now form sites for adventures. In such a campaign, you could decide that many of the strange creatures found in the world result from ancient genetic engineering. Finally, perhaps members of some advanced civilization have come to the campaign world with their advanced science and now serve as patrons or overlords. They dole out their technology in small doses to those who serve them well.

No matter what way you use to place high-tech items in your game, they should always be like very rare magic items or artifacts—difficult or impossible to reproduce. Treating them as artifacts (see Chapter 8: Magic Items) is most appropriate. They shouldn't dominate the game, but should serve as an occasional diversion. It's fun for some players for their characters to occasionally use a big gun against the dragon rather than a sword, and it's an interesting diversion to run into a warbot in a dungeon rather than a band of trolls. But in a fantasy game, most players don't want to do that every day.

Some advanced technological weapons are detailed below. These weapons have no cost listed, because they cannot be manufactured. They can only be found as artifacts.

These weapon statistics also show how to rate something in your game that you might not know how to handle. Since you probably have a good idea what a pistol is like, or a laser, you can deal with such situations on firmer ground. For example, you might want to develop a trap that fires large needles rapidly. You could use the statistics for an automatic rifle or extrapolate from them to get what you want. When explaining the trap, you could even describe it to the players as resembling a machine gun to help them understand it.

Modern Era Firearms

Firearms should be treated like other ranged projectile weapons. Exotic Weapon Proficiency (firearms) gains a creature proficiency with all firearms; otherwise, a –4 penalty is assessed against all attack rolls. A firearm cannot be constructed to take advantage of a user's exceptional Strength as part of the damage it deals (no mighty automatic rifles, for instance).

Grenade Launcher: The grenade launcher can fire fragmentation or smoke grenades using its range, but must be reloaded each time it fires, requiring a standard action. The grenade launcher is a tube set on a metal tripod and equipped with a sighting mechanism. A single smoke grenade or fragmentation grenade easily slips into the tube.

Metal Cartridge: These lead bullets are jacketed in copper and held in a brass shell.

Metal Cartridge Clip: These lead bullets are jacketed in copper and held in a brass shell. They are found in either a 20-round metal clip (for automatic pistols) or a 30-round metal clip (for automatic rifles). The clip is inserted into the butt of an automatic pistol or the stock of an automatic rifle.

Pistol, Automatic: An automatic pistol can fire twenty times before reloading and can be used to attack more than once per round if the user has the ability to make multiple attacks. Reloading is a standard action.

Pistol, Revolver: A revolver fires once a round maximum, but it can fire six times before it needs reloading (which requires a full-round action).

Rifle, Automatic: An automatic rifle can fire thirty times before reloading and can be used to attack more than once per round if the user has the ability to make multiple attacks. Reloading is a standard action.

Rifle, Repeater: A repeater rifle fires once a round maximum, but it can fire six times before it needs reloading (which requires a full-round action).

Scattergun: The scattergun deals 3d6 points of damage to a target in the first range increment, 2d6 to a target in the second range increment, and 1d6 to anyone in a 5-foot-wide path beyond that distance out to maximum range. It can fire once a round maximum, but it can fire five times before it needs reloading. Reloading up to two shells is a standard action. Reloading more shells than that (up to all five) is a full-round action.

Scattergun Shells: These cylindrical cartridges have a built-in firing cap at their base. They are packed with a mixture of gunpowder and small lead pellets.

Modern Era Grenadelike Weapons

These explosive grenadelike weapons work just like Renaissance grenadelike weapons (see above).

Dynamite: This short, thin cylinder of explosive must be lit before it is thrown or set. Lighting the dynamite is a standard action. The explosive has a blast radius of 5 feet and deals 3d6 points of fire damage. Those caught within the blast radius can make a Reflex save (DC 20) to take half damage.

Grenade, Smoke: A smoke grenade looks like a squat cylinder on a 1-foot-long stick with small fins. If thrown, it uses its range increment, but if launched from a grenade launcher, it uses that weapon's range increment. One round after it lands or hits its target, this nondamaging explosive emits a cloud of smoke in a 20-foot radius that persists in still conditions for 1d3+6 rounds and in windy conditions for 1d3+1 rounds. Visibility within the smoke is limited to 2 feet. Everything within the cloud has 90% concealment.

Grenade, Fragmentation: A fragmentation grenade looks like a large egg on a 1-foot-long stick with small fins. If thrown, it uses its range increment, but if launched from a grenade launcher, it uses that weapon's range increment. Fragmentation grenades are advanced antipersonnel explosives that deal damage that is half piercing damage and half fire damage in a 20-foot radius. Those caught within the blast radius can make a Reflex save (DC 20) to take half damage.

TABLE 6–5: MODERN ERA WEAPONS

	Damage	Critical	Range Increment	Weight	Type
Exotic Weapons (Firearms)—Ranged					
Small					
Pistol, automatic	1d10	×3	150 ft.	5 lb.	Piercing
Metal cartridge, pistol (20)	—	—	—	1/2 lb.	—
Pistol, revolver	1d10	×3	100 ft.	3 lb.	Piercing
Metal cartridge, pistol (20)	—	—	—	1/2 lb.	—
Medium-size					
Rifle, automatic	1d12	×3	250 ft.	12 lb.	Piercing
Metal cartridge clip, rifle (30)	—	—	—	1/2 lb.	—
Rifle, repeater	1d12	×3	200 ft.	10 lb.	Piercing
Metal cartridge, rifle (20)	—	—	—	1/2 lb.	—
Scattergun	*	*	10 ft.	10 lb.	Piercing
Scattergun shells (20)	—	—	—	1/2 lb.	—
Large					
Grenade launcher	*	*	200 ft.	12 lb.	**

*See description.
**Fires fragmentation or smoke grenades. See Table 6–6: Modern Era Grenadelike Weapons.

TABLE 6–6: MODERN ERA GRENADELIKE WEAPONS

	Blast	Range		
Weapon*	Damage	Radius	Increment	Weight
Dynamite	3d6**	5 ft.	10 ft.	1 lb.
Grenade, fragmentation	6d6	20 ft.	10 ft.	1 lb.
Grenade, smoke	Smoke	**	10 ft.	1 lb.

*Grenadelike weapons require no proficiency to use.
**See description.

Futuristic Weapons

Futuristic weapons are like other ranged projectile weapons, though the type of damage they deal is special. Exotic Weapon Proficiency (futuristic) gains a creature proficiency with all futuristic weapons; otherwise, a –4 penalty is assessed against all attack rolls. Futuristic weapons do not take advantage of a user's exceptional Strength as part of the damage they deal (no mighty laser rifles, for instance).

Antimatter Rifle: The antimatter rifle is a devastating short-range attack weapon that can be fired no more than once per round. It holds two shots. Reloading it is a standard action.

Energy Pack: This small pack fits snugly into the butt of a laser rifle, laser pistol, or antimatter rifle. It powers a laser pistol or laser rifle for fifty shots or an antimatter rifle for two shots.

Fuel Pack: This extremely sturdy pack clips snugly onto the barrel of a flamer near its base. It contains enough concentrated flamer fuel for ten shots.

Laser Pistol: Laser pistols fire fifty times before they need to be reloaded and have a rate of fire equal to the attacker's number of attacks. Reloading is a standard action.

Laser Rifle: Laser rifles fire fifty times before they need to be reloaded and have a rate of fire equal to the attacker's number of attacks. Reloading is a standard action.

Flamer: The flamer can only be fired once per round and must be reloaded after firing ten times. Reloading is a standard action.

TABLE 6–7: FUTURISTIC WEAPONS

	Damage	Critical	Range Increment	Weight	Type
Exotic Weapons (Futuristic)—Ranged					
Small					
Laser pistol	2d10	×2	100 ft.	2 lb.	Special
Energy pack, laser pistol	—	—	—	1/2 lb.	—
Medium-size					
Antimatter rifle	6d10	×2	10 ft.	10 lb.	Special
Energy pack, antimatter rifle	—	—	—	1/2 lb.	—
Flamer	3d6‡	—	20 ft.	8 lb.	Special
Fuel pack, flamer	—	—	—	1/2 lb.	—
Laser rifle	3d10	×2	200 ft.	7 lb.	Special
Energy pack, laser rifle	—	—	—	1/2 lb.	—

‡Damage dealt in a 5-foot-wide stream extending to the maximum range.

DIFFERING MAGIC

Another way to create a divergent game is to change the amount of magic available.

Low Magic: In a low-magic game, spellcasters and magic treasure are about twice as rare as normal. Magic items aren't for sale because they're too rare to ever think of parting with for mere gold. The occasional trade of an item or its sale for gold is possible, of course, but it is a rarity in the economic structure.

Common people almost never see magic. Some might not even believe in it. A spell or a magic-using creature completely bedevils the common folk and terrifies them. All magic-using creatures, including characters, may be thought of as "demons." They might be persecuted. Witch trials and the like could be a common fate for wizards and sorcerers. Clerics and other divine spellcasters are probably safer than arcane spellcasters, but they might not be, depending on the culture.

High Magic: Spellcasters and magic treasures are twice as common as presented in these rules, if not more so. Most characters have a level or two of wizard or sorcerer. Even a shopkeeper might be at least a 1st-level spellcaster. Magic items are bought and sold in clearly marked shops like any other commodity. Spells are used to light homes, keep people warm, and communicate. The function they serve is as commonplace as modern-day technology is in the real world.

This sort of campaign can be directed one of two ways. The first is to take the world of the utterly fantastic route, where magic is sophisticated and common, and to create a world unlike anything anyone but you has ever imagined. The second is to take the comical route, where magic simply becomes technology—little imps in boxes perform calculations like computers, and people have magical transmission television sets. The second route can be fun, but the sort of light-hearted parody it leads to is probably not a good basis for a long-term campaign.

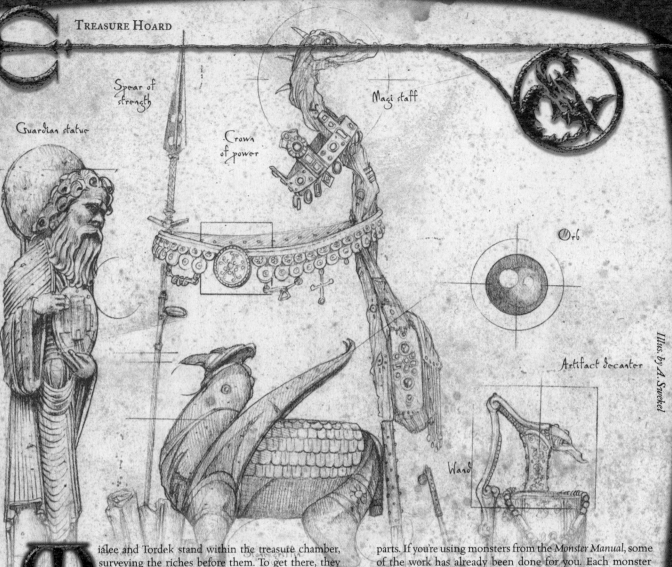

Guardian statue

Spear of strength

Crown of power

Magi staff

Orb

Artifact decanter

Wand

Illus. by A. Swekel

ialee and Tordek stand within the treasure chamber, surveying the riches before them. To get there, they slew three trolls, bypassed several devious traps, and solved the riddle of the golden golem before it crushed them. Now they are not only richer, but through their experiences they have grown in knowledge and power.

Experience points are a measure of accomplishment. They represent training and learning by doing, and they illustrate the fact that, in fantasy, the more experienced a character is, the more power he or she possesses. Experience points allow a character to gain levels. Gaining levels heightens the fun and excitement.

Experience points can also be spent by spellcasters to power some of their most potent spells. Experience points also represent the personal puissance that a character must imbue an object with in order to create a magic item.

In addition to experience, characters also earn treasure on their adventures. They find gold and other valuables that allow them to buy bigger and better equipment, and they find magic items that give them new and better abilities.

EXPERIENCE AWARDS

When the party defeats monsters, the DM awards them experience points (XP). The more dangerous the monsters, compared to the party's level, the more XP the characters earn. The PCs split the XP between themselves, and each character increases in level as his or her personal XP total increases.

STANDARD AWARDS

In order to give PCs experience points, you need to break the game down into encounters and then break the encounters down into

Magical horn

parts. If you're using monsters from the *Monster Manual*, some of the work has already been done for you. Each monster there has been given a Challenge Rating (CR) that, when compared to party level, translates directly into XP awards.

A Challenge Rating is a measure of how easy or difficult a monster or trap is to overcome. Challenge Ratings are used in Chapter 4: Adventures to determine Encounter Levels (EL), which in turn indicate how difficult an entire encounter (often with multiple monsters) is to overcome. A monster is usually overcome by defeating it in battle, a trap by being disarmed, and so forth.

As the DM, you must decide when a challenge is overcome. Usually, this is simple to do. Did the PCs defeat the enemy in battle? Then they met the challenge and earned experience points. Other times it can be trickier. Suppose the PCs sneak by the sleeping minotaur to get into the magical vault—did they overcome the minotaur encounter? If their goal was to get into the vault and the minotaur was just a guardian, then the answer is probably yes. It's up to you to make such judgments.

Only characters who take part in an encounter should gain the commensurate awards. Characters who died or were incapacitated before the encounter earn nothing, even if they are raised or healed later on.

To determine the XP award for an encounter, follow these steps:

1. Determine the party level (average level of the party members).

Jewel encrusted chest

2. For each monster defeated, determine that single monster's Challenge Rating.
3. Use Table 7–1: Experience Point Awards (Single Monster) to cross-reference the party level with the Challenge Rating to find the XP award.
4. Add up the XP award for each monster defeated to find the party's award.
5. Divide the total XP among all the characters who started the encounter. (Even if they are knocked unconscious, everyone who took part in an encounter gains experience for that encounter.)

Do not award XP for creatures that enemies summon or otherwise add to their forces with magic powers. An enemy's ability to summon or add these creatures is part of the enemy's CR already.

(You don't give PCs more XP if a drow cleric casts *unholy blight* on them, so don't give them more XP if she casts *summon monster IV* instead.)

Example: A party of five 4th-level PCs defeats two ogres. An ogre is Challenge Rating 2, so the party earns 600 XP per monster, for a total of 1,200 XP. There are five characters in the party, so they each get 240 XP (1,200 ÷ 5 = 240).

Monsters Below CR 1

Some monsters are fractions of a Challenge Rating. For instance, a single orc is not a good challenge for even a 1st-level party, although two might be. You could think of an orc as approximately CR 1/2. For these cases, calculate XP as if the creature were CR 1, then divide the result by 2.

TABLE 7–1: EXPERIENCE POINT AWARDS (SINGLE MONSTER)

Party Level	Challenge Rating									
	CR 1	CR 2	CR 3	CR 4	CR 5	CR 6	CR 7	CR 8	CR 9	CR 10
1st–3rd	**300**	**600**	**900**	1,350	1,800	2,700	3,600	5,400	7,200	10,800
4th	300	600	800	**1,200**	1,600	2,400	3,200	4,800	6,400	9,600
5th	300	500	750	1,000	**1,500**	2,250	3,000	4,500	6,000	9,000
6th	300	450	600	900	1,200	**1,800**	2,700	3,600	5,400	7,200
7th	263	394	525	700	1,050	1,400	**2,100**	3,150	4,200	6,300
8th	200	300	450	600	800	1,200	1,600	**2,400**	3,600	4,800
9th	*	225	338	506	675	900	1,350	1,800	**2,700**	4,050
10th	*	*	250	375	563	750	1,000	1,500	2,000	**3,000**
11th	*	*	*	275	413	619	825	1,100	1,650	2,200
12th	*	*	*	*	300	450	675	900	1,200	1,800
13th	*	*	*	*	*	325	488	731	975	1,300
14th	*	*	*	*	*	*	350	525	788	1,050
15th	*	*	*	*	*	*	*	375	563	844
16th	*	*	*	*	*	*	*	*	400	600
17th	*	*	*	*	*	*	*	*	*	425
18th	*	*	*	*	*	*	*	*	*	*
19th	*	*	*	*	*	*	*	*	*	*
20th	*	*	*	*	*	*	*	*	*	*

Party Level	Challenge Rating									
	CR 11	CR 12	CR 13	CR 14	CR 15	CR 16	CR 17	CR 18	CR 19	CR 20
1st–3rd	**	**	**	**	**	**	**	**	**	**
4th	12,800	**	**	**	**	**	**	**	**	**
5th	12,000	18,000	**	**	**	**	**	**	**	**
6th	10,800	14,400	21,600	**	**	**	**	**	**	**
7th	8,400	12,600	16,800	25,200	**	**	**	**	**	**
8th	7,200	9,600	14,400	19,200	28,800	**	**	**	**	**
9th	5,400	8,100	10,800	16,200	21,600	32,400	**	**	**	**
10th	4,500	6,000	9,000	12,000	18,000	24,000	36,000	**	**	**
11th	**3,300**	4,950	6,600	9,900	13,200	19,800	26,400	39,600	**	**
12th	2,400	**3,600**	5,400	7,200	10,800	14,400	21,600	28,800	43,200	**
13th	1,950	2,600	**3,900**	5,850	7,800	11,700	15,600	23,400	31,200	46,800
14th	1,400	2,100	2,800	**4,200**	6,300	8,400	12,600	16,800	25,200	33,600
15th	1,125	1,500	2,250	3,000	**4,500**	6,750	9,000	13,500	18,000	27,000
16th	900	1,200	1,600	2,400	3,200	**4,800**	7,200	9,600	14,400	19,200
17th	638	956	1,275	1,700	2,550	3,400	**5,100**	7,650	10,200	15,300
18th	450	675	1,013	1,350	1,800	2,700	3,600	**5,400**	8,100	10,800
19th	*	475	713	1,069	1,425	1,900	2,850	3,800	**5,700**	8,550
20th	*	*	500	750	1,000	1,500	2,000	3,000	4,000	**6,000**

For monsters with CRs above 20, double the reward for a CR two levels below the desired CR. Thus, a CR 21 reward equals double the CR 19 reward, CR 22 is double the CR 20 reward, CR 23 is double the CR 21 reward, and so on.

Bold numbers indicate the amount of XP that a standard encounter for a party of that level should provide.

*The XP chart doesn't support XP for monsters that individually are eight Challenge Ratings lower than the party level, since an encounter with multiple weak creatures is hard to measure. See Assigning Ad Hoc XP Awards.

**The XP chart doesn't support awards for encounters eight or more Challenge Ratings above the party's level. If the party is taking on challenges that far above their level, something strange is going on, and the DM needs to think carefully about the awards rather than just taking them off a table. See Assigning Ad Hoc XP Awards.

or NPCs

...s has a Challenge Rating equal to the NPC's ...l sorcerer is an 8th-level encounter. As a rule ...he number of foes adds 2 to the Encounter ...8th-level fighters are an EL 10 encounter. A ...-level characters is an EL 12 encounter.

...eatures are more of a challenge than their level ...ow, for example, has spell resistance and other ...s equal to her level + 1.

...ave monster levels in addition to their class lev- ...r ranger. In this case, add the creature's base CR ...els to get its overall CR. For example, a centaur is CR 1, so a centaur who's also a 7th-level ranger is CR 8.

Since NPC classes (see Chapter 2: Classes) are weaker than PC classes, levels in an NPC class contribute less to a creature's CR than levels in a PC class. For an NPC with an NPC class, determine her Challenge Rating as if she had a PC class with 1 fewer level. For a creature with monster levels in addition to NPC class levels, add the NPC levels – 1 to the creature's base CR (always adding at least +1).

For example, when adding class levels to some sample charac- ters, the resulting CRs would be as presented in the following example chart. Remember that warrior is an NPC class, and fighter is a PC class.

Creature	—Class Levels—		
	1	2	10
Dwarven warrior	1/2	1	9
Dwarven fighter	1	2	10
Orc warrior*	1/2	1	9
Orc fighter*	1	2	10
Drow warrior	1	2	10
Drow fighter	2	3	11
Ogre warrior**	3	3	11
Ogre fighter	3	4	12

*The orc with no class levels has a CR of 1/2

**The ogre with no class levels has a CR of 2. Ogres with class levels retain their original 4 HD, attack bonuses and other aspects of their monster levels.

Challenge Ratings for Traps

Traps vary considerably. Those presented in this book (see Chapter 4: Adventures) have Challenge Ratings assigned to them. For traps you and your players create, assign +1 CR for every 2d6 points of damage the trap deals. For magic traps, start at CR 1 and then assign +1 CR for every 2d6 points of damage the trap deals or +1 for every level of the spell. Traps generally shouldn't have a Challenge Rating above 10.

Overcoming the challenge of a trap involves encountering the trap, either by disarming it, avoiding it, or simply surviving the damage it deals. A trap never discovered or never bypassed was not encountered (and hence grants no XP award).

MODIFYING ENCOUNTER LEVELS

An orc warband that attacks the PCs by flying over them on prim- itive hang gliders and dropping large rocks is not the same encounter as one in which the orcs just charge in with spears. Sometimes, the circumstances give the characters' opponents a dis- tinct advantage. Other times, the PCs have an advantage. Adjust the XP award and the EL depending on how greatly circumstances change the encounter's difficulty.

Circumstance	XP Award Adjustment	EL Adjustment
Half as difficult	×1/2 XP	–2 EL
Significantly less difficult	×2/3 XP	–1 EL
Significantly more difficult	×3/2 XP	+1 EL
Twice as difficult	×2 XP	+2 EL

ELs of 2 or lower are the exception. They increase and decrease in proportion to the change in XP. For example, an encounter

that's normally EL 1 but that's twice as tough as normal is EL 2, not EL 3.

You can, of course, increase or decrease XP by smaller amounts, such as +10% or –10%, and just eyeball the EL.

See Chapter 4: Adventures for examples of the sorts of factors that make an encounter easier or more difficult.

Modify all ELs and experience rewards as you see fit, but keep a few points in mind:

- Experience points drive the game. Don't be too stingy or too generous.
- Most encounters do not need modifying. Don't waste a lot of time worrying about the minutia. Don't worry about modifying encounters until after you have played the game a while.
- Bad rolls or poor choices on the PCs' part should not modify ELs or XP. If the encounter is hard because the players were unlucky or careless, they don't get more experience.
- Just because the PCs are worn down from prior encounters does not mean that later (more difficult) encounters should gain high- er awards. Judge the difficulty of an encounter on its own merits.

Assigning Ad Hoc XP Awards

Sometimes the XP chart doesn't quite cover a given situation ade- quately. If two orcs are an EL 1 encounter, four orcs EL 3, eight orcs EL 5, and sixteen orcs EL 7 (maybe), are thirty-two orcs an EL 9 encounter? A party of 9th-level characters almost certainly can wipe them out with ease. By 9th level a character's defenses are so good that the standard orc cannot hit him or her, and one or two spells cast by a character at that level could easily destroy all thirty- two orcs. At such a point, your judgment as the DM overrules whatever the XP table would say.

An encounter so easy that it uses up none or almost none of the PCs' resources shouldn't result in any XP award at all, while a dan- gerous encounter that the PCs defeat handily through luck or excellent strategy is worth full XP. However, an encounter in which the PCs defeat something far above their own level (CRs higher than their level by eight or more) was probably the result of fantastic luck or a unique set of circumstances, and thus a full XP award may not be appropriate. As the DM, you're going to have to make these decisions. As a guideline, the minimum and maximum awards given on Table 7–1: Experience Point Awards (Single Mon- ster) for a group of a given level are the least and most you should award a group. Circumstances in your campaign may alter this, however. You might decide that an EL 2 encounter is worth at least a little to your 10th-level party since it caused them to waste some major spells, so you give them half the amount an EL 3 encounter would have garnered, or 125 XP. Or you might judge that a vast number of CR 1 monsters are indeed an appropriate equal chal- lenge for the same 10th-level party because the group had lost all their equipment before the fight started.

Sometimes, you may want to estimate experience point awards for actions that normally don't result in XP under the standard sys- tem. These are called story awards (see below) and should only be used by an experienced DM.

VARIANT: FASTER OR SLOWER EXPERIENCE

You control the pace of character progress, and the easiest way to do that is through experience point awards. Obviously, if you want the characters to progress faster, simply make every award 10%, 20%, or even 50% larger. If you want characters to progress more slowly, give awards that are some suitable fraction of the original award.

When modifying awards in this way, keep track of the amount of change you impose on the PCs' progress. You need to balance this with the pace of treasure awarded. For example, if you increase the amount of experience earned by the characters by 20% across the board, treasure also needs to increase by 20%, or the PCs end up poor and underequipped for their level.

Modifying Challenge Ratings

The other way to modify character progress is to modify the Challenge Ratings of monsters encountered. If you increase the CRs, you increase the experience awards and speed up advancement.

Of course, whether or not you want to change character progress, you may decide to modify various Challenge Ratings. If you think that a certain monster is worth more (or less) than its *Monster Manual* rating, feel free to change it. Keep in mind, however, that just because the PCs in your campaign happen to all have bane weapons useful against aberrations, that doesn't necessarily make beholders actually a lower challenge overall. It just means that your party is well equipped to deal with their challenge.

VARIANT: FREE-FORM EXPERIENCE

Instead of calculating experience points, just hand out about 75 XP times the average party level for each character in the party per balanced encounter. Hand out more for tough encounters: 100 XP per level per character, or even 150 XP. Award less for easy ones: 25 to 50 XP. Alternatively, you could give out 300 XP times the average party level for each character per session, modified slightly for tough or easy sessions.

It's very simple to track how quickly characters gain levels using this system. The drawback is that it generalizes PC rewards, rather than granting them based on specific accomplishments. You risk players becoming dissatisfied by gaining the same reward every session.

VARIANT: STORY AWARDS

The PCs have rescued the constable's son from the troll lair. They leave the lair and stop their current quest so they can return the young boy to his home and parents. Do they get experience points for this?

Some DMs want the answer to be "Of course they do." To accomplish this, you need to set up a system in which you can award XP for accomplishing goals and for actions and encounters that don't involve combat.

Challenge Ratings for Noncombat Encounters

You could award experience points for solving a puzzle, learning a secret, convincing an NPC to help, or escaping from a powerful foe. Mysteries, puzzles, and roleplaying encounters (such as negotiations) can be assigned Challenge Ratings, but these sorts of awards require more ad hoc ruling on the DM's part.

Challenge Ratings for noncombat encounters are even more of a variable than traps. A roleplaying encounter should only be considered a challenge at all if there's some risk involved and success or failure really matters. For example, the PCs encounter an NPC who knows the secret password to get into a magical prison that holds their companion. The PCs must get the information out of her—if they don't, their

Ember takes a moment to reflect on her victory over an umber hulk.

friend remains trapped forever. In another instance, the characters must cross a raging river by wading, swimming, or climbing across a rope. If they fail, they can't get to where the magic gem lies, and if they fail spectacularly they are washed away down the river.

You might see such situations as having a Challenge Rating equal to the level of the party. Simple puzzles and minor encounters should have a CR lower than the party's level if they are worth an award at all. They should never have a CR higher than the party's level. As a rule, you probably don't want to hand out a lot of experience for these types of encounters unless you intentionally want to run a low-combat game.

In the end, this type of story award feels pretty much like a standard award. Don't ever feel obligated to give out XP for an encounter that you don't feel was much of a challenge. Remember that the key word in "experience award" is *award*. The PCs should have to do something impressive to get an award.

Mission Goals

Often an adventure has a mission or a goal that pulls the PCs into the action. Should the PCs accomplish their goal, they may get a story award. No Challenge Ratings are involved here: The XP award is entirely up to the DM.

Such rewards should be fairly large—large enough to seem significant when compared to the standard awards earned along the way toward achieving the mission goal. The mission award should be more than the XP for any single encounter on the mission, but not more than all standard awards for encounters for the mission put together (see Story Awards and Standard Awards, below). Potentially, you could give out only story awards and no standard awards. In this nonstandard game, the mission award would be the main contributor for XP.

It's possible that in a single adventure a party can have multiple goals. Sometimes the goals are all known at the outset: Unchain the gold dragon, destroy or imprison the two black dragons, and find the lost *staff of healing*. Sometimes the next goal is discovered when the first one is accomplished: Now that the illithid is dead, find the people who were under its mental control and bring them back to town.

Some players will want to set up personal goals for their characters. Perhaps the PC paladin holds a grudge against the night hag from when they encountered her before. Although it's not critical to the adventure at hand, it becomes his personal goal to avenge the wrongs she committed by destroying her. Or, another character wants to find the magic item that will enable her to return to her home village and stop the plague. These are worthy goals, and the individual character who achieves them should get a special award. "I want to get more powerful" is not an individual goal, since that's what just about everyone wants to accomplish.

Remember: A goal that's easy to accomplish is worth little or no award. Likewise, goals that merely reflect standard awards (such as "Kill all the monsters in this cavern complex") should be treated as standard awards.

Roleplaying Awards

A player who enjoys playing a role well may sometimes make decisions that fit his or her character but don't necessarily lead to the most favorable outcome for that character. Good roleplayers might perform some deeds that seem particularly fitting for their characters. Someone playing a bard might compose a short poem about events in the campaign. A smart-aleck sorcerer might crack an in-game joke that sends the other players to the floor laughing. Another player might have his character fall in love with an NPC and then devote some portion of his time to playing out that love affair. Such roleplaying should be rewarded, since it enhances the game. (If it doesn't enhance the game, don't give an award.)

Roleplaying XP awards are purely ad hoc. That is, there is no system for assigning Challenge Ratings to bits of roleplaying. The awards should be just large enough for the player to notice them, probably no more than 50 XP per character level per adventure.

Story Awards and Standard Awards

You can handle story awards in one of two ways. The first is to make all awards story awards. Thus, killing monsters would earn no experience in and of itself—although it may allow characters to achieve what they need to do in order to earn the story awards. If you follow this method, you should still pay attention to how many experience points the characters would be earning by defeating enemies so that you can make sure the PCs' treasure totals are in line with what they should be earning.

The second way is to use standard awards for defeating enemies but award only half the normal amount for doing so, making up the other half through story awards. This method has the virtue of keeping the treasure earned at about the same rate as XP.

Don't simply add story awards to standard awards (even if you compensate by giving out more treasure as well) unless you want to speed up character progression.

EXPERIENCE PENALTIES

Characters can lose experience points by casting certain spells or creating magical items. This allocation of personal power serves a specific game function: It limits and controls these activities, as well as making them interesting choices for players. In general, however, you shouldn't use experience penalties in any other situation. While awards can be used to encourage behavior, penalties don't serve to discourage bad behavior. They usually only lead to arguments and anger. If a player behaves in a way you don't want him to behave, talk to him about it. If he continues, stop playing with him.

DEATH AND EXPERIENCE POINTS

If a character takes part in an encounter, even if she is incapacitated or dies during the encounter, that character gets a share of the experience points. If a character dies and is raised, the awarded experience points are granted to her after she comes back from the dead (and after she loses the level from death, if appropriate).

TREASURE

A close second in importance to experience points, treasure provides an important motivator for PCs to go on adventures. As with experience points, treasure empowers the PCs. The more they get, the more powerful they become.

MONSTERS WITH TREASURE

The standard way to acquire treasure is to defeat enemies who possess it, guard it, or happen to be near it. In the *Monster Manual*, every monster has a treasure rating (indicating how much treasure it has), although for some creatures the rating is "None." The tables found in this section enable you to determine the specifics. Referencing the level and type of treasure (coins, goods, items) found in the creature's description, roll on the appropriate row and columns of the table.

When generating an encounter dealing with monsters away from their lair (a patrol, a wandering creature, and so on), remember that a creature only takes what it can easily carry with it. In the case of something such as a displacer beast, that generally means nothing. The monster safeguards or hides its treasure as well as it can, but it leaves it behind when outside the lair.

Example: Gnolls that live in a dungeon often leave their lair to wage war on nearby orc brigands to steal treasure and food. The PCs encounter and defeat the gnolls while the bestial humanoids on their way to raid the orcs. Each gnoll has a smattering of coins or gems on its person. The leader has the masterwork greatsword from the group's hoard and uses it in the battle. The majority of the gnolls' treasure, however, remains in their lair, guarded by a few gnolls left behind and two well-concealed pit traps.

Treasure per Encounter

Table 7–4: Treasure has been created so that if PCs face enough encounters of their own level to gain a level, they will have also gained enough treasure to keep them apace with the wealth-by-level information found in Chapter 5: Campaigns (page 145). Just as gaining a level requires between thirteen and fourteen encounters of a party's level, so too fourteen average rolls on the table at the party's level will get them the treasure they need to gain the appropriate amount for the next highest level. To make up for the fact that some monsters in the *Monster Manual* typically have no

BEHIND THE CURTAIN: EXPERIENCE POINTS

The experience point award for encounters is based on the concept that 13.33 encounters of an EL equal to the player characters' level allow them to gain a level.

Thirteen to fourteen encounters sometimes seem to go by very quickly. This is particularly true at low levels, where most of the encounters that characters take part in are appropriate for their levels. At higher levels, the PCs face a varied range of Encounter Levels (more lower than higher, if they're to survive) and thus gain levels somewhat more slowly. Higher-level characters also tend to spend more and more time interacting with each other and with NPCs, which results in fewer experience points over time.

With this information in mind, you can roughly gauge how quickly the PCs in your game will advance. In fact, you can control it. You are in charge of what encounters happen and the circumstances in which they occur. You can predict at what level the characters will reach the dark

temple and prepare accordingly. If it turns out that you predicted incorrectly, you can engineer encounters to allow them to reach the appropriate level or increase the difficulty of the temple encounters as needed.

Published adventures always provide a guideline for which levels of characters are appropriate to play. Keep in mind that this information is based on character power as well as expected treasure. Chapter 5: Campaigns gives a guideline for about how much treasure a character of a certain level should possess. This guideline is based on the (slightly more than) thirteen-encounters-per-level formula and assumes average treasures were given out. If you use a published adventure but tend to be generous with experience points, you might find that the characters in your group don't have as much treasure as the scenario assumes. Likewise, if you're stingy with experience points, the characters will probably gain treasure faster than levels. Of course, if you're stingy or generous with both treasure and experience points, it might just all even out.

treasure, other monsters have been given ratings of double the normal treasure for their encounter level.

On average, the PCs should earn one treasure suitable to their level for each encounter they overcome. The key, of course, is "average." Some monsters might have less treasure than average, some might have more, and some might have none at all. Monitor the progress of treasure into the hands of the PCs. For instance, you may want to use lots of high-treasure or low-treasure monsters, yet still hand out a normal amount of treasure overall.

Building a Treasure

You can use any of several methods for determining what treasures to include in your encounters or adventures.

An easy approach is to determine treasure randomly using the treasure information given in the *Monster Manual* for each kind of creature. Some creatures have more than average treasure and some less. If you use this system, the kind of creatures in an adventure determines how rich the treasures are. An adventure with lots of intelligent creatures has higher than average treasure, and one with mostly oozes, vermin, and dire animals has poor treasure. Balance the treasure by balancing the kinds of creatures or simply by adjusting the treasures toward the average.

If you want to include a balanced amount of treasure, you can just roll on Table 7–4: Treasure for each encounter according to its Encounter Level. If you want the treasures to make sense, roll for them randomly but then assign them to the encounters based on your best judgment. Double or triple up for some encounters, giving them two or three rolled treasures, and leave some others without treasure. In this way, you're sure that the treasures are balanced to the encounters overall, even if some encounters have lots of treasure and others have

none. For example, if your adventure has seven encounters of Encounter Level 5 each, just roll on the 5th-level row on Table 7–4: Treasure seven times and assign the seven treasures among the encounters.

You can also bypass Table 7–4 and base treasures on what their overall value should be. For example, since each 5th-level trea-

TABLE 7–2: TREASURE VALUES PER ENCOUNTER

Encounter Level	Treasure per Encounter
1	300 gp
2	600 gp
3	900 gp
4	1,200 gp
5	1,600 gp
6	2,000 gp
7	2,600 gp
8	3,400 gp
9	4,500 gp
10	5,800 gp
11	7,500 gp
12	9,800 gp
13	13,000 gp
14	17,000 gp
15	22,000 gp
16	28,000 gp
17	36,000 gp
18	47,000 gp
19	61,000 gp
20	80,000 gp

TABLE 7–3: AVERAGE TREASURE RESULTS

Type	Average Result
Gem	275 gp
Art object	1,100 gp
Mundane item	350 gp
Minor magic item	1,000 gp
Medium magic item	10,000 gp
Major magic item	40,000 gp

TABLE 7–4: TREASURE

Level	d%	—— Coins ——	d%	Goods	d%	Items
1st	01–14	—	01–90	—	01–71	—
	15–29	1d6×1,000 cp	91–95	1 gem	72–95	1 mundane
	30–52	1d8×100 sp	96–100	1 art	96–100	1 minor
	53–95	2d8×10 gp				
	96–100	1d4×10 pp				
2nd	01–13	—	01–81	—	01–49	—
	14–23	1d10×1,000 cp	82–95	1d3 gems	50–85	1 mundane
	24–43	2d10×100 sp	96–100	1d3 art	86–100	1 minor
	44–95	4d10×10 gp				
	96–100	2d8×10 pp				
3rd	01–11	—	01–77	—	01–49	—
	12–21	2d10×1,000 cp	78–95	1d3 gems	50–79	1d3 mundane
	22–41	4d8×100 sp	96–100	1d3 art	80–100	1 minor
	42–95	1d4×100 gp				
	96–100	1d10×10 pp				
4th	01–11	—	01–70	—	01–42	—
	12–21	3d10×1,000 cp	71–95	1d4 gems	43–62	1d4 mundane
	22–41	4d12×1,000 sp	96–100	1d3 art	63–100	1 minor
	42–95	1d6×100 gp				
	96–100	1d8×10 pp				
5th	01–10	—	01–60	—	01–57	—
	11–19	1d4×10,000 cp	61–95	1d4 gems	58–67	1d4 mundane
	20–38	1d6×1,000 sp	96–100	1d4 art	68–100	1d3 minor
	39–95	1d8×100 gp				
	96–100	1d10×10 pp				
6th	01–10	—	01–56	—	01–54	—
	11–18	1d6×10,000 cp	57–92	1d4 gems	55–59	1d4 mundane
	19–37	1d8×1,000 sp	93–100	1d4 art	60–99	1d3 minor
	38–95	1d10×100 gp			100	1 medium
	96–100	1d12×10 pp				
7th	01–11	—	01–48	—	01–51	—
	12–18	1d10×10,000 cp	49–88	1d4 gems	52–97	1d3 minor
	19–35	1d12×1,000 sp	89–100	1d4 art	98–100	1 medium
	36–93	2d6×100 gp				
	94–100	3d4×10 pp				
8th	01–10	—	01–45	—	01–48	—
	11–15	1d12×10,000 cp	46–85	1d6 gems	49–96	1d4 minor
	16–29	2d6×1,000 sp	86–100	1d4 art	97–100	1 medium
	30–87	2d8×100 gp				
	88–100	3d6×10 pp				
9th	01–10	—	01–40	—	01–43	—
	11–15	2d6×10,000 cp	41–80	1d8 gems	44–91	1d4 minor
	16–29	2d8×1,000 sp	81–100	1d4 art	92–100	1 medium
	30–85	5d4×100 gp				
	86–100	2d12×10 pp				
10th	01–10	—	01–35	—	01–40	—
	11–24	2d10×1,000 sp	36–79	1d8 gems	41–88	1d4 minor
	25–79	6d4×100 gp	80–100	1d6 art	89–99	1 medium
	80–100	5d6×10 pp			100	1 major

sure is worth 1,600 gp (on average), seven of them should be worth about 11,200 gp (on average). You can go right to the other tables (Table 7–5: Gems, Table 7–6: Art Objects, and so on) and roll on them instead. To balance these rolls, you need to know the average value of each table; see Table 7–3: Average Treasure Results. So for a treasure worth about 11,200 gp, you could roll for a medium magic item (10,000 gp) and an art object (1,100 gp) or roll for four minor items (1,000 gp each) and five gems (275 gp each), giving the rest in coins of the appropriate value. Depending on your rolls, you can get a treasure worth less than average or much more, but over the course of a campaign you should get pretty close to average results overall.

Finally, you could avoid rolling altogether and choose treasures. For treasures totaling 11,200 gp, you could just invent coins and gems worth 5,000 to 6,000 gp, and choose magic items from Chapter 8: Magic Items to fill the rest of the total.

NPCs with Treasure

The gear that NPCs carry serves as the bulk of their treasure. The average value of an NPC's gear is listed on Table 2–44: NPC Gear Value (page 58), and examples of what specific gear a character of a given class and level would have are in the sample NPC descriptions, pages 49–57. NPCs may have treasure in addition to their gear, at your discretion, but an NPC's gear is already worth about three times the average value of a treasure of his or her level. Defeating NPC foes brings about great reward for treasure-seekers, but since the gear is mostly magic that the NPC can use against the characters (some of which is one-use), it all evens out.

OTHER TREASURE

At times you're going to want to generate a treasure on the fly that's not directly related to a monster. You might, for example, have created a devious dungeon full of traps and puzzles with no monsters at all, and now you have to generate the grand treasury that the traps were protecting. You can still use the table. Just pick an appropriate level and roll. In situations where you are making an ad hoc adjudication, the appropriate level is usually the level of the party.

Using the Treasure Table

Cross-reference the level of the treasure on the left with the type of treasure. A standard treasure (one that includes coins, goods, and items) requires three rolls, one for each category. On a roll of 96–100, roll again on the next higher-level table in addition to the value listed. At 20th level, roll again on the same table.

TYPES OF TREASURE

Treasure comes in many forms: piles of coins, pouches of gems, useful adventuring equipment, and magic items.

Coins: The most basic sort of treasure is money. Table 7–4: Treasure generates anything from common copper pieces to rare platinum pieces. When placing coin hoards, remember the volume and weight of tens of thousands of coins is considerable (50 coins weigh 1 pound, so 10,000 coins weigh 200 pounds).

Gems: Smart PCs love gems because they're small, lightweight, and easily concealed compared with the same value in coins. Gem treasures are more interesting when you describe them and provide names. "A lustrous black pearl" is more interesting than "a 100 gp gem."

Art: Idols of solid gold, necklaces dripping with gems, old paintings of ancient kings, a bejeweled golden flagon—the category "art" includes all these and more. Portability is a major concern here. A jeweled comb is easy to carry, but a life-sized bronze statue of a knight is not. In general, most treasure you place in encounters should be easy for the PCs to carry (weighing 10 pounds or less). Treasure impossible to take out of the dungeon isn't really treasure.

Mundane Items: While nonmagical, these items are worthwhile as treasure because they are useful or valuable or both. Many of these treasures are used by intelligent opponents rather than just stored away as coins or gems are.

TABLE 7–4: TREASURE

Level	d%	— Coins —	d%	Goods	d%	Items
11th	01–08	—	01–24	—	01–31	—
	09–14	3d10×1,000 sp	25–74	1d10 gems	32–84	1d4 minor
	15–75	4d8×1,000 gp	75–100	1d6 art	85–98	1 medium
	76–100	4d10×10 pp			99–100	1 major
12th	01–08	—	01–17	—	01–27	—
	09–14	3d12×1,000 sp	18–70	1d10 gems	28–82	1d6 minor
	15–75	1d4×1,000 gp	71–100	1d8 art	83–97	1 medium
	76–100	1d4×100 pp			98–100	1 major
13th	01–08	—	01–11	—	01–19	—
	09–75	1d4×1,000 gp	12–66	1d12 gems	20–73	1d6 minor
	76–100	1d10×100 pp	67–100	1d10 art	74–95	1 medium
					96–100	1 major
14th	01–08	—	01–11	—	01–19	—
	09–75	1d6×1,000 gp	12–66	2d8 gems	20–58	1d6 minor
	76–100	1d12×100 pp	67–100	2d6 art	59–92	1 medium
					93–100	1 major
15th	01–03	—	01–09	—	01–11	—
	04–74	1d8×1,000 gp	10–65	2d10 gems	12–46	1d10 minor
	75–100	3d4×100 pp	66–100	2d8 art	47–90	1 medium
					91–100	1 major
16th	01–03	—	01–07	—	01–40	—
	04–74	1d12×1,000 gp	08–64	4d6 gems	41–46	1d10 minor
	75–100	3d4×100 pp	65–100	2d10 art	47–90	1d3 medium
					91–100	1 major
17th	01–03	—	01–04	—	01–33	—
	04–68	3d4×1,000 gp	05–63	4d8 gems	34–83	1d3 medium
	69–100	2d10×100 pp	64–100	3d8 art	84–100	1 major
18th	01–02	—	01–04	—	01–24	—
	03–65	3d6×1,000 gp	05–54	3d12 gems	25–80	1d4 medium
	66–100	5d4×100 pp	55–100	3d10 art	81–100	1 major
19th	01–02	—	01–03	—	01–04	—
	03–65	3d8×1,000 gp	04–50	6d6 gems	05–70	1d4 medium
	66–100	3d10×100 pp	51–100	6d6 art	71–100	1 major
20th	01–02	—	01–02	—	01–25	—
	03–65	4d8×1,000 gp	03–38	4d10 gems	26–65	1d4 medium
	66–100	4d10×100 pp	39–100	7d6 art	66–100	1d3 major

For treasures above 20th level, use the 20th-level row and then add a number of random major items.

Level	Magic Items	Level	Magic Items	Level	Magic Items
21st	+1	25th	+9	28th	+23
22nd	+2	26th	+12	29th	+31
23rd	+4	27th	+17	30th	+42
24th	+6				

TABLE 7–5: GEMS

d%	Value	Average	Examples
01–25	4d4 gp	10 gp	Banded, eye, or moss agate; azurite; blue quartz; hematite; lapis lazuli; malachite; obsidian; rhodochrosite; tiger eye turquoise; freshwater (irregular) pearl
26–50	2d4×10 gp	50 gp	Bloodstone; carnelian; chalcedony; chrysoprase; citrine; iolite, jasper; moonstone; onyx; peridot; rock crystal (clear quartz); sard; sardonyx; rose, smoky, or star rose quartz; zircon
51–70	4d4×10 gp	100 gp	Amber; amethyst; chrysoberyl; coral; red or brown-green garnet; jade; jet; white, golden, pink, or silver pearl; red spinel, red-brown or deep green spinel; tourmaline
71–90	2d4×100 gp	500 gp	Alexandrite, aquamarine, violet garnet, black pearl, deep blue spinel, golden yellow topaz
91–99	4d4×100 gp	1,000 gp	Emerald; white, black, or fire opal; blue sapphire; fiery yellow or rich purple corundum; blue or black star sapphire; star ruby
100	2d4×1,000 gp	5,000 gp	Clearest bright green emerald; blue-white, canary, pink, brown, or blue diamond; jacinth

TABLE 7–6: ART OBJECTS

d%	Value	Average	Examples
01–10	1d10×10 gp	55 gp	Silver ewer; carved bone or ivory statuette; finely wrought small gold bracelet
11–25	3d6×10 gp	105 gp	Cloth of gold vestments; black velvet mask with numerous citrines; silver chalice with lapis lazuli gems
26–40	1d6×100 gp	350 gp	Large well-done wool tapestry; brass mug with jade inlays
41–50	1d10×100 gp	550 gp	Silver comb with moonstones; silver-plated steel longsword with jet jewel in hilt
51–60	2d6×100 gp	700 gp	Carved harp of exotic wood with ivory inlay and zircon gems; solid gold idol (10 lb.)
61–70	3d6×100 gp	1,050 gp	Gold dragon comb with red garnet eye; gold and topaz bottle stopper cork; ceremonial electrum dagger with a star ruby in the pommel
71–80	4d6×100 gp	1,400 gp	Eyepatch with mock eye of sapphire and moonstone; fire opal pendant on a fine gold chain; old masterpiece painting
81–85	5d6×100 gp	1,750 gp	Embroidered silk and velvet mantle with numerous moonstones; sapphire pendant on gold chain
86–90	1d4×1,000 gp	2,500 gp	Embroidered and bejeweled glove; jeweled anklet; gold music box
91–95	1d6×1,000 gp	3,500 gp	Golden circlet with four aquamarines; a string of small pink pearls (necklace)
96–99	2d4×1,000 gp	5,000 gp	Jeweled gold crown; jeweled electrum ring
100	2d6×1,000 gp	7,000 gp	Gold and ruby ring; gold cup set with emeralds

TABLE 7–7: MUNDANE ITEMS

d%	Mundane Item
01–05	Alchemist's fire (1d4 flasks, 20 gp each)
06–10	Acid (2d4 flasks, 10 gp each)
11–12	Smokesticks (1d4 sticks, 20 gp each)
13–18	Holy water (1d4 flasks, 25 gp each)
19–20	Thunderstones (1d4 stones, 30 gp each)
21–22	Chain shirt (100 gp)*
23–27	Antitoxin (1d4 doses, 50 gp each)
28–29	Tanglefoot bag (1d4 bags, 50 gp each)
30–34	Masterwork studded leather (175 gp)**
35–39	Mighty composite shortbow†
40–43	Breastplate (200 gp)*
44–48	Banded mail (250 gp)*
49–66	Masterwork common melee weapon (roll on Table 8–12: Common Melee Weapons, page 184)
67–68	Masterwork uncommon weapon (roll on Table 8–13: Uncommon Weapons, page 184)
69–73	Masterwork ranged weapon (roll on Table 8–14: Common Ranged Weapons, page 185)
74–83	Mighty composite longbow††
84–93	Half-plate (600 gp)*
94–100	Full plate (1,500 gp)*

*Roll d%: 01–10 = Small, 11–100 = Medium-size. (Mundane armor is sized to fit its wearer. Magic armor resizes to its wearer's size.)

**Roll d%: 01–50 = Small, 51–100 = Medium-size. (Mundane armor is sized to fit its wearer. Magic armor resizes to its wearer's size.)

†Roll on Table 7–8: Random Mighty Composite Shortbow for bonus.

††Roll on Table 7–9: Random Mighty Composite Longbow for bonus.

TABLE 7–8: RANDOM MIGHTY COMPOSITE SHORTBOW

d%	Str Bonus	Value
01–60	+1	150 gp
61–100	+2	225 gp

TABLE 7–9: RANDOM MIGHTY COMPOSITE LONGBOW

d%	Str Bonus	Value
01–45	+1	200 gp
46–75	+2	300 gp
76–90	+3	400 gp
91–00	+4	500 gp

Minor, Medium, and Major Magic Items: Refer to the appropriate column on Table 8–2: Random Magic Item Generation (page 179) and use it to generate the specified number of magic items. Keep in mind that intelligent creatures use the magic items in their treasure if they're aware of the items' powers.

OTHER REWARDS

With great deeds and increasing reputation come the gratitude and admiration of those around you. Heroes are often awarded grants of land (which aid in the building of strongholds), decrees of friendship from communities they have rescued, and even honorary titles of nobility. As PCs gain levels and complete adventure after adventure, their notoriety (good or bad) spreads throughout the land so that NPCs may recognize them on sight.

Once PCs establish a reputation, it becomes easier to attract like-minded allies and admiring followers. Cohorts arrive who wish to share in their adventures, as do apprentices eager to be trained by such legendary figures. Villains begin to consider the PCs' possible actions when concocting their evil schemes. The player characters have left their mark and made a place for themselves in the campaign world with their grand exploits.

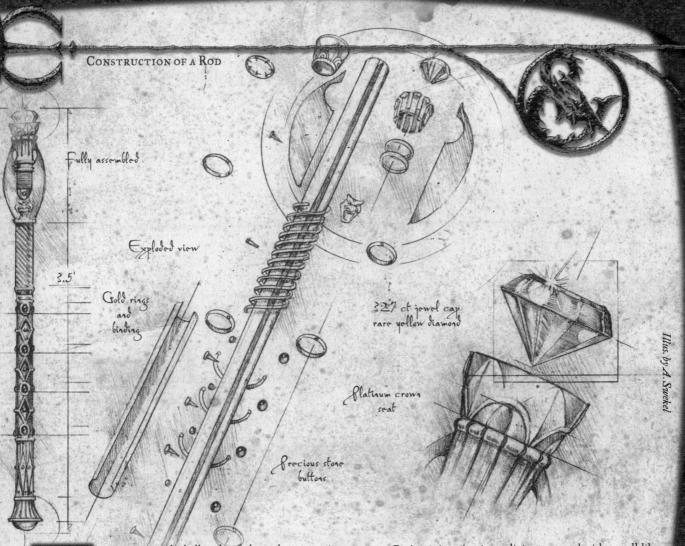

CONSTRUCTION OF A ROD

Fully assembled

3.5'

Exploded view

Gold rings
and
binding

Precious stone
buttons

32'7 ct jewel cap
rare yellow diamond

Platinum crown
seat

Illus. by A. Swekel

Magic items are the hallmarks of a legendary campaign. They are gleaned from the hoards of conquered monsters, taken from fallen foes, and sometimes crafted by the characters themselves. The most valuable and coveted of all the sorts of treasure that an adventurer could hope to find, magic items grant abilities to a character that he could never have otherwise, or complement his existing capabilities in wondrous ways. Some magic items even have intelligence and are almost NPCs in their own right.

Magic items are divided into categories: armor, weapons, potions, rings, rods, scrolls, staffs, wands, and wondrous items. In addition, some magic items are cursed or intelligent. Finally, a few magic items are of such rarity and power that they are considered to belong to a category of their own: artifacts. Artifacts are classified in turn as minor (extremely rare but not one-of-a-kind items) or major (each one unique and extremely potent).

Armor and Shields: Armor (including shields) offers improved, magical protection to the wearer. Some of these items confer abilities beyond a benefit to Armor Class. A character wearing a *+2 breastplate of etherealness* is not only protected by this magically enhanced armor (+2 enhancement bonus to AC) but can transform her body into an ethereal form.

Weapons: Weapons are enchanted with a variety of combat powers and almost always improve the attack and damage rolls of the wielder as well. A *+3 frost dwarven waraxe* named Durandil ("stone cleaver") adds +3 to attack rolls and damage rolls, and also inflicts an additional 1d6 points of bonus cold damage. Durandil was once a valued weapon of the dwarves of Durast, but it has long been lost and now rests on an island in the middle of a pool of lava in a cavern deep below the surface. Durandil is buried under a pile of various coins, a forgotten treasure of the red wyrm Nath.

Potions: A potion is an elixir concocted with a spell-like effect that affects only the drinker. A *potion of gaseous form* is a purplish, oily liquid in a frosted glass vial. It allows a character to dissolve into a wispy mist and float through cracks.

Rings: A ring is a circular metal band worn on the finger (no more than two rings per character) that contains a spell-like power (often a constant effect that affects the wearer). A *ring of three wishes* has three rubies, each of which holds the power needed to grant the wearer a single *wish*, while a *ring of invisibility* can render its wearer invisible an unlimited number of times.

Rods: A rod is a unique, scepterlike item with a special power unlike any known spell. The *rod of lordly might*, for example, can transform into various weapons at the push of a button, as well as become a ladder, a battering ram, and more.

Scrolls: A scroll is a spell magically inscribed onto paper or parchment so that it can be used later. A scroll of *searing light* allows a cleric to cast *searing light* once, as though she had prepared the spell herself, except that any level-based effects—such as range and damage—are based on the level of the scroll's creator (in this case Uthan, the high priest of Pelor in the Duchy of Urnst). Uthan is willing to give the scroll to any who would challenge his rival: Red Willapir, the head of the assassins' guild operating out of the nearby hills.

Staffs: A staff looks like a large wand but is always enchanted to cast a number of different (often related) spells. The *staff of the deathsong* is a long shaft of hardened wood, emblazoned with cryptic,

mystic runes and capped by a forked piece of dark metal at one end. It hums when picked up or when swung like a quarterstaff by its owner, presently the dark elf Yrinthakis. The *staff of the deathsong* has the ability to produce sonic vibrations that act as either a *shatter* spell (DC 12) or a *shout* spell (DC 14). Since it has 50 charges, Yrinthakis can use its powers for a total of fifty times. When Mialee, Tordek, and Jozan defeat the drow wizard after a bitter fight, the staff has only 34 charges left.

Wands: A wand is a short stick imbued with the power to cast a specific spell fifty times. The *wand of magic missile* is a useful weapon for a wizard or sorcerer. Fully charged, it allows its user to cast a *magic missile* spell fifty times. Nosh the Mighty, a wizard of great skill, keeps one secreted on his person at all times.

Wondrous Items: All wondrous items belong to a catch-all category that includes magic jewelry, tools, books, clothing, and much more. They range from the *hat of disguise*, which allows the wearer to take on the appearance of others, to the monstrous *apparatus of Kwalish*, a metallic, crablike construct that characters can ride within and control.

HANDLING MAGIC ITEMS

The DM should keep all the following information in mind when dealing with magic items.

PLACEMENT AS TREASURE

Including magic items as part of a treasure is a vital task of the DM. It's also a delicately difficult one. It can be tempting to hand out powerful or particularly interesting items too soon or too often. (A smaller number of DMs make the opposite mistake, being too stingy and handing out too few magic items.) A single overpowering item can ruin a whole campaign—but if the PCs don't get enough magic items, they won't be powerful enough to deal with the challenges that have been balanced for characters of their level. The treasure tables were designed to help in this regard (see Generating Random Magic Items, page 179). Occasionally, however, you'll want to give your players items you have hand-picked as especially suitable for their characters. Feel free to do this more and more as you gain experience as a DM and—most important—as you become familiar with what the items can and can't do.

Remember that magic items can and probably will be used by the NPCs who own them. If an orc chief has a *+2 longsword* in his treasure hoard, most likely he'll use it in that final battle with the PCs' champion. Creatures such as a medusa or a lammasu might be able to use a *necklace of adaptation*, and even a dragon can drink a potion.

APPEARANCE

Most magic items come into the campaign as treasure found by the PCs. When they find a new item, you have to describe it to them. Describing magic items to the players verbally requires a little forethought on your part. You don't want to say "You see a *+2 short sword* and a *wand of web* on the table." That gives away too much information. Presumably, a character can't tell what bonus a magic weapon has by looking at it, and can't know a wand's spell by its shape. Even if he or she could identify an item in this way, that should be because the ability to do so is something that you have consciously decided to incorporate into your game.

You have three choices when describing magic items:

Magic Items Appear Mundane: Magic items don't look like anything special. Only *detect magic* or a suspicious/curious/lucky player (see Trial and Error, below) allows the PC to discover that the stick he's been using as a backscratcher is really a *staff of the magi*. The benefit to this method is that players are always curiously examining everything. The drawback is that the players are *always* curiously examining everything, taking a great deal of time away from the action. You also run the risk of making magic seem dull because magic items are nothing special to look at.

Magic Items Appear Distinctive: Magic items glow, pulse with power, and are covered in runes, gems, and ornate workmanship. In this flashy sort of campaign, appearance usually has a direct relationship to the power of the item. Magic swords glow, and particularly powerful magic swords (encrusted with gems or carved entirely from a single pure gemstone) glow particularly bright. The item's appearance also may be a clue to its powers. A *wand of burning hands* could be carved from cedar or redwood with a fiery pattern etched into its surface in gold leaf. *Boots of speed* might be stitched with the image of a runner on

Yrinthakis the dark elf uses the staff of the deathsong to devastating effect.

their sides. The benefit of this approach is that magic items always seem grand and marvelous. The drawback is that they also become obvious, to the point of being ostentatious.

Magic Items Vary in Appearance: Magic items vary greatly in appearance, from unremarkable to exotic-looking. (This is the default method. Magic items described in this chapter were handled in this way.) Sometimes great power lies hidden within modest housing. Other times, items indicate their function or level of power in obvious ways. This case-by-case approach has the benefits and drawbacks of both methods above and allows you to focus your level of detail where and when you want to.

IDENTIFYING ITEMS

When PCs find magic items as treasure, they're going to need to figure out what to do. The following methods are available to identify magic items.

Trial and Error: This is often the first approach that a group of PCs tries once they believe they've found a magic item. It's a fun part of any game. Without access to spells that tell what an item does, PCs are free to experiment. This usually entails a PC attempting to use the item. "I put the ring on and jump up and down, flapping my arms," a player might say. If the item happens to be a *ring of flying*, then the experiment (and good guesswork) should be rewarded. Or, the player might put the same ring on and ask if she feels anything. In this case, a DM might say, "You feel light-headed and your stomach lurches upward," or even "You feel particularly light on your feet." With items that are normally completely consumed, allow for minor experimentation. A sip of a potion, for example, might be enough to give the character a tingling sensation and some clue to its function.

Close study of an item might provide some information. A command word could be etched in tiny letters on the inside of the ring, or a feathered design might hint that it allows one to fly. In such a case, a Search check (DC 15 or maybe 20) should reveal the clue.

You might also permit a character to attempt a Spellcraft or Knowledge (arcana) check (DC 30) to determine if she can attune herself with the item's power or if she remembers reading of it once in her studies. The PCs may want to consult bards, sages, or high-level spellcasters who might be able to identify items either through their own spell use, prior knowledge and experience, or research. They might know some details or rumors about an item's history as well. Such consultants always want something in return for the information, of course.

Spells: Obviously, the easiest way for characters to discern whether an object is magic is to use *detect magic*. That spell can also be used to find out a little about an item. When focused on an item, it can determine the school of the spell or spells embedded within, as well as the general power level of the item (based on the caster level). When a character uses *detect magic* on a magic item, the information you provide often serves as a clue to a smart player for identifying the item. Because of this, always be clear about the school of the spell and the caster level. (See the spell description for exact details.)

The *identify* and *analyze dweomer* spells provide much more information. See their descriptions in the *Player's Handbook*.

DM Explanation: Eventually, you might just break down and tell the players what an item is. That's okay, particularly in the instance where the item adds a bonus to actions the PC is already taking. A PC using a +2 *sword*, for example, eventually notices the amount that the sword is helping him and can thereby determine its bonus. Use this option if it becomes a pain for you to keep mentally adding +2 to all the character's attack and damage rolls with that unidentified (to him) item.

Magic Items and *Detect Magic*

When *detect magic* identifies a magic item's school of magic, this information refers to the school of the spell placed within the potion, scroll, or wand, or the prerequisite given for the item. If more than one spell is given as a prerequisite, use the highest-level spell. If no spells are included in the prerequisites, use the following default guidelines:

Item Nature	School
Armor and protection items	Abjuration
Weapons or offensive items	Invocation
Bonus to ability score, skill check, etc.	Transmutation

USING ITEMS

To use a magic item, it must be activated, although sometimes activation simply means putting a ring on your finger. Some items, once donned, function constantly. In most cases, using an item requires an activate magic item action that does not provoke attacks of opportunity. By contrast, spell completion items are treated like spells in combat and do provoke attacks of opportunity.

Activating a magic item is a standard action unless the item indicates otherwise. However, the casting time of a spell is the time required to activate the same power in an item, whether it's a scroll, a wand, or a pair of boots, unless the item description specifically states otherwise.

The four ways to activate magic items are:

Spell Completion: This is the activation method for scrolls. A scroll is a spell that is mostly finished. The preparation is done for the caster, so no preparation time is needed beforehand as with normal spellcasting. All that's left to do is perform the short, simple, finishing parts of the spellcasting (the final gestures, words, and so on.). To use a spell completion item safely, a character must be high enough level in the right class to cast the spell already. If he can't already cast the spell, there's a chance he'll make a mistake (see Scroll Mishaps, page 203, for possible consequences). Activating a spell completion item is a standard action and provokes attacks of opportunity exactly as casting a spell does.

Spell Trigger: Spell trigger activation is similar to spell completion, but it's even simpler. No gestures or spell finishing is needed, just a special knowledge of spellcasting that an appropriate character would know and a single word that must be spoken. This means that if a wizard picks up a spell trigger activation item (such as a wand or a staff) and that item stores a wizard spell, she knows how to use it. Specifically, anyone with a spell on his or her spell list knows how to use a spell trigger item that stores that spell. (This is the case even for a character who can't actually cast spells, such as a 3rd-level paladin.) The user must still determine what spell is stored in the item before she can and activate it. Activating a spell trigger item is a standard action and does not provoke attacks of opportunity.

Command Word: If no activation method is suggested either in the magic item description or by the nature of the item, assume that a command word is needed to activate it. Command word activation means that a character speaks the word and the item activates. No other special knowledge is needed.

A command word is the key to the item's lock, as it were. It can be a real word such as "Vibrant," "Square," or "Horse," but when this is the case, the holder of the item runs the risk of activating the item accidentally by speaking the word in normal conversation. More often, the command word is some seemingly nonsensical word, or a word or phrase from an ancient language no longer in common use. Activating a command word magic item is a standard action and does not provoke attacks of opportunity.

As mentioned above, sometimes the command word to activate an item is written right on the item. Occasionally, it might be hidden within a pattern or design engraved on, carved into, or built into the item, or the item might bear a clue to the command word. For example, if the command word is "King," the item might have the image of a king or a crown etched in its surface. A more difficult version of the same clue might be the name of the local king when the item was made. In this case, the character has to conduct some historical research to identify the name.

Knowledge (arcana) or Knowledge (history) skills might be useful in helping to identify command words or deciphering clues regarding them. A successful check (DC 30) is needed to come up with the word itself. If that check is failed, succeeding at a second check (DC 25) might provide some insight into a clue.

The spells *identify* and *analyze dweomer* both reveal command words.

Use Activated: This type of item simply has to be used in order to activate it. A character has to drink a potion, swing a sword, interpose a shield to deflect a blow in combat, look through a lens, sprinkle dust, wear a ring, or don a hat. Use activation is generally straightforward and self-explanatory.

Many use-activated items are objects that a character wears. Continually functioning items, such as a *cloak of resistance* or a *headband of intellect*, are practically always items that one wears. A few, such as a *pearl of power*, must simply be in the character's possession (on his person, not at home in a locked trunk). However, some items made for wearing, such as a *ring of invisibility*, must still be activated. Although this activation sometimes requires a command word (see above), usually it means mentally willing the activation to happen. The description of an item usually states whether a command word is needed in such a case.

Unless stated otherwise, activating a use-activated magic item is either a standard action or not even an action and does not provoke attacks of opportunity, unless the use involves committing an action that provokes an attack of opportunity in itself, such as running through a threatened area with magic boots. If the use of the item takes time (such as drinking a potion or putting on or taking off a ring or hat) before a magical effect occurs, then use activation is a standard action. If the item's activation is subsumed in use and takes no extra time (such as swinging a magic sword that has a built-in enhancement bonus), use activation is usually not even an action.

Use activation doesn't mean that if you use an item you automatically know what it can do. Just putting on a *ring of jumping* does not immediately activate it. You must know (or at least guess) what the item can do and then use the item in order to activate it, unless the benefit of the item comes automatically, such from drinking a potion or swinging a sword.

Size and Magic Items

When an article of magic clothing, jewelry, or armor is discovered, most of the time size shouldn't be an issue. Many magic garments are made to be easily adjustable, or they adjust themselves magically to the wearer. As a rule, size should not keep overweight characters, characters of various genders, or characters of various kinds from using magic items. Players shouldn't be penalized for choosing a halfling character or deciding that their character is especially tall.

Only say "It doesn't fit" if there's a good reason. Cloaks made specifically by the selfish, self-absorbed drow elves might fit only elves. Dwarves might make items usable only by dwarf-sized and dwarf-shaped characters to keep their items from being used against them. Such items should be the exceptions, however, not the rule.

Limit on Magic Items Worn

Characters are limited in their ability to use certain magic items, based on the item's type. Just as it doesn't make sense to wear multiple pairs of glasses or shoes simultaneously, so too characters can't stack items meant to be worn on a particular part of the body. Only so many items of a certain kind can be worn and be effective at the same time. The limits include the following:

1 headband, hat, or helmet
1 pair of eye lenses or goggles

1 cloak, cape, or mantle
1 amulet, brooch, medallion, necklace, periapt, or scarab
1 suit of armor
1 robe
1 vest, vestment, or shirt
1 pair of bracers or bracelets
1 pair of gloves or gauntlets
2 rings
1 belt
1 pair of boots

Of course, a character may carry or possess as many items of the same type as he wishes. He can have a pouch jammed full of magic rings, for example. But he can only benefit from two rings at a time. If he puts on a third ring, it doesn't work. This general rule applies to other attempts to "double up" on magic items—for instance, if a character puts on another magic cloak on top of the one he is already wearing, the second cloak's power does not work.

SAVING THROWS AGAINST MAGIC ITEM POWERS

Magic items produce spells or spell-like effects. For a saving throw against a spell or spell-like effect from a magic item, the DC is always 10 + the level of the spell or effect + the ability bonus of the minimum ability score needed to cast that level of spell. For example, a 2nd-level spell's DC would be 10 + 2 (for being 2nd level) + 1 (for needing at least a 12 in the relevant ability score to cast a 2nd-level spell), or a total of 13. Another way to figure this number is to multiply the spell's level by 1.5 and add 10 to the result.

Most item descriptions give saving throw DCs for various effects, particularly when the effect has no exact spell equivalent (making its level otherwise difficult to determine quickly).

DAMAGING MAGIC ITEMS

Magic items should always get a saving throw against spells that might deal damage to them—even against attacks from which a mundane item would normally get no chance to save. Magic items use the same saving throw bonus for all saves, no matter what the type (Fortitude, Reflex, or Will). A magic item's saving throw bonus equals 2 + one-half its caster level (round down). For example, a *lantern of revealing*, with a caster level of 5, has a +4 saving throw bonus if it is caught in a *fireball*, and the same bonus if someone attempts to *disintegrate* it. The only exceptions to this are intelligent magic items, which make Will saves based on their own Wisdom scores.

Magic items, unless otherwise noted, take damage as normal items of the same type. A damaged magic item continues to function, but if it is destroyed, all its magical power is lost.

BONUSES FROM MAGIC

Many magic items offer a bonus on attack rolls, damage rolls, saving throws, Armor Class, ability scores, or skill checks. Most items that add to saving throws, attack rolls, damage rolls, or AC are restricted to a maximum bonus of +5. (*Bracers of armor* are an exception.) Most items that add to ability scores are restricted to a maximum bonus of +6, and the bonus usually comes in multiples of 2 (+2, +4, or +6). Skill check bonuses do not have a maximum.

Bonuses of different types always stack. So a +1 *cloak of resistance* (adds a resistance bonus to saving throws) works with a paladin's general +2 bonus to saving throws. Identical types of bonuses do not stack, so a +3 *longsword* (+3 enhancement bonus for a +3 to attack, +3 to damage) would not be affected by a *magic weapon* spell that grants a weapon a +1 enhancement bonus to attack and damage.

Different named bonus types all stack, but usually a named bonus does not stack with another bonus of the same name (except for enhancement bonuses to armor and shields, enhancement bonuses to ranged weapons and their ammunition, dodge bonuses, synergy bonuses, and some circumstance bonuses).

Armor: This is the same type of bonus that mundane armor gives a character. A spell that gives an armor bonus typically creates an invisible, tangible field of force around the affected character.

Circumstance: A bonus or penalty based on situational factors, which may apply either to a check or the DC for that check. Circumstance modifiers stack with each other, unless they arise from essentially the same circumstance. Example: *robe of blending*.

Competence: When a character has a competence bonus, he actually gets better at what he's doing, such as with the spell *guidance*.

Deflection: A deflection bonus increases a character's AC by making attacks veer off, such as with the spell *shield of faith*.

Dodge: An enhancement of a character's ability to get out of the way quickly. Dodge bonuses *do* stack with other dodge bonuses. However, spells and magic items never grant dodge bonuses. Only feats and special abilities can do that.

Enhancement: An enhancement bonus represents an increase in the strength or effectiveness of a character's armor or weapon, as with the spells *magic vestment* and *magic weapon*, or a general bonus to an ability score, such as with the spell *cat's grace*.

Enlargement: When a character gets bigger, his Strength increases (as might his Constitution). That's an enlargement bonus. Example: *enlarge*.

Haste: A haste bonus improves a character's AC because he is moving faster, as in the spell *haste*.

Inherent: An inherent bonus is a bonus to an ability score that results from powerful magic, such as a *wish*. A character is limited to a total inherent bonus of +5 to any ability score.

Insight: An insight bonus makes a character better at what he's doing because he has an almost precognitive knowledge of factors pertinent to the activity, as with the spell *true strike*.

Luck: A luck bonus is a general bonus that represents good fortune, such as from the spell *divine favor*.

Morale: A morale bonus represents the effects of greater hope, courage, and determination, such as from the *bless* spell.

Natural Armor: A natural armor bonus is the type of bonus that many monsters get because of their tough or scaly hides. A natural armor bonus bestowed by a spell (such as *barkskin*) indicates that the subject's skin has become tougher.

Profane: A profane bonus represents the power of evil, such as granted by the spell *desecrate*.

Resistance: A resistance bonus is a general bonus against magic or harm.

Sacred: The opposite of a profane bonus, a sacred bonus relates to the power of good, such as granted by the spell *consecrate*.

Synergy: A bonus resulting from an unusually beneficial interaction between two related skills. Synergy bonuses are not granted by magic items.

INTELLIGENCE

Some magic items, particularly weapons, have an intelligence all their own. Only permanent magic items (as opposed to those with a single use or those with charges) can be intelligent. (This means that potions, scrolls, and wands, among other items, are never intelligent.)

In general, melee weapons have intelligence 15% of the time, ranged weapons have intelligence 5% of the time, and items of other sorts are intelligent 1% of the time.

See Intelligent Items, page 228, for more information.

CURSED ITEMS

Some items are cursed—incorrectly made, or corrupted by outside forces. Cursed items might be particularly dangerous to the user, or they might be normal items with a minor flaw, an inconvenient

TABLE 8–1: BONUSES FROM MAGIC

Bonus Type	Improves	Sample Spell	Sample Magic Item
Armor	AC	Mage armor	Bracers of armor
Circumstance	Attacks, checks	—	Robe of blending
Competence	Attacks, saves, checks	Tenser's transformation	Potion of heroism
Deflection	AC	Cloak of chaos	Ring of protection
Dodge	AC	Never	Never
Enhancement	Armor's bonus	Magic vestment	+1 armor
Enhancement	Attacks, damage	Magic weapon	+1 sword
Enhancement	Ability scores	Cat's grace	Gauntlets of ogre power
Enlargement	Str, Con	Righteous might	Potion of enlarge
Haste	AC	Haste	Monk's belt
Inherent	Ability scores	Wish	Tome of clear thought
Insight	Attacks, AC, saves, checks	True strike	—
Luck	Attacks, weapon damage, AC, saves, checks	Divine favor	Stone of good luck
Morale	Attacks, weapon damage, checks, saves	Bless	Ring of elemental command
Natural armor	AC	Barkskin	Amulet of natural armor
Profane	AC, saves, checks	Unhallow	Horn of evil
Resistance	Saves	Resistance	Cloak of resistance
Sacred	AC, saves, checks	Consecrate	Horn of goodness
Synergy	Checks	—	—

BEHIND THE CURTAIN: STACKING BONUSES

Keeping track of the different types of bonuses a character gets from different sources may seem like a real bother. There are good reasons to do this, however.

Balance: The main reason to keep track of what stacks and what doesn't stack is to keep total bonuses from getting out of hand. If a character wears a *belt of giant strength*, it's unbalancing to allow the cleric to cast *bull's strength* on her as well and allow both bonuses to add up. Likewise, a character with *mage armor*, magic plate armor, a *ring of protection*, a *cloak of protection*, a *barkskin* spell, and an *amulet of natural armor* would be unbalanced if all his bonuses were cumulative. Stacking restrictions keep the game within manageable limits, while still allowing characters to benefit from multiple magic items. For instance, note that half of the items from the previous example—the *mage armor*, the *ring of protection*, and the *barkskin*, for example—could all work together, because they provide bonuses of different types.

Consistency and Logic: The system of bonus types provides a way to make sense out of what can work together and what can't. At some point, when adding types of protection together, a reasonable player realizes that some protections are just redundant. This system logically portrays how it all makes sense together.

Encouraging Good Play: Categorizing bonuses by type allows players to put together suites of effects that do work in conjunction in a consistent manner—encouraging smart play rather than pile-it-on play.

requirement, or an unpredictable nature. Randomly generated items are cursed 5% of the time. If you wish to include faulty and/or dangerous magic items in your campaign, see Cursed Items, page 231, for more information.

CHARGES, DOSES, AND MULTIPLE CHARGES AND USES

Many items, particularly wands and staffs, are limited in power by the number of charges they hold. Normally, charged items have 50 charges at most. If such an item is found as a random part of a treasure, roll d% and divide by 2 to determine the number of charges left (round down, minimum 1). If the item has a maximum number of charges other than 50, roll randomly to determine how many charges are left. For example, a random *ring of three wishes* has 1d3 *wishes* left.

Prices listed are always for fully charged items. (When an item is created, it is fully charged.) For an item that's worthless when its charges run out (which is the case for almost all charged items), the value of the partially used item is proportional to the number of charges left. A wand with 20 charges, for example, is worth 40% of the value of a fully charged wand (with 50 charges). For an item the has usefulness in addition to its charges, only part of the item's value is based on the number of charges left (DM's discretion).

Some items, such as arrows, sticks of incense, pinches of magic dust, and potions, are single-use and expendable. Such items can often be found in sets or groups. For example, it's common to come upon a pouch with more than one pinch of *dust of disappearance*, or a flask with multiple 1-ounce doses of a *potion of cure light wounds*. (Potions are priced by the vial.) These are priced and weighted in the random tables individually, but you can allow more of such items when they are determined. For example, if three minor magic items are indicated in a treasure hoard and you get *incense of meditation* on the first roll, you might decide that all three items are sticks of incense. Such placement makes for more logical hoards of treasure and more useful finds for adventurers.

NEW MAGIC ITEMS

In the same way that you can invent new spells and monsters for your campaign, you can invent new magic items. In the same way that a PC spellcaster can research a new spell, a PC may be able to invent a new kind of magic item. And just as you have to be careful about new spells, you need to be careful with new magic items.

Use the magic item descriptions in this chapter as examples on which to base new magic items. A new magic item needs all the information that similar, existing magic items have, possibly including activation type, activation time, and caster level. You should also be ready to determine the market value of a new magic item, even one that the PCs simply find, in case a character wants to sell it or duplicate it.

MAGIC ITEM DESCRIPTIONS

In the following sections, each general type of magic item, such as armor or potions, gets an overall description, followed by descriptions of specific items.

General descriptions include notes on activation, random generation, and other material. The AC, hardness, hit points, and break DC are listed for typical examples of some types of magic items. The AC assumes that the item is unattended and includes a –5 penalty for the item's effective Dexterity of 0. If a creature holds the item, use the creature's Dexterity modifier in place of the –5 penalty.

Some individual items, notably those that simply store spells and nothing else, don't get full-blown descriptions. Simply reference the spell's description in the *Player's Handbook* for details, modified by the form of the item (potion, scroll, wand, and so on).

Assume that the spell is cast at the minimum level required to cast it, unless you choose to make it higher for some reason (which increases the cost of the item; see Table 8–40: Calculating Magic Item Gold Piece Values). The main reason to make it higher, of course, would be to increase the power of the spell. This decision is common for spells dependent on level, such as *fireball*, for which damage is everything, or *summon monster*, in which duration can increase the power of the spell dramatically.

Items with full descriptions have their powers detailed, and each of the following topics is covered in notational form at the end of the description.

Caster Level: The power of the item (just as a spell's caster level measures its power). The caster level determines the item's saving throw bonus, as well as range or other level-dependent aspects of the powers of the item (if variable). It also determines the level that must be contended with should the item come under the effect of a *dispel magic* spell or similar situation.

For potions, scrolls, and wands, the creator can set the caster level of the item at any number high enough to cast the stored spell and not higher than her own caster level. For example, at 5th level, Mialee could scribe a scroll of *invisibility* at caster level 3 (making it last 30 minutes), caster level 4 (40 minutes), or caster level 5 (50 minutes). For other magic items, the caster level is determined by the item itself. In this case, the creator's caster level must be as high as the item's caster level (and prerequisites may effectively put a higher minimum on the creator's level).

Prerequisites: The requirements that must be met in order for a character to create the item. These include feats, spells, and miscellaneous requirements such as level, alignment, and race or kind. Note that a spell prerequisite may be provided by a character who has prepared the spell (or who knows the spell, in the case of a sorcerer or bard), or through the use of a spell completion or spell trigger magic item or a spell-like ability that produces the desired spell effect. For each day that passes in the creation process, the creator must expend one spell completion item (such as a scroll) or one charge from a spell trigger item (such as a wand), if either of those objects is used to supply a prerequisite.

It is possible for more than one character to cooperate in the creation of an item, with each participant providing one or more of the prerequisites. In some cases, cooperation may even be necessary, such as if one character knows some of the spells necessary to create an item and another character knows the rest.

If two or more characters cooperate to create an item, they must agree among themselves who will be considered the creator for the purpose of determinations where the creator's level must be known. (It's generally sensible, although not mandatory, for the highest-level character involved to be considered the creator.)

Typically, a list of prerequisites includes one feat and one or more spells (or some other requirement in addition to the feat). When two spells at the end of a list are separated by "or," one of those spells is required in addition to every other spell mentioned prior to the last two. For example, the prerequisites for a *ring of three wishes* are "Forge Ring, *wish* or *miracle*," meaning that either *wish* or *miracle* is required as well as the Forge Ring feat.

Market Price: The going rate if a character wants to buy the item. Market price is also included on the random tables for easy reference. The market price for an item that can be constructed with the item creation feats is usually equal to the base price plus the price for any components (material or experience point).

Cost to Create: The cost in gp and XP to create the item. This entry appears only for items with components (material or experience points), which make their market prices higher than their base prices. The cost to create includes the costs derived from the base cost plus the costs of the components. Items without components do not have a "Cost to Create" entry. For them, the market price and the base price are the same. The cost in gp is 1/2 the market price, and the cost in XP is 1/25 the market price.

Weight: Wondrous items have their weight listed. An entry of "—" indicates an item that has no weight worth noting (for purposes of determining how much of a load a character can carry).

MAGIC ITEM NAMES

Spell-storing magic items—primarily potions and wands—have names that simply reflect the spell stored within them, such as a *wand of fireball* or *potion of haste*. In the game world, these may be replaced by more sophisticated or evocative names (see Chapter 6: World-Building). The straightforward names of spell-storing items also distinguish them from more powerful items with more interesting names such as the *staff of power*, the *robe of the archmagi*, or a *holy avenger* sword.

RANDOM MAGIC ITEMS

The adventurers have slain the evil lich and now plunder her ancient tomb. What wonders does it hold? Well, the DM has already used Table 7–4: Treasure (pages 170–171), some of the results of which then referred him or her to Table 8–2: Random Magic Item Generation, below (a good reason to always prepare treasure hoards ahead of time). Chapter 7 also contains references to minor, medium, and major magic treasures. Minor magic treasures are fairly meager, medium magic treasures are the most standard (worth about ten to twelve times that of a minor), and major treasures are the greatest of hauls (worth about four times as much as a medium treasure, on average).

Follow this procedure to generate a magic item as part of a treasure hoard:

1. When Table 7–2 indicates a minor, medium, or major magic treasure, you can use Table 8–2: Random Magic Item Generation to determine the specific type of magic item—such as a scroll, wand, or weapon. Optionally, you can roll d%: On a result of 01–05, refer to Table 8–38: Cursed Items rather than rolling on the standard tables.

2. Refer to the table that corresponds to the type of item indicated in step 1. These tables produce an appropriate item for each type (scroll, wand, wondrous item, and so on) and rating (minor, medium, or major).

3. Once the item has been determined, roll d% for special qualities:

   Staffs and Wands: If the item is a wand, a 01–30 result indicates that something (a design, inscription, etc.) provides a clue to its function, and 31–100 indicates no special qualities.

   Armors, Shields, Rings, Rods, Staffs, and Wondrous Items: If the item is a rod, staff, ring, wondrous item, armor, or shield, a 01 result indicates the item is intelligent, a 02–31 result indicates that something (a design, inscription, etc.) provides a clue to its function, and 32–100 indicates no special qualities.

   Ranged Weapons: If the item is a ranged weapon, a 01–05 result indicates the item is intelligent, a 06–25 result indicates that something (a design, inscription, etc.) provides a clue to its function, and 26–100 indicates no special qualities.

   Melee Weapons: If the item is a melee weapon, a 01–20 result indicates that the item sheds light, a 21–25 result indicates that the item is intelligent, 26–35 indicates that the item is both intelligent and sheds light, 36–50 indicates that something (a design, inscription, etc.) provides a clue to its function, and 51–100 indicates no special qualities.

4. If the item has charges or uses, roll randomly to determine how many charges or uses it has (as described in Charges, Doses, and Multiple Charges and Uses, above).

Sometimes you want to pick an item rather than generating it randomly. In this case, simply skim through the listings until you find one to your liking. Note that no artifacts (minor or major) appear anywhere on the random tables. This is deliberate: You must place artifacts intentionally at appropriate places within your campaign.

TABLE 8–2: RANDOM MAGIC ITEM GENERATION

Minor	Medium	Major	Item
01–04	01–10	01–10	Armor and shields (Table 8–3)
05–09	11–20	11–20	Weapons (Table 8–10)
10–44	21–30	21–25	Potions (Table 8–18)
45–46	31–40	26–35	Rings (Table 8–19)
—	41–50	36–45	Rods (Table 8–20)
47–81	51–65	46–55	Scrolls (Table 8–21)
—	66–68	56–75	Staffs (Table 8–26)
82–91	69–83	76–80	Wands (Table 8–27)
92–100	84–100	81–100	Wondrous items (Tables 8–28, 8–29, and 8–30)

ARMOR

Magic armor is a common but vital type of enchanted item. In general, it protects the wearer to a greater extent than armor without any enchantment. Magic armor bonuses are referred to as enhancement bonuses, never rise above +5, and stack with regular armor bonuses (and with shield and magic shield enhancement bonuses). Further, all magic armor is also masterwork armor, so armor check penalties are reduced by 1.

In addition to an enhancement bonus, armor may have special abilities, such as the ability to resist critical hits or to help the wearer hide. Special abilities count as additional bonuses for determining the market value of an item, but do not improve AC. A suit of armor cannot have an effective bonus (enhancement plus special ability bonus equivalents) higher than +10. A suit of armor with a special ability must have at least a +1 enhancement bonus.

Armor is always created so that even if the type of armor comes with boots or gauntlets, these pieces can be switched for other magic boots or gauntlets. Magic armor, like almost all magic items, resizes itself to fit the wearer.

Caster Level for Armor and Shields: The caster level of a magic shield or magic armor with a special ability is given in the item description. For an item with only an enhancement bonus, the caster level is three times the enhancement bonus. If an item has both an enhancement bonus and a special ability, the higher of the two caster level requirements must be met.

Shields: Shield enhancement bonuses stack with armor enhancement bonuses, so that a *+1 large steel shield* and *+1 chainmail* grant a total of bonus of +9 to AC. Shield enhancement bonuses do not act as attack or damage bonuses when the shield is used in a bash. The *bashing shield* enchantment, however, does grant a +1 bonus to attacks and damage (see the item description). You could, in fact, build a shield that also acted as a magic weapon, but the magic offensive bonus cost would need to be added into the defensive bonus cost of the shield.

As with armor, special abilities built into the shield add to the market value in the form of additions to the bonus of the shield, although they do not improve AC. A shield cannot have an effective bonus (enhancement plus special ability bonus equivalents) higher than +10. A shield with a special ability must have at least a +1 enhancement bonus.

Shields' Hardness and Hit Points: An attacker cannot damage a magic shield with an enhancement bonus unless his own weapon has at least as high an enhancement bonus as the shield struck. Each +1 of enhancement bonus also adds 1 to the shield's hardness and hit points. (See Attack an Object in Chapter 8: Combat, page 135 in the *Player's Handbook* for common shield hardness and hit points.)

Activation: Usually a character benefits from magic armor and shields in exactly the way a character benefits from mundane armor and shields—by wearing them. If armor or a shield has a special ability that the user needs to activate (such as with an *animated shield*), then the user usually needs to utter the command word (a standard action).

Random Generation: To generate magic armor and shields randomly, first roll on Table 8–3: Armor and Shields, and then roll on Table 8–4: Random Armor Type or Table 8–5: Random Shield Type as indicated. Use Table 8–6: Armor Special Abilities, Table 8–7: Shield Special Abilities, Table 8–8: Specific Magic Armors, or Table 8–9: Specific Magic Shields as further indicated. For example, on Table 8–3, rolling a 94 on the Medium column indicates a special ability and another roll. The second roll is a 29, indicating +2 *armor*. A roll of 64 on Table 8–6: Armor Special Abilities indicates acid resistance. Finally, a roll of 44 on Table 8–4: Random Armor Type indicates chainmail, so the result is *+2 chainmail of acid resistance*.

Special Qualities: Roll d%. An 01 result indicates the armor or shield is intelligent, a 02–31 result indicates that something (a design, inscription, etc.) provides a clue to its function, and 32–100 indicates no special qualities. Intelligent items have extra abilities and sometimes also extraordinary powers and special purposes. Use Table 8–31: Item Intelligence, Wisdom, Charisma, and Capabilities as indicated if armor or a shield is intelligent.

TABLE 8–3: ARMOR AND SHIELDS

Minor	Medium	Major	Item	Market Price
01–60	01–05	—	+1 shield	+1,000 gp
61–80	06–10	—	+1 armor	+1,000 gp
81–85	11–20	—	+2 shield	+4,000 gp
86–87	21–30	—	+2 armor	+4,000 gp
—	31–40	01–08	+3 shield	+9,000 gp
—	41–50	09–16	+3 armor	+9,000 gp
—	51–55	17–27	+4 shield	+16,000 gp
—	56–57	28–38	+4 armor	+16,000 gp
—	—	39–49	+5 shield	+25,000 gp
—	—	50–57	+5 armor	+25,000 gp
—	—	—	+6 armor/shield*	+36,000 gp
—	—	—	+7 armor/shield*	+49,000 gp
—	—	—	+8 armor/shield*	+64,000 gp
—	—	—	+9 armor/shield*	+81,000 gp
—	—	—	+10 armor/shield*	+100,000 gp
—	58–60	58–60	Specific armor**	—
—	61–63	61–63	Specific shield†	—
88–100	64–100	64–100	Special ability and roll again‡	—

*Armor and shields can't actually have bonuses this high. Use these lines to determine price when special abilities are added in. *Example:* A suit of *+5 armor* that also has the shadow special ability (+1 modifier) is treated as *+6 armor* for pricing purposes and is priced at 36,000 gp.

**Roll on Table 8–8: Specific Armors.

†Roll on Table 8–9: Specific Shields.

‡Roll on Table 8–6: Armor Special Abilities or Table 8–7: Shield Special Abilities.

TABLE 8–4: RANDOM ARMOR TYPE

d%	Armor	Armor Cost*
01	Padded	+155 gp
02	Leather	+160 gp
03–12	Hide	+165 gp
13–27	Studded leather	+175 gp
28–42	Chain shirt	+250 gp
43	Scale mail	+200 gp
44	Chainmail	+300 gp
45–57	Breastplate	+350 gp
58	Splint mail	+350 gp
59	Banded mail	+400 gp
60	Half-plate	+750 gp
61–100	Full plate	+1,650 gp

All magic armor is masterwork armor (with an armor check penalty 1 lower than normal).

*Add to enhancement bonus on Table 8–3: Armor and Shields to determine total market price.

TABLE 8–5: RANDOM SHIELD TYPE

d%	Shield	Shield Cost*
01–10	Buckler	+165 gp
11–15	Shield, small, wooden	+153 gp
16–20	Shield, small, steel	+159 gp
21–30	Shield, large, wooden	+157 gp
31–95	Shield, large, steel	+170 gp
96–100	Shield, tower	+180 gp

All magic shields are masterwork shields (with an armor check penalty 1 lower than normal).

*Add to enhancement bonus on Table 8–3: Armor and Shields to determine total market price.

TABLE 8–6: ARMOR SPECIAL ABILITIES

Minor	Medium	Major	Special Ability	Market Price Modifier*
—	01–02	01–02	Fortification, light	+1 bonus
01–30	03–07	03–08	Glamered	+1 bonus
31–52	08–19	09	Slick	+1 bonus
53–74	20–30	10–11	Shadow	+1 bonus
75–96	31–49	12–14	Silent moves	+1 bonus
—	50–50	15–16	Spell resistance (13)	+2 bonus
—	51–60	17–21	Ghost touch	+3 bonus
—	—	22–23	Invulnerability	+3 bonus
97–98	61–65	24–27	Fortification, moderate	+3 bonus
—	66	28–29	Spell resistance (15)	+3 bonus
—	67–71	30–31	Acid resistance	+3 bonus
—	72–76	32–41	Cold resistance	+3 bonus
—	77–81	42–51	Fire resistance	+3 bonus
—	82–86	52–61	Lightning resistance	+3 bonus
—	87–91	62–64	Sonic resistance	+3 bonus
—	92–94	65–67	Spell resistance (17)	+4 bonus
—	95	68–69	Etherealness	+5 bonus
—	96–98	70–72	Fortification, heavy	+5 bonus
—	—	73–74	Spell resistance (19)	+5 bonus
99–100	99–100	75–100	Roll twice again**	—

*Add to enhancement bonus on Table 8–3: Armor and Shields to determine total market price.

**If you roll a special ability twice, only one counts. If you roll two versions of the same special ability, use the better.

TABLE 8–7: SHIELD SPECIAL ABILITIES

Minor	Medium	Major	Special Ability	Market Price Modifier*
01–30	—	—	Bashing	+1 bonus
31–50	—	—	Blinding	+1 bonus
51–60	—	—	Fortification, light	+1 bonus
61–99	01–10	—	Arrow deflection	+2 bonus
—	11–16	01–15	Animated	+2 bonus
—	17–20	16–20	Spell resistance (13)	+2 bonus
—	21–25	21–25	Ghost touch	+3 bonus
—	26–30	26–35	Fortification, moderate	+3 bonus
—	31–40	36–38	Acid resistance	+3 bonus
—	41–50	39–41	Cold resistance	+3 bonus
—	51–60	42–44	Fire resistance	+3 bonus
—	61–70	45–47	Lightning resistance	+3 bonus
—	71–80	48–50	Sonic resistance	+3 bonus
—	—	51–55	Spell resistance (15)	+3 bonus
—	—	56–60	Spell resistance (17)	+4 bonus
—	—	61–65	Fortification, heavy	+5 bonus
—	81–90	66–70	Reflecting	+5 bonus
—	—	71–80	Spell resistance (19)	+5 bonus
100	91–100	81–100	Roll twice again**	—

*Add to enhancement bonus on Table 8–3: Armor and Shields to determine total market price.

**If you roll a special ability twice, only one counts. If you roll two versions of the same special ability, use the better.

Armor and Shield Special Abilities Descriptions

Most magic armor and shields only have enhancement bonuses. Such items can also have the special abilities detailed here. Armor or a shield with a special ability must have at least a +1 enhancement bonus.

Acid Resistance: A suit of armor or a shield with this enchantment normally has a dull gray appearance. The armor absorbs the first 10 points of acid damage per round that the wearer would normally take (similar to the *resist elements* spell).

Caster Level: 5th; *Prerequisites:* Craft Magic Arms and Armor, *resist elements*; *Market Price:* +3 bonus.

Animated: Upon command, an animated shield floats within 2 feet of the wielder, protecting her as if she were using it herself but freeing up both her hands. Only one shield can protect a character at a time.

Caster Level: 12th; *Prerequisites:* Craft Magic Arms and Armor, *animate objects*; *Market Price:* +2 bonus.

Arrow Deflection: This shield protects the wielder as if he had the Deflect Arrows feat. Once per round when he would normally be struck by a ranged weapon, he can make a Reflex saving throw (DC 20). If the ranged weapon has an enhancement bonus, the DC increases by that amount. If he succeeds, the shield deflects the weapon. He must be aware of the attack and not flat-footed. Attempting to deflect a ranged weapon doesn't count as an action. Exceptional ranged weapons, such as boulders hurled by giants or *Melf's acid arrows*, can't be deflected.

Caster Level: 5th; *Prerequisites:* Craft Magic Arms and Armor, *shield*; *Market Price:* +2 bonus.

Bashing: This shield is made to make a shield bash. No matter what the size of the attacker, a large bashing shield deals 1d8 points of damage and a small bashing shield deals 1d6 points of damage. The shield acts as a +1 *weapon* when used to bash. (Tower shields cannot be bashing shields.)

Caster Level: 8th; *Prerequisites:* Craft Magic Arms and Armor, *bull's strength*; *Market Price:* +1 bonus.

Blinding: A shield with this enchantment flashes with a brilliant light up to twice per day upon command of the wielder. All within 20 feet except the wielder must make a Reflex saving throw (DC 14) or be blinded for 1d4 rounds.

Caster Level: 7th; *Prerequisites:* Craft Magic Arms and Armor, *blindness/deafness, searing light*; *Market Price:* +1 bonus.

Cold Resistance: A suit of armor or a shield with this enchantment normally has a bluish, icy hue or is adorned with furs and shaggy pelts. The armor absorbs the first 10 points of cold damage per round that the wearer would normally take (similar to the *resist elements* spell).

Caster Level: 5th; *Prerequisites:* Craft Magic Arms and Armor, *resist elements*; *Market Price:* +3 bonus.

Etherealness: On command, this enchantment allows the wearer of the armor to become ethereal (see the *ethereal jaunt* spell) once per day. The character can remain ethereal for as long as desired, but once he returns to normal, he cannot become ethereal again that day.

Caster Level: 15th; *Prerequisites:* Craft Magic Arms and Armor, *ethereal jaunt*; *Market Price:* +5 bonus.

Fire Resistance: A suit of armor with this enchantment normally has a reddish hue and often is decorated with a draconic motif. The armor absorbs the first 10 points of heat damage per round that the wearer would normally take (similar to the *resist elements* spell).

Caster Level: 5th; *Prerequisites:* Craft Magic Arms and Armor, *resist elements*; *Market Price:* +3 bonus.

Fortification: This suit of armor or shield produces a magical force that protects vital areas of the wearer more effectively. When a critical hit or sneak attack is scored on the wearer, there is a chance that the critical hit or sneak attack is negated and damage is instead rolled normally:

Fortification Type	Chance for Normal Damage	Market Price
Light	25%	+1 bonus
Moderate	75%	+3 bonus
Heavy	100%	+5 bonus

Caster Level: 13th; *Prerequisites:* Craft Magic Arms and Armor, *limited wish* or *miracle*; *Market Price:* varies (see above).

Ghost Touch: This armor or shield seems almost translucent. Both its enhancement bonus and its armor bonus count against the attacks of incorporeal creatures. Further, it can be picked up, moved, and worn by incorporeal creatures at any time. Incorporeal creatures gain the armor or shield's enhancement bonus against both corporeal and incorporeal attacks, and they can still pass freely through solid objects.

Caster Level: 15th; *Prerequisites:* Craft Magic Arms and Armor, *etherealness*; *Market Price:* +3 bonus.

Glamered: A suit of armor with this capability appears normal. Upon command, the armor changes shape and form to assume the appearance of a normal set of clothing. The armor retains all its properties (including weight) when glamered. Only a *true seeing* spell or similar magic reveals the true nature of the armor when disguised.

Caster Level: 10th; *Prerequisites:* Craft Magic Arms and Armor, *alter self*; *Market Price:* +1 bonus.

Invulnerability: This suit of armor grants the wearer damage reduction of 5/+1.

Caster Level: 18th; *Prerequisites:* Craft Magic Arms and Armor, *stoneskin, wish* or *miracle*; *Market Price:* +3 bonus.

Lightning Resistance: A suit of armor or a shield with this enchantment normally has a bluish hue and often bears a storm or lightning motif. The armor absorbs the first 10 points of electrical damage per round that the wearer would normally take (similar to the *resist elements* spell).

Caster Level: 5th; *Prerequisites:* Craft Magic Arms and Armor, *resist elements*; *Market Price:* +3 bonus.

Reflection: This shield seems like a mirror. Its surface is completely reflective. Once per day as a free action, it can be called on to reflect a spell back at its caster exactly like the *spell turning* spell.

Caster Level: 14th; *Prerequisites:* Craft Magic Arms and Armor, *spell turning*; *Market Price:* +5 bonus.

Shadow: This type of armor is jet black and blurs the wearer whenever she tries to hide, granting a +10 circumstance bonus to Hide checks (essentially a bonus for an extremely favorable condition). This bonus does not stack with the Hide bonus granted by a *cloak of elvenkind* or obscuring or blinding-based Hide check bonuses. (The armor's armor check penalty still applies normally.)

Caster Level: 5th; *Prerequisites:* Craft Magic Arms and Armor, *invisibility*; *Market Price:* +1 bonus.

Silent Moves: This armor is well oiled and magically constructed so that it not only makes little sound, but it dampens sound around it. It adds a +10 circumstance bonus to its wearer's Move Silently checks. (The armor's armor check penalty still applies normally.)

Caster Level: 5th; *Prerequisites:* Craft Magic Arms and Armor, *silence*; *Market Price:* +1 bonus.

Slick: Slick armor seems coated at all times with a slightly greasy oil. It adds a +10 circumstance bonus to its wearer's Escape Artist checks. (The armor's armor check penalty still applies normally.)

Caster Level: 4th; *Prerequisites:* Craft Magic Arms and Armor, *grease*; *Market Price:* +1 bonus.

Sonic Resistance: A suit of armor or a shield with this enchantment normally has a glistening appearance. The armor absorbs the first 10 points of sonic damage per round that the wearer would normally take (similar to the *resist elements* spell).

Caster Level: 5th; *Prerequisites:* Craft Magic Arms and Armor, *resist elements*; *Market Price:* +3 bonus.

Spell Resistance: This enchantment grants the armor's wearer spell resistance while the armor is worn. The spell resistance can be SR 13, SR 15, SR 17, or SR 19, depending on the armor.

Caster Level: 15th; *Prerequisites:* Craft Magic Arms and Armor, *spell resistance; Market Price:* +2 bonus (SR 13), +3 bonus (SR 15), +4 bonus (SR 17), or +5 bonus (SR 19).

TABLE 8–8: SPECIFIC ARMORS

Medium	Major	Specific Armor	Market Price
01–10	—	Mithral shirt	1,100 gp
11–25	—	Elven chain	4,150 gp
26–35	—	*Rhino hide*	5,165 gp
36–45	—	Adamantine breastplate	5,350 gp
46–70	—	Dwarven plate	10,500 gp
71–80	01–10	*Plate armor of the deep*	16,650 gp
81–90	11–40	*Banded mail of luck*	18,900 gp
91–100	41–60	*Breastplate of command*	21,600 gp
—	61–80	*Celestial armor*	25,300 gp
—	81–100	*Demon armor*	41,650 gp

Specific Armors

The following specific suits of armor usually are preconstructed with exactly the qualities described here.

Adamantine Breastplate: This nonmagical breastplate is made of adamantine, giving it a natural +2 enhancement bonus.

Caster Level: —; *Prerequisites:* —; *Market Price:* 5,350 gp.

Banded Mail of Luck: Ten 100-gp gems adorn this +3 banded mail. Once per week, the armor allows its wearer to require that an attack roll made against him be rerolled. He must take whatever consequences come from the second roll, since not all luck is good. The wearer's player must decide whether to have the attack roll rerolled before damage is rolled.

Caster Level: 12th; *Prerequisites:* Craft Magic Arms and Armor, *bless; Market Price:* 18,900 gp; *Cost to Create:* 10,150 gp + 700 XP.

Breastplate of Command: This finely crafted +2 *breastplate* radiates a powerful aura of magic. When worn, the armor bestows a dignified and commanding aura upon its owner. The wearer gains a +2 circumstance bonus on Charisma checks, checks using skills for which Charisma is the key ability, and turning checks. Friendly troops within 360 feet of the user become braver than normal (for example, more willing than normal to follow a leader into battle against dangerous foes). Since the effect arises in great part from the distinctiveness of the armor, the wearer cannot hide or conceal herself in any way and still have the effect function.

Caster Level: 15th; *Prerequisites:* Craft Magic Arms and Armor, *mass charm; Market Price:* 21,600 gp; *Cost to Create:* 10,975 gp + 850 XP.

Celestial Armor: This bright silver or gold +1 *chainmail* is so fine and light that it can be worn under normal clothing without revealing its presence. It has a maximum Dexterity bonus of +8, an armor check penalty of −2, and an arcane spell failure chance of 15%. It is considered light armor, and it allows the wearer to *fly* on command (as the spell) once per day.

Caster Level: 5th; *Prerequisites:* Craft Magic Arms and Armor, creator must be good; *Market Price:* 25,300 gp; *Cost to Create:* 12,800 gp + 1,000 XP.

Demon Armor: This plate armor is fashioned to make the wearer appear to be a demon. The helmet is shaped to look like a horned demon head, and its wearer looks out of the open, tooth-filled mouth. This +4 *full plate* allows the wearer to make claw attacks that deal 1d10 (×2 critical) points of damage, strike as +1 weapons, and afflict the target as if she had been struck by a *contagion* spell (Fortitude negates DC 14). The "claws" are built into the armor's vambraces and gauntlets.

The armor bestows one negative level on any nonevil creature wearing it. This negative level persists as long as the armor is worn and disappears when the armor is removed. The negative level never results in actual level loss, but it cannot be overcome in any way (including *restoration* spells) while the armor is worn.

Caster Level: 13th; *Prerequisites:* Craft Magic Arms and Armor, *contagion; Market Price:* 41,650 gp; *Cost to Create:* 21,650 gp + 1,600 XP.

Dwarven Plate: This full plate is made of mithral. This armor has an arcane spell failure chance of 25%, a maximum Dexterity bonus of +3, and an armor check penalty of −4. It is considered medium armor and weighs 25 pounds.

Caster Level: —; *Prerequisites:* —; *Market Price:* 10,500 gp.

Elven Chain: This very light chainmail is made of very fine mithral links. Speed while wearing elven chain is 30 feet for Medium-size creatures, or 20 feet for Small. The armor has an arcane spell failure chance of 20%, a maximum Dexterity bonus of +4, and an armor check penalty of −2. It is considered light armor and weighs 20 pounds.

Caster Level: —; *Prerequisites:* —; *Market Price:* 4,150 gp.

Mithral Shirt: This very light chain shirt is made of very fine mithral links. Speed while wearing a *mithral shirt* is 30 feet for Medium-size creatures, or 20 feet for Small. The armor has an arcane spell failure chance of 10%, a maximum Dexterity bonus of +6, and no armor check penalty. It is still considered light armor (see Mithral, page 242). The shirt weighs 10 pounds.

Caster Level: —; *Prerequisite:* —; *Market Price:* 1,100 gp.

Plate Armor of the Deep: This +1 full plate armor is decorated with a wave and fish motif. The wearer takes no pressure damage from being deep underwater and is treated as unarmored for purposes of Swim checks. The wearer can also breathe underwater and can converse with any creature that breathes water.

Caster Level: 11th; *Prerequisites:* Craft Magic Arms and Armor, *freedom of movement, water breathing, tongues; Market Price:* 16,650 gp; *Cost to Create:* 9,150 gp + 600 XP.

Rhino Hide: This +2 *hide* armor is made from rhinoceros hide. In addition to granting a +2 enhancement AC bonus, it has a −1 armor check penalty and doubles all damage dealt by a charge attack made by the wearer.

Caster Level: 9th; *Prerequisites:* Craft Magic Arms and Armor, *haste; Market Price:* 5,165 gp; *Cost to Create:* 2,665 gp + 200 XP.

Demon armor

Specific Shields

The following specific shields usually are preconstructed with exactly the qualities described here.

Absorbing Shield: This +1 *large steel shield* is flat black in color and seems to absorb light. Every other day, it can be commanded to absorb a single Large or smaller object or creature that touches its front, annihilating the thing that touches it as a *sphere of anni-*

TABLE 8–9: SPECIFIC SHIELDS

Medium	Major	Specific Shield	Market Price
01–10	—	Darkwood shield	257 gp
11–18	—	Mithral large shield	1,020 gp
19–25	—	Adamantine shield	2,170 gp
26–45	01–20	*Spined shield*	2,670 gp
46–65	21–40	*Caster's shield*	3,153 gp
66–90	41–60	*Lion's shield*	9,170 gp
91–100	61–80	*Winged shield*	15,159 gp
—	81–100	*Absorbing shield*	50,170 gp

hilation does. A successful touch attack in combat is all that's needed to absorb a target. The shield therefore can deliver devastating shield bashes, but it is also useful for destroying an opponent's weapon.

Caster Level: 17th; *Prerequisites:* Craft Magic Arms and Armor, *disintegrate; Market Price:* 50,170 gp; *Cost to Create:* 25,170 gp + 2,000 XP.

Adamantine Shield: This large nonmagical shield is made from adamantine, giving it a natural +1 enhancement bonus.

Caster Level: —; *Prerequisites:* —; *Market Price:* 2,170 gp.

Caster's Shield: This *+1 small wooden shield* has a small leather strip on the back on which a spellcaster can scribe a single spell as on a scroll. A spell so scribed has only half the normal materials cost. (Experience point and component costs remain the same.) The user can cast the spell scribed on the back of the shield with no chance of arcane spell failure due to the shield.

A random *caster's shield* has a 50% chance of having a single medium scroll spell on it. The spell is divine (01–80 on d%) or arcane (81–100).

Caster Level: 6th; *Prerequisites:* Craft Magic Arms and Armor, Scribe Scroll, creator must be at least 6th level; *Market Price:* 3,153 gp (plus the value of the scroll spell if one is currently scribed); *Cost to Create:* 1,653 gp + 120 XP.

Darkwood Shield: This large nonmagical wooden shield is made out of darkwood. It has no enhancement bonus, but its construction material makes it lighter than a normal wooden shield. It weighs 5 pounds and has no armor check penalty.

Caster Level: —; *Prerequisites:* —; *Market Price:* 257 gp.

Lion's Shield: This *+2 large steel shield* is fashioned to appear to be a roaring lion's head. Three times per day, the lion's head can be commanded to attack (independently of the shield wearer), biting with the wielder's base attack bonus (including multiple attacks, if the wielder has them) and dealing 2d6 points of damage (×2 critical). This attack is in addition to any actions performed by the wielder.

Lion's shield

Caster Level: 10th; *Prerequisites:* Craft Magic Arms and Armor, *summon nature's ally IV; Market Price:* 9,170 gp; *Cost to Create:* 4,670 gp + 360 XP.

Mithral Large Shield: This very light large shield is made of mithral. It has a 5% arcane spell failure chance and no armor check penalty. It weighs 5 pounds.

Caster Level: —; *Prerequisite:* —; *Market Price:* 1,020 gp.

Spined Shield: This *+1 large steel shield* is covered in spines. It acts as a normal spiked shield. On command up to three times per day, the shield's wearer can fire one of the shield's spines. A fired spine has a +1 enhancement bonus, a range increment of 120 feet, and deals 1d10 points of damage (19–20/×2 critical). Fired spines regenerate each day.

Caster Level: 6th; *Prerequisites:* Craft Magic Arms and Armor, *magic missile; Market Price:* 2,670 gp; *Cost to Create:* 1,420 gp + 100 XP.

Winged Shield: This round, large wooden shield has a +3 enhancement bonus. Small, feathered wings encircle the shield. Once per day it can be commanded to *fly* (as the spell), carrying the wielder. The shield can *fly* up to 2 hours and carry 400 pounds while doing so.

Caster Level: 5th; *Prerequisites:* Craft Magic Arms and Armor, *fly; Market Price:* 15,159 gp; *Cost to Create:* 7,659 gp + 600 XP.

WEAPONS

As magic items go, magic weapons are a staple of all campaigns. Magic weapons have enhancement bonuses ranging from +1 to +5. They apply these bonuses to both attack and damage rolls when used in combat. All magic weapons are also masterwork weapons, but their masterwork bonus to attack does not stack with their enhancement bonus to attack.

Weapons come in two basic categories: melee and ranged. Some of the weapons listed as melee weapons (for example, daggers) can also be used as ranged weapons. In this case, their enhancement bonus applies to either type of attack.

In addition to an enhancement bonus, weapons may have special abilities, such as the ability to flame or the ability to attack on their own. Special abilities count as additional bonuses for determining the market value of the item, but do not modify attack or damage bonuses (except where specifically noted). A single weapon cannot have a modified bonus (enhancement bonus plus special ability bonus equivalents) higher than +10. A weapon with a special ability must have at least a +1 enhancement bonus.

Caster Level for Weapons: The caster level of a weapon with a special ability is given in the item description. For an item with only an enhancement bonus and no other abilities, the caster level is three times the enhancement bonus. If an item has both an enhancement bonus and a special ability, the higher of the two caster level requirements must be met.

Bonus Damage Dice: Some magic weapons deal bonus dice of damage. Unlike other modifiers to damage, bonus dice of damage are not multiplied when the attacker scores a critical hit.

Ranged Weapons and Ammunition: Masterwork ranged weapon bonuses to attack and masterwork ammunition (arrows, crossbow bolts, and sling bullets) attack bonuses stack with each other (but not with enhancement bonuses).

Unlike most enhancement bonuses, but similar to the way in which armor and shields work together, the enhancement bonuses of magic ranged weapons and magic ammunition stack for attack and damage purposes. So a *+1 longbow* firing a *+1 arrow* contributes a +2 attack bonus to the ranged attack roll and a +2 bonus to any damage dealt by the attack. However, for purposes of damage reduction, the enhancement bonuses of a magic ranged weapon and magic ammunition do not stack. Only the ammunition's enhancement bonus is applied against the damage reduction, since it is the only part of the weapon actually striking the creature. So, a *+1 longbow* firing a *+1 arrow* contributes a +2 attack bonus to hit a creature with damage resistance 5/+2, but since the arrow itself only has a +1 enhancement bonus, the damage reduction is still effective: 5 points of any damage dealt are subtracted from the damage the creature actually sustains.

Magic Ammunition and Breakage: When a magic arrow, crossbow bolt, or sling bullet misses its target, there is a 50% chance it breaks or otherwise is rendered useless. A magic arrow, bolt, or bullet that hits is destroyed.

TABLE 8–10: WEAPONS

Minor	Medium	Major	Weapon Bonus	Base Price*
01–70	01–10	—	+1	2,000 gp
71–85	11–20	—	+2	8,000 gp
—	21–58	01–20	+3	18,000 gp
—	59–62	21–38	+4	32,000 gp
—	—	39–49	+5	50,000 gp
—	—	—	+6**	72,000 gp
—	—	—	+7**	98,000 gp
—	—	—	+8**	128,000 gp
—	—	—	+9**	162,000 gp
—	—	—	+10**	200,000 gp
—	63–68	50–63	Specific weapon†	—
86–100	69–100	64–100	Special ability and roll again‡	—

*This price is for 50 arrows, crossbow bolts, or sling bullets.

**A weapon can't actually have a bonus higher than +5. Use these lines to determine price when special abilities are added in.

Example: A +3 dagger that also has the speed special ability (+4 modifier; see Table 8–15: Melee Weapon Special Abilities) is treated as a +7 dagger for pricing purposes and is priced at 98,000 gp.

†See Table 8–17: Specific Weapons.

‡See Table 8–15: Melee Weapon Special Abilities for melee weapons or Table 8–16: Ranged Weapon Special Abilities for ranged weapons.

TABLE 8–11: WEAPON TYPE DETERMINATION

d%	Weapon Type
01–70	Common melee weapon (see Table 8–12)
71–80	Uncommon weapon (see Table 8–13)
81–100	Common ranged weapon (see Table 8–14)

TABLE 8–12: COMMON MELEE WEAPONS

d%	Weapon	Weapon Cost*
01–04	Dagger	+302 gp
05–14	Greataxe	+320 gp
15–24	Greatsword	+350 gp
25–28	Kama	+302 gp
29–41	Longsword	+315 gp
42–45	Mace, light	+305 gp
46–50	Mace, heavy	+312 gp
51–54	Nunchaku	+302 gp
55–57	Quarterstaff**	+600 gp
58–61	Rapier	+320 gp
62–66	Scimitar	+315 gp
67–70	Shortspear	+302 gp
71–74	Siangham	+303 gp
75–84	Sword, bastard	+335 gp
85–89	Sword, short	+310 gp
90–100	Waraxe, dwarven	+330 gp

All magic weapons are masterwork weapons.

*Add to enhancement bonus on Table 8–10: Weapons to determine total market price.

**Masterwork double weapons incur double the masterwork cost to account for each head (+300 gp masterwork cost per head for a total of +600 gp). Double weapons have separate magical bonuses for their different heads. If randomly determined, the second head of a double weapon has the same enhancement bonus as the main head (01–50 on d%), doubling the cost of the bonus, or its enhancement bonus is one less (51–100 on d%) and it has no special abilities.

Light Generation: Fully 30% of magic weapons shed light equivalent to a torch (20-foot radius). These glowing weapons are quite obviously magical. Such a weapon can't be concealed when drawn, nor can its light be shut off. Some of the specific weapons detailed below always or never glow, as defined in their descriptions.

Hardness and Hit Points: An attacker cannot damage a magic weapon with an enhancement bonus unless his own weapon has at least as high an enhancement bonus as the weapon or shield struck. Each +1 of enhancement bonus also adds 1 to the weapon's or shield's hardness and hit points. (See Attack an Object in Chapter 8: Combat, page 135 in the *Player's Handbook* for common weapon hardnesses and hit points.)

Activation: Usually a character benefits from a magic weapon in exactly the way a character benefits from a mundane

TABLE 8–13: UNCOMMON WEAPONS

d%	Weapon	Weapon Cost*
01–03	Axe, orc double**	+660 gp
04–07	Battleaxe	+310 gp
08–10	Chain, spiked	+325 gp
11–12	Club	+300 gp
13–16	Crossbow, hand	+400 gp
17–19	Crossbow, repeating	+550 gp
20–21	Dagger, punching	+302 gp
22–23	Falchion	+375 gp
24–26	Flail, dire**	+690 gp
27–31	Flail, heavy	+315 gp
32–35	Flail, light	+308 gp
36–37	Gauntlet	+302 gp
38–39	Gauntlet, spiked	+305 gp
40–41	Glaive	+308 gp
42–43	Greatclub	+305 gp
44–45	Guisarme	+309 gp
46–48	Halberd	+310 gp
49–51	Halfspear	+301 gp
52–54	Hammer, gnome hooked**	+620 gp
55–56	Hammer, light	+301 gp
57–58	Handaxe	+306 gp
59–61	Kukri	+308 gp
62–63	Lance, heavy	+310 gp
64–65	Lance, light	+306 gp
66–67	Longspear	+305 gp
68–70	Morningstar	+308 gp
71–72	Net	+320 gp
73–74	Pick, heavy	+308 gp
75–76	Pick, light	+304 gp
77–78	Ranseur	+310 gp
79–80	Sap	+301 gp
81–82	Scythe	+318 gp
83–84	Shuriken	+301 gp
85–86	Sickle	+306 gp
87–89	Sword, two-bladed**	+700 gp
90–91	Trident	+315 gp
92–94	Urgrosh, dwarven**	+650 gp
95–97	Warhammer	+312 gp
98–100	Whip	+301 gp

All magic weapons are masterwork weapons.

*Add to enhancement bonus on Table 8–10: Weapons to determine total market price.

**Masterwork double weapons incur double the masterwork cost to account for each head (+300 gp masterwork cost per head for a total of +600 gp). Double weapons have separate magical bonuses for their different heads. If randomly determined, the second head of a double weapon has the same enhancement bonus as the main head (01–50 on d%), doubling the cost of the bonus, or its enhancement bonus is one less (51–100 on d%) and it has no special abilities.

weapon—by attacking with it. If a weapon has a special ability that the user needs to activate (such as the *sunbeam* power of a *sun blade*), then the user usually needs to utter the command word (a standard action).

Random Generation: To generate magic weapons randomly, first roll on Table 8–10: Weapons, and then roll on Table 8–11: Weapon Type Determination. Use Table 8–15: Melee Weapon Special Abilities, Table 8–16: Ranged Weapon Special Abilities, or Table 8–17: Specific Weapons if indicated by the roll on Table 8–10.

Special Qualities: Roll d%. If the item is a melee weapon, a 01–20 result indicates that the item sheds light, 21–25 indicates that the weapon is intelligent, 26–35 indicates that the weapon is both intelligent and sheds light, 36–50 indicates that something (a design, inscription, etc.) provides a clue to the weapon's function, and 51–100 indicates no special qualities. If the item is a ranged weapon, a 01–05 result indicates the weapon is intelligent, 06–25 indicates that something (a design, inscription, etc.) provides a clue to the weapon's function, and 26–100 indicates no special qualities. Intelligent weapons have extra abilities and sometimes also extraordinary powers and special purposes. Use Table 8–31: Item Intelligence, Wisdom, Charisma, and Capabilities as indicated if a magic weapon is intelligent.

TABLE 8–14: COMMON RANGED WEAPONS

d%	Weapon	Weapon Cost*
01–10	Ammunition	
01–50	Arrows (50)	+350 gp
51–80	Bolts, crossbow (50)	+350 gp
81–100	Bullets, sling (50)	+350 gp
11–15	Axe, throwing	+308 gp
16–25	Crossbow, heavy	+350 gp
26–35	Crossbow, light	+335 gp
36–39	Dart	+300 gp 5 sp
40–41	Javelin	+301 gp
42–46	Shortbow	+330 gp
47–51	Shortbow, composite	+375 gp
52–56	Shortbow, mighty composite (+1 Str bonus)	+450 gp
57–61	Shortbow, mighty composite (+2 Str bonus)	+525 gp
62–65	Sling	+300 gp
66–75	Longbow	+375 gp
76–80	Longbow, composite	+400 gp
81–85	Longbow, mighty composite (+1 Str bonus)	+500 gp
86–90	Longbow, mighty composite (+2 Str bonus)	+600 gp
91–95	Longbow, mighty composite (+3 Str bonus)	+700 gp
96–100	Longbow, mighty composite (+4 Str bonus)	+800 gp

All magic weapons are masterwork weapons.

*Add to enhancement bonus on Table 8–10: Weapons to determine total market price.

Magic Weapon Special Abilities Descriptions

Most magic weapons only have enhancement bonuses. They can also have the special abilities detailed here. A weapon with a special ability must have at least a +1 enhancement bonus.

Bane: A bane weapon excels at attacking one type of creature. Against its designated foe, its effective enhancement bonus is +2 better than its normal enhancement bonus (so a *+1 longsword* is a *+3 longsword* against its foe). Further, it deals +2d6 points of bonus damage against the foe. To randomly determine a weapon's designated foe, roll on the following table:

(Text continues on page 186)

TABLE 8–15: MELEE WEAPON SPECIAL ABILITIES

Minor	Medium	Major	Special Ability	Market Price Modifier*
01–15	01–10	—	Defending	+1 bonus
16–25	11–15	01–03	Flaming	+1 bonus
26–35	16–20	04–06	Frost	+1 bonus
36–45	21–25	07–09	Shock	+1 bonus
46–55	26–30	10–12	Ghost touch	+1 bonus
56–70	31–40	—	Keen‡	+1 bonus
71–80	41–50	13–17	Mighty cleaving	+1 bonus
81–89	51	18–19	Spell storing	+1 bonus
90–99	52–56	20–21	Throwing	+1 bonus
—	57–59	22–26	Bane	+2 bonus
—	60–62	27–29	Disruption†	+2 bonus
—	63–65	30–33	Flaming burst	+2 bonus
—	66–68	34–37	Icy burst	+2 bonus
—	69–71	38–41	Shocking burst	+2 bonus
—	72–76	42–44	Thundering	+2 bonus
—	77–79	46–47	Wounding	+2 bonus
—	80–82	48–52	Holy	+2 bonus
—	83–85	53–57	Unholy	+2 bonus
—	86–88	58–62	Lawful	+2 bonus
—	89–91	63–67	Chaotic	+2 bonus
—	92	68–71	Brilliant energy	+4 bonus
—	93	70–73	Dancing	+4 bonus
—	94–95	74–76	Speed	+4 bonus
—	—	77–80	Vorpal‡	+5 bonus
100	96–100	81–100	Roll again twice**	—

*Add to enhancement bonus on Table 8–10: Weapons to determine total market price.

**Reroll if you get a duplicate special ability, an ability incompatible with an ability that you've already rolled, or if the extra ability puts you over the +10 limit. A weapon's enhancement bonus and special ability bonus equivalents can't total more than +10.

†Bludgeoning weapons only. Reroll if randomly generated for a piercing or slashing weapon.

‡Slashing weapons only. Reroll if randomly generated for a non-slashing weapon.

TABLE 8–16: RANGED WEAPON SPECIAL ABILITIES

Minor	Medium	Major	Special Ability	Market Price Modifier*
01–20	01–15	—	Returning	+1 bonus
21–40	16–30	—	Distance	+1 bonus
41–60	31–35	01–10	Flaming	+1 bonus
61–80	36–40	11–20	Shock	+1 bonus
81–100	41–45	21–30	Frost	+1 bonus
—	46–50	31–40	Flaming burst	+2 bonus
—	51–55	41–50	Icy burst	+2 bonus
—	56–60	51–60	Shocking burst	+2 bonus
—	61–66	61–65	Bane	+2 bonus
—	67–74	66–70	Holy	+2 bonus
—	75–82	71–75	Unholy	+2 bonus
—	83–90	76–80	Lawful	+2 bonus
—	91–98	81–85	Chaotic	+2 bonus
—	—	86–90	Speed	+4 bonus
—	—	91–97	Brilliant energy	+4 bonus
—	99–100	98–100	Roll again twice**	—

*Add to enhancement bonus on Table 8–10: Weapons to determine total market price.

**Reroll if you get a duplicate special ability, an ability incompatible with an ability that you've already rolled, or if the extra ability puts you over the +10 limit. A weapon's enhancement bonus and special ability bonus equivalents can't total more than +10.

d%	Designated Foe
01–05	Aberrations
06–08	Animals
09–13	Beasts
14–20	Constructs
21–25	Dragons
26–30	Elementals
31–35	Fey
36–40	Giants
41–45	Magical beasts
46–50	Monstrous humanoids
51–53	Oozes
54–58	Outsiders, chaotic
59–65	Outsiders, evil
66–70	Outsiders, good
71–75	Outsiders, lawful
76–77	Plants
78–85	Shapechangers
86–92	Undead
93–94	Vermin
95–100	Humanoids (choose subtype)

Caster Level: 8th; *Prerequisites:* Craft Magic Arms and Armor, *summon monster I*; *Market Price:* +2 bonus.

Brilliant Energy: A brilliant energy weapon has its significant portion—such as its blade, axe head, or arrowhead—transformed into light, although this does not modify the item's weight. It gives off light as a torch (20-foot radius). A brilliant energy weapon ignores nonliving matter. Armor and enhancement AC bonuses do not count against it because the weapon passes through armor. (Dexterity, deflection, dodge, natural armor, and other such bonuses still apply.) A brilliant energy weapon cannot harm undead, constructs, and objects. Bows, crossbows, and slings cannot be enchanted with this ability.

Caster Level: 16th; *Prerequisites:* Craft Magic Arms and Armor, *gaseous form, continual flame*; *Market Price:* +4 bonus.

Chaotic: A chaotic weapon is chaotically aligned and infused with the power of chaos. It deals +2d6 points of bonus chaotic damage against all of lawful alignment. It bestows one negative level on any lawful creature attempting to wield it. The negative level remains as long as the weapon is in hand and disappears when the weapon is no longer wielded. This negative level never results in actual level loss, but it cannot be overcome in any way (including *restoration* spells) while the weapon is wielded. Bows, crossbows, and slings so enchanted bestow the chaotic power upon their ammunition.

Caster Level: 7th; *Prerequisites:* Craft Magic Arms and Armor, *chaos hammer*, creator must be chaotic; *Market Price:* +2 bonus.

Dancing: A dancing weapon can be loosed (requiring a standard action) to attack on its own. It fights for 4 rounds using the base attack bonus of the one who loosed it and then drops. It never leaves the side of the one who loosed it (never straying more than 5 feet) and fights on even if that creature falls. The wielder who loosed it can grasp it while it is attacking on its own as a free action, but when so retrieved it can't dance (attack on its own) again for 4 rounds.

Caster Level: 15th; *Prerequisites:* Craft Magic Arms and Armor, *animate objects*; *Market Price:* +4 bonus.

Defending: A defender weapon allows the wielder to transfer some or all of the sword's enhancement bonus to his AC as a special bonus that stacks with all others. As a free action, the wielder chooses how to allocate the weapon's enhancement bonus at the start of his turn before using the weapon, and the effect to AC lasts until his next turn.

Caster Level: 8th; *Prerequisites:* Craft Magic Arms and Armor, *shield* or *shield of faith*; *Market Price:* +1 bonus.

Disruption: A weapon of disruption is the bane of all undead. Any undead creature struck in combat must succeed at a Fortitude save (DC 14) or be destroyed. A weapon of disruption must be a bludgeoning weapon. (If you roll this property randomly for a piercing or slashing weapon, reroll.)

Caster Level: 14th; *Prerequisites:* Craft Magic Arms and Armor, *heal*; *Market Price:* a+2 bonus.

Distance: This enchantment can only be placed on a ranged weapon. A weapon of distance doubles its range increment.

Caster Level: 6th; *Prerequisites:* Craft Magic Arms and Armor, *clairaudience/clairvoyance*; *Market Price:* +1 bonus.

Flaming: Upon command, a flaming weapon is sheathed in fire. The fire does not harm the hands that hold the weapon. Flaming weapons deal +1d6 points of bonus fire damage on a successful hit. Bows, crossbows, and slings so enchanted bestow the fire energy upon their ammunition.

Caster Level: 10th; *Prerequisites:* Craft Magic Arms and Armor and *flame blade, flame strike,* or *fireball*; *Market Price:* +1 bonus.

Flaming Burst: A flaming burst weapon functions as a flaming weapon that also explodes with flame upon striking a successful critical hit. The fire does not harm the hands that hold the weapon. Flaming burst weapons deal +1d10 points of bonus fire damage on a successful critical hit. If the weapon's critical multiplier is ×3, add +2d10 points of bonus fire damage instead, and if the multiplier is ×4, add +3d10 points of bonus fire damage. Bows, crossbows, and slings so enchanted bestow the fire energy upon their ammunition.

Caster Level: 12th; *Prerequisites:* Craft Magic Arms and Armor and *flame blade, flame strike,* or *fireball*; *Market Price:* +2 bonus.

Frost: Upon command, a frost weapon is sheathed in icy cold. The cold does not harm the hands that hold the weapon. Frost weapons deal +1d6 points of bonus cold damage on a successful hit. Bows, crossbows, and slings so enchanted bestow the cold energy upon their ammunition.

Caster Level: 8th; *Prerequisites:* Craft Magic Arms and Armor, *chill metal* or *ice storm*; *Market Price:* +1 bonus.

Ghost Touch: A ghost touch weapon deals damage normally against incorporeal creatures, regardless of its bonus. (An incorporeal creature's 50% chance to avoid damage does not apply to ghost touch weapons.) Further, it can be picked up and moved by incorporeal creatures at any time. A manifesting ghost can wield the weapon against corporeal foes. Essentially, a ghost touch weapon counts as either corporeal or incorporeal at any given time, whichever is more beneficial to the wielder.

Caster Level: 9th; *Prerequisites:* Craft Magic Arms and Armor, *plane shift*; *Market Price:* +1 bonus.

Holy: A holy weapon is good aligned and blessed with holy power. It deals +2d6 points of bonus holy (good) damage against all of evil alignment. It bestows one negative level on any evil creature attempting to wield it. The negative level remains as long as the weapon is in hand and disappears when the weapon is no longer wielded. This negative level never results in actual level loss, but it cannot be overcome in any way (including *restoration* spells) while the weapon is wielded. Bows,

Brilliant energy battleaxe

crossbows, and slings so enchanted bestow the holy power upon their ammunition.

Caster Level: 7th; *Prerequisites:* Craft Magic Arms and Armor, *holy smite,* creator must be good; *Market Price:* +2 bonus.

Icy Burst: An icy burst weapon functions as a frost weapon that also explodes with frost upon striking a successful critical hit. The frost does not harm the hands that hold the weapon. Icy burst weapons deal +1d10 points of bonus cold damage on a successful critical hit. If the weapon's critical multiplier is ×3, add +2d10 points of bonus cold damage instead, and if the multiplier is ×4, add +3d10 points of bonus cold damage. Bows, crossbows, and slings so enchanted bestow the cold energy upon their ammunition.

Caster Level: 10th; *Prerequisites:* Craft Magic Arms and Armor, *chill metal* or *ice storm; Market Price:* +2 bonus.

Keen: This enchantment doubles the threat range of a weapon. For instance, if it is placed on a longsword (which has a normal threat range of 19–20), the keen longsword scores a threat on a 17–20. Only slashing weapons can be enchanted to be keen. (If you roll this property randomly for an inappropriate weapon, reroll.)

Caster Level: 10th; *Prerequisites:* Craft Magic Arms and Armor, *keen edge; Market Price:* +1 bonus.

Lawful: A lawful weapon is lawfully aligned and infused with the power of law. It deals +2d6 points of bonus lawful damage against all of chaotic alignment. It bestows one negative level on any chaotic creature attempting to wield it. The negative level remains as long as the weapon is in hand and disappears when the weapon is no longer wielded. This negative level never results in actual level loss, but it cannot be overcome in any way (including *restoration* spells) while the weapon is wielded. Bows, crossbows, and slings so enchanted bestow the lawful power upon their ammunition.

Caster Level: 7th; *Prerequisites:* Craft Magic Arms and Armor, *order's wrath,* creator must be lawful; *Market Price:* +2 bonus.

Mighty Cleaving: A mighty cleaving weapon allows a wielder with the Cleave feat to make one additional cleave attempt in a round. Only one extra cleave attempt is allowed per round.

Caster Level: 8th; *Prerequisites:* Craft Magic Arms and Armor, *divine power; Market Price:* +1 bonus.

Returning: This enchantment can only be placed on a weapon that can be thrown. A returning weapon returns through the air back to the creature that threw it. It returns on the round following the round that it was thrown just before its throwing creature's turn. It is therefore ready to use again that turn.

Caster Level: 7th; *Prerequisites:* Craft Magic Arms and Armor, *telekinesis; Market Price:* +1 bonus.

Shock: Upon command, a shock weapon is sheathed in crackling electricity. The electricity does not harm the hands that hold the weapon. Shock weapons deal +1d6 points of bonus electricity damage on a successful hit. Bows, crossbows, and slings so enchanted bestow the electricity energy upon their ammunition.

Caster Level: 8th; *Prerequisites:* Craft Magic Arms and Armor, *call lightning* or *lightning bolt; Market Price:* +1 bonus.

Shocking Burst: A shocking burst weapon functions as a shock weapon that also explodes with electricity upon striking a successful critical hit. The electricity does not harm the hands that hold the weapon. Shocking burst weapons deal +1d10 points of bonus electricity damage on a successful critical hit. If the weapon's critical multiplier is ×3, add +2d10 points of bonus electricity damage instead, and if the multiplier is ×4, add +3d10 points of bonus electricity damage. Bows, crossbows, and slings so enchanted bestow the electricity energy upon their ammunition.

Caster Level: 10th; *Prerequisites:* Craft Magic Arms and Armor, *call lightning* or *lightning bolt; Market Price:* +2 bonus.

Speed: A weapon of speed allows the wielder one single extra attack each round at his highest bonus. It is not cumulative with *haste.* The extra attack must be with this weapon, not with some other weapon. The weapon does not grant the benefits of a *haste* spell, so an additional partial action is not what is granted, simply an extra single attack with this weapon.

Caster Level: 7th; *Prerequisites:* Craft Magic Arms and Armor, *haste; Market Price:* +4 bonus.

Spell Storing: A spell-storing weapon allows a spellcaster to store a single targeted spell of up to 3rd level in the weapon. (The spell must have a casting time of 1 action.) Any time the weapon strikes a creature and the creature takes damage from it, the weapon can immediately cast the spell on that creature as a free action if the wielder desires. (This ability is a special exception to the general rule that casting a spell from an item takes at least as long as casting that spell normally.) *Inflict serious wounds, contagion, blindness,* and *hold person* are all common choices for the stored spell. Once the spell has been cast, the weapon is empty of spells, and a spellcaster can cast any other targeted spell of up to 3rd level into it. The weapon magically imparts to the wearer the name of the spell currently stored within it. A randomly rolled spell-storing weapon has a 50% chance to have a spell stored in it already.

Caster Level: 8th; *Prerequisites:* Craft Magic Arms and Armor, creator must be a caster of at least 12th level; *Market Price:* +1 bonus.

Thundering: A thundering weapon creates a cacophonous roar like thunder upon striking a successful critical hit. The sonic energy does not harm the wielder of the weapon. Thundering weapons deal +1d8 points of bonus sonic damage on a successful critical hit. If the weapon's critical multiplier is ×3, add +2d8 points of bonus sonic damage instead, and if the multiplier is ×4, add +3d8 points of bonus sonic damage. Bows, crossbows, and slings so enchanted bestow the sonic energy upon their ammunition. Subjects dealt a critical hit by a thundering weapon must make a Fortitude save (DC 14) or be deafened permanently.

Caster Level: 5th; *Prerequisites:* Craft Magic Arms and Armor, *blindness/deafness; Market Price:* +2 bonus.

Throwing: This enchantment can only be placed on a melee weapon. A melee weapon enchanted with this ability gains a range increment of 10 feet and can be thrown by a wielder proficient in its normal use.

Caster Level: 5th; *Prerequisites:* Craft Magic Arms and Armor, *magic stone; Market Price:* +1 bonus.

Unholy: An unholy weapon is evilly aligned and blessed with unholy power. It deals +2d6 points of bonus unholy (evil) damage against all of good alignment. It bestows one negative level on any good creature attempting to wield it. The negative level remains as long as the weapon is in hand and disappears when the weapon is no longer wielded. This negative level never results in actual level loss, but it cannot be overcome in any way (including *restoration* spells) while the weapon is wielded. Bows, crossbows, and slings so enchanted bestow the unholy power upon their ammunition.

Caster Level: 7th; *Prerequisites:* Craft Magic Arms and Armor, *unholy blight,* creator must be evil; *Market Price:* +2 bonus.

Vorpal: This potent and feared enchantment allows the weapon to sever the heads of those it strikes. Upon a successful critical hit, the weapon severs the opponent's head (if it has one) from its body. Some creatures, such as many abominations and all oozes, have no heads. Others, such as golems and undead creatures other than vampires, are not affected by the loss of their heads. Most other creatures, however, die when their heads are cut off. The DM may have to make judgment calls about this sword's effect. A vorpal weapon must be a slashing weapon. (If you roll this property randomly for an inappropriate weapon, reroll.)

Caster Level: 18th; *Prerequisites:* Craft Magic Arms and Armor, *keen edge, death spell; Market Price:* +5 bonus.

Wounding: A weapon of wounding deals damage to a creature such that a wound it inflicts bleeds for 1 point of damage per round thereafter in addition to the normal damage the weapon deals. Multiple wounds from the weapon result in cumulative bleeding loss (two wounds for 2 points of damage per round, and so on). The bleeding can only be stopped by a successful Heal check (DC 15) or the application of any *cure* spell or other healing spell (*heal, healing circle*, and so on).

Caster Level: 10th; *Prerequisites:* Craft Magic Arms and Armor, *Mordenkainen's sword; Market Price:* +1 bonus.

TABLE 8–17: SPECIFIC WEAPONS

Medium	Major	Specific Weapon	Market Price
01–20	—	Sleep arrow	132 gp
21–40	—	Screaming bolt	257 gp
41–55	01–04	Javelin of lightning	751 gp
56–65	05–09	Slaying arrow	2,282 gp
66–70	—	Adamantine dagger	3,302 gp
71–72	10–11	Trident of fish command	3,815 gp
—	12–13	Slaying arrow (greater)	4,057 gp
73–74	14–17	Dagger of venom	9,302 gp
75–76	18–20	Adamantine battleaxe	9,310 gp
77–79	21–25	Trident of warning	9,815 gp
80–82	26–30	Assassin's dagger	10,302 gp
83–85	31–35	Sword of subtlety	15,310 gp
86–88	36–40	Mace of terror	17,812 gp
89–91	41–45	Nine lives stealer	25,315 gp
92–94	46–50	Oathbow	27,875 gp
95–96	51–55	Sword of life stealing	30,315 gp
97–98	56–60	Flame tongue	32,315 gp
99–100	61–66	Life-drinker	40,320 gp
—	67–72	Frost brand	49,350 gp
—	73–78	Rapier of puncturing	50,320 gp
—	79–81	Sun blade	50,335 gp
—	82–83	Sword of the planes	52,315 gp
—	84–85	Sylvan scimitar	55,815 gp
—	86–87	Dwarven thrower	60,312 gp
—	88–90	Mace of smiting	75,312 gp
—	91–96	Holy avenger	120,315 gp
—	97–100	Luck blade	170,560 gp

Specific Weapons

The following specific weapons usually are preconstructed with exactly the qualities described here.

Adamantine Battleaxe: This nonmagical axe is made out of adamantine, giving it a natural +2 enhancement bonus.

Caster Level: —; *Prerequisites:* —; *Market Price:* 9,310 gp.

Adamantine Dagger: This nonmagical dagger is made out of adamantine, giving it a natural +1 enhancement bonus.

Caster Level: —; *Prerequisites:* —; *Market Price:* 3,302 gp.

Assassin's Dagger: This wicked-looking, curved +2 *dagger* adds a +1 bonus to the DC of a Fortitude save forced by the death attack of an assassin.

Caster Level: 9th; *Prerequisites:* Craft Magic Arms and Armor, *slay living; Market Price:* 10,302 gp; *Cost to Create:* 5,302 gp + 400 XP.

Dagger of Venom: This black +1 *dagger* has a serrated edge. It allows the wielder to inflict a *poison* spell (DC 14) upon a creature struck by the blade once per day. The wielder can decide to use the power after he has struck. Doing so is a a free action, but the *poison* spell must be inflicted on the same round that the dagger strikes.

Caster Level: 5th; *Prerequisites:* Craft Magic Arms and Armor, *poison; Market Price:* 9,302 gp; *Cost to Create:* 4,802 gp + 360 XP.

Dwarven Thrower: This weapon commonly functions as a +2 *warhammer*. If in the hands of a dwarf, the warhammer gains an additional +1 enhancement bonus (for a total enhancement bonus of +3) and can be hurled with a 30-foot range increment. It returns to its thrower on the round after it was thrown and is then ready to be wielded or thrown again. When hurled, it deals +1d8 points of bonus damage or +2d8 points of bonus damage against giants.

Dagger of venom

Caster Level: 10th; *Prerequisites:* Craft Magic Arms and Armor, creator must be a dwarf of at least 10th level; *Market Price:* 60,312 gp; *Cost to Create:* 30,312 gp + 2,400 XP.

Flame Tongue: This +1 *flaming longsword* (+1d6 points of fire damage with each hit) is also a flaming burst weapon (+1d10 points of bonus fire damage on a critical; see flaming burst, above).

Caster Level: 11th; *Prerequisites:* Craft Magic Arms and Armor and *flame blade, flame strike*, or *fireball; Market Price:* 32,315 gp; *Cost to Create:* 16,315 + 1,280 XP.

Frost Brand: This +3 *frost greatsword* (+1d6 points of bonus cold damage with each hit) does not shed any light except when the air temperature is below 0°F. Its wielder is protected from fire, since the sword absorbs the first 10 points of fire damage each round that the wielder would otherwise suffer.

The *frost brand* sword also has a 50% chance of extinguishing any fire into which its blade is thrust. This power extends to a 10-foot radius and includes lasting effects such as *wall of fire* but excludes instantaneous effects such as *fireball, meteor swarm*, and *flame strike*.

Caster Level: 14th; *Prerequisites:* Craft Magic Arms and Armor, *ice storm, dispel magic, protection from elements; Market Price:* 49,350 gp; *Cost to Create:* 24,850 gp + 1,960 XP.

Holy Avenger: In the hands of any character other than a paladin, this sword performs only as a +2 *longsword*. In the hands of a paladin, this holy (+1d6 points of bonus holy damage against evil creatures) becomes a +5 *longsword*, creates a spell resistance of 15 in a 5-foot radius, and casts *dispel magic* (usable every round as a standard action) in a 5-foot radius at the class level of the paladin. (Only the area dispel is possible, not the targeted dispel or counterspell versions of *dispel magic*.)

Holy avenger

Caster Level: 18th; *Prerequisites:* Craft Magic Arms and Armor, *holy aura*, creator must be good; *Market Price:* 120,315 gp; *Cost to Create:* 60,315 gp + 4,800 XP.

Javelin of Lightning: This javelin becomes a 5d6 *lightning bolt* when thrown (DC 14). It is consumed in the attack.

Caster Level: 5th; *Prerequisites:* Craft Magic Arms and Armor, *lightning bolt; Market Price:* 751 gp; *Cost to Create:* 526 gp + 18 XP.

Life-Drinker: This +1 *greataxe* bestows two negative levels on its target whenever it deals damage, just as if its target had been struck by an undead creature. One day after being struck, subjects must make a Fortitude save (DC 23) for each negative level or lose a character level. However, each time a *life-drinker* deals damage to a foe, it also bestows one negative level on the wielder. The negative level gained by the wielder lasts until the axe is put down. The axe can't be used again for 1 hour without the wielder once again gaining the negative level.

Caster Level: 13th; *Prerequisites:* Craft Magic Arms and Armor, *enervation; Market Price:* 40,320 gp; *Cost to Create:* 20,320 gp + 1,600 XP.

Luck Blade: This +1 *short sword* gives its possessor a +1 luck bonus to all saving throws and contains five *wish* spells when newly created. When randomly rolled, the *luck blade* can contain fewer than five *wishes* (1d6–1, minimum 0). The DM should keep the number of *wishes* left a secret. When the last wish is

WAN

used, the sword remains a *+1 short sword*, and it still grants the +1 luck bonus.

Caster Level: 17th; *Prerequisites:* Craft Magic Arms and Armor, *wish* or *miracle*; *Market Price:* 170,560 gp; *Cost to Create:* 22,935 gp + 26,810 XP.

Mace of Smiting: This *+3 heavy mace* has a +5 enhancement bonus against constructs, and any critical hit dealt to a construct completely destroys it (no saving throw). Furthermore, a critical hit dealt to an outsider deals ×4 critical damage rather than ×2.

Caster Level: 13th; *Prerequisites:* Craft Magic Arms and Armor, *finger of death*; *Market Price:* 75,312 gp; *Cost to Create:* 37,812 gp + 3,000 XP.

Mace of Terror: This *+2 heavy mace* has a potent spell-like ability allowing the wielder to envelop himself in a terrifying aura. His clothes and appearance are transformed into an illusion of darkest horror, such that all within 20 feet who view him must roll successful Will saving throws (DC 16) or be struck motionless with terror (treat as *hold person*). Those who succeed on their saves are shaken. Each time the mace is used to cause terror, there is a 20% chance the wielder permanently loses 1 point from his Charisma score.

Caster Level: 13th; *Prerequisites:* Craft Magic Arms and Armor, *fear*, *hold person*; *Market Price:* 17,812 gp; *Cost to Create:* 9,062 gp + 700 XP.

Nine Lives Stealer: This longsword always performs as a *+2 longsword*, but it also has the power to draw the life force from an opponent. It can do this nine times before the ability is lost. At that point, the sword becomes a simple *+2 longsword* (with perhaps a hint of evil about it). A critical hit must be dealt for the sword's death-dealing ability to function. The victim is entitled to a Fortitude saving throw (DC 17) to avoid death. If the save is successful, the sword's death-dealing ability does not function, no charge is used, and normal critical damage is determined. This sword is evil, and any good character attempting to wield it gains two negative levels. These negative levels remain as long as the sword is in hand and disappear when the sword is no longer wielded. These negative levels never result in actual level loss, but they cannot be overcome in any way (including *restoration* spells) while the sword is wielded.

Caster Level: 13th; *Prerequisites:* Craft Magic Arms and Armor, *finger of death*; *Market Price:* 25,315 gp; *Cost to Create:* 12,815 gp + 1,000 XP.

Oathbow: Of elven make, this white *+1 longbow* whispers "Swift defeat to my enemies" in Elven when nocked and pulled. If the firer swears aloud to slay her target, the bow's whisper becomes the low shout "Swift death to those who have wronged me." Against such a sworn enemy, the bow has a +3 enhancement bonus, and arrows launched from it deal double normal damage (and ×4 on a critical hit instead of the normal ×3). However, if the firer does not deal the killing blow on the sworn enemy within 24 hours, the bow falls inert for one week, during which it possesses no magical abilities or bonuses at all. Further, the character is demoralized and suffers a −1 morale penalty to attack rolls, saving throws, and skill checks during that week.

Caster Level: 15th; *Prerequisites:* Craft Magic Arms and Armor, creator must be an elf; *Market Price:* 27,875 gp; *Cost to Create:* 14,125 gp + 1,100 XP.

Rapier of Puncturing: Three times per day, this *+2 rapier of wounding* allows the wielder to make a touch attack with the weapon that deals 1d6 points of temporary Constitution damage by draining blood.

Caster Level: 13th; *Prerequisites:* Craft Magic Arms and Armor, *harm*; *Market Price:* 50,320 gp; *Cost to Create:* 25,320 gp + 2,000 XP.

Life-drinker

Screaming Bolt: One of these *+2 bolts* screams when fired, forcing all enemies of the firer within 20 feet of the path of the bolt to succeed at a Will save (DC 14) or become shaken. This is a mind-affecting fear effect.

Caster Level: 5th; *Prerequisites:* Craft Magic Arms and Armor, *scare*; *Market Price:* 257 gp; *Cost to Create:* 132 gp + 10 XP.

Slaying Arrow: This *+1 arrow* is keyed to a particular type of creature. If it strikes such a creature, the target must make a Fortitude save (DC 20) or die (or, in the case of unliving targets, be destroyed) instantly. Note that even creatures normally exempt from Fortitude saves (undead and constructs) are subject to this attack. When keyed to a living creature, this is a death effect (and thus *death ward* protects a target). To determine the type of creature the arrow is keyed to, roll on the following table:

d%	Target Type
01–05	Aberrations
06–08	Animals
09–13	Beasts
14–20	Constructs
21–25	Dragons
26–30	Elementals
31–35	Fey
36–40	Giants
41–45	Magical beasts
46–50	Monstrous humanoid
51–53	Oozes
54–58	Outsiders, chaotic
59–65	Outsiders, evil
66–70	Outsiders, good
71–75	Outsiders, lawful
76–77	Plants
78–85	Shapechangers
86–92	Undead
93–94	Vermin
95–100	Humanoid (choose subtype)

A *greater slaying arrow* functions just like a normal *slaying arrow*, but the DC to avoid the death effect is 23.

Caster Level: 13th; *Prerequisites:* Craft Magic Arms and Armor, *finger of death* (slaying arrow) or heightened *finger of death* (greater slaying arrow); *Market Price:* 2,282 gp (slaying arrow) or 4,057 gp (greater slaying arrow); *Cost to Create:* 1,144 gp 5 sp + 91 XP (slaying arrow) or 2,032 gp + 162 XP (greater slaying arrow).

Sleep Arrow: This strange *+1 arrow* is painted white and has white fletching. If it strikes a foe so that it would normally deal damage, it instead bursts into magical energy that deals subdual damage (in the same amount as would be normal damage) and forces the target to make a Will save (DC 11) or fall asleep.

Caster Level: 5th; *Prerequisites:* Craft Magic Arms and Armor, *sleep*; *Market Price:* 132 gp; *Cost to Create:* 69 gp 5 sp + 5 XP.

Sun Blade: This sword is the size of a bastard sword. However, its enchantment enables the *sun blade* to be wielded as if it were a short sword with respect to weight and ease of use. (In other words, the weapon appears to all viewers to be a bastard sword, and deals bastard sword damage, but the wielder feels and reacts as if the weapon were a short sword.) Any individual able to use either a bastard sword or a short sword with proficiency is proficient in the use of a *sun blade*. Likewise, Weapon Focus and Weapon Specialization in short sword and bastard sword apply equally.

Illus. by W. Reynolds

In normal combat, the glowing golden blade of the weapon is equal to a +2 *bastard sword*. Against evil creatures, its enhancement bonus is +4. Against Negative Energy Plane creatures or undead creatures, the sword deals double damage (and ×3 on a critical hit instead of the usual ×2).

Furthermore, the blade has a special *sunbeam* power. Once a day, the wielder can swing the blade vigorously above her head while speaking a command word. The *sunblade* then sheds a bright yellow radiance that is like full daylight. The radiance begins shining in a 10-foot radius around the sword wielder and spreads outward at 5 feet per round for 10 rounds thereafter, to create a globe of light with a 60-foot radius. When the wielder stops swinging, the radiance fades to a dim glow that persists for another minute before disappearing entirely. All *sun blades* are of good alignment, and any evil creature attempting to wield one gains one negative level. The negative level remains as long as the sword is in hand and disappears when the sword is no longer wielded. This negative level never results in actual level loss, but it cannot be overcome in any way (including *restoration* spells) while the sword is wielded.

Caster Level: 10th; *Prerequisites:* Craft Magic Arms and Armor, *continual light*, creator must be good; *Market Price:* 50,335 gp; *Cost to Create:* 25,335 gp + 2,000 XP.

Sword of Life Stealing: This black iron +2 *longsword* bestows a negative level when it deals a critical hit. The sword wielder gains 1d6 temporary hit points each time a negative level is bestowed on another. These temporary hit points last 24 hours.

Caster Level: 17th; *Prerequisites:* Craft Magic Arms and Armor, *energy drain*; *Market Price:* 30,315 gp; *Cost to Create:* 15,315 gp + 1,200 XP.

Sword of the Planes: This longsword has an enhancement bonus of +1 on the Material Plane, but on any Elemental Plane its enhancement bonus increases to +2. (The +2 enhancement bonus also applies on the Material Plane when the weapon is used against elementals.) It operates as a +3 *longsword* on the Astral or Ethereal plane or when used against opponents from either of those planes. On any other plane, or against any outsider, it functions as a +4 *longsword*.

Caster Level: 15th; *Prerequisites:* Craft Magic Arms and Armor, *plane shift*; *Market Price:* 52,315 gp; *Cost to Create:* 26,315 gp + 2,080 XP.

Sword of Subtlety: A +1 *short sword* with a thin, dull gray blade, this sword adds a +4 bonus to its wielder's attack roll and damage when he is making a sneak attack with it.

Caster Level: 7th; *Prerequisites:* Craft Magic Arms and Armor, *blur*; *Market Price:* 15,310 gp; *Cost to Create:* 7,810 gp + 600 XP.

Sylvan Scimitar: This +3 *scimitar*, when used outdoors in a temperate climate, grants its wielder the use of the Cleave feat and deals +1d6 points of bonus damage.

Caster Level: 11th; *Prerequisites:* Craft Magic Arms and Armor; *divine power* or caster must be druid level 7th+; *Market Price:* 55,815 gp; *Cost to Create:* 28,065 gp + 2,220 XP.

Trident of Fish Command: The magical properties of this +1 *trident* with a 6-foot-long haft enable its wielder to cause all water-dwelling animals within a 60-foot radius to make a Will saving throw (DC 12). This uses 1 charge of the trident. Animals failing this save are completely under the empathic command of the wielder and will not attack her or any of her allies within 10 feet of her. The wielder can make the controlled marine animals move in

whatever direction she desires and convey messages of emotion to them (in other words, fear, hunger, anger, indifference, repletion, and so on). Animals making their saving throw are free of empathic control, but they will not approach within 10 feet of the trident. A school of fish should be checked as a single entity.

A newly created trident has 50 charges. When all the charges are used, it remains a +1 *trident*.

Caster Level: 7th; *Prerequisites:* Craft Magic Arms and Armor, *speak with animals*; *Market Price:* 3,815 gp; *Cost to Create:* 2,065 gp + 140 XP.

Trident of Warning: A weapon of this type enables its wielder to determine the location, depth, species, and number of hostile or hungry marine predators within 240 feet. A *trident of warning* must be grasped and pointed in order for the character using it to gain such information, and it requires 1 round to scan a hemisphere with a radius of 240 feet. The weapon is otherwise a +2 *trident*.

Caster Level: 7th; *Prerequisites:* Craft Magic Arms and Armor, *detect magic*; *Market Price:* 9,815 gp; *Cost to Create:* 5,065 gp + 380 XP.

POTIONS

A potion is a magic liquid that produces its effect when imbibed. Potions are also sometimes called elixirs. Magic oils are similar to potions, except that oils are applied externally rather than imbibed. A potion, oil, or elixir can be used only once.

Potions are like spells cast upon the imbiber. The character taking the potion doesn't get to make any decisions about the effect—the caster who brewed the potion has already done so. For example, a *potion of protection from elements* is always designed to protect against a specific element chosen by the creator, not the drinker.

Physical Description: A typical potion or oil consists of 1 ounce of liquid held in a ceramic or glass vial fitted with a tight stopper. The stoppered container is usually no more than 1 inch wide and 2 inches high. The vial has an AC of 13, 1 hit point, a hardness of 1, and a break DC of 12. Vials hold 1 ounce of liquid.

Identifying Potions: In addition to the standard methods of identification, PCs can sample from each container they find to attempt to determine the nature of the liquid inside. An experienced character learns to identify potions by memory—for example, the last time she tasted a liquid that reminded her of almonds, it turned out to be a *potion of cure moderate wounds*. (You can reward players who keep records of potion sampling by always having the same type of potion taste the same—or you can cross them up by occasionally having the almond-flavored potion be something other than a *potion of cure moderate wounds*.)

Activation: Drinking a potion or applying an oil requires no special skill. The user merely removes the stopper and swallows the potion or smears on the oil. The following rules govern potion and oil use:

Potions

- Drinking a potion or applying an oil is a standard action. The potion or oil takes effect immediately.
- Using a potion or oil provokes attacks of opportunity. A successful attack (including grappling attacks) against the character forces a Concentration check (as with casting a spell). If the character fails this check, she cannot drink the potion. An attacker may direct the attack of opportunity against the potion

or oil container rather than against the character. A successful attack on the potion can destroy the container (see Attack an Object, page 135 in Chapter 8: Combat in the *Player's Handbook*).

- A creature must be able to swallow a potion or smear on an oil. Because of this, incorporeal creatures cannot use potions or oils.
- Any corporeal creature can imbibe a potion. The potion must be swallowed. Any corporeal creature can use an oil.
- A character can carefully administer a potion to an unconscious creature as a full-round action, trickling the liquid down the creature's throat. Likewise, it takes a full-round action to apply an oil to an unconscious creature.

TABLE 8–18: POTIONS

Minor	Medium	Major	Potion	Market Price
01–05	—	—	Jump	50 gp
06–10	—	—	Spider climb	50 gp
11–19	—	—	Cure light wounds	50 gp
20	01	—	Love	150 gp
21–24	02	—	Vision	150 gp
25–28	03	—	Swimming	150 gp
29–32	04	—	Hiding	150 gp
33–36	05	—	Sneaking	150 gp
37	06	—	Oil of timelessness	150 gp
38–42	07	—	Reduce (at 5th level)	250 gp
43–47	08	—	Enlarge (at 5th level)	250 gp
48–50	09	—	Speak with animals	300 gp
51–53	10	01	Clairaudience/clairvoyance	300 gp
54–56	11–12	02	Charisma	300 gp
57–59	13–14	03	Intelligence	300 gp
60–62	15–16	04	Wisdom	300 gp
63–65	17–18	05	Alter self	300 gp
66–68	19–21	06–07	Blur	300 gp
69–71	22–24	08	Darkvision	300 gp
72–74	25–26	09	Ghoul touch	300 gp
75–77	27–29	10	Delay poison	300 gp
78–80	30–32	11–13	Endurance	300 gp
81–83	33–40	14–16	Cure moderate wounds	300 gp
84–86	41–45	17–19	Detect thoughts	300 gp
87–89	46–50	20–22	Levitate	300 gp
90–91	51–55	23–25	Aid	300 gp
92–93	56–60	26–30	Invisibility	300 gp
94	61–65	31–35	Lesser restoration	300 gp
95	66–70	36–40	Cat's grace	300 gp
96	71–75	41–45	Bull's strength	300 gp
97	76–77	46	Truth	500 gp
98	78–79	47	Glibness	500 gp
99	80–84	48–49	Nondetection	750 gp
100	85–87	50–51	Tongues	750 gp
—	88–91	52–53	Water breathing	750 gp
—	92	54–55	Remove paralysis	750 gp
—	93	56–57	Remove blindness/deafness	750 gp
—	94	58–59	Remove disease	750 gp
—	95–96	60–69	Neutralize poison	750 gp
—	97	70–73	Cure serious wounds	750 gp
—	98	74–75	Fly	750 gp
—	—	76–77	Protection from elements (cold)	750 gp
—	—	78–79	Protection from elements (electricity)	750 gp
—	—	80–83	Protection from elements (fire)	750 gp
—	—	84–85	Protection from elements (acid)	750 gp
—	—	86–87	Protection from elements (sonic)	750 gp
—	—	88–90	Haste	750 gp
—	—	91–93	Gaseous form	750 gp
—	—	94–95	Oil of slipperiness	900 gp
—	99–100	96–98	Heroism	900 gp
—	—	99–100	Fire breath	900 gp

Random Generation: To generate potions randomly, roll on Table 8–18: Potions.

Potion Descriptions

For those standard potions that are spells in liquid form, simply refer to the spell description in the *Player's Handbook* for all pertinent details. The caster level for a standard potion is the minimum caster level needed to cast the spell (unless otherwise specified). Nonstandard potions are described below.

Charisma: This potion allows the character to speak eloquently and persuasively as well as exude an aura of personality and charm, adding a 1d4+1 enhancement bonus to her Charisma score for 3 hours.

Caster Level: 3rd; *Prerequisites:* Brew Potion, spellcaster level 4th+; *Market Price:* 300 gp.

Fire Breath: This strange elixir bestows upon the drinker the ability to spit gouts of flame. He can breathe fire up to three times, each time dealing 3d6 points of fire damage to a single target up to 25 feet away. The victim can attempt a Reflex save (DC 12) for half damage. Unused blasts dissipate 1 hour after the potion is consumed. Most drinkers suffer from terrible heartburn afterward.

Caster Level: 3rd; *Prerequisites:* Brew Potion, spellcaster level 8th+; *Market Price:* 900 gp.

Glibness: This potion enables the imbiber to speak fluently and even to tell lies smoothly, believably, and undetectably for 1 hour (add +30 to Bluff checks). Even magic investigation, such as the *discern lies* spell, does not register the speaker's lies as such.

Caster Level: 4th; *Prerequisites:* Brew Potion, spellcaster level 8th+; *Market Price:* 500 gp.

Heroism: This potion grants the drinker a +2 competence bonus to attacks, saves, and skill checks for 1 hour.

Caster Level: 4th; *Prerequisites:* Brew Potion, spellcaster level 8th+; *Market Price:* 900 gp.

Hiding: A character drinking this potion gains an intuitive ability to hide (+10 competence bonus to Hide checks for 1 hour).

Caster Level: 2nd; *Prerequisites:* Brew Potion, spellcaster level 6th+; *Market Price:* 150 gp.

Intelligence: The clarity of mind and quicker wit granted by this potion results in an enhancement bonus of 1d4+1 to the drinker's Intelligence score for 3 hours.

Caster Level: 3rd; *Prerequisites:* Brew Potion, spellcaster level 4th+; *Market Price:* 300 gp.

Love: This potion causes the character drinking it to become *charmed* with the first creature she sees after consuming the draft (as *charm person*—the drinker must be a humanoid of Medium-size or smaller, Will save, DC 14). She actually becomes enamored if the creature is of similar race or kind. The charm effects wear off in 1d3 hours, but the enamoring effect is permanent.

Caster Level: 2nd; *Prerequisites:* Brew Potion, *charm person*; *Market Price:* 150 gp.

Oil of Slipperiness: This oil adds a +30 bonus to all Escape Artist checks, meaning that it is almost impossible to grapple such a character or to tie or chain him up. In addition, such obstructions as webs (magical or otherwise) do not affect an anointed individual. Magic ropes and the like do not avail against this oil. If the oil is poured on a floor or on steps, the spill should be treated as a long-lasting *grease* spell. The oil requires 8 hours to wear off normally, or it can be wiped off with an alcohol solution (even wine!).

Oil of slipperiness is needed to coat the inside of a container that is meant to hold *sovereign glue* (see page 226).

Caster Level: 6th; *Prerequisites:* Brew Potion, *grease*, spellcaster level 6th+; *Market Price:* 900 gp.

Oil of Timelessness: When applied to any matter that was once alive (leather, leaves, paper, wood, dead flesh, and so on), this oil allows that substance to resist the passage of time. Each year of actual time affects the substance as if only a day had passed. The coated object has a +1 resistance bonus on all saving throws. The oil never wears off, although it can be magically removed (by dispelling the effect, for instance). One flask contains enough oil to coat eight Medium-size objects or an equivalent area.

Caster Level: 2nd; *Prerequisite:* Brew Potion; *Market Price:* 150 gp.

Sneaking: This potion grants the drinker the ability to walk softly and dampens sound around her slightly, granting a +10 circumstance bonus to her Move Silently checks for 1 hour.

Caster Level: 2nd; *Prerequisites:* Brew Potion, spellcaster level 6th+; *Market Price:* 150 gp.

Swimming: This potion bestows swimming ability. An almost imperceptible magic sheath surrounds the drinker, allowing him to glide through the water easily (+10 circumstance bonus to Swim checks for 1 hour).

Caster Level: 2nd; *Prerequisites:* Brew Potion, spellcaster level 6th+; *Market Price:* 150 gp.

Truth: This potion forces the individual drinking it to say nothing but the truth for 10 minutes (Will negates DC 12). Further, she is compelled to answer any questions put to her in that time, but with each question she is free to make a separate Will save (DC 12). If one of these secondary saves is successful, she doesn't break free of the truth-compelling enchantment but also doesn't have to answer that particular question. No more than one question can be asked each round. This is a mind-affecting compulsion enchantment.

Caster Level: 4th; *Prerequisites:* Brew Potion, spellcaster level 8th+; *Market Price:* 500 gp.

Vision: Drinking this potion grants the imbiber the ability to notice acute details with great accuracy (+10 to his Search checks for 1 hour).

Caster Level: 2nd; *Prerequisites:* Brew Potion, spellcaster level 6th+; *Market Price:* 150 gp.

Wisdom: Imbuing her with intuition, this potion adds a 1d4+1 enhancement bonus to the drinker's Wisdom score for 3 hours.

Caster Level: 3rd; *Prerequisites:* Brew Potion, spellcaster level 4th+; *Market Price:* 300 gp.

RINGS

Rings bestow magical powers upon their wearers. Only a rare few have charges. Anyone can use a ring.

A character can only effectively wear two magic rings. A third magic ring doesn't work if the wearer is already wearing two magic rings.

Physical Description: Rings have no appreciable weight. Although there are exceptions crafted from glass or bone, the vast majority of rings are forged from metal—usually precious metals such as gold, silver, and platinum. A ring has an AC of 13, 2 hit points, a hardness of 10, and a break DC of 25.

Activation: Usually, a ring's ability is activated by a command word (a standard action that does not provoke attacks of opportunity) or it works continually. Some rings have exceptional activation methods, according to their descriptions.

Random Generation: To generate rings randomly, roll on Table 8–19: Rings.

Special Qualities: Roll d%. An 01 result indicates the ring is intelligent, 02–31 indicates that something (a design, inscription, etc.) provides a clue to its function, and 32–100 indicates no special qualities. Intelligent items have extra abilities and sometimes also extraordinary powers and special purposes. Use Table 8–31: Item Intelligence, Wisdom, Charisma, and Capabilities as indicated if a ring is intelligent. Rings with charges can never be intelligent.

Ring Descriptions

Rings are some of the most coveted and generally useful magic items. Standard rings are described below.

Animal Friendship: On command, this ring affects an animal as if the wearer had cast *animal friendship.* The ring wearer can befriend 12 HD worth of animals (see the spell description). If

TABLE 8–19: RINGS

Minor	Medium	Major	Potion	Market Price
01–05	—	—	Climbing	2,000 gp
06–10	—	—	Jumping	2,000 gp
11–25	—	—	Protection +1	2,000 gp
26–30	—	—	Warmth	2,100 gp
31–40	—	—	Feather falling	2,200 gp
41–45	—	—	Swimming	2,300 gp
46–50	—	—	Sustenance	2,500 gp
51–55	01–05	—	Counterspells	4,000 gp
56–60	06–10	—	Mind shielding	8,000 gp
61–70	11–20	—	Protection +2	8,000 gp
71–75	21–25	—	Force shield	8,500 gp
76–80	26–30	01	Ram	8,600 gp
81–85	31–35	02	Animal friendship	9,500 gp
86–90	36–40	03	Chameleon power	12,000 gp
91–95	41–45	04	Water walking	15,000 gp
96–100	46–50	05–06	Elemental resistance, minor	16,000 gp
—	51–60	07–10	Protection +3	18,000 gp
—	61–70	11–15	Invisibility	20,000 gp
—	71–75	16–20	Wizardry (I)	20,000 gp
—	76–80	21–25	Elemental resistance, major	24,000 gp
—	81–82	26–30	X-ray vision	25,000 gp
—	83–84	31–35	Evasion	25,000 gp
—	85–86	36–40	Blinking	30,000 gp
—	87–88	41–45	Protection +4	32,000 gp
—	89–90	46–50	Wizardry (II)	40,000 gp
—	91–92	51–55	Freedom of movement	40,000 gp
—	93–94	56–60	Friend shield	50,000 gp
—	95–96	61–65	Protection +5	50,000 gp
—	97–98	66–70	Shooting stars	50,000 gp
—	99	71–75	Telekinesis	75,000 gp
—	100	76–80	Wizardry (III)	80,000 gp
—	—	81–84	Spell storing	90,000 gp
—	—	85–87	Regeneration	90,000 gp
—	—	86–89	Three wishes	97,950 gp
—	—	90–92	Wizardry (IV)	100,000 gp
—	—	93–94	Djinni calling	125,000 gp
—	—	95–96	Spell turning	150,000 gp
—	—	97	Air elemental command	200,000 gp
—	—	98	Earth elemental command	200,000 gp
—	—	99	Fire elemental command	200,000 gp
—	—	100	Water elemental command	200,000 gp

animal friendship is already on the character's spell list, this ring allows the character to befriend additional animals.

Caster Level: 6th; *Prerequisites:* Forge Ring, *animal friendship;* *Market Price:* 9,500 gp.

Blinking: On command, this ring makes the wearer blink, as with the *blink* spell.

Caster Level: 7th; *Prerequisites:* Forge Ring, *blink;* *Market Price:* 30,000 gp.

Chameleon Power: As a free action, the wearer of this ring can gain the ability to magically blend in with the surroundings. This adds a +15 bonus to her Hide checks. As a standard action, she can also command the ring to utilize the spell *change self* as often as she wants.

Caster Level: 3rd; *Prerequisites:* Forge Ring, *change self, invisibility;* *Market Price:* 12,000 gp.

Climbing: This ring is actually a magic leather cord that ties around a finger. It continually grants the wearer a +10 competence bonus to Climb checks.

Caster Level: 5th; *Prerequisites:* Forge Ring, creator must have 5 ranks of the Climb skill; *Market Price:* 2,000 gp.

Counterspells: This ring might seem to be a *ring of spell storing* upon first examination. However, while it allows a single spell of 1st through 6th level to be cast into it, that spell cannot be cast out of it again. Instead, should that spell ever be cast upon the wearer, the spell is immediately countered, as a counterspell action, requiring no action (or even knowledge) on the wearer's part. Once so used, the spell cast within the ring is gone. A new spell (or the same one as before) may be placed in it again.

Caster Level: 11th; *Prerequisites:* Forge Ring, *spell turning; Market Price:* 4,000 gp.

Djinni Calling: One of the many rings of fable, this "genie" ring is most useful indeed. It serves as a special gate by means of which a specific djinni can be called from the Elemental Plane of Air. When the ring is rubbed, the call goes out, and the djinni appears on the next round. The djinni faithfully obeys and serves the wearer of the ring, but never for more than 1 hour per day. If the djinni of the ring is ever killed, the ring becomes nonmagical and worthless. See the *Monster Manual* for details of a djinni's abilities.

Caster Level: 17th; *Prerequisites:* Forge Ring, *gate; Market Price:* 125,000 gp.

Elemental Command: All four types of *elemental command* rings are very powerful. Each appears to be nothing more than a lesser magic ring until fully activated (see below), but each has certain other powers as well as the following common properties:

- Elementals of the plane to which the ring is attuned can't attack the wearer, or even approach within 5 feet of him. If the wearer desires, he may forego this protection and instead attempt to charm the elemental (as *charm monster,* Will save DC 17). If the charm attempt fails, however, absolute protection is lost and no further attempt at charming can be made.
- Creatures from the plane to which the ring is attuned who attack the wearer suffer a –1 penalty to their attack rolls. The ring wearer makes applicable saving throws from the extraplanar creature's attacks with a +2 resistance bonus. He gains a +4 morale bonus to all attacks against such creatures. Any weapon he uses bypasses the damage reduction of such creatures, regardless of any qualities the weapon may or may not have.
- The wearer of the ring is able to converse with creatures from the plane to which his ring is attuned. These creatures recognize that he wears the ring. They show a healthy respect for the wearer if alignments are similar. If alignments are opposed, creatures fear the wearer if he is strong. If he is weak, they hate and desire to slay him. Fear, hatred, and respect are determined by the DM.
- The possessor of a *ring of elemental command* suffers a saving throw penalty as follows:

Element	Saving Throw Penalty
Air	–2 against earth-based effects
Earth	–2 against air- or electricity-based effects
Fire	–2 against water- or cold-based effects
Water	–2 against fire-based effects

In addition to the powers described above, each specific ring gives its wearer the following abilities according to its type:

Ring of Elemental Command (Air)
- *Feather fall* (unlimited use, wearer only)
- *Resist elements* (*electricity*) (unlimited use, wearer only)
- *Gust of wind* (twice per day)
- *Wind wall* (unlimited use)
- *Air walk* (once per day, wearer only)
- *Chain lightning* (once per week)

The ring appears to be a *ring of feather fall* until a certain condition is met, such as having the ring *blessed,* single-handedly slaying an air elemental, or whatever the DM determines necessary to

activate its full potential. It must be reactivated each time a new wearer acquires it.

Ring of Elemental Command (Earth)
- *Meld into stone* (unlimited use, wearer only)
- *Soften earth or stone* (unlimited use)
- *Stone shape* (twice per day)
- *Stoneskin* (once per week, wearer only)
- *Passwall* (twice per week)
- *Wall of stone* (once per day)

The ring appears to be a *ring of meld into stone* until the DM-established condition is met.

Ring of Elemental Command (Fire)
- *Resist elements* (*fire*) (as a *major ring of elemental resistance* [*fire*])
- *Burning hands* (unlimited use)
- *Flaming sphere* (twice per day)
- *Pyrotechnics* (twice per day)
- *Wall of fire* (once per day)
- *Flame strike* (twice per week)

The ring appears to be a *major ring of elemental resistance (fire)* until the DM-established condition is met.

Ring of Elemental Command (Water)
- *Water walk* (unlimited use)
- *Create water* (unlimited use)
- *Water breathing* (unlimited use)
- *Wall of ice* (once per day)
- *Ice storm* (twice per week)
- *Control water* (twice per week)

The ring appears to be a *ring of water walking* until the DM-established condition is met.

Caster Level: 15th; *Prerequisites:* Forge Ring, *summon monster VI,* all appropriate spells; *Market Price:* 200,000 gp.

Elemental Resistance, Minor: This reddish iron ring continually protects the wearer from damage from one type of energy—fire, cold, electricity, acid, or sonic. When the wearer would normally take such damage, subtract 15 points of damage per round from the total to account for the ring's effect.

Caster Level: 5th; *Prerequisites:* Forge Ring, *protection from elements; Market Price:* 16,000 gp.

Elemental Resistance, Major: This reddish iron ring continually protects the wearer from even greater damage from one type of energy—fire, cold, electricity, acid, or sonic. When the wearer would normally take such damage, subtract 30 points of damage per round from the amount before applying. This amount is enough to survive even on the Elemental Plane corresponding to the energy type (if applicable), but it still won't completely absorb the breath of a nasty dragon or completely negate a powerful *fireball.*

Caster Level: 7th; *Prerequisites:* Forge Ring, *protection from elements; Market Price:* 24,000 gp.

Evasion: This ring continually grants the wearer extreme nimbleness, allowing her to avoid damage as if she had the evasion ability. Whenever she makes a Reflex saving throw to determine whether she takes half damage from an attack, a successful save results in no damage.

Caster Level: 7th; *Prerequisites:* Forge Ring, *jump; Market Price:* 25,000 gp.

Feather Falling: This ring is crafted with a feather pattern all around its edge. It acts exactly like a *feather fall* spell, activated immediately if the wearer falls more than 3 feet.

Ring of feather falling

Caster Level: 1st; *Prerequisites:* Forge Ring, *feather fall*; *Market Price:* 2,200 gp.

Force Shield: An iron band, this simple ring generates a large shield-sized (and shield-shaped) *wall of force* that stays with the ring and can be wielded by the wearer as if it were a normal shield (+2 AC). This special creation, since it can be activated and deactivated at will (a free action), has no armor check penalty or arcane spell failure chance.

Caster Level: 9th; *Prerequisites:* Forge Ring, *wall of force*; *Market Price:* 8,500 gp.

Freedom of Movement: This gold ring allows the wearer to act as if continually under the effect of a *freedom of movement* spell.

Caster Level: 7th; *Prerequisites:* Forge Ring, *freedom of movement*; *Market Price:* 40,000 gp.

Friend Shield: These curious rings always comes in pairs. A *friend shield* ring without its mate is useless. Either wearer of one of a pair of the rings can, at any time, command his or her ring to cast a *shield other* spell with the wearer of the mated ring as the recipient. There is no range limitation on this effect.

Caster Level: 10th; *Prerequisites:* Forge Ring, *shield other*; *Market Price:* 50,000 gp (for a pair).

Invisibility: By activating this simple silver ring, the wearer can become *invisible*, as the spell.

Caster Level: 3rd; *Prerequisites:* Forge Ring, *invisibility*; *Market Price:* 20,000 gp.

Jumping: This ring continually allows the wearer to leap about as if a *jump* spell had been cast upon him, adding a +30 bonus to all his Jump checks and eliminating his usual maximum distances.

Caster Level: 1st; *Prerequisites:* Forge Ring, *jump*; *Market Price:* 2,000 gp.

Mind Shielding: This ring is usually of fine workmanship and wrought from heavy gold. The wearer is continually immune to *detect thoughts*, *discern lies*, and any attempt to magically discern her alignment.

Caster Level: 3rd; *Prerequisites:* Forge Ring, *nondetection*; *Market Price:* 8,000 gp.

Protection: This ring offers continual magical protection in the form of a deflection bonus of +1 to +5 to AC.

Caster Level: 5th; *Prerequisites:* Forge Ring, *shield of faith*, caster must be of a level three times that of the bonus of the ring; *Market Price:* 2,000 gp (ring +1); 8,000 gp (ring +2); 18,000 gp (ring +3); 32,000 gp (ring +4); or 50,000 gp (ring +5).

Ram: The *ring of the ram* is an ornate ring forged of hard metal, usually iron or an iron alloy. It has the head of a ram (or a buck goat) as its device.

The wearer can command the ring to give forth a ramlike force, manifested by a vaguely discernible shape that resembles the head of a ram or a goat. This force strikes a single target, dealing 1d6 points of damage if 1 charge is expended, 2d6 points if 2 charges are used, or 3d6 points if 3 charges (the maximum) are used. Treat this as a ranged attack with a 50-foot maximum range and no penalties for distance. The ring is quite useful for knocking opponents off parapets or ledges, among other things.

The force of the blow is considerable, and those struck by the ring are subject to a bull rush if within 30 feet of the ring-wearer. (The ram has Strength 25 and is Large.) The ram gains a +1 bonus to the bull rush attempt if 2 charges are expended, or +2 if 3 charges are expended.

In addition to its attack mode, the *ring of the ram* also has the power to open doors as if it were a character with Strength 25. If 2 charges are expended, the effect is equivalent to a character with Strength 27. If 3 charges are expended, the effect is that of a character with Strength 29.

A newly created ring has 50 charges. When all the charges are expended, the ring becomes a nonmagical item.

Caster Level: 9th; *Prerequisites:* Forge Ring, *bull's strength*, *telekinesis*; *Market Price:* 8,600 gp.

Regeneration: This white gold ring continually allows a living wearer to heal 1 point of damage per level every hour rather than every day. (This ability cannot be aided by the Heal skill.) Subdual damage heals at a rate of 1 point of damage per level every 5 minutes. If the wearer loses a limb, an organ, or any other body part while wearing this ring, the ring *regenerates* it like the spell. In either case, only damage taken while wearing the ring is regenerated.

Caster Level: 15th; *Prerequisites:* Forge Ring, *regenerate*; *Market Price:* 90,000 gp.

Shooting Stars: This ring has two modes of operation—at night and underground—both of which work only in relative darkness.

During the night under the open sky, the *ring of shooting stars* can perform the following functions on command:

- *Dancing lights* (once per hour)
- *Light* (twice per night)
- *Ball lightning* (special, once per night)
- *Shooting stars* (special, three per week)

The first special function, *ball lightning*, releases one to four balls of lightning (ring wearer's choice). These glowing globes resemble *dancing lights*, and the ring wearer controls them in the same fashion (see the *dancing lights* spell description in the *Player's Handbook*). The spheres have a 120-foot range and a duration of 4 rounds. They can be moved at 120 feet per round. Each sphere is about 3 feet in diameter, and any creature who comes within 5 feet of one causes its charge to dissipate, taking electricity damage in the process according to the number of balls created.

Number of Balls	Damage per Ball
4 lightning balls	1d6 points of damage each
3 lightning balls	2d6 points of damage each
2 lightning balls	3d6 points of damage each
1 lightning ball	4d6 points of damage

Once the *ball lightning* function is activated, the balls can be released at any time before the sun rises. (Multiple balls can be released in the same round.)

The second special function, *shooting stars*, produces glowing projectiles with fiery trails, much like a *meteor swarm*. Three *shooting stars* can be released from the ring each week, simultaneously or one at a time. They impact for 12 points of damage and spread (as a *fireball*) in a 5-foot-radius sphere for 24 points of fire damage.

Any creature struck by a *shooting star* takes full damage from impact plus full damage from the spread. Creatures not struck but within the spread ignore the impact damage and take only half damage from the fire spread on a successful Reflex save (DC 13). Range is 70 feet, at the end of which the *shooting star* explodes, unless it strikes a creature or object before that. A *shooting star* always follows a straight line, and any creature in its path must make a save or be hit by the projectile.

Indoors at night, or underground, the *ring of shooting stars* has the following properties:

- *Faerie fire* (twice per day)
- *Spark shower* (special, once per day)

The *spark shower* is a flying cloud of sizzling purple sparks that fan out from the ring for a distance of 20 feet in an arc 10 feet wide. Creatures within this area take 2d8 points of damage each if not wearing metal armor or carrying a metal weapon. Those wearing metal armor and/or carrying a metal weapon take 4d8 points of damage.

Caster Level: 12th; *Prerequisites:* Forge Ring, *light*, *faerie fire*, *lightning bolt*, *meteor swarm*; *Market Price:* 50,000 gp.

Spell Storing: A *ring of spell storing* contains up to ten levels of spells that the wearer can cast. Each spell has a caster level equal to the minimum level needed to cast that spell. As with a wand (see the Wands section later in this chapter), the user need not provide any material components or focus, or pay an XP cost to cast the spell, and there is no arcane spell failure chance for wearing armor (since the ring user need not gesture).

For a randomly generated ring, treat it as a scroll to determine what spells are stored in it (see the Scrolls section later in this chapter). If you roll a spell that would put the ring over the ten-level limit, ignore that roll; the ring has no more spells in it. (Not every newly discovered ring need be fully charged.)

A spellcaster can cast any spells into the ring, so long as the total spell levels do not add up to more than ten. A wizard could cast two *fireball* spells and a *stoneskin* spell into the ring (3 + 3 + 4 = 10). She could then give the ring to a druid, who casts the *stoneskin* spell from the ring and then puts four *calm animal* spells into the ring. The druid could give the ring to a barbarian, who could use all the spells but could not replace any.

The ring magically imparts to the wearer the names of all spells currently stored within it.

Caster Level: Varies (minimum needed to cast each stored spell); *Prerequisites:* Forge Ring, *imbue with spell ability; Market Price:* 90,000 gp.

Spell Turning: On command, this simple platinum band automatically reflects spells cast at the wearer, exactly as if *spell turning* had been cast upon the wearer.

Caster Level: 15th; *Prerequisites:* Forge Ring, *spell turning; Market Price:* 150,000 gp.

Sustenance: This ring continually provides its wearer with life-sustaining nourishment. The ring also refreshes the body and mind, so that its wearer needs only sleep 2 hours per day to gain the benefit of 8 hours of sleep. The ring must be worn for a full week before it begins to work. If it is removed, the owner must wear it for another week to reattune it to himself.

Caster Level: 5th; *Prerequisites:* Forge Ring, *create food and water; Market Price:* 2,500 gp.

Swimming: This silver ring has a wave pattern etched into the band. It continually grants the wearer a +10 competence bonus to Swim checks.

Caster Level: 5th; *Prerequisites:* Forge Ring, creator must have 5 ranks of the Swim skill; *Market Price:* 2,300 gp.

Telekinesis: This ring allows the caster to use the spell *telekinesis* on command.

Caster Level: 9th; *Prerequisites:* Forge Ring, *telekinesis; Market Price:* 75,000 gp.

Three Wishes: This ring is set with three rubies. Each ruby stores a *wish* spell, activated by the ring. When a wish is used, that ruby disappears. For a randomly generated ring, roll 1d3 to determine the remaining number of rubies. When all the wishes are used, the ring becomes a nonmagical item.

Caster Level: 20th; *Prerequisites:* Forge Ring, *wish* or *miracle; Market Price:* 97,950 gp; *Cost to Create:* 11,475 gp + 15,918 XP.

Warmth: This ring is brass and set with a single red stone. It continually keeps the wearer comfortably warm, allowing her to withstand cold weather and cold damage as if she had *endure elements* (cold) cast upon her (negating 5 points of cold damage per round).

Caster Level: 7th; *Prerequisites:* Forge Ring, *endure elements; Market Price:* 2,100 gp.

Water Walking: This ring, set with an opal, allows the wearer to continually utilize the effects of the spell *water walk*.

Caster Level: 9th; *Prerequisites:* Forge Ring, *water walk; Market Price:* 15,000 gp.

WAI

Ring of three wishes

Wizardry: This special ring come in four types (*ring of wizardry I, ring of wizardry II, ring of wizardry III,* and *ring of wizardry IV*), all of them useful only to arcane spellcasters. The wearer's arcane spells per day are doubled for one specific spell level. A *ring of wizardry I* doubles 1st-level spells, a *ring of wizardry II* doubles 2nd-level spells, a *ring of wizardry III* doubles 3rd-level spells, and a *ring of wizardry IV* doubles 4th-level spells. Bonus spells from high ability scores or school specialization are not doubled.

Caster Level: 11th (*wizardry I*), 14th (*wizardry II*), 17th (*wizardry III*), or 20th (*wizardry IV*); *Prerequisites:* Forge Ring, *limited wish* (*wizardry I–wizardry IV*); *Market Price:* 20,000 gp (*wizardry I*), 40,000 gp (*wizardry II*), 70,000 gp (*wizardry III*), or 100,000 gp (*wizardry IV*).

X-Ray Vision: On command, this ring gives its possessor the ability to see into and through solid matter. Vision range is 20 feet, with the viewer seeing as if he were looking at something in normal light even if there is no illumination. (For example, if the wearer looks into a locked chest, he can see inside even if there's no light within.) X-ray vision can penetrate 20 feet of cloth, wood, or similar animal or vegetable material. It can see through up to 10 feet of stone or some metals. Some metals can't be penetrated at all.

Substance Scanned	Thickness Penetrated per Round of X-Raying	Maximum Thickness
Organic matter (animal)	4 ft.	20 ft.
Organic matter (vegetable)	2 1/2 ft.	20 ft.
Stone	1 ft.	10 ft.
Iron, steel, copper, brass, etc.	1 in.	10 in.
Lead, gold, platinum	Cannot penetrate	—

It's possible to scan an area of up to 100 square feet during 1 round. For example, during 1 round the wearer of the ring could scan an area of stone 10 feet wide and 10 feet high. Alternatively, he could scan an area 5 feet wide and 20 feet high.

Secret compartments, drawers, recesses, and doors are 90% likely to be located by X-ray vision scanning. Using the ring is physically exhausting, causing the wearer 1 point of temporary Constitution damage per minute after the first 10 minutes of use in a single day.

Caster Level: 6th; *Prerequisites:* Forge Ring, *true seeing; Market Price:* 25,000 gp.

RODS

Rods are scepterlike devices that have unique magic powers and do not usually have charges. Anyone can use a rod.

Physical Description: Rods weigh approximately 5 pounds. They range from 2 feet to 3 feet long and are usually made of iron or some other metal. (Many can function as light maces or clubs due to their sturdy construction.) These sturdy items have an AC of 9, 10 hit points, a hardness of 10, and a break DC of 27.

Activation: Details relating to rod use vary from item to item. See the individual descriptions for specifics.

Random Generation: To generate rods randomly, roll on Table 8–20: Rods.

Special Qualities: Roll d%. An 01 result indicates the rod is intelligent, 02–31 indicates that something (a design, inscription, etc.) provides a clue to its function, and 32–100 indicates no special qualities.

TABLE 8—20: RODS

Medium	Major	Rod	Market Price
01–06	—	Immovable	7,500 gp
07–12	—	Metal and mineral detection	10,500 gp
13–20	01–05	Cancellation	11,000 gp
21–25	06–10	Wonder	12,000 gp
26–29	11–15	Python	13,000 gp
30–34	16–20	Flame extinguishing	15,000 gp
35–40	21–27	Withering	17,000 gp
41–45	28–33	Viper	19,000 gp
46–52	34–40	Thunder and lightning	23,000 gp
53–60	41–50	Enemy detection	23,500 gp
61–68	51–55	Splendor	25,000 gp
69–78	56–65	Negation	35,000 gp
79–90	66–80	Flailing	40,000 gp
91–96	81–85	Absorption	50,000 gp
97–99	86–90	Rulership	60,000 gp
100	91–94	Security	61,000 gp
—	95–98	Lordly might	70,000 gp
—	99–100	Alertness	72,000 gp

Intelligent items have extra abilities and sometimes also extraordinary powers and special purposes. Use Table 8–31: Item Intelligence, Wisdom, Charisma, and Capabilities as indicated if a rod is intelligent. Rods with charges can never be intelligent.

Rod Descriptions

Although all rods are generally scepter-like, their configurations and abilities run the magical gamut. Standard rods are described below.

Absorption: This rod acts as a magnet, drawing spells or spell-like abilities into itself. The magic absorbed must be a single-target spell or a ray directed either at the character possessing the rod or her gear. The rod then nullifies the spell's effect and stores its potential until the wielder releases this energy in the form of spells of her own. She can instantly detect a spell's level as the rod absorbs that spell's energy. Absorption requires no action on the part of the user if the rod is in hand at the time.

A running total of absorbed (and used) spell levels should be kept. For example, a rod that absorbs a 6th-level spell and a 3rd-level spell has a total of nine absorbed spell levels. The wielder of the rod can use captured spell energy to cast any spell she has prepared, without expending the preparation itself. The only restrictions are that the levels of spell energy stored in the rod must be equal to or greater than the level of the spell the wielder wants to cast, that any material components required for the spell be present, and that the rod be in hand when casting. Continuing the example above, the rod wielder could use the nine absorbed spell levels to cast one 9th-level spell, or one 5th-level and one 4th-level spell, or nine 1st-level spells, and so on. For casters such as bards or sorcerers who do not prepare spells, the rod's energy can be used to cast any spell of the appropriate level or levels that they know.

The *rod of absorption* absorbs a maximum of fifty spell levels and can thereafter only discharge any remaining potential it might have. The rod cannot be recharged. The wielder knows the rod's remaining absorbing potential and current amount of stored energy.

A more specific example: Jozan the cleric uses a brand-new *rod of absorption* to nullify the effect of a *suggestion* spell cast at

Using multiple immovable rods

him by a sorcerer. The rod has now absorbed three spell levels and can absorb forty-seven more. Jozan can cast any 1st-, 2nd-, or 3rd-level spell he has prepared, without loss of that preparation, by using the stored potential of the rod. Let's assume he casts *hold person* back at the sorcerer who just attacked him. This spell is 2nd level for him, so the rod still holds one spell level of potential, can absorb forty-seven more, and has disposed of two spell levels permanently.

To determine the absorption potential remaining in a newly found rod, roll d% and divide the result by 2. Then roll d% again: On a result of 01–30, half the levels already absorbed by the rod are still stored within. For example, if the first roll determines that the rod has thirty-four levels of absorption potential remaining, that means the rod has absorbed sixteen levels' worth of spells. Half of sixteen is eight, so there's a 30% chance that it still holds eight absorbed spell levels ready for use.

Caster Level: 15th; *Prerequisites:* Craft Rod, *spell turning; Market Price:* 50,000 gp.

Alertness: This rod is indistinguishable from a +1 *light mace*. It has eight flanges on its macelike head. The rod bestows a +1 initiative bonus. If grasped firmly, the rod enables the holder to *detect evil, detect good, detect chaos, detect law, detect magic, discern lies,* or *see invisibility.* The use of these powers can be done freely with the rod, each different use taking a separate standard action.

If the head of a *rod of alertness* is planted in the ground, and the possessor wills it to alertness (a standard action), the rod senses any creature within 120 feet who intends to harm the possessor. Each of the flanges on the rod's head then casts a *light* spell along the direction it faces (usually north, northeast, east, southeast, south, southwest, west, and northwest) out to a 60-foot range. At the same time, the rod creates the effect of a *prayer* spell upon all creatures friendly to the possessor in a 20-foot radius. Immediately thereafter, the rod sends forth a mental alert to these friendly creatures, warning them of possible danger from the unfriendly creature or creatures within the 120-foot radius. These effects last for 10 minutes, and the rod can perform this function once per day.

Last, the rod can be used to simulate the casting of an *animate objects* spell, utilizing any eight (or fewer) objects located roughly around the perimeter of a 5-foot-radius circle centered on the rod when planted in the ground. Objects remain animated for 10 minutes. The rod can perform this function once per day.

Caster Level: 14th; *Prerequisites:* Craft Rod, *light, detect magic, alarm, detect chaos, detect evil, detect good, detect law, discern lies, see invisibility, prayer, animate objects; Market Price:* 72,000 gp.

Cancellation: This dreaded rod is a bane to magic items, for its touch drains an item of all magical properties. The item touched gets a saving throw (DC 19). If a creature is holding it at the time, then the item can use the holder's Will save bonus in place of its own if the holder's is better. In such cases, contact is made by making a melee touch attack roll. Upon draining an item, the rod itself becomes brittle and cannot be used again. Drained items are only restorable by *wish* or *miracle.* (If a *sphere of annihilation* and a *rod of cancellation* negate each other, nothing can restore either of them.)

Caster Level: 15th; *Prerequisites:* Craft Rod, *dispel magic; Market Price:* 11,000 gp.

Enemy Detection: This device pulses in the wielder's hand and points in the direction of any creature or creatures hostile to the bearer of the device (nearest ones first). These creatures can be invisible, ethereal, hidden, disguised, or in plain sight. Detection range is 60 feet. The rod can be used three times each day, each use lasting up to 10 minutes. Activating the rod is a standard action.

Caster Level: 10th; *Prerequisites:* Craft Rod, *discern lies; Market Price:* 23,500 gp.

Flailing: Upon the command of its possessor, the rod activates, changing from a normal-seeming rod to a +3 *dire flail.* The dire flail is a double weapon, which means that each of the weapon's heads can be used to attack (see the weapon description in Chapter 7: Equipment, page 100 in the *Player's Handbook*). The wielder can gain an extra attack (with the second head) at the cost of making all attacks at a −2 penalty (as if she had the Two-Weapon Fighting and Ambidexterity feats).

Once per day the wielder can use a free action to cause the rod to grant her a +4 deflection bonus to Armor Class and a +4 resistance bonus to saving throws for 10 minutes. The rod need not be in weapon form to grant this benefit. Transforming it into a weapon or back into a rod is a move-equivalent action.

Caster Level: 9th; *Prerequisites:* Craft Rod, Craft Magic Arms and Armor, *bless; Market Price:* 40,000 gp.

Flame Extinguishing: This rod can extinguish Medium-size or smaller nonmagical fires with simply a touch (a standard action). Extinguishing a Large or larger nonmagical fire, or a magic fire of Medium-size or smaller (such as that of a flaming weapon or a *burning hands* spell), expends 1 charge. Continual magic flames, such as those of a weapon or a fire creature, are suppressed for 6 rounds and flare up again after that time. To extinguish an instantaneous fire spell, the rod must be within the area of the effect and the wielder must have used a ready action, effectively countering the entire spell. When applied to Large or larger magic fires, such as those caused by *fireball, flame strike,* or *wall of fire,* extinguishing the flames expends 2 charges from the rod.

If the device is used upon a fire creature, a successful attack roll deals 6d6 points of damage to the creature. This requires 3 charges.

The rod has 10 charges, renewed each day.

Caster Level: 12th; *Prerequisites:* Craft Rod, *pyrotechnics; Market Price:* 15,000 gp.

Immovable Rod: This rod is a flat iron bar with a small button on one end. When the button is pushed (a move-equivalent action), the rod does not move from where it is, even if staying in place defies gravity. Thus, the owner can lift or place the rod wherever he wishes, push the button, and let go. Adventurers have found the *immovable rod* useful for holding ropes, barring doors, and all sorts of other utilitarian tasks. Many adventurers have found it useful to have more than one. Several *immovable rods* can even make a ladder when used together (although only two are needed). An *immovable rod* can support up to 8,000 pounds before falling to the ground. If a creature pushes against an *immovable rod,* it must make a Strength check (DC 30) to move it up to 10 feet in a single round.

Caster Level: 10th; *Prerequisites:* Craft Rod, *levitate; Market Price:* 7,500 gp.

Lordly Might: This rod has functions that are spell-like, and it can also be used as a magic weapon of various sorts. It also has several more mundane uses. The *rod of lordly might* is metal, thicker than other rods, with a flanged ball at one end and six studlike buttons along its length. (Pushing any of the rod's buttons is equivalent to drawing a weapon.) It weighs 10 pounds.

The following spell-like functions of the rod can each be used once per day:

- *Hold person* upon touch, if the wielder so commands (DC 14). The wielder must choose to use this power and then succeed with a melee touch attack to activate the power. If the attack fails, the effect is lost.
- *Fear* upon all enemies viewing it, if the wielder so desires (10-foot maximum range, DC 16). Invoking this power is a standard action.
- Deal 2d4 hit points of damage to an opponent on a successful touch attack and cure the wielder of a like amount of damage (DC 17). The wielder must choose to use this power before attacking, as with *hold person.*

The following weapon uses of the rod have no limits on their use:

- In its normal form, the rod can be used as a +2 *light mace.*
- When button 1 is pushed, the rod becomes a +1 *flaming longsword.* A blade springs from the ball, with the ball itself becoming the sword's hilt. The weapon lengthens to an overall length of 4 feet.
- When button 2 is pushed, the rod becomes a +4 *battleaxe.* A wide blade springs forth at the ball, and the whole lengthens to 4 feet.
- When button 3 is pushed, the rod becomes a +3 *shortspear or longspear.* The spear blade springs forth, and the handle can be lengthened up to 12 feet (wielder's choice), for an overall length of from 6 feet to 15 feet. At its 15-foot length, the rod is suitable for use as a lance.

The following mundane uses of the rod also have no limits on their use:

- Climbing pole/ladder. When button 4 is pushed, a spike that can anchor in granite is extruded from the ball, while the other end sprouts three sharp hooks. The rod lengthens to anywhere between 5 and 50 feet in a single round, stopping when button 4 is pushed again. Horizontal bars three inches long fold out from the sides, 1 foot apart, in staggered progression. The rod is firmly held by the spike and hooks and can bear up to 4,000 pounds. The wielder can retract the pole by pushing button 5.
- The ladder function can be used to force open doors. The wielder plants the rod's base 30 feet or less from the portal to be forced and in line with it, then pushes button 4. The force exerted has a +12 Strength bonus.
- When button 6 is pushed, the rod indicates magnetic north and gives the wielder a knowledge of his approximate depth beneath the surface or height above it.

Rod of lordly might

Caster Level: 19th; *Prerequisites:* Craft Rod, Craft Magic Arms and Armor, *inflict light wounds, bull's strength, flame blade, hold person, fear; Market Price:* 70,000 gp.

Metal and Mineral Detection: This rod pulses in the wielder's hand and points to the largest mass of metal within 30 feet. However, the wielder can concentrate on a specific metal or mineral (gold, platinum, quartz, beryl, diamond, corundum, and so on). If the specific mineral is within 30 feet, the rod points to any places it is located, and the rod wielder knows the approximate quantity as well. If more than one deposit of the specified metal or mineral is within range, the rod points to the largest cache first. Each operation requires a full-round action.

Caster Level: 9th; *Prerequisites:* Craft Rod, *locate object; Market Price:* 10,500 gp.

Negation: This device negates the spell or spell-like function or functions of magic items. The wielder points the rod at the magic item, and a pale gray beam shoots forth to touch the target device, attacking as a ray (a ranged touch attack). The ray negates any currently active item function and has a 75% chance to negate any other spell or spell-like functions of that device, regardless of the level or power of the functions, for 2d4 rounds. To negate instantaneous effects, the rod wielder needs to have used a ready action. The target item gets no saving throw or means to resist this effect, although the rod can't negate artifacts (even minor artifacts). The rod can function three times per day.

Caster Level: 16th; *Prerequisites:* Craft Rod, *dispel magic,* and *limited wish* or *miracle; Market Price:* 44,600 gp.

Python: This rod is longer than normal rods. It is about 4 feet long and weighs 10 pounds. It strikes as a +2 *quarterstaff.* If the user throws the rod to the ground (a standard action), it grows to become a 25-foot-long Huge constrictor snake (see the *Monster Manual* for complete statistics) by the end of the round. The python obeys all commands of the owner. (In animal form, it lacks the +2 enhancement bonus to attacks and damage possessed by the rod form.) The serpent returns to rod form (a full-round action) whenever the wielder desires, or whenever it moves farther than 100 feet from the owner. If the snake form is slain, it returns to rod form and cannot be activated again for three days. A python rod only functions if the possessor is good.

Caster Level: 10th; *Prerequisites:* Craft Rod, Craft Magic Arms and Armor, *polymorph other,* creator must be good; *Market Price:* 13,000 gp.

Rulership: This rod looks like a royal scepter worth at least 5,000 gp in materials and workmanship alone. The wielder can command the obedience and fealty of creatures within 120 feet when she activates the device (a standard action). Creatures totaling 300 Hit Dice can be ruled, but creatures with Intelligence scores of 12 or higher are entitled to a Will saving throw (DC 16) to negate the effect. Ruled creatures obey the wielder as if she were their absolute sovereign. Still, if the wielder gives a command that is contrary to the nature of the creatures commanded, the magic is broken. The rod can be used for 500 total minutes before crumbling to dust. This duration need not be continuous.

Caster Level: 20th; *Prerequisites:* Craft Rod, *mass charm; Market Price:* 60,000 gp.

Security: This item creates a nondimensional space, a pocket paradise. There the rod's possessor and as many as 199 other creatures can stay in complete safety for a period of time, up to 200 days divided by the number of creatures affected. Thus, one creature (the rod's possessor) can stay for 200 days, four creatures can stay for 50 days, or a group of 60 creatures can stay for three days. All fractions are rounded down, so that a group numbering between 101 and 200 inclusive can stay for one day only.

In this pocket paradise, creatures don't age, and natural healing take place at twice the normal rate. Fresh water and food (fruits and vegetables only) are in abundance. The climate is comfortable for all creatures involved.

Activating the rod (a standard action) causes the wielder and all creatures touching the rod to be transported instantaneously to the paradise. Members of large groups can hold hands or otherwise maintain physical contact, allowing all connected creatures in a circle or a chain to be affected by the rod. Unwilling creatures get a Will saving throw (DC 17) to negate the effect. If such a creature succeeds at its save, other creatures beyond that point in a chain can still be affected by the rod.

When the rod's effect expires or is dispelled, all the affected creatures instantly reappear in the location they occupied when the rod was activated. If something else occupies the space that a traveler would be returning to, then his body is displaced a sufficient distance to provide the space required for reentry. The rod's possessor

can dismiss the effect whenever he wishes before the maximum time period expires, but the rod can only be activated once per week.

Caster Level: 20th; *Prerequisites:* Craft Rod, *gate; Market Price:* 61,000 gp.

Splendor: The possessor of this rod gains a +4 enhancement bonus to her Charisma score for as long as she holds or carries the item. Once per day, the rod creates and garbs her in clothing of the finest fabrics, plus adornments of furs and jewels.

Apparel created by the magic of the rod remains in existence for 12 hours. However, if she attempts to sell or give away any part of it, to use it for a spell component, or the like, all the apparel immediately disappears. The same applies if any of it is forcibly taken from her.

The value of noble garb created by the rod ranges from 7,000 to 10,000 gp (1d4+6 times 1,000 gp)—1,000 gp for the fabric alone, 5,000 gp for the furs, and the rest for the jewel trim (maximum of twenty gems, maximum value 200 gp each).

In addition, the rod has a second special power, usable once per week. Upon command, it creates a palatial tent—a huge pavilion of silk 60 feet across. Inside the tent are temporary furnishings and food suitable to the splendor of the pavilion and sufficient to entertain as many as one hundred persons. The tent and its trappings last for one day. At the end of that time, the tent and all objects associated with it (including any items that were taken out of the tent) disappear.

Caster Level: 12th; *Prerequisites:* Craft Rod, *fabricate, major creation; Market Price:* 25,000 gp.

Thunder and Lightning: Constructed of iron set with silver rivets, this rod has the properties of a +2 *light mace.* Its other magical powers are as follows:

- *Thunder:* Once per day, the rod can strike as a +3 *light mace,* and the opponent struck is stunned from the noise of the rod's impact (Fortitude negates DC 13). Activating this power counts as a free action, and it works if the wielder strikes an opponent within 1 round.

- *Lightning:* Once per day, a short spark of electricity can leap forth when the rod strikes an opponent to deal the normal damage for a +2 *light mace* (1d6) and +2d6 points of bonus electricity damage. Even when the rod might not score a normal hit in combat, if the roll was good enough to count as a successful melee touch attack hit, then the +2d6 points of bonus electrical damage still applies. The wielder activates this power as a free action, and it works if he strikes an opponent within 1 round.

- *Thunderclap:* Once per day as a standard action, the rod can create a deafening noise, just as a *shout* spell (DC 14, 2d6 points of sonic damage, target deafened for 2d6 rounds).

- *Lightning Stroke:* Once per day as a standard action, a 5-foot-wide *lightning bolt* (9d6 points of damage, DC 14) can blast from the rod to a range of 200 feet.

- *Thunder and Lightning:* Once per week as a standard action, the rod can combine the *thunderclap* described above with a forked lightning bolt, as in the *lightning stroke.* The thunderclap affects all within 10 feet of the bolt. The lightning alone deals 9d6 points of damage (count rolls of 1 or 2 as rolls of 3, for a range of 27 to 54 points), plus 2d6 more for the thunderclap. A single Reflex saving throw applies for both effects (DC 14), with deafness and half damage suffered by those who are successful.

Caster Level: 9th; *Prerequisites:* Craft Rod, Craft Magic Arms and Armor, *lightning bolt, shout; Market Price:* 23,000 gp.

Viper: This rod strikes as a +1 *heavy mace.* Once per day, upon command (a free action), the head of the rod becomes that of an actual serpent for 10 minutes. During this period, any successful strike with the rod deals normal damage and poisons the creature

Rod of the viper

hit. The poison deals 1d10 points of temporary Constitution damage immediately (Fortitude negates DC 14) and another 1d10 points of temporary Constitution damage 1 minute later (Fortitude negates DC 14). The rod only functions if the possessor is evil.

Caster Level: 10th; *Prerequisites:* Craft Rod, Craft Magic Arms and Armor, *poison*, creator must be evil; *Market Price:* 19,000 gp.

Withering: The *rod of withering* acts as a +1 light mace that deals no hit point damage. Instead, the wielder deals 1d4 points of temporary Strength damage and 1d4 points of temporary Constitution damage to any creature she touches with the rod (by making a melee touch attack). If she scores a critical hit, the damage from that hit is actually permanent ability drain. In either case, the defender negates the effect with a Fortitude save (DC 14).

Caster Level: 13th; *Prerequisites:* Craft Rod, Craft Magic Arms and Armor, *contagion*; *Market Price:* 17,000 gp.

Wonder: The *rod of wonder* is a strange and unpredictable device that randomly generates any number of weird effects each time it is used. (Activating the rod is a standard action.) The usual effects are shown on the table below, but you may alter these for any or all of these as you see fit for your own campaign. Typical powers of the rod include all of the following:

ROD OF WONDER

d%	Wondrous Effect
01–05	*Slow* creature pointed at for 10 rounds (DC 13).
06–10	*Faerie fire* surrounds the target (DC 11).
11–15	Deludes wielder for 1 round into believing the rod functions as indicated by a second die roll (no save).
16–20	*Gust of wind*, but at windstorm force; see Weather Hazards, page 87 (DC 13).
21–25	Wielder learns target's surface thoughts (as with *detect thoughts*) for 1d4 rounds (no save).
26–30	*Stinking cloud* at 30-ft. range (DC 12).
31–33	Heavy rain falls for 1 round in 60-ft. radius centered on rod wielder.
34–36	*Summon* an animal—a rhino (01–25 result on d%), elephant (26–50), or mouse (51–100).
37–46	*Lightning bolt* (70 ft. long, 5 ft. wide), 6d6 points of damage (DC 13).
47–49	Stream of 600 large butterflies pours forth and flutters around for 2 rounds, blinding everyone (including wielder) within 25 ft. (Reflex save DC 14 to avoid).
50–53	*Enlarge* target 50% if within 60 ft. of rod (DC 11).
54–58	*Darkness*, 30-ft.-diameter hemisphere, centered 30 ft. away from rod.
59–62	Grass grows in 160-sq.-ft. area before the rod, or grass existing there grows to ten times normal size.
63–65	Turn ethereal any nonliving object of up to 1,000 lb. mass and up to 30 cu. ft. in size.
66–69	*Reduce* wielder to 1/12 height (no save).
70–79	*Fireball* at target or 100 ft. straight ahead, 6d6 damage (DC 13).
80–84	*Invisibility* covers rod wielder.
85–87	Leaves grow from target if within 60 ft. of rod. These last 24 hours.
88–90	10–40 gems, value 1 gp each, shoot forth in a 30-ft.-long stream. Each gem causes 1 point of damage to any creature in its path: roll 5d4 for the number of hits and divide them among the available targets.
91–95	Shimmering colors dance and play over a 40-ft.-by-30-ft. area in front of rod. Creatures therein are blinded for 1d6 rounds (Fortitude negates DC 12).
96–97	Wielder (50% chance) or target (50% chance) turns permanently blue, green, or purple (no save).
98–100	*Flesh to stone* (or *stone to flesh* if target is stone already) if target is within 60 ft.

Caster Level: 10th; *Prerequisites:* Craft Rod, *confusion*, creator must be chaotic; *Market Price:* 12,000 gp.

SCROLLS

A scroll is a spell (or collection of spells) that has been stored in written form. A spell on a scroll can be used only once. The writing vanishes from the scroll when the spell is activated. Using a scroll is basically like casting a spell.

Physical Description: A scroll is a heavy sheet of fine vellum or high-quality paper roughly the size of a piece of modern notepaper (about 8 1/2 inches wide and 11 inches long), which is sufficient to hold one spell. The sheet is reinforced at the top and bottom with strips of leather slightly longer than the sheet is wide. A scroll holding more than one spell has the same width (about 8 1/2 inches) but is an extra foot or so long for each extra spell. Scrolls that hold three or more spells are usually fitted with reinforcing rods at each end rather than simple strips of leather. A scroll has an AC of 9, 1 hit point, a hardness of 0, and a break DC of 8.

To protect the scroll from wrinkling or tearing, the scroll is rolled up from both ends to form a double cylinder. (This also helps the user unroll the scroll quickly.) The scroll is placed in a tube of ivory, jade, leather, metal, or wood. Most scroll cases are inscribed with magic symbols (see the *arcane mark* spell and Arcane Magical Writings, page 155 in Chapter 10: Magic in the *Player's Handbook*), which often identify the owner or the spells stored on the scrolls inside. The symbols often hide magic traps such as *glyph of warding* or *fire trap* spells.

Activation: To activate a scroll, a spellcaster must read the spell written on it. Doing so involves several steps and conditions.

Decipher the Writing: The writing on a scroll must be deciphered (Text continues on page 203)

Using a scroll with a spell that is beyond her, Mialee suffers painful consequences.

TABLE 8–24: ARCANE SPELL SCROLLS

1st-Level Arcane Spells

d%	Spell	Market Price
01–05	Burning hands	25 gp
06–10	Change self	25 gp
11–15	Charm person	25 gp
16–18	Color spray	25 gp
19–22	Detect secret doors	25 gp
23–25	Detect undead	25 gp
26–28	Enlarge	25 gp
29–31	Erase	25 gp
32–36	Feather fall	25 gp
37–39	Grease	25 gp
40–44	Identify	125 gp
45–47	Jump	25 gp
48–51	Mage armor	25 gp
52–54	Magic weapon	25 gp
55–57	Mount	25 gp
58–60	Ray of enfeeblement	25 gp
61–63	Reduce	25 gp
63–66	Shield	25 gp
67–69	Shocking grasp	25 gp
70–73	Silent image	25 gp
74–78	Sleep	25 gp
79–81	Spider climb	25 gp
82–84	Summon monster I	25 gp
85–87	Tenser's floating disk	25 gp
88–92	Unseen servant	25 gp
93–95	Ventriloquism	25 gp
96–100	DM's choice of any 1st-level arcane spell	—

2nd-Level Arcane Spells

d%	Spell	Market Price
01–03	Arcane lock	175 gp
04–08	Blindness/deafness	150 gp
09–13	Blur	150 gp
14–18	Bull's strength	150 gp
19–22	Cat's grace	150 gp
23–25	Darkvision	150 gp
26–30	Detect thoughts	150 gp
31–33	Flaming sphere	150 gp
34–38	Invisibility	150 gp
39–41	Knock	150 gp
42–46	Levitate	150 gp
47–51	Locate object	150 gp
52–54	Melf's acid arrow	150 gp
55–59	Minor image	150 gp
60–64	Mirror image	150 gp
65–69	Misdirection	150 gp
70–72	Protection from arrows	150 gp
73–77	See invisibility	150 gp
78–80	Spectral hand	150 gp
81–83	Stinking cloud	150 gp
84–87	Summon monster II	150 gp
88–92	Summon swarm	150 gp
93–95	Web	150 gp
96–100	DM's choice of any 2nd-level arcane spell	—

3rd-Level Arcane Spells

d%	Spell	Market Price
01–05	Blink	375 gp
06–10	Clairaudience/clairvoyance	375 gp
11–15	Dispel magic	375 gp
16–20	Displacement	375 gp
21–25	Fireball	375 gp
26–28	Flame arrow	375 gp
29–31	Fly	375 gp
32–33	Gaseous form	375 gp
34–36	Greater magic weapon	375 gp
37–39	Halt undead	375 gp
40–42	Haste	375 gp
43–45	Hold person	375 gp
46–47	Invisibility sphere	375 gp
48–53	Lightning bolt	375 gp
54	Magic circle against chaos	375 gp
55	Magic circle against evil	375 gp
56	Magic circle against good	375 gp
57	Magic circle against law	375 gp
58–60	Nondetection	425 gp
61–65	Slow	375 gp
66–70	Spectral hand	375 gp
71–75	Suggestion	375 gp
76–79	Summon monster III	375 gp
80–84	Tongues	375 gp
85–87	Vampiric touch	375 gp
88–90	Water breathing	375 gp
91–100	DM's choice of any 3rd-level arcane spell	—

4th-Level Arcane Spells

d%	Spell	Market Price
01–05	Charm monster	700 gp
06–10	Confusion	700 gp
11–15	Contagion	700 gp
16–20	Detect scrying	700 gp
21–23	Dimensional anchor	700 gp
24–28	Dimension door	700 gp
29–33	Emotion	700 gp
34–36	Enervation	700 gp
37–39	Evard's black tentacles	700 gp
40–44	Fear	700 gp
45–47	Fire shield	700 gp
48–50	Ice storm	700 gp
51–55	Improved invisibility	700 gp
56–58	Lesser geas	700 gp
59–61	Minor globe of invulnerability	700 gp
65–67	Phantasmal killer	700 gp
68–70	Polymorph other	700 gp
71–73	Polymorph self	700 gp
74–76	Remove curse	700 gp
77–79	Shadow conjuration	700 gp
80–82	Stoneskin	950 gp
83–84	Summon monster IV	700 gp
85–87	Wall of fire	700 gp
88–90	Wall of ice	700 gp
91–100	DM's choice of any 4th-level arcane spell	—

5th-Level Arcane Spells

d%	Spell	Market Price
01–04	Bigby's interposing hand	1,125 gp
05–08	Cloudkill	1,125 gp
09–13	Cone of cold	1,125 gp
14–17	Dismissal	1,125 gp
18–21	Domination	1,125 gp
22–24	Feeblemind	1,125 gp
25–27	Greater shadow conjuration	1,125 gp
28–31	Hold monster	1,125 gp
32–35	Major creation	1,125 gp
36–40	Mind fog	1,125 gp
41–44	Passwall	1,125 gp
45–49	Persistent image	1,125 gp
50–53	Shadow evocation	1,125 gp
54–56	Stone shape	1,125 gp
57–60	Summon monster V	1,125 gp
61–64	Telekinesis	1,125 gp

d%	Spell	Market Price
65–69	Teleport	1,125 gp
70–73	Transmute mud to rock	1,125 gp
74–77	Transmute rock to mud	1,125 gp
78–81	Wall of force	1,125 gp
82–86	Wall of iron	1,175 gp
87–90	Wall of stone	1,125 gp
91–100	DM's choice of any 5th-level arcane spell	—

6th-Level Arcane Spells

d%	Spell	Market Price
01–04	Acid fog	1,650 gp
05–07	Analyze dweomer	1,650 gp
08–11	Antimagic field	1,650 gp
12–15	Bigby's forceful hand	1,650 gp
16–19	Chain lightning	1,650 gp
20–23	Circle of death	2,150 gp
24–26	Control water	1,650 gp
27–30	Disintegrate	1,650 gp
31–33	Eyebite	1,650 gp
34–37	Flesh to stone	1,650 gp
38–41	Globe of invulnerability	1,650 gp
42–45	Greater shadow evocation	1,650 gp
46–49	Mass suggestion	1,650 gp
50–52	Mislead	1,650 gp
53–57	Move earth	1,650 gp
58–61	Otiluke's freezing sphere	1,650 gp
62–65	Programmed image	1,650 gp
66–70	Project image	1,650 gp
71–75	Repulsion	1,650 gp
76–78	Shades	1,650 gp
79–82	Stone to flesh	1,650 gp
83–86	Summon monster VI	1,650 gp
87–90	True seeing	1,900 gp
91–100	DM's choice of any 6th-level arcane spell	—

7th-Level Arcane Spells

d%	Spell	Market Price
01–05	Bigby's grasping hand	2,275 gp
06–10	Control undead	2,275 gp
11–15	Delayed blast fireball	2,275 gp
16–20	Ethereal jaunt	2,275 gp
21–25	Finger of death	2,275 gp
26–30	Forcecage	3,775 gp
31–35	Limited wish	3,775 gp*
36–40	Mass invisibility	2,275 gp
41–45	Mordenkainen's sword	2,275 gp
46–50	Power word, stun	2,275 gp
51–55	Prismatic spray	2,275 gp
56–60	Reverse gravity	2,275 gp
61–65	Sequester	2,275 gp
66–70	Spell turning	2,275 gp
71–75	Summon monster VII	2,275 gp
76–80	Teleport without error	2,275 gp
81–85	Vanish	2,275 gp
86–90	Vision	3,025 gp
91–100	DM's choice of any 7th-level arcane spell	—

*Assumes no material component cost in excess of 1,000 gp and no XP cost in excess of 300 XP.

8th-Level Arcane Spells

d%	Spell	Market Price
01–03	Antipathy	3,000 gp
04–08	Bigby's clenched fist	3,000 gp
09–13	Clone	4,000 gp
14–18	Demand	3,000 gp
19–23	Horrid wilting	3,000 gp
24–28	Incendiary cloud	3,000 gp
29–33	Mass charm	3,000 gp
34–38	Maze	3,000 gp
39–43	Mind blank	3,000 gp
44–48	Otiluke's telekinetic sphere	3,000 gp
49–53	Otto's irresistible dance	3,000 gp
54–58	Polymorph any object	3,000 gp
59–63	Power word, blind	3,000 gp
64–68	Prismatic wall	3,000 gp
69–73	Protection from spells	3,500 gp
74–78	Screen	3,000 gp
79–83	Summon monster VII	3,000 gp
84–88	Sunburst	3,000 gp
89–90	Sympathy	4,500 gp
91–100	DM's choice of any 8th-level arcane spell	—

9th-Level Arcane Spells

d%	Spell	Market Price
01–07	Bigby's crushing hand	3,825 gp
08–14	Energy drain	3,825 gp
15–21	Imprisonment	3,825 gp
22–28	Meteor swarm	3,825 gp
29–35	Mordenkainen's disjunction	3,825 gp
43–49	Prismatic sphere	3,825 gp
50–56	Shapechange	3,825 gp
57–63	Summon monster IX	3,825 gp
64–69	Time stop	3,825 gp
70–76	Wail of the banshee	3,825 gp
77–83	Weird	3,825 gp
84–90	Wish	28,825 gp*
91–100	DM's choice of any 9th-level arcane spell	—

*Assumes no material component cost in excess of 10,000 gp and no XP cost in excess of 5,000 XP.

TABLE 8–25: DIVINE SPELL SCROLLS

1st-Level Divine Spells

d%	Spell	Market Price
01–05	Bless	25 gp
06–10	Calm animals	25 gp
11–14	Command	25 gp
15–19	Cure light wounds	25 gp
20–22	Detect chaos	25 gp
23–25	Detect evil	25 gp
26–28	Detect good	25 gp
29–31	Detect law	25 gp
32–34	Detect snares and pits	25 gp
35–39	Doom	25 gp
40–44	Entangle	25 gp
43–49	Faerie fire	25 gp
50–54	Inflict light wounds	25 gp
55–59	Invisibility to animals	25 gp
60–64	Invisibility to undead	25 gp
65–67	Magic fang	25 gp
68–70	Magic stone	25 gp
71–73	Magic weapon	25 gp
74–77	Sanctuary	25 gp
78–82	Shillelagh	25 gp
83–86	Summon monster I	25 gp
87–90	Summon nature's ally I	25 gp
91–100	DM's choice of any 1st-level divine spell	—

2nd-Level Divine Spells

d%	Spell	Market Price
01–05	Aid	150 gp
06–10	Augury	150 gp
11–15	Barkskin	150 gp
16–20	Bull's strength	150 gp
21–25	Charm person or animal	150 gp

d%	Spell	Market Price
26–28	Chill metal	150 gp
29–31	Cure moderate wounds	150 gp
32–36	Delay poison	150 gp
37–39	Flame blade	150 gp
40–42	Flaming sphere	150 gp
43–47	Heat metal	150 gp
48–50	Hold animal	150 gp
51–55	Hold person	150 gp
56–58	Inflict moderate wounds	150 gp
59–63	Lesser restoration	150 gp
64–67	Silence	150 gp
68–70	Speak with animals	150 gp
71–75	Spiritual weapon	150 gp
76–79	Summon monster II	150 gp
80–83	Summon nature's ally II	150 gp
84–85	Summon swarm	150 gp
86–90	Undetectable alignment	150 gp
91–100	DM's choice of any 2nd-level divine spell	—

3rd-Level Divine Spells

d%	Spell	Market Price
01–02	Call lightning	375 gp
03–09	Cure serious wounds	375 gp
10–13	Dispel magic	375 gp
14–15	Dominate animal	375 gp
16–17	Greater magic fang	375 gp
18–19	Inflict serious wounds	375 gp
20–22	Invisibility purge	375 gp
23–26	Locate object	375 gp
27–28	Magic circle against chaos	375 gp
29–30	Magic circle against evil	375 gp
31–32	Magic circle against good	375 gp
33–34	Magic circle against law	375 gp
35–38	Negative energy protection	375 gp
39–41	Neutralize poison	375 gp
42–43	Plant growth	375 gp
44–46	Prayer	375 gp
47–51	Protection from elements	375 gp
52–53	Remove blindness/deafness	375 gp
54–56	Remove curse	375 gp
57–59	Remove disease	375 gp
60–62	Searing light	375 gp
63–65	Speak with dead	375 gp
66–67	Spike growth	375 gp
68–72	Stone shape	375 gp
73–75	Summon monster III	375 gp
76–78	Summon nature's ally III	375 gp
79–80	Water breathing	375 gp
81–90	Water walk	375 gp
91–100	DM's choice of any 3rd-level divine spell	—

4th-Level Divine Spells

d%	Spell	Market Price
01–02	Antiplant shell	700 gp
03–05	Control water	700 gp
06–12	Cure critical wounds	700 gp
13–19	Discern lies	700 gp
20–24	Dispel magic	700 gp
25–27	Divine power	700 gp
28–34	Flame strike	700 gp
35–41	Freedom of movement	700 gp
42–47	Giant vermin	700 gp
48–50	Greater magic weapon	700 gp
51–53	Inflict critical wounds	700 gp
54–55	Lesser planar ally	700 gp
56–62	Neutralize poison	700 gp
63–66	Quench	700 gp
67–68	Restoration	800 gp
69–71	Rusting grasp	700 gp
72–74	Spell immunity	700 gp
75–76	Spike stones	700 gp
77–80	Summon monster IV	700 gp
81–82	Summon nature's ally IV	700 gp
83–90	Tongues	700 gp
91–100	DM's choice of any 4th-level divine spell	—

5th-Level Divine Spells

d%	Spell	Market Price
01–07	Break enchantment	1,125 gp
08–13	Commune	1,625 gp
14–15	Control winds	1,125 gp
16–22	Cure critical wounds	1,125 gp
23–26	Dispel evil	1,125 gp
27–29	Dispel good	1,125 gp
30–35	Flame strike	1,125 gp
36–38	Greater command	1,125 gp
39–40	Hallow	6,125 gp*
41–43	Healing circle	1,125 gp
44–45	Ice storm	1,125 gp
46–50	Insect plague	1,125 gp
51–57	Raise dead	1,625 gp
58–60	Righteous might	1,125 gp
61–63	Slay living	1,125 gp
64–65	Spell resistance	1,125 gp
66–67	Summon monster V	1,125 gp
68–69	Summon nature's ally V	1,125 gp
70–72	Transmute rock to mud	1,125 gp
73–74	True seeing	1,375 gp
75	Unhallow	6,125 gp*
76–78	Wall of fire	1,125 gp
79–80	Wall of stone	1,125 gp
81–90	Wall of thorns	1,125 gp
91–100	DM's choice of any 5th-level divine spell	—

*Allows for up to a 4th-level spell to be tied to the *hallowed* or *unhallowed* area.

6th-Level Divine Spells

d%	Spell	Market Price
01–08	Antilife shell	1,650 gp
09–14	Blade barrier	1,650 gp
15–19	Find the path	1,650 gp
20–23	Fire seeds	1,650 gp
24–28	Geas/Quest	1,650 gp
29–34	Harm	1,650 gp
35–41	Heal	1,650 gp
42–47	Heroes' feast	1,650 gp
48–55	Planar ally	1,650 gp
56–57	Repel wood	1,650 gp
58–60	Stone tell	1,650 gp
61–68	Summon monster VI	1,650 gp
69–71	Transport via plants	1,650 gp
72–77	Wall of stone	1,650 gp
78–80	Wind walk	1,650 gp
81–90	Word of recall	1,650 gp
91–100	DM's choice of any 6th-level divine spell	—

7th-Level Divine Spells

d%	Spell	Market Price
01–11	Control weather	2,275 gp
12–18	Creeping doom	2,275 gp
19–25	Destruction	2,275 gp
26–32	Dictum	2,275 gp

33–36	Fire storm	2,275 gp
37–40	Greater restoration	4,775 gp
41–47	Holy word	2,275 gp
48–54	Regenerate	2,275 gp
55–61	Repulsion	2,275 gp
62–68	Resurrection	2,775 gp
69–72	Summon monster VII	2,275 gp
73–76	Transmute metal to wood	2,275 gp
77–80	True seeing	2,525 gp
81–90	Word of chaos	2,275 gp
91–100	DM's choice of any 7th-level divine spell	—

8th-Level Divine Spells

d%	Spell	Market Price
01–06	Antimagic field	3,000 gp
07–12	Creeping doom	3,000 gp
13–18	Discern location	3,000 gp
19–25	Earthquake	3,000 gp
26–30	Finger of death	3,000 gp
31–35	Fire storm	3,000 gp
36–44	Holy aura	3,000 gp
45–50	Mass heal	3,000 gp
51–56	Repel metal or stone	3,000 gp
57–62	Reverse gravity	3,000 gp
63–68	Summon monster VIII	3,000 gp
69–74	Sunburst	3,000 gp
75–80	Unholy aura	3,000 gp
81–90	Whirlwind	3,000 gp
91–100	DM's choice of any 8th-level divine spell	—

9th-Level Divine Spells

d%	Spell	Market Price
01–07	Earthquake	3,825 gp
08–14	Elemental swarm	3,825 gp
15–26	Energy drain	3,825 gp
27–38	Implosion	3,825 gp
39–50	Miracle	28,825 gp*
51–57	Shapechange	3,825 gp
58–68	Storm of vengeance	3,825 gp
69–80	Summon monster IX	3,825 gp
81–90	True resurrection	8,825 gp
91–100	DM's choice of any 9th-level divine spell	—

*Assumes powerful request but no expensive material components in excess of 100 gp and no additional XP cost.

before a character can use it or know exactly what spell it contains. This requires a *read magic* spell or a successful Spellcraft check (DC 15 + spell level).

Deciphering a scroll to determine its contents does not activate its magic unless it is a specially prepared cursed scroll. A character can decipher the writing on a scroll in advance so that he or she can proceed directly to the next step when the time comes to use the scroll.

Activate the Spell: Activating a scroll requires reading the spell from the scroll. The character must be able to see and read the writing on the scroll.

Activating a scroll spell requires no material components or focus. (The creator of the scroll provided these when scribing the scroll.) Note that some spells are effective only when cast on an item or items (for example, *Drawmij's instant summons* and *snare*). In such a case, the scroll user must provide the item when activating the spell. Activating a scroll spell is subject to disruption just as casting a normally prepared spell would be (see Cast a Spell in Chapter 8: Combat, page 125 in the *Player's Handbook*).

To have any chance of activating a scroll spell, the caster must meet the following requirements:

- The spell must be of the correct type (arcane or divine). Arcane spellcasters (wizards, sorcerers, and bards) cannot cast divine spells from a scroll, nor can divine spellcasters (clerics, druids, paladins, and rangers) cast arcane spells in this manner. (The type of scroll a character creates is determined by his or her class. For example, clerics create scrolls of divine spells, wizards create scrolls of arcane spells, and so forth.)
- The user must have the spell on his or her class list (see Chapter 11: Spells in the *Player's Handbook* for which classes can cast which spells).
- The user must have the requisite ability score (for example, Intelligence 15 for a wizard casting a 5th-level spell).

If the user meets all the requirements noted above, and her caster level is at least equal to the spell's caster level, she can automatically activate the spell without a check. If she meets all three requirements but her own caster level is lower than the scroll spell's caster level, then she has to make a caster level check (DC = scroll's caster level + 1) to cast the spell successfully. If she fails, she must make a Wisdom check (DC 5) to avoid a mishap (see Scroll Mishaps, below). A natural roll of 1 always fails, whatever the modifiers.

Determine Effect: A spell successfully activated from a scroll works exactly like a spell prepared and cast the normal way. Assume the scroll spell's caster level is always the minimum level required to cast the spell for the character who scribed the scroll (usually twice the spell's level, minus 1), unless the caster specifically desire otherwise. For example, a 10th-level cleric might want to create a *cure critical wounds* scroll at caster level 10 rather than the minimum for the spell (caster level 7), in order to get more benefit from the scroll spell. (This scroll would, however, be more costly to scribe.)

The writing for an activated spell disappears from the scroll.

Scroll Mishaps: In a mishap, the spell on the scroll has a reversed or harmful effect. The DM determines what sort of mishap occurs, with a surge of uncontrolled magic energy that deals 1d6 points of per spell level being the default. The DM can use the default, decide what happens, or select an effect from the following list:

- Spell strikes the caster or an ally instead of the intended target, or a random target nearby if the caster was the intended recipient.
- Spell takes effect at some random location within spell range.
- Spell's effect on the target is contrary to the spell's normal effect. For example, a *fireball* might produce a blast of nondamaging cold or release a burst of healing energy.
- The caster suffers some minor but bizarre effect related to the spell in some way. For example, a *fireball* might cause smoke to pour from the caster's ears, a *fly* spell might turn the caster's arms into nonfunctional wings, or a *clairaudience/clairvoyance* spell might cause the caster's eyes and ears to grow to 10 times their normal size. Most such effects should last only as long as the original spell's duration, or 2d10 minutes for instantaneous spells.
- Some innocuous item or items appear in the spell's area. For example, a *fireball* might cause a rain of lit torches to fall in the target area; a *feather fall* spell might produce a cloud of feathers; a *passwall* spell might cause a (nonfunctional) door to appear.
- Spell has delayed effect. Within the next 1d12 hours, the spell activates. If the caster was the intended recipient, the spell takes effect normally. If the caster was not the intended recipient, the spell goes off in the general direction of the original recipient or target, up to the spell's maximum range, if the target has moved away.

Random Generation: To generate scrolls randomly, first roll on Table 8–21: Scroll Types to determine whether the spells are

TABLE 8–21: SCROLL TYPES

d% roll	Type
01–70	Arcane
71–100	Divine

TABLE 8–22: NUMBER OF SPELLS ON A SCROLL

Scroll Type	Number of Spells
Minor scroll	1d3 spells
Medium scroll	1d4 spells
Major scroll	1d6 spells

TABLE 8–23: SCROLL SPELL LEVELS

Minor	Medium	Major	Spell Level	Spell's Caster Level*
01–50	—	—	1st	1st
51–95	01–05	—	2nd	3rd
96–100	06–65	—	3rd	5th
—	66–95	01–05	4th	7th
—	96–100	06–50	5th	9th
—	—	51–70	6th	11th
—	—	71–85	7th	13th
—	—	86–95	8th	15th
—	—	95–100	9th	17th

*These numbers assume that the creator is a cleric, druid, or wizard. The tables for random generation of scrolls likewise assume that the scroll was prepared by a member of one of those classes. For other classes that cast spells (bard, paladin, ranger, and sorcerer), the experience level at which certain spells become available, and sometimes the level of the spell itself, differs.

arcane or divine. Then randomly determine how many spells are on the scroll, according to Table 8–22: Number of Spells on a Scroll. For each spell, roll on Table 8–23: Scroll Spell Levels to determine its level and then on the appropriate subtable of Table 8–24: Arcane Spell Scrolls or of Table 8–25: Divine Spell Scrolls to determine the specific spell.

STAFFS

A staff is a long shaft of wood that stores several spells. Unlike wands (see the Wands section later in this chapter), each staff is of a specific type. A spellcaster can't stick any combination of spells in a staff. A staff has 50 charges when created.

Physical Description: A typical staff is 4 feet to 7 feet long and 2 inches to 3 inches thick, weighing about 5 pounds. Most staffs are wood, but a rare few are bone, metal, or even glass. (These are extremely exotic.) Staffs often have a gem or some device at their tip or are shod in metal at one or both ends. Staffs are often decorated with carvings or runes. A typical staff is like a walking stick, quarterstaff, or cudgel. It has an AC of 7, 10 hit points,

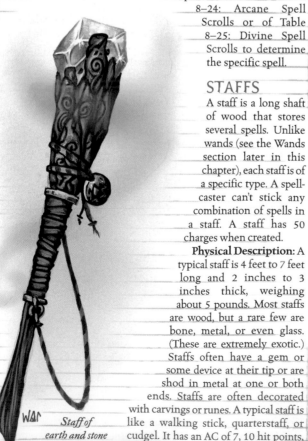

Staff of earth and stone

a hardness of 5, and a break DC of 24.

Activation: Staffs use the spell trigger activation method, so casting a spell from a staff is usually a standard action that doesn't provoke attacks of opportunity. (If the spell being cast, however, has a longer casting time than 1 action, it takes that long to cast the spell from a staff.) To activate a staff, a character must hold it forth in at least one hand (or whatever passes for a hand, for nonhumanoid creatures).

Random Generation: To generate staffs randomly, roll on Table 8–26: Staffs.

Special Qualities: Roll d%. A 01–30 result indicates that something (a design, inscription, etc.) provides some clue to the staff's function, and 31–100 indicates no special qualities.

Staff of frost

TABLE 8–26: STAFFS

Medium	Major	Staff	Market Price
01–10	—	Size alteration	6,500 gp
11–20	01–05	Charming	12,000 gp
21–30	06–15	Healing	33,000 gp
31–40	16–30	Fire	29,000 gp
41–50	31–40	Swarming insects	20,000 gp
51–60	41–50	Frost	70,000 gp
61–70	51–60	Earth and stone	85,000 gp
71–80	61–70	Defense	80,000 gp
81–89	71–80	Woodlands	90,000 gp
90–95	81–90	Life	130,000 gp
96–100	91–96	Passage	180,000 gp
—	97–100	Power	200,000 gp

Staff Descriptions

Staffs have immense utility because they pack so many capabilities into one item. This compact might, plus a certain stately charm that many have, makes them appealing to all spellcasters. Standard staffs are described below.

Charming: Made of twisting wood ornately shaped and carved, this staff allows use of the following spells:

- *Charm person* (1 charge, DC 11)
- *Charm monster* (2 charges, DC 16)

Caster Level: 7th; *Prerequisites:* Craft Staff, *charm person*, *charm monster*; *Market Price:* 12,000 gp.

Healing: This white ash staff, with inlaid silver runes, allows use of the following spells:

- *Lesser restoration* (1 charge)
- *Cure serious wounds* (1 charge)
- *Remove blindness/deafness* (1 charge)
- *Remove disease* (1 charge)

Caster Level: 7th; *Prerequisites:* Craft Staff, *lesser restoration*, *cure serious wounds*, *remove blindness/deafness*, *remove disease*; *Market Price:* 33,000 gp.

Defense: The *staff of defense* is a simple-looking staff that throbs with power when held defensively. It allows use of the following spells:

- *Shield* (1 charge)
- *Shield of faith* (+5 deflection bonus to AC) (1 charge)
- *Shield other* (1 charge)
- *Shield of law* (2 charges)

Caster Level: 15th; *Prerequisites:* Craft Staff, *shield, shield of faith, shield other, shield of law,* creator must be lawful; *Market Price:* 80,000 gp.

Earth and Stone: This staff is topped with a fist-sized emerald that gleams with smoldering power. It allows the use of the following spells:

- *Passwall* (1 charge)
- *Move earth* (1 charge)

Caster Level: 11th; *Prerequisites:* Craft Staff, *passwall, move earth; Market Price:* 85,000 gp.

Fire: Crafted from bronzewood with brass bindings, this staff allows use of the following spells:

- *Burning hands* (1 charge, DC 11)
- *Fireball* (8d6, DC 14) (1 charge)
- *Wall of fire* (2 charges, DC 16)

Caster Level: 8th; *Prerequisites:* Craft Staff, *burning hands, fireball, wall of fire; Market Price:* 29,000 gp.

Frost: Tipped on either end with a glistening diamond, this rune-covered staff allows the use of the following spells:

- *Ice storm* (1 charge, DC 16)
- *Wall of ice* (1 charge, DC 16)
- *Cone of cold* (10d6, DC 17) (1 charge)

Caster Level: 10th; *Prerequisites:* Craft Staff, *ice storm, wall of ice, cone of cold; Market Price:* 70,000 gp.

Life: Made of thick oak shod in gold, this staff allows use of the following spells:

- *Heal* (1 charge)
- *Resurrection* (1 charge)

Caster Level: 13th; *Prerequisites:* Craft Staff, *heal, resurrection; Market Price:* 130,000 gp.

Passage: This potent item allows the use of the following spells:

- *Dimension door* (1 charge)
- *Passwall* (1 charge)
- *Phase door* (2 charges)
- *Teleport without error* (2 charges)
- *Astral projection* (2 charges)

Caster Level: 17th; *Prerequisites:* Craft Staff, *dimension door, passwall, phase door, teleport without error, astral projection; Market Price:* 180,000 gp.

Power: The *staff of power* is a very potent magic item, with offensive and defensive abilities. It is usually topped with a glistening gem, its shaft straight and smooth. It has the following powers:

- *Magic missile* (5 missiles) (1 charge)
- *Ray of enfeeblement* (heightened to 5th level, DC 17) (1 charge)
- *Continual flame* (1 charge)
- *Levitate* (1 charge)
- *Lightning bolt* (heightened to 5th level, 10d6, DC 17) (1 charge)
- *Fireball* (heightened to 5th level, 10d6, DC 17) (1 charge)
- *Cone of cold* (15d6, DC 15) (2 charges)
- *Hold monster* (2 charges, DC 14)
- *Wall of force* (in a 10-foot-diameter hemisphere around the caster only) (2 charges)
  - *Globe of invulnerability* (2 charges)

The wielder of a *staff of power* gains a +2 luck bonus to AC and saving throws. The staff is also a +2 *quarterstaff,* and its wielder may use it to smite opponents. If 1 charge is expended (as a free action), the staff causes double damage (×3 on a critical hit) for 1 round.

A *staff of power* can be broken for a retributive strike. The breaking of the staff must be purposeful and declared by the wielder. All charges currently in the staff are instantly released in a 30-foot- radius globe. All within 10 feet of the broken staff take hit points of damage equal to eight times the number of charges in the staff, those between 11 feet and 20 feet away take six times the number of charges in damage, and those 21 feet to 30 feet distant take four times the number of charges in damage. Successful Reflex saving throws (DC 17) reduce the damage sustained by half.

The character breaking the staff has a 50% chance of traveling to another plane of existence, but if he does not, the explosive release of spell energy destroys him. Only certain items, including the *staff of the magi* (see Minor Artifacts) and the *staff of power,* are capable of a retributive strike.

After all charges are used up from the staff, it remains a +2 *quarterstaff.* (Once empty of charges, it cannot be broken in a retributive strike.)

Caster Level: 15th; *Prerequisites:* Craft Staff, Craft Magic Arms and Armor, *magic missile,* heightened *ray of enfeeblement, continual flame, levitate,* heightened *fireball,* heightened *lightning bolt, cone of cold, hold monster, wall of force, globe of invulnerability; Market Price:* 200,000 gp.

Size Alteration: Stout and sturdy, this staff of dark wood allows use of the following spells:

- *Enlarge* (1 charge)
- *Reduce* (1 charge)

Caster Level: 5th; *Prerequisites:* Craft Staff, *enlarge, reduce; Market Price:* 6,500 gp.

Swarming Insects: Made of twisted dark wood with dark spots resembling crawling insects (which occasionally seem to move), this staff allows use of the following spells:

- *Summon swarm* (1 charge)
- *Insect plague* (2 charges)

Staff of swarming insects

Caster Level: 9th; *Prerequisites:* Craft Staff, *summon swarm, insect plague; Market Price:* 20,000 gp.

Woodlands: Appearing to have grown naturally into its shape, this oak, ash, or yew staff allows use of the following spells:

- *Animal friendship* (1 charge)
- *Barkskin* (1 charge)
- *Speak with animals* (1 charge)
- *Wall of thorns* (1 charge)
- *Summon nature's ally VI* (2 charges)

Further, the staff may be used as a weapon, functioning as a +2 *quarterstaff*. The *staff of the woodlands* also allows its wielder to *pass without trace* at will, with no charge cost.

Caster Level: 9th; Prerequisites: Craft Staff, Craft Magic Arms and Armor, *pass without trace, animal friendship, barkskin, speak with animals, wall of thorns, summon nature's ally VI*; Market Price: 90,000 gp.

WANDS

A wand is a thin baton that contains a single spell. Each wand has 50 charges when created, and each charge expended allows the user to use the wand's spell one time. A wand that runs out of charges is just a stick.

Physical Description: A typical wand is 6 inches to 12 inches long and about 1/4 inch thick, and often weighs no more than 1 ounce. Most wands are wood, but some are bone. A rare few are metal, glass, or even ceramic, but these are quite exotic. Occasionally, a wand has a gem or some device at its tip, and most are decorated with carvings or runes. A typical wand has an AC of 7, 5 hit points, a hardness of 5, and a break DC of 16.

Activation: Wands use the spell trigger activation method, so casting a spell from a wand is usually a standard action that doesn't provoke attacks of opportunity. (If the spell being cast, however, has a longer casting time than 1 action, it takes that long to cast the spell from a wand.) To activate a wand, a character must hold it in hand (or whatever passes for a hand, for nonhumanoid creatures) and point it in the general direction of the target or area.

Random Generation: To generate wands randomly, roll on Table 8–27: Wands.

Special Qualities: Roll d%. A 01–30 result indicates that something (a design, inscription, etc.) provides some clue to the wand's function, and 31–100 indicates no special qualities.

Wand of lightning

TABLE 8–27: WANDS

Minor	Medium	Major	Wand	Market Price
01–05	—	—	Detect magic	375 gp
06–10	—	—	Light	375 gp
11–15	—	—	Detect secret doors	750 gp
16–20	—	—	Color spray	750 gp
21–25	—	—	Burning hands	750 gp
26–30	01–03	—	Charm person	750 gp
31–35	04–06	—	Enlarge	750 gp
36–40	07–09	—	Magic missile (1st-level caster)	750 gp
41–45	10–12	—	Shocking grasp	750 gp
46–50	13–15	—	Summon monster I	750 gp
51–55	16–18	—	Cure light wounds	750 gp
56–58	19–21	—	Magic missile (3rd-level caster)	2,250 gp
59	22–23	01–02	Magic missile (5th-level caster)	3,750 gp
60–63	24–26	03	Levitate	4,500 gp
64–66	27–29	04	Summon monster II	4,500 gp
67–69	30–32	05	Silence	4,500 gp
70–72	33–35	06	Knock	4,500 gp
73–75	36–38	07	Daylight	4,500 gp
76–78	39–41	08–10	Invisibility	4,500 gp
79–81	42–44	11–12	Shatter	4,500 gp
82–84	45–48	13–15	Bull's strength	4,500 gp
85–87	49–50	16–17	Mirror image	4,500 gp
88–90	51–53	18–19	Ghoul touch	4,500 gp
91–93	54–60	20–21	Cure moderate wounds	4,500 gp
94–96	61–63	22–23	Hold person	4,500 gp
97–98	64–66	24–25	Melf's acid arrow	4,500 gp
99	67–69	26–27	Web	4,500 gp
100	60–71	28–30	Darkness	4,500 gp
—	72	31–33	Magic missile (7th-level caster)	5,250 gp
—	—	34–36	Magic missile (9th-level caster)	6,750 gp
—	73–75	37–39	Fireball (3rd-level caster)	11,250 gp
—	76–80	40–41	Lightning bolt (3rd-level caster)	11,250 gp
—	81–82	42–43	Summon monster III	11,250 gp
—	83–84	44–45	Keen edge	11,250 gp
—	85–86	46–47	Major image	11,250 gp
—	87–88	48–49	Slow	11,250 gp
—	89–90	50–51	Suggestion	11,250 gp

Minor	Medium	Major	Wand	Market Price
—	91–92	52–53	Dispel magic	11,250 gp
—	93–94	54–55	Cure serious wounds	11,250 gp
—	95	55–57	Contagion	11,250 gp
—	96	58	Charm person (heightened to 3rd-level spell)	11,250 gp
—	97	59	Fireball (6th-level caster)	13,500 gp
—	98–99	60–61	Searing light (6th-level caster)	13,500 gp
—	100	62–63	Lightning bolt (6th-level caster)	13,500 gp
—	—	64–65	Fireball (8th-level caster)	18,000 gp
—	—	66–67	Lightning bolt (8th-level caster)	18,000 gp
—	—	68–69	Charm monster	21,000 gp
—	—	70–71	Fear	21,000 gp
—	—	72–73	Improved invisibility	21,000 gp
—	—	74–75	Polymorph self	21,000 gp
—	—	76–77	Polymorph other	21,000 gp
—	—	78–79	Ice storm	21,000 gp
—	—	80–81	Summon monster IV	21,000 gp
—	—	82–83	Wall of ice	21,000 gp
—	—	84	Wall of fire	21,000 gp
—	—	85	Ray of enfeeblement (heightened to 4th-level spell)	21,000 gp
—	—	86	Poison	21,000 gp
—	—	87	Suggestion (heightened to 4th-level spell)	21,000 gp
—	—	88–89	Neutralize poison	21,000 gp
—	—	90	Inflict critical wounds	21,000 gp
—	—	91–92	Cure critical wounds	21,000 gp
—	—	93	Restoration	21,100 gp
—	—	94	Fireball (10th-level caster)	22,500 gp
—	—	95	Lightning bolt (10th-level caster)	22,500 gp
—	—	96	Holy smite (8th-level caster)	24,000 gp
—	—	97	Chaos hammer (8th-level caster)	24,000 gp
—	—	98	Unholy blight (8th-level caster)	24,000 gp
—	—	99	Order's wrath (8th-level caster)	24,000 gp
—	—	100	Stoneskin	37,700 gp*

*The cost to create a *wand of stoneskin* is 10,500 gp, 840 XP, plus 12,500 gp for the material components.

Wand Descriptions

All wands are simply storage devices for spells and thus have no special descriptions. Refer to the spell descriptions in Chapter 11: Magic in the *Player's Handbook* for all pertinent details.

WONDROUS ITEMS

This is a catch-all category for anything that doesn't fall into the other groups. Anyone can use a wondrous item (unless specified otherwise in the description).

Physical Description: Varies.

Activation: Usually use activated or command word, but details vary from item to item.

Random Generation: To generate wondrous items randomly, roll on Table 8–28: Minor Wondrous Items, Table 8–29: Medium Wondrous Items, or Table 8–30: Major Wondrous Items. (These tables appear on pages 208–210.)

Special Qualities: Roll d%. An 01 result indicates the wondrous item is intelligent, 02–31 indicates that something (a design, inscription, etc.) provides a clue to its function, and 32–100 indicates no special qualities. Intelligent items have extra abilities and sometimes also extraordinary powers and special purposes. Use Table 8–31: Item Intelligence, Wisdom, Charisma, and Capabilities as indicated if a wondrous item is intelligent. Wondrous items with charges can never be intelligent.

Wondrous Item Descriptions

Wondrous items can be configured to do just about anything from create a breeze to improve ability scores. Standard wondrous items are described below.

Amulet of Health: This amulet is a golden disk on a chain. It usually bears the image of a lion or other powerful animal. The amulet grants the wearer an enhancement bonus to Constitution of +2, +4, or +6.

Caster Level: 8th; *Prerequisites:* Craft Wondrous Item, *endurance; Market Price:* 4, 000 gp (+2), 16,000 gp (+4), or 36,000 gp (+6); *Weight:* —.

Amulet of Natural Armor: This amulet, usually crafted from bone or beast scales, toughens the wearer's body and flesh, giving him a natural armor bonus to his AC of from +1 to +5, depending on the type of amulet.

Caster Level: 5th; *Prerequisites:* Craft Wondrous Item, *barkskin,* creator's caster level must be at least three times the amulet's bonus; *Market Price:* 2,000 gp (+1), 8,000 gp (+2), 18,000 gp (+3), 32,000 gp (+4), or 50,000 gp (+5); *Weight:* —.

Amulet of the Planes: This strange device usually appears to be a black circular amulet, although any character looking closely at it sees a dark, moving swirl of color. The amulet allows its wearer to utilize *plane shift.* However, this is a difficult item to master. The user must make an Intelligence check (DC 15) in order to get the amulet to take her to the plane (and the specific location on that plane) that she wants. If she fails, the amulet transports her and all those traveling with her to a random location on that plane (a 01–60 result on d%) or to a random plane (61–100).

Caster Level: 15th; *Prerequisites:* Craft Wondrous Item, *plane shift; Market Price:* 80,000 gp; *Weight:* —.

Amulet of Proof against Detection and Location: This silver amulet protects the wearer from scrying and magical location just as a *nondetection* spell does. If a divination is attempted against the wearer, the caster of the divination must succeed at a caster level check (1d20 + caster level) against a DC of 19 (as if the caster had cast *nondetection* on herself).

Caster Level: 8th; *Prerequisites:* Craft Wondrous Item, *nondetection; Market Price:* 35,000 gp; *Weight:* —.

Amulet of Undead Turning: This holy item allows a cleric or paladin to turn undead as if she were four levels higher than her actual class level.

Caster Level: 10th; *Prerequisites:* Craft Wondrous Item, 10th-level cleric; *Market Price:* 11,000 gp; *Weight:* —.

Apparatus of Kwalish: This item appears to be a large, sealed iron barrel, but it has a secret catch (Search DC 20 to locate) that opens a hatch in one end. Anyone who crawls inside finds ten (unlabeled) levers:

Lever (1d10)	Lever Function
1	Extend/retract legs and tail
2	Uncover/cover forward porthole
3	Uncover/cover side portholes
4	Extend/retract pincers and feelers
5	Snap pincers
6	Move forward/backward
7	Turn left/right
8	Open "eyes" with *continual flame* inside/close "eyes"
9	Rise/sink in water
10	Open/close hatch

The device has the following characteristics:

Speed:	Forward 10 ft., backward 20 ft.
AC:	20 (–1 size, 11 natural)
Hit Points:	200
Attacks:	2 pincers, +12 melee
Damage:	2d8 each
Special Qualities:	Hardness 15

Operating a lever is a full-round action, and no lever may be operated more than once per round. However, since two Medium-size characters can fit inside, the apparatus can move and attack in the same round. The device can function in water up to 900 feet deep. It holds enough air for a crew of two to survive 1d4+1 hours (twice as long for a single occupant). When activated, the apparatus looks something like a giant lobster.

Caster Level: 19th; *Prerequisites:* Craft Wondrous Item, *animate objects,* 8 ranks of Knowledge (architecture and engineering); *Market Price:* 130,000 gp; *Weight:* 500 lb.

Apparatus of Kwalish

Bag of Holding: This appears to be a common cloth sack about 2 feet by 4 feet in size. The *bag of holding* opens into a nondimensional space: Its inside is larger than its outside dimensions. Regardless of what is put into the bag, it weighs a fixed amount. This weight, and the limits in weight and volume of the bag's contents, depend on the bag's type, as shown on the table below:

Bag Type	Bag Weight	Contents Weight Limit	Contents Volume Limit	Market Price
Bag 1	15 lb.	250 lb.	30 cu. ft.	2,500 gp
Bag 2	25 lb.	500 lb.	70 cu. ft.	5,000 gp
Bag 3	35 lb.	1,000 lb.	150 cu. ft.	7,400 gp
Bag 4	60 lb.	1,500 lb.	250 cu. ft.	10,000 gp

(Text continues on page 210)

TABLE 8–28: MINOR WONDROUS ITEMS

d%	Item	Market Price
01	Ioun stone (dull gray)	25 gp
02	Quaal's feather token (anchor)	50 gp
03	Everburning torch	90 gp
04	Quaal's feather token (tree)	100 gp
05	Quaal's feather token (fan)	200 gp
06	Dust of tracelessness	250 gp
07	Quaal's feather token (bird)	300 gp
08	Quaal's feather token (swan boat)	450 gp
09	Dust of illusion	500 gp
10	Necklace of prayer beads (blessing)	500 gp
11	Quaal's feather token (whip)	500 gp
12	Scarab, golembane (flesh)	800 gp
13	Bag of tricks (gray)	900 gp
14	Dust of dryness	900 gp
15	Bracers of armor (+1)	1,000 gp
16	Cloak of resistance (+1)	1,000 gp
17	Eyes of the eagle	1,000 gp
18	Goggles of minute seeing	1,000 gp
19	Hand of the mage	1,000 gp
20	Pearl of power (1st-level spell)	1,000 gp
21	Phylactery of faithfulness	1,000 gp
22	Scarab, golembane (clay)	1,000 gp
23	Stone of alarm	1,000 gp
24	Pipes of the sewers	1,150 gp
25	Scarab, golembane (stone)	1,200 gp
26	Brooch of shielding	1,500 gp
27	Scarab, golembane (iron)	1,600 gp
28	Necklace of fireballs (Type I)	1,650 gp
29	Pipes of sounding	1,800 gp
30	Quiver of Ehlonna	1,800 gp
31	Scarab, golembane (flesh and clay)	1,800 gp
32	Horseshoes of speed	1,900 gp
33	Amulet of natural armor (+1)	2,000 gp
34	Bead of force	2,000 gp
35	Boots of elvenkind	2,000 gp
36	Cloak of elvenkind	2,000 gp
37	Hat of disguise	2,000 gp
38	Heward's handy haversack	2,000 gp
39	Horn of fog	2,000 gp
40	Slippers of spider climbing	2,000 gp
41	Universal solvent	2,000 gp
42	Vest of escape	2,000 gp
43	Dust of appearance	2,100 gp
44	Glove of storing	2,200 gp
45	Sovereign glue	2,400 gp
46	Candle of truth	2,500 gp
47	Bag of holding (Bag 1)	2,500 gp
48	Boots of the winterlands	2,500 gp
49	Boots of striding and springing	2,500 gp
50	Scarab, golembane (any golem)	2,500 gp
51	Helm of comprehending languages and reading magic	2,600 gp
52	Necklace of fireballs (Type II)	2,700 gp
53	Bag of tricks (rust)	3,000 gp
54	Chime of opening	3,000 gp
55	Rope of climbing	3,000 gp
56	Horseshoes of a zephyr	3,000 gp
57	Dust of disappearance	3,500 gp
58	Lens of detection	3,500 gp
59	Figurine of wondrous power (silver raven)	3,800 gp
60	Bracers of armor (+2)	4,000 gp
61	Cloak of resistance (+2)	4,000 gp
62	Gloves of arrow snaring	4,000 gp
63	Ioun stone (dusty rose prism)	4,000 gp
64	Keoghtom's ointment	4,000 gp
65	Pearl of power (2nd-level spell)	4,000 gp
66	Periapt of proof against poison	4,000 gp
67	Stone salve	4,000 gp
68	Gauntlets of ogre power	4,000 gp
69	Bracers of health (+2)	4,000 gp
70	Gloves of Dexterity (+2)	4,000 gp
71	Headband of intellect (+2)	4,000 gp
72	Periapt of Wisdom (+2)	4,000 gp
73	Cloak of Charisma (+2)	4,000 gp
74	Necklace of fireballs (Type III)	4,350 gp
75	Circlet of persuasion	4,500 gp
76	Bracelet of friends	4,550 gp
77	Incense of meditation	4,900 gp
78	Bag of holding (Bag 2)	5,000 gp
79	Ioun stone (clear spindle)	5,000 gp
80	Necklace of prayer beads (karma)	5,000 gp
81	Bracers of archery	5,100 gp
82	Eversmoking bottle	5,200 gp
83	Necklace of fireballs (Type IV)	5,400 gp
84	Murlynd's spoon	5,500 gp
85	Nolzur's marvelous pigments	5,500 gp
86	Wind fan	5,500 gp
87	Wings of flying	5,500 gp
88	Vestment, druid's	5,800 gp
89	Cloak of arachnida	6,000 gp
90	Gloves of swimming and climbing	6,000 gp
91	Horn of goodness/evil	6,000 gp
92	Necklace of fireballs (Type V)	6,150 gp
93	Bag of tricks (tan)	6,300 gp
94	Circlet of blasting, minor	6,480 gp
95	Pipes of haunting	6,500 gp
96	Robe of useful items	7,000 gp
97	Hand of glory	7,200 gp
98	Bag of holding (Bag 3)	7,400 gp
99	DM's choice	—
100	DM's choice	—

TABLE 8–29: MEDIUM WONDROUS ITEMS

d%	Item	Market Price
01	Boots of levitation	7,500 gp
02	Harp of charming	7,500 gp
03	Periapt of health	7,500 gp
04	Candle of invocation	7,800 gp
05	Amulet of natural armor (+2)	8,000 gp
06	Boots of speed	8,000 gp
07	Ioun stone (dark blue rhomboid)	8,000 gp
08	Ioun stone (deep red sphere)	8,000 gp
09	Ioun stone (incandescent blue sphere)	8,000 gp
10	Ioun stone (pale blue rhomboid)	8,000 gp
11	Ioun stone (pink rhomboid)	8,000 gp
12	Ioun stone (pink and green sphere)	8,000 gp
13	Ioun stone (scarlet and blue sphere)	8,000 gp
14	Goggles of night	8,000 gp
15	Necklace of fireballs (Type VI)	8,100 gp
16	Belt, monk's	9,000 gp
17	Bracers of armor (+3)	9,000 gp
18	Cloak of resistance (+3)	9,000 gp
19	Decanter of endless water	9,000 gp
20	Pearl of power (3rd-level spell)	9,000 gp
21	Talisman of the sphere	9,000 gp
22	Figurine of wondrous power (serpentine owl)	9,100 gp
23	Necklace of fireballs (Type VII)	9,150 gp
24	Deck of illusions	9,200 gp
25	Boccob's blessed book	9,500 gp
26	Bag of holding (Bag 4)	10,000 gp
27	Figurine of wondrous power (bronze griffon)	10,000 gp
28	Figurine of wondrous power (ebony fly)	10,000 gp
29	Necklace of prayer beads (healing)	10,000 gp

d%	Item	Market Price
30	Robe of blending	10,000 gp
31	Stone of good luck (luckstone)	10,000 gp
32	Stone horse (courser)	10,000 gp
33	Boat, folding	10,500 gp
34	Amulet of undead turning	11,000 gp
35	Gauntlet of rust	11,500 gp
36	Boots, winged	12,000 gp
37	Horn of blasting	12,000 gp
38	Ioun stone (vibrant purple prism)	12,000 gp
39	Medallion of thoughts	12,000 gp
40	Pipes of pain	12,000 gp
41	Cape of the mountebank	12,960 gp
42	Lyre of building	13,000 gp
43	Portable hole	14,000 gp
44	Bottle of air	14,500 gp
45	Stone horse (destrier)	14,800 gp
46	Belt of dwarvenkind	14,900 gp
47	Ioun stone (iridescent spindle)	15,000 gp
48	Necklace of prayer beads (smiting)	15,000 gp
49	Periapt of wound closure	15,000 gp
50	Scabbard of keen edges	15,000 gp
51	Broom of flying	15,100 gp
52	Horn of the tritons	15,100 gp
53	Gem of brightness	15,200 gp
54	Pearl of the sirines	15,300 gp
55	Figurine of wondrous power (onyx dog)	15,500 gp
56	Chime of interruption	15,800 gp
57	Bracers of armor (+4)	16,000 gp
58	Cloak of resistance (+4)	16,000 gp
59	Pearl of power (4th-level spell)	16,000 gp
60	Belt of giant strength (+4)	16,000 gp
61	Gloves of Dexterity (+4)	16,000 gp
62	Bracers of health (+4)	16,000 gp
63	Headband of intellect (+4)	16,000 gp
64	Periapt of Wisdom (+4)	16,000 gp
65	Cloak of Charisma (+4)	16,000 gp
66	Figurine of wondrous power (golden lions)	16,500 gp
67	Figurine of wondrous power (marble elephant)	17,000 gp
68	Amulet of natural armor (+3)	18,000 gp
69	Carpet of flying (3 ft. by 5 ft.)	18,000 gp
70	Necklace of adaptation	19,000 gp
71	Cloak of the manta ray	20,000 gp
72	Ioun stone (pale green prism)	20,000 gp
73	Ioun stone (pale lavender ellipsoid)	20,000 gp
74	Ioun stone (pearly white spindle)	20,000 gp
75	Figurine of wondrous power (ivory goats)	21,000 gp
76	Rope of entanglement	21,000 gp
77	Cube of frost resistance	22,000 gp
78	Mattock of the titans	23,000 gp
79	Circlet of blasting, major	23,760 gp
80	Cloak of the bat	24,000 gp
81	Helm of underwater action	24,000 gp
82	Eyes of doom	24,500 gp
83	Cloak of displacement, minor (20% miss chance)	25,000 gp
84	Cloak of resistance (+5)	25,000 gp
85	Mask of the skull	25,000 gp
86	Maul of the titans	25,000 gp
87	Pearl of power (5th-level spell)	25,000 gp
88	Bracers of armor (+5)	25,000 gp
89	Dimensional shackles	26,000 gp
90	Iron bands of Bilarro	26,000 gp
91	Robe of scintillating colors	27,000 gp
92	Manual of bodily health +1	27,500 gp
93	Manual of gainful exercise +1	27,500 gp
94	Manual of quickness in action +1	27,500 gp
95	Tome of clear thought +1	27,500 gp
96	Tome of leadership and influence +1	27,500 gp
97	Tome of understanding +1	27,500 gp
98	Figurine of wondrous power (obsidian steed)	28,500 gp
99	Carpet of flying (4 ft. by 6 ft.)	29,000 gp
100	DM's choice	—

Table 8–30: Major Wondrous Items

d%	Item	Market Price
01–02	Lantern of revealing	30,000 gp
03–04	Necklace of prayer beads (wind walking)	30,000 gp
05–06	Drums of panic	30,000 gp
07–08	Helm of telepathy	31,000 gp
09–10	Amulet of natural armor (+4)	32,000 gp
11–12	Amulet of proof against detection and location	35,000 gp
13–14	Bracers of armor (+6)	36,000 gp
15	Belt of giant strength (+6)	36,000 gp
16	Gloves of Dexterity (+6)	36,000 gp
17	Bracers of health (+6)	36,000 gp
18	Headband of intellect (+6)	36,000 gp
19	Periapt of Wisdom (+6)	36,000 gp
20	Cloak of Charisma (+6)	36,000 gp
21–22	Pearl of power (6th-level spell)	36,000 gp
23–24	Orb of storms	38,000 gp
25–26	Scarab of protection	38,000 gp
27–28	Ioun stone (lavender and green ellipsoid)	40,000 gp
29–30	Ring gates	40,000 gp
31	Carpet of flying (5 ft. by 7 ft.)	41,000 gp
32	Crystal ball	42,000 gp
33	Helm of teleportation	48,600 gp
34	Bracers of armor (+7)	49,000 gp
35	Pearl of power (7th-level spell)	49,000 gp
36	Amulet of natural armor (+5)	50,000 gp
37	Cloak of displacement, major (50% miss chance)	50,000 gp
38	Crystal ball with detect invisibility	50,000 gp
39	Horn of Valhalla	50,000 gp
40	Necklace of prayer beads (summons)	50,000 gp
41	Crystal ball with detect thoughts	51,000 gp
42	Cloak of etherealness	52,000 gp
43	Carpet of flying (6 ft. by 9 ft.)	53,000 gp
44	Daern's instant fortress	55,000 gp
45	Manual of bodily health +2	55,000 gp
46	Manual of gainful exercise +2	55,000 gp
47	Manual of quickness in action +2	55,000 gp
48	Tome of clear thought +2	55,000 gp
49	Tome of leadership and influence +2	55,000 gp
50	Tome of understanding +2	55,000 gp
51	Eyes of charming	56,000 gp
52	Robe of stars	58,000 gp
53	Darkskull	60,000 gp
54	Cube of force	62,000 gp
55	Bracers of armor (+8)	64,000 gp
56	Pearl of power (8th-level spell)	64,000 gp
57	Crystal ball with telepathy	70,000 gp
58	Pearl of power (two spells)	70,000 gp
59	Gem of seeing	75,000 gp
60	Robe of the archmagi	75,000 gp
61	Vestments of faith	76,000 gp
62	Amulet of the planes	80,000 gp
63	Crystal ball with true seeing	80,000 gp
64	Pearl of power (9th-level spell)	81,000 gp
65	Well of many worlds	82,000 gp
66	Manual of bodily health +3	82,500 gp
67	Manual of gainful exercise +3	82,500 gp
68	Manual of quickness in action +3	82,500 gp
69	Tome of clear thought +3	82,500 gp
70	Tome of leadership and influence +3	82,500 gp
71	Tome of understanding +3	82,500 gp
72	Mantle of spell resistance	90,000 gp

73	Robe of eyes	90,000 gp
74	Mirror of opposition	92,000 gp
75	Chaos diamond	93,000 gp
76	Eyes of petrification	98,000 gp
77	Bowl of commanding water elementals	100,000 gp
78	Brazier of commanding fire elementals	100,000 gp
79	Censer of controlling air elementals	100,000 gp
80	Stone of controlling earth elementals	100,000 gp
81	Manual of bodily health +4	110,000 gp
82	Manual of gainful exercise +4	110,000 gp
83	Manual of quickness in action +4	110,000 gp
84	Tome of clear thought +4	110,000 gp
85	Tome of leadership and influence +4	110,000 gp
86	Tome of understanding +4	110,000 gp

87	Apparatus of Kwalish	130,000 gp
88	Manual of bodily health +5	137,500 gp
89	Manual of gainful exercise +5	137,500 gp
90	Manual of quickness in action +5	137,500 gp
91	Tome of clear thought +5	137,500 gp
92	Tome of leadership and influence +5	137,500 gp
93	Tome of understanding +5	137,500 gp
94	Efreeti bottle	150,000 gp
95	Mirror of life trapping	152,000 gp
96	Cubic gate	156,000 gp
97	Helm of brilliance	157,000 gp
98	Iron flask	170,000 gp
99	Mirror of mental prowess	175,000 gp
100	DM's choice	—

If the bag is overloaded, or if sharp objects pierce it (from inside or outside), the bag ruptures and is ruined. All contents are lost forever. If a *bag of holding* is turned inside out, its contents spill out, unharmed, but the bag must be put right before it can be used again. If living creatures are placed within the bag, they can survive for up to 10 minutes, after which time they suffocate. Retrieving a specific item from a *bag of holding* is a move-equivalent action—unless the bag contains more than an ordinary backpack would hold, in which case retrieving a specific item is a full-round action.

If a *bag of holding* is placed within a *portable hole*, a rift to the Astral Plane is torn in the space: Bag and hole alike are sucked into the void and forever lost. If a *portable hole* is placed within a *bag of holding*, it opens a gate to the Astral Plane: The hole, the bag, and any creatures within a 10-foot radius are drawn there, destroying the *portable hole* and *bag of holding* in the process.

Caster Level: 9th; *Prerequisites:* Craft Wondrous Item, *Leomund's secret chest.*

Bag of Tricks: This small sack appears normal and empty. However, anyone reaching into the bag feels a small, fuzzy ball. If the ball is removed and tossed up to 20 feet away, it turns into an animal. The animal serves the character who drew it from the bag for 10 minutes (or until slain or ordered back into the bag), at which point it disappears. There are three drab colors of bags, each producing a different set of animals. Use the following tables to determine what animals can be drawn out of each.

Belt of giant strength

Gray		Rust		Tan	
d%	Animal	d%	Animal	d%	Animal
01–30	Bat	01–30	Wolverine	01–30	Brown bear
31–60	Rat	31–60	Wolf	31–60	Lion
61–75	Cat	61–85	Boar	61–80	Warhorse
76–90	Weasel	86–100	Black bear	81–90	Tiger
91–100	Badger			91–100	Rhinoceros

Animals produced are always random, and only one may exist at a time. Up to ten animals can be drawn from the bag each week.

Caster Level: 3rd (gray), 5th (rust), or 9th (tan); *Prerequisites:* Craft Wondrous Item; *summon nature's ally II* (gray), *summon nature's ally III* (rust), or *summon nature's ally V* (tan); *Market Price:* 900 gp (gray); 3,000 gp (rust); 6,300 gp (tan); *Weight:* —.

Bead of Force: This small black sphere appears to be a lusterless pearl. Upon sharp impact, however, the bead explodes, sending forth a burst of force that deals 5d6 points of damage to all creatures within a 10-foot radius. Each victim is allowed a Reflex saving throw (DC 16). Those who fail are then encapsulated in a sphere of force with a radius of 10 feet. Those trapped inside cannot escape except by those methods that can bypass or destroy a *wall of force.* The

sphere persists for 3d6 minutes and then disappears. The explosion completely consumes the bead, making this a one-use item.

Caster Level: 11th; *Prerequisites:* Craft Wondrous Item, *wall of force; Market Price:* 2,000 gp; *Weight:* —.

Belt, Monk's: This simple rope belt, when wrapped around a character's waist, confers great ability in unarmed combat. Any time the wearer engages in unarmed combat, the belt grants him the ability to use both hands as though he possessed the Ambidexterity and Two-Weapon Fighting feats. He may also make a stunning attack (as a monk) once per day. If donned by a monk, the belt grants one additional stunning attack per day and allows the monk to *haste* herself once per day for up to 10 consecutive rounds.

Caster Level: 12th; *Prerequisites:* Craft Wondrous Item, *haste, righteous might* or *Tenser's transformation; Market Price:* 9,000 gp; *Weight:* 1 lb.

Belt of Dwarvenkind: This belt gives the wearer a +4 competence bonus on all Charisma checks (such as Charisma checks for NPC attitude) and Charisma-keyed skill checks such as Bluff, Diplomacy, Disguise, Gather Information, Intimidate and Perform as they relate to dealing with dwarves, a +2 competence bonus on similar checks when dealing with gnomes and halflings, and a –2 competence penalty on similar checks when dealing with anyone else. The wearer can understand, speak, and read Dwarven. If the wearer is not a dwarf, he gains darkvision (range 60 feet), dwarven stonecunning, a +2 enhancement bonus to Constitution, and +2 resistance bonuses against poison, spells, and spell-like effects.

Caster Level: 12th; *Prerequisites:* Craft Wondrous Item, *tongues,* and either *polymorph self* or the creator must be a dwarf; *Market Price:* 14,900 gp; *Weight:* 1 lb.

Belt of Giant Strength: This wide belt is made of thick leather and studded with iron. The belt adds to the wearer's Strength score in the form of an enhancement bonus of +4 or +6.

Caster Level: 10th; *Prerequisites:* Craft Wondrous Item, *bull's strength; Market Price:* 16,000 gp (+4) or 36,000 gp (+6); *Weight:* 1 lb.

Boat, Folding: A folding boat looks like a small wooden box—about 12 inches long, 6 inches wide, and 6 inches deep. It can be used to store items like any other box. If a command word is given, however, the box unfolds itself to form a boat 10 feet long, 4 feet wide, and 2 feet in depth. A second (different) command word causes it to unfold to a ship 24 feet long, 8 feet wide, and 6 feet deep. Any objects formerly stored in the box now rest in the bottom of the boat or ship.

In its smaller form, the boat has one pair of oars, an anchor, a mast, and a lateen sail. In its larger form, the boat has a deck, single rowing seats, five sets of oars, a steering oar, an anchor, a deck cabin, and a mast with a square sail. The boat can hold three or four people comfortably, while the ship carries fifteen with ease.

A third word of command causes the boat or ship to fold itself into a box once again. The words of command may be inscribed visibly or invisibly on the box, or they may be written elsewhere—perhaps on an item within the box.

Caster Level: 6th; *Prerequisites:* Craft Wondrous Item, *fabricate,* 2 ranks of Craft (shipmaking); *Market Price:* 10,500 gp; *Weight:* 4 lb.

Boccob's Blessed Book: This well-made tome is always of small size, typically no more than 12 inches tall, 8 inches wide, and 1 inch thick. All such books are durable, waterproof, bound with iron overlaid with silver, and locked.

The pages of a *Boccob's blessed book* freely accept spells scribed upon them, and any such book can contain up to forty-five spells of any level. The book is thus highly prized by wizards as a spellbook. This book is never found as randomly generated treasure with spells already inscribed in it.

Winged boots

Caster Level: 7th; *Prerequisites:* Craft Wondrous Item, *secret page; Market Price:* 9,500 gp; *Weight:* 1 lb.

Boots of Elvenkind: These soft boots enable the wearer to move quietly in virtually any surroundings, granting a +10 circumstance bonus to Move Silently checks.

Caster Level: 5th; *Prerequisites:* Craft Wondrous Item, creator must be an elf; *Market Price:* 2,000 gp; *Weight:* 1 lb.

Boots of Levitation: These leather boots allow the wearer to levitate as if she had cast *levitate* on herself.

Caster Level: 3rd; *Prerequisites:* Craft Wondrous Item, *levitate; Market Price:* 7,500 gp; *Weight:* 1 lb.

Boots of Speed: On command, these boots enable the wearer to act as though *hasted* for up to 10 rounds each day. The duration of the *haste* need not be consecutive rounds.

Caster Level: 10th; *Prerequisites:* Craft Wondrous Item, *haste; Market Price:* 8,000 gp; *Weight:* 1 lb.

Boots of Striding and Springing: The wearer of these boots moves at double her normal speed. In addition to this striding ability, these boots allow the wearer to make great leaps. She can jump with a +10 competence bonus to Jump checks, and the wearer's jumping distance is not limited by her height.

Caster Level: 3rd; *Prerequisites:* Craft Wondrous Item, *expeditious retreat, jump; Market Price:* 2,500 gp; *Weight:* 1 lb.

Boots, Winged: These boots appear to be ordinary footgear. On command, the boots sprout wings at the heel and let the wearer fly, without having to maintain concentration, as if affected by a *fly* spell. He can fly for a total of up to 2 hours each day.

Caster Level: 9th; *Prerequisites:* Craft Wondrous Item, *fly; Market Price:* 12,000 gp; *Weight:* 1 lb.

Boots of the Winterlands: This footgear bestows many powers upon the wearer. First, he is able to travel across snow at his normal speed, leaving no tracks. The boots also enable him to travel at half normal speed across the most slippery ice (horizontal surfaces only, not vertical or sharply slanted ones) without falling or slipping. Finally, *boots of the winterlands* warm the wearer, as if he were affected by an *endure elements* (cold) spell.

Caster Level: 5th; *Prerequisites:* Craft Wondrous Item, *endure elements, pass without trace, cat's grace; Market Price:* 2,500 gp; *Weight:* 1 lb.

Bottle of Air: This item appears to be a normal glass bottle with a cork. When taken to any airless environment (such as underwater or in a vacuum), it retains air within it at all times, continually renewing its contents. This means that a character can draw air out of the bottle in order to breathe. The bottle can even be shared by multiple characters who pass it around. Breathing out of the bottle requires a standard action, but a character so doing can then act for as long as she can hold her breath.

Caster Level: 7th; *Prerequisites:* Craft Wondrous Item, *control wind; Market Price:* 14,500 gp; *Weight:* 2 lb.

Bowl of Commanding Water Elementals: This large container is usually fashioned from blue or green semiprecious stone (malachite, lapis lazuli, azurite, turquoise, or peridot, or sometimes jade). It is about 1 foot in diameter, half that deep, and relatively fragile. When the bowl is filled with fresh water, and certain words are spoken, a Large water elemental appears. The summoning words require 1 full round to speak. In all ways the bowl functions as the *summon monster VI* spell. Only one elemental can be called at a time. A new elemental requires the bowl to be filled with new water, which cannot happen until after the first elemental disappears (is dispelled, dismissed, or slain).

If salt water is used, the elemental is Huge rather than Large (as if *summon monster VII* had been cast). See the *Monster Manual* for details on water elementals.

Caster Level: 13th; *Prerequisites:* Craft Wondrous Item, *summon monster VI, summon monster VII; Market Price:* 100,000 gp; *Weight:* 3 lb.

Bracelet of Friends: This silver charm bracelet has seven charms upon it. The owner may designate one person known to him to be keyed to one charm. (This designation takes a standard action, but once done it lasts forever or until changed.) When a charm is grasped and the name of the keyed individual is spoken, that person is called to the spot (another standard action) along with his or her gear. Unwilling characters are allowed a Will saving throw (DC 19). Once a charm is activated, it disappears, so such bracelets discovered as treasure may have fewer than a full complement of charms when found.

Caster Level: 15th; *Prerequisites:* Craft Wondrous Item, *refuge; Market Price:* 4,550 gp; *Weight:* —.

Bracers of Archery: These wristbands look like normal protective wear. The bracers empower the wearer to use any bow (not including crossbows) as if she were proficient in its use. If she already has proficiency with any type of bow, she gains a +2 competence bonus to attack rolls and a +1 competence bonus to damage dealt whenever using that type of bow. The bonus to damage only applies if the target is within 30 feet. Both bracers must be worn for the magic to be effective.

Caster Level: 4th; *Prerequisites:* Craft Wondrous Item, Craft Magic Arms and Armor; *Market Price:* 5,100 gp; *Weight:* 1 lb.

Bracers of Armor: These items appear to be wrist or arm guards. They surround the wearer with an invisible but tangible field of force, granting him an armor bonus of +1 to +8, just as though he were wearing armor. Both bracers must be worn for the magic to be effective.

Caster Level: 7th; *Prerequisites:* Craft Wondrous Item, *mage armor,* creator's class level must be twice that of the bonus placed in the bracers; *Bracers of armor*

Market Price: 1,000 gp (+1), 4,000 gp (+2), 9,000 gp (+3), 16,000 gp (+4), 25,000 gp (+5), 36,000 gp (+6), 39,000 gp (+7), or 64,000 gp (+8); *Weight:* 1 lb.

Brazier of Commanding Fire Elementals: This device appears to be a normal container for holding burning coals. When a fire is lit in the brazier and the proper summoning words are spoken, a Large fire elemental appears. The summoning words require 1 full round to speak. In all ways the brazier functions as the *summon monster VI* spell. If brimstone is added, the elemental is Huge instead of Large, and the brazier works as a *summon monster VII* spell. Only one elemental can be summoned at a time. A new elemental requires a new fire, which cannot be lit until after the first elemental disappears (is dispelled, dismissed, or slain). See the *Monster Manual* for details on fire elementals.

Caster Level: 13th; *Prerequisites:* Craft Wondrous Item, *summon monster VI, summon monster VII; Market Price:* 100,000 gp; *Weight:* 5 lb.

Brooch of Shielding: This appears to be a piece of silver or gold jewelry used to fasten a cloak or cape. In addition to this mundane task, it can absorb magic missiles of the sort generated by spell or spell-like ability. A brooch can absorb up to 101 points of *magic missile* damage before it melts and becomes useless.

Caster Level: 1st; *Prerequisites:* Craft Wondrous Item, *shield; Market Price:* 1,500 gp; *Weight:* —.

Broom of Flying: This broom is able to fly through the air as if affected by a *fly* spell with unlimited duration. The broom can carry 200 pounds. In addition, the broom can travel alone to any destination named by the owner as long as she has a good idea of the location and layout of that destination. It comes to its owner from as far away as 300 yards when she speaks the command word.

Caster Level: 5th; *Prerequisites:* Craft Wondrous Item, *fly, permanency; Market Price:* 15,100 gp; *Weight:* 3 lb.

Candle of Invocation: Each of these specially blessed tapers is dedicated to one of the nine alignments. Simply burning the candle generates a favorable aura for the individual so doing if the candle's alignment matches that of the character. Characters of the same alignment as the burning candle add a +2 morale bonus to attack rolls, saving throws, and skill checks while within 30 feet of the flame.

A cleric whose alignment matches the candle's operates as if 2 levels higher for purposes of determining spells per day if he burns the candle during or just prior to his spell preparation time. He can even cast spells normally unavailable to him, as if he were of that higher level, but only so long as the candle continues to burn. Except in special cases (see below), the candle burns for 4 hours.

In addition, burning the candle also allows the owner to cast a *gate* spell, the respondent being of the same alignment as the candle, but the taper is immediately consumed in the process. It is possible to extinguish the candle simply by blowing it out, so users often place it in a lantern to protect it from drafts and the like. Doing this doesn't interfere with its magical properties.

Caster Level: 17th; *Prerequisites:* Craft Wondrous Item, *gate*, creator must be same alignment as candle created; *Market Price:* 7,800 gp; *Weight:* 1/2 lb.

Candle of Truth: This white tallow candle, when burned, calls into place a *zone of truth* spell in a 30-foot radius centered on the candle. The zone lasts for 1 hour, as the candle burns. If the candle is snuffed before that time, the effect is canceled and the candle ruined.

Caster Level: 5th; *Prerequisites:* Craft Wondrous Item, *zone of truth; Market Price:* 2,500 gp; *Weight:* 1/2 lb.

Cape of the Mountebank: On command, this bright red and gold cape allows the wearer to use the magic of the *dimension door* spell once per day. When he disappears, he leaves behind a cloud of smoke, appearing in a similar fashion at his destination.

Caster Level: 9th; *Prerequisites:* Craft Wondrous Item, *dimension door; Market Price:* 12,960 gp; *Weight:* 1 lb.

Carpet of Flying: This rug is able to fly through the air as if affected by a *fly* spell of unlimited duration. The size, carrying capacity, and speed of the different *carpets of flying* are shown on the table below. Beautifully and intricately made, each carpet has its own command word to activate it—if the device is within voice range, the command word activates it, whether the speaker is on the rug or not. The carpet is then controlled by spoken directions.

Size	Capacity	Speed	Weight	Market Price
3 ft. by 5 ft.	300 lb.	210 ft.	5 lb.	18,000 gp
4 ft. by 6 ft.	600 lb.	180 ft.	8 lb.	29,000 gp
5 ft. by 7 ft.	900 lb.	150 ft.	10 lb.	41,000 gp
6 ft. by 9 ft.	1200 lb.	120 ft.	15 lb.	53,000 gp

Caster Level: 7th; *Prerequisites:* Craft Wondrous Item, *fly, permanency.*

Censer of Controlling Air Elementals: This 6-inch-wide, 1-inch-high perforated golden vessel resembles thuribles found in places of worship. If it is filled with incense and lit, summoning words spoken over it summon forth a Large air elemental. The summoning words require 1 full round to speak. In all ways the censer functions as the *summon monster VI* spell. If *incense of meditation* is burned within the censer, the air elemental is an elder air elemental instead (as if *summon monster IX* had just been cast). Only one elemental can be summoned at a time. A new elemental requires a new piece of incense, which cannot be lit until after the first elemental disappears (is dispelled, dismissed, or slain). See the *Monster Manual* for details on air elementals.

Censer of controlling air elementals

Caster Level: 17th; *Prerequisites:* Craft Wondrous Item, *summon monster VI, summon monster IX; Market Price:* 100,000 gp; *Weight:* 1 lb.

Chaos Diamond: This lustrous gemstone is uncut and about the size of a human fist. The gem grants its possessor the following powers:

- *Random action*
- *Magic circle against law*
- *Word of chaos*
- *Cloak of chaos*

Each power is usable 1d4 times per day. (The DM rolls secretly each day for each power separately.)

A nonchaotic character who possesses a *chaos diamond* gains one negative level. Although this level never results in actual level loss, it remains as long as the diamond is in the character's possession and cannot be overcome in any way (including *restoration* spells).

Caster Level: 19th; *Prerequisites:* Craft Wondrous Item, *random action, magic circle against law, word of chaos, cloak of chaos*, creator must be chaotic; *Market Price:* 93,000 gp; *Weight:* 1 lb.

Chime of Interruption: This instrument can be struck once every 10 minutes, and its resonant tone lasts for 3 full minutes. While the chime is resonating, no spell requiring a verbal component can be cast within a 30-foot radius of it unless the caster can make a Concentration check (DC = 15 + the spell's level).

Caster Level: 7th; *Prerequisites:* Craft Wondrous Item, *shout; Market Price:* 15,800 gp; *Weight:* 1 lb.

Chime of Opening: A *chime of opening* is a hollow mithral tube about 1 foot long. When struck, it sends forth magic vibrations that cause locks, lids, doors, valves, and portals to open. The device functions against normal bars, shackles, chains, bolts, and so on. The *chime of opening* also automatically dispels a *hold portal* spell or even an *arcane lock* cast by a wizard of less than 15th level.

The chime must be pointed at the item or gate to be loosed or opened (which must be visible and known to the user). The chime is then struck, a clear tone rings forth, and in 1 round the target lock is unlocked, the shackle is loosed, the secret door is opened, or the lid of the chest is lifted. Each sounding only opens one form of locking, so if a chest is chained, padlocked, locked, and *arcane locked*, it takes four uses of the chime of opening to get it open. A *silence* spell negates the power of the device. A brand-new chime can be used a total of 50 times before it cracks and becomes useless.

Caster Level: 11th; *Prerequisites:* Craft Wondrous Item, *knock*; *Market Price:* 3,000 gp; *Weight:* 1 lb.

Circlet of Blasting, Minor: On command, this simple golden headband projects a blast of *searing light* (3d8 points of damage) once per day.

Caster Level: 6th; *Prerequisites:* Craft Wondrous Item, *searing light*; *Market Price:* 6,480 gp; *Weight:* —.

Circlet of Blasting, Major: On command, this elaborate golden headband projects a blast of *searing light* (5d8 maximized for 40 points of damage) once per day.

Caster Level: 17th; *Prerequisites:* Craft Wondrous Item, Maximize Spell, *searing light*; *Market Price:* 23,760 gp; *Weight:* —.

Circlet of Persuasion: This silver headband grants a +2 competence bonus to the wearer's Charisma checks and Charisma-based skill checks.

Caster Level: 5th; *Prerequisites:* Craft Wondrous Item, *charm person*; *Market Price:* 4,500 gp; *Weight:* —.

Cloak of Arachnida: This black garment, embroidered with a weblike pattern in silk, gives the wearer the ability to climb as if a *spider climb* spell had been placed upon her. In addition, the cloak grants her immunity to entrapment by *web* spells or webs of any sort—she can actually move in webs at half her normal speed.

Cloak of arachnida

Once per day, the wearer of this cloak can cast *web*. She also gains a +2 luck bonus to all Fortitude saves against poison from spiders.

Caster Level: 6th; *Prerequisites:* Craft Wondrous Item, *spider climb*, *web*; *Market Price:* 6,000 gp; *Weight:* 1 lb.

Cloak of the Bat: Fashioned of dark brown or black cloth, this cloak bestows a +10 circumstance bonus to Hide checks. The wearer is also able to hang upside down from the ceiling, like a bat.

By holding the edges of the garment, the wearer is able to *fly* as per the spell. If he desires, the wearer can actually polymorph himself into an ordinary bat and fly accordingly. (All possessions worn or carried are part of the transformation.) Flying, either with the cloak or in bat form, can be accomplished only in darkness (either under the night sky or in a lightless or near-lightless environment underground). Either of the flying powers is usable for up to 1 hour at a time, but after a flight of any duration the cloak cannot bestow any flying power for a like period of time.

Finally, the cloak also provides a +2 deflection bonus to Armor Class. This benefit extends to the wearer even when he is in bat form.

Caster Level: 9th; *Prerequisites:* Craft Wondrous Item, *fly, polymorph self*; *Market Price:* 24,000 gp; *Weight:* 1 lb.

Cloak of Charisma: This lightweight and fashionable cloak has a highly decorative silver trim. When in a character's possession, it adds a +2, +4, or +6 enhancement bonus to her Charisma score.

Caster Level: 8th; *Prerequisites:* Craft Wondrous Item, *charm monster*; *Market Price:* 4, 000 gp (+2), 16,000 gp (+4), or 36,000 gp (+6); *Weight:* 2 lb.

Cloak of Displacement, Minor: This item appears to be a normal cloak, but when worn by a character its magic properties distort and warp light waves. This displacement works similar to the *displacement* spell except that it only grants a 20% miss chance (the same as one-half concealment). It functions continually.

Caster Level: 3rd; *Prerequisites:* Craft Wondrous Item, *displacement*; *Market Price:* 25,000 gp; *Weight:* 1 lb.

Cloak of Displacement, Major: This item appears to be a normal cloak, but when worn by a character its magic properties distort and warp light waves. This displacement works just like the *displacement* spell and functions continually.

Caster Level: 5th; *Prerequisites:* Craft Wondrous Item, *displacement*; *Market Price:* 50,000 gp; *Weight:* 1 lb.

Cloak of Elvenkind: This cloak of neutral gray cloth is indistinguishable from an ordinary cloak of the same color. However, when worn with the hood drawn up around the head, it gives the wearer a +10 circumstance bonus on Hide checks.

Caster Level: 3rd; *Prerequisites:* Craft Wondrous Item, *invisibility*, creator must be an elf; *Market Price:* 2,000 gp; *Weight:* 1 lb.

Cloak of Etherealness: This silvery-gray cloak seems to absorb light rather than be illuminated by it. On command, the cloak makes its wearer ethereal (as the spell *ethereal jaunt*). The effect is dismissible. The cloak works for a total of up to 10 minutes per day. This duration need not be continuous.

Caster Level: 15th; *Prerequisites:* Craft Wondrous Item, *ethereal jaunt*; *Market Price:* 52,000 gp; *Weight:* 1 lb.

Cloak of the Manta Ray: This cloak appears to be made of leather until the wearer enters salt water. At that time the *cloak of the manta ray* adheres to the individual, and he appears nearly identical to a manta ray. (A Spot check against DC 20 is needed to determine otherwise.) He gains a +3 natural armor bonus, the ability to breathe underwater, and a speed of 60 feet, exactly like a real manta ray.

Although the cloak does not enable the wearer to bite opponents as a manta ray does, it does have a tail spine that can be used to strike at opponents behind him, dealing 1d6 points of damage. This attack can be used in addition to any other attack the character has, using his highest melee attack bonus. The wearer can release his arms from the cloak without sacrificing underwater movement if so desired.

Caster Level: 9th; *Prerequisites:* Craft Wondrous Item, *water breathing, freedom of movement*; *Market Price:* 20,000 gp; *Weight:* 1 lb.

Cloak of Resistance: These garments offer magic protection in the form of a +1 to +5 resistance bonus for all saving throws (Fortitude, Reflex, Will).

Caster Level: 5th; *Prerequisites:* Craft Wondrous Item, *resistance*, caster level must be three times that of the cloak's bonus; *Market Price:* 1, 000 gp (+1), 4,000 gp (+2), 9,000 gp (+3), 16,000 gp (+4), or 25,000 gp (+5); *Weight:* 1 lb.

Crystal Ball: This is the most common form of scrying device, a crystal sphere about 6 inches in diameter. A character can use the device to see over virtually any distance or into other planes of existence, as with the spell *scrying*.

Certain *crystal balls* have additional powers that can be used through the *crystal ball* at targets viewed.

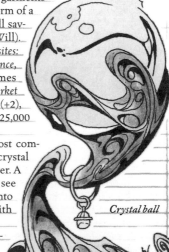

Crystal ball

Crystal Ball Type	Market Price
Crystal ball	42,000 gp
Crystal ball with *see invisibility*	50,000 gp
Crystal ball with *detect thoughts*	51,000 gp
Crystal ball with *telepathy**	70,000 gp
Crystal ball with *true seeing*	80,000 gp

*The viewer is able to send and receive silent mental messages with the person appearing in the crystal ball. Once per day the character may attempt to implant a *suggestion* (as the spell, DC 14) as well.

Caster Level: 10th; *Prerequisites:* Craft Wondrous Item, *scrying* (plus any additional spells put into item); *Weight:* 7 lb.

Cube of Force: This device can be made of ivory, bone, or any hard mineral. About the size of a large die (perhaps 3/4 inch across), it enables its possessor to put up a special *wall of force* 10 feet per side around her person. This cubic screen moves with the character and is impervious to the attack forms shown on the table below. The cube has 36 charges, which are renewed each day. The character presses one face of the cube to activate or deactivate the field:

Cube Face	Charge Cost per Minute	Maximum Speed	Effect
1	1	30 ft.	Keeps out gases, wind, etc.
2	2	20 ft.	Keeps out nonliving matter
3	3	15 ft.	Keeps out living matter
4	4	10 ft.	Keeps out magic
5	6	10 ft.	Keeps out all things
6	0	As normal	Deactivates

When the force screen is up, attacks dealing more than 30 points of damage drain 1 charge for every 10 points of damage beyond 30 that they deal (40 points of damage drains 1 charge, 50 points drains 2 charges, and so forth). Spells that affect the integrity of the screen, such as *disintegrate* or *passwall*, also drain extra charges. These spells (in the following list) cannot be cast into or out of the cube:

Attack Form	Extra Charges
Horn of blasting	6
Wall of fire	2
Passwall	3
Disintegrate	6
Phase door	5
Prismatic spray	7

Caster Level: 10th; *Prerequisites:* Craft Wondrous Item, *wall of force*; *Market Price:* 62,000 gp; *Weight:* —.

Cube of Frost Resistance: When this cube is activated, it encloses a cube-shaped area 10 feet per side. The temperature within this area is always at least 65°F. The field absorbs all cold-based attacks (such as *ice storm, cone of cold*, and white dragon breath). However, if the field is subjected to more than 50 points of cold damage in 1 round (from one or multiple attacks), it collapses and cannot be renewed for 1 hour. If the field receives over 100 points of damage in a 10-round period, the cube is destroyed.

Cold below 0°F deals the field 2 points of cold damage per round, +2 points per each 10° below 0 (2 points at −1° to −9°, 4 points at −10° to −19°, and so on).

Caster Level: 7th; *Prerequisites:* Craft Wondrous Item, *protection from elements*; *Market Price:* 22,000 gp; *Weight:* —.

Cubic Gate: This item is fashioned from carnelian. Each of the six sides of the cube is keyed to a plane, one of which is the Material Plane. The character creating the item should choose the planes to which the other five sides are keyed. If such a cube is found as treasure, the DM can determine the planes accessed by the device in any manner he or she chooses.

If a side of the *cubic gate* is pressed once, it opens a *gate* to the plane keyed to that side. There is a 10% chance per minute that an outsider from that plane (determine randomly) comes through it looking for food, fun, or trouble. Pressing the side a second time closes the *gate*. It is impossible to open more than one *gate* at a time.

If a side is pressed twice in quick succession, the character so doing is transported to the other plane, along with all creatures in a 5-foot radius. (Those others may avoid this fate by succeeding at Will saves against DC 23).

Caster Level: 18th; *Prerequisites:* Craft Wondrous Item, *gate*; *Market Price:* 156,000 gp; *Weight:* —.

Daern's Instant Fortress: This metal cube is small, but when activated it grows to form a tower 20 feet square and 30 feet high, with arrow slits on all sides and a crenellated battlement atop it. The metal walls extend 10 feet into the ground, rooting it to the spot and preventing it from being tipped over. The fortress has a small door that opens only at the command of the owner of the fortress—even *knock* spells can't open the door.

The adamantine walls of *Daern's instant fortress* have 100 hit points and a hardness of 20. The fortress cannot be repaired except by a *wish* or a *miracle*, which restores 50 points of damage sustained.

The fortress springs up in just 1 round, with the door facing the device's owner. The door opens and closes instantly at his command. People and creatures nearby (except the owner) must be careful not to be caught by the fortress's sudden growth. Anyone so caught sustains 10d10 points of damage (Reflex half DC 19).

Daern's instant fortress

Caster Level: 12th; *Prerequisites:* Craft Wondrous Item, *Mordenkainen's magnificent mansion*; *Market Price:* 55,000 gp; *Weight:* —.

Darkskull: This skull, carved from ebony, is wholly evil. Wherever the skull goes, the area around it is treated as though an *unhallow* spell had been cast with the skull as the touched point of origin (except that there is no additional spell effect tied or fixed to the *darkskull*).

Caster Level: 9th; *Prerequisites:* Craft Wondrous Item, *unhallow*, creator must be evil; *Market Price:* 60,000 gp; *Weight:* 5 lb.

Decanter of Endless Water: If the stopper is removed from this ordinary-looking flask and a command word spoken, a stream of fresh or salt water pours out. Separate command words determine the type as well as the volume and velocity:

- *Stream:* pours out 1 gallon per round
- *Fountain:* 5-foot-long stream at 5 gallons per round
- *Geyser:* 20-foot-long, 1-foot-wide stream at 30 gallons per round

The geyser causes considerable back pressure, requiring the holder to make a Strength check (DC 12) to avoid being knocked down. The force of the geyser deals 1d4 points of damage but can only affect one target per round. The command word must be spoken to stop it.

Caster Level: 9th; *Prerequisites:* Craft Wondrous Item, *control water*; *Market Price:* 9,000 gp; *Weight:* 2 lb.

Deck of Illusions: This set of parchment cards is usually found in an ivory, leather, or wooden box. A full deck consists of thirty-four cards. When a card is drawn at random and thrown to the ground, a *major image* of a creature is formed. The figment lasts until dispelled. The illusory creature cannot move more than 30 feet away from where the card landed, but otherwise moves and acts as if it were real. At all times it obeys the desires of the character who drew the card. When the illusion is dispelled, the card becomes blank and cannot be used again. If the card is picked up, the illusion is automatically and instantly dispelled. The cards in a deck and the illusions they bring forth are summarized on the following table. (Use one of the first two columns to simulate the contents of a full deck using either ordinary playing cards or tarot cards.)

DECK OF ILLUSIONS

Playing Card	Tarot Card	Creature
Ace of hearts	IV. The Emperor	Red dragon
King of hearts	Knight of swords	Human fighter (male) and four guards
Queen of hearts	Queen of staves	Human wizard (female)
Jack of hearts	King of staves	Human druid (male)
Ten of hearts	VII. The Chariot	Cloud giant
Nine of hearts	Page of staves	Ettin
Eight of hearts	Ace of cups	Bugbear
Two of hearts	Five of staves	Goblin

Playing Card	Tarot Card	Creature
Ace of diamonds	III. The Empress	Beholder
King of diamonds	Two of cups	Elven wizard (male) and apprentice (female)
Queen of diamonds	Queen of swords	Half-elven ranger (female)
Jack of diamonds	XIV. Temperance	Harpy
Ten of diamonds	Seven of staves	Half-orc barbarian (male)
Nine of diamonds	Four of pentacles	Ogre mage
Eight of diamonds	Ace of pentacles	Gnoll
Two of diamonds	Six of pentacles	Kobold

Playing Card	Tarot Card	Creature
Ace of spades	II. The High Priestess	Lich
King of spades	Three of staves	Three human clerics (male)
Queen of spades	Four of cups	Medusa
Jack of spades	Knight of pentacles	Dwarven paladin (male)
Ten of spades	Seven of swords	Frost giant
Nine of spades	Three of swords	Troll
Eight of spades	Ace of swords	Hobgoblin
Two of spades	Five of cups	Goblin

Playing Card	Tarot Card	Creature
Ace of clubs	VIII. Strength	Iron golem
King of clubs	Page of pentacles	Three halfling rogues (male)
Queen of clubs	Ten of cups	Pixies
Jack of clubs	Nine of pentacles	Half-elven bard (female)
Ten of clubs	Nine of staves	Hill giant
Nine of clubs	King of swords	Ogre
Eight of clubs	Ace of staves	Orc
Two of clubs	Five of cups	Kobold

Playing Card	Tarot Card	Creature
Joker	Two of pentacles	Illusion of deck's owner
Joker	Two of staves	Illusion of deck's owner (sex reversed)

A randomly generated deck may be discovered (a 01–10 result on d%) with 1d20 of its cards missing. (On a result of 11–100, it is complete.)

Caster Level: 6th; *Prerequisites:* Craft Wondrous Item, *major image*; *Market Price:* 9,200 gp; *Weight:* 1/2 lb.

Dimensional Shackles: These shackles have golden runes traced across their cold iron surface. Any creature bound within them is affected as if a *dimensional anchor* spell were cast upon her (no save). They fit any Small to Large creature. The DC to break or slip out of the shackles is 30.

Caster Level: 11th; *Prerequisites:* Craft Wondrous Item, *dimensional anchor*; *Market Price:* 26,000 gp; *Weight:* 5 lb.

Drums of Panic: These drums are kettle drums (hemispheres about 1 1/2 feet in diameter on stands). They come in pairs and are unremarkable in appearance. If both of the pair are sounded, all creatures within 120 feet (with the exception of those within a 20-foot-radius safe zone around the drums) are affected as by a *fear* spell (Will negates DC 16).

Caster Level: 7th; *Prerequisites:* Craft Wondrous Item, *fear*; *Market Price:* 30,000 gp; *Weight:* 10 lb.

Dust of Appearance: This fine powder appears to be a very fine, very light metallic dust. A single handful of this substance flung into the air coats surrounding objects, making them visible even if they are invisible—just like the *glitterdust* spell. (The *dust of appearance*, however, doesn't blind creatures.) The dust also reveals figments, *mirror images*, and *projected images* for what they are. It likewise negates the effects of *blur* and *displacement*. (In this, it works just like the *faerie fire* spell). A creature coated with the dust cannot hide. The dust's effect lasts for 2d% minutes.

Dust of appearance is typically stored in small silk packets or hollow bone blow-tubes.

Caster Level: 5th; *Prerequisites:* Craft Wondrous Item, *glitterdust*; *Market Price:* 2,100 gp; *Weight:* —.

Dust of Disappearance: This dust looks just like *dust of appearance* and is typically stored in the same manner. A creature or object touched by it becomes invisible (as *improved invisibility*). Normal vision can't see dusted creatures or objects, nor can they be detected by magical means, including *see invisibility* or *invisibility purge*. *Dust of appearance*, however, does reveal people and objects made invisible by *dust of disappearance*. Other factors, such as sound and smell, also allow possible detection.

The *improved invisibility* bestowed by the dust lasts for 2d10 minutes (1d10+10 if sprinkled carefully upon an object).

Caster Level: 7th; *Prerequisites:* Craft Wondrous Item, *improved invisibility*; *Market Price:* 3,500 gp; *Weight:* —.

Dust of Dryness: This special dust has many uses. If it is thrown into water, up to a cubic yard of the water is instantly transformed to nothingness, and the dust becomes a marble-sized pellet, floating or resting where it was thrown. If this pellet is hurled down, it breaks and releases the same volume of water. The dust affects only water (fresh, salt, alkaline), not other liquids.

If the dust is employed against a water creature, the creature must make a Fortitude save (DC 18) or be destroyed. The dust deals 5d6 points of damage to the water creature even if its saving throw succeeds.

Caster Level: 11th; *Prerequisites:* Craft Wondrous Item, *control water*; *Market Price:* 850 gp; *Weight:* —.

Dust of Illusion: This unremarkable powder resembles chalk dust or powdered graphite. Stare at it, however, and the dust changes color and form. Put the *dust of illusion* on a creature, and that creature is affected as if by a *change self* glamer, with the individual who sprinkles the dust envisioning the illusion desired. An unwilling recipient is allowed a Reflex saving throw (DC 11) to escape the effect. The glamer lasts for 1d6+6 hours.

Caster Level: 2nd; *Prerequisites:* Craft Wondrous Item, *change self*; *Market Price:* 500 gp; *Weight:* —.

Illus. by W. Reynolds

Dust of Tracelessness: This normal-seeming dust is actually a magic powder that can conceal the passage of its possessor and his companions. Tossing a pinch of this dust into the air causes a chamber of up to 1,000 square feet of floor space to become as dusty, dirty, and cobweb-laden as if it had been abandoned and disused for a decade.

A pinch of dust sprinkled along a trail causes evidence of the passage of as many as a dozen men and horses to be obliterated for a mile back into the distance. The results of the dust are instantaneous, so no magical aura lingers afterward from this use of the dust. Tracking checks across an area affected by this dust are made against a DC 20 higher than normal.

Caster Level: 3rd; *Prerequisites:* Craft Wondrous Item, *pass without trace; Market Price:* 250 gp; *Weight:* —.

Efreeti Bottle: This item is typically fashioned of brass or bronze, with a lead stopper bearing special seals. A thin stream of smoke is often seen issuing from it. The bottle can be opened once per day. When opened, the efreeti imprisoned within issues from the bottle instantly. There is a 10% chance (a 01–10 result on d%) that the efreeti is insane and attacks immediately upon being released. There is also a 10% chance (91–100) that the efreeti of the bottle grants three *wishes.* In either case, the efreeti afterward disappears forever. The other 80% of the time (11–90), the inhabitant of the bottle loyally serves the character for up to 10 minutes per day (or until the efreeti's death), doing as she commands. (See the *Monster Manual* for efreeti statistics.) Roll each day the bottle is opened for that day's effect.

Caster Level: 14th; *Prerequisites:* Craft Wondrous Item, *summon monster VII; Market Price:* 150,000 gp; *Weight:* 1 lb.

Everburning Torch: This torch has a *continual flame* cast upon it.

Caster Level: 3rd; *Prerequisite: Continual flame* (no feat needed); *Market Price:* 90 gp; *Weight:* 1 lb.

Eversmoking Bottle: This metal urn is identical in appearance to an *efreeti bottle,* except that it does nothing but smoke. The amount of smoke is great if the stopper is pulled out, pouring from the bottle and totally obscuring vision across a spread of 50 feet in 1 round. If the bottle is left unstopped, the smoke spreads another 10 feet per round until it has spread 100 feet. This area remains smoke-filled until the *eversmoking bottle* is stoppered. The bottle must be resealed by a command word, after which the smoke dissipates normally.

Caster Level: 3rd; *Prerequisites:* Craft Wondrous Item, *pyrotechnics; Market Price:* 5,200 gp; *Weight:* 1 lb.

Eyes of Charming: These two crystal lenses fit over the user's eyes. The wearer is able to *charm person* (one target per round) merely by meeting a target's gaze. Those failing a Will saving throw (DC 16) are *charmed* as per the spell. If the wearer has only one lens, the DC of the saving throw is reduced to 10.

Caster Level: 7th; *Prerequisites:* Craft Wondrous Item, Heighten Spell, *charm person; Market Price:* 56,000 gp; *Weight:* —.

Eyes of Doom: These crystal lenses fit over the user's eyes, enabling him to cast *doom* upon those around him (one target per round) merely by meeting their gaze. Those failing a Will saving throw (DC 11) are *doomed* as per the spell. If the wearer has only one lens, the DC of the saving throw is reduced to 10. However, if the wearer has both lenses, he gains the additional power of continual *deathwatch* vision and can enact an *eyebite* (DC 19) once per week.

Caster Level: 11th; *Prerequisites:* Craft Wondrous Item, *doom, deathwatch, eyebite; Market Price:* 24,500 gp; *Weight:* —.

Eyes of the Eagle: These items are made of special crystal and fit over the eyes of the wearer. These lenses grant a +5 circumstance bonus to Spot checks. Wearing only one of the pair causes a character to become dizzy and, in effect, stunned for 1 round.

Thereafter, the wearer can use the single lens without being stunned so long as she covers her other eye. Of course, she can remove the single lens and see normally at any time, or wear both lenses to end or avoid the dizziness.

Caster Level: 3rd; *Prerequisites:* Craft Wondrous Item, *clairaudience/clairvoyance; Market Price:* 1,000 gp; *Weight:* —.

Eyes of Petrification: These items are made of special crystal and fit over the eyes of the wearer. They allow her to use a petrification gaze attack (DC 19), such as that of a basilisk, for 10 rounds per day (see the *Monster Manual* for details on the basilisk's gaze attack). Both lenses must be worn for the magic to be effective.

Caster Level: 11th; *Prerequisites:* Craft Wondrous Item, *flesh to stone; Market Price:* 98,000 gp; *Weight:* —.

Figurines of Wondrous Power: Each of the several kinds of *figurines of wondrous power* appears to be a tiny statuette of an creature an inch or so high (with one exception). When the figurine is tossed down and the correct command word spoken, it becomes a living creature of normal size (except when noted otherwise below). The creature obeys and serves its owner.

If a *figurine of wondrous power* is broken or destroyed in its statuette form, it is forever ruined. All magic is lost, its power departed. If slain in animal form, the figurine simply reverts to a statuette that can be used again at a later time.

Bronze Griffon: When animated, the *bronze griffon* acts in all ways like a normal griffon under the command of its possessor. The item can be used twice per week for up to 6 hours per use. When 6 hours have passed or when the command word is spoken, the *bronze griffon* once again becomes a tiny statuette.

Caster Level: 11th; *Prerequisites:* Craft Wondrous Item, *animate objects; Market Price:* 10,000 gp; *Weight:* —.

Ebony Fly: When animated, the *ebony fly* is the size of a pony and has all the statistics of a hippogriff (Hit Dice, AC, carrying capacity, speed, and so on) but can make no attacks. The item can be used three times per week for up to 12 hours per use. When 12 hours have passed or when the command word is spoken, the *ebony fly* again becomes a tiny statuette.

Caster Level: 11th; *Prerequisites:* Craft Wondrous Item, *animate objects; Market Price:* 10,000 gp; *Weight:* —.

Golden Lions: These come in pairs. They become normal adult male lions (see the *Monster Manual*). If slain in combat, the lions cannot be brought back from statuette form for one full week. Otherwise, they can be used once per day for up to 1 hour. They enlarge and shrink upon speaking the command word.

Caster Level: 11th; *Prerequisites:* Craft Wondrous Item, *animate objects; Market Price:* 16,500 gp; *Weight:* —.

Ivory Goats: These come in threes. Each goat of this trio looks slightly different from the others, and each has a different function:

- *The Goat of Traveling:* This statuette provides a speedy and enduring mount equal to that of a draft horse in every way except appearance. The goat can travel for a maximum of one day each week—continuously or in any combination of periods totaling 24 hours. At this point, or when the command word is uttered, it returns to its statuette form for not less than one day before it can again be used.
- *The Goat of Travail:* This statuette becomes an enormous creature, larger than a bull, with the statistics of a nightmare except for the addition of a pair of wicked horns of exceptional size (damage 1d8+4/1d8+4). If it is charging to attack, it may only use its horns (but add +6 points of damage to each successful attack on that round). It can be called to life just once per month for up to 12 hours at a time.

Ebony fly

- *The Goat of Terror*: When called upon with the proper command word, this statuette becomes a destrierlike mount, with the statistics of a light warhorse (but hairier). However, its rider can employ the goat's horns as weapons (one horn as a +3 *lance*, the other as a +5 *longsword*). When ridden in an attack against an opponent, the *goat of terror* radiates *fear* as the spell in a 30-foot radius (DC 16). It can be used once every two weeks for up to 3 hours per use.

After three uses, each of the *ivory goats* loses its magical ability forever.

Caster Level: 11th; *Prerequisites:* Craft Wondrous Item, *animate objects*; *Market Price:* 21,000 gp; *Weight:* —.

Marble Elephant: This is the largest of the figurines, the statuette being about the size of a human hand. Upon utterance of the command word, a *marble elephant* grows to the size and specifications of a true elephant. The animal created from the statuette is fully obedient to the figurine's owner, serving as a beast of burden, a mount, or a combatant.

Details of the elephant are found in the *Monster Manual*. The statuette can be used four times per month for up to 24 hours at a time.

Caster Level: 11th; *Prerequisites:* Craft Wondrous Item, *animate objects*; *Market Price:* 17,000 gp; *Weight:* —.

Obsidian Steed: An obsidian steed appears to be a small, nearly shapeless lump of black stone. Only careful inspection reveals that it vaguely resembles some form of quadruped. On command, the near-formless piece of obsidian becomes a fantastic mount. Treat it as a heavy warhorse with the following additional powers usable once per round at will: *fly*, *plane shift*, and *etherealness*. The steed allows itself to be ridden, but if the rider is of good alignment, the steed is 10% likely per use to carry him to the Lower Planes and then return to its statuette form. The statuette can be used once per week for one continuous period of up to 24 hours. Note that when the obsidian steed becomes ethereal or *plane shifts*, its rider and his gear follow suit. Thus, the user can travel to other planes via this means.

Caster Level: 15th; *Prerequisites:* Craft Wondrous Item, *animate objects, fly, plane shift, etherealness*; *Market Price:* 28,500 gp; *Weight:* —.

Onyx Dog: When commanded, this statuette changes into a creature with the same properties as a war dog, except that it is endowed with an Intelligence score of 8, can communicate in Common, and has exceptional olfactory and visual abilities. (It has the scent ability and adds +4 to its Spot and Search checks.) It has darkvision (range 60 feet) and it can *see invisible*. An *onyx dog* can be used once per week for up to 6 hours. It obeys only its owner.

Caster Level: 11th; *Prerequisites:* Craft Wondrous Item, *animate objects*; *Market Price:* 15,500 gp; *Weight:* —.

Serpentine Owl: A *serpentine owl* becomes either a normal-sized horned owl or a giant owl, according to the command word used. The transformation can take place once per day, with a maximum duration of 8 continuous hours. However, after three transformations into giant owl form, the statuette loses all of its magical properties. The owl communicates with its owner by telepathic means, informing her of all it sees and hears. (Remember the limitations of its Intelligence.)

Caster Level: 11th; *Prerequisites:* Craft Wondrous Item, *animate objects*; *Market Price:* 9,100 gp; *Weight:* —.

Silver Raven: This figurine turns into a raven on command (but it retains its silver consistency, which gives it a hardness of 10). Another command sends it off into the air, bearing a message just like a creature affected by an *animal messenger* spell. If not commanded to carry a message, the raven obeys the commands of its owner, although it has no special powers or telepathic abilities. It can maintain its nonfigurine status for only 24 hours per week, but the duration need not be continuous.

Caster Level: 6th; *Prerequisites:* Craft Wondrous Item, *animal messenger*; *Market Price:* 3,800 gp; *Weight:* —.

Gauntlets of Ogre Power: These gauntlets are made of tough leather with iron studs running across the back of the hands and fingers. They grant the wearer great strength, adding a +2 enhancement bonus to his Strength score. Both gauntlets must be worn for the magic to be effective.

Caster Level: 6th; *Prerequisites:* Craft Wondrous Item, *bull's strength*; *Market Price:* 4,000 gp; *Weight:* 2 lb.

Gauntlet of Rust: This single metal gauntlet looks rusted and pitted but is actually quite powerful. Once per day, it can affect an object as with the *rusting grasp* spell. It also completely protects the wearer and her gear from rust (magical or otherwise), including the attack of a rust monster.

Caster Level: 7th; *Prerequisites:* Craft Wondrous Item, *rusting grasp*; *Market Price:* 11,500 gp; *Weight:* 2 lb.

Gem of Brightness: This crystal appears to be a long, rough prism. Upon utterance of a command word, the crystal emits bright light of one of three sorts.

- One command word causes the gem to shed a pale light in a cone 10 feet long. This use of the gem does not expend any charges.
- Another command word causes the *gem of brightness* to send out a very bright ray 1 foot in diameter and 50 feet long. This strikes as a ranged touch attack, and any creature struck by this beam is blinded for 1d4 rounds unless it succeeds at a Reflex save (DC 14). This use of the gem expends 1 charge.
- The third command word causes the gem to flare in a blinding flash of light in a cone 30 feet long Although this glare lasts but a moment, all creatures within its area must make a Reflex save (DC 14) or be blinded for 1d4 rounds and thereafter suffer a penalty of −1 to attack rolls, Spot checks, and Search checks due to permanent eye damage. This use expends 5 charges.

Eye damage can be cured by a *remove blindness* or a *heal* spell. A newly created *gem of brightness* has 50 charges. When all its charges are expended, the gem becomes nonmagical.

Caster Level: 6th; *Prerequisites:* Craft Wondrous Item, *daylight, blindness/deafness*; *Market Price:* 15,200 gp; *Weight:* —.

Gem of Seeing: This finely cut and polished stone is indistinguishable from an ordinary jewel in appearance. When gazed through, the *gem of seeing* enables the user to see as though she were affected by a *true seeing* spell.

Caster Level: 10th; *Prerequisites:* Craft Wondrous Item, *true seeing*; *Market Price:* 75,000 gp; *Weight:* —.

Gloves of Arrow Snaring: Once snugly worn, these gloves seem to meld with the hands, becoming almost invisible. (They are undetectable unless the viewer is within 5 feet of the wearer.) The wearer can act as if he had the Deflect Arrows feat, except that he catches the thrown weapons and projectiles instead of deflecting them. Both gloves must be worn for the magic to be effective. At least one hand must be free to take advantage of the magic.

Caster Level: 3rd; *Prerequisites:* Craft Wondrous Item, *shield*; *Market Price:* 4,000 gp; *Weight:* —.

Gloves of Dexterity: These tight-fitting, thin leather gloves are very flexible and allow for delicate manipulation. They add to the wearer's Dexterity score in the form of an enhancement bonus of +2, +4, or +6. Both gloves must be worn for the magic to be effective.

Caster Level: 8th; *Prerequisites:* Craft Wondrous Item, *cat's grace*; *Market Price:* 4,000 gp (+2), 16,000 gp (+4), or 36,000 gp (+6); *Weight:* —.

Glove of Storing: This device is a simple leather glove. On command, one item held in the hand wearing the glove disappears. The item can weigh no more than 20 pounds and must be able to be held in one hand. With a snap of the fingers wearing the glove, the item reappears. A glove can only store one item at a time. The item is held in stasis and shrunk down so small within the palm of the glove that it cannot be seen. Many owners of *gloves of storing* find them to be useful and dramatic ways to store weapons, wands, and—because the item is stored in stasis—even lit torches. If the effect is suppressed or dispelled, the stored item appears instantly. Although it is handy to have two of these gloves, the creation process yields only one.

Caster Level: 6th; *Prerequisites:* Craft Wondrous Item, *shrink item*; *Market Price:* 2,200 gp; *Weight:* —.

Gloves of Swimming and Climbing: These apparently normal lightweight gloves grant a +10 competence bonus to Swim and Climb checks. Both gloves must be worn for the magic to be effective.

Caster Level: 5th; *Prerequisites:* Craft Wondrous Item, *cat's grace*; *Market Price:* 6,000 gp; *Weight:* —.

Goggles of Minute Seeing: The lenses of this item are made of special crystal. When placed over the eyes of the wearer, they enable her to see much better than normal at distances of 1 foot or less, granting her a +5 bonus to Search checks to locate or identify features such as tiny seams, marks, cracks, or imperfections. Both lenses must be worn for the magic to be effective.

Caster Level: 3rd; *Prerequisites:* Craft Wondrous Item, *true seeing*; *Market Price:* 1,000 gp; *Weight:* —.

Goggles of Night: The lenses of this item are made of dark crystal. Even though the lenses are opaque, when placed over the eyes of the wearer they enable him to see normally and also grant him darkvision (range 60 feet). Both lenses must be worn for the magic to be effective.

Caster Level: 3rd; *Prerequisites:* Craft Wondrous Item, *darkvision*; *Market Price:* 8,000 gp; *Weight:* —.

Hand of Glory: This mummified human hand hangs by a leather cord around a character's neck (taking up space as a magic necklace would). If a magic ring is placed on one of the fingers of the hand, the wearer benefits from the ring as if wearing it herself, and it does not count against her two-ring limit. The hand can wear only one ring at a time.

Even without a ring, the hand itself allows its wearer to use *daylight* and *see invisibility* each once per day.

Caster Level: 9th; *Prerequisites:* Craft Wondrous Item, *daylight*, *detect invisibility*, *animate dead*; *Market Price:* 7,200 gp; *Weight:* 2 lb.

Hand of the Mage: This mummified elven hand hangs by a golden chain around a character's neck (taking up space as a magic necklace would). It allows the wearer to utilize the spell *mage hand* at will.

Caster Level: 3rd; *Prerequisites:* Craft Wondrous Item, *mage hand*; *Market Price:* 1,000 gp; *Weight:* 2 lb.

Harp of Charming: This instrument is a golden, intricately carved harp. When played, it enables the performer to cast one *suggestion* (Will negates DC 14) for each 10 minutes of playing if he can succeed at a Perform check (DC 15). On a die roll of a natural 1, the harpist has played so poorly that he enrages all those within earshot.

Caster Level: 5th; *Prerequisites:* Craft Wondrous Item, *suggestion*;

Hand of glory

Helm of brilliance

Market Price: 7,500 gp; **Weight:** 5 lb.

Hat of Disguise: This apparently normal hat allows its wearer to alter her appearance as with a *change self* spell. As part of the disguise, the hat can be changed to appear as a comb, ribbon, headband, cap, coif, hood, helmet, and so on.

Caster Level: 2nd; *Prerequisites:* Craft Wondrous Item, *change self*; *Market Price:* 2,000 gp; *Weight:* —.

Headband of Intellect: This device is a light cord with a small gem set so that it rests upon the forehead of the wearer. The headband adds to the wearer's Intelligence score in the form of an enhancement bonus of +2, +4, or +6.

Caster Level: 8th; *Prerequisites:* Craft Wondrous Item, *commune or legend lore*; *Market Price:* 4,000 gp (+2), 16,000 gp (+4), or 36,000 gp (+6); *Weight:* —.

Helm of Brilliance: This normal-looking helm takes its true form and manifests its powers when the user dons it and speaks the command word. Made of brilliant silver and polished steel, a newly created helm is set with ten diamonds, twenty rubies, thirty fire opals, and forty opals, each of large size and enchanted. When struck by bright light, the helm scintillates and sends forth reflective rays in all directions from its crownlike, gem-tipped spikes. The jewels' functions are as follows:

Jewel	Effect
Diamond	*Prismatic spray* (DC 17)
Ruby	*Wall of fire*
Fire opal	*Fireball* (10d6)
Opal	*Light*

The helm may be used once per round, but each gem can perform its spell-like power just once. Until all of its jewels are depleted, a *helm of brilliance* also has the following magical properties when activated:

- It emanates a bluish light when undead are within 30 feet. This light causes pain and 1d6 points of damage per round to all such creatures within that range.
- The wearer may command any weapon he wields to become a flaming weapon (see page 186). This is in addition to whatever abilities the weapon may already have (unless the weapon already is a flaming weapon). The command takes 1 round to take effect.
- Each round, the helm absorbs the first 30 points of fire damage the wearer would otherwise take. This protection does not stack with similar protection from other sources, such as *endure elements*.

Once all of its jewels have lost their magic, the helm loses all its powers and the gems turn to worthless powder. Removing a jewel destroys it.

If a creature wearing the helm is damaged by magic fire (after the fire protection is taken into account) and fails an additional Will saving throw (DC 15), the remaining gems on the helm overload and detonate.

Caster Level: 13th; *Prerequisites:* Craft Wondrous Item, *light, fireball, prismatic spray, wall of fire, flame blade, detect undead, protection from elements; Market Price:* 157,000 gp; *Weight:* 3 lb.

Helm of Comprehending Languages and Reading Magic: Appearing as a normal helmet, a *helmet of comprehending languages and reading magic* grants its wearer a 90% chance to understand any strange tongue or writing she encounters and an 80% chance to understand any magic writings. Note that understanding does not necessarily imply spell use.

Caster Level: 4th; *Prerequisites:* Craft Wondrous Item, *comprehend languages, read magic; Market Price:* 2,600 gp; *Weight:* 3 lb.

Helm of Telepathy: The wearer can use *detect thoughts* at will. Furthermore, he can send a telepathic message to anyone whose surface thoughts he is reading (allowing two-way communication). Once per day, the wearer of the helm can implant a *suggestion* (as the spell, Will negates, DC 14) along with his telepathic message.

Caster Level: 8th; *Prerequisites:* Craft Wondrous Item, *detect thoughts, suggestion; Market Price:* 31,000 gp; *Weight:* 3 lb.

Helm of Teleportation: Any character wearing this device may *teleport* three times per day, exactly as if he had cast the spell of the same name.

Caster Level: 9th; *Prerequisites:* Craft Wondrous Item, *teleport; Market Price:* 48,600 gp; *Weight:* 3 lb.

Helm of Underwater Action: The wearer of this helmet can see underwater. Drawing the small lenses in compartments on either side into position before the wearer's eyes activates the visual properties of the helm, allowing her to see five times farther than water and light conditions would allow for normal human vision. (Weeds, obstructions, and the like block vision in the usual manner.) If the command word is spoken, the *helm of underwater action* creates a globe of air around the wearer's head and maintains it until the command word is spoken again, enabling her to breathe freely.

Caster Level: 7th; *Prerequisites:* Craft Wondrous Item, *freedom of movement, water breathing; Market Price:* 24,000 gp; *Weight:* 3 lb.

Heward's Handy Haversack: A backpack of this sort appears to be well made, well used, and quite ordinary. It is constructed of finely tanned leather, and the straps have brass hardware and buckles. It has two side pouches, each of which appears large enough to hold about a quart of material. In fact, each is like a *bag of holding* and can actually hold material equal to as much as 2 cubic feet in volume or 20 pounds in weight. The large central portion of the pack can contain up to 8 cubic feet or 80 pounds of material. Even when so filled, the backpack always weighs only 5 pounds.

While such storage is useful enough, the pack has an even greater power in addition. When the wearer reaches into it for a specific item, that item is always on top. Thus, no digging around and fumbling is ever necessary to find what a haversack contains. Retrieving any specific item from a haversack is a move-equivalent action. *Heward's handy haversack* and whatever it contains gain a +2 resistance bonus to all saving throws.

Caster Level: 5th; *Prerequisites:* Craft Wondrous Item, *Leomund's secret chest; Market Price:* 2,000 gp; *Weight:* 5 lb.

Horn of Blasting: This horn appears to be a normal trumpet. It can be sounded as a normal horn, but if the command word is spoken and the instrument is then played, it has the following effects, both of which happen at once:

- A 100-foot cone of sound issues forth from the horn. All within this area must make a Fortitude saving throw (DC 16). Those who succeed are stunned for 1 round and deafened for 2 rounds. Those failing the saving throw take 1d10 points of damage, are stunned for 2 rounds, and are deafened for 4 rounds.
- An ultrasonic wave 1 foot wide and 100 feet long issues from the horn. The wave weakens such materials as metal, stone, and wood. This effect deals 1d10 points of damage to objects within the area, ignoring their hardness.

If a *horn of blasting* is used magically more than once in a given day, there is a 10% cumulative chance with each extra use that it explodes and deals 5d10 points of damage to the person sounding it.

Caster Level: 7th; *Prerequisites:* Craft Wondrous Item, *shout; Market Price:* 12,000 gp; *Weight:* 1 lb.

Horn of Fog: This small bugle allows its possessor to blow forth a thick cloud of heavy fog similar to that of an *obscuring mist* spell. The fog spreads 10 feet each round that the user continues to blow the horn. The device makes a deep, foghornlike noise, with the note dropping abruptly to a lower register at the end of each blast.

Caster Level: 3rd; *Prerequisites:* Craft Wondrous Item, *obscuring mist; Market Price:* 2,000 gp; *Weight:* 1 lb.

Horn of Goodness/Evil: This trumpet adapts itself to its owner, so it produces either a good or an evil effect depending on the owner's alignment. If the owner is neither good nor evil, the horn has no power whatsoever. If he is good, then blowing the horn has the effect of a *magic circle against evil.* If he is evil, then blowing the horn has the effect of a *magic circle against good.* In either case, this ward lasts for 10 rounds. The horn can be blown once per day.

Caster Level: 7th; *Prerequisites:* Craft Wondrous Item, *magic circle against good* or *magic circle against evil; Market Price:* 6,000 gp; *Weight:* 1 lb.

Horn of the Tritons: This device is a conch shell that can be blown once per day (except by a triton, who can sound it three times per day). A *horn of the tritons* can do any one of the following functions when blown:

Horn of Valhalla

- Calm rough waters in a one-mile radius. This dispels a summoned water elemental if it fails its Will saving throw (DC 16).
- Attract 5d4 Large sharks (a 01–30 result on d%), 5d6 Medium-size sharks (31–80), or 1d10 sea lions (81–100) if the character is in a body of water in which such creatures dwell. The creatures are friendly and obey, to the best of their ability, the one who sounded the horn.
- Panic and demoralize aquatic creatures with Intelligence scores of 1 or 2 within 500 feet as if they had been targeted by a *fear* spell (DC 16). Those who do save are shaken for 3d6 rounds.

Any sounding of a *horn of the tritons* can be heard by all tritons within a three-mile radius.

Caster Level: 8th; *Prerequisites:* Craft Wondrous Item, *fear, summon monster V, water control,* creator must be a triton or get construction aid from a triton; *Market Price:* 15,100 gp; *Weight:* 2 lb.

Horn of Valhalla: This magic instrument comes in four varieties. Each appears to be normal until someone speaks its command word and blows the horn. Then the horn summons a number of human barbarians to fight for the character who summoned them. Each horn can be blown just once every seven days. Roll d% to see what type of horn is found. The horn's type determines what barbarians are summoned and what prerequisite is needed to use the horn. Any character who uses a *horn of Valhalla* but doesn't have the prerequisite is attacked by the barbarians she herself summoned.

d%	Type of Horn	Barbarians Summoned	Prerequisites
01–40	Silver	2d4+2, 2nd level	None
41–75	Brass	2d4+1, 3rd level	Spellcaster level 1st+
76–90	Bronze	2d4, 4th level	Proficiency with all martial weapons or bardic music ability
91–100	Iron	1d4+1, 5th level	Proficiency with all martial weapons or bardic music ability

Summoned barbarians are magic constructs, not actual people (though they seem to be), and they arrive with the starting equipment for barbarians found in the *Player's Handbook* (page 26). They gladly attack anyone the possessor of the horn commands them to fight until they or their opponents are slain or until 1 hour has elapsed, whichever comes first.

Caster Level: 13th; *Prerequisites:* Craft Wondrous Item, *summon monster VI; Market Price:* 50,000 gp; *Weight:* 2 lb.

Horseshoes of Speed: These iron shoes come in sets of four like ordinary horseshoes. When affixed to a horse's hooves, they double the animal's speed. All four shoes must be worn by the same animal for the magic to be effective.

Caster Level: 5th; *Prerequisites:* Craft Wondrous Item, *haste; Market Price:* 1,900 gp; *Weight:* 3 lb. each.

Horseshoes of a Zephyr: These four iron shoes are affixed like normal horseshoes. They allow a horse to travel without actually touching the ground. The horse must still run above (always around 4 inches above) a roughly horizontal surface. This means that nonsolid or unstable surfaces, such as water or lava, can be crossed, and that movement is possible without leaving tracks on any sort of ground. The horse moves at normal speed. All four shoes must be worn by the same animal for the magic to be effective.

Caster Level: 3rd; *Prerequisites:* Craft Wondrous Item, *levitate; Market Price:* 3,000 gp; *Weight:* 1 lb. each.

Incense of Meditation: This small rectangular block of sweet-smelling incense is visually indistinguishable from nonmagical incense until lit. When it is burning, the special fragrance and pearly-hued smoke of this special incense are recognizable by anyone making a Spellcraft check (DC 15).

When a divine spellcaster lights a block of *incense of meditation* and then spends 8 hours praying and meditating nearby, the incense enables him to prepare all of his spells as though affected by the Maximize Spell metamagic feat. However, all the spells prepared in this way are at their normal level, not at three levels higher (as with the regular metamagic feat).

Each block of incense burns for 8 hours, and the effects remain for 24 hours.

Caster Level: 7th; *Prerequisites:* Craft Wondrous Item, Maximize Spell, *bless; Market Price:* 4,900 gp; *Weight:* 1 lb. each.

Ioun Stones: These stones always float in the air and must be within 3 feet of their owner to be of any use. When a character first acquires a stone, she must hold it and then release it, whereupon it takes up a circling orbit 1d3 feet from her head. Thereafter, a stone must be grasped or netted to separate it from its owner. The owner may voluntarily seize and stow a stone (while sleeping, for example) to keep it safe, but she loses the benefits of the stone during that time. *Ioun stones* have an AC of 24, 10 hit points, and a hardness of 5.

Regeneration from the pearly white *Ioun stone* works like a *ring of regeneration.* (It only cures damage taken while the character is using the stone.) The pale lavender and lavender and green stones work like a *rod of absorption,* but absorbing a spell requires a readied action, and these stones cannot be used to empower spells. Stored spells in the vibrant purple stone must be placed by a spellcaster but can be used by anyone (see *ring of spell storing*).

Caster Level: 12th; *Prerequisites:* Craft Wondrous Item, creator must be 12th level; *Weight:* —.

Iron Bands of Bilarro: When initially discovered, this very potent item appears to be a rusty iron sphere. Close examination reveals that there are bandings on the 3-inch-diameter globe.

When the proper command word is spoken and the spherical iron device is hurled at an opponent, the bands expand and tightly constrict the target creature on a successful ranged touch attack. A single creature of Large size or smaller can be captured thus and held immobile until the command word is spoken to bring the bands into globular form again. The creature can break (and ruin) the bands with a successful Strength check (DC 30) or escape them with a successful Escape Artist check (also DC 30).

Caster Level: 10th; *Prerequisites:* Craft Wondrous Item, *Bigby's grasping hand; Market Price:* 26,000 gp; *Weight:* 1 lb.

Iron Flask: These special containers are typically inlaid with runes of silver and stoppered by a brass plug bearing a seal engraved with sigils, glyphs, and special symbols. When the user

IOUN STONES

Color	Shape	Effect	Market Price
Dull gray	Any	Merely orbits without further powers	25 gp
Dusty rose	Prism	+1 deflection bonus to AC	4,000 gp
Clear	Spindle	Sustains creature without food or water	5,000 gp
Pale blue	Rhomboid	+2 enhancement bonus to Strength	8,000 gp
Scarlet and blue	Sphere	+2 enhancement bonus to Intelligence	8,000 gp
Incandescent blue	Sphere	+2 enhancement bonus to Wisdom	8,000 gp
Deep red	Sphere	+2 enhancement bonus to Dexterity	8,000 gp
Pink	Rhomboid	+2 enhancement bonus to Constitution	8,000 gp
Pink and green	Sphere	+2 enhancement bonus to Charisma	8,000 gp
Dark blue	Rhomboid	Alertness (as the feat)	8,000 gp
Vibrant purple	Prism	Stores six levels of spells	12,000 gp
Iridescent	Spindle	Sustains creature without air	15,000 gp
Pale green	Prism	+1 competence bonus to attack rolls, saves, and checks	20,000 gp
Pearly white	Spindle	Regenerate 1 point of damage/hour	20,000 gp
Pale lavender	Ellipsoid	Absorb spells up to 4th level*	20,000 gp
Lavender and green	Ellipsoid	Absorb spells up to 8th level**	40,000 gp

*After absorbing 20 spell levels, the stone burns out and turns to dull gray, forever useless.
**After absorbing 50 spell levels, the stone burns out and turns dull gray, forever useless.

speaks the command word, he can force any creature from another plane into the container, provided that creature fails a Will saving throw (DC 19). The range of this effect is 60 feet. Only one creature at a time can be so contained. Loosing the stopper frees the captured creature.

If the individual freeing the captured creature speaks the command word, the creature can be forced to serve for 1 hour. If freed without the command word, the creature acts according to its natural inclinations. (It usually attacks the user, unless it perceives a good reason not to.) Any attempt to force the same creature into the flask a second time allows it a +2 bonus on its saving throw and makes it very angry and totally hostile. A newly discovered bottle might contain any of the following:

d%	Contents	d%	Contents
01–50	Empty	89	Demon (glabrezu)
51–54	Large air elemental	90	Demon (succubus)
55–58	Arrowhawk	91	Devil (osyluth)
59–62	Large earth elemental	92	Devil (barbazu)
63–66	Xorn	93	Devil (erinyes)
67–70	Large fire elemental	94	Devil (cornugon)
71–74	Salamander	95	Celestial (avoral)
75–78	Large water elemental	96	Celestial (ghaele)
79–82	Adult tojanida	97	Formian myrmarch
83–84	Red slaad	98	Blue slaad
85–86	Formian taskmaster (alone)	99	Rakshasa
87	Demon (vrock)	100	Demon (balor) or devil
88	Demon (hezrou)		(pit fiend)—equal chance for either

Caster Level: 20th; *Prerequisites:* Craft Wondrous Item, *trap the soul; Market Price:* 170,000 gp (empty); *Weight:* 1 lb.

Keoghtom's Ointment: A jar of this unguent is small—3 inches in diameter and 1 inch deep—but contains five applications. Placed upon a poisoned wound or swallowed, the ointment detoxifies any poison (as *neutralize poison*). Applied to a diseased area, it removes disease (as *remove disease*). Rubbed on a wound, the ointment cures 1d8+5 points of damage (as *cure light wounds*).

Caster Level: 5th; *Prerequisites:* Craft Wondrous Item, *cure light wounds, neutralize poison, remove disease; Market Price:* 4,000 gp; *Weight:* 1/2 lb.

Lantern of Revealing: This lantern operates as a normal hooded lantern. While it is lit, it also reveals all invisible creatures and objects within 25 feet of it, just like the spell *invisibility purge*.

Caster Level: 5th; *Prerequisites:* Craft Wondrous Item, *invisibility purge; Market Price:* 30,000 gp; *Weight:* 2 lb.

Lens of Detection: This circular prism enables its user to detect minute details, granting a +10 bonus to Search checks. It also aids in following tracks, adding a +10 bonus to Wilderness Lore checks when tracking. The lens is about 6 inches in diameter and set in a frame with a handle.

Caster Level: 5th; *Prerequisites:* Craft Wondrous Item, *true seeing; Market Price:* 3,500 gp; *Weight:* 1 lb.

Lyre of Building: If the proper chords are struck, a single use of this lyre negates any attacks made against all inanimate construction (walls, roof, floor, and so on) within 300 feet. This includes the effects of a *horn of blasting*, a *disintegrate* spell, or an attack from a ram or similar siege weapon. The lyre can be used in this way once per day, with the protection lasting for 30 minutes.

Lyre of building

The lyre is also useful with respect to building. Once a week its strings can be strummed so as to produce chords that magically construct buildings, mines, tunnels, ditches, or whatever. The effect produced in but 30 minutes of playing is equal to the work of 100 humans laboring for three days. Each hour after the first, a character playing the lyre must make a Perform check (DC 18). If it fails, she must stop and cannot play it again for this purpose until a week has passed.

Caster Level: 6th; *Prerequisites:* Craft Wondrous Item, *fabricate; Market Price:* 13,000 gp; *Weight:* 5 lb.

Mantle of Spell Resistance: This embroidered garment is worn over normal clothing or armor. It grants the wearer spell resistance of 21.

Caster Level: 9th; *Prerequisites:* Craft Wondrous Item, *spell resistance; Market Price:* 90,000 gp; *Weight:* —.

Manual of Bodily Health: This thick tome contains tips on health and fitness, but entwined within the words is a powerful magical effect. If anyone reads this book, which takes a total of 48 hours over a minimum of six days, he gains an inherent bonus of from +1 to +5 (depending on the type of manual) to his Constitution score. Once the book is read, the magic disappears from the pages and it becomes a normal book.

Caster Level: 17th; *Prerequisites:* Craft Wondrous Item, *wish* or *miracle; Market Price:* 27,500 gp (+1), 55,000 gp (+2), 82,500 gp (+3), 110,000 gp (+4), or 137,500 gp (+5); *Cost to Create:* 1,250 gp + 5,100 XP (+1), 2,500 gp + 10,200 XP (+2), 3,750 gp + 15,300 XP (+3), 5,000 gp + 20,400 XP (+4), or 6,250 gp + 25,500 XP (+5); *Weight:* 5 lb.

Manual of Gainful Exercise: This thick tome contains exercise descriptions and diet suggestions, but entwined within the words is a powerful magical effect. If anyone reads this book, which takes a total of 48 hours over a minimum of six days, she gains an inherent bonus of from +1 to +5 (depending on the type of manual) to her Strength score. Once the book is read, the magic disappears from the pages and it becomes a normal book.

Caster Level: 17th; *Prerequisites:* Craft Wondrous Item, *wish* or *miracle; Market Price:* 27,500 gp (+1), 55,000 gp (+2), 82,500 gp (+3), 110,000 gp (+4), or 137,500 gp (+5); *Cost to Create:* 1,250 gp + 5,100 XP (+1), 2,500 gp + 10,200 XP (+2), 3,750 gp + 15,300 XP (+3), 5,000 gp + 20,400 XP (+4), or 6,250 gp + 25,500 XP (+5); *Weight:* 5 lb.

Manual of Quickness of Action: This thick tome contains tips on coordination exercises and balance, but entwined within the words is a powerful magical effect. If anyone reads this book, which takes a total of 48 hours over a minimum of six days, he gains an inherent bonus of from +1 to +5 (depending on the type of manual) to his Dexterity score. Once the book is read, the magic disappears from the pages and it becomes a normal book.

Caster Level: 17th; *Prerequisites:* Craft Wondrous Item, *wish* or *miracle; Market Price:* 27,500 gp (+1), 55,000 gp (+2), 82,500 gp (+3), 110,000 gp (+4), or 137,500 gp (+5); *Cost to Create:* 1,250 gp + 5,100 XP (+1), 2,500 gp + 10,200 XP (+2), 3,750 gp + 15,300 XP (+3), 5,000 gp + 20,400 XP (+4), or 6,250 gp + 25,500 XP (+5); *Weight:* 5 lb.

Mask of the Skull: This ivory mask has been fashioned into the likeness of a human skull. Once per day, after it has been worn for at least 1 hour, the mask can be loosed to fly from the wearer's face. It travels up to 50 feet away from the wearer and attacks a target assigned to it. The grinning skull mask makes a touch attack against the target. If it succeeds, the target must make a Fortitude saving throw (DC 20) or be struck dead, as if affected by a *finger of death* spell. If the target succeeds at his saving throw, he nevertheless takes 3d6+13 points of damage. After attacking (whether successful or not), the mask flies back to its user.

Caster Level: 13th; *Prerequisites:* Craft Wondrous Item, *finger of death*, *animate objects*, *fly*; *Market Price:* 25,000 gp; *Weight:* 3 lb.

Mattock of the Titans: This digging tool is 10 feet long. Any creature of at least Huge size can use it to loosen or tumble earth or earthen ramparts (a 10-foot cube every 10 minutes). It also smashes rock (a 10-foot cube per hour). If used as a weapon, it is the equivalent of a +3 *Gargantuan morningstar*, dealing 4d6 points of base damage.

Caster Level: 16th; *Prerequisites:* Craft Wondrous Item, Craft Magic Arms and Armor, *dig*; *Market Price:* 23,000 gp; *Weight:* 120 lb.

Maul of the Titans: This mallet is 8 feet long. If used as a weapon, it is the equivalent of a +3 *greatclub* and deals triple damage against inanimate objects. However, the wielder must have a Strength score of at least 18 to wield it properly. Otherwise, she suffers a –4 attack penalty.

Caster Level: 15th; *Prerequisites:* Craft Wondrous Item, Craft Magic Arms and Armor, *Bigby's clenched fist*; *Market Price:* 25,000 gp; *Weight:* 160 lb.

Medallion of Thoughts: This appears to be a normal pendant disk hung from a neck chain. Usually fashioned from bronze, copper, or nickel-silver, the medallion allows the wearer to read the thoughts of others, as with the spell *detect thoughts*.

Caster Level: 5th; *Prerequisites:* Craft Wondrous Item, *detect thoughts*; *Market Price:* 12,000 gp; *Weight:* —.

Mirror of Life Trapping: This crystal device is usually about 4 feet square and framed in metal or wood. It can be affixed to a surface and activated by giving a command word. The same command word deactivates the mirror. A *mirror of life trapping* has from thirteen to eighteen nonspatial extradimensional compartments within it. Any creature coming within 30 feet of the device and looking at its reflection must make a Will save (DC 19) or be trapped within the mirror in one of the cells. A creature not aware of the nature of the device always sees its reflection. The probability of a creature seeing its reflection, and thus needing to make the saving throw, drops to 50% if the creature is aware that the mirror traps life and seeks to avoid looking at it (treat as a gaze attack; see page 77).

When a creature is trapped, it is taken bodily into the mirror. Size is not a factor, but constructs and undead are not trapped, nor are inanimate objects and other nonliving matter. A victim's equipment (including clothing and anything being carried) remains behind. If the mirror's owner knows the right command word, he can call the reflection of any creature trapped within to its surface and engage his powerless prisoner in conversation. Another command word frees the trapped creature. Each pair of command words is specific to each prisoner.

If the mirror's capacity is exceeded, one victim (determined randomly) is set free in order to accommodate the latest one. If the mirror is broken, all victims currently trapped in it are freed and usually promptly attack the possessor of the device in revenge for their imprisonment.

Caster Level: 15th; *Prerequisites:* Craft Wondrous Item, *imprisonment*; *Market Price:* 152,000 gp; *Weight:* 50 lb.

Mirror of Mental Prowess: This mirror resembles an ordinary looking glass 5 feet tall by 2 feet wide. The possessor who knows the proper commands can cause it to perform as follows:

- Read the thoughts of any creature reflected therein, as long as the owner is within 25 feet of the mirror, even if those thoughts are in an unknown language.
- Scry with it as if it were a *crystal ball*, able to view even into other planes if the viewer is sufficiently familiar with them.
  - Use it as a portal to visit other places. The user first scries the place normally and then steps through the mirror to the place pictured. An invisible portal remains on the other side where she arrives, and she can return through that portal. Once she returns, the portal closes. The portal closes on its own after 24 hours (trapping the user if she's still in the other place), and the user can also close it with a command word. Creatures with Intelligence scores of 12 or greater might notice the portal just as they might notice a magical sensor from a *scrying* spell. Any creature who steps through the portal appears in front of the mirror.
  - Once per week the mirror accurately answers one short question regarding a creature whose image is shown on its surface.

Caster Level: 18th; *Prerequisites:* Craft Wondrous Item, *detect thoughts*, *scrying*, *clairaudience/clairvoyance*, *gate*, *commune*; *Market Price:* 175,000 gp; *Weight:* 40 lb.

Mirror of Opposition: This item resembles a normal mirror about 4 feet long and 3 feet wide. It can be affixed to a surface and activated by speaking a command word. The same command word deactivates the mirror. If a creature sees its reflection in the mirror's surface, an exact duplicate of that creature comes into being. This opposite immediately attacks the original. The duplicate has all the possessions and powers of its original (including magic). Upon the defeat or destruction of either the duplicate or the original, the duplicate and her items disappear completely. The mirror functions up to four times per day.

Caster Level: 15th; *Prerequisites:* Craft Wondrous Item, *clone*; *Market Price:* 92,000 gp; *Weight:* 45 lb.

Murlynd's Spoon: This unremarkable eating utensil is typically fashioned from horn. If the spoon is placed in an empty container—a bowl, a cup, or a dish, for example—the vessel fills with a thick, pasty gruel. Although this substance has a flavor similar to that of warm, wet cardboard, it is highly nourishing and contains everything necessary to sustain any herbivorous, omnivorous, or carnivorous creature. The spoon can produce sufficient gruel each day to feed up to four humans.

Caster Level: 5th; *Prerequisites:* Craft Wondrous Item, *create food and water*; *Market Price:* 5,500 gp; *Weight:* —.

Necklace of Adaptation: This necklace is a heavy chain with a platinum medallion. The magic of the necklace wraps the wearer in a shell of fresh air, making him immune to all gases and allowing him to breathe, even underwater or in a vacuum.

Caster Level: 7th; *Prerequisites:* Craft Wondrous Item, *water breathing*; *Market Price:* 19,000 gp; *Weight:* —.

Necklace of Fireballs: This device appears to be nothing but a cheap medallion or piece of valueless jewelry. If a character places it about her neck, however, all can see the necklace as it really is—a golden chain from which hang a number of golden spheres. The spheres are detachable by the wearer (and only by the wearer), who can easily hurl them up to a 70-foot distance. When a sphere arrives at the end of its trajectory, it bursts as a magic *fireball* (DC 14). The number of spheres on each type of necklace, and their respective Hit Dice of *fireball* damage, are as follows:

Mask of the skull

Necklace	10d6	9d6	8d6	7d6	6d6	5d6	4d6	3d6	2d6	Market Price
Type I	—	—	—	—	—	1	—	2	—	1,650 gp
Type II	—	—	—	—	1	—	2	—	2	2,700 gp
Type III	—	—	—	1	—	2	—	4	—	4,350 gp
Type IV	—	—	1	—	2	—	2	—	4	5,400 gp
Type V	—	1	—	2	—	2	—	2	—	6,150 gp
Type VI	1	—	2	—	2	—	4	—	—	8,100 gp
Type VII	1	2	—	2	—	2	—	2	—	9,150 gp

For example, a Type III necklace has seven spheres—one 7-dice, two 5-dice, and four 3-dice *fireballs*.

The more dice of damage a sphere deals, the bigger it is. If the necklace is being worn or carried by a character who fails her saving throw against a magic fire attack, the item must make a saving throw as well (with a bonus of +7). If the necklace fails to save, all of its remaining spheres detonate simultaneously, often with regrettable consequences for the wearer.

Caster Level: 11th; *Prerequisites:* Craft Wondrous Item, *fireball; Weight:* 2 lb.

Necklace of Prayer Beads: A necklace of this sort appears to be a normal piece of nonvaluable jewelry until it is placed about a character's neck and the wearer casts a divine spell. The *necklace of prayer beads* consists of 1d6+24 semiprecious stones (total value 1,000 gp) along with one special bead:

Special Bead Type	Special Bead Ability
Bead of blessing	Wearer can cast *bless.*
Bead of healing	Wearer can cast *remove blindness, remove disease,* or *cure serious wounds.*
Bead of karma	Wearer can cast his spells at +4 caster level (with respect to range, duration, etc.). Effect lasts 10 minutes.
Bead of smiting	Wearer can cast *holy smite, chaos hammer, order's wrath,* or *unholy blight*— if appropriate to his alignment. (A neutral wearer can't use this bead.)
Bead of summons	Calls the wearer's deity (90% probability) to come to him in material form. (It had better be for a good reason.) Usable only once.
Bead of wind walking	Wearer can cast *wind walk.*

Each special bead can be used once per day, except for the *bead of summons.* If the wearer uses that bead to summon his deity frivolously, the deity takes the character's items and places a *geas* upon him as punishment at the very least. The power of a special bead is lost if it is removed from the necklace. Sometimes necklaces are found with multiple special beads.

Caster Level: 17th; *Prerequisites:* Craft Wondrous Item, *gate, wind walk,* and one of the following spells: *bless, cure blindness, cure disease, cure serious wounds, holy smite, chaos hammer, order's wrath,* or *unholy blight* (whichever is appropriate); *Market Price:* 500 gp (*bead of blessing*), 5,000 gp (*bead of karma*), 10,000 gp (*bead of healing*), 15,000 gp (*bead of smiting*), 30,000 gp (*bead of wind walking*), or 50,000 gp (*bead of summons*), plus 1,000 gp for the nonmagical beads for each necklace; *Weight:* —.

Nolzur's Marvelous Pigments: These magic emulsions enable their possessor to create actual, permanent objects simply by depicting their form in two dimensions. The pigments are applied by a stick tipped with bristles, hair, or fur. The emulsion flows from the application to form the desired object as the artist concentrates on the desired image. One pot of *Nolzur's marvelous pigments* is sufficient to create a 1,000-cubic-foot object by depicting it two-dimensionally over a

Periapt of health

100-square-foot surface. Thus, a 10-foot-by-10-foot rendition of a pit would result in an actual 10-foot-by-10-foot-by-10-foot pit; a 10-foot-by-10-foot depiction of a room would result in a 10-foot-by-10-foot-by-10-foot room; and so on.

Only normal, inanimate objects can be created—doors, pits, flowers, trees, cells, and so on. Creatures can't be created. The pigments must be applied to a surface (a floor, wall, ceiling, door, etc.). It takes 10 minutes to depict an object with the pigments. *Nolzur's marvelous pigments* cannot create magic items. Objects of value depicted by the pigments—precious metals, gems, jewelry, ivory, and so on—appear to be valuable but are really made of tin, lead, paste, brass, bone, and other such inexpensive materials. The user can create normal weapons, armor, and other mundane items whose value does not exceed 2,000 gp.

Items created are not magical; the effect is instantaneous.

Caster Level: 15th; *Prerequisites:* Craft Wondrous Item, *major creation; Market Price:* 5,500 gp; *Weight:* —.

Orb of Storms: This glass sphere is 8 inches in diameter. The possessor can call forth all manner of weather, even supernaturally destructive storms. Once per day she can call upon the orb to access a *control weather* spell. Once per month, she can bring upon a *storm of vengeance.* The owner of the orb gains a +2 luck bonus to all saves and checks concerning the weather (including surviving in great heat or cold, but not including walking through fire, *cones of cold,* and other such conditions).

Caster Level: 18th; *Prerequisites:* Craft Wondrous Item, *control weather, storm of vengeance; Market Price:* 38,000 gp; *Weight:* 6 lb.

Pearl of Power: This seemingly normal pearl of average size and luster is a potent aid to all spellcasters who prepare spells (clerics, druids, rangers, paladins, and wizards). Once per day on command, a *pearl of power* enables the possessor to recall any one spell that she had prepared and then cast. The spell is then prepared again, just as if it hadn't been cast. The spell must be of a particular level, depending on the pearl. Different pearls exist for recalling one spell per day of each level from 1st through 9th and for the recall of two spells per day (each of a different level, up to 6th).

Caster Level: 17th; *Prerequisites:* Craft Wondrous Item, creator must be able to cast spells of the spell level to be recalled; *Market Price:* 1,000 gp (1st), 4,000 gp (2nd), 9,000 gp (3rd), 16,000 gp (4th), 25,000 gp (5th), 36,000 gp (6th), 49,000 gp (7th), 64,000 gp (8th), 81,000 gp (9th), or 70,000 gp (two spells); *Weight:* —.

Pearl of the Sirines: This normal-seeming pearl is beautiful and worth at least 1,000 gp on that basis alone. If it is clasped firmly in hand or held to the breast while the possessor attempts actions related to the pearl's powers, she understands and is able to employ the item.

The pearl enables its possessor to breathe in water as if she were in clean, fresh air. Her underwater swim speed is 60 feet, and she can cast spells and act underwater without hindrance.

Caster Level: 8th; *Prerequisites:* Craft Wondrous Item, *water breathing, freedom of movement; Market Price:* 15,300 gp; *Weight:* —.

Periapt of Health: The wearer of this blue gem on a silver chain is immune to disease, including supernatural diseases (see Table 3–14: Diseases, page 75).

Caster Level: 5th; *Prerequisites:* Craft Wondrous Item, *remove disease;* *Market Price:* 7,500 gp; *Weight:* —.

Periapt of Proof against Poison: This item is a brilliant-cut black gem on a delicate silver chain. The wearer gains a +4 luck saving throw bonus against any type of poison.

Caster Level: 5th; *Prerequisites:* Craft Wondrous Item, *neutralize poison;* *Market Price:* 4,000 gp; *Weight:* —.

Periapt of Wisdom: Although it appears to be a normal pearl on a light chain, a *periapt of wisdom* actually increases the possessor's Wisdom score in the form of an enhancement bonus of +2, +4, or +6 (depending on the individual item).

Caster Level: 8th; *Prerequisites:* Craft Wondrous Item, *commune* or *legend lore; Market Price:* 4,000 gp (+2), 16,000 gp (+4), or 36,000 gp (+6); *Weight:* —.

Periapt of Wound Closure: This stone is bright red and dangles on a gold chain. The wearer does not lose hit points when brought to negative hit points. The periapt doubles the normal rate of healing or allows normal healing of wounds that would not do so normally. Bleeding damage, such as that from a *weapon of wounding,* is negated, but the periapt doesn't prevent active blood drain (such as that caused by a stirge).

Caster Level: 10th; *Prerequisites:* Craft Wondrous Item, *heal; Market Price:* 15,000 gp; *Weight:* —.

Phylactery of Faithfulness: This item is a small box containing holy scripture affixed to a leather cord. There is no mundane way to determine what function this religious item performs until it is worn. The wearer of a *phylactery of faithfulness* is aware of any action or item that could adversely affect his alignment and standing with his deity, including magical effects. He acquires this information prior to performing the action or becoming associated with such an item if he takes a moment to contemplate the action.

Caster Level: 1st; *Prerequisites:* Craft Wondrous Item plus either *detect evil, detect good, detect chaos,* or *detect law; Market Price:* 1,000 gp; *Weight:* —.

Pipes of Haunting: This magic item appears to be a small set of pan pipes. When played by a person who has the Perform (pan pipes) skill, the pipes create an eerie, spellbinding tune. A listener thinks the source of the music is somewhere within 30 feet of the musician. Those hearing the tune but not aware of the piper must make a Will saving throw (DC 13). Those who fail become shaken for 10 minutes.

Portable hole

Caster Level: 4th; *Prerequisites:* Craft Wondrous Item, *scare; Market Price:* 6,500 gp; *Weight:* 3 lb.

Pipes of Pain: These appear to be like any other standard set of pipes with nothing to reveal their true nature. When played by a person who has the Perform (pan pipes) skill, the pipes create a wondrous melody. All within 30 feet, including the piper, must make a Will save (DC 14) or be enchanted by the sound. (This is a mind-affecting sonic enchantment.) So long as the pipes are played, none of the creatures so enchanted attack or attempt any action (as if they are dazed). If the piper is enchanted, however, he plays on for 1d10 rounds.

As soon as the piping stops, all those affected are stricken by intense pain at even the slightest noise. Unless a character is in a totally silent area, she takes 1d4 points of damage per round for 2d4 rounds. During this time, damage from sonic attacks, such as *sound burst,* is doubled. Thereafter, the least noise causes an affected character to wince, giving her a −2 penalty to attack rolls, skill checks, and saving throws (except when she is in a totally silent area). This hypersensitivity is a curse and therefore hard to remove (see the *bestow curse* spell).

Caster Level: 6th; *Prerequisites:* Craft Wondrous Item, *charm person, sound burst; Market Price:* 12,000 gp; *Weight:* 3 lb.

Pipes of the Sewers: These wooden pipes appear ordinary, but if the possessor learns the proper tune, he can attract 1d6×10 dire rats (01–80 result on d%) or 3d6×10 normal rats (81–100) if either or both are within 400 feet. For each 50-foot distance the rats have to travel, there is a 1-round delay. The piper must continue playing until the rats appear, and when they do so, the piper must make a Perform (pan pipes) check (DC 10). Success means that they obey the piper's telepathic commands so long as he continues to play. Failure indicates that they turn on the piper. If for any reason the piper ceases playing, the rats leave immediately. If they are called again within a day, the Perform check is against DC 15.

If the rats are under the control of another creature, add the HD of the controller to the Perform check DC. Once control is assumed, another check is required each round to maintain it if the other creature is actively seeking to reassert its control.

Caster Level: 2nd; *Prerequisites:* Craft Wondrous Item, *summon nature's ally I, animal friendship; Market Price:* 1,150 gp; *Weight:* 3 lb.

Pipes of Sounding: When played by a character who has the Perform (pan pipes) skill, these pipes create a variety of sounds. The figment sounds are the equivalent of *ghost sound* (caster level 2).

Caster Level: 2nd; *Prerequisites:* Craft Wondrous Item, *ghost sound; Market Price:* 1,800 gp; *Weight:* 3 lb.

Portable Hole: A portable hole is a circle of cloth spun from the webs of a phase spider interwoven with strands of ether and beams of starlight. When opened fully, a portable hole is 6 feet in diameter, but it can be folded up to be as small as a pocket handkerchief. When spread upon any surface, it causes an extradimensional space 10 feet deep to come into being. This hole can be picked up from inside or out by simply taking hold of the edges of the cloth and folding it up. Either way, the entrance disappears, but anything inside the hole remains.

The only air in the hole is that which enters when the hole is opened. It contains enough air to supply one Medium-size creature or two Small creatures for 10 minutes. (See Suffocation, page 88.) The cloth does not accumulate weight even if its hole is filled (with gold, for example). Each *portable hole* opens on its own particular nondimensional space. If a *bag of holding* is placed within a *portable hole,* a rift to the Astral Plane is torn in that place. Both the bag and the cloth are sucked into the void and forever lost. If a *portable hole* is placed within a *bag of holding,* it opens a gate to the Astral Plane. The hole, the bag, and any creatures within a 10-foot radius are drawn there, the *portable hole* and *bag of holding* being destroyed in the process.

Caster Level: 12th; *Prerequisites:* Craft Wondrous Item, *plane shift; Market Price:* 14,000 gp; *Weight:* —.

Quaal's Feather Token: Each of these items is a small feather that has a power to suit a special need. The types of tokens are described below. Each token is usable but once.

Anchor: A token useful to moor a craft in water so as to render it immobile for up to one day.

Bird: A token that can be used to deliver a small written message unerringly to a designated target as would a carrier pigeon. The token lasts as long as it takes to carry the message.

Fan: A token that forms a huge flapping fan, causing a breeze of sufficient strength to propel one ship (about 25 mph). This wind is not cumulative with existing wind speed—if a severe wind is already blowing, this wind cannot be added to it to create a windstorm. The token can, however, be used to lessen existing winds, creating an area of relative calm or lighter winds (but wave size in a storm is not affected). The fan can be used up to 8 hours. It does not function on land.

Swan Boat: A token that forms a huge swanlike boat capable of moving on water at a speed of 60 feet. It can carry eight horses and gear or thirty-two Medium-size characters or any equivalent combination. The boat lasts for one day.

Tree: A token that causes a great oak to spring into being (6-foot-diameter trunk, 60-foot height, 40-foot top diameter). This is an instantaneous effect.

Whip: A token that forms into a huge leather whip and wields itself against any opponent desired just like a dancing weapon (see page 186). The weapon has a +10 base attack bonus, does 1d6+1 points of base damage, has a +1 enhancement bonus to attacks and damage, and a makes a free grapple attack (at a +15 attack bonus) if it hits. The whip lasts no longer than 1 hour.

Caster Level: 12th; *Prerequisites:* Craft Wondrous Item, *major creation; Market Price:* 50 gp (anchor), 300 gp (bird), 200 gp (fan), 450 gp (swan boat), 100 gp (tree), or 500 gp (whip); *Weight:* —.

Quiver of Ehlonna: This appears to be a typical arrow container capable of holding about 20 arrows. Examination shows that it has three distinct portions, each with an extradimensional space allowing it to store far more than would normally be possible. The first and smallest one can contain up to 60 objects of the same general size and shape as an arrow. The second slightly longer compartment holds up to 18 objects of the same general size and shape as a javelin. The third and longest portion of the case contains as many as six objects of the same general size and shape as a bow (spears, staffs, etc.). Once the owner has filled it, she can command the quiver each round to produce any stored items she wishes.

Caster Level: 9th; *Prerequisites:* Craft Wondrous Item, *Leomund's secret chest; Market Price:* 1,800 gp; *Weight:* —.

Ring Gates: These always come in pairs—two iron rings, each about 14 inches in diameter. The rings must be within 100 miles of each other to function. Whatever is put through one ring comes out the other, and up to 100 pounds of material can be transferred each day. (Objects only partially pushed through do not count.) This useful device allows for instantaneous transport of items, messages, and even attacks. A character can reach through to grab things near the other ring, or even stab a weapon through if so desired. Alternatively, a character could stick his head through to look around. A spellcaster could even cast a spell through a *ring gate.* A Small character can make an Escape Artist check (DC 13) to slip through. Creatures of Tiny, Diminutive, or Fine size can pass through easily. Each ring has a "entry side" and an "exit side," both marked with appropriate symbols.

Caster Level: 17th; *Prerequisites:* Craft Wondrous Item, *gate; Market Price:* 40,000 gp; *Weight:* 1 lb. each.

Robe of the Archmagi: This normal-appearing garment can be white (a 01–45 result on d%, good alignment), gray (46–75, neither good nor evil alignment), or black (76–100, evil alignment). Its wearer, if an arcane spellcaster, gains the following powers:

- +5 armor bonus to AC.
- Spell resistance 17.
- +1 resistance bonus to all saving throws.
- Ability to overcome the spell resistance of others as if she had the feat Spell Penetration.

If a white robe is donned by an evil character, she immediately gains three negative levels. The reverse is true with respect to a black robe donned by a good character. An evil or good character who puts on a gray robe, or a neutral character who dons either a white or black robe, gains two negative levels. While negative levels never result in lost levels, they remain as long as the garment is worn and cannot be overcome in any way (including *restoration* spells).

Caster Level: 14th; *Prerequisites:* Craft Wondrous Item, *mage armor, bless, spell resistance,* creator must be same alignment as robe; *Market Price:* 75,000 gp; *Weight:* 1 lb.

Robe of Blending: When this robe is put on, the wearer intuitively knows that the garment has very special properties. A *robe of blending* enables its wearer to appear to be part of his surroundings. This allows her to add a +15 circumstance bonus to her Hide check. Further, the wearer can adopt the appearance of another creature as in the spell *change self* at will. All creatures acquainted with and friendly to the wearer see him normally.

Caster Level: 10th; *Prerequisites:* Craft Wondrous Item, *change self; Market Price:* 10,000 gp; *Weight:* 1 lb.

Robe of Eyes: This valuable garment appears to be a normal robe until it is put on. Its wearer is able to see in all directions at the same moment due to scores of visible, magical eyelike patterns that adorn the robe. She also gains darkvision (range 120 feet). The *robe of eyes* sees all forms of invisible or ethereal things within 120 feet.

The *robe of eyes* grants its wearer a +15 circumstance bonus to Search and Spot checks. She retains her Dexterity bonus to AC even when flat-footed and can't be flanked. The wearer can't avert her eyes from or close her eyes to a creature with a gaze attack.

A *light* or *continual flame* spell thrown directly on a *robe of eyes* blinds it for 1d3 minutes. A *daylight* spell blinds it for 2d4 minutes.

Caster Level: 11th; *Prerequisites:* Craft Wondrous Item, *true seeing; Market Price:* 90,000 gp; *Weight:* 1 lb.

Robe of Scintillating Colors: The wearer can cause the garment to become a shifting pattern of incredible hues, color after color cascading from the upper part of the robe to the hem in sparkling rainbows of dazzling light. The colors daze those near the wearer, conceal the wearer, and illuminate the surroundings. It takes 1 full round after the wearer speaks the command word for the colors to start flowing on the robe.

The colors create the equivalent of a gaze attack with a 30-foot range. Those who look at the wearer are dazed for 1d4+1 rounds (Will negates DC 14). This is a mind-affecting pattern.

Every round of continuous scintillation of the robe gives the wearer better concealment. Miss chances start at 10% (one-quarter concealment) and increase another 10% each round until they reach 50% (full concealment).

The robe illuminates a 30-foot radius.

The effect can last no longer than a total of 10 rounds per day.

Caster Level: 15th; *Prerequisites:* Craft Wondrous Item, *hypnosis, color spray; Market Price:* 27,000 gp; *Weight:* 1 lb.

Robe of Stars: This garment is typically black or dark blue and embroidered with small white or silver stars. The robe has three magical powers.

- The robe enables its wearer to travel physically to the Astral Plane, along with all that she is wearing or carrying.
- The robe gives its wearer a +1 luck bonus to all saving throws.
- The robe's wearer can use up to six of the embroidered stars on the chest portion of the robe as *+5 shuriken.* The robe grants its wearer proficiency with such weapons. Each shuriken disappears after it is used.

Robe of eyes

Caster Level: 17th; *Prerequisites:* Craft Wondrous Item, *astral projection* or *plane shift, magic missile; Market Price:* 58,000 gp; *Weight:* 1 lb.

Robe of Useful Items: This appears to be an unremarkable robe, but a character who dons it notes that it is adorned with small cloth patches of various shapes. Only the wearer of the robe can see these patches, recognize them for what items they become, and detach them. One patch can be detached each round. Detaching a patch causes it to become an actual item, as indicated below. A newly created *robe of useful items* always has two each of the following patches:

- dagger
- bullseye lantern (filled and lit)
- mirror (a highly polished 2-foot-by-4-foot steel mirror)
- pole (10-foot length)
- hemp rope (50-foot coil)
- sack

In addition, the robe has 4d4 other items:

d%	Result
01–08	Bag of 100 gold pieces
09–15	Coffer, silver (6 in. by 6 in. by 1 ft.), 500 gp value
16–22	Door, iron (up to 10 ft. wide and 10 ft. high and barred on one side—must be placed upright, attaches and hinges itself)
23–30	Gems, 10 (100 gp value each)
31–44	Ladder, wooden (24 ft. long)
45–51	Mule (with saddle bags)
52–59	Pit, open (10 cubic ft.)
60–68	*Potion of cure serious wounds*
69–75	Rowboat (12 ft. long)
76–83	Minor scroll of one randomly determined spell
84–90	War dogs, pair (treat as riding dogs)
91–96	Window (2 ft. by 4 ft., up to 2 ft. deep)
97–100	Roll twice more

Multiple items of the same kind are permissible. Once removed, items cannot be replaced.

Caster Level: 9th; *Prerequisites:* Craft Wondrous Item, *fabricate; Market Price:* 7,000 gp; *Weight:* 1 lb.

Rope of Climbing: A 60-foot-long *rope of climbing* is no thicker than a slender wand, but it is strong enough to support 3,000 pounds. Upon command, the rope snakes forward, upward, downward, or in any other direction at 10 feet per round, attaching itself securely wherever its owner desires. It can unfasten itself and return in the same manner.

A *rope of climbing* can be commanded to knot or unknot itself. This causes large knots to appear at 1-foot intervals along the rope. Knotting shortens the rope to a 50-foot length until the knots are untied but lowers the DC of Climb checks while using it by 10. A creature must hold one end of the rope when its magic is invoked.

Caster Level: 3rd; *Prerequisites:* Craft Wondrous Item, *animate rope; Market Price:* 3,000 gp; *Weight:* 3 lb.

Rope of Entanglement: A *rope of entanglement* looks just like any other hemp rope about 30 feet long. Upon command, the rope lashes forward 20 feet or upward 10 feet to entangle a victim, using a grapple attack with a +15 attack bonus (including +4 for being Large and +6 for its Strength score of 22).

The rope cannot be broken by sheer strength. It must be severed by an edged weapon. The rope has an AC of 22, 12 hit points, and a hardness of 10. Damage repairs itself at a rate of 1 point per 5 minutes, but if a *rope of entanglement* is severed (all 12 hit points lost to damage), it is destroyed.

Caster Level: 12th; *Prerequisites:* Craft Wondrous Item, *entangle, animate rope, animate objects; Market Price:* 21,000 gp; *Weight:* 5 lb.

Scabbard of Keen Edges: This scabbard is fashioned from cured leather and fine silver. It can shrink or enlarge to accommodate any knife, dagger, sword, or similar weapon up to and including a greatsword. Up to three times per day on command, the scabbard casts *keen edge* on any blade placed within it.

Caster Level: 7th; *Prerequisites:* Craft Wondrous Item, *keen edge; Market Price:* 15,000 gp; *Weight:* 1 lb.

Scarab of Protection: This device appears to be a silver medallion in the shape of a beetle. It gives off a faint magical aura. If it is held for 1 round, an inscription appears on its surface letting the holder know that it is a protective device.

The scarab's possessor gains spell resistance 15. The scarab can also absorb up to twelve energy-draining attacks or death effects (such as *finger of death*). (An attack that would bestow two negative levels counts as two attacks.) However, upon absorbing twelve such attacks, the scarab turns to powder and is destroyed.

Caster Level: 18th; *Prerequisites:* Craft Wondrous Item, *bless, death ward, negative energy protection,* and *wish* or *miracle; Market Price:* 38,000 gp; *Weight:* —.

Scarab, Golembane: This beetle-shaped pin enables its wearer to detect any golem within 60 feet, although he must concentrate in order for the detection to take place. Furthermore, the scarab enables its possessor to combat a golem with weapons or unarmed attacks as if the golem had no damage reduction. Each scarab has this effect with regard to a different sort of golem.

Caster Level: 8th; *Prerequisites:* Craft Wondrous Item, *detect magic,* and *keen edge* or *holy power; Market Price:* 800 gp (flesh), 1,000 gp (clay), 1,200 gp (stone), 1,600 gp (iron), 1,800 gp (flesh and clay), or 2,500 gp (any golem); *Weight:* —.

Slippers of Spider Climbing: When worn, a pair of these slippers enable movement on vertical surfaces or even upside down along ceilings, leaving the wearer's hands free. Her speed is 15 feet. Extremely slippery surfaces—icy, oiled, or greased surfaces— make these slippers useless.

Caster Level: 4th; *Prerequisites:* Craft Wondrous Item, *spider climb; Market Price:* 2,000 gp; *Weight:* 1/2 lb.

Sovereign Glue: This pale amber substance is thick and viscous. Because of its particular powers, it can be contained only in a flask whose inside has been coated with 1 ounce of *oil of slipperiness,* and each time any of the bonding agent is poured from the flask, a new application of the *oil of slipperiness* must be put in the flask within 1 round to prevent the remaining glue from adhering to the side of the container. A flask of *sovereign glue,* when found, holds anywhere from 1 to 7 ounces of the stuff (1d8–1, minimum 1), with the other ounce of the flask's capacity taken up by the *oil of slipperiness.*

One ounce of this adhesive covers 1 square foot of surface, bonding virtually any two substances together in a permanent union. The glue takes 1 round to set. If the objects are pulled apart before that time has elapsed, that application of the glue loses its stickiness and is worthless. If the glue is allowed to set, then attempting to separate the two bonded objects only results in the rending of one or the other, except when *universal solvent* is applied to the bond. (*Sovereign glue* is dissolved by *universal solvent.*)

Caster Level: 20th; *Prerequisites:* Craft Wondrous Item, *make whole; Market Price:* 2,400 gp (per ounce); *Weight:* —.

Stone of Alarm: This stone cube, when given the command word, affixes itself to any object. If that object is touched thereafter by anyone who does not first speak that same command word, the stone emits a piercing screech for 1 hour that can be heard up to a quarter-mile away (assuming no intervening barriers).

Caster Level: 3rd; *Prerequisites:* Craft Wondrous Item, *alarm; Market Price:* 1,000 gp; *Weight:* 2 lb.

Stone of Controlling Earth Elementals: A stone of this nature is typically an oddly shaped bit of roughly polished rock. The possessor of such a stone need but utter a few words of summoning, and a Huge earth elemental comes to the summoner if earth, mud, or clay is available. The summoning words require

1 full round to speak, and in all ways the stone functions as the *summon monster VII* spell. (If sand or rough, unhewn stone is the summoning medium, the elemental that comes is Large instead, and the stone functions as the *summon monster VI* spell.) The area of summoning for an earth elemental must be at least 4 feet square and have a volume of 4 cubic yards. The elemental appears in 1d4 rounds. For detailed information about elementals, see the *Monster Manual*. Only one elemental can be summoned at a time. A new elemental requires a new patch of earth or stone, which cannot be accessed until after the first elemental disappears (is dispelled, dismissed, or slain).

Caster Level: 13th; *Prerequisites:* Craft Wondrous Item, *summon monster VI, summon monster VII; Market Price:* 100,000 gp; *Weight:* 5 lb.

Stone of Good Luck (Luckstone): This stone is typically a bit of rough polished agate or some similar mineral. Its possessor gains a +1 luck bonus on saving throws, ability checks, and skill checks.

Caster Level: 5th; *Prerequisites:* Craft Wondrous Item, *divine favor; Market Price:* 10,000 gp; *Weight:* —.

Stone Horse: Each item of this nature appears to be a full-sized, roughly hewn statue of a horse, carved from some type of hard stone. A command word brings the steed to life, enabling it to carry a burden and even to attack as if it were a real horse of the appropriate type.

A *stone horse* can carry 1,000 pounds tirelessly and never needs to rest or feed. Damage dealt to it can be repaired by first using a *stone to flesh* spell, thus causing the *stone horse* to become a normal horse that can be healed normally. When fully healed, it automatically reverts to its stone form. While in its stone form, it can be fed gemstones, healing 1 point of damage for each 50 gp worth of mineral it is given.

There are two sorts of *stone horses:*

Courser: This *stone horse* has all the same statistics as a heavy horse, as well as having a hardness of 10.

Destrier: This *stone horse* has all the same statistics as a heavy warhorse, as well as having a hardness of 10.

Caster Level: 14th; *Prerequisites:* Craft Wondrous Item, *flesh to stone, animate objects; Market Price:* 10,000 gp (courser) or 14,800 gp (destrier); *Weight:* 6,000 lb.

Stone Salve: This strange ointment has two uses. If an ounce of it is applied to the flesh of a petrified creature, it returns the creature to flesh (as the spell *stone to flesh*). If an ounce of it is applied to the flesh of a nonpetrified creature, it protects the creature as a *stoneskin* spell.

Caster Level: 13th; *Prerequisites:* Craft Wondrous Item, *flesh to stone, stoneskin; Market Price:* 4,000 gp per ounce; *Weight:* —.

Talisman of the Sphere: This small adamantine loop and handle are useless to those unable to cast arcane spells. Characters who cannot cast arcane spells take 5d6 points of damage merely from picking up and holding a talisman of this sort. However, when held by an arcane spellcaster who is concentrating on control of a *sphere of annihilation* (see page 238), a *talisman of the sphere* doubles the bonus for Intelligence and level for determining control.

If the wielder of a talisman establishes control, he need check for continual control only every other round thereafter. If control is not established, the sphere moves toward him. Note that while many spells and effects of cancellation have no effect upon a *sphere of annihilation*, the talisman's power of control can be suppressed or canceled.

Caster Level: 16th; *Prerequisites:* Craft Wondrous Item, *telekinesis; Market Price:* 9,000 gp; *Weight:* 1 lb.

Tome of Clear Thought: This heavy book contains instruction on improving memory and logic, but entwined within the words is a powerful magical effect. If anyone reads this book, which takes a total of 48 hours over a minimum of six days, she gains an inherent bonus of from +1 to +5 (depending on the type of tome) to her Intelligence score. Once the book is read, the magic disappears from the pages and it becomes a normal book.

Caster Level: 17th; *Prerequisites:* Craft Wondrous Item, *wish* or *miracle; Market Price:* 27,500 gp (+1), 55,000 gp (+2), 82,500 gp (+3), 110,000 gp (+4), or 137,500 gp (+5); *Cost to Create:* 1,250 gp + 5,100 XP (+1), 2,500 gp + 10,200 XP (+2), 3,750 gp + 15,300 XP (+3), 5,000 gp + 20,400 XP (+4), or 6,250 gp + 25,500 XP (+5); *Weight:* 5 lb.

Tome of Leadership and Influence: This ponderous book details suggestions for persuading and inspiring others, but entwined within the words is a powerful magical effect. If anyone reads this book, which takes a total of 48 hours over a minimum of six days, he gains an inherent bonus of from +1 to +5 (depending on the type of tome) to his Charisma score. Once the book is read, the magic disappears from the pages and it becomes a normal book.

Caster Level: 17th; *Prerequisites:* Craft Wondrous Item, *wish* or *miracle; Market Price:* 27,500 gp (+1), 55,000 gp (+2), 82,500 gp (+3), 110,000 gp (+4), or 137,500 gp (+5); *Cost to Create:* 1,250 gp + 5,100 XP (+1), 2,500 gp + 10,200 XP (+2), 3,750 gp + 15,300 XP (+3), 5,000 gp + 20,400 XP (+4), or 6,250 gp + 25,500 XP (+5); *Weight:* 5 lb.

Tome of Understanding: This thick book contains tips for improving instinct and perception, but entwined within the words is a powerful magical effect. If anyone reads this book, which takes a total of 48 hours over a minimum of six days, she gains an inherent bonus of from +1 to +5 (depending on the type of tome) to her Wisdom score. Once the book is read, the magic disappears from the pages and it becomes a normal book.

Tome of understanding

Caster Level: 17th; *Prerequisites:* Craft Wondrous Item, *wish* or *miracle; Market Price:* 27,500 gp (+1), 55,000 gp (+2), 82,500 gp (+3), 110,000 gp (+4), or 137,500 gp (+5); *Cost to Create:* 1,250 gp + 5,100 XP (+1), 2,500 gp + 10,200 XP (+2), 3,750 gp + 15,300 XP (+3), 5,000 gp + 20,400 XP (+4), or 6,250 gp + 25,500 XP (+5); *Weight:* 5 lb.

Universal Solvent: This strange liquid appears to be some sort of minor oil or potion and always comes in containers of 1 ounce. Upon first examination, it seems to have the properties of *oil of slipperiness*. However, if it is applied to any form of adhesive or sticky material, the solution immediately dissolves the other material. It immediately negates the effect of *sovereign glue*, as well as any other form of cement, glue, or adhesive. An ounce affects 1 cubic foot.

If the liquid is carefully distilled to bring it down to one-third of its original volume, each dose (1/3 ounce, having been a full ounce before distillation) dissolves 1 cubic foot of organic or inorganic material, just as if a *disintegrate* spell had been employed. To find out if a resisting target is affected by this concentrated solution, a touch attack roll is required, and the subject is entitled to a Fortitude saving throw (DC 19).

Caster Level: 20th; *Prerequisites:* Craft Wondrous Item, *disintegrate; Market Price:* 2,000 gp (per ounce); *Weight:* —.

Vest of Escape: Hidden within secret pockets of this simple silk vest are lockpicks that add a +4 competence bonus to Open Lock checks. If the lockpicks are separated by more than 15 feet from the vest, they lose their competence bonus, but the bonus returns when they are returned to the pockets of the vest. Further, the vest grants the wearer a +6 competence bonus to Escape Artist checks.

Illus. by W. Reynolds

Caster Level: 4th; *Prerequisites:* Craft Wondrous Item, *knock, grease; Market Price:* 2,000 gp; *Weight:* —.

Vestment, Druid's: This light garment is worn over normal clothing or armor. Most such vestments are green, embroidered with plant or animal motifs. When worn by a druid with the wild shape ability, the character can use that ability one additional time each day.

Caster Level: 10th; *Prerequisites:* Craft Wondrous Item, *polymorph self* or creator must be at least a 10th-level druid; *Market Price:* 5,800 gp; *Weight:* —.

Vestments of Faith: This holy garment, worn over normal clothing, grants a special protection (damage reduction 5/+5) to the character wearing it.

Caster Level: 20th; *Prerequisites:* Craft Wondrous Item, *stoneskin; Market Price:* 76,000 gp; *Weight:* —.

Well of Many Worlds: This strange, interdimensional device looks just like a *portable hole.* Anything placed within it is immediately cast to another world—a parallel world, another planet, or a different plane, at the DM's option or by random determination. If the well is moved, the random factor again comes into play. It can be picked up, folded, or rolled, just like a *portable hole.* Objects from the world the well touches can come through the opening just as easily as from the initiating place. (It is a two-way portal.)

Caster Level: 17th; *Prerequisites:* Craft Wondrous Item, *gate; Market Price:* 82,000 gp; *Weight:* —.

Wind Fan: A *wind fan* appears to be nothing more than a wood and papyrus or cloth instrument with which to create a cooling breeze. By uttering the command word, its possessor causes the fan to generate air movement duplicating a *gust of wind* spell. The fan can be used once per day with no risk. If it is used more frequently, there is a 20% cumulative chance per usage that the device tears into useless, nonmagical tatters.

Caster Level: 5th; *Prerequisites:* Craft Wondrous Item, *gust of wind; Market Price:* 5,500 gp; *Weight:* —.

Wings of Flying: A pair of these wings might appear to be nothing more than a plain cloak of old, black cloth, or they could be as elegant as a long cape of blue feathers. When the wearer speaks the command word, the cloak turns into a pair of gigantic wings (bat or bird, 20-foot span) and empower her to fly as with a *fly* spell.

Caster Level: 5th; *Prerequisites:* Craft Wondrous Item, *fly; Market Price:* 5,500 gp; *Weight:* 2 lb.

INTELLIGENT ITEMS

Magic items sometimes possess intelligence of their own. Magically imbued with sentience, these items think and feel the same way characters do and should be treated as NPCs. They can be many things to characters—valued ally, wily foe, or continual thorn in their side. Intelligent items have extra abilities and sometimes extraordinary powers and special purposes. Only permanent magic items (rather than those with one use or with charges) can be intelligent. (This means that potions, scrolls, and wands, among other items, are never intelligent.) Melee weapons have intelligence 15% of the time (a 01–15 result on d%), ranged weapons have intelligence 5% of the time (a 01–05 result on d%), and items of other sorts are intelligent only 1% of the time (a 01 result on d%). Intelligent items can actually be considered creatures since they have Intelligence, Wisdom, and Charisma scores. (See the entry on constructs in the *Monster Manual.*)

The tables below should be used to determine the properties of an intelligent item: the number of powers, unusual properties, alignment, and special purpose of the item (if any). Of the three mental ability scores, two scores are favored (2d6 + some number) and one is completely random (3d6). Choose which scores get assigned which number, or roll 1d4 and determine randomly according to the following table:

1d4	High Score	Medium Score	Low Score
1	Intelligence	Charisma	Wisdom
2	Intelligence	Wisdom	Charisma
3	Wisdom	Intelligence	Charisma
4	Charisma	Intelligence	Wisdom

The DM is encouraged to design unusual magic items along special themes and for specific campaign purposes, using the tables as guidelines and for inspiration. Just because a power is rolled does not mean it must be given out. If you feel a combination is too bizarre or too powerful, simply change or ignore it.

The first step in determining the properties of a random intelligent item is to determine its general capabilities. These are found by rolling d% and consulting Table 8–31: Item Intelligence, Wisdom, Charisma, and Capacities.

INTELLIGENT ITEM ALIGNMENT

Any item with Intelligence has an alignment. Note that intelligent weapons already have alignments, either stated or by implication. (A foekiller mace made to kill chaotic outsiders would hardly be chaotic itself; it would be lawful.) If you're generating a random intelligent weapon, that weapon's alignment must fit with any alignment-oriented special properties it has (such as "holy").

TABLE 8–31: ITEM INTELLIGENCE, WISDOM, CHARISMA, AND CAPABILITIES

d%	Mental Ability Scores	Communication	Capabilities	Market Price Modifier
01–34	Two at 2d6+5, one at 3d6	Semiempathy*	One primary ability	+10,000 gp
35–59	Two at 2d6+6, one at 3d6	Empathy**	Two primary abilities	+15,000 gp
60–79	Two at 2d6+7, one at 3d6	Speech†	Two primary abilities	+17,500 gp
80–91	Two at 2d6+8, one at 3d6	Speech†	Three primary abilities	+25,000 gp
92–97	Two at 2d6+9, one at 3d6	Speech†	Three primary abilities‡	+32,000 gp
98	Two at 2d6+10, one at 3d6	Speech, telepathy††	Three primary abilities‡ and one extraordinary power	+55,000 gp
99	Two at 2d6+11, one at 3d6	Speech, telepathy††	Three primary abilities‡‡ and two extraordinary powers	+78,000 gp
100	Two at 2d6+12, one at 3d6	Speech, telepathy††	Four primary abilities‡‡ and two extraordinary powers	+90,000 gp

*The possessor receives some signal (a throb or tingle, for example) when the item's ability functions.

**The possessor feels urges and sometimes emotions from the item that encourage or discourage certain courses of action.

†Like a character, an intelligent item speaks Common plus one language per point of Intelligence bonus.

††The item can use either communication mode at will, with language use as any speaking item.

‡The item can also read any languages it can speak.

‡‡The item can read all languages as well as *read magic.*

TABLE 8–32: ITEM ALIGNMENT

d%	Alignment of Item
01–05	Chaotic good
06–15	Chaotic neutral*
16–20	Chaotic evil
21–25	Neutral evil*
26–30	Lawful evil
31–55	Lawful good
56–60	Lawful neutral*
61–80	Neutral good*
81–100	Neutral

*The item can also be used by any character whose alignment corresponds to the nonneutral portion of the item's alignment (in other words, chaotic, evil, good, or lawful). Thus, any chaotic character (CG, CN, CE) can use an item with chaotic neutral alignment.

Any character whose alignment does not correspond to that of the item (except as noted by the asterisk on Table 8–32), gains one negative level if he or she so much as picks up the item. Although this never results in actual level loss, the negative level remains as long as the item is in hand and cannot be overcome in any way (including *restoration* spells). This negative level is cumulative with any other penalties the item might already place on inappropriate wielders. Items with Egos (see below) of 20 to 30 bestow two negative levels. Items with Egos of 30 or higher bestow three negative levels.

LANGUAGES SPOKEN BY ITEM

Like a character, an intelligent item speaks Common plus one language per point of Intelligence bonus. Choose appropriate languages, taking into account the item's origin and purposes For instance, an intelligent drow weapon would probably speak Elven, and a holy weapon might speak Celestial.

INTELLIGENT ITEM ABILITIES

Using the number of capabilities determined above, find the item's specific abilities by rolling on the appropriate tables below.

TABLE 8–33: INTELLIGENT ITEM PRIMARY ABILITIES

d%	Primary Ability
01–04	Item can Intuit Direction (10 ranks)
05–08	Item can Sense Motive (10 ranks)
09–12	Wielder has free use of Combat Reflexes
13–16	Wielder has free use of Blind-Fight
17–20	Wielder has free use of Improved Initiative
21–24	Wielder has free use of Mobility
25–28	Wielder has free use of Sunder
29–32	Wielder has free use of Expertise
33–39	*Detect [opposing alignment]* at will
40–42	*Find traps* at will
43–47	*Detect secret doors* at will
48–54	*Detect magic* at will
55–57	Wielder has free use of uncanny dodge (as a 5th-level barbarian)
58–60	Wielder has free use of evasion
61–65	Wielder can *see invisible* at will
66–70	*Cure light wounds* (1d8+5) on wielder 1/day
71–75	*Feather fall* on wielder 1/day
76	*Locate object* in a 120-ft. radius
77	Wielder does not need to sleep
78	Wielder does not need to breathe
79	*Jump* for 20 minutes on wielder 1/day
80	*Spider climb* for 20 minutes on wielder 1/day
81–90	Roll twice again on this table
91–100	Roll on Table 8–34: Intelligent Item Extraordinary Powers instead

If the same ability is rolled twice or more, the range, frequency, or effectiveness of the power is doubled, tripled, and so on.

All abilities function only when the item is held, drawn, or otherwise brandished and the possessor is concentrating on the desired result. Activating a power is a standard action, but using a free feat is not. Feats may be used regardless of prerequisites, but the item still must be held and drawn. At the DM's discretion, an intelligent item might activate a power on its own.

TABLE 8–34: INTELLIGENT ITEM EXTRAORDINARY POWERS

d%	Extraordinary Power	Times Per Day
01–05	*Charm person* (DC 11) on contact	3/day
06–10	*Clairaudience/clairvoyance* (100-ft. range, 1 minute per use)	3/day
11–15	*Magic missile* (200-ft. range, 3 missiles)	3/day
16–20	*Shield* on wielder	3/day
21–25	*Detect thoughts* (100-ft. range, 1 minute per use)	3/day
26–30	*Levitation* (wielder only, 10 minute duration)	3/day
31–35	*Invisibility* (wielder only, up to 30 minutes per use)	3/day
36–40	*Fly* (30 minutes per use)	2/day
41–45	*Lightning bolt* (8d6 points of damage, 200-ft. range, DC 13)	1/day
46–50	*Summon monster III*	1/day
51–55	*Telepathy* (100 ft. range)	2/day
56–60	*Cat's grace* (wielder only)	1/day
61–65	*Bull's strength* (wielder only)	1/day
66–70	*Haste* (wielder only, 10 rounds)	1/day
71–73	*Telekinesis* (250 lb. maximum, 1 minute each use)	2/day
74–76	*Heal*	1/day
77	*Teleport*, 600 lb. maximum	1/day
78	*Globe of invulnerability*	1/day
79	*Stoneskin* (wielder only, 10 minutes per use)	2/day
80	*Feeblemind* by touch	2/day
81	*True seeing*	At will
82	*Wall of force*	1/day
83	*Summon monster VI*	1/day
84	*Finger of death* (100 ft. range, DC 17)	1/day
85	*Passwall*	At will
86–90	Roll twice again on this table	—
91–100	Roll again on this table, and then roll for a special purpose on Table 8–35: Intelligent Item Purpose	—

If the same power is rolled twice, the uses per day are doubled. If *true seeing* or *passwall* is rolled twice, roll again.) Powers chosen by the possessor are then set and never again changing for that character.

Powers function only when the item is drawn and held, and the possessor is concentrating upon the desired effect. Activating a power is a standard action. At the DM's discretion, an intelligent item might activate a power on its own.

SPECIAL PURPOSE ITEMS

Items with special purposes are a challenge to run. However, they are worth the trouble, because they can deeply enrich a campaign.

Purpose

An item's purpose must suit the type and alignment of the item and should always be treated reasonably. A purpose of "defeat/slay arcane spellcasters" doesn't mean that the sword forces the wielder to kill every wizard she sees. Nor does it mean that the sword believes it is possible to kill every wizard, sorcerer, and bard in the world. It does mean that the item hates arcane spellcasters and wants to bring the local wizard's cabal to ruin, as well as end the rule of a sorceress-queen in a nearby land. Likewise, a purpose of "defend elves" doesn't mean that if the wielder is an elf, he only wants to help himself. It means that the item wants to be used in furthering the cause of elves, stamping out their enemies and aiding their leaders. A purpose of "defeat/slay all" isn't just a matter of self-preservation. It means that the item won't rest (or let its wielder rest) until it places itself above all others. A lofty—and probably unrealistic—goal, to be sure.

TABLE 8–35: INTELLIGENT ITEM PURPOSE

d%	Purpose
01–20	Defeat/slay diametrically opposed alignment*
21–30	Defeat/slay arcane spellcasters (including spellcasting monsters and those that use spell-like abilities)
31–40	Defeat/slay divine spellcasters (including divine entities and servitors)
41–50	Defeat/slay nonspellcasters
51–55	Defeat/slay a particular creature type (see *Monster Manual* for choices)
56–60	Defeat/slay a particular race or kind of creature
61–70	Defend a particular race or kind of creature
71–80	Defeat/slay the servants of a specific deity
81–90	Defend the servants and interests of a specific deity
91–95	Defeat/slay all (other than the item and the wielder)
96–100	DM's or character's choice

*The purpose of the neutral (N) version of this item is to preserve the balance by defeating/slaying powerful beings of the extreme alignments (LG, LE, CG, CE).

Special Purpose Power

A special purpose power operates only when the item is in pursuit of its special purpose. This is always up to the purview of the item. It should always be easy and straightforward to see how the ends justify the means. That is to say that if the player's reasoning for how a particular action serves the item's purpose is not completely believable, the item won't allow it.

TABLE 8–36: INTELLIGENT ITEM SPECIAL PURPOSE POWERS

d%	Special Purpose Power
01–10	*Blindness** (DC 12) for 2d6 rounds
11–20	*Confusion** (DC 14) for 2d6 rounds
21–25	*Fear** (DC 14) for 1d4 rounds
26–55	*Hold monster** (DC 14) for 1d4 rounds
56–65	*Slay living** (DC 15)
66–75	*Disintegrate** (DC 16)
76–80	*True resurrection* on wielder, one time only
81–100	+2 luck bonus to all saving throws, +2 deflection AC bonus, spell resistance 15

*This power affects the opponent of the item's wielder on a successful hit unless the opponent makes a Will save at the listed DC.

ITEM EGO

Ego is a measure of the total power and force of personality that an item possesses. Only after all aspects of an item have been generated and recorded can its Ego score be determined. Ego is a factor with regard to the dominance of item over character, as detailed below.

TABLE 8–37: ITEM EGO

Attribute of Item	Ego Points
Each +1 enhancement of item	1
Each +1 bonus of special abilities	1
Each primary ability*	1
Each extraordinary power*	2
Special purpose	4
Telepathic ability	1
Read languages ability	1
Read magic ability	1
Each +1 of Intelligence bonus	1
Each +1 of Wisdom bonus	1
Each +1 of Charisma bonus	1

*If double ability, double Ego points.

Thus, a *+2 short sword* (2 Ego points) with an Intelligence score of 10, Wisdom score of 13 (1 Ego point), and Charisma score of 11, plus the primary ability of finding traps (1 Ego point) has an Ego score of 4. By contrast, imagine a *+1 flaming longsword* (3 Ego points, 1 for the +1 enhancement bonus and 2 for the +2 bonus value of flaming [see Table 8–15: Weapon Special Abilities]) with an Intelligence score of 16 (3 Ego points), Wisdom of 15 (2 Ego points), and Charisma of 19 (4 Ego points). Add the primary abilities of *detect magic*, Sunder, and Evasion (3 Ego points), the extraordinary powers to *heal* (2 Ego points) and *fly* (2 Ego points), and the special purpose power to disintegrate spellcasters (4 Ego points). Also include the fact that the weapon is telepathic (1 Ego point) and reads languages (1 Ego point), and the sword has a total Ego score of 25.

ITEMS AGAINST CHARACTERS

When an item has an Ego of its own, it has a will of its own. The item is, of course, absolutely true to its alignment. If the character who possesses the item is not true to that alignment's goals or the item's special purpose, personality conflict—item against character—results. Similarly, any item with an Ego score of 20 or higher always considers itself superior to any character, and a personality conflict results if the possessor does not always agree with the item.

When a personality conflict occurs, the possessor must make a Will saving throw (DC = item's Ego). If the possessor succeeds, she is dominant. If she fails, the item is dominant. Dominance lasts for one day or until a critical situation occurs (such as a major battle, a serious threat to either item or character, and so on—DM discretion). Should a item gain dominance, it resists the character's desires and demands concessions such as any of the following:

- Removal of associates or items whose alignment or personality is distasteful to the item.
- The character divesting herself of all other magic items or items of a certain type.
- Obedience from the character so the item can direct where they go for its own purposes.
- Immediate seeking out and slaying of creatures hateful to the item.
- Magical protections and devices to protect the item from molestation when it is not in use.
- That the character carry the item with her on all occasions.
- That the character relinquish the item in favor of a more suitable possessor due to alignment differences or conduct.

In extreme circumstances, the item can resort to even harsher measures:

- Force its possessor into combat.
- Refuse to strike opponents.
- Strike at its wielder or her associates.
- Force its possessor to surrender to an opponent.
- Cause itself to drop from the character's grasp.

Naturally, such actions are unlikely when harmony reigns between the character's and item's alignments or when their purposes and personalities are well matched. Even so, an item might wish to have a lesser character possess it in order to easily command him, or a higher-level possessor so as to better accomplish its goals.

All magic items with personalities desire to play an important role in whatever activity is under way, particularly combat. Such items are rivals of each other, even if they are of the same alignment. No intelligent item wants to share its wielder with others. An intelligent item is aware of the presence of any other intelligent item within 60 feet, and most intelligent items try their best to mislead or distract their host so that she ignores or destroys the rival. Of course, alignment might change this sort of behavior. A *holy avenger*, for example, would certainly not allow destruction of any other lawful good item and might encourage their discovery, even at the risk of having to face grim odds to do so.

Items with personalities are never totally controlled or silenced by the characters who possess them, even though they may never successfully control their possessor. They may be powerless to force their demands but remain undaunted and continue to air their wishes and demands. Even a humble +1 weapon of unusual nature can be a vocal martyr, denigrating its own abilities and asking only that the character give it the chance to shatter itself against some hated enemy.

Note: You should assume the personality of the item as you would with any NPC. Refer to Chapter 5: Campaigns, especially Table 5–5: One Hundred Traits (page 150), for ideas on personality quirks to make an intelligent item's persona more memorable.

CURSED ITEMS

In the process of crafting a magic item, so many delicate factors have to be taken into account that occasionally things are bound to go awry. These small errors are often readily apparent and usually show up immediately. Sometimes, however, they are more subtle and don't emerge until days, months, or even years later.

Other factors can make a magic item go wrong as well—things not the fault of its creator in any way. The forces of chaos and general entropy can cause magic to decay or become corrupted. Time corrodes all things—even magic. Long exposure to powerful magical forces, gateways to other planes, or even the proximity of other magic items or creatures can alter a magic item in odd ways.

Finally, items with unpredictable or cursed effects can be created by the devious intention of spellcasters who are malicious, chaotic, or simply insane. These are the most dangerous cursed items of all.

Cursed items are magic items with some sort of potentially negative impact. Sometimes they're directly bad for the user, sometimes they're just inconvenient. Occasionally they mix bad with good, forcing characters to make difficult choices. If you want to include the chance for cursed items in your game, determine treasure randomly as usual. Whenever you roll for a magic item, however, make a second secret d% roll. On a result of 01–05, the item generated is cursed in some way. To determine how the item is cursed, consult the table below.

TABLE 8–38: CURSED ITEM COMMON CURSES

d%	Curse
01–15	Delusion
16–35	Opposite effect or target
36–45	Intermittent functioning
46–60	Requirement
61–75	Drawback
76–90	Completely different effect
91–100	Substitute specific cursed item

COMMON CURSE DESCRIPTIONS

The most common curses that items can possess are described below.

Delusion: The user believes the item is what it appears to be, yet it actually has no magical power other than to deceive. The user is mentally fooled into thinking the item is functioning (making him invisible, emitting lightning bolts, or whatever) and cannot be convinced otherwise without the help of a *remove curse*.

Opposite Effect or Target: These cursed items malfunction, so that either they do the opposite of what the creator intended, or they target the user instead of someone else. For example, *eyes of charming* with the opposite effect enrage targets rather than charm them. A *rod of curing* inflicts wounds. *Eyes of petrification* turn the wearer to stone. A magic arrow curves around to strike the archer. The interesting point to keep in mind here is that these items aren't

always bad to have. A *wand of lightning bolt* that heals rather than harms can be used as a potent healing item.

Opposite-effect items include weapons that impose penalties on attack and damage rolls rather than bonuses. Just as a character shouldn't necessarily immediately know what the bonus of a good magic item is, she shouldn't immediately know that the weapon is so cursed. Once she knows, however, the item can be discarded unless some sort of enchantment is placed upon it that compels the wielder to keep and use it. In such cases, a *remove curse* spell is generally needed to get rid of such an item.

Intermittent Functioning: The three varieties of intermittent functioning items all function perfectly as described—at least some of the time. The three types include unreliable, dependent, and uncontrolled items.

Unreliable: Each time the item is activated, there is a 5% chance (a 01–05 result on d%) that it does not function. At the DM's option, the failure chance can be altered to be anything from 1% to 10%, depending on the item and the campaign.

Dependent: The item only functions in certain situations. To determine what the situation is, either select an activation condition or roll on the following table.

d%	Situation
01–03	Temperature below freezing
04–05	Temperature above freezing
06–10	During the day
11–15	During the night
16–20	In direct sunlight
21–25	Out of direct sunlight
26–34	Underwater
35–37	Out of water
38–45	Underground
46–55	Aboveground
56–60	Within 10 feet of a random creature type
61–64	Within 10 feet of a random race or kind of creature
65–72	Within 10 feet of an arcane spellcaster
73–80	Within 10 feet of a divine spellcaster
81–85	In the hands of a nonspellcaster
86–90	In the hands of a spellcaster
91–95	In the hands of a creature of a particular alignment
96	In the hands of a creature of particular gender
97–99	On nonholy days or during particular astrological events
100	More than 100 miles from a particular site (holy, magical, etc.)

Uncontrolled: An uncontrolled item occasionally activates at random times. Roll d% every day. On a result of 01–05 (or whatever range the DM determines as appropriate), the item activates at some random point during that day. Results range from the humorous, such as when the wearer of a *ring of invisibility* suddenly disappears right in the middle of bargaining in the market, to the disastrous, such as when the wielder's *wand of fireball* discharges in the middle of her friends—er, former friends.

Requirement: In a sense, a command word is a requirement. Nevertheless, some items have much more stringent requirements to be used. To keep the item functioning, one (or more) of the following conditions must be met:

- Character must eat twice as much as normal.
- Character must sleep twice as much as normal.
- Character must undergo a specific quest (one time only, and then item functions normally thereafter).
- Character must sacrifice (destroy) 100 gp worth of valuables per day.
- Character must sacrifice (destroy) 2,000 gp worth of magic items each week.
- Character must swear fealty to a particular noble or his family.
- Character must discard all other magic items.

- Character must worship a particular deity.
- Character must change her name to a specific name. (The item only works for characters of that name.)
- Character must change his class to a specific class if not of that class already.
- Character must have a minimum number of ranks in a particular skill.
- Character must sacrifice some part of her life energy (2 points of Constitution) one time. If the character gets the Constitution points back (such as from *restoration*), the item ceases functioning. (The item does not cease functioning if the character receives a Constitution increase caused by level gain, a *wish*, or the use of a magic item.)
- Item must be cleansed with holy water each day.
- Item must be used to kill a living creature each day.
- Item must be bathed in volcanic lava once per month.
- Item must be used at least once a day, or it won't function again for its current possessor.
- Item must draw blood when wielded (weapons only). It can't be put away or exchanged for another weapon until it has scored a hit.
- Item must have a particular spell cast upon it each day (such as *bless*, *atonement*, or *animate objects*).

Requirements are so dependent upon suitability to the item that they should never be determined randomly. An item with a requirement that is also intelligent often imposes its requirement through its personality. If the requirement is not met, the item ceases to function. If it is met, usually the item functions for one day before the requirement must be met again (although some requirements are one-time-only, others monthly, and still others continuous).

Drawback: Items with drawbacks are usually beneficial to the possessor (for instance, a weapon with an enhancement bonus still benefits its wielder in combat), but they also carry some negative aspect. You might think of them as "give and take" items. Although sometimes drawbacks occur only when the item is used (or held, in the case of some items such as weapons), usually the drawback remains with the character for as long as she has it.

The following are drawbacks that remain in effect as long as the item is in the character's possession:

d%	Drawback
01–04	Character's hair grows 1 inch longer (only happens once).
05–09	Character either shrinks a half-inch (a 01–50 result on d%) or grows that much taller (a 51–100 result). This event only happens once.

d%	Drawback
10–13	Temperature around item is 10°F cooler than normal.
14–17	Temperature around item is 10°F warmer than normal.
18–21	Character's hair color changes.
22–25	Character's skin color changes.
26–29	Character now bears some identifying mark (tattoo, strange glow, etc.).
30–32	Character's gender changes.
33–34	Character's race or kind changes.
35	Character is afflicted with a random disease that cannot be cured.
36–39	Item continually emits a disturbing sound (moaning, weeping, screaming, cursing, insults).
40	Item looks ridiculous (garishly colored, silly shape, glows bright pink, etc.).
41–45	Character becomes selfishly possessive about the item.
46–49	Character becomes paranoid about losing the item and afraid of damage occurring to it.
50–51	Character's alignment changes.
52–54	Character must attack nearest creature (5% chance [a 01–05 result on d%] each day).
55–57	Character is stunned for 1d4 rounds once item function is finished (or randomly, 1/day).
58–60	Character's vision is blurry (–2 penalty to attacks, saves, and skill checks requiring vision).
61–64	Character gains one negative level.
65	Character gains two negative levels.
66–70	Character must make a Will save each day or take 1 point of temporary Intelligence damage.
71–75	Character must make a Will save each day or take 1 point of temporary Wisdom damage.
76–80	Character must make a Will save each day or take 1 point of temporary Charisma damage.
81–85	Character must make a Fortitude save each day or take 1 point of temporary Constitution damage.
86–90	Character must make a Fortitude save each day or take 1 point of temporary Strength damage.
91–95	Character must make a Fortitude save each day or take 1 point of temporary Dexterity damage.
96	Character is polymorphed into a specific creature (5% chance [a 01–05 result on d%] each day).
97	Character cannot cast arcane spells.
98	Character cannot cast divine spells.
99	Character cannot cast any spells.
100	DM's choice: DM either picks one of the above that's appropriate or creates a drawback specifically for that item.

BEHIND THE CURTAIN: PUTTING CURSED ITEMS IN YOUR GAME

Some DMs decide not to use cursed items because they complicate the discovery process, since everyone is nervous about trying to use a new item. Other DMs include them for a variation of the same reason: Discovering new items becomes more exciting, because there's always at least a minor hint of danger.

Items with requirements and drawbacks force players to make difficult decisions, which makes for interesting roleplaying opportunities: "Do I want the *+5 sword,* even though it occasionally makes me attack my friends?" "Do I keep the *rod of curing,* even though it puts me at –1 to attacks, saves, and checks?"

Don't give out a lot of cursed items that characters can't get rid of—that only becomes annoying to players. While some cursed items are meant to hassle the players a little, too much annoyance detracts from fun game play. Once a player has figured out that her

character has a cursed item, most of the time she should just be able to rid herself of it.

And of course, some cursed items aren't really that bad. *Dust of sneezing and choking,* once it's identified, can be a potent weapon. Some, players who identify cursed items for what they really are will still try to think of some use for them. Some DMs assume that players automatically discard cursed items, which is not necessarily the case. Expect most to do so, but don't step on the creativity of those who think of some ingenious use for a cursed item.

Some of the items on the regular magic item tables have drawbacks or limitations but aren't mentioned in this section. That's because either the item is still so good to have that no one would think twice about using it, or the item is too interesting to automatically exclude it from a campaign, even if cursed items aren't used.

Completely Different Effect: The DM should choose a negative effect for the item, perhaps using the specific cursed items (see below) as examples. The item may seem to be the item that was originally determined, but at some juncture it displays different properties altogether.

TABLE 8–39: SPECIFIC CURSED ITEMS

d%	Item	Market Price
01–05	Incense of obsession	200 gp
06–15	Ring of clumsiness	500 gp
16–20	Amulet of inescapable location	1,000 gp
21–25	Stone of weight	1,000 gp
26–30	Bracers of defenselessness	1,200 gp
31–35	Gauntlets of fumbling	1,300 gp
36–40	–2 sword, cursed	1,500 gp
41–43	Armor of rage	1,600 gp
44–46	Medallion of thought projection	1,800 gp
47–50	Spear, cursed backbiter	2,000 gp
51–55	Flask of curses	2,100 gp
56–57	Dust of sneezing and choking	2,400 gp
58	Helm of opposite alignment	4,000 gp
59–64	Potion of poison	5,000 gp
65	Broom of animated attack	5,200 gp
66–67	Robe of powerlessness	5,500 gp
68	Vacuous grimoire	6,000 gp
69–70	Armor of arrow attraction	9,000 gp
71–72	Net of snaring	10,000 gp
73–75	Bag of devouring	15,500 gp
76–80	Mace of blood	16,000 gp
81–85	Robe of vermin	16,500 gp
86–88	Periapt of foul rotting	17,000 gp
89–92	Sword, berserking	17,500 gp
93–96	Boots of dancing	30,000 gp
97	Crystal hypnosis ball	—
98	Necklace of strangulation	60,000 gp
99	Cloak of poisonousness	62,000 gp
100	Scarab of death	80,000 gp

SPECIFIC CURSED ITEMS

The following items are provided as examples of cursed items. They are given creation prerequisites, should someone want to intentionally create them (although that does not need to be the origin of the item if you choose otherwise). Note, however, two exceptions: The *crystal hypnosis ball* and the *bag of devouring* cannot be created by any known means. The *bag of devouring* is a creature, and the *crystal hypnosis ball* is the tool of powerful NPCs such as liches. Market prices are listed to facilitate construction of the items, but players will generally not be able to sell cursed items.

All of the following are relatively common cursed items. They may be used as is, or may serve as good examples you to create your own.

Amulet of Inescapable Location: This device is typically worn on a chain or as a brooch. It appears, to magical analysis, to prevent location, scrying (*crystal ball* viewing and the like), or detection or influence by *detect thoughts* or telepathy. Actually, the amulet doubles the likelihood and/or range of these location and detection modes. Item identification attempts, including *identify*, *analyze dweomer*, *detect magic*, and so on, do not reveal its true nature.

Caster Level: 10th; *Prerequisites:* Create Wondrous Item, *bestow curse; Market Price:* 1,000 gp.

Armor of Arrow Attraction: Magical analysis indicates that this armor is a normal suit of *+3 full plate*. However, the armor is cursed. It works normally in regard to melee attacks but actually serves to attract ranged weapons. The wearer has twice the normal chance to be selected as a random target of a ranged weapon. In cases where each individual in a group is the target of a set number of ranged weapons (such as in large-scale combats with multiple archers), the wearer has twice as many weapons fired at him. Furthermore, the magical protection of the armor does not apply for ranged attacks. The true nature of the armor does not reveal itself until the character is fired upon in earnest—simple experiments (throwing rocks, for example) do not suffice.

Caster Level: 16th; *Prerequisites:* Craft Magic Arms and Armor, *bestow curse; Market Price:* 9,000 gp.

Armor of Rage: This armor is similar in appearance to *armor of command* and functions as a suit of *+1 full plate*. However, when it is worn, the armor causes the character to suffer a –4 Charisma penalty. All unfriendly characters within 300 feet have a +1 morale bonus on attacks against her. The effect is not noticeable to the wearer or those affected. (In other words, the wearer does not immediately notice that donning the armor is the cause of her problems, nor do foes understand the reason for the depth of their enmity.)

Caster Level: 16th; *Prerequisites:* Craft Magic Arms and Armor, *bestow curse; Market Price:* 1,600 gp.

Bag of Devouring: This bag appears to be an ordinary sack. Detection for magical properties makes it seem as if it were a *bag of holding*. The sack is, however, a lure used by an extradimensional creature—in fact, one of its feeding orifices.

Any substance of animal or vegetable nature is subject to "swallowing" if thrust within the bag. The *bag of devouring* is 90% likely to ignore any initial intrusion, but any time thereafter that it senses living flesh within (such as if someone reaches into the bag to pull something out), it is 60% likely to close around the offending member and attempt to draw the whole victim in. The bag has a Strength of 23 for purposes of pulling someone in.

The bag radiates magic and can hold up to 30 cubic feet of matter. It acts as a *bag of holding* (bag 1), but each hour it has a 5% cumulative chance of swallowing the contents and then spitting the stuff out in some nonspace or other plane. Creatures drawn within are consumed in 1 round, eaten, and gone forever.

Caster Level: 17th; *Prerequisites:* In effect, this is a minor artifact and cannot be created; *Market Price:* 15,500 gp (but note that the bag cannot be created, since it is a creature).

Boots of Dancing: These boots initially function as one of the other types of useful boots (DM's choice) and are indistinguishable from other magic boots. But when the wearer is in (or fleeing from) melee combat, the *boots of dancing* impede movement, making him behave as if *Otto's irresistible dance* had been cast upon him. Only a *remove curse* enables the boots to be removed once their true nature is revealed.

Caster Level: 16th; *Prerequisites:* Create Wondrous Item, *Otto's irresistible dance; Market Price:* 30,000 gp.

Bracers of Defenselessness: These appear to be *+5 bracers of armor* and actually serve as such until the wearer is attacked in anger by an enemy with a Challenge Rating equal to or greater than her level. At that moment and thereafter, the bracers inflict a –5 penalty to AC. Once their curse is activated, *bracers of defenselessness* can be removed only by means of a *remove curse* spell.

Caster Level: 16th; *Prerequisites:* Create Wondrous Item, *mage armor, bestow curse; Market Price:* 1,200 gp.

Broom of Animated Attack: This is indistinguishable in appearance from a normal broom, except that detection

Bag of devouring

spells reveal it to be magical. It is identical to a *broom of flying* by all tests short of attempted use. Using it reveals that a *broom of animated attack* is a very nasty item.

If a command ("Fly," "Go," "Giddy-up," or some similar command) is spoken, the broom does a loop-the-loop with its hopeful rider, dumping him on his head from 1d4+5 feet off the ground (no falling damage, since the fall is less than 10 feet). The broom then attacks the victim, swatting the face with the straw or twig end and beating him with the fhandle end.

The broom gets two attacks per round with each end (two swats with the straw and two with the handle, for a total of four attacks per round). It attacks with a +5 bonus on each attack. The straw end causes blindness for 1 round if it hits. The handle causes 1d6 points of damage when it hits. The broom has an AC of 13, 18 hit points, and a hardness of 4.

Caster Level: 10th; *Prerequisites:* Create Wondrous Item, *fly, animate objects; Market Price:* 5,200 gp.

Cloak of Poisonousness: This cloak is usually made of a wool-like material, although it can be made of leather. It radiates magic. The cloak can be handled without harm, but as soon as it is actually donned the wearer is stricken stone dead unless she succeeds at a Fortitude save (DC 28). A *detect poison* spell registers the poison impregnated in the fabric.

Once donned, a *cloak of poisonousness* can be removed only with a *remove curse* spell—this destroys the magical properties of the cloak. If a *neutralize poison* spell is then used, it may be possible to revive the victim with a *raise dead* or *resurrection* spell, but not before.

Caster Level: 15th; *Prerequisites:* Create Wondrous Item, *poison,* and *limited wish* or *miracle; Market Price:* 62,000 gp.

Crystal Hypnosis Ball: This cursed item is indistinguishable from a normal *crystal ball.* It radiates magic, but not evil, to appropriate detection spells. In fact, it doesn't function as a *crystal ball* at all. However, anyone attempting to use the scrying device becomes hypnotized, and a telepathic *suggestion* is implanted in his mind (Will negates DC 19).

The user of the device believes that the desired creature or scene was viewed, but actually he came under the influence of a powerful wizard, lich, or even some power or being from another plane. (The DM should choose the controller to fit his or her campaign.) Each further use brings the *crystal hypnosis ball* gazer deeper under the influence of the controller, either as a servant or a tool. The DM decides whether to make this a gradual or sudden affair, according to the surroundings and circumstances peculiar to the finding of the *crystal hypnosis ball* and the character locating it. Note that throughout this time, the user remains unaware of his subjugation.

Caster Level: 17th; *Prerequisites:* In effect, this is a minor artifact and cannot be created by a player character; *Market Price:* — (cannot be created).

Dust of Sneezing and Choking: This fine dust appears to be either *dust of appearance* or *dust of disappearance.* If cast into the air, however, it causes those within a 20-foot spread to fall into fits of sneezing and coughing. Those failing a Fortitude save (DC 15) take 2d6 points of temporary Constitution damage immediately. In addition, those failing a second Fortitude save (DC 15) 1 minute later are dealt 1d6 points of temporary Constitution damage. Those who succeed on either saving throw are nonetheless disabled by choking (treat as stunned) for 5d4 rounds.

Caster Level: 7th; *Prerequisites:* Create Wondrous Item, *poison; Market Price:* 2,400 gp.

Flask of Curses: This item looks like an ordinary beaker, bottle, container, decanter, flask, or jug. It has magical properties, but detection does not reveal the nature of the *flask of curses.* It may contain a liquid, or it may emit smoke. When the flask is first unstoppered, all within 30 feet must make a Will save (DC 17) or be cursed, suffering a –2 penalty to attack rolls, saving throws, and skill checks until a *remove curse* spell is cast upon them.

Caster Level: 7th; *Prerequisites:* Create Wondrous Item, *bestow curse; Market Price:* 2,100 gp.

Gauntlets of Fumbling: These gauntlets may be of supple leather or heavy protective material suitable for use with armor (ring, scale, chain, and so on). In the former instance, they appear to be *gloves of Dexterity.* In the latter case, they appear to be *gauntlets of ogre power.* The gauntlets perform according to every test as if they were *gloves of Dexterity* or *gauntlets of ogre power* until the wearer finds herself under attack or in a life-and-death situation. At that time, the curse is activated. The wearer becomes fumble-fingered, with a 50% chance each round of dropping anything held in either hand. (If items are held in both hands, roll only once. If the d% result is 01–50, roll again: even = right hand, odd = left hand). The gauntlets also lower Dexterity by 2 points. Once the curse is activated, the gloves can be removed only by means of a *remove curse* spell, a *wish,* or a *miracle.*

Caster Level: 7th; *Prerequisites:* Create Wondrous Item, *bestow curse; Market Price:* 1,300 gp.

Helm of Opposite Alignment: This metal hat looks like a typical helmet. When placed upon the head, however, its curse immediately takes effect (Will save negates DC 15). The alignment of the wearer is radically altered—good to evil, chaotic to lawful, neutral to some extreme commitment (LE, LG, CE, or CG)—to an alignment as different as possible from the former alignment. Alteration in alignment is mental as well as moral, and the individual changed by the magic thoroughly enjoys his new outlook.

Only a *wish* or a *miracle* can restore former alignment, and the affected individual does not make any attempt to return to the former alignment. (In fact, he views the prospect with horror and avoids it in any way possible.) If a character of a class with an alignment requirement is affected, an *atonement* spell is needed as well if the curse is to be obliterated. Note that this is a one-use item: once a *helm of opposite alignment* has functioned, it loses all magical properties.

Caster Level: 12th; *Prerequisites:* Create Wondrous Item, creator must be 12th level; *Market Price:* 4,000 gp; *Weight:* 3 lb.

Incense of Obsession: These blocks of incense exactly resemble *incense of meditation.* If meditation and prayer are conducted while *incense of obsession* is burning nearby, its odor and smoke cause the priest to become totally confident that her spell ability is superior, due to the magic incense. The priest is determined to use her spells at every opportunity, even when not needed or when useless. The priest remains obsessed with her abilities and spells until all are cast or until 24 hours have elapsed.

Caster Level: 6th; *Prerequisites:* Create Wondrous Item, *confusion* or *bestow curse; Market Price:* 200 gp.

Mace of Blood: This +3 *heavy mace* must be coated in blood every day, or its bonus fades away (until the mace is coated again). The character using this mace must make a Will save (DC 13) every day it is within his possession or become chaotic evil.

Caster Level: 8th; *Prerequisites:* Craft Magic Arms and Armor, creator must be at least 9th level and chaotic evil; *Market Price:* 16,000 gp.

Medallion of Thought Projection: This device seems like a *medallion of thoughts,* even down to the range at which it functions, except that the thoughts overheard are muffled and distorted, requiring a successful Will save (DC 15) to sort out. However, while the user thinks she is picking up the thoughts of others, all she is really hearing are figments created by the medallion itself. These illusory thoughts always seem plausible and thus can seriously mislead any who rely upon them. What's worse, unknown to her, the cursed medallion actually broadcasts her thoughts to creatures in the path of the beam, thus alerting them of her presence.

Caster Level: 7th; *Prerequisites:* Create Wondrous Item, *detect thoughts, ghost sound; Market Price:* 1,800 gp.

Necklace of Strangulation: A *necklace of strangulation* appears to be a rare and wondrous piece of valuable jewelry and, short of the use of something as powerful as a *miracle* or a *wish*, can only be identified as a cursed item when placed around a character's neck. The necklace immediately constricts, inflicting 6 points of strangulation damage per round. It cannot be removed by any means short of a *limited wish*, *wish*, or *miracle* and remains clasped around the victim's throat even after his death. Only when he has decayed to a dry skeleton (after approximately one month) does it loosen, ready for another victim.

Caster Level: 18th; *Prerequisites:* Create Wondrous Item, *slay living*; *Market Price:* 60,000 gp.

Net of Snaring: This net offers a +3 bonus to attack rolls but can only be used underwater, thus making it a limited item rather than what most would really call a "curse." Underwater, it can be commanded to shoot forth up to 30 feet to trap a creature.

Caster Level: 8th; *Prerequisites:* Craft Magic Arms and Armor, *freedom of movement*; *Market Price:* 10,000 gp.

Periapt of Foul Rotting: This engraved gem appears to be of little value. If any character keeps the periapt in her possession for more than 24 hours, she contracts a terrible rotting disease that can be removed only by application of a *remove curse* spell followed by a *cure disease* and then a *heal*, *miracle*, *limited wish*, or *wish* spell. The rotting can also be countered by crushing a *periapt of health* and sprinkling its dust upon the afflicted character. Otherwise, the afflicted loses 1 point each of Dexterity, Constitution, and Charisma per week (as if permanently drained).

Caster Level: 10th; *Prerequisites:* Create Wondrous Item, *contagion*; *Market Price:* 17,000 gp.

Potion of Poison: This potion has lost its once potent magical abilities and has become a potent poison. The imbiber must make a Fortitude save (DC 16) or take 1d10 points of temporary Constitution damage. A minute later he must save again (DC 16) or take 1d10 points of temporary Constitution damage.

Caster Level: 12th; *Prerequisites:* Brew Potion, *poison*; *Market Price:* 5,000 gp.

Robe of Powerlessness: A *robe of powerlessness* appears to be a robe of another sort, and detection discovers nothing more than the fact that it has a magical aura. As soon as a character dons this garment, she suffers an immediate –10 effective penalty to Strength and Intelligence scores, forgetting all spells and magic knowledge. The robe can be removed easily, but in order to restore mind and body, the character must receive a *remove curse* spell followed by a *heal*.

Caster Level: 13th; *Prerequisites:* Create Wondrous Item, *bestow curse*, *permanency*; *Market Price:* 5,500 gp.

Robe of Vermin: The wearer notices nothing unusual when the robe is donned, other than that it offers great magical defense (as a *cloak of protection +4*). However, as soon as he is in a situation requiring concentration and action against hostile opponents, the true nature of the garment is revealed: The wearer immediately suffers a multitude of bites from the insects that magically infest the garment. He must cease all other activities in order to scratch, shift the robe, and generally show signs of the extreme discomfort caused by the bites and movement of these pests.

The wearer suffers a –5 initiative penalty and a –2 penalty on all attack rolls, saves, and skill checks. If he tries to cast a spell, he must make a Concentration check (DC 20 + spell level) or lose the spell.

Caster Level: 13th; *Prerequisites:* Create Wondrous Item, *summon swarm*, creator must be at least 8th level; *Market Price:* 16,500 gp.

Ring of Clumsiness: This ring operates exactly like a *ring of feather falling*. However, it also makes the wearer clumsy. She suffers a –4 penalty to Dexterity and has a 20% chance of spell failure for all arcane spells that require a somatic component. (Note: This chance of spell failure stacks with other types of arcane spell failure chances.)

Caster Level: 15th; *Prerequisites:* Forge Ring, *feather fall*, *bestow curse*; *Market Price:* 500 gp.

Scarab of Death: This small pin appears to be any one of the various beneficial amulets, brooches, or scarabs. However, if it is held for more than 1 round or placed within a soft container (bag, pack, etc.) within 1 foot of a warm, living body for 1 minute, it changes into a horrible burrowing beetlelike creature. The thing tears through any leather or cloth, burrows into flesh, and reaches the victim's heart in 1 round, causing death. A Reflex save (DC 25) allows the wearer to tear the scarab away before it burrows out of sight, but he still takes 3d6 points of damage. The beetle then returns to its scarab form. Note that placing the scarab in a container of hard wood, ceramic, bone, ivory, or metal prevents the monster from coming to life and allows for long-term storage of the item.

Caster Level: 19th; *Prerequisites:* Create Wondrous Item, *slay living*; *Market Price:* 80,000 gp.

Spear, Cursed Backbiter: This is a +2 *shortspear*, but each time it is used in melee against a foe and the attack roll is a natural 1, it damages its wielder instead of her intended target. When the curse takes effect, the spear curls around to strike its wielder in the back, automatically striking her for normal damage. The curse even functions when the spear is hurled, but in that case the damage to the hurler is doubled.

Caster Level: 10th; *Prerequisites:* Craft Magic Arms and Armor, *bestow curse*; *Market Price:* 2,000 gp.

Stone of Weight (Loadstone): This stone appears to be a dark, smoothly polished stone. It reduces the possessor's speed to one-half of normal. Furthermore, once picked up, the stone cannot be disposed of by any nonmagical means—if it is thrown away or smashed, it reappears somewhere on his person. If a *remove curse* spell is cast upon a *loadstone*, the item may be discarded normally and no longer haunts the individual.

Caster Level: 5th; *Prerequisites:* Create Wondrous Item, *slow*; *Market Price:* 1,000 gp.

–2 Sword, Cursed: This longsword gives off a magical aura and performs well against targets in practice, but when used against an opponent in combat, it penalizes its wielder's attack rolls by –2. Only by careful observation can this penalty be detected.

All damage dealt is also reduced by 2 points, but never below a minimum of 1 point of damage on any successful hit. After one week in the character's possession, the sword always forces her to employ it rather than another weapon. The sword's owner automatically draws and fights with it even when she meant to draw or ready some other weapon. It can be gotten rid of only by means of *limited wish*, *wish*, or *miracle*.

Caster Level: 15th; *Prerequisites:* Craft Magic Arms and Armor, *bestow curse*, and *limited wish* or *miracle*; *Market Price:* 1,500 gp.

Sword, Berserking: This performs by every test, except that of the heat of battle, as a +2 *greatsword*. However, in actual battle its wielder goes berserk (gaining all benefits and drawbacks of a barbarian rage). He attacks the nearest creature and continues to fight until unconscious or dead or until no living thing remains within 30 feet. Although many see this sword as a curse, others see it as a boon.

Caster Level: 8th; *Prerequisites:* Craft Magic Arms and Armor, *feeblemind*; *Market Price:* 17,500 gp.

Vacuous Grimoire: A book of this sort is identical in appearance to a normal one on some mildly interesting topic, although a *detect magic* spell reveals it to have a magical aura. Any character who opens the work and reads so much as a single glyph therein must make two Will saving throws (DC 15 each). The first is to determine if 1 point of Intelligence is permanently drained. The second is to find out if 2 points of Wisdom are permanently drained. To destroy the book, a character must burn it while casting *remove curse*. If the grimoire is placed with other books, its appearance instantly alters to conform to the look of these other works.

Caster Level: 20th; *Prerequisites:* Create Wondrous Item, *feeblemind*; *Market Price:* 6,000 gp.

ARTIFACTS

The misty past holds many secrets. Great wizards and powerful clerics, not to mention the deities themselves, used spells and created items that are beyond the ken of modern knowledge. These items survive as artifacts, but their means of creation are long gone.

Artifacts are very powerful. Rather than magic equipment, they are the sorts of legendary relics that whole campaigns can be based around. Each could be the center of a whole set of adventures—a quest to recover it, a fight against a opponent wielding it, a mission to cause its destruction, and so on.

No table has been included for you to randomly generate specific artifacts, since these items should only enter a campaign through deliberate choice on your part.

MINOR ARTIFACTS

Minor artifacts are not necessarily unique items, Instead, they are magic items that no longer can be made, at least by common mortal means.

Minor Artifact Descriptions

Described below is a selection of the most famous minor artifacts.

Book of Exalted Deeds: This holy book is sacred to divine spellcasters of good alignment (LG, NG, CG). Study of the work requires one week, but upon completion the good spellcaster gains a +1 inherent bonus to Wisdom and experience points sufficient to place him halfway into the next level of experience. Divine spellcasters neither good nor evil (LN, N, CN) lose 2d6×1,000 experience points for perusing the work. Evil divine spellcasters (LE, NE, CE) lose twice that amount. Furthermore, they have to atone (see the *atonement* spell) in order to gain further experience.

Nonspellcasters who handle or read the book are unaffected. Arcane spellcasters who read it have 1 point of Intelligence permanently drained and lose 1d6×1,000 experience points unless they make a Will save (DC 15).

Except as indicated above, the writing in a *book of exalted deeds* can't be distinguished from any other magic book, libram, tome, or so on until perused. Once read, the book vanishes, never to be seen again, nor can the same character ever benefit from reading a similar tome a second time.

Caster Level: 19th; *Weight:* 3 lb.

Book of Infinite Spells: This work bestows upon any character of any class the ability to use the spells within its pages. However, upon first reading the work, any character not already able to use spells gains one negative level for as long as the book is in her possession or while she uses its power. The *book of infinite spells* contains 1d8+22 pages. The nature of each page is determined by die roll:

d%	Page Contents
01–30	Blank page
31–60	Divine spell
61–100	Arcane spell

If a spell is written on a page, determine the spell by using the tables for determining major scroll spells (the third column on Table 8–23: Scroll Spell Levels, along with Table 8–24: Arcane Spell Scrolls and Table 8–25: Divine Spell Scrolls).

Once a page is turned, it can never be flipped back—paging through a *book of infinite spells* is a one-way trip. If the book is closed, it always opens again to the page it was on before the book was closed. When the last page is turned, the book vanishes.

Once per day the owner of the book can cast the spell to which the book is opened. If that spell happens to be one that is on the character's class spell list, she can cast it up to four times per day. The pages cannot be ripped out without destroying the book. Similarly, the spells cannot be cast as scroll spells, nor can they be copied into a spellbook—their magic is bound up permanently within the book itself.

The owner of the book need not have the book on her person in order to use its power. The book can be stored in a place of safety while the owner is adventuring and still allow its owner to cast spells by means of its power.

Each time a spell is cast, there is a chance that the energy connected with its use causes the page to magically turn despite all precautions. The owner knows this and may even benefit from the turning by gaining access to a new spell. The chance of a page turning is as follows:

Condition	Chance of Page Turning
Spellcaster employing spells usable by own class and/or level	10%
Spellcaster using spells foreign to own class and/or level	20%
Nonspellcaster using divine spell	25%
Nonspellcaster using arcane spell	30%

Treat each spell use as if a scroll were being employed, for purposes of determining casting time, spell failure, and so on.

Caster Level: 18th; *Weight:* 3 lb.

Book of Vile Darkness: This is a work of ineffable evil—meat and drink to divine spellcasters of that alignment (LE, NE, CE). To fully consume the contents requires one week of study. Once this has been accomplished, the evil spellcaster gains a +1 inherent bonus to Wisdom and enough experience points to place him halfway into the next experience level.

Divine spellcasters neither good nor evil (LN, N, CN) who read the book either lose 2d6×1,000 XP (a 01–50 result on d%) or become evil without benefit from the book (51–100). Good divine spellcasters (LG, NG, CG) perusing the pages of the *book of vile darkness* have to make a Fortitude save (DC 16) or die. If they do not die, they must succeed on a Will save (DC 15) or become permanently insane. In the latter event, even if the save is successful, the character loses 20,000 experience points, minus 1,000 for each point of Wisdom he has. (This calculation cannot result in an XP gain.)

Book of vile darkness

Other characters of good alignment take 5d6 points of damage from just handling the tome. If such a character looks inside, there is an 80% chance that an evil outsider attacks the character that night. Nonevil neutral characters take 5d4 points of damage from handling the book, and reading its pages causes them to become evil (Fortitude negates DC 13). Such converts immediately seek out an evil cleric to confirm their new alignment (with an *atonement* spell).

Caster Level: 19th; *Weight:* 3 lb.

Deck of Many Things: A *deck of many things* (both beneficial and baneful) is usually found in a box or leather pouch. Each deck contains a number of cards or plaques made of ivory or vellum. Each is engraved with glyphs, characters, and sigils. As soon as one of these cards is drawn from the pack, its magic is bestowed upon the person who drew it, for better or worse.

The character with a *deck of many things* who wishes to draw a card must announce how many cards she will draw before she begins. Cards must be drawn within 1 hour of each other, and a character can never again draw from this deck any more cards than she has announced. If the character does not willingly draw her allotted number (or if she is somehow prevented from doing so), the cards flip out of the deck on their own. Exception: If a jester is drawn, the possessor of the deck may elect to draw two additional cards.

Each time a card is taken from the deck, it is replaced (making it possible to draw the same card twice) unless the draw is a jester or fool, in which case the card is discarded from the pack. A *deck of many things* contains 22 cards. To simulate the magic cards, you may want to use tarot cards, as indicated by the second column in the accompanying table. If no tarot deck is available, substitute ordinary playing cards instead, as indicated by the third column.

Balance: As in "weighed in the balance and found wanting," the character must change to a radically different alignment. If the character fails to act according to the new alignment, she gains a negative level.

Comet: The character must single-handedly defeat the next hostile monster or monsters encountered, or the benefit is lost. If successful, the character moves to the midpoint of the next experience level.

Donjon: This signifies imprisonment—either by the *imprisonment* spell or by some powerful being, at the DM's option. All gear and spells are stripped from the victim in any case. Whether these items are recoverable is, likewise, up to the DM. Draw no more cards.

Euryale: The medusalike visage of this card brings a curse that only the Fates card or a deific being can remove. The –1 penalty to all saving throws is otherwise permanent.

Deck of many things

Fates: This card enables the character to avoid even an instantaneous occurrence if so desired, for the fabric of reality is unraveled and respun. Note that it does not enable something to happen. It can only stop something from happening or reverse a past occurrence. The reversal is only for the character who drew the card; other party members may have to endure the confrontation.

Flames: Hot anger, jealousy, and envy are but a few of the possible motivational forces for the enmity. The enmity of the outsider can't be ended until one of the parties has been slain. Determine the outsider randomly, and assume that it attacks the character (or plagues her life in some way) within 1d20 days.

Fool: The payment of XP and the redraw are mandatory! This card is always discarded when drawn, unlike all others except the jester.

Gem: This card indicates wealth. The jewelry is all gold set with gems, each piece worth 2,000 gp each, the gems all of 1,000 gp value each.

Idiot: This card causes the loss of 1d4+1 points of Intelligence immediately. The additional draw is optional.

Jester: This card is always discarded when drawn, unlike all others except the fool. The redraws are optional.

Key: The magic weapon granted must be one usable by the character; use the weapon tables beginning with Table 8–11: Weapon Type Determination until a useful item is awarded. It suddenly appears out of nowhere in the character's hand.

Knight: The fighter appears out of nowhere and serves loyally until death. He or she is a magic construct (not a real person) but appears to be of the same race (or kind) and gender as the character. He or she is equipped with the starting fighter package found in the *Player's Handbook* (page 37).

Moon: This is sometimes represented by a moonstone gem with the appropriate number of wishes shown as

DECK OF MANY THINGS

Plaque	Tarot Card	Playing Card	Effect
Balance	XI. Justice	Two of spades	Change alignment instantly.
Comet	Two of swords	Two of diamonds	Defeat the next monster you meet to gain one level.
Donjon	Four of swords	Ace of spaces	You are *imprisoned* (see above).
Euryale	Ten of swords	Queen of spades	–1 penalty to all saving throws henceforth.
The Fates	Three of cups	Ace of hearts	Avoid any situation you choose . . . once.
Flames	XV. The Devil	Queen of clubs	Enmity between you and an outsider.
Fool	0. The Fool	Joker (with trademark)	Lose 10,000 experience points and you must draw again.
Gem	Seven of cups	Two of hearts	Gain your choice of twenty-five pieces of jewelry or fifty gems.
Idiot	I. The Juggler	Ace of clubs	Lose Intelligence (permanent drain). You may draw again.
Jester	XII. The Hanged Man	Joker (without trademark)	Gain 10,000 XP or two more draws from the deck.
Key	V. The Hierophant	Queen of hearts	Gain a major magic weapon.
Knight	Page of swords	Jack of hearts	Gain the service of a 4th-level fighter.
Moon	XVIII. The Moon	Queen of diamonds	You are granted 1d4 wishes.
Rogue	Five of swords	Jack of spades	One of your friends turns against you.
Ruin	XVI. The Tower	King of spades	Immediately lose all wealth and real property.
Skull	XIII. Death	Jack of clubs	Defeat Death or be forever destroyed.
Star	XVII. The Star	Jack of diamonds	Immediately gain a +2 inherent bonus to one ability.
Sun	XIX. The Sun	King of diamonds	Gain beneficial medium wondrous item and 50,000 XP.
Talons	Queen of pentacles	Two of clubs	All magic items you possess disappear permanently.
Throne	Four of staves	King of hearts	Gain 6 ranks in Diplomacy plus a small keep.
Vizier	IX. The Hermit	Ace of diamonds	Know the answer to your next dilemma.
The Void	Eight of swords	King of clubs	Body functions, but soul is trapped elsewhere

gleams therein, sometimes by a moon with its phase indicating the number of wishes (full = four; gibbous = three; half = two; quarter = 1). These wishes are the same as those granted by the 9th-level wizard spell and must be used in a number of minutes equal to the number received.

Rogue: When this card is drawn, one of the character's NPC friends (preferably a cohort) is totally alienated and forever after hostile. If the character has no cohorts, the enmity of some powerful personage (or community, or religious order) can be substituted. The hatred is secret until the time is ripe for it to be revealed with devastating effect.

Ruin: As implied, when this card is drawn every bit of money (including all gems, jewelry, treasure, and art objects) is lost (disintegrated). All land owned is struck by blight and forever ruined, buildings collapse into dust, etc.

Skull: A minor death appears. Treat this minor death as an unturnable spectre with a *ghost touch scythe* that never misses and deals 2d8 points of damage. The character must fight it alone—if others help, they get minor deaths to fight as well. If the character is slain, she is slain forever and cannot be revived, even with a *wish* or a *miracle*.

Star: The 2 points are added to any ability the character chooses. They cannot be divided among two abilities.

Sun: Roll for a medium wondrous item (Table 8–29: Medium Wondrous Items) until a useful item is indicated. The XP granted are immediately available.

Talons: When this card is drawn, every magic item owned or possessed by the character is instantly and irrevocably gone (disintegrated).

Throne: The character becomes a true leader in people's eyes. The castle gained appears in any open area she wishes (but the decision where to place it must be made immediately).

Vizier: This card empowers the character drawing it with the one-time ability to call upon supernatural wisdom to solve any single problem or answer fully any question upon her request. Whether the information gained can be successfully acted upon is another question entirely.

The Void: This black card spells instant disaster. The character's body continues to function, as though in a coma, but her psyche is trapped in a prison somewhere—in an object on a far plane or planet, possibly in the possession of an outsider. A *wish* or a *miracle* does not bring the character back, instead merely revealing the plane of entrapment. Draw no more cards.

Caster Level: 20th; Weight: —.

Hammer of Thunderbolts: This appears to be an oversized, extra-heavy warhammer. A character smaller than Large finds it too unbalanced to wield properly in combat (–2 penalty to attack). However, a character of sufficient size finds that the hammer functions with a +3 enhancement bonus and deals double damage on any hit.

If the wielder (of any size) wears a *belt of giant strength* and *gauntlets of ogre power* and he knows that the hammer is a *hammer of thunderbolts* (not just a +3 warhammer), the weapon can be used to full effect: When swung or hurled, it gains a total +5 enhancement bonus, deals double damage, allows all *girdle* and *gauntlet* bonuses to stack (only when using this weapon), and strikes dead any giant upon whom it scores a hit (Fortitude save DC 16 to survive).

When hurled, on a successful hit the hammer emits a great noise, like a clap of thunder, stunning all crea-

tures within 90 feet for 1 round (Fortitude save DC 12 to resist). The hammer's throwing range is 180 feet, and its range increment is 30 feet.

Caster Level: 20th.

Philosopher's Stone: This rare and magic substance appears to be an ordinary, sooty piece of blackish rock. If the stone is broken open, a cavity is revealed at the stone's heart. This cavity is lined with a magical quicksilver that enables any wizard to transmute base metals (iron and lead) into silver and gold. A single *philosopher's stone* can turn from 500 to 5,000 pounds of iron into silver, or from 100 to 1,000 pounds of lead into gold. However, the magical quicksilver becomes unstable once the stone is opened and sublimates within 24 hours, so all transmutations must take place within that period.

The quicksilver found in the center of the stone may also be put to another use. If mixed with any *cure* potion, it creates a special *potion of life* that acts as a *true resurrection* for any dead body it is sprinkled upon.

Caster Level: 20th; Weight: 3 lb.

Sphere of Annihilation: A *sphere of annihilation* is a globe of absolute blackness, a ball of nothingness 2 feet in diameter. A sphere is actually a hole in the continuity of the multiverse. Any matter that comes in contact with a sphere is instantly sucked into the void, gone, and utterly destroyed. Only the direct intervention of a deity can restore an annihilated character.

A *sphere of annihilation* is static, resting in some spot as if it were a normal hole. It can be caused to move, however, by mental effort. The brain waves of the individual concentrating on moving it bend spatial fabrics, causing the hole to slide. The range of this control is 40 feet initially, then 40 feet +10 feet per character level once control is established. Control is based on the character's Intelligence and level of experience. (The higher his level, the greater his mental discipline.) The character adds his Intelligence bonus and character level and then applies the total to a 1d20 roll. To control the sphere, the DC is 30. The sphere's speed is 10 feet per round +1 foot for every point by which the control check result exceeds 30.

Any attempt to control the sphere causes it to move, but if control is not established, the sphere slides toward the character attempting to move it. It continues to move in the direction he wills it to (or toward the character, if the attempt failed) for 1d4 rounds or for as long as the character is within 30 feet, whichever is greater. Control must be checked each round.

If two or more wizards vie for control of a *sphere of annihilation*, the rolls are opposed. If none are successful, the sphere slips toward the one who rolled lowest.

Sphere of annihilation

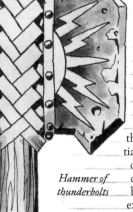

Hammer of thunderbolts

Should a *gate* spell be cast upon a *sphere of annihilation*, there is a 50% chance (a 01–50 result on d%) that the spell destroys it, a 35% chance (51–85) that the spell does nothing, and a 15% chance (86–100) that a gap is torn in the spatial fabric, catapulting everything within a 180-foot radius into another plane. If a *rod of cancellation* touches a sphere, they negate each other in a tremendous explosion. Everything within a 60-foot radius takes 2d6×10 points of damage. *Dispel magic* and *Mordenkainen's disjunction* have no effect on the sphere.

See also *talisman of the sphere* (page 227).

Caster Level: 20th; Weight: —.

Staff of the Magi: A long wooden staff, shod in iron and inscribed with sigils and runes of all types, this potent artifact contains many spell powers and other functions. Some of its powers drain charges, while others don't. The following powers do not drain charges:

- *detect magic*
- *enlarge*
- *hold portal*
- *light*
- *mage armor*
- *mage hand*

The following powers drain 1 charge per usage:
- *dispel magic*
- *fireball* (10d6 points of damage, DC 13)
- *ice storm*
- *invisibility*
- *knock*
- *lightning bolt* (10d6 points of damage, DC 13)
- *passwall*
- *pyrotechnics*
- *wall of fire*
- *web*

These powers drain 2 charges per usage:
- *monster summoning IX*
- *plane shift*
- *telekinesis* (400 pounds maximum weight)
- *whirlwind*

The *staff of the magi* gives the wielder spell resistance 23. If this is willingly lowered, however, the staff can also be used to absorb arcane spell energy directed at its wielder exactly like a *rod of absorption* (page 196). The staff uses spell levels as charges, not as spell energy usable by a spellcaster. If the staff absorbs spell levels beyond its charge limit (50), it explodes as if a retributive strike had been made (see below). Note that the wielder has no idea how many spell levels are cast at her, for the staff does not communicate this knowledge as a *rod of absorption* does. Absorbing spells is risky, but absorption is the *only* way this staff can be recharged.

Retributive Strike: A *staff of the magi* can be broken for a retributive strike. Such an act must be purposeful and declared by the wielder. All charges in the staff are released in a 30-foot spread. All within 10 feet of the broken staff take hit points of damage equal to 8 times the number of charges in the staff, those between 11 feet and 20 feet away take points equal to 6 times the number of charges, and those 21 feet to 30 feet distant take 4 times the number of charges. Successful Reflex saving throws (DC 17) reduce damage by half.

The character breaking the staff has a 50% chance (a 01–50 result on d%) of traveling to another plane of existence, but if she does not (51–100), the explosive release of spell energy destroys her.

Staff of the magi

Only specific items, including the *staff of the magi* and the *staff of power* (page 205), are capable of a retributive strike.

Caster Level: 20th; Weight: 5 lb.

Talisman of Pure Good: A good (LG, NG, CG) divine spellcaster who possesses this item can cause a flaming crack to open at the feet of an evil (LE, NE, CE) divine spellcaster who is up to 100 feet away. The intended victim is swallowed up forever and sent hurtling to the center of the earth. The wielder of the talisman must be good, and if he is not exceptionally pure in thought and deed (DM's discretion), the evil character gains a Reflex saving throw (DC 19) to leap away from the crack. Obviously, the target must be standing on solid ground for this item to function. (In the air, in a high tower, or on a ship are all places of safety against this otherwise potent item.)

A *talisman of pure good* has 7 charges. If a neutral (LN, N, CN) divine spellcaster touches one of these stones, he takes 6d6 points of damage. If an evil divine spellcaster touches one, he takes 8d6 points of damage. All other characters are unaffected by the device.

Caster Level: 18th; Weight: —.

Talisman of Ultimate Evil: An evil (LE, NE, CE) divine spellcaster who possesses this item can cause a flaming crack to open at the feet of a good (LG, NG, CG) divine spellcaster who is up to 100 feet away. The intended victim is swallowed up forever and sent hurtling to the center of the earth. The wielder of the talisman must be evil, and if she is not exceptionally foul and perverse in the sights of her evil deity (DM's discretion), the good character gains a Reflex saving throw (DC 19) to leap away from the crack. Obviously, the target must be standing on solid ground for this item to function. (In the air, in a high tower, or on a ship are all places of safety against this otherwise potent item.)

A *talisman of ultimate evil* has 6 charges. If a neutral (LN, N, CN) divine spellcaster touches one of these stones, she takes 6d6 points of damage. If a good divine spellcaster touches one, she takes 8d6 points of damage. All other characters are unaffected by the device.

Caster Level: 18th; Weight: —.

Talisman of Zagy: A talisman of this sort appears the same as a *stone of controlling earth elementals*. Its powers are quite different, however, and dependent on the Charisma of the individual holding the talisman. Whenever a character touches a *talisman of Zagy*, he must make a Charisma check (DC 15).

If he fails, the device acts as a *stone of weight* (see page 235). Discarding or destroying it results in 5d6 points of damage to the character and the disappearance of the talisman.

If he succeeds, the talisman remains with the character for 5d6 hours, or until a *wish* is made with it, whichever comes first. It then disappears.

If he rolls a natural 20, the character finds it impossible to be rid of the talisman for as many months as he has points of Charisma. In addition, the artifact grants him one *wish* for every 6 points of the character's Charisma. It also grows warm and throbs whenever its possessor comes within 20 feet of a mechanical or magic trap. (If the talisman is not held, its warning heat and pulses are of no avail.)

Regardless of which reaction results, the talisman disappears when its time period expires, leaving behind a 10,000 gp diamond in its stead.

Caster Level: 20th; Weight: 1 lb.

MAJOR ARTIFACTS

Major artifacts are unique items—only one of each such item exists. Each has a long history, and the tales told of them are fantastic . . . and usually fraught with error and misconception. Major artifacts are secretive things, their current whereabouts unknown, waiting to be found and once again unleashed upon the world.

Talisman of pure good

Never introduce a major artifact into a campaign without careful consideration. These are the most potent of magic items, capable of altering the balance of a campaign.

Unlike all other magic items, major artifacts are not easily destroyed. Each should have only a single, specific means of destruction, determined ahead of time by you. For example, a specific artifact might be undone by one of the following means:

• Throwing it into the volcano lair of the dragon Uthrax.
• Crushed under the heel of a demideity.
• Buried in the Rift of Corrosion in the Abyss.
• Disintegrated while placed at the base of the Infinite Staircase.
• Devoured by Talos, the triple iron golem.
• Immersed in the Fountain of Light in the holy Halls of Heironeous himself.

Because the means of destruction of a major artifact are so difficult, such an item is often buried in a deep vault, thrown into the Astral Plane, or placed behind extremely powerful and untiring guardians by those without the power, knowledge, or wherewithal to destroy it.

Major Artifact Descriptions

The artifacts presented here are meant to be examples. Artifacts should be tailored to fit your individual campaign and its history: The discovery of a major artifact should be a campaign-defining moment. Feel free to change the powers given here in order to customize these artifacts to your campaign.

The Hand and Eye of Vecna: The archlich Vecna may have been the most powerful wizard ever to have lived. He may also have been the most evil. Apparently risen now to deityhood, he left behind relics embodying remnants of his power—the mummified remains of his hand and his eye.

Powers of the Eye: In order to function, the *Eye of Vecna* must be placed in the empty socket of a character's skull. The bearer of the *Eye* loses two points of Charisma, and these points may never be restored. The *Eye* may not thereafter be removed without resulting in the death of its host. It grants the host continuous *darkvision* and *true seeing*. Three times per day each, the host can use the spell *eyebite* and *domination*. Once per day, the bearer of the *Eye* can call forth *destruction* and *unhallow*. A nonevil character must make a Will save each week (DC 17) to avoid becoming evil. All powers are at a caster level of 20th, and all DCs to resist their effects are 20.

Powers of the Hand: In order to function, the *Hand of Vecna* must be placed on the end of a left arm whose original hand has been severed. The bearer of the *Hand* loses two points of Dexterity that may never be regained. Removal of the hand thereafter always results in the death of the host. The touch of the *Hand*, once so placed, deals 1d10 points of cold damage to a target. Three times per day, its touch can permanently drain one ability score point (host's choice of ability) from a victim. The host gains the points drained for the rest of that day. (They last until the next sunrise.) Once per day, the bearer of the *Hand* can call upon *blasphemy* and *unholy aura*. A nonevil character must make a Will save each week (DC 17) to avoid becoming evil. All powers are at a caster level of 20th and all DCs to resist their effects are 20.

The Hand and Eye of Vecna

Powers with Both Artifacts: If a single character bears both the *Hand of Vecna* and the *Eye of Vecna*, all powers have a DC of 25 to resist. The host is granted +2 Strength and +2 Intelligence but suffers a −2 penalty to Wisdom. Further, she can call upon *summon monster IX* once per day (to summon evil outsiders only). A nonevil character must make a Will save each week (DC 23) to avoid becoming evil.

The Mace of Cuthbert: St. Cuthbert, tales say, once walked the earth as a man. When he did, he used a potent weapon to strike against the infidels and evil beings he encountered everywhere he went. Today, this relic appears to be a simple, well-used cudgel, but its simple appearance hides great power. The *Mace of Cuthbert* has a +5 enhancement bonus and functions as a holy, lawful, disruption weapon. Further, the wielder can project *searing light* from the mace at will, at 20th caster level.

The Mace of Cuthbert

The Moaning Diamond: Said to have been ripped from the ground in a ritual that tortured the earth itself, the *Moaning Diamond* appears to be an uncut diamond the size of a human fist. At all times, it gives forth a baleful moaning sound, as if in pain. Despite the noise, the *Moaning Diamond* is not evil (although it was birthed in torture). The wielder of the stone can, three times per day, call upon it to reshape earth and stone as if by the spell *stone shape*, affecting 5,000 cubic feet of material. Further, the *Moaning Diamond* can summon an elder earth elemental with maximum hit points that serves the caster until it is slain. Only one such elemental can be summoned at a time; if it is slain, a new creature cannot be summoned for 24 hours. Tales from the past tell of the *Moaning Diamond* creating stone structures, opening underground chambers where there had been none before, and collapsing entire castles.

The Orbs of Dragonkind: These fabled *Orbs* were created eons ago in order to master dragons in the great Dragon Wars. Each contains the essence and personality of an ancient dragon of a different variety (one for each of the major ten different chromatic and metallic dragons). The bearer of an *Orb* can *dominate* dragons of its particular variety within 500 feet (as *dominate monster*), the dragon being forced to make a Will save (DC 25) to resist. (Spell resistance has no power against this effect.) Each *Orb of Dragonkind* bestows upon the wielder the AC and saving throw bonuses of the dragon within (see the *Monster Manual* for details on each dragon variety). These values replace whatever values the character would otherwise have, regardless whether they are better or worse. These values cannot be modified by any means short of ridding the character of the *Orb*. Further, a character possessing an *Orb of Dragonkind* is immune to the breath weapon—but only the breath weapon—of the dragon variety keyed to the *Orb*. Thus, the possessor of the *Red Dragon Orb of Dragonkind* is immune to red dragon breath, but not fire of any other sort. Finally, a character possessing an *Orb* can herself use the breath weapon of the dragon in the *Orb* three times per day (see the *Monster Manual*).

All *Orbs of Dragonkind* can be used to communicate verbally and visually with the possessors of the other *Orbs*. The owner of an *Orb* knows whether there are dragons within ten miles at all times. For dragons of the *Orb's* particular variety, the range is one hundred miles. If within one mile of a dragon of the *Orb's* variety, the wielder can determine the exact location and age of the creature. The bearer of one of these *Orbs* earns the enmity forever of all dragonkind for profiting by the enslavement of one of their kin, even if she later loses the item.

Each *Orb* also has an individual power that can be invoked once per round at 10th caster level:

- *Black Dragon Orb: fly.*
- *Blue Dragon Orb: haste.*
- *Brass Dragon Orb: teleport.*
- *Bronze Dragon Orb: scrying.*
- *Copper Dragon Orb: suggestion.*
- *Gold Dragon Orb:* Special. The owner of the gold *Orb* can call upon any power possessed by one of the other orbs—including the *dominate* and breath weapon abilities but not AC, saves or breath weapon immunity—but can only use an individual power once per day. Further, she can *dominate* any other possessor of an *Orb* within one mile (DC 16).
- *Green Dragon Orb: spectral force.*
- *Red Dragon Orb: wall of fire.*
- *Silver Dragon Orb: cure critical wounds.*
- *White Dragon Orb: protection from elements (cold only).*

The Shadowstaff: The wizard Malhavoc crafted this artifact centuries ago, weaving together the wispy strands of shadow itself into a twisted black staff. The *Shadowstaff* makes the wielder slightly shadowy and incorporeal, granting him a +4 bonus to AC and Reflex saves (stackable with any other bonuses). However, in bright light (such as that of the sun, but not a torch) or in absolute darkness, the wielder suffers a –2 penalty to all attack rolls, saves, and checks. The *Shadowstaff* also has these powers:

Summon Shadows: Three times per day the staff may summon 2d4 shadows. Immune to turning, they serve the wielder as if called by a *summon monster V* spell cast at 20th level.

The Shadowstaff

Summon Nightshade: Once per month, the staff can summon a nightcrawler nightshade that serves the wielder as if called by a *summon monster IX* spell cast at 20th level.

Shadow Form: Three times per day the wielder can become a living shadow, with all the movement powers granted by the *gaseous form* spell.

Shadow Bolt: Three times per day the staff can project a ray attack that deals 10d6 points of cold damage to a single target. The shadow bolt has a range of 100 feet.

The Shield of Prator: A hero of old, the paladin Prator bore this relic in many a valiant battle. The *Shield of Prator* is said to have disappeared when Prator fell in the Battle of the Three Hells, although it has reportedly surfaced briefly from time to time since then. This *+5 large shield*, emblazoned with the symbol of the sun, allows the wielder to cast spells as if she were a 20th-level paladin with a Wisdom score of 20. The spells gained are cumulative with any existing spells per day that the character might have, even if she's already a paladin. The *Shield of Prator* also grants spell resistance 15 to its wielder. Furthermore, it absorbs the first 10 points of damage each round from fire, cold, acid, electricity, and sonic attacks. (Each element has its own limit of 10 points of damage per round.) In return for all this, once per year the shield's owner must undertake a quest (no

The Shield of Prator

saving throw to avoid this) at the behest of a lawful good deity.

A character who is evil or chaotic (LE, NE, CE, CN, CG) gains four negative levels if she attempts to use this artifact. Although these levels never results in actual level loss, they remain as long as the shield is in hand and cannot be overcome in any way (including *restoration* spells). The negative levels disappear when the shield is stowed or leaves the wearer's possession.

The Sword of Kas: The vampire Kas was the dreaded lieutenant of Vecna. He used this mighty blade, created by his master, to betray and attack the archlich, cutting off his hand and eye in a terrible battle before Vecna destroyed him. Only his sword survived, and it is said to forever seek vengeance against Vecna. The *Sword of Kas* is a *+6 unholy keen vorpal longsword.* It grants the wielder a +10 enhancement bonus to Strength. The sword is intelligent (Int 15, Wis 13, Cha 16, Ego 34) and chaotic evil. It can be used to cast the following spells, once per day each: *call lightning* (10d6 points of damage, DC 14), *blasphemy,* and *unhallow.* Once per week it can be used to *slay living.*

CREATING MAGIC ITEMS

To create magic items, spellcasters use special feats. They invest time, money, and their own personal energy (in the form of experience points) in an item's creation. For details on creating the different types of magic items, see the appropriate section below as well as the information on item creation feats in Chapter 5: Feats, page 77 in the *Player's Handbook.*

Note that all items have prerequisites in their descriptions. These prerequisites must be met for the item to be created. Most of the time, they take the form of spells that must be known by the item's creator (although access through another magic item or spellcaster is allowed).

While item creation costs are handled in detail elsewhere, note that normally the two primary factors are the caster level of the creator and the level of the spell or spells put into the item. A creator can create an item at a lower caster level than her own, but never lower than the minimum level needed to cast the needed spell. For example, a 15th-level wizard could craft a *wand of fireball* at 10th caster level, or even as low as 5th level (the minimum caster level for *fireball,* a 3rd-level spell), but no lower. If she did this, the *fireball* would in all ways be treated as if the caster was of the lower specified level (for damage, range, and so on). Using metamagic feats, a caster can place spells in items at a higher level than normal. For example, a caster could heighten a spell's level to increase its effectiveness, or quicken a spell to allow it to be used as a free action, placing it within an item at the higher metamagic level. See Chapter 5: Feats, page 78 in the *Player's Handbook* for more on metamagic feats.

Base creation costs for items are always half of the base price in gp and 1/25 of the base price in XP. For most items, the market price equals the base price. For example, a *cloak of elvenkind* has a market price (and base price) of 2,000 gp. Making one costs 1,000 gp in raw materials plus 80 XP.

Some items, however, cast or replicate spells with costly material components or with XP components. For these items, the market price equals the base price plus an extra price for the components. (Each XP in the components adds 5 gp to the market price.) The cost to create these items is the base raw material cost and the base XP cost (both determined by the base price) plus the costs for

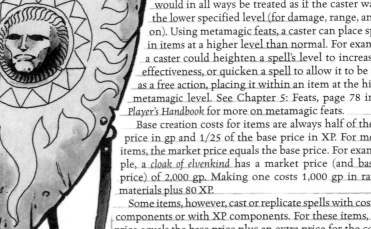

The Sword of Kas

the components. For example, a *ring of three wishes* has a market price of 97,950 gp, which includes 75,000 gp for the extra 15,000 XP that the creator must expend to forge the ring. The ring's base price is only 22,950 gp (the market price minus the extra cost for the XP expenditure). These items have a "Cost to Create" entry that lists the total cost to create the item. (You don't have to calculate creation costs for these items. It's done for you.)

The creator also needs a fairly quiet, comfortable, and well-lit place in which to work. Any place suitable for preparing spells (see Chapter 10: Magic in the *Player's Handbook*) is suitable for making items. Creating an item requires one day per 1,000 gp in the item's base price, with a minimum of at least one day. Potions are an exception to this rule; they always take just one day to brew. The caster is assumed to work for 8 hours each day. He cannot rush the process by working longer. A character can only work on one item at a time. He can do nothing else while working. During rest periods, he can engage in light activity such as talking or walking but cannot fight, cast spells, use magic items, conduct research, or perform any other physically or mentally demanding task. The caster can take a short break from working (for naps and the like) as often as he likes, so long as he spends at least 8 hours out of every 24 working on the item. He cannot take a day off: Once the process has started, he must see it through to the end or admit defeat. If the caster is disturbed while making the item, or spends less than 8 hours working in any period of 24 hours, the process is ruined. All materials used and XP spent are wasted.

The secrets to creating artifacts are long lost.

MASTERWORK ITEMS

As detailed in Chapter 7: Equipment in the *Player's Handbook*, masterwork items are extraordinarily well-made items. They are more expensive, but they benefit the user with improved quality. They are not magical in any way. However, only masterwork items may be enchanted to become magic armor and weapons. (Items that are not weapons or armor may or may not be masterwork items.)

SPECIAL MATERIALS

In addition to magic items enchanted with spells, some substances have innate special properties. While only three such materials are presented here, other special materials may exist in a given campaign.

Adamantine: Found only in meteorites and the rarest of veins in magical areas, this ultrahard metal adds to the quality of a weapon or suit of armor based on how much of the material is used. Thus, adamantine plate offers a greater increase in protection (as well as a higher cost) than adamantine chainmail, and an adamantine battleaxe offers a greater increase in offensive capability than an adamantine dagger. Weapons fashioned from adamantine have a

TABLE 8–40: CALCULATING MAGIC ITEM GOLD PIECE VALUES

Effect	Base Price	Example
Ability enhancement bonus	Bonus squared × 1,000 gp	*Gloves of Dexterity +2*
Armor enhancement bonus	Bonus squared × 1,000 gp	*+1 chainmail*
Bonus spell	Spell level squared × 1,000 gp	*Pearl of power*
Deflection bonus	Bonus squared × 2,000 gp	*Ring of protection +3*
Luck bonus	Bonus squared × 2,500 gp	*Staff of power*
Natural armor bonus	Bonus squared × 2,000 gp	*Amulet of natural armor +1*
Resistance bonus	Bonus squared × 1,000 gp	*Cloak of resistance +5*
Save bonus (limited)	Bonus squared × 250 gp	*Periapt of proof against poison +4*
Skill bonus	Bonus squared × 20 gp	*Ring of climbing*
Spell resistance	10,000 gp per point over SR 12; SR 13 minimum	*Mantle of spell resistance*
Weapon enhancement bonus	Bonus squared × 2,000 gp	*+1 longsword*

Spell Effect	Base Price	Example
Single use, spell completion	Spell level × caster level × 25 gp	*Scroll of haste*
Single use, use-activated	Spell level × caster level × 50 gp	*Potion of cure light wounds*
50 charges, spell trigger	Spell level × caster level × 750 gp	*Wand of fireball*
Command word	Spell level × caster level × 1,800 gp	*Cape of the mountebank*
Use-activated	Spell level × caster level × 2,000 gp	*Lantern of revealing*

Special	Base Price Adjustment	Example
Charges per day	Divide by (5 ÷ charges per day)	*Helm of teleportation*
No space limitation*	Multiply entire cost by 2	*Ioun stone*
Charged (50 charges)	1/2 unlimited use base price	*Ring of the ram*

Component	Extra Cost	Example
Armor, shield, or weapon	Add cost of masterwork item	*+1 composite longbow*
Spell has material component cost	Add directly into price of item per charge**	*Wand of stoneskin*
Spell has XP cost	Add 5 gp per 1 XP per charge**	*Ring of three wishes*

Spell Level: A 0-level spell is half the value of a 1st-level spell for determining price.

*See Limit on Magic Items Worn, page 176. Basically, an item that does not take up one of these limited spaces costs double.

**If item is continuous or unlimited, not charged, determine cost as if it had 100 charges. If it has some daily limit, determine cost as if it had 50 charges.

natural enhancement bonus to attack and damage. Armor fashioned from adamantine has a natural enhancement bonus to AC. These bonuses do not stack with any other enhancement bonuses. Thus, an adamantine (+2) sword enchanted with a +5 enhancement bonus effectively has a +5 enhancement bonus. In an area where magic does not function, it still retains its natural +2 enhancement bonus. Weapons and armor fashioned from adamantine are treated as masterwork items with regard to creation times, but the masterwork quality does not affect the enhancement bonus of weapons or the armor check penalty of armor.

Adamantine has a hardness of 20 and 40 hit points per inch of thickness.

Item	Enhancement Bonus	Market Price Modifier
Light armor	+1	+2,000 gp
Medium armor	+2	+5,000 gp
Heavy armor	+3	+10,000 gp
Shield	+1	+2,000 gp
Weapon damage 1d4 or 1d6	+1	+3,000 gp
Weapon damage 1d8, 1d10, or 1d12	+2	+9,000 gp

Mithral: Mithral is a very rare silvery, glistening metal that is lighter than iron but just as hard. When worked like steel, it becomes a wonderful material from which to create armor and is occasionally used for other items as well. Most mithral armors are one category lighter than normal for purposes of movement and other limitations (for example, whether a barbarian can use her fast movement ability while wearing the armor or not). Heavy armors are treated as medium, and medium armors are treated as light, but light armors are still treated as light. Spell failure chances for armors and shields made from mithral are decreased by 10%, maximum Dexterity bonus is increased by 2, and armor check penalties are decreased by 3. Nonarmor or nonshield items made from mithral weigh half as much as the same item made from other metals. Note that items not primarily of metal are not meaningfully affected. (A longsword is affected, while a spear is not.)

Weapons or armors fashioned from mithral are treated as masterwork items with regard to creation times, but the masterwork quality does not affect the enhancement bonus of weapons or the armor check penalty of armor.

Mithral has a hardness of 15 and 30 hit points per inch of thickness.

Item	Market Price Modifier
Light armor	+1,000 gp
Medium armor	+4,000 gp
Heavy armor	+9,000 gp
Shield	+1,000 gp
Other items	+500 gp/lb.

Darkwood: This rare magic wood is as hard as normal wood but very light. Any wooden or mostly wooden item (such as a bow, an arrow, or a spear) made from darkwood is considered a masterwork item and weighs only half as much as a normal wooden item of that type. Items not normally made of wood or only partially of wood (such as a battleaxe or a mace) either cannot be made from darkwood or do not gain any special benefit from being made of darkwood. Armor check penalties for darkwood shields are reduced by 2. To determine the price of darkwood items, use the original weight but add +10 gp per pound to the price of a masterwork version of that item.

Darkwood has a hardness of 5 and 10 hit points per inch of thickness.

CREATING ARMOR

To create magic armor, a character needs a heat source and some iron, wood, or leatherworking tools. He also needs a supply of materials, the most obvious being the armor or the pieces of the armor to be assembled. Armor to be enchanted must be masterwork armor, and its cost is added to the total enchantment cost to determine final market value. Additional costs for the materials are subsumed in the cost for creating the magic armor—half the market value presented in the tables in this chapter.

Creating magic armor has a special prerequisite: The creator's caster level must be at least three times the enhancement bonus of the armor. Thus, a 6th-level creator can make a +2 *breastplate*, a 9th-level creator can create the same breastplate and make it +3, and a 15th-level caster can make it +5. If an item has both an enhancement bonus and a special ability (such as cold resistance), the higher of the two caster level requirements must be met.

Magic armor or a magic shield must have at least a +1 enhancement bonus to have any of the abilities listed on Table 8–6: Armor Special Abilities and Table 8–7: Shield Special Abilities. A character can't create, for example, simply *shadow chainmail*. In order to have a special magical ability, the chainmail needs first to have an enhancement bonus of at least +1.

If spells are involved in the prerequisites for making the armor, the creator must have prepared the spells to be cast (or must know the spells, in the case of a sorcerer or bard) but need not provide any material components or focuses the spells require, nor are any XP costs inherent in a prerequisite spell incurred in the creation of the item. The act of working on the armor triggers the prepared spells, making them unavailable for casting during each day of the armor's creation. (That is, those spell slots are expended from his currently prepared spells, just as if they had been cast.)

Creating some armor may entail other prerequisites beyond or other than spellcasting. See the individual descriptions on pages 181–183 for details.

BEHIND THE CURTAIN: MAGIC ITEM GOLD PIECE VALUES

Many factors must be considered when determining the price of magic items you invent. The easiest way to come up with a price is to match the new item to an item priced in this chapter and use its price as a guide. Otherwise, use the guidelines summarized on Table 8–40: Calculating Magic Item Gold Piece Values.

Multiple Similar Abilities: For items with multiple similar abilities that don't take up a limited space (see Limit on Magic Items Worn, page 176), use the following formula: Calculate the price based on the single most costly ability, then add 75% of the value of the next most costly ability, plus one-half the value of any other abilities. (The many spell-like powers of a *staff of power* are a good example of multiple similar abilities). However, abilities such as an attack or saving throw bonus and a spell-like function are not similar, and their values are simply added together to determine the cost. For items that do take up a limited space (such as a ring or a necklace), each additional power not only has no discount but instead has a 10% increase in price. A *belt of Strength +4 and Dexterity +4* is more valuable than a *belt of Strength* worn with *gauntlets of Dexterity*, since it takes up only one space on a character's body.

When multiplying spell levels to determine value, 0-level spells should be treated as a half-level.

Other factors can reduce the cost of an item:

- **Item Requires Skill to Use.** Some items require a specific skill (such as Scry for the *crystal ball* or Perform for a musical instrument) to get them to function. This factor should reduce the cost about 10%. Requiring a skill barred to most classes (such as Scry) is even more restrictive and might reduce the cost about 20%.

- **Item Requires Specific Class or Alignment to Function.** Even more restrictive, such a requirement cuts the price by 30%.

Prices presented in the magic item descriptions in this book are the market value, which is generally twice what it costs the creator to make the item. Since different classes get the same spells at different levels, the prices for them to make the same item might actually be different. Take *hold person*, for example. A cleric casts it as a 2nd-level spell, so a clerical *wand of hold person* costs him 2 (2nd-level spell) × 3 (3rd-level caster) × 750 gp, divided in half, or 2,250 gp. However, a wizard casts *hold person* as a 3rd-level spell, so her wand costs her 3 (3rd-level spell) × 5 (5th-level caster) × 750 gp, divided in half, or 5,625 gp. A sorcerer also casts *hold person* as a 3rd-level spell, but he doesn't get the spell until 6th level, so his wand costs 3 (3rd-level spell) × 6 (6th-level caster) × 750 gp, divided in half, or 6,750 gp. The wand is only worth two times what the most efficient caster can make it for, however, so the market value of a *wand of hold person* is 4,500 gp, no matter who makes it.

You'll notice, however, that not all the items presented here adhere to these formulas directly. The reasons for this are several. First and foremost, these few formulas aren't enough to truly gauge the exact differences between, say, a *ring of fire resistance* and *boots of speed*—two very different items. Each of the magic items presented here was examined and modified based on its actual worth. The formulas only provide a starting point. Scrolls, potions, and wands follow the formulas exactly. Staffs follow the formulas closely, and other items require at least some DM judgment calls. Use good sense when assigning prices, along with the items here as examples.

Creating magic items requires time and money as well as skill.

Crafting magic armor requires one day for each 1,000 gp value of the completed item.

Item Creation Feat Required: Craft Magic Arms and Armor.

ties. For example, a dire flail could have a +1 *flaming* head and a +3 *disruption* head.

Creating some weapons may entail other prerequisites beyond or other than spellcasting. See the individual descriptions on pages 186–190 for details.

Crafting a magic weapon requires one day for each 1,000 gp value of the completed weapon.

Item Creation Feat Required: Craft Magic Arms and Armor.

CREATING WEAPONS

To create a magic weapon, a character needs a heat source and some iron, wood, or leather-working tools. She also needs a supply of materials, the most obvious being the weapon or the pieces of the weapon to be assembled. Only a masterwork weapon can be enchanted to become a magic weapon, and its cost is added to the total enchantment cost to determine final market value. Additional costs for the materials are subsumed in the cost for creating the magic weapon—half the base price listed on Table 8–10: Weapons, according to the weapon's total effective bonus.

Creating a magic weapon has a special prerequisite: The creator's caster level must be at least three times the enhancement bonus of the weapon. Thus, a 6th-level creator can make a +2 *longsword*, a 9th-level creator can create the same sword and make it +3, and a 15th-level caster can make it +5. If an item has both an enhancement bonus and a special ability (such as ghost touch), the higher of the two caster level requirements must be met.

A magic weapon must have at least a +1 enhancement bonus to have any of the abilities listed on Table 8–15: Weapon Special Abilities. A character can't create, for example, simply a *keen rapier*. A *keen rapier* needs an enhancement bonus of at least +1.

If spells are involved in the prerequisites for making the weapon, the creator must have prepared the spells to be cast (or must know the spells, in the case of a sorcerer or bard) but need not provide any material components or focuses the spells require, nor are any XP costs inherent in a prerequisite spell incurred in the creation of the item. The act of working on the weapon triggers the prepared spells, making them unavailable for casting during each day of the weapon's creation. (That is, those spell slots are expended from his currently prepared spells, just as if they had been cast.)

At the time of creation, the creator must decide if the weapon glows or not as a side-effect of the magic imbued within it. This decision does not affect the price or the creation time, but once the item is finished, the decision is binding.

Creating magic double-headed weapons is treated as creating two weapons when determining cost, time, XP, and special abili-

CREATING POTIONS

The creator needs a level working surface and at least a few containers in which to mix liquids, as well as a source of heat to boil the brew. In addition, he needs ingredients. The costs for materials and ingredients are subsumed in the cost for brewing the potion—25 gp per level of the spell times the level of the caster. All ingredients and materials used to brew a potion must be fresh and unused. The character must pay the full cost for brewing each potion. (Economies of scale do not apply.)

The creator must have prepared the spell to be placed in the potion (or must know the spell, in the case of a sorcerer or bard) and must provide any material components or focuses the spell requires. If casting the spell would reduce the caster's XP total, he pays the XP cost upon beginning the brew in addition to the XP cost for making the potion itself. Material components are consumed when he begins working, but focuses are not. (A focus used in brewing a potion can be reused.) The act of brewing triggers the prepared spell, making it unavailable for casting until the character has rested and regained spells. (That is, that spell slot is expended from his currently prepared spells, just as if it had been cast.)

Brewing the potion requires one day.

Item Creation Feat Required: Brew Potion.

TABLE 8–41: POTION BASE PRICES (BY BREWER'S CLASS)

Spell Level	Clr, Drd, Wiz	Sor	Brd	Pal, Rgr*
0	25 gp	25 gp	25 gp	—
1	50 gp	50 gp	100 gp	100 gp
2	300 gp	400 gp	400 gp	400 gp
3	750 gp	900 gp	1,050 gp	750 gp

*Caster level is half class level.

Prices assume that the potion was made at the minimum caster level.

TABLE 8–42: BASE COST TO BREW A POTION (BY BREWER'S CLASS)

Spell Level	Clr, Drd, Wiz	Sor	Brd	Pal, Rgr*
0	12 gp 5 sp +1 XP	12 gp 5 sp +1 XP	12 gp 5 sp +1 XP	—
1	25 gp +2 XP	25 gp +2 XP	50 gp +4 XP	50 gp +4 XP
2	150 gp +12 XP	200 gp +16 XP	200 gp +16 XP	200 gp +16 XP
3	375 gp +30 XP	450 gp +36 XP	525 gp +42 XP	375 gp +30 XP

*Caster level is half class level.

Costs assume that the creator makes the potion at the minimum caster level.

CREATING RINGS

To create a magic ring, a character needs a heat source. He also needs a supply of materials, the most obvious being a ring or the pieces of the ring to be assembled. The cost for the materials is subsumed in the cost for creating the ring. Ring costs are difficult to formularize. Refer to the sidebar on page 243 and use the ring prices in this chapter as a guideline. Creating a ring costs half the market value listed.

If spells are involved in the prerequisites for making the ring, the creator must have prepared the spells to be cast (or must know the spells, in the case of a sorcerer or bard) but need not provide any material components or focuses the spells require, nor are any XP costs inherent in a prerequisite spell incurred in the creation of the item. The act of working on the ring triggers the prepared spells, making them unavailable for casting during each day of the ring's creation. (That is, those spell slots are expended from his currently prepared spells, just as if they had been cast.)

Creating some rings may entail other prerequisites beyond or other than spellcasting. See the individual descriptions on pages 192–195 for details.

Forging a ring requires one day for each 1,000 gp value of the completed ring.

Item Creation Feat Required: Forge Ring.

CREATING SCROLLS

The character needs a supply of choice writing materials, the cost of which is subsumed in the cost for scribing the scroll—12.5 gp per level of the spell times the level of the caster. All writing implements and materials used to scribe a scroll must be fresh and unused. The character must pay the full cost for scribing each spell scroll no matter how many times she previously has scribed the same spell.

The creator must have prepared the spell to be scribed (or must know the spell, in the case of a sorcerer or bard) and must provide any material components or focuses the spell requires. If casting the spell would reduce the caster's XP total, she pays the cost upon beginning the scroll in addition to the XP cost for making the scroll itself. Likewise, material components are consumed when she begins writing, but focuses are not. (A focus used in scribing a scroll can be reused.) The act of writing triggers the prepared spell, making it unavailable for casting until the character has rested and regained spells. (That is, that spell slot is expended from her currently prepared spells, just as if it had been cast.)

Scribing a scroll requires one day per each 1,000 gp value of the completed scroll.

Item Creation Feat Required: Scribe Scroll.

TABLE 8–43: SCROLL BASE PRICES (BY SCRIBER'S CLASS)

Spell Level	Clr, Drd, Wiz	Sor	Brd	Pal, Rgr*
0	12 gp 5 sp	12 gp 5 sp	12 gp 5 sp	—
1	25 gp	25 gp	50 gp	50 gp
2	150 gp	200 gp	200 gp	200 gp
3	375 gp	450 gp	525 gp	375 gp
4	700 gp	800 gp	1,000 gp	700 gp
5	1,125 gp	1,250 gp	1,625 gp	—
6	1,650 gp	1,800 gp	2,400 gp	—
7	2,275 gp	2,450 gp	—	—
8	3,000 gp	3,200 gp	—	—
9	3,825 gp	4,050 gp	—	—

*Caster level is half class level.

Prices assume that the scroll was made at the minimum caster level.

TABLE 8–44: BASE COST TO SCRIBE A SCROLL (BY SCRIBER'S CLASS)

Spell Level	Clr, Drd, Wiz	Sor	Brd	Pal, Rgr*
0	6 gp 2 sp 5 cp +1 XP	6 gp 2 sp 5 cp +1 XP	6 gp 2 sp 5 cp +1 XP	—
1	12 gp 5 sp +1 XP	12 gp 5 sp +1 XP	25 gp +2 XP	25 gp +2 XP
2	75 gp +6 XP	100 gp +8 XP	100 gp +8 XP	100 gp +8 XP
3	187 gp 5 sp +15 XP	225 gp +18 XP	262 gp 5 sp +21 XP	187 gp 5 sp +15 XP
4	350 gp +28 XP	400 gp +32 XP	500 gp +40 XP	350 gp +28 XP
5	562 gp 5 sp +45 XP	625 gp +50 XP	812 gp 5 sp +65 XP	—
6	826 gp +66 XP	900 gp +72 XP	1,200 gp +96 XP	—
7	1,135 gp 5 sp +91 XP	1,225 gp +98 XP	—	—
8	1,500 gp +120 XP	1,600 gp +128 XP	—	—
9	1,912 gp 5 sp +153 XP	2, 025 gp +162 XP	—	—

*Caster level is half class level.

Costs assume that the creator makes the scroll at the minimum caster level.

CREATING RODS

The character needs a supply of materials, the most obvious being a rod or the pieces of the rod to be assembled. The cost for the materials is subsumed in the cost for creating the rod. Rod costs are difficult to formularize. Refer to the sidebar on page 243 and use the rod prices in this chapter as a guideline. Creating a rod costs half the market value listed.

If spells are involved in the prerequisites for making the rod, the creator must have prepared the spells to be cast (or must know the spells, in the case of a sorcerer or bard) but need not provide any material components or focuses the spells require, nor are any XP costs inherent in a prerequisite spell incurred in the creation of the item. The act of working on the rod triggers the prepared spells, making them unavailable for casting during each day of the rod's creation. (That is, those spell slots are expended from his currently prepared spells, just as if they had been cast.)

Creating some rods may entail other prerequisites beyond or other than spellcasting. See the individual descriptions on pages 195–199 for details.

Crafting a rod requires one day for each 1,000 gp value of the completed rod.

Item Creation Feat Required: Craft Rod.

CREATING STAFFS

The character needs a supply of materials, the most obvious being a staff or the pieces of the staff to be assembled. The cost for the materials is subsumed in the cost for creating the staff—375 gp per level of the highest-level spell times the level of the caster, plus 75% of the value of the next most costly ability (281.25 gp per level of the spell times the level of the caster), plus one-half of the value of any other abilities (187.5 gp per level of the spell times the level of the caster). To get the final price, the results can be modified by the DM by up to 20% based on the number and types of spells placed together in the same staff. Staffs are always fully charged (50 charges) when created.

If desired, a spell can be placed into the staff at only half the normal cost, but then activating that particular spell costs 2 charges from the staff. A single function can cost no more than 2 charges. The caster level of all spells in a staff must be the same.

The creator must have prepared the spells to be stored (or must know the spell, in the case of a sorcerer or bard) and must provide any material components or focuses the spells require. Fifty of each needed component are required (one for each charge). If casting the spells would reduce the caster's XP total, he pays the cost (multiplied by 50) upon beginning the staff in addition to the XP cost for making the staff itself. Likewise, material components are consumed when he begins working, but focuses are not. (A focus used in creating a staff can be reused.) The act of working on the staff triggers the prepared spells, making them unavailable for casting during each day of the staff's creation. (That is, those spell slots are expended from his currently prepared spells, just as if they had been cast.)

Creating a few staffs may entail other prerequisites beyond spellcasting. See the individual descriptions on pages 204–206 for details.

Crafting a staff requires one day for each 1,000 gp value of the completed staff.

Item Creation Feat Required: Craft Staff.

CREATING WANDS

The character needs a small supply of materials, the most obvious being a baton or the pieces of the wand to be assembled. The cost for the materials is subsumed in the cost for creating the wand—375 gp per level of the spell times the level of the caster. Wands are always fully charged (50 charges) when created.

The creator must have prepared the spell to be stored (or must know the spell, in the case of a sorcerer or bard) and must provide any material components or focuses the spell requires. Fifty of each needed component are required, one for each charge. If casting the spell would reduce the caster's XP total, she pays the cost (multiplied by 50) upon beginning the wand in addition to the XP cost for making the wand itself. Likewise, material components are consumed when she begins working, but focuses are not. (A focus used in creating a wand can be reused.) The act of working on the wand triggers the prepared spell, making it unavailable for casting during each day devoted to the wand's creation. (That is, that spell slot is expended from her currently prepared spells, just as if it had been cast.)

Crafting a wand requires one day per each 1,000 gp value of the completed wand.

Item Creation Feat Required: Craft Wand.

TABLE 8–45: WAND BASE PRICES (BY CRAFTER'S CLASS)

Spell Level	Clr, Drd, Wiz	Sor	Brd	Pal, Rgr*
0	375 gp	375 gp	375 gp	—
1	750 gp	750 gp	1,500 gp	1,500 gp
2	4,500 gp	6,000 gp	6,000 gp	6,000 gp
3	11,250 gp	13,500 gp	15,750 gp	11,250 gp
4	21,000 gp	24,000 gp	30,000 gp	21,000 gp

*Caster level is half class level.
Prices assume that the wand was made at the minimum caster level.

TABLE 8–46: BASE COST TO CRAFT A WAND (BY CRAFTER'S CLASS)

Spell Level	Clr, Drd, Wiz	Sor	Brd	Pal, Rgr*
0	187 gp 5 sp	187 gp 5 sp	187 gp 5 sp	—
	+15 XP	+15 XP	+15 XP	
1	325 gp	325 gp	1,250 gp	1,250 gp
	+30 XP	+30 XP	+60 XP	+60 XP
2	2,250 gp	3,000 gp	3,000 gp	3,000 gp
	+180 XP	+240 XP	+240 XP	+240 XP
3	5,625 gp	6,750 gp	7,875 gp	5,625 gp
	+450 XP	+540 XP	+630 XP	+450 XP
4	10,500 gp	12,000 gp	15,000 gp	10,500 gp
	+840 XP	+960 XP	+1,200 XP	+840 XP

*Caster level is half class level.
Costs assume that the creator makes the wand at the minimum caster level.

CREATING WONDROUS ITEMS

To create a wondrous item, a character usually needs some sort of equipment or tools to work on the item. She also needs a supply of materials, the most obvious being the item itself or the pieces of the item to be assembled. The cost for the materials is subsumed in the cost for creating the item. Wondrous item costs are difficult to formularize. Refer to the sidebar on page 243 and use the item prices in this chapter as a guideline. Creating an item costs half the market value listed.

If spells are involved in the prerequisites for making the item, the creator must have prepared the spells to be cast (or must know the spells, in the case of a sorcerer or bard) but need not provide any material components or focuses the spells require, nor are any XP costs inherent in a prerequisite spell incurred in the creation of the item. The act of working on the item triggers the prepared spells, making them unavailable for casting during each day of the item's creation. (That is, those spell slots are expended from his currently prepared spells, just as if they had been cast.)

Creating some items may entail other prerequisites beyond or other than spellcasting. See the individual descriptions beginning on page 207 for details.

Crafting a wondrous item requires one day for each 1,000 gp value of the completed item.

Item Creation Feat Required: Craft Wondrous Item.

INTELLIGENT ITEM CREATION

To create an intelligent item the, creator's caster level must be at least 15th. Time and creation cost are based on the normal item creation rules, with the market price values on Table 8–31: Item Intelligence, Wisdom, Charisma, and Capabilities (page 228) treated as additions to both time, gold piece cost, and XP cost. Determine the item's Intelligence, Wisdom, and Charisma randomly, as outlined on page 228 (though no ability score may be higher than the creator's score in that ability). The item's alignment is the same as its creator's. Determine other features randomly, following the guidelines in the relevant sections of this chapter.

ADDING NEW ABILITIES

A creator can add new magical abilities to a magic item with no restrictions. The cost to do this is the same as if the item was not magical. Thus, a +1 longsword can be made into a +2 vorpal longsword, with the cost of creation being equal to that of a +2 vorpal sword minus the cost of a +1 sword.

If the item is one that takes up a specific space on a character (see Limit on Magic Items Worn, page 176), any additional power added to that item doubles the cost. For example, if a character adds the power to confer invisibility to her +2 ring of protection, the cost of adding this ability is the same as for creating a ring of invisibility multiplied by 2.

Appendix: Quick Reference Tables

Magic Items and Special Items of up to 3,000 gp Market Price

Weapons

Weapons	Market Price
Masterwork weapon	Cost of ordinary weapon plus 300 gp
Masterwork double weapon	Cost of ordinary weapon plus 600 gp
+1 weapon	Cost of ordinary weapon plus 1,300 gp
+1 double weapon	Cost of ordinary weapon plus 2,600 gp
Silvered arrow, bolt, or bullet	1 gp
Masterwork arrow, bolt, or bullet	7 gp
Silvered dagger	10 gp
Sleep arrow	132 gp
Mighty composite shortbow (+1 Str bonus)	150 gp
Mighty composite longbow (+1 Str bonus)	200 gp
Mighty composite shortbow (+2 Str bonus)	225 gp
Screaming bolt	257 gp
Mighty composite longbow (+2 Str bonus)	300 gp
Mighty composite longbow (+3 Str bonus)	400 gp
Mighty composite longbow (+4 Str bonus)	500 gp
Javelin of lightning	751 gp
Slaying arrow	2,282 gp

Armor and Shields

Armor and Shields	Market Price
Masterwork armor or shield	Cost of ordinary armor or shield plus 150 gp
+1 armor or shield	Cost of ordinary armor or shield plus 1,150 gp
Darkwood shield	257 gp
Mithral large shield	1,020 gp
Mithral shirt	1,100 gp
Adamantine shield	2,170 gp
Spined shield	2,670 gp

Potions

Potions	Market Price
Potion, 0-level spell (caster level 1–20)	Caster level × 25 gp
Potion, 1st-level spell (caster level 1–20)	Caster level × 50 gp
Potion, 2nd-level spell (caster level 3–20)	Caster level × 100 gp
Potion, 3rd-level spell (caster level 5–20)	Caster level × 150 gp
Potion of hiding	150 gp
Potion of love	150 gp
Potion of sneaking	150 gp
Potion of swimming	150 gp
Potion of vision	150 gp
Potion of Charisma	300 gp
Potion of Intelligence	300 gp
Potion of Wisdom	300 gp
Potion of glibness	500 gp
Potion of truth	500 gp
Potion of fire breath	900 gp
Potion of heroism	900 gp

Rings

Rings	Market Price
Ring of climbing	2,000 gp
Ring of jumping	2,000 gp
Ring of protection +1	2,000 gp
Ring of warmth	2,100 gp
Ring of feather falling	2,200 gp
Ring of swimming	2,300 gp
Ring of sustenance	2,500 gp

Scrolls

Scrolls	Market Price
Scroll, 0-level spell (caster level 1–20)	Caster level × 12 gp 5 sp
Scroll, 1st-level spell (caster level 1–20)	Caster level × 25 gp
Scroll, 2nd-level spell (caster level 3–20)	Caster level × 50 gp
Scroll, 3rd-level spell (caster level 5–20)	Caster level × 75 gp
Scroll, 4th-level spell (caster level 7–20)	Caster level × 100 gp
Scroll, 5th-level spell (caster level 9–20)	Caster level × 125 gp
Scroll, 6th-level spell (caster level 11–20)	Caster level × 150 gp
Scroll, 7th-level spell (caster level 13–17)	Caster level × 175 gp
Scroll, 8th-level spell (caster level 15)	Caster level × 200 gp

Wands

Wands	Market Price
Wand, 0-level spell (caster level 1–8)	Caster level × 375 gp
Wand, 1st-level spell (caster level 1–4)	Caster level × 750 gp

Minor Wondrous Items

Minor Wondrous Items	Market Price
Ioun stone (dull gray)	25 gp
Quaal's feather token (anchor)	50 gp
Everburning torch	90 gp
Quaal's feather token (tree)	100 gp
Oil of timelessness	150 gp
Quaal's feather token (fan)	200 gp
Dust of tracelessness	250 gp
Quaal's feather token (bird)	300 gp
Quaal's feather token (swan boat)	450 gp
Dust of illusion	500 gp
Necklace of prayer beads (blessing)	500 gp
Quaal's feather token (whip)	500 gp
Scarab, golembane (flesh)	800 gp
Bag of tricks (gray)	900 gp
Dust of dryness	900 gp
Oil of slipperiness	900 gp
Bracers of armor (+1)	1,000 gp
Cloak of resistance (+1)	1,000 gp
Eyes of the eagle	1,000 gp
Goggles of minute seeing	1,000 gp
Hand of the mage	1,000 gp
Pearl of power (1st-level spell)	1,000 gp
Phylactery of faithfulness	1,000 gp
Scarab, golembane (clay)	1,000 gp
Stone of alarm	1,000 gp
Pipes of the sewers	1,150 gp
Scarab, golembane (stone)	1,200 gp
Brooch of shielding	1,500 gp
Scarab, golembane (iron)	1,600 gp
Necklace of fireballs (Type I)	1,650 gp
Pipes of sounding	1,800 gp
Quiver of Ehlonna	1,800 gp
Scarab, golembane (flesh and clay)	1,800 gp
Horseshoes of speed	1,900 gp
Amulet of natural armor (+1)	2,000 gp
Bead of force	2,000 gp
Boots of elvenkind	2,000 gp
Cloak of elvenkind	2,000 gp
Hat of disguise	2,000 gp
Heward's handy haversack	2,000 gp
Horn of fog	2,000 gp
Slippers of spider climbing	2,000 gp
Universal solvent	2,000 gp
Vest of escape	2,000 gp
Dust of appearance	2,100 gp
Glove of storing	2,200 gp
Sovereign glue	2,400 gp
Bag of holding (Bag 1)	2,500 gp
Boots of striding and springing	2,500 gp
Boots of the winterlands	2,500 gp
Candle of truth	2,500 gp
Scarab, golembane (any golem)	2,500 gp
Helm of comprehending languages and reading magic	2,600 gp
Necklace of fireballs (Type II)	2,700 gp
Bag of tricks (rust)	3,000 gp

MAGIC ITEMS AND SPECIAL ITEMS OF UP TO 3,000 GP MARKET PRICE (CONT.)

Chime of opening	3,000 gp
Horseshoes of a zephyr	3,000 gp

Cursed Items	Market Price
Incense of obsession	200 gp
Ring of clumsiness	500 gp
Amulet of inescapable location	1,000 gp
Stone of weight	1,000 gp
Bracers of defenselessness	1,200 gp
Gauntlets of fumbling	1,300 gp
–2 sword, cursed	1,500 gp
Armor of rage	1,600 gp
Medallion of thought projection	1,800 gp

Spear, cursed backbiter	2,000 gp
Flask of curses	2,100 gp
Dust of sneezing and choking	2,400 gp

Special Substances and Items	Market Price
Tindertwig	1 gp
Sunrod	2 gp
Acid (flask)	10 gp
Alchemist's fire (flask)	20 gp
Smokestick	20 gp
Holy water (flask)	25 gp
Thunderstone	30 gp
Antitoxin (vial)	50 gp
Tanglefoot bag	50 gp

ALPHABETICAL LISTING OF STANDARD WEAPONS

Weapon [Size]	Category	Cost	Damage	Critical	Range Increment	Weight	Type
Arrows (20)*	—	1 gp	—	—	—	3 lb.	—
Axe, orc double* [Large]	Exotic melee	60 gp	1d8/1d8	×3	—	25 lb.	Slashing
Axe, throwing [Small]	Martial melee	8 gp	1d6	×2	10 ft.	4 lb.	Slashing
Battleaxe [Medium-size]	Martial melee	10 gp	1d8	×3	—	7 lb.	Slashing
Bolts, crossbow (10)*	—	1 gp	—	—	—	1 lb.	—
Bolts, repeating crossbow (5)*	—	1 gp	—	—	—	1 lb.	—
Bullets, sling (10)	—	1 sp	—	—	—	5 lb.	—
Chain, spiked*† [Large]	Exotic melee	25 gp	2d4	×2	—	15 lb.	Piercing
Club [Medium-size]	Simple melee	—	1d6	×2	10 ft.	3 lb.	Bludgeoning
Crossbow, hand* [Tiny]	Exotic ranged	100 gp	1d4	19–20/×2	30 ft.	3 lb.	Piercing
Crossbow, heavy* [Medium-size]	Simple ranged	50 gp	1d10	19–20/×2	120 ft.	9 lb.	Piercing
Crossbow, light* [Small]	Simple ranged	35 gp	1d8	19–20/×2	80 ft.	6 lb.	Piercing
Crossbow, repeating* [Medium-size]	Exotic ranged	250 gp	1d8	19–20/×2	80 ft.	16 lb.	Piercing
Dagger* [Tiny]	Simple melee	2 gp	1d4	19–20/×2	10 ft.	1 lb.	Piercing
Dagger, punching [Tiny]	Simple melee	2 gp	1d4	×3	—	2 lb.	Piercing
Dart [Small]	Simple ranged	5 sp	1d4	×2	20 ft.	1/2 lb.	Piercing
Falchion [Large]	Martial melee	75 gp	2d4	18–20/×2	—	16 lb.	Slashing
Flail, dire* [Large]	Exotic melee	90 gp	1d8/1d8	×2	—	20 lb.	Bludgeoning
Flail, heavy* [Large]	Martial melee	15 gp	1d10	19–20/×2	—	20 lb.	Bludgeoning
Flail, light* [Medium-size]	Martial melee	8 gp	1d8	×2	—	5 lb.	Bludgeoning
Gauntlet (unarmed)	Simple melee	2 gp	*	*	—	2 lb.	Bludgeoning
Gauntlet, spiked* [Tiny]	Simple melee	5 gp	1d4	×2	—	2 lb.	Piercing
Glaive*† [Large]	Martial melee	8 gp	1d10	×3	—	15 lb.	Slashing
Greataxe [Large]	Martial melee	20 gp	1d12	×3	—	20 lb.	Slashing
Greatclub [Large]	Martial melee	5 gp	1d10	×2	—	10 lb.	Bludgeoning
Greatsword [Large]	Martial melee	50 gp	2d6	19–20/×2	—	15 lb.	Slashing
Guisarme*† [Large]	Martial melee	9 gp	2d4	×3	—	15 lb.	Slashing
Halberd*ª [Large]	Martial melee	10 gp	1d10	×3	—	15 lb.	Piercing and slashing
Halfspearª [Medium-size]	Simple melee	1 gp	1d6	×3	20 ft.	3 lb.	Piercing
Hammer, gnome hooked* [Medium-size]	Exotic melee	20 gp	1d6/1d4	×3/×4	—	6 lb.	Bludgeoning and piercing
Hammer, light [Small]	Martial melee	1 gp	1d4	×2	20 ft.	2 lb.	Bludgeoning
Handaxe [Small]	Martial melee	6 gp	1d6	×3	—	5 lb.	Slashing
Javelin [Medium-size]	Simple ranged	1 gp	1d6	×2	30 ft.	2 lb.	Piercing
Kama* [Small]	Exotic melee	2 gp	1d6	×2	—	2 lb.	Slashing
Kama, halfling* [Tiny]	Exotic melee	2 gp	1d4	×2	—	1 lb.	Slashing
Kukri [Tiny]	Exotic melee	8 gp	1d4	18–20/×2	—	3 lb.	Slashing
Lance, heavy*† [Medium-size]	Martial melee	10 gp	1d8	×3	—	10 lb.	Piercing
Lance, light* [Small]	Martial melee	6 gp	1d6	×3	—	5 lb.	Piercing
Longbow* [Large]	Martial ranged	75 gp	1d8	×3	100 ft.	3 lb.	Piercing
Longbow, composite* [Large]	Martial ranged	100 gp	1d8	×3	110 ft.	3 lb.	Piercing
Longspear*†ª [Large]	Martial melee	5 gp	1d8	×3	—	9 lb.	Piercing
Longsword [Medium-size]	Martial melee	15 gp	1d8	19–20/×2	—	4 lb.	Slashing
Mace, heavy [Medium-size]	Simple melee	12 gp	1d8	×2	—	12 lb.	Bludgeoning
Mace, light [Small]	Simple melee	5 gp	1d6	×2	—	6 lb.	Bludgeoning
Morningstar [Medium-size]	Simple melee	8 gp	1d8	×2	—	8 lb.	Bludgeoning and piercing
Net* [Medium-size]	Exotic ranged	20 gp	*	*	10 ft.*	10 lb.	*
Nunchaku* [Small]	Exotic melee	2 gp	1d6	×2	—	2 lb.	Bludgeoning

ALPHABETICAL LISTING OF STANDARD WEAPONS (CONT.)

Weapon [Size]	Category	Cost	Damage	Critical	Range Increment	Weight	Type
Nunchaku, halfling* [Tiny]	Exotic melee	2 gp	1d4	×2	—	1 lb.	Bludgeoning
Pick, heavy* [Medium-size]	Martial melee	8 gp	1d6	×4	—	6 lb.	Piercing
Pick, light* [Small]	Martial melee	4 gp	1d4	×4	—	4 lb.	Piercing
Quarterstaff*‡ [Large]	Simple melee	—	1d6/1d6	×2	—	4 lb.	Bludgeoning
Ranseur*† [Large]	Martial melee	10 gp	2d4	×3	—	15 lb.	Piercing
Rapier* [Medium-size]	Martial melee	20 gp	1d6	18–20/×2	—	3 lb.	Piercing
Sap [Small]	Martial melee	1 gp	1d6∫	×2	—	3 lb.	Bludgeoning
Scimitar [Medium-size]	Martial melee	15 gp	1d6	18–20/×2	—	4 lb.	Slashing
Scythe [Large]	Martial melee	18 gp	2d4	×4	—	12 lb.	Piercing and slashing
Shortbow* [Medium-size]	Martial ranged	30 gp	1d6	×3	60 ft.	2 lb.	Piercing
Shortbow, composite* [Medium-size]	Martial ranged	75 gp	1d6	×3	70 ft.	2 lb.	Piercing
Shortspearᵃ [Large]	Simple melee	2 gp	1d8	×3	20 ft.	5 lb.	Piercing
Shuriken* [Tiny]	Exotic ranged	1 gp	1	×2	10 ft.	1/10 lb.	Piercing
Siangham* [Small]	Exotic melee	3 gp	1d6	×2	—	1 lb.	Piercing
Siangham, halfling* [Tiny]	Exotic melee	2 gp	1d4	×2	—	1 lb.	Piercing
Sickle [Small]	Simple melee	6 gp	1d6	×2	—	3 lb.	Slashing
Sling [Small]	Simple ranged	—	1d4	×2	50 ft.	0 lb.	Bludgeoning
Strike, unarmed (Medium-size being)	Simple melee	—	1d3∫	×2	—	—	Bludgeoning
Strike, unarmed (Small being)	Simple melee	—	1d2∫	×2	—	—	Bludgeoning
Sword, bastard* [Medium-size]	Exotic melee	35 gp	1d10	19–20/×2	—	10 lb.	Slashing
Sword, short [Small]	Martial melee	10 gp	1d6	19–20/×2	—	3 lb.	Piercing
Sword, two-bladed* [Large]	Exotic melee	100 gp	1d8/1d8	19–20/×2	—	30 lb.	Slashing
Tridentᵃ [Medium-size]	Martial melee	15 gp	1d8	×2	10 ft.	5 lb.	Piercing
Urgrosh, dwarven*ᵃ [Large]	Exotic melee	50 gp	1d8/1d6	×3	—	15 lb.	Slashing and piercing
Waraxe, dwarven* [Medium-size]	Exotic melee	30 gp	1d10	×3	—	15 lb.	Slashing
Warhammer [Medium-size]	Martial melee	12 gp	1d8	×3	—	8 lb.	Bludgeoning
Whip* [Small]	Exotic ranged	1 gp	1d2∫	×2	15 ft.*	2 lb.	Slashing

*See the description of this weapon for special rules.

†Reach weapon.

∫The weapon deals subdual damage rather than normal damage.

ᵃ If you use a ready action to set this weapon against a charge, you deal double damage if you score a hit against a charging character.

GRENADELIKE WEAPONS

Weapon	Cost	Damage Direct Hit	Damage Splash	Range Increment	Weight
Acid (flask)	10 gp	1d6	1 pt	10 ft.	1 1/4 lb.
Alchemist's fire (flask)	20 gp	1d6	1 pt	10 ft.	1 1/4 lb.
Holy water (flask)	25 gp	2d4	1 pt	10 ft.	1 1/4 lb.
Tanglefoot bag	50 gp	Entangles	—	10 ft.	4 lb.
Thunderstone	30 gp	Sonic attack	—	20 ft.	1 lb.

SIEGE ENGINES

Item	Cost	Damage	Critical	Range Increment	Crew
Catapult, heavy	800 gp	5d6	—	200 ft. (100 ft. minimum)	5
Catapult, light	550 gp	3d6	—	150 ft. (100 ft. minimum)	2
Ballista	500 gp	3d6	×3	120	1
Ram	2,000 gp	4d6	×3	—	10

ALPHABETICAL LISTING OF STANDARD ARMOR FOR MEDIUM-SIZE CREATURES

Armor [Category]	Cost	Armor Bonus	Maximum Dex Bonus	Armor Check Penalty	Arcane Spell Failure	Speed (30 ft.)	Speed (20 ft.)	Weight
Armor spikes	+50 gp	—	—	—	—	—	—	+10 lb.
Banded mail [Heavy]	250 gp	+6	+1	–6	35%	20 ft.	15 ft.	35 lb.
Breastplate [Medium]	200 gp	+5	+3	–4	25%	20 ft.	15 ft.	30 lb.
Buckler	15 gp	+1	—	–1	5%	—	—	5 lb.
Chain shirt [Light]	100 gp	+4	+4	–2	20%	30 ft.	20 ft.	25 lb.
Chainmail [Medium]	150 gp	+5	+2	–5	30%	20 ft.	15 ft.	40 lb.
Full plate [Heavy]	1,500 gp	+8	+1	–6	35%	20 ft.	15 ft.	50 lb.
Gauntlet, locked	8 gp	—	—	Special	—	—	—	+5 lb.
Half-plate [Heavy]	600 gp	+7	+0	–7	40%	20 ft.	15 ft.	50 lb.
Hide armor [Medium]	15 gp	+3	+4	–3	20%	20 ft.	15 ft.	25 lb.
Leather armor [Light]	10 gp	+2	+6	0	10%	30 ft.	20 ft.	15 lb.
Padded armor [Light]	5 gp	+1	+8	0	5%	30 ft.	20 ft.	10 lb.
Scale mail [Medium]	50 gp	+4	+3	–4	25%	20 ft.	15 ft.	30 lb.
Shield spikes	+10 gp	—	—	—	—	—	—	+5 lb.
Shield, large, steel	20 gp	+2	—	–2	15%	—	—	15 lb.
Shield, large, wooden	7 gp	+2	—	–2	15%	—	—	10 lb.
Shield, small, steel	9 gp	+1	—	–1	5%	—	—	6 lb.
Shield, small, wooden	3 gp	+1	—	–1	5%	—	—	5 lb.
Shield, tower	30 gp	**	—	–10	50%	—	—	45 lb.
Splint mail [Heavy]	200 gp	+6	+0	–7	40%	20 ft.	15 ft.	45 lb.
Studded leather armor [Light]	25 gp	+3	+5	–1	15%	30 ft.	20 ft.	20 lb.

ALPHABETICAL LISTING OF GOODS AND SERVICES

Item	Cost	Weight
Alchemist's lab‡	500 gp	40 lb.
Ale		
Gallon	2 sp	8 lb.
Mug	4 cp	1 lb.
Artisan's outfit	1 gp	4 lb.†
Artisan's tools‡	5 gp	5 lb.
Artisan's tools, masterwork‡	55 gp	5 lb.
Backpack (empty)	2 gp	2 lb.†
Banquet (per person)	10 gp	—
Barding		
Medium-size creature	×2	×1
Large creature	×4	×2
Barrel (empty)	2 gp	30 lb.
Basket (empty)	4 sp	1 lb.
Bedroll	1 sp	5 lb.†
Bell	1 gp	*
Bit and bridle	2 gp	1 lb.
Blanket, winter	5 sp	3 lb.†
Block and tackle	5 gp	5 lb.
Bottle, wine, glass	2 gp	*
Bread, per loaf	2 cp	1/2 lb.
Bucket (empty)	5 sp	2 lb.
Caltrops	1 gp	2 lb.
Candle	1 cp	*
Canvas (sq. yd.)	1 sp	1 lb.
Cart	15 gp	200 lb.
Case, map or scroll	1 gp	1/2 lb.
Castle	500,000 gp	—
Castle, huge	1,000,000 gp	—
Chain (10 ft.)	30 gp	2 lb.
Chalk, 1 piece	1 cp	*
Cheese, hunk of	1 sp	1/2 lb.
Chest (empty)	2 gp	25 lb.
Chicken	2 cp	—
Cinnamon	1 gp	1 lb.
Cleric's vestments	5 gp	6 lb.†
Climber's kit	80 gp	5 lb.†
Cloves	15 gp	1 lb.
Cold weather outfit	8 gp	7 lb.†
Copper	5 sp	1 lb.
Courtier's outfit	30 gp	6 lb.†
Cow	10 gp	—
Crowbar	2 gp	5 lb.
Disguise kit	50 gp	8 lb.†
Dog	25 gp	—
Dog, riding	150 gp	—
Donkey or mule	8 gp	—
Entertainer's outfit	3 gp	4 lb.†
Explorer's outfit	10 gp	8 lb.†
Feed (per day)	5 cp	10 lb.
Firewood (per day)	1 cp	20 lb.
Fishhook	1 sp	*
Fishing net, 25 sq. ft.	4 gp	5 lb.
Flask	3 cp	*
Flint and steel	1 gp	*
Flour	2 cp	1 lb.
Galley	30,000 gp	—
Ginger	2 gp	1 lb.
Goat	1 gp	—
Gold	50 gp	1 lb.
Grappling hook	1 gp	4 lb.
Hammer	5 sp	2 lb.
Healer's kit	50 gp	1 lb.
Holly and mistletoe	—	*
Holy symbol, wooden	1 gp	**
Holy symbol, silver	25 gp	1 lb.
Horse		
Horse, heavy	200 gp	—
Horse, light	75 gp	—
Pony	30 gp	—
Warhorse, heavy	400 gp	—
Warhorse, light	150 gp	—
Warpony	100 gp	—
Hourglass	25 gp	1 lb.
House, grand	5,000 gp	—
House, simple	1,000 gp	—
Ink (1 oz. vial)	8 gp	*
Inkpen	1 sp	*
Inn stay (per day)‡		
Good	2 gp	—
Common	5 sp	—
Poor	2 sp	—
Iron	1 sp	1 lb.
Jug, clay	3 cp	9 lb.
Keelboat	3,000 gp	—
Keep	150,000 gp	—
Ladder, 10-foot	5 cp	20 lb.
Lamp, common	1 sp	1 lb.
Lantern, bullseye	12 gp	3 lb.
Lantern, hooded	7 gp	2 lb.
Linen (sq. yard)	4 gp	1 lb.
Lock‡		1 lb.
Very simple	20 gp	1 lb.
Average	40 gp	1 lb.
Good	80 gp	1 lb.
Amazing	150 gp	1 lb.
Longship	10,000 gp	—
Magnifying glass‡	100 gp	*
Manacles	15 gp	2 lb.
Manacles, masterwork	50 gp	2 lb.
Mansion	100,000 gp	—
Meals (per day)‡		
Good	5 sp	—
Common	3 sp	—
Poor	1 sp	—
Meat, chunk of	3 sp	1/2 lb.
Mirror, small steel	10 gp	1/2 lb.
Moat with bridge	50,000 gp	—
Monk's outfit	5 gp	2 lb.†
Mug/tankard, clay	2 cp	1 lb.
Musical instrument, common	5 gp	3 lb.†
Musical instrument, masterwork	100 gp	3 lb.†
Noble's outfit	75 gp	10 lb.†
Oar	2 gp	—
Oil (1-pint flask)	1 sp	1 lb.
Ox	15 gp	—
Paper (sheet)	4 sp	*
Parchment (sheet)	2 sp	*
Peasant's outfit	1 sp	2 lb.†
Pepper	2 gp	1 lb.
Pick, miner's	3 gp	10 lb.
Pig	3 gp	—
Pitcher, clay	2 cp	5 lb.
Piton	1 sp	1/2 lb.
Pole, 10-foot	2 sp	8 lb.
Pot, iron	5 sp	10 lb.
Pouch, belt	1 gp	3 lb.†
Ram, portable	10 gp	20 lb.
Rations, trail (per day)	5 sp	1 lb.†
Rope, hemp (50 ft.)	1 gp	10 lb.
Rope, silk (50 ft.)	10 gp	5 lb.
Rowboat	50 gp	—
Royal outfit	200 gp	15 lb.†
Sack (empty)	1 sp	1/2 lb.†
Saddle		
Military	20 gp	30 lb.
Pack	5 gp	15 lb.
Riding	10 gp	25 lb.
Saddle, Exotic		
Military	60 gp	40 lb.
Pack	15 gp	20 lb.
Riding	30 gp	30 lb.
Saddlebags	4 gp	8 lb.
Saffron	15 gp	1 lb.
Sailing ship	10,000 gp	—
Salt	5 gp	1 lb.
Scale, merchant's‡	2 gp	1 lb.
Scholar's outfit	5 gp	6 lb.†
Sealing wax	1 gp	1 lb.
Sewing needle	5 sp	*
Sheep	2 gp	—
Siege tower	1,000 gp	—
Signal whistle	8 sp	**
Signet ring‡	5 gp	*
Silk (2 sq. yards)	20 gp	1 lb.
Silver	5 gp	1 lb.
Sled	20 gp	300 lb.
Sledge	1 gp	10 lb.
Soap (per lb.)	5 sp	1 lb.
Spade or shovel	2 gp	8 lb.
Spell component pouch	5 gp	3 lb.†
Spellbook, wizard's (blank)	15 gp	3 lb.†
Spyglass	1,000 gp	1 lb.
Stabling (per day)	5 sp	—
Tea leaves	2 sp	1 lb.
Tent	10 gp	20 lb.†
Thieves' tools	30 gp	1 lb.
Thieves' tools, masterwork	100 gp	2 lb.
Tobacco	5 sp	1 lb.
Torch	1 cp	1 lb.
Tower	50,000 gp	—
Traveler's outfit	1 gp	5 lb.†
Vial, ink or potion	1 gp	*
Wagon	35 gp	400 lb.
Warship	25,000 gp	—
Water clock‡	1,000 gp	200 lb.
Waterskin	1 gp	4 lb.†
Wheat	1 cp	1 lb.
Whetstone	2 cp	1 lb.
Wine		
Common (pitcher)	2 sp	6 lb.
Fine (bottle)	10 gp	1 1/2 lb.

*No weight worth noting.
**Ten of these items together weigh 1 pound.
†These items weigh one-quarter this amount when made for Small characters. Containers for Small characters also carry one-quarter the normal amount.
‡See description.

FUNDAMENTAL ACTIONS IN COMBAT

Attack Actions	Move	Attack of Opportunity*
Attack (melee)	Yes	No
Attack (ranged)	Yes	Yes
Attack (unarmed)	Yes	Maybe
Charge	speed ×2 (special)†	No
Full attack	5-ft. step	No

Magic Actions	Move	Attack of Opportunity*
Cast a spell		
1-action spell	Yes	Yes
Full-round spell	5-ft. step	Yes
Concentrate to maintain	Yes	No
Activate magic item	Yes	Maybe
Use special ability		
Use spell-like ability	Usually**	Yes
Use supernatural ability	Usually**	No
Use extraordinary ability††	Usually**	No

Movement-Only Actions	Move	Attack of Opportunity*
Double move	speed ×2	Maybe
Run	speed ×4	Yes

*Regardless of the action, if you move within or out of a threatened area, you usually provoke an attack of opportunity. This column indicates whether the action itself, not moving, provokes an attack of opportunity.

**You can move unless the action is defined as a full-round action, in which case you normally get a 5-foot step.

†You can move up to twice your normal speed, but only before the attack, not after. You must move at least 10 feet, and the entire move must be in a straight line.

††Most extraordinary abilities aren't actions. This applies to those that are.

MISCELLANEOUS ACTIONS

No Action	Attack of Opportunity*
Delay	No

Free Actions	Attack of Opportunity*
Cast a quickened spell or *feather fall* spell	No
Cease concentration on a spell	No
Prepare spell components to cast a spell**	No
Change form (*shapechange*)	No
Drop an item	No
Drop to the floor	No
Speak	No
Make Spellcraft check on counterspell attempt	No
Make Listen check to find invisible creature	No

Move-Equivalent Actions	Attack of Opportunity*
Climb (one-quarter your speed)	No
Draw a weapon†	No
Sheathe a weapon	Yes
Ready a shield†	No
Loose a shield†	No
Open a door	No
Pick up an item	Yes
Retrieve a stored item	Yes
Move a heavy object	Yes
Stand up from prone	No
Load a hand crossbow or a light crossbow	Yes
Control a frightened mount	Yes
Mount a horse or dismount	No

Standard Actions	Attack of Opportunity*
Ready (triggers a partial action)	No
Dismiss a spell	No
Aid another	No
Bull rush (charge)	No
Bull rush (attack)	No
Change form (shapeshifter)	No
Use touch spell on self	No
Escape a grapple	No
Issue command to animated rope	No
Overrun (charge)	No
Heal a dying friend	Yes
Light a torch with a tindertwig	Yes
Use a skill that takes 1 action	Usually
Rebuke undead (use special ability)	No
Turn undead (use special ability)	No
Strike a weapon (attack)	Yes
Strike an object (attack)	Maybe††
Total defense	No
Voluntarily lower one's own spell resistance	No
Drink a potion	Yes
Apply an oil	Yes
Activate a power of an intelligent item	No

Full-Round Actions	Attack of Opportunity*
Climb (one-half your speed)	No
Use a skill that takes 1 round	Usually
Coup de grace	Yes
Light a torch	Yes
Change form (*polymorph self*)	Yes
Extinguish flames manually	No
Load a heavy crossbow	Yes
Load a repeating crossbow	Yes
Lock or unlock weapon in locked gauntlet	Yes
Prepare to throw oil	Yes
Throw a two-handed weapon with one hand	Yes
Use touch spell on up to six friends	Yes
Refocus (no move)	No
Escape from a net, *entangle* spell, *Otiluke's freezing sphere*, etc.	Yes
Administer a potion or oil to an unconscious creature	Yes

Action Type Varies	Attack of Opportunity*
Disarm‡	Yes
Grapple‡	Yes
Trip an opponent‡	No
Use feat‡‡	Varies

*Regardless of the action, if you move within or out of a threatened area, you usually provoke an attack of opportunity. This column indicates whether the action itself (not the moving) provokes an attack of opportunity.

**Unless the component is an extremely large or awkward item (DM's call).

†If you have a base attack bonus of +1 or higher, you can combine one of these actions with a regular move. If you have the Two-Weapon Fighting feat, you can draw two light or one-handed weapons in the time it would normally take you to draw one.

††If the object is being held, carried, or worn by a creature, yes. If not, no.

‡These attack forms substitute for a melee attack, not an action. As melee attacks, they can be used once in an attack or charge action, one or more times in a full attack action, or even as an attack of opportunity.

‡‡The description of a feat defines its effect.

Partial Actions

Attack Partial Actions	Move	Attack of Opportunity*
Attack (melee)	5-ft. step	No
Attack (ranged)	5-ft. step	Yes
Attack (unarmed)	5-ft. step	Maybe
Partial charge	Yes (special)†	No

Magic Partial Actions		
Cast a spell‡	5-ft. step	Yes
Activate magic item	5-ft. step	Maybe
Use special ability‡	5-ft. step	Maybe
Concentrate to maintain a spell	5-ft. step	No
Dismiss a spell	5-ft. step	No

Movement-Only Partial Actions		
Single move	Yes	No
Partial run	×2	Yes

Miscellaneous Partial Actions**	5-ft. step	Maybe

Special Partial Action		
Start full-round action	No	Maybe

*Regardless of the action, if you move within or out of a threatened area, you usually provoke an attack of opportunity. This column indicates whether the action itself (not the moving) provokes an attack of opportunity.

†You must move in a straight line before attacking and must move at least 10 feet.

‡Unless doing so is a full-round action, in which case you could start a full-round action and then finish it the next round with a cast a spell action. Spells that take longer than 1 full round to cast take twice as long to cast.

**Those actions on Table 8–4: Miscellaneous Actions defined as standard or move-equivalent actions. Most allow a 5-foot step, though actions that are variant charge actions follow the move for partial charge.

Attack Roll Modifiers

Circumstance	Melee	Ranged
Attacker flanking defender*	+2	—
Attacker on higher ground	+1	+0
Attacker prone	−4	**
Attacker invisible	+2†	+2†
Defender sitting or kneeling	+2	−2
Defender prone	+4	−4
Defender stunned, cowering, or off balance	+2†	+2†
Defender climbing (cannot use shield)	+2†	+2†
Defender surprised or flat-footed	+0†	+0†
Defender running	+0†	−2†
Defender grappling (attacker not)	+0†	+0††
Defender pinned	+4†	−4†
Defender has cover	——— See Cover ———	
Defender concealed or invisible	— See Concealment —	
Defender helpless	See Helpless Defenders	
(such as paralyzed, sleeping, or bound)		

*You flank a defender when you have an ally on the opposite side of the defender threatening him. Rogues can sneak attack defenders that they flank.

**Most ranged weapons can't be used while the attacker is prone, but you can use a crossbow while prone.

†The defender loses any Dexterity bonus to AC.

††Roll randomly to see which grappling combatant you strike. That defender loses any Dexterity bonus to AC.

Base Save and Base Attack Bonuses

Class Level	Base Save Bonus	Warrior, Fighter, Barbarian, Paladin, or Ranger Base Attack Bonus	Aristocrat, Expert, Cleric, Druid, Rogue, Bard, or Monk Base Attack Bonus	Adept, Commoner, Wizard, or Sorcerer Base Attack Bonus
1	+0/+2	+1	+0	+0
2	+0/+3	+2	+1	+1
3	+1/+3	+3	+2	+1
4	+1/+4	+4	+3	+2
5	+1/+4	+5	+3	+2
6	+2/+5	+6/+1	+4	+3
7	+2/+5	+7/+2	+5	+3
8	+2/+6	+8/+3	+6/+1	+4
9	+3/+6	+9/+4	+6/+1	+4
10	+3/+7	+10/+5	+7/+2	+5
11	+3/+7	+11/+6/+1	+8/+3	+5
12	+4/+8	+12/+7/+2	+9/+4	+6/+1
13	+4/+8	+13/+8/+3	+9/+4	+6/+1
14	+4/+9	+14/+9/+4	+10/+5	+7/+2
15	+5/+9	+15/+10/+5	+11/+6/+1	+7/+2
16	+5/+10	+16/+11/+6/+1	+12/+7/+2	+8/+3
17	+5/+10	+17/+12/+7/+2	+12/+7/+2	+8/+3
18	+6/+11	+18/+13/+8/+3	+13/+8/+3	+9/+4
19	+6/+11	+19/+14/+9/+4	+14/+9/+4	+9/+4
20	+6/+12	+20/+15/+10/+5	+15/+10/+5	+10/+5

Experience and Level-Dependent Benefits

Character Level	XP	Class Skill Max Ranks	Cross-Class Skill Max Ranks	Feats	Ability Increases
1	0	4	2	1st	—
2	1,000	5	2 1/2	—	—
3	3,000	6	3	2nd	—
4	6,000	7	3 1/2	—	1st
5	10,000	8	4	—	—
6	15,000	9	4 1/2	3rd	—
7	21,000	10	5	—	—
8	28,000	11	5 1/2	—	2nd
9	36,000	12	6	4th	—
10	45,000	13	6 1/2	—	—
11	55,000	14	7	—	—
12	66,000	15	7 1/2	5th	3rd
13	78,000	16	8	—	—
14	91,000	17	8 1/2	—	—
15	105,000	18	9	6th	—
16	120,000	19	9 1/2	—	4th
17	136,000	20	10	—	—
18	153,000	21	10 1/2	7th	—
19	171,000	22	11	—	—
20	190,000	23	11 1/2	—	5th

Access to Spells (By Class Level)

Spell Level	Clr, Drd, Wiz Level	Sor Level	Brd Level*	Pal, Rgr Level*	Adp Level*
0	1	1	1	—	1
1	1	1	2	4	1
2	3	4	4	8	4
3	5	6	7	11	8
4	7	8	10	14	12
5	9	10	13		16
6	11	12	16		
7	13	14			
8	15	16			
9	17	18			

*Provided character has bonus spells.

Size and AC of Objects

Size (Example)	AC Modifier	Size (Example)	AC Modifier
Colossal (broad side of a barn)	−8	Medium-size (barrel	+0
		Small (chair)	+1
Gigantic (narrow side of a barn)	−4	Tiny (tome)	+2
		Diminutive (scroll)	+4
Huge (wagon)	−2	Fine (potion in a vial)	+8
Large (big door)	−1		

Substance Hardness and Hit Points

Substance	Hardness	Hit Points
Paper	0	2/inch of thickness
Rope	0	2/inch of thickness
Glass	1	1/inch of thickness
Ice	0	3/inch of thickness
Wood	5	10/inch of thickness
Stone	8	15/inch of thickness
Iron	10	30/inch of thickness
Mithral	15	30/inch of thickness
Adamantite	20	40/inch of thickness

Common Weapon and Shield Hardness and Hit Points

Weapon	Example	Hardness	HP
Tiny blade	Dagger	10	1
Small blade	Short sword	10	2
Medium-size blade	Longsword	10	5
Large blade	Greatsword	10	10
Small metal-hafted weapon	Light mace	10	10
Medium-size metal-hafted weapon	Heavy mace	10	25
Small hafted weapon	Handaxe	5	2
Medium-size hafted weapon	Battleaxe	5	5
Large hafted weapon	Greataxe	5	10
Huge club	Ogre's club	5	60
Buckler	—	10	5
Small wooden shield	—	5	10
Large wooden shield	—	5	15
Small steel shield	—	10	10
Large steel shield	—	10	20
Tower shield	—	5	20

DCs to Break or Burst Items

Strength Check to:	DC		
Break down simple door	13	Bend iron bars	24
Break down good door	18	Break down barred door	25
Break down strong door	23	Burst chain bonds	26
Burst rope bonds	23	Break down iron door	28

Object Hardness and Hit Points

Object	Hardness	Hit Points	Break DC
Rope (1 inch diam.)	0	2	23
Simple wooden door	5	10	13
Spear	5	2	14
Small chest	5	1	17
Good wooden door	5	15	18
Treasure chest	5	15	23
Strong wooden door	5	20	23
Masonry wall (1 ft. thick)	8	90	35
Hewn stone (3 ft. thick)	8	540	50
Chain	10	5	26
Manacles	10	10	26
Masterwork manacles	10	10	28
Iron door (2 in. thick)	10	60	28

Example Opposed Checks

Task	Skill (Key Ability)	Opposing Skill (Key Ability)
Sneak up behind someone	Move Silently (Dex)	Listen (Wis)
Con someone	Bluff (Cha)	Sense Motive (Wis)
Hide from someone	Hide (Dex)	Spot (Wis)
Tie a prisoner securely	Use Rope (Dex)	Escape Artist (Dex)
Win a horserace	Ride (Dex)	Ride (Dex)
Pass as someone else	Disguise (Cha)	Spot (Wis)
Steal a coin pouch	Pick Pockets (Dex)	Spot (Wis)
Create a false map	Forgery (Int)	Forgery (Int)

Example Door DCs

DC	Door
10 or lower	A door just about anyone can bash open.
11 to 15	A door that a strong person could bash with one try and an average person might bash with one try.
13	Typical DC for a simple wooden door.
16 to 20	A door that almost anyone could bash, given time.
18	Typical DC for a good wooden door.
21 to 25	A door that only a strong or very strong person has a hope of bashing, and probably not on the first try.
23	Typical DC for a strong wooden door.
25	Typical DC for an iron-barred wooden door.
26 or higher	A door that only an exceptionally strong person has a hope of bashing.
28	Typical DC for an iron door.
+5*	Hold portal (increases DC by 5).
+10*	Arcane lock (increases DC by 10).

*Not cumulative; if both apply, use the larger number.

Skills that Can Be Used Untrained

Skill	Ability	Skill	Ability
Appraise	Int	Intimidate	Cha
Balance	Dex*	Jump	Str*
Bluff	Cha	Listen	Wis
Climb	Str*	Move Silently	Dex*
Concentration	Con	Perform	Cha
Craft	Int	Ride	Dex
Diplomacy	Cha	Scry	Int
Disguise	Cha	Search	Int
Escape Artist	Dex*	Sense Motive	Wis
Forgery	Int	Spot	Wis
Gather Information	Cha	Swim	Str
Heal	Wis	Use Rope	Dex
Hide	Dex*	Wilderness Lore	Wis

*The PC's armor check penalty, if any, also applies.

Light Sources

Object	Light	Duration
Candle	5 ft.	1 hr.
Lamp, common	15 ft.	6 hr./pint
Lantern, bullseye	60-ft. cone*	6 hr./pint
Lantern, hooded	30 ft.	6 hr./pint
Sunrod	30 ft.	6 hr.
Torch	20 ft.	1 hr.

Spell	Light	Duration
Continual flame	20 ft.	Permanent
Dancing lights (torches)	20 ft. (each)	1 min.
Daylight	60 ft.	30 min.
Light	20 ft.	10 min.

*A cone 60 feet long and 20 feet wide at the far end.

Index